Privatisation in Developing Countries
Volume I

The International Library of Critical Writings in Economics

Series Editor: Mark Blaug

Professor Emeritus, University of London, UK
Professor Emeritus, University of Buckingham, UK
Visiting Professor, University of Amsterdam, The Netherlands

This series is an essential reference source for students, researchers and lecturers in economic It presents by theme a selection of the most important articles across the entire spectrum economics. Each volume has been prepared by a leading specialist who has written a authoritative introduction to the literature included.

A full list of published and future titles in this series is printed at the end of this volume.

Wherever possible, the articles in these volumes have been reproduced as originally publishe using facsimile reproduction, inclusive of footnotes and pagination to facilitate ease of referenc

For a list of all Edward Elgar published titles visit our site on the World Wide Web at
http://www.e-elgar.co.uk

Privatisation in Developing Countries Volume I

Edited by

Paul Cook

Reader in Economics, Institute for Development Policy and Management, University of Manchester, UK

and

Colin Kirkpatrick

Professor of Development Economics and Director, Institute for Development Policy and Management, University of Manchester, UK

THE INTERNATIONAL LIBRARY OF CRITICAL WRITINGS IN ECONOMICS

An Elgar Reference Collection
Cheltenham, UK • Northampton, MA, USA

Published by
Edward Elgar Publishing Limited
Glensanda House
Montpellier Parade
Cheltenham
Glos GL50 1UA
UK

Edward Elgar Publishing, Inc.
136 West Street
Suite 202
Northampton
Massachusetts 01060
USA

A catalogue record for this book is available from the British Library.

Library of Congress Cataloguing in Publication Data

Privatisation in developing countries / edited by Paul Cook and Colin Kirkpatrick.
(The International library of critical writings in economics)
Includes index.
1. Privatization—Developing countries. 2. Government ownership—Developing countries. 3. Industrial policy—Developing countries. I. Cook, Paul, 1944– II. Kirkpatrick, C. H. (Colin H.), 1944– III. Series.

HD4420.8 .P698 2000
338.9'009172'4—dc21 00–34797

ISBN 1 85898 358 4 (2 volume set)

Printed and bound in Great Britain by Biddles Ltd, *www.biddles.co.uk*

Contents

Acknowledgements

The editors and publishers wish to thank the authors and the following publishers who have kindly given permission for the use of copyright material.

Blackwell Publishers Ltd for article: Maxim Boycko, Andrei Shleifer and Robert W. Vishny (1996), 'A Theory of Privatisation', *Economic Journal*, **106** (435), March, 309–19.

Dieter Bös, Wolfgang Peters, Attiat F. Ott and Keith Hartley for excerpt: Dieter Bös and Wolfgang Peters (1991), 'A Principal–Agent Approach on Manager Effort and Control in Privatized and Public Firms', in Attiat F. Ott and Keith Hartley (eds), *Privatization and Economic Efficiency: A Comparative Analysis of Developed and Developing Countries*, Chapter 3, 26–52.

Cambridge University Press for excerpts: Leroy P. Jones and Edward S. Mason (1982), 'Role of Economic Factors in Determining the Size and Structure of the Public-Enterprise Sector in Less-Developed Countries with Mixed Economies', in Leroy P. Jones (ed.), *Public Enterprise in Less-Developed Countries*, Chapter 2, 17–47; Yair Aharoni (1982), 'State-Owned Enterprise: An Agent Without a Principal', in Leroy P. Jones (ed.), *Public Enterprise in Less-Developed Countries*, Chapter 4, 67–76.

Elsevier Science Ltd for articles: Nicolas van de Walle (1989), 'Privatization in Developing Countries: A Review of the Issues', *World Development*, **17** (5), May, 601–15; Heidi Vernon-Wortzel and Lawrence H. Wortzel (1989), 'Privatization: Not the Only Answer', *World Development*, **17** (5), May, 633–41; William Glade (1989), 'Privatization in Rent-Seeking Societies', *World Development*, **17** (5), May, 673–82; George Yarrow (1999), 'A Theory of Privatization, or Why Bureaucrats are Still in Business', *World Development*, **27** (1), 157–68.

HarperCollins Publishers, Inc. for excerpt: Yair Aharoni (1986), 'Measuring the Performance of State-Owned Enterprises', in *The Evolution and Management of State Owned Enterprises*, Chapter 5, 161–216, references.

Institute of Latin American Studies, University of Texas at Austin for excerpt: John F. Coburn and Lawrence H. Wortzel (1986), 'The Problem of Public Enterprise in Developing Countries: Is Privatization the Solution?', in W.P. Glade (ed.), *State Shrinking: A Comparative Inquiry into Privatization*, Chapter 2, 24–39.

Intereconomics for article: Peter Nunnenkamp (1986), 'State Enterprises in Developing Countries', *Intereconomics*, **21** (4), July/August, 186–93.

Macmillan Press Ltd for excerpt: Nicholas Kaldor (1980), 'Public or Private Enterprise – the Issues to be Considered', in William J. Baumol (ed.), *Public and Private Enterprise in a Mixed Economy: Proceedings of a Conference held by the International Economic Association in Mexico City*, Chapter 1, 1–12.

MIT Press for excerpts: David E.M. Sappington and Joseph E. Stiglitz (1987), 'Information and Regulation', in Elizabeth E. Bailey (ed.), *Public Regulation: New Perspectives on Institutions and Policies*, Chapter 1, 3–43; John Vickers and George Yarrow (1988), 'Ownership and Incentives', in *Privatization: An Economic Analysis*, Chapter 2, 7–44, references; John Vickers and George Yarrow (1988), 'Competitive Forces', in *Privatization: An Economic Analysis*, Chapter 3, 45–77, references.

Pearson Education Ltd for excerpts: Robert Millward and David M. Parker (1983), 'Public and Private Enterprise: Comparative Behaviour and Relative Efficiency', in Robert Millward, David Parker, Leslie Rosenthal, Michael T. Sumner and Neville Topham (eds), *Public Sector Economics*, Chapter 5, 199–274; Paul Cook and Colin Kirkpatrick (1988), 'Privatisation in Less Developed Countries: An Overview', in Paul Cook and Colin Kirkpatrick (eds), *Privatisation in Less Developed Countries*, Chapter 1, 3–44; Robert Millward (1988), 'Measured Sources of Inefficiency in the Performance of Private and Public Enterprises in LDCs', in Paul Cook and Colin Kirkpatrick (eds), *Privatisation in Less Developed Countries*, Chapter 6, 143–61.

Routledge, Taylor & Francis Books Ltd for excerpt: Stephen Martin and David Parker (1997), 'Privatisation: The Conceptual Framework', in *The Impact of Privatisation: Ownership and Corporate Performance in the UK*, Chapter 1, 1–30, references.

Ezra N. Suleiman for excerpt: Carl Shapiro and Robert D. Willig (1990), 'Economic Rationales for the Scope of Privatization', in Ezra N. Suleiman and John Waterbury (eds), *The Political Economy of Public Sector Reform and Privatization*, Chapter 3, 55–87.

John Wiley & Sons Ltd for article: David Heald (1990), 'The Relevance of Privatization to Developing Economies', *Public Administration and Development*, **10** (1), January–March, 3–18.

World Bank for excerpts and articles: World Bank (1983), 'Managing State-Owned Enterprises', in *World Development Report 1983*, Chapter 8, 74–87; Mahmood A. Ayub and Sven O. Hegstad (1987), 'Management of Public Industrial Enterprises', *World Bank Research Observer*, **2** (1), January, 79–101; Robert D. Willig (1993), 'Public versus Regulated Private Enterprise', in *Proceedings of the World Bank Annual Conference on Development Economics 1993*, 155–70; Leroy P. Jones (1993), 'Appropriate Regulatory Technology: The Interplay of Economic and Institutional Conditions', in *Proceedings of the World Bank Annual Conference on Development Economics 1993*, 181–204; Jose Edgardo Campos and Hadi Salehi Esfahani (1996), 'Why and When Do Governments Initiate Public Enterprise Reform?', *World Bank Economic Review*, **10** (3), September, 451–85.

Every effort has been made to trace all the copyright holders but if any have been inadvertently overlooked the publishers will be pleased to make the necessary arrangement at the first opportunity.

In addition the publishers wish to thank the Library of the London School of Economics and Political Science, the Marshall Library of Economics, Cambridge University and the Library of Indiana University at Bloomington, USA, for their assistance in obtaining these articles.

Introduction

Paul Cook and Colin Kirkpatrick

Privatisation, defined as the transfer of productive assets from public to private ownership and control, has been at the forefront of economic policy debate in all parts of the developing world for several decades and has been seen as a key policy instrument in the move to more market based economic systems. Privatisation was initially implemented in developing countries in the absence of a literature that had either theoretically or empirically convincingly proved that private ownership was superior to public ownership. The theoretical treatment of the subject that has subsequently developed has not fully incorporated the factors that make the debate different in developing countries to that found in the industrialised countries. Empirical studies comparing public and private sector performances have grown since the early 1980s and indicate that the balance of evidence has shifted in favour of the private sector.

Privatisation featured prominently in the structural adjustment programmes adopted by most developing countries in the 1980s and 1990s. Privatisation, however, was not necessarily accompanied by an increase in market competition. Many public utilities were privatised as monopolies, and regulatory systems have been developed to curb their market power and protect consumer interests while, at the same time, attempting to maintain incentives to achieve higher efficiency and investment.

Policy makers have had a variety of objectives in mind for privatisation. First, with widespread evidence of poor economic performance of many public enterprises, privatisation has been seen as a means of improving economic efficiency, which will be reflected in lower consumer prices and improved product quality. Second, faced with large net financial deficits in the public enterprise sector, privatisation has been perceived as a means of reducing fiscal deficits, by increased tax revenues on enterprise output, reduction in central government transfers to the enterprise sector, and receipts from privatisation sales. Third, privatisation has been used as a means of shifting the balance between the public and private sectors and promoting market forces within the economy. This is a more ideological, and hence controversial, argument for privatisation, since it rests on the idea that the economic role of the state should be defined (i.e. reduced), with the state concentrating on its core functions and responsibilities for creating a stable economic, legal and institutional environment within which the private sector can flourish. Other objectives for privatisation have included the generation of new investment (including foreign investment), wider share ownership and the deepening of the domestic financial system.

The process of privatising public enterprises began slowly in developing countries, but in the late 1980s the pace accelerated and by the early 1990s there had been almost 3000 separate privatisations in the developing world. Developing countries accounted for 86 per cent of all transactions by the mid 1990s but, as a share of global privatisation in value terms, their share was only 35 per cent.

In the early stages, privatisation sales in developing countries were predominantly of small public enterprises, primarily agribusinesses, services and light manufacturing. The privatisations were largely trade sales and employee and management buyouts, with fewer stockmarket flotations and limited foreign capital participation. However, in the 1990s privatisation in developing countries included a growing number of large public enterprises, particularly in the utilities and industrial sectors, using public flotations and with foreign capital participation. Nevertheless, in 1994 direct private sales still accounted for 86 per cent of all transactions. Share issues in domestic and international capital markets accounted for only 10 per cent of transactions, representing 47 per cent of sales in 1994. Between 1988 and 1993, the largest share of public revenue from privatisation sales came from infrastructure.

There are also marked regional differences in the scale of privatisation in developing countries. Latin America accounted for over 60 per cent of the value of sales between 1988 and 1994. By contrast, African involvement has been marginal in terms of both volume and value, accounting for less than 3 per cent of revenue.

The body of evidence on the impact of privatisation in developing countries is rather limited. In part, this may reflect the various methodological difficulties that arise in impact assessment analysis. It also reflects a failure on the part of policy makers to specify clearly the objectives of privatisation, and to rely on implementation measures rather than performance outcomes. Performance indicators for privatisation in developing countries can be grouped into two broad categories, covering macro- and micro-level results. The impact of privatisation on the macro economy can be assessed by a change in the state's share in the economy, a reduction in the fiscal imbalance, and development of capital markets and resource mobilisation, including foreign investment. There are four main micro indicators: technical (or productive) efficiency, cost efficiency, financial profitability and real prices.

In terms of macro indicators, the share of the public enterprises sector has shown little change over the period of privatisation. Despite the fiscal gains from privatisation, this does not appear to have reduced the overall fiscal deficit. Privatisation has contributed to the inflow of foreign investment to developing countries.

Micro-level evidence on the impact of privatisation is derived from enterprise data with 'before–after' comparisons of performance for the same enterprise. Other studies have also compared the performance of public and private sector enterprises that operate side by side in the same industry. In general these studies do not provide unequivocal support for the view that privatisation improves performance. Perhaps a clearer message emerging from this body of evidence is that private ownership is favoured but only in competitive markets. When markets are less competitive, then the case for superior performances is less clear cut.

Most studies show an improvement in profitability after privatisation. However, this financial performance improvement need not be accompanied by an increase in efficiency, where, for example, the now privately owned monopoly is able to exploit its position of market dominance, protected from competition by natural barriers to entry or by tariff protection. Evidence on employment and productivity gains is more mixed.

The available evidence suggests, therefore, that the scale of privatisation in developing countries, in the narrow sense of divestiture, has been much less than is commonly supposed. The reasons for this are both practical and political. In a low income economy where markets are imperfect, where the private sector is uncompetitive and underdeveloped, and where the administrative capacity of government is limited, the technical and institutional barriers to implementing a privatisation programme are considerable. The political constraints on the adoption of privatisation arise from the distributional impact. The divestiture of enterprises has an immediate impact on those interest groups that currently benefit from the public enterprise sector's inefficiencies, either in terms of surplus workforce levels, uneconomical prices or excessive factor payments. In contrast, the gains from privatisation are diffused throughout the economy and may only arise after the immediate costs have been incurred. The short-term political costs of privatisation may outweigh the longer-term economic and political benefits and act as a brake on the pace of privatisation in developing countries.

A second conclusion to be drawn from experience is that divestiture alone is unlikely to result in a significant reduction in the size of the public enterprise sector 'burden' in the developing countries. Other measures to improve the performance of the enterprises which remain in the public sector have an important role to play in an overall reform programme. Broader forms of privatisation, such as management contracts and contracting out, combined with market liberalisation and competition policy and the establishment of a sound regulatory framework, will be important components of such a reform programme. The choice of measures to be used and the relative weight which is given to each of them will depend on the objectives set for the public enterprise reform programme and on a realistic assessment of the economic, institutional and political constraints on policy design and implementation.

The library of critical writings on privatisation in developing countries is contained in two volumes. Each volume is divided into four parts. Each part covers a separate aspect of the privatisation experience in developing countries, and the papers selected reflect the major contributions to each topic.

In the first volume, Part I incorporates papers that capture the historical evolution of the debate over the role of enterprises under public and private ownership. The second Part presents some of the papers that have influenced the theoretical debate. Few of these addressed directly the issues faced by developing countries, but nevertheless they have had a profound influence on the process of decision making and implementation. The third Part presents some of the papers that have provided new theoretical and policy insights into the issues surrounding the need for post-privatisation regulation. The fourth Part of this volume incorporates a selection of papers that have reviewed the comparative performance between enterprises under private and public ownership.

The first Part of the second volume encompasses a set of papers that explore the political, as well as the economic, explanations for privatisation. The second Part presents two papers that review the experience with regulation. The third Part incorporates papers that have attempted to assess the impact of privatisation. These cover micro and macro indicators, as well as different sectoral and geographical perspectives. They reveal the complexity of assessment and the difficulties raised in interpreting the evidence. The final Part presents a set of papers that have attempted to assess the evidence and provide lessons for policy makers.

In conclusion, privatisation is a policy instrument that can be used in developing countries to bring about significant economic gains. However, it needs to be used in a selective and pragmatic manner, not for ideological gains. Experience has shown that there is a host of constraints to successful privatisation that need to be recognised and controlled, that a variety of forms and types of privatisation are required, and that serious consequences for the credibility of the broader economic reform process arise if privatisation is mismanaged.

Privatisation also needs to be seen as part of a broader strategy aimed at improving the performance of the public enterprise sector. Privatisation alone is unlikely to be sufficient to ease significantly the economic burden which the public enterprise sector places on the economy of many developing countries. Other forms of public enterprise reform, where ownership remains with the state but the contractual relationship between the enterprises and government is redefined, are needed.

Ultimately, the contribution that privatisation makes to economic advancement in developing countries will be determined by political will and commitment. There is now sufficient experience and evidence for economists to advise, with some confidence, on the appropriate design and execution of privatisation proposals, as part of a programme of public enterprise reform. This knowledge is the first prerequisite for successful privatisation; the second is a government's commitment to the use of privatisation as one of the means of advancing the nation's developmental goals.

Part I
Privatisation and Public Enterprise in Developing Countries

[1]

Public or Private Enterprise – the Issues to be Considered

Nicholas Kaldor
PROFESSOR EMERITUS, CAMBRIDGE UNIVERSITY

INTRODUCTORY

The subject matter of this meeting concerns the relative advantages of public and private enterprise in mixed economies.

This problem has a large number of aspects and it is one that cannot be analysed universally without taking into account the framework of political and social institutions, traditions and history, and the stage of economic development, of the particular country to which the analysis is applied.

For good or ill the world is divided into separate states which differ from one another in many things, not just in language, culture and historical image, but also in the nature of their political and social institutions which are a legacy of their past history. It is usual to distinguish among three broad groups of countries: socialist, capitalist and those of the 'third world'.

I. THE SOCIALIST COUNTRIES

In the first group we have the so-called Socialist states or 'centrally-planned economies' such as the USSR and the Peoples' Democracies of Eastern Europe, as well as China and some other countries of South-East Asia. The main feature of these countries is that private enterprise has more or less been abolished except perhaps in agriculture and in small enterprises employing not more than one or two workers. Yet, as one of the papers before us shows, the question of the type of enterprise to be preferred and to be expanded is a live problem even in the case of these economies, since, apart from state enterprises, they contain a large sector of co-operatives which, to a greater or lesser degree, are under the self-management of their worker-members, who are also collectively the owners of the enterprises though they cannot 'withdraw' their share individually. Within limits the members of the co-operatives, directly or through their elected committees, decide on the main policy issues concerning the type of products to be produced and the types of activity to which the enterprise should extend, as well as on the share of the current income which should be ploughed back into the enterprise rather than distributed. There are no clear principles to determine where the boundary line between state enterprises and co-operative enterprises should be drawn. The fact that co-operative enterprise is dominant in agriculture whilst state enterprise dominates industry and services is the outcome of a historical development which leaves open the question whether the co-operative type of enterprise should be extended to the industrial field or state enterprise be extended to agriculture, or whether it would be best to have both types of enterprise in all the main sectors of the economy, operating side by side. The Socialist countries also possess a privately owned sector producing for the market, but consisting mainly of small enterprises or of people working on their own account. Here again there is the question whether the limits of private enterprise should be constrained or loosened and what are the types of activities or the sectors of the economy for which they are best suited. All these matters are the subject of continuing discussion.

II. THE DEVELOPED CAPITALIST COUNTRIES

The mixed economies of the rest of the world raise problems of a different character. The world of the developed capitalist states of Western Europe, North America and Oceania is one in which private enterprise is dominant but where some public enterprise is also universal – they necessarily exist in those institutions which are charged with law and order, defence, public administration, and so on. In most countries they also extend to education, health and related social services, communications by road, rail, air and sea and public utilities. Many of these services could be (and partially are) provided by private enterprise – for example, education and medical services – others are a public monopoly mainly on the ground that they are natural monopolies, or that they can best be provided by a single organisation on a national scale – such as the provision of post and telecommunications, electricity, gas, railways, as well as the services which are generally provided by local authorities such as water supplies, sewage systems, street lighting, etc.

In addition to all these which we might broadly denote under the name of 'infrastructure', there is also in most countries public ownership of a varying number of industrial enterprises which are either directly or indirectly in competition with private enterprise, and where the question whether public enterprise performs better or worse than private enterprise is a matter of considerable controversy. In some countries (as in France at the present moment) the expansion of this 'optional' public sector (if I may use that term) is in the forefront of political discussion.

The individual capitalist countries show a great deal of variation in respect of the importance of this 'optional' public sector. At one extreme there are countries which have had a Social Democratic Government for a very long period and yet refrained from nationalising private enterprise or creating public enterprise in sectors where it would compete with private enterprise. The best example of this is Sweden which had a Socialist Government in power continually for forty-four years, during which the country was brought to the forefront of all others in the matter of the provision of public education and health services, social security, etc., but where the state refrained from either taking over existing firms or creating new public enterprises in competition with private ones. At the opposite end of the scale is Italy, which never had a Socialist or even a Social-Democratic government (though Social-Democrats or Socialists were often part of a coalition dominated by non-Socialists) but where nevertheless the state-owned sector of industry is very large and extensive, as we shall learn from Dr Marsan's paper.

Then we have countries which occupy a mid-position: such as Austria, France and Britain, each of which has an important group of publicly owned enterprises. In the case of Austria, which is perhaps economically the most successful of these countries, the public sector (resulting from large-scale nationalisations immediately after the war) extends to the three largest banks and to the 'heavy industries' – coal, iron, steel, engineering, shipbuilding, oil refineries and the heavy chemicals. The industrial state enterprises are thus complementary to rather than competitive with the private sector and they have provided through their own steady expansion the indispensable base for a large expansion of manufacturing industry in general. (It is not, perhaps, generally known that next to Japan, Austria had the fastest rate of economic growth since the Second World War, and the fastest increase in real income per head – in sharp contrast to the inter-war period when her economy was stagnant through most of the period, with heavy unemployment.) The public sector of Austria, accounting for 16 per cent of all employees, 20 per cent of total output and 25 per cent of exports, is the largest (in relative terms) among the developed countries of the West.[1]

Then there is the case of France and Britain where the nationalised sector of industries is mostly the product of the post-war period. Both in Britain and France the 'infrastructure' services – electricity, gas, railways and air services – were mainly nationalised after the Second World War. In addition, in Britain the first post-war Labour Government nationalised the coal industry and also the steel industry, though the latter was later denationalised by a Conservative government, only to be renationalised again – though with a much narrower scope – by the Labour Government of 1964–70. In addition, the British National Oil Corporation is a recently created state-owned enterprise for the production and distribution of North Sea oil, operating in co-operation with private firms. The Government has also recently nationalised the shipbuilding and aircraft industries. The road haulage industry has also been partially nationalised. In France, in addition to the public utilities – gas, electricity,

[1]In Great Britain the nationalised industries and enterprises account for 10 per cent of output and of employment.

railways and air services – nationalisation extended to parts of the oil-producing and refining industry, the chemical industry, the aeronautical construction industry and the motor car industry as well as some of the large banks and insurance companies. Two enterprises discussed in detail in M. Dreyfus's paper are La Régie Renault and Elf-Aquitaine, both of which are in direct competition with privately owned enterprises.

The individual firms which are nationalised in France, like Renault, are mainly the historical result of their having been owned by collaborators with the enemy during the war. In Britain on the other hand there is a group of state-owned firms where state-ownership has much more in common with the state-owned firms of Italy – that is to say, it is public ownership 'by default', occasioned by the insolvency or bankruptcy of important enterprises which would have ceased to exist unless they were taken over by the state; and where their continued existence was considered to be a national interest. This is the case of Rolls Royce, one of the largest aero engine manufacturers of the world, and the motor car firm of British Leyland, which only recently was the largest producer of motor cars in Britain and the only large motor car firm in British ownership.

In both these countries, Britain and France, the question of whether nationalisation should be extended or otherwise is a matter of acute public discussion. In France the parties of the Left are united in wishing to extend nationalisation considerably, the acute difference between the Socialist and Communist parties concerns only how large this extension should be. In Britain on the other hand the professed aim of the Tory party is to restrict the scope of public enterprises, but (apart from the BNOC), as far as I know, they have no concrete plans for the denationalisation of any particular part of the existing public sector.

The evidence concerning the relative efficiency of the public sector varies according to country, period and the particular criteria chosen. In Britain, for example, according to Mr Pryke, the public sector had a clear lead over the private sector in terms of output and productivity growth up to 1968[1] while according to his present paper, the experience was the reverse one for the period after 1968. The same appears to be true of Italy and for much the same reasons: with the deterioration of the economic situation and the acceleration of inflation, the State enterprises became the recipients of open-ended subsidies (mainly to hold down prices) with the usual demoralising effects on management and workers which that involves. There can be no doubt, however, of the success of the public sector in Austria and (at least partially) in France. In Austria the growth of output of the public sector was more than sixfold, and the growth employment threefold in 30 years.[2]

[1]See his book, *Public Enterprise in Practice: British Experience over Two Decades* (London, 1971).

[2]For France, cf. the evidence in M. Dreyfus's paper.

III. THE DEVELOPING COUNTRIES

The experience of the countries of Western Europe with public enterprise is, however, only of limited relevance for the question which should be at the centre of our discussions this week – the question, that is, how far the 'third world countries' of Latin America, Asia and Africa should develop their industries through public enterprise or through private enterprise.

This is a highly complex question, and all I can do within the compass of an introductory paper is to indicate which, in my view, are the main considerations relevant to the issue.

I assume that the main aim of all these countries is to have a maximum attainable rate of economic development so as to raise the standard of living of their populations. It is also agreed that such development is not attainable without a large manufacturing industry capable of absorbing a considerable part of the available labour force.

The main issues to be considered are:

(1) *The extent and continuity of development.* Here the argument in favour of nationalisation is that state enterprise can take its decisions on long-run considerations and these are not, or need not, be governed by the profit motive which should not necessarily be regarded as relevant from the point of view of investment decisions.

(2) *National or foreign ownership of large industrial enterprises.* While in principle this is independent of the choice between public or private enterprise, in practice in many of the developing countries, private enterprise means enterprise under the control of foreign countries.

(3) *Efficiency of operation.* Both from a technological and a managerial point of view.

(4) *Long-run effects on the general social structure.* I.e. the degree of equality or inequality in the distribution of wealth and power.

I would like to say something on each of these four points.

(1) Public enterprise and economic development

Private enterprise is actuated by the profit motive. Firms only invest in a particular 'project' when the profit which they expect from it (looked at either in isolation or as part of an interconnected plan of investments) is at least as high as any alternative way of investing the same funds. There are a number of reasons which can be adduced to show that such profit-guided investment will tend to be smaller than the social optimum.

(i) The profitability associated with the project is based on expectations, and as the future is uncertain these may be heavily discounted on account of uncertainty. This is particularly true in cases where it is a question of extending enterprises into a 'new field', either into a new industry which comes into existence as the result of new technical knowledge, or into a country in which an industry, existing elsewhere, has not yet been developed, and where the circumstances surrounding its future operations are uncertain (availability of skilled labour, management supporting public services, etc.). It normally cannot take into account either the static or dynamic economies which result from the expansion of the scale of industrial activities.

(ii) The theory which suggests that the profit criterion secures the best allocation of resources is only applicable under highly unreal assumptions under which the market mechanism operates perfectly, where both the amount of labour available for employment and the amount and the size of funds available for investment are to be taken as given, and where the profit resulting from any particular investment provides a measure of the net addition to the national output which can be attributed to that investment. There are a number of powerful reasons for rejecting such postulates. The additional flow of output which results from a given amount of investment may be very much greater than the stream of profits which result from it, and may be more reasonably measured by the value of the net output stream (or the stream of 'value-added') which results from that investment. When productive capacity is enlarged, it will in general be possible to increase the volume of employment, or to transfer labour from occupations where its net contribution to the national output is very small or zero to a new employment where its productivity is positive and large and where the earnings of labour are also much higher. For these reasons the measure of social profitability should not be the profit that is imputed to the owners of the capital invested in an enterprise, but should comprise also the addition to other types of income generated by the new investment. In principle, therefore, public investment can make use of better criteria for deciding on the amounts and kinds of investment to be undertaken than is the case with private investment.

(iii) This will be true also on account of the fact that when public investment is part of a national plan it is possible to take all kinds of criss-cross effects (or indirect effects) into consideration which would not be possible with private investment. Keynes once said that in the face of complete uncertainty investors generally rely on a convention that the future will be just like the present, and for that reason 'the effects of the existing situation enter, in a sense disproportionately, into the formation of long-term expectations'. Hence capacity is only likely to be created in so far as its use appears to be profitable at the *existing state of demand*. Since the demand for commodities depends on the level of incomes which are generated in production, the additional production generated in the future by the sum of the investment decisions of the present will itself increase the demand for commodities in comparison with the present level – a factor which private investors cannot take into account (or can do so only very imperfectly) since they take their decisions independently of each other. Investment by public enterprise, on the other hand, can take the comprehensive effect of all investments into account in judging the social profitability of any particular investment project. (It should be noted, however, that a State Plan is capable of doing this even when investment is undertaken by private enterprise, as the Japanese example shows. What is required is that there should be a fairly comprehensive state investment plan for industrial development, and that the state should be capable of giving effect to this plan, through the 'administrative guidance' of privately owned firms – provided that, as in Japan, these are native and not foreign-owned firms.)

(2) National or foreign ownership

In principle the question whether a particular country's industries should be developed by national or by foreign enterprise is a different one from whether the enterprise should be privately or publicly run. In some countries (such as Japan or Sweden) the scope for foreign-owned or foreign-controlled enterprises was firmly restricted from the start. However in the developing countries the standards and attainments of education are not normally sufficient for self-generated development of modern industry by native entrepreneurs, since they lack the knowledge and ability to run such enterprises, and/or the willingness to bear the risks. Hence, in practice, public enterprise may be the only alternative to foreign-owned and foreign-controlled private enterprise. It should be pointed out, however, that the absence of the necessary know-how presents an obstacle to the development of industry under public enterprise in the same way as to native private enterprise, i.e. that public enterprises will also be dependent on foreign know-how for their operation, so that in practice it may not make so much difference whether an enterprise is formally owned by the state or whether it is owned by a foreign parent company. It is also argued in favour of a foreign-controlled private enterprise that there will normally be much greater willingness to provide the necessary know-how for efficient operation – both from a technical and a managerial point of view – to a subsidiary than to provide the same in the form of technical assistance for the running of a nationalised enterprise.

In my view this presents a very real dilemma to many developing countries. It is generally agreed that foreign domination of a country's industries leads to highly undesirable results, both socially and politically, and may be creative of tensions, both domestic and international. There are several distinguished economists in the United States (such as Professor Hirschmann) who advocate that the United States should divest itself entirely from the enterprises it owns in Latin American countries, and that this is an essential prerequisite for the development both of more satisfactory international relationships and also for the sound evolution of political institutions within the countries. The best solution might be (a suggestion once made by Myrdal) that the governments of developing countries should aim at the creation of *joint enterprises* in which the developing country would provide the greater part of the capital, while the parent company of the developed country would provide the technical and managerial know-how, and they would both have equal participation in the shares of, and equal say in the running of, the enterprise, but with the proviso that the government of the developing country should have the option of acquiring the foreign parent country's share of the enterprise after a stated number of years.

(3) Efficiency of operation

The strongest argument in favour of private enterprise in developing countries is that it is generally better managed and technically more efficient than public enterprise. In the developed countries, as we have seen, there is no clear presumption on present evidence one way or the other. But it could be argued that the case against public enterprise is stronger on efficiency grounds in the less developed countries where considerations other than fitness and efficiency for a job may play an important role in appointments for the top posts in state-owned enterprises – these may be decided as a matter of political patronage, in the same way as the top posts in government services. (This does not mean that private enterprise is free of such patronage; in the case of enterprises owned or controlled by the family of the founder, family members receive undue preference for top appointments.) However, I think on balance it would be conceded that in less developed countries privately run firms may be more efficient in that they involve less bureaucracy and have a better quality of management than public enterprises.

Both this consideration and the one preceding may argue in favour of private enterprise or of joint private and public enterprises as the main vehicle for development. But it should be kept in mind that any such judgement can only be made on the basis of the existing situation the continuation of which cannot be taken for granted. It is possible for a country to develop native talents to a high degree of technical skill through education in the same way as a number of countries such as Japan or the USSR have done and it is possible also to develop a cadre of administrators both for government services and for the running of public enterprises who would bring to their task the same qualities of selfless devotion and incorruptibility as that of the public servants of many of the developed countries of Western Europe.

(4) Long-run considerations

While it cannot be demonstrated that private enterprise is superior to public enterprise in the majority of cases and the majority of countries, there are reasons for supposing that public enterprise is inferior in terms of efficiency of operation, technical dynamism etc. in countries which are less developed economically and also less mature politically – these two things generally go together.

It would also not be contested by unbiased observers that the establishment of fully fledged socialist states in the Soviet Union and various countries of Eastern Europe has not produced the results which were expected of it, not only by those who were the fervent advocates of a Socialist state, but of the more numerous group of Western intellectuals who looked favourably on the idea of a socialist state, and who hoped that the countries where such régimes were established would provide, through their success, an example for others to follow.

The Soviet Union has now been in existence for sixty years. Very few people would have expected that after such a long period the results should be so meagre – either in terms of an increase in living standards of the working classes or in terms of the creation of a free society in which the powers of compulsion exercised by the state authority have vanished or at least were reduced to a minimum. No one (certainly not Lenin) expected that the 'dictatorship of the proletariat' would last for sixty years or anything like it. Some Communist leaders, like Rosa Luxembourg, questioned the need or the justification for such dictatorship from the start. And no one expected that a Socialist society would retain so many features of the class conflict of capitalist states. (Some of the difficulties and complications that beset the organisation and control of production of a centrally-run socialist state are well brought out in the analysis of Rezsó Nyers and Márton Tardos relating to the economic reforms of Hungary.)

In some fields no doubt the Soviet Union has made enormous strides – in the development of science-based technology in certain fields (mainly those related to defence); in others, however, there is a surprising lack of technical dynamism and continued dependence on western technology to secure industrial progress. Hungary is probably the most successful of the Socialist countries economically and manages to run its affairs with less restriction on individual freedom than is the case with other socialist countries of the Warsaw Pact. Yet in terms of the increase in real income per head over the last 20–25 years Hungary's record with 65 per cent of employees in state enterprises is much inferior to that of neighbouring Austria which is a mixed economy in which the share of employees in state industry is only 16–20 per cent. In the period after the Second World War there can be no doubt that the mixed economies of the type of Austria and Sweden have proved far more successful than the socialist economies of Eastern Europe – irrespective of whether success is judged purely by the criterion of the increase in material living standards, or also by the criterion of the general freedom and contentment of the population, and its effective participation in decision-making.

The greatest problem of the Socialist countries which has not so far been resolved is connected with the centralisation of power which appears to be an inevitable adjunct of universal state ownership. Again, I do not think that many people would dissent from the view that centralisation of power is undesirable in human society, as it generally leads to both moral and material corruption of those who exercise power.

On the other hand, looking at the development of capitalism since the Second World War, one cannot believe that the kind of society which has emerged in the developed countries of the West (and which is imitated with greater or lesser success in the developing countries) is either viable or desirable as the destination of humanity. The concentration on material welfare of the successful modern consumer societies in the West is not only highly wasteful in terms of exhaustible resources, but creates a socially restless and basically frustrated competitive society which fosters a scale of values that moralists and religions throughout human history have regarded as reprehensible. Moreover it also leads, through the process of industrial concentration – which in some of the leading countries of the West has accelerated considerably since the Second World War – to a concentration of power in the hands of the owners and managers of giant enterprises which is no less distasteful than state power: indeed in some ways it is more so, since it is power without responsibility. I cannot see that there is any long-run future for a society where some men are extremely powerful in relation to their fellow men simply because they possess a great deal of money or have the power of dismissal or patronage over a large number of employees. The more capitalism develops into a corporate state dominated by a small number of giant enterprises the less likely it is that it can survive. As biological evolution shows, nature abhors giantism.

It is the power conferred by the possession of wealth, far more than the inequalities of living standards occasioned by it, which makes modern capitalism so unsatisfactory as a method of organisation of human societies. (Capitalist consumption, though highly conspicuous, may not amount to much, at least in the developed countries, in terms of consumption foregone by wage and salary earners.) For that reason, it is at most inconceivable that it should continue to exist indefinitely. Sooner or later it is inevitable that it should give way to, or be replaced by, or develop into, something else. But in the light of the history of the present century it is far less clear than it appeared at the end of the nineteenth century what that something else is going to be. In the light of the experience of the Communist countries of Eastern Europe (perhaps it is too early to come to any definite judgement on the Chinese experiment) it can confidently be predicted that it will not be centralised Socialism that provides the alternative.

IV. WORKERS' CO-OPERATIVES

There is a small but growing group of people who put their faith in workers' co-operatives operating through the framework of a regulated market economy as the best solution to the problem of the economic organisation of human societies.

There are a number of isolated examples suggesting that it is possible to run enterprises under workers' control and/or ownership, and that this form of organisation avoids the main defects of both capitalist enterprise and of a centrally directed Socialist economy. For it secures a high degree of decentralisation in decision-making, and avoids the conflict of interest between workers and capitalists or workers and management – which events have shown can be the plague of state enterprise in Socialist states or of the public sector of mixed economies as well as of capitalist private enterprise. Among the Socialist countries, Yugoslavia alone has been entirely restructured along co-operative lines. The intention has been to create a system of 'self-management' of business undertakings by their workers and this has recently been extended to include the separate control of 'work units' within an enterprise. However, the workers are not the owners of the enterprises – the initiation of a co-operative is the task of the local authorities and the workers have no beneficial interest in the assets of the enterprises. Hence under that system the material incentive to develop through reinvestment of profits is a weak one. Moreover, it is not clear how far in the case of Yugoslavia the decentralisation of decision-making in the economic sphere has led to an abatement in the exercise of centralised power in the political sphere.

Co-operatives exist in the agricultural sector of most Socialist countries, and in at least one, Hungary, they have proved more successful in improving productivity and real earnings than State-operated manufacturing industry. Agricultural co-operatives extend also in the field of banking in a number of countries where production is in the hands of individual private enterprises. The co-operative Credit Agricole of France is the largest bank in Europe and the third largest bank in the world. In Germany also co-operative banking has made great strides since the Second World War through the Bank fuer Gemeinwirtschaft. In Britain, under the recent Labour Government some industrial enterprises have been rescued from extinction through the creation of workers' co-operatives as in the motor bicycle factory, Meriden, and the Kirkby engineering factory. These enterprises now appear to have reached a stage at which they can operate without loss; and in both cases they secured the full identification of the workers with the success of the enterprise which ended demarcation disputes or union squabbles which mar the rest of British industry. There is also the much publicised Basque experiment at Mondragon (near Bilbao in Spain) started by a Basque priest, Jose Maria Anizmendi (who died in 1976). Thanks to him, fifty-eight industrial co-operatives have been created in the last twenty years with a combined turnover of roughly $300 million a year and a labour force of nearly 14,500.

And last but not least there is the experience of the Kibbutzim of Israel going back over fifty years which shows (as Professor Barkai's paper relates) that co-operative enterprise, given the right ideological motivation, is capable of producing results in terms of output and productivity growth which are comparable with the best results of capitalist enterprise in manufacturing and not just in agriculture.

In comparison with the huge enterprises of modern industry, publicly or privately owned, the size of most workers' co-operatives is very small. Experience also tends to suggest that the effective involvement of workers in the management of enterprises – which is essential to their success – is only possible when the number of workers involved in decision-making is not too large. This fact alone makes it improbable that workers' co-operatives could effectively displace other forms of enterprise within a measurable period of time. There is also the fact that this type of enterprise appears more promising when it emerges in replacement of other types of enterprise which have failed – whether capitalist (as in Britain) or Socialist (as in Yugoslavia). Thus even if co-operative enterprises were to be regarded, *faute de mieux*, as the most promising ultimate solution of the problem of organising human societies, this is not likely to obviate the need of developing countries having to choose in the interim stages between public ownership or private enterprise or of forms of joint control of the state and private interests.

[2]

Role of economic factors in determining the size and structure of the public-enterprise sector in less-developed countries with mixed economies

Leroy P. Jones and Edward S. Mason

2.1 Introduction

The issues

What is to be explained is the size and structure of the public-enterprise sector[1] in mixed economies, in particular those in less-developed countries (LDCs). The numerous reasons for establishing or retaining public enterprises can be consolidated into four groups:

1. Ideological predilection
2. Acquisition or consolidation of political or economic power
3. Historical heritage and inertia
4. Pragmatic response to economic problems

Although we will be concerned primarily with the fourth (economic) group of factors, we begin by briefly considering the competing–complementary explanations. Causation is multiple, and it is necessary to be explicit about what is being left out as we focus on economic determinants.

Ideological predilection

What does it mean to say that ideology has influenced the choice of public enterprise? We take it to mean that the decision rests not upon an unbiased examination of means in relation to ends in a particular case but upon a prior belief that certain forms of organization are generally preferable to others.

Work on this chapter was partially supported by a Ford Foundation grant to the Boston University Public Enterprise Program. We are indebted to Peter Evans, Richard D. Mallon, Jan Tinbergen, and John Sheahan for their comments on an earlier draft.

This does not imply that all choices influenced by ideology are irrational. In some cases the decision would be the same if based on an unbiased examination of the relation of means to ends. More important, ideology can influence ends as well as means. A belief in the merits of a "socialist pattern of society" can lend extra value to expansion of employment or redistribution of income, favoring investment decisions promoting those ends. But whatever the ends, there remains the choice of appropriate means. For example, income can be redistributed by taxation as well as by public ownership. The Scandinavian countries have chosen the former means, with relatively small public-enterprise sectors but very high levels of income redistribution via taxes to finance transfers and public services. Eastern Europe, on the other hand, chooses public production as the means of satisfying consumption requirements. Given the aim of income redistribution, which mix of means is preferable in a particular setting? Ideology biases this difficult decision in a particular direction and may lead to choices in which inferior means are chosen to attain particular ends. It is only if public or private enterprise is regarded as an end in itself (e.g., a capitalist concern for freedom of opportunity or the preference among some socialists for nonhierarchical production relationships) that the pragmatic choice among alternative forms of organization becomes moot.

There is no economy in which a dominant ideology does not exercise some influence. Ideologies favorable to public enterprise in LDCs may be described simply as socialism but are more commonly associated with a modifier – Arab, African, or Burmese socialism or the pursuit of a socialist pattern of society. The modifiers are intended to convey a nondoctrinaire recognition of specific local conditions, but there can be little doubt that such ideologies provide facilitating environments for public enterprises. Conversely, the establishment of public enterprise is much more difficult in a country such as the Republic of the Philippines, which has inherited the United States' antipublic bias.

Acquisition or consolidation of political or economic power

This is obviously related to ideology but is conceptually distinct as decisions are made not according to some preconceived position but according to the consequences of particular actions. Decisions to establish, retain, or divest a public enterprise are not made in a political vacuum. In the struggle for power among various interest groups, ownership and control of economic units are instruments for advancing certain interests and frustrating others.

The nationalization of foreign-owned enterprises in Egypt following the Suez War in 1956 eliminated potential centers of opposition to Nasser's revolutionary government. Although ideology certainly had some influence in 1960 and 1961, it is significant that Nasser's promulgation of the Charter of Arab Socialism came after nationalization rather than before. The dominant motivation can be interpreted to have been a consolidation of political power through the elimination of the economic base of political components.[2]

The quest for economic power may also play a role. Ahmad (Chapter 3) sees various classes struggling over the surplus generated by the public enterprises. Evans argues that there is a symbiotic relationship between multinationals and public enterprises that supports capitalist interests.[3] He also emphasizes the role of public enterprise in furthering the interests of the "state bourgeoisie," which controls and manages the enterprises.[4] Sobhan and Ahmad describe a situation in Bangladesh where the interests of the capitalist class were served by public enterprises whose pricing policies allowed capitalist middlemen to usurp surplus in a system that was ostensibly operated to benefit the masses.[5]

Financial and political interests of course interact. It has been argued that in India the existence of a strong business class (which must be relied on for political funding) has exerted its influence in retarding progress toward the "socialist pattern of society" advocated by the dominant political party. In Korea under the Rhee regime, the public banking system was used to channel campaign funds to the ruling political party.[6]

Historical heritage and inertia

In the wake of colonial exodus (Korea in 1945) or a liberation war (Bangladesh in 1972), new governments often have little short-term alternative but to take over substantial responsibilities in the industrial sphere. Once an enterprise is in public hands for any significant period of time, there then develops a strong inertia (defended by various interest groups) that tends to keep it in the public sector regardless of ideology or performance. The influence of inertia is particularly visible in situations in which the locus of political power changes drastically. Post-Allende Chile is one of the few cases of broad-based divestiture of public enterprises. Elsewhere, public enterprises established under one regime or philosophy exhibit remarkable staying power even in the face of later antagonistic governments. Employees, as well as civil servants (and sometimes consumers), have clear vested interests whose defense can impede denationalization. Less dramatic evidence of the operation of inertia occurs with economic development. A country might establish its first fertilizer plant in the public sector on the legitimate grounds of inadequate private entrepreneurship. It may well remain public 15 years later when the private sector has proven itself capable of running far larger and more complicated projects.

Pragmatic response to economic problems

In their pursuit of economic goals, governments have a variety of centralized and decentralized institutional arrangements to choose from. These range from purely competitive market organizations through private enterprises guided by taxes, subsidies, and various kinds of direct controls and joint and cooperative ventures of various sorts to publicly owned and controlled enterprises. A pragmatic, non-ideological government would view public enterprise neutrally as simply one tool among many. It would then select a tool on the basis of institutional comparative advantage derived from evaluation of the benefits and costs of each form for dealing with a particular problem in a particular industry.

Now, no country operates in such pristine isolation from political and historical conditions, but conversely, no country can totally ignore economic factors. Even the USSR places truck gardening in the private sector and even the United States uses public enterprise for the postal system. Less ideologically biased mixed economies – particularly in the LDCs – might be expected to be much more heavily influenced by pragmatic considerations. That, at least, is the first major theme of this chapter. In the words of Talcott Parsons: "The balance between governmentally controlled and free-enterprise industry is to a far larger degree than is generally held a pragmatic question and not one of fundamental principles."[7]

The second major theme of this chapter is that economic factors must be understood to include both costs and benefits of public operation and that these must be evaluated in comparison with those of institutional alternatives. Public enterprises are sometimes inefficient, but the alternatives create their own problems. Large family groups in LDCs, regulated monopolies in the United States, and credit-subsidized or tariff-protected private firms also create distortions.

Our third major theme is that the net benefits of public operation – and the resulting institutional comparative advantage – are sufficiently uniform across countries to have both predictive and prescriptive value in determining the structure and, to a lesser extent, the size of the public-enterprise sector.

None of this should be misconstrued as an argument for economic determinism in which political, sociological, and historical factors are impotent. Far from it; as already stated, causation is multiple. The limited role of this chapter, however, is to analyze only the contribution of economic factors.

2.2 Evidence on size and structure

a. The question

To the extent that the choice of public enterprise is pragmatic, and to the extent that the determinants of institutional comparative advantage apply across countries, then similar countries facing similar problems will choose public enterprise to a similar extent. The result would be identifiable regularities in the size and structure of the public-enterprise sector across countries. To what extent do such regularities exist?

b. India versus Korea

A comparison of India and the Republic of Korea provides a useful starting point, as the public-enterprise sectors of both are well developed and well documented but spring from quite different ideological predilections.[8] In India the prevailing view has been that

> the adoption of the socialist pattern of society as the national objective, as well as the need for planned and rapid development require that all industries of basic and strategic importance, or in the nature of public utility services should be in the public sector.[9]

In Korea, on the other hand:

> private ownership of production should unconditionally be encouraged except in instances where it is necessary to control it to stimulate national development and protect the interests of the people.[10]

In short, public enterprise is typically viewed as a "necessary evil" in Korea, an appellation reserved for private enterprise in India. What difference does this make in practice?

In the early 1970s the share of GDP originating in the public-enterprise sector was virtually identical in India and Korea at about 9%. If this result is surprising, part of the explanation may be due to differences in sectoral structure: India is much more agrarian and public ownership is universally less prevalent in agriculture than in industry. This is reflected in the fact that as a share of nonagricultural GDP, India's public-enterprise sector becomes somewhat larger than Korea's (15% vs. 13%). If this remains surprising, it might be because a simple static comparison of levels disguises quite different trends. True, from 1960-1 to 1972-3 the Indian public-enterprise sector increased its share of the economy by 80%, whereas from 1963 to 1972 the Korean sector share expanded by only 50%. However, because the Korean economy was growing more than twice as fast as India's during this period, the Korean public-enterprise sector actually grew much faster than India's (14% real annual growth rate vs. 8%).

Perhaps ideology reveals itself in structure rather than in size. Table 2.1 gives a single-digit comparison of the industrial composition of public-enterprise output in the two countries. There is only one really striking difference – in transport and communication. This is due primarily to the share of railways: In both countries railways are public, but Korean railways are a much smaller share of total transportation than in India, as Korea is geographically a very small country and India a very large one.[11] The difference is thus not due to a different public–private choice but to different industrial structures. In sum, and even allowing for errors in measurement, the impact of ideology seems undetectable: The dominant feature of a comparison of the size, trend, and structure of the public-enterprise sectors in India and Korea is one of similarities rather than differences.

c. *Other countries: size*

The reader who suspects that India and Korea are atypical in their similarities and that the set of LDCs as a whole exhibits substantially more diversity is correct. In the absence of careful statistical work using common definitions it is difficult to be

Table 2.1. *Percentage of public-enterprise sector in value added of various industries: Korea and India, 1971–2*

Industry	Korea[a]	India[b]
Agriculture, forestry, fishing	0.2	1.8
Mining	32.6	36.3
Manufacturing	16.4	13.3
Electricity, water, etc.	71.7	83.8
Construction	4.9	4.8
Trade	1.2	3.2
Transport, communication	30.8	61.4
Finance	83.5	84.0[c]
Other	0.5	1.6
Total	9.1	9.4

[a] Leroy Jones, *Public Enterprise and Economic Development: The Korean Case* (Seoul: Korean Development Institute, 1975), p. 78.

[b] N. S. Ramaswamy, V. J. Kesary, P. V. George, G. K. Nayar, V. G. Kamath, and P. D. Deenadayalu, *Performance of Indian Public Enterprise* (New Delhi: Standing Conference on Public Enterprises, 1978), p. 96. These shares are reported in constant prices, but current price shares are identical because deflation of public enterprise current price data was done at the single-digit level using national accounts deflators (Ramaswamy et.al., pp. 98–104).

[c] The source gives 25.4%, but there is an incompatibility as "ownership of dwellings" is grouped with "finance." As a rough adjustment we use a figure of 84%, which is the 1973 share of loans plus deposits in the public banks. Vadilal Dagli, ed., *Commerce Yearbook of Public Sector: 1974–1975* (Bombay: Mahatme, 1974), pp. 90–1.

precise, but in terms of size, the sector's contribution to GNP would seem to range from lows in the vicinity of from 2 to 3% (Philippines, Nepal) to highs that may approach or exceed 50% (Saudi Arabia). Further, diversity within the manufacturing sector is probably even greater. As already noted, agriculture has a low publicization[12] propensity, so that even wholesale public ownership of industry may leave only a modest share of GNP in the public-enterprise sector in a largely agrarian economy. For example, in Bangladesh public enterprises are estimated to account for 56% of value added in mining and manufacturing (and for 80% of large-scale manufacturing) but for only 8% of GDP.[13]

A substantial part of this diversity, however, is explained by differences in resource endowments. Most important in this regard is mining, which has a relatively high publicization propensity (one-third in India and Korea and three-fourths or more where oil is a prominent resource). The largest public-enterprise sectors therefore occur where large-scale mining generates a large share of GNP.

The size difference between such countries as Iran, Bolivia, and Saudi Arabia, on the one hand, and those such as India and Korea, on the other, are thus due not to ideology or history but to differences in resource endowments.

Available data suggest that the bulk of mixed-economy LDCs fall in a much narrower range. In an International Development Research Centre sponsored study of seven Asian nations, the size of the public-enterprise sector ranged from a low of 2% of GDP in Nepal to a high of 12% in Sri Lanka, with Thailand intermediate at 4% and India, Bangladesh, Pakistan, and Korea in the 8% to 9% range.[14] On the basis of this evidence plus scattered impressions elsewhere we suggest that the bulk of public-enterprise sectors in LDCs fall in the fairly narrow range of 7% to 15% of GDP.[15] This modal range appears to include such diverse countries as Korea, India, Taiwan, Brazil, Pakistan, Bangladesh, Singapore, Sri Lanka, and Mexico. Outlying observations are explained by differences in both resource endowment and ideology and history, as is variance within the modal range. The Philippines is at the low end for ideological reasons, whereas Nepal is there because of a particularly primitive economic structure. The bulk of the high observations occur for economic reasons (high national-resource extraction) with a few for ideological (Tanzania) or historical (Egypt, Turkey) reasons.

Other countries: structure

The similarities in structure in India and Korea have even wider applicability than do the similarities in size. Pryor has compared Eastern and Western Europe where the *level* of public-sector activity ranged from 9% to 71%[16]. There was nonetheless great similarity in the *pattern* of nationalization as measured by a high and statistically significant rank correlation coefficient of ownership shares in a one-digit industry classification and a significant correlation within a two-digit mining and manufacturing ranking. That is, although countries differed markedly in the *level* of public-enterprise use, there were marked similarities in *structure* with the same industries having the highest publicization propensities across ideological boundaries. Sakong Il has produced similar results at the one-digit level for a seven-nation sample of Asian countries.[17]

In sum, the exceptional similarity of the public-enterprise sectors in India and Korea is due to a constellation of factors – history, ideology, interest-group struggle, and pragmatic responses to different economic conditions – which act in offsetting directions and just happen to balance out in these two countries. Elsewhere, national differences often act in reinforcing, rather than offsetting, directions and create much greater variance of outcome. Nonetheless, our survey of the available empirical evidence suggests that this variance is much less than might be expected and that much of it is due to differences in economic conditions. This supports the notion that underlying economic factors play a significant causal role. We now explain why this might be so.

2.3 Benefits and costs of public enterprise in an optimal economic order

a. Market failure versus organization failure

To focus on pragmatic economic considerations we assume away the influence of ideological, historical, and political factors and imagine a rational decision-making entity exclusively concerned with maximizing social welfare through a choice among a wide variety of centralized and decentralized institutions.[18] Public enterprise is then simply one among many tools available for achieving the government's goals, and the choice of this tool is a function of the costs and benefits associated with its use as compared to those of other institutional forms.

Discussion of the behavior of such a mythical beast by no means implies its existence. It is nonetheless of interest for at least three reasons. First, some governments sometimes try to make some decisions on pragmatic grounds and in these cases the availability of a cost–benefit framework has both predictive and prescriptive value. Second, at the opposite extreme where pragmatic considerations are likely to be totally ignored, there is some interest in being able to distinguish situations where the net cost of the public-enterprise choice is low from those where it is high. Finally, in the most common case where all factors enter into the decision, the pragmatic cost–benefit calculus may play a substantial role at the margin. In most mixed-economy LDCs there will be pressures both for and against further extensions or contractions of the public-enterprise sectors. The pro public-enterprise forces are more likely to win those battles where they also have pragmatic arguments on their side and vice versa. Occasionally, the imbalance between the forces will provoke a wholesale shift in one direction or the other, but subsequent adjustments at the margin may still follow predictable patterns. In Pakistan ideological nationalizations in 1972–4 were followed in 1977 by *selective* denationalization along lines predictable on pragmatic grounds.[19]

We are engaged in what Tinbergen terms a quest for the "optimum organization of the economy."[20] The first step is the specification of an interdependent set of desirable *outcomes,* one subset of which is the marginal conditions of pareto efficiency. The second step is the choice of a set of *institutions* to achieve the desired outcome. Two polar institutional possibilities are a perfectly centralized planning system and a perfectly decentralized market system. Our particular concern is with an intermediate mixed institution (public enterprise) that combines the potential for centralized direction of some decisions with response to market signals in others.

Under what conditions will public enterprise be part of the optimal economic order? We structure our answer to this question in terms of the costs and benefits associated with this choice. These could be classified in many ways, but we utilize two broad categories:

1. Benefits can be had from government intervention where market failures lead a profit-maximizing private producer to behavior incompatible

with social-welfare maximization;

2. Costs occur as a result of *organizational failures* associated with a specific intervention mechanism. A particular institutional tool (say public enterprise) may achieve an *intended* deviation from private behavior (say, willingness to price at marginal cost rather than marginal revenue in a natural monopoly) but may at the same time produce *unintended* deviations (say, cost inefficiency) that must be compared with the costs associated with other intervention mechanisms (say, price and profit regulation under private ownership).

This classification reflects the notion that enterprise outcomes can deviate from the welfare norm for two reasons:

1. Incorrect *external* signals of economic opportunity
2. Incorrect *internal* responses because organizational and/or behavioral characteristics create nonmaximizing behavior by the firm (individuals or coalitions *within* the firm may of course still be maximizing)

Economists have traditionally been most concerned with the former problem, leaving the latter to management and public-administration scientists. There are, however, several rapidly evolving bodies of economic literature that address the organizational-failure problem under such headings as ''*X*-efficiency theory,'' ''behavioral theories of the firm,'' ''property rights,'' and the ''economics of internal organization.''[21] It is our contention that the insights from these materials must be brought to bear in assessing the costs of the choice of public enterprise relative to other organization forms.

We approach the problem of an optimum organization from the point of view of a laissez-faire economy, examining the areas in which market failures may call for some type of intervention. It could be approached equally well from the point of view of a fully centralized economy, asking in what areas a decentralization of decision making or a limitation of controls on economic units may be desirable. The only difference is that the costs of centralization (organizational failures) become the benefits of decentralization and vice versa.

b. Benefits: market failures

The concept of market failures in the context of welfare economics is well known and here we provide only an overview. Pareto efficiency is a condition whereby no one can be made better off without making someone else worse off. As such, it is a necessary, but not a sufficient, condition for a ''good'' economic system. It is necessary because, regardless of our value judgments,[22] it is desirable to undertake a reallocation if it makes someone better off without harming anyone else. It is not sufficient because we may reject a *particular* pareto efficient allocation if we:

1. Do not accept the initial wealth (and subsequent income) distribution with which it is associated

2. Reject consumer preferences (e.g., for drugs over nutritious food or for child labor over education or for current consumption over savings for old age)
3. Consider the social relations of production to have value independent of the value of inputs and outputs

Such a specification of *outcomes* thus constitutes part of Stage 1 of Tinbergen's scheme for selection of the "optimum organization of the economy."

Stage 2 consists of specifying a set of instruments for achieving the marginal conditions. Under certain highly restrictive conditions (discussed later) perfectly decentralized decision making (either via private ownership or market socialism as per Lange–Lerner) can achieve the marginal conditions and thus serve public welfare without intervention by centralized authority. Any deviation from these conditions can be broadly defined as a market failure (to achieve the marginal conditions via decentralized decisions) and creates the *potential* for improvement via government intervention. We utilize a somewhat narrower definition of market failure by decomposing the broad definition into organizational failures (internal to the firm) and (narrow) market failures (external to the firm).

Pareto efficiency is attained when marginal social costs equal marginal social benefits for all activities. The two most commonly cited circumstances in which markets fail to produce these results are decreasing cost technology and external effects. In the first case, the larger the firm, the greater the cost advantage, so that profit-seeking activity leads to exit of all but the single largest firm, creating a natural monopoly. In less extreme cases the result is oligopoly, with resulting opportunities for concerted action to constrain production, raise prices, and enjoy excess profits. In the second case, activities generate costs (e.g., pollution) and benefits (e.g., some forms of worker training) to society that do not enter the firm's calculus, which means that even where marginal costs equal marginal benefits from the narrow enterprise perspective, they will not do so from the broader social perspective. There is then an argument for replacing the invisible hand of the market with the visible hand of government to increase social welfare by restoring the social marginal conditions.

These considerations lead Tinbergen to conclude (in part) that "a mixed order seems to be optimal showing the following structure: (a) a public sector of considerable extent takes care of all activities showing external effects or indivisibilities of some importance, while activities that show neither of these characteristics can be carried out by a private sector."[23]

This statement is of course only a first approximation and needs to be both modified and extended. The modification is that the specified conditions create only a *motive* for intervention and not a case for a particular *means* of intervention. Public enterprise is only one way of restoring the marginal conditions and alternatives (regulation, taxes, and subsidies, etc) must be considered. Further, the benefits must be set against the costs (see the following subsection). The extension is that additional sources of market failure need to be appended to the Tinbergen pair. Although there is no widely accepted morphology of market failures, other commonly cited categories include public goods, merit goods, information imperfections, and lumpy capital. Two additional reasons that deserve mention in the context of LDCs are dynamic considerations and artificial monopoly, topics to which we now briefly turn.

The pareto-efficiency conditions are generally stated in static (single-period) terms, but there is in principle no difficulty in extending it to a dynamic multi-period formulation. Now costs and benefits occur in different time periods and what must be equated is the net present vparticular decision. The practical difficulty is that as these costs and benefits recede into the future they need to be discounted not only for forgone opportunities and preferences but also for increasing uncertainty in an unknowable future. In LDCs the future is particularly uncertain because of information imperfections, political instability, and the absence of vehicles for risk spreading. An investment may then be socially desirable but perceived as privately undersirable because of a low expected rate of private return.

These problems become greater as we move from small-scale traditional activities to large-scale modern activities with long gestation and payback periods and unknown production technology and marketing conditions. It is the function of entrepreneurs to solve these problems, but entrepreneurial failure will be greater in LDCs. Economies advance in large part through innovations in technology, marketing, management, and so on, and optimal levels of innovation cannot be achieved if left solely to private initiative in LDCs. Further, innovation often requires abandonment of traditional ways so that Schumpeter's "creative destruction" is an essential part of the development process. If private entrepreneurs prefer a low, but certain, return in traditional activities to a larger expected return with higher variance in modern activities, there is again room for positive government intervention.

Monopoly can be artificial as well as natural, that is, created by the efforts of man rather than dictated by the necessities of technology. There can be conspiracies among firms, individuals, and governments, producing unfair practices designed to force the exit of, and preclude the entrance of, competitors; efforts that are sometimes accompanied by bribery and strong-arm tactics. These practices are certainly significant in many LDCs. It is commonly held that the wholesale rice trade in some southeast nations in some periods has been controlled by ethnic Chinese using force and political payoffs. Perhaps more important, monopoly enforced by political influence can occur in factor markets, most noticeably in those for credit and foreign exchange. If large family groups control existing industry and exert political power as a result, they can influence factor allocations, reduce entry, and distort marginal conditions across many product markets.

This last observation leads to a critical compounding factor in the theory of government intervention. Markets are interdependent so that distortions in one market are transmitted to others, creating divergences between private and social

28 **Why public enterprise?**

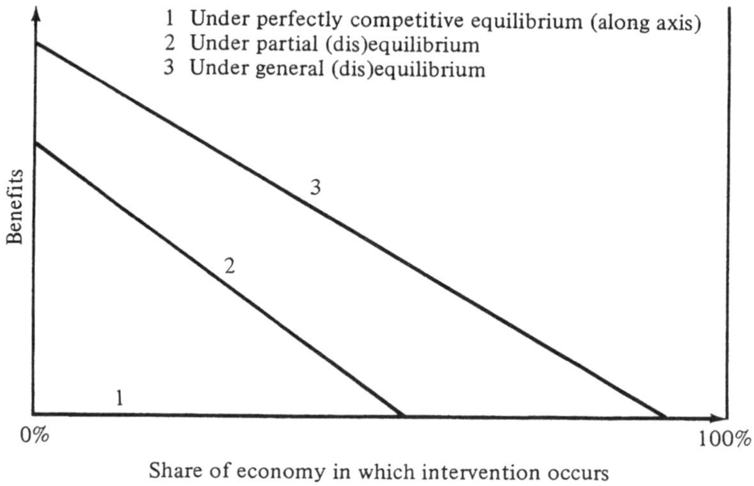

Figure 2.1. Potential benefits from government intervention.

marginal costs and benefits even in markets that are themselves otherwise undistorted. Recognition of such constrained general equilibrium considerations, where there exist unremedied distortions in some uncontrollable markets, can justify intervention in other controllable (but themselves undistorted) markets as a second-best solution. For example, the existence of public goods plus the impossibility of a poll tax means that other markets must be distorted by taxes to generate the revenue to finance the public good.[24]

The argument of this subsection can be summarized in terms of Figure 2.1 and the following propositions:

1. Under certain highly restrictive assumptions, decentralized markets yield pareto efficiency and there are no benefits to be had from intervention (curve 1, along axis)
2. Violation of any of these conditions creates market failures whose removal by government intervention could yield benefits in those markets. The potential-benefit curve slopes downward, as some markets are more distorted than others. It intersects the abscissa, as not all markets are distorted in the partial-equilibrium sense (curve 2)
3. In constrained general (dis)equilibrium, the interdependence of markets can justify intervention in virtually all markets (curve 3).

Costs of intervention

Although a rational case can thus be made for intervention in virtually any market, our pragmatic government will set the benefits of such intervention against its costs. These costs may be of two sorts. First, there are the resource costs – largely manpower and intertemporal delays – involved in central planning boards, regulatory agencies, tax bureaus, and like institutions at the center, plus those incurred at the enterprise level in providing information, bargaining, and designing a means of circumventing the intervention mechanism. The second set of costs, probably much more important, is the tendency of intervention institutions to generate new problems in attempting to solve old ones. A tool is selected to achieve *intended* deviations from idealized private behavior and ends up creating *unintended* deviations as well: A public enterprise is created to avoid the problems of private monopoly but ends up producing with excessive costs as well; a system of price and profit regulation of private enterprise is set up for the same reason but also results in excessively capital-intensive investment decisions; a credit subsidy is designed to encourage exports but also results in interest arbitrage and land speculation; jawboning may temporarily reduce price increases but incur implicit government commitments that create new problems when due. Examples of such costly unintended deviations associated with various intervention institutions could be expanded indefinitely. Our purpose, here, however, is merely to stress that such costs are by no means confined to the public-enterprise problems discussed here but are associated to one degree or another with *all* intervention mechanisms.

Around the world public enterprises are often accused of inefficiency. This is not surprising. Public enterprises are a hybrid, sharing characteristics of government bureaucracies, on the one hand, and private enterprises, on the other. As an "enterprise," they must face a market test of the acceptability of their product, and this imposes one set of pressures on management. As a "public" organization, they must be responsive to the needs of dominant political forces and are subject to the constraints and opportunities afforded by being part of the civil-service chain of command. Given the necessity of trade-offs between these two sets of pressures, it is not only unsurprising but positively predictable that the outcome will often be suboptimal by the standards of one side or the other or both. This is not to excuse the result or suggest that its most deleterious consequences cannot be mitigated but only to suggest that certain efficiency costs are likely to be incurred in choosing the public-enterprise tool.

The inefficiency to which we refer is not so much that associated with traditional allocative efficiency (choice of the wrong price–quantity bundle) as with failure to minimize costs of production for the quantity actually chosen. Both the popular and academic literature on public enterprise are replete with instances of this form of behavior; here we only outline the more important causal antecedents.

Public enterprises often operate under bureaucratic systems that control processes rather than outcomes. Procurement patterns, for example, typically mandate formal bidding procedures and multiple official ministerial approvals regardless of economic cost. An Asian fertilizer plant was shut down for more than a month by bureaucratic impediments in obtaining replacement parts from

Europe, which could otherwise have been gotten in a few days. The cost? Roughly $200,000 *per day* of downtime. The benefits? Avoidance of corruption and overcharging on equipment worth $100,000 at most. Assume 30 days excess downtime and 100% corruption via kickback. It then cost $6 million to save $100,000[25]. The time-consuming traditional rules of government are difficult to reconcile with the needs of an organization that must operate in a dynamic market.

A second kind of problem involves the use of political influence to transfer income from the public to various special-interest groups, be it unemployed brothers-in-law, retired generals, politically potent unions, constituents back home, or industrialists who want the public output at a low price. There is a narrow line here between the legitimate and the illegitimate. A major function of government is to transfer income from one group to another. The difficulty with public enterprises is that the transfers can be so readily hidden from those who pay the freight in terms of increased taxes, higher inflation, or lower government expenditures on health, education, or welfare.

A third difficulty is that public-enterprise decision makers often have little incentive to control costs. In part this can result from recruitment practices (short-term political appointees as chief executives) and in part from civil-service pay structures that preclude merit bonuses. More fundamentally, however, it is seldom possible to distinguish ''good'' from ''bad'' performance. If there are both legitimate and illegitimate reasons for losing money and no techniques for distinguishing between the two, managerial performance cannot be judged. A public manager under pressure to hire unproductive workers has little reason to resist, as any effect on profit can be hidden by attribution to government pricing policies on inputs or outputs.

A list of this sort could be extended indefinitely; our purpose is merely suggestive. There are no necessary reasons for public enterprises to fail to minimize costs but a host of sufficient ones. Although such costs of public enterprise are real, they must be compared with the costs of alternatives.

Private firms also experience managerial failures, and the resulting costs must be taken into account in determining the net advantage (or disadvantage) of public enterprises in particular industries. As Comanor and Leibenstein argue, the major disadvantages of monopoly may not be the social cost of misallocation – ''too little production and too high a price'' – but that the absence of competitive pressure yields excess costs for what *is* produced.[26] In the less-developed countries the prevalence of family firms with accompanying nepotism may produce similar results. Further, Sheahan argues that the unwillingness of some LDC entrepreneurs to dilute family control can lead to suboptimal investment in large-scale projects unless the government intervenes.[27] This list could again be both extended and debated, but the general point is clear. Private enterprise, like public enterprise, may not behave as profit maximizers, and these internal organizational failures must also be considered in assessing the costs and benefits of intervention.

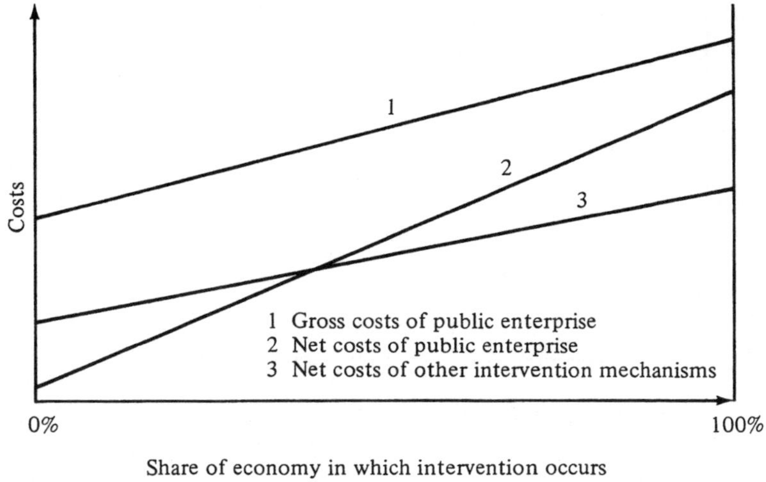

Figure 2.2. Costs of public intervention.

The argument of this subsection may be summarized in terms of Figure 2.2,[28] which incorporates the following propositions:

1. Gross costs of public enterprise: If the problems of public enterprise are greater in some sectors than others, the slope of the curve will be positive, reflecting increasing marginal costs as increasingly inappropriate activities are brought into the public domain. The level of the curve is a function of the efficacy of the public-enterprise control system.
2. Net costs of public enterprise: Private organizations also suffer organizational failures and these must be netted out in evaluating public enterprises. This curve necessarily lies below the gross cost curve by an amount varying with the efficacy of private enterprises in particular countries and particular industries.
3. Net costs of alternative forms of intervention: This is defined as with number 2 but for the best alternative form of intervention. It is sometimes above and sometimes below the public-enterprise curve on the assumption that one institutional form will have a comparative advantage in some activities and another form in others.

Equilibrium

Equilibrium occurs at the intersection of the various cost and benefit curves, partitioning the economy into public-enterprise and controlled and uncontrolled private sectors as shown in Figure 2.3.[29] For some activities, the costs of any form

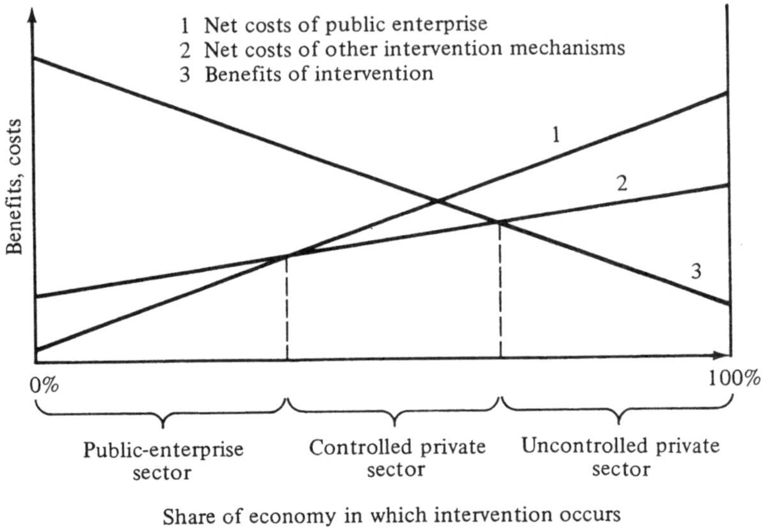

Figure 2.3. Partitioning of economy according to costs and benefits of intervention.

of intervention exceed the benefits and these can best be left in the uncontrolled private sector. For other activities, the costs of public enterprise are less than both the benefits and the costs of alternatives, thus determining a public enterprise sector. In the remainder of the economy, the costs of alternative intervention mechanisms are below both public-enterprise costs and the benefits of intervention, thus suggesting a controlled private sector.

Insofar as (1) countries face identical economic conditions (i.e., have identically positioned curves), (2) ideological, historical, and political influences are neutral, so that decisions are made on the basis of social-welfare maximization, (3) information on relative costs and benefits are widely available, and (4) distributional considerations are neutral, the equilibrium will be uniform across countries and national institutional partitionings will be identical. As these conditions are nowhere fulfilled, uniformity is not to be expected, but insofar as pragmatic considerations have influence, there will be at least pressures in this direction. This is the notion behind "convergence theory," which predicts and finds increasing similarities between economic institutions in the United States and the USSR.[30] Even if economic conditions are identical and distributional considerations are ignored, however, complete convergence is still not to be expected because in the middle range net benefits minus costs will be not only small but indeterminate because of information imperfections. There is thus likely to be a substantial range over which ideological and political predilection can and will operate at no great economic cost, and the United States and the USSR could be expected to settle at opposite ends of this band of indeterminancy.

Our contention is that this argument applies to the public-enterprise sector in LDCs. In similar countries there would be a common realm of institutional comparative advantage for public enterprise. There would also be a band of indeterminancy in which ideological and political factors would alter the outcome at no great expense, but economic pressures would over time force countries within this band. Countries differ, however, so that even purely pragmatic governments might still differ in their use of public enterprise. How might these differences affect the appropriate realm for public enterprise in LDCs as opposed to more-developed countries (MDCs)?

Costs and benefits in LDCs

How do the relative positions of the curves vary between MDCs and LDCs and within the LDC set? We make no pretense to being able to answer this question, as so little systematic comparative work has been done on the cost side. For example, consider the fact that the United States uses regulation and formal antitrust to deal with monopoly and oligopoly, whereas most of the rest of the world's mixed economies handle the same problems through a mixture of public enterprise and informal ''administrative guidance'' (the latter exemplified by countries as diverse as France and Japan). Why is this so? Is it because ideological bias blinds one set of countries to the institutional advantages of alternatives? Is it because the cost differences are really negligible as between forms of intervention? Or is it because the costs vary in different historical, political, and cultural nexuses and each country has chosen an optimal solution for its own environment? The comparative systems literature, in focusing on the polar extremes of planning and markets, has tended to ignore such issues of institutional choice, which are most relevant at the margin in mixed economies. We do not propose to redress this sort of imbalance here but merely to suggest a few factors that may be germane in determining the outcome.

A pragmatic choice as to the optimal organization of production is likely to differ substantially between LDCs and MDCs. Differences on the benefit side are clear-cut in favoring more intervention in LDCs, whereas those on the cost side probably argue in the opposite direction, making the net results indeterminant on a priori grounds without detailed study of relative magnitudes.

It is virtually tautological to argue that potential gross benefits from intervention are greater in LDCs, as extensive and pervasive market failures are part of the definition of underdevelopment. Information is absent, impacted, or costly. There is a shortage of capable entrepreneurs and managers. Externalities abound. Markets are small, so natural monopolies and oligopolies (which are a function of scale relative to market size) are much more common. Factors such as these affect the ability of markets to allocate resources and achieve the marginal conditions.

In MDCs both supply and demand curves are likely to be smoother, facilitating marginal adjustments as consumer tastes and better information, together with higher incomes and a greater variety of products, encourage substitution and easier adaption to price and quantity changes. On the supply side the greater mobility of factors geographically, and among various types of activity, tends to equalize factor prices and accommodate factor use to changing profit opportunities. In LDCs, on the other hand, the relative absence of these conditions tends to produce more and greater market failures and lack of opportunity for exploiting potential innovations. Demand and supply curves are not smooth and differences are discrete rather than marginal. On the demand side, handicaps of communication, transportation, and information yield different prices for similar products and the absence of variety discourages substitution. On the supply side, lack of factor mobility and the relative absence of market intermediaries tend to produce large differences in factor prices and factor availability both geographically and among different activities. In sum, market failures are more widespread and significant in LDCs.

Taken alone, the foregoing would argue for greater government intervention in LDCs. Consideration of cost factors, however, argues in the opposite direction. Shortages of entrepreneurial and managerial talent and of information constrain the public sector as well as the private. As a consequence, LDCs typically lack the competent and relatively uncorrupt civil services required to effectively administer controls and do not command the pool of experienced administrators and managers required to run public enterprises efficiently. As a consequence, our imagined body of pragmatic decision makers at the top do not have the same set of choices among various forms of organization that their counterparts might be expected to have in developed countries. Administrative cost considerations of this sort have led some experts to be much more skeptical of the wisdom of giving as large a role to public enterprise in LDCs as in MDCs. Administrative weakness is as much a characteristic of underdevelopment as market failure.

If gross costs of intervention are thus higher in LDCs, net costs are certainly less so because the organizational failures of private enterprise are also greater. Public enterprises may be far from exhibiting cost-minimizing behavior, but what of the family-run conglomerates that are often the institutional alternative?

The relative positions of the two net cost curves also might be expected to vary between LDCs and MDCs. If intervention in small-scale decentralized activities is more costly via public ownership as compared to tax–subsidy combinations, and if such activities - notably agriculture - constitute a larger fraction of output in LDCs, the public-enterprise tool will dominate alternative intervention mechanisms over a smaller fraction of national output. On the industry side, relative factor endowment may argue for more small-scale, labor-intensive activities where public-enterprise intervention is similarly more costly.

The various curves will also differ substantially across the highly heterogeneous set of LDCs. In part this will be due to differences in economic conditions. Large deposits of extractable natural resources will lift gross benefits in some sectors in countries so endowed and raise the left-hand side of the gross benefit curve. Small countries will have a greater fraction of the economy susceptible to natural monopoly and oligopoly than will larger countries at similar stages of development. Finally, the level of development varies greatly across the LDCs with some much closer to the MDC pole than to other LDCs.

Cost curves may also vary as a result of differences in political and cultural heritage, though this is far more hypothetical. ''Hard'' political structures may enable more effective control of public enterprises and reduce their costs relative to alternative means of intervention. The hierarchical orientation of East Asian Sinitic cultures may shift curves in the same direction if these cultures are more capable of handling the centralized forms of large-scale organizations as compared to more individualistic cultures. Differences in bureaucratic tradition – say British, French, American, and Sinitic – may have profound effects on the relative efficacy of different intervention mechanisms. Also, the degree of political, economic, religious, and ethnic homogeneity may alter the degree to which it is possible for a government to concern itself with such mundane matters as relative economic costs and benefits.

Finally, the relative positions of the cost curves are not immutable even within a particular country. Indeed, much of the public-enterprise literature is concerned with investigation of institutional structures that will reduce the gross costs of public enterprise. Although the historical record suggests skepticism as to the potential for rapid change, the possibility remains that better documented research can convince top decision makers to make the changes necessary to lower the gross cost curve.

If the net effect of this bewildering set of offsetting considerations is a priori agnosticism, sobeit. This merely points to the need for careful research leading to country- and industry-specific decisions rather than guidance by ideological predilection or historical inertia.

Ranking of activities

It is obviously of considerable practical interest to be able to rank activities according to their appropriateness for public operation. Three sorts of classification scheme might be used:

1. Industrial classification (e.g., cement on the left, truck gardening on the right)
2. Popular classification (e.g., basic or heavy industry on the left; light industry on the right)
3. Technical classification (e.g., those industries that are large relative to the product and factor markets on the left)

It is our contention that the technical form has far more normative and predictive power, and that the other two forms are useful only insofar as they serve as proxies in particular countries at particular times.

36 **Why public enterprise?**

Consider the cement industry, which is certainly "basic" in the sense that its output is critical to the growth of most modern sectors. Yet the net benefits from its nationalization are likely to be high (or even positive) only in those countries where its scale is large relative to product and factor markets. By modern standards, cement establishments are relatively small in absolute size and require only a relatively simple mechanical mixing technology. A medium-size economy is therefore capable of sustaining a fairly large number of such plants and it should be one of the earlier industries that private entrepreneurs are capable of financing and operating. A small economy, on the other hand, may be capable of sustaining only a single plant; and a very primitive economy may find finance and operation beyond the capacity of indigenous entrepreneurs and managers. Korea has 20 cement establishments, and these are all private. Sri Lanka has only 3 units and these are all public. Although ideological, historical, and political factors have played a role in determining these different outcomes, they are both quite consistent with a pragmatic solution. Popular and industrial descriptions are thus useful primarily as proxies for underlying technical characteristics. As the latter vary with national economic circumstance, the former are likely to be misleading in particular cases.

Consider the steel industry. Here scale with modern technology is large relative to product and factor markets in all but the largest and most developed economies. Here the "basic" and "industrial" proxies would seem to serve well. Although this is true if we confine ourselves to LDCs, the analysis does not extend to MDCs. To be sure, steel has been increasingly subject to nationalization (or other major forms of government intervention) in MDCs, but this has little to do with its "basic" nature or even its scale. Rather, it is because a combination of technological obsolescence and shifting relative prices makes its production increasingly noncompetitive in countries that were previously dominant. If there is a divergence between the social and private costs of exit (costs of reallocating labor and the presence of interest obligations, which represent private costs but social benefits), there is an economic argument for government intervention to defer bankruptcy until social marginal costs fall below social marginal benefits. Steel may be heavily public in both MDCs and LDCs, but the reasons are quite different, as are the policy implications. In one the goal is to manage decline systematically and in the other to manage growth. Hiring, training, and investment decisions are accordingly quite different.

"Nationalism" is another popular category that needs to be looked at in terms of its underlying technical motivations. As a political or ideological description it has explanatory value, but as an economic category, it is a rather broad proxy. Although expropriation of foreign firms is occasionally undertaken on a wholesale basis for ideological reasons, selective nationalization is far more common. What explains this is the differential industrial propensities to publicization. It is no accident that natural-resources extraction has the highest propensity. First, there is often a large pure economic rent to be extracted, and if institutional constraints (bookkeeping practices, transfer prices) make problematic the domestic expropriation of these rents via taxation, there is an economic argument for nationalization on the benefit side. Second, as pointed out by Vernon and Levy (Chapter 9), the costs of nationalization are a function of the existence and availability of alternative managerial and engineering skills (either through the training of nationals or the existence of an international factor market where such skills can be hired). The timing as well as the pattern of nationalization is thus explicable in part in terms of the underlying technical characteristics of the industry.

As another example of the importance of going beyond industrial classifications, consider export-oriented mineral extraction. For reasons just given, such activities are particularly likely to be in public enterprises. Sri Lanka, however, has left gemstone mining largely in private hands, despite its economic importance, economic rents, and countervailing ideological predilection. Why? Because these gems are typically found in alluvial deposits, requiring mining by a few men working in small widely separated pits. The technology of production is similar to truck gardening and its very small scale makes for high net costs of centralization. The rent is accordingly extracted by a monopsonistic public-marketing organization, but production is quite naturally left in private hands.

In sum, traditional and industrial descriptors can be useful proxies, especially in particular national settings. They are nonetheless only proxies, and serious attempts at ranking activities requires attention to underlying technical characteristics. We now consider some partial evidence on just what these characteristics are.

2.4 Evidence on revealed institutional advantage of public enterprise

The issues

In Section 2.2 we presented evidence suggesting that public enterprises are not randomly distributed but concentrated in particular industrial sectors. We now go a step deeper to ascertain the underlying technical characteristics of those industries chosen for public operation. The question is whether or not those characteristics define areas where the net benefits minus costs of public enterprise are liable to be particularly high. To the extent that they are, we have further confirmation of the role of pragmatic economic considerations in determining the size and structure of the public-enterprise sector. These revealed preferences also provide some preliminary guidance on the ranking of activities in terms of their appropriateness for public operation. The Korean case is first examined in some detail.

Korea: size relative to product market

The single most striking characteristic of the Korean public-enterprise sector is output-market concentration.[31] In 1972, 76% of public-enterprise value added was in markets that were egregiously imperfect (i.e., monopoly, monpsony, bilateral monopoly, or regulated oligopoly). Three-quarters of the remaining public-enterprise output was in manufacturing sectors with an output-weighted, International Standard Industrial Classification four-digit, four-company concentration ratio of 0.73, compared with 0.51 for the manufacturing sector as a whole. Public enterprises thus operated overwhelmingly in imperfect output markets, with at most 10% of value added sold in reasonably competitive markets.

The converse also held, with public enterprises dominating highly concentrated industries. For the mining and manufacturing sector, this is readily documented. Among all four-digit industries with four-firm concentration ratios of 0.70 or greater, there was at least one public enterprise in each of seven sectors, which together accounted for 73% of sales in the concentrated industries. Outside manufacturing no comparable statistics are available, but it is difficult to think of any major concentrated activity in Korea that does not have substantial public-enterprise participation.

Given this high correlation between public enterprise and imperfect competition, what was the direction of causation? One possibility is that the government used its power to protect its enterprises from competitive pressures. This is clearly the case with the Office of Monopoly (cigarettes and ginseng) where the goal was straightforward revenue maximization. In virtually all the other cases, however, enterprises have been in the public sector because they operate in imperfect markets rather than vice versa.

In sum, the single characteristic of size relative to product markets thus provides striking support for the hypothesis of economic pragmatism.[32] Virtually the entire sector in Korea consists of activities where gross benefits are likely to be particularly large for this reason alone.

Korea: size relative to factor market

Size relative to factor markets is a second technical characteristic defining activities where gross benefits are likely to be large. Using absolute enterprise size as a proxy, the correlation is notable but less impressive than for output-market concentration. Twenty of Korea's 50 largest enterprises were in the public sector in 1972, including 12 of the 16 largest. How might this result be explained in terms of cost and benefits? Gross benefits of intervention are liable to be high in such activities for two reasons:

1. Private entrepreneurial market failures will be greater the larger the scale of the activity relative to the accumulated stock of entrepreneurial capital and experience.
2. The dangers to the public of extensions of private market power increase with size.

Both these factors are only imperfectly reflected in our proxy measure, the first because our unit of observation is too large, the second because it is too small. The relevant measure for many entrepreneurial market failures is the establishment (rather than the enterprise), as it determines the technologically minimal scale. Some large Korean private enterprises consist of many establishments that have accrued sequentially in activities that are essentially small scale (trade, plywood, sugar, textiles, miscellaneous foodstuffs, highway transport, etc). Large enterprises need not exceed entrepreneurial capacities even when large establishments do. In addition, the rapidly expanding entrepreneurial capacity has meant that by the 1970s even relatively large establishments were within the capacity of private entrepreneurs (e.g., the first oil refinery was built in the early 1960s with public participation, the next two with private participation).

The relevant measure of economic power is the conglomerate family group, so that the enterprise measure used above substantially understates their influence. In fact, the size of such groups in Korea is growing rapidly and the government has made only the most modest efforts to restrict that growth. However, there has been a major effort to constrain the *influence* of this size by keeping the banks in the public-enterprise sector. By controlling credit allocation to the highly leveraged conglomerates, the government is able to constrain their influence.[33]

The foregoing gives a partial explanation of why enterprise size is a significant but imperfect predictor of inclusion in the public-enterprise sector. However, it covers only gross benefits, and net costs must also be considered. Many of the large private enterprises are in activities that are decentralized (e.g., trade) or produce export-oriented products requiring innovative foreign marketing (e.g., clothing), and in these sectors the costs of centralized, risk-averse decision making may be high.

Korea: capital intensity

Entrepreneurial market failures, and thus gross benefits of intervention, are likely to be higher in the most modern, capital-intensive, high-technology industries. Capital intensity (as measured by the ratio of the capital stock to employee compensation at the 117-sector level in 1972) for the public-enterprise sector is more than three times that of the Korean economy, almost triple that of the nonagricultural economy, and almost double that of Korean manufacturing. Public-enterprise manufacturing enterprises are themselves roughly twice as capital intensive as manufacturing as a whole. Public enterprises are thus overwhelmingly capital intensive in Korea.

The converse also holds, though to a somewhat lesser extent, with the capital-intensive sectors generally influenced by public operation. Of the 11 most capital-intensive sectors in the Korean economy, public enterprises produce virtually all output in 4 and are significant (10 to 50% of the market share) in 6. The single capital-intensive sector without public participation – cement – is instructive. Here high capital–labor ratios are combined with relatively small scale and relatively simple technology, so that entrepreneurial failures are likely to be absent.

Korea: high forward linkages

If the costs of administering intervention are significant, and rise with the size of the sector being centrally directed, it makes sense to concentrate intervention in those "basic" sectors where removal of distortions is particularly beneficial so that transmission to downstream users can be avoided. This can be measured using the Hirschmanian concept of linkages. Forward linkages represent sales to intermediate (rather than final) users, and backward linkages reflect purchases from intermediate producers. Industries with high linkages may thus have greater impact on other productive sectors and might be taken as representing "the commanding heights" of the economy.[34] In Korea, the public-enterprise sector as a whole has high forward linkages but modest backward linkages relative to the entire nonagricultural economy. Further, the public-enterprise manufacturing sector (excluding the consumer-oriented Office of Monopoly) has very high forward linkages relative to Korean manufacturing as a whole and virtually identical backward linkages.

Korea: export orientation

The Korean economy is heavily export oriented, yet the public-enterprise sector plays a negligible direct role. Only about 4.9% of public-enterprise output is exported, accounting for only 5.3% of total exports. In part this reflects the fact that Korean exports on the average are labor intensive, whereas public-enterprise production is capital intensive. It may also, however, reflect high organizational costs of public operation in an area where quick decisions, rapid adjustments, and innovative marketing are prerequisites to success (Jones and Wortzel, Chapter 11).

Korea: multicollinearity

The technical factors just described correlate with one another, of course, as well as with the dependent variable of publicness. When all the cross-correlations are positive, the characteristics just discussed, taken as a group, come very close to being both necessary and sufficient for publicness. Virtually all industries that are large relative to product and factor markets, are capital intensive, have high forward linkages, and are not export oriented have public participation. Where the cross-correlations are negative, trade-offs emerge. For example, consider those manufacturing sectors that are both highly concentrated (concentration ratios greater than 0.70) and large (1977 sales greater than $15 billion Korean dollars). Of 15 such sectors there is no public participation in 9, all of which have very low forward linkages (sugar, beer, candies, soft drinks, dairy products, paint, watches and clocks, meat processing).

In sum, the revealed determinants of the costs and benefits of publicness are multiple. Product-market concentration has a very large single-factor explanatory power, but the other elements also play an identifiable role.

Other countries: similarities

Because Korea has a particularly pragmatic, growth-oriented government, the explanatory power of the foregoing variables might be expected to be particularly large. Although we know of no other country where sufficiently detailed work has been done to permit similar quantification, casual empiricism suggests that technical factors play a major role in most countries. A few scattered pieces of evidence supporting this notion are:

1. Trebat, writing on Brazil and Mexico, observes that "in both countries (we can identify) a core group of 30–50 enterprises which, because of their size or influence on resource allocation, are the backbone of the respective public enterprise sectors. With some exceptions (e.g., CONASUPO in Mexico), these tend to be public enterprise monopolies or oligopolies."[35] He further reports that in 1978 the 10 largest enterprises in Brazil were all public enterprises, as were 7 of the next 15 largest firms.
2. Of the 52 largest LDC firms listed in *Fortune's* 1979 list of the 500 largest non-U.S. industrials, 34 were public enterprises. Further, these public enterprises accounted for three-quarters of total sales by listed LDC firms, as opposed to less than 10% for public enterprises among listed MDC firms.[36]
3. In Indian manufacturing in 1977–8, the 7 largest enterprises were public as were 12 of the top 16.[37] A list of the public-enterprise share of output in 135 mining and manufacturing product lines gives no less than 78 in which public enterprises produced from 90 to 100%, with 37 more in the 50 to 90% range.[38] The 100% category includes an impressive array of commodities ranging from petroleum to turbines to vitamin B_2.

Although these data are hardly definitive, they are certainly suggestive. The alternative to public enterprise is not the perfectly competitive private enterprise of economic theory but private monopoly or oligopoly. Writ large, the pattern of public enterprises in LDCs does not on the average seem inconsistent with pragmatic choices based on a cost–benefit calculus.

Based on theory, careful examination of the Korean data, and casual perusal of limited data elsewhere, we would propose the following hypothesis: The sectors where the benefits minus costs of public ownership are likely to be highest in mixed-economy LDCs are those with the following characteristics:

1. Large in scale relative to product market
2. Large relative to factor markets
3. Capital intensive
4. High forward linkages
5. High rent, natural-resource export

42 **Why public enterprise?**

6. Standardized products, easily marketed
7. Not requiring decentralized establishments

Other countries: exceptions

Although all countries are liable to have many individual exceptions to the foregoing hypothesis (e.g., small, sick companies taken over through conversion of debt to equity by public banks), their aggregate output would seem to generally be small relative to the public-enterprise sector as a whole. There are nonetheless a number of countries where, in addition to the sectors defined above, there is substantial aggregate output from small, differentiated producers of consumer goods.

In Malaysia, the government has a conscious policy of improving the lot of the ethnic Malay population, in part by integrating them into the entrepreneurial class (Mallon, Chapter 16). One major vehicle has been the establishment of large numbers of small public enterprises with a view to turning them over eventually to emergent Malay entrepreneurs. There is thus an ethnic distributional dimension to entrepreneurial failure. Available stocks of ethnic Chinese and Indian entrepreneurs could readily have undertaken such activities without public-enterprise intervention. The simple distribution-neutral efficiency conditions that we have focused on have thus been subordinated to what is perceived as a higher social goal.

In Bangladesh, wholesale nationalization at liberation resulted in large numbers of small, consumer-oriented enterprises moving into government hands, where they remain.[39] Two factors seem to have been at work. First, there was an ideological predisposition toward public enterprise on the part of some decision makers. Second, on the pragmatic side, the exodus of West Pakistanis and Biharis may have left inadequate numbers of domestic entrepreneurs and managers. To the extent the latter factor was operative, one would expect eventual divestiture of the smaller-scale activities as a domestic entrepreneurial class develops, as per the Malaysian plan.

Indonesia, like Malaysia and Bangladesh, has large numbers of small-scale public enterprises; unlike them, it is difficult to discern any pattern of explanation.[40] They are scattered across the literal and figurative landscape in a plethora of industries that combine public and private activity in a most eclectic pattern. If our analytic benefit–cost framework has any value, this is likely to entail rather substantial social costs.

These three examples serve to reemphasize two features of our approach. First, although economic factors explain a great deal, they do not come close to explaining everything. Second, where cost–benefit factors are ignored, or overridden, economic loss is likely to accrue. In Malaysia, these extra costs may be offset by distributional benefits, but in Indonesia, there would seem to be largely deadweight loss.

2.5 Conclusion

Our analytic framework may be summarized in the following propositions:[41]

1. The share of the public-enterprise sector in GNP is (by definition) the product of the industrial structure (the share of GNP generated in each sector) and the publicization propensity (the share of public enterprise in each sector).
2. The overall publicization propensity is a function of underlying economic, historical, political, and ideological propensities.
3. The economic publicization propensity in turn depends upon a purely pragmatic comparison of benefits and costs of public enterprise.
4. Benefits are conceived as flowing from the removal of imperfections resulting from market failures external to the enterprise.
5. Costs are conceived as following from organizational failures internal to the enterprise; and costs associated with public enterprise must be compared with those of alternative institutional intervention mechanisms.
6. Benefits and costs are a function of technical characteristics that have *both* an industry-specific and a country-specific environmental component – such as minimal efficient scale (an industry characteristic) relative to market size (a country characteristic).

Our low-order empirical survey suggests the following hypotheses for mixed-economy LDCs:

7. The share of the public-enterprise sector falls in a narrow range, with the majority of countries in the 7 to 15% region.
8. Much of the variance in GNP shares is explained by differential industrial structure (especially the share of large-scale mining) and this makes the publicization propensities even more uniform across countries than the GNP shares.
9. The historical, political, and ideological factors operate largely as country-specific shift parameters, meaning still greater uniformity across countries in the economic publicization propensities.
10. The economic propensities still vary across the countries for the same industry, primarily because the environmental characteristics differ[42] (e.g., the minimum efficient scale of cement is large relative to Sri Lanka's market but small relative to Korea's).
11. More controversially, in most countries, the economic propensities seem to dominate the historical, political, and ideological factors in determining the overall publicization propensity.

As an illustration, India and Korea generate virtually identical shares of GDP in the public-enterprise sector. This is due not to identical levels of the entire first layer of explanatory variables (industrial structure and the publicization propensity) but to rough correspondence, with differences that happen to offset one another. In the same vein, the similarity of the overall publicization propensity subsumes offsetting differences at lower levels of explanation. However, major differences between the two countries in ideology, history, and political factors seem to us to play only a minor role in explaining the overall publicization propensities, leaving the major role to be played by economic propensities.

Thus the major theme of this paper has been that economic factors – reflected in the costs and benefits of institutional choice – explain a great deal of the observed size and structure of public-enterprise sectors. There are, of course, countries in which other factors are quite important. Malaysia has established many small public enterprises to help ethnic Malays. Bangladesh took over many small-scale enterprises after its liberation struggle. Although economic considerations explain much, they do not explain everything.

We have made statements that are at once descriptive, predictive, and normative. This linkage can be justified only through some form of economic Darwinism: Governments do best that are rational and in the long run make choices consistent with pragmatic welfare maximization. A strong version would amount to single-causal economic determinism. This is absurd. The evidence clearly shows substantial divergence in the size, and to a lesser extent the structure, of public-enterprise sectors. Whereas a very important share of these differences is attributable to international variations in economic conditions, much is also clearly due to non-economic factors. There is nonetheless sufficient similarity across countries to support a weak version of economic Darwinism in which causation is multiple but in which there is a clear contribution from governments that respond *as if* they were rational welfare maximizers. Although this may be because decisions, in fact, are made on the basis of careful cost–benefit calculations, it more often results because economic conditions serve to constrain alternative decisions at the margin. For some activities the net costs of a wrong decision are so great that ideological predilection is eventually overcome. For other activities the net costs are smaller but still sufficient to tip the balance one way or the other when decisions are the result of political compromise between competing interest groups. In such circumstances a normative theory of the costs and benefits of public ownership and control also has descriptive–predictive value.

One major implication of our analysis is that institutional choices do matter a great deal in determining economic outcomes. Organizational failures are as important as market failures in explaining suboptimal economic performance. The failure of mainstream economists to direct much attention toward this source of economic inefficiency suggests a supoptimal allocation of professional resources.[43]

Our analysis implies a need for interdisciplinary studies of the effect of institutional choices on economic outcomes. Economists' empirical work generally explains outcomes only in terms of market variables. Other social scientists examine the behavior of various institutional structures without examining the economic costs and benefits of that behavior. Research strategies that recognize outcomes as a function of both markets and institutions are needed. This is particularly true of those institutional forms intermediate between market and plan, which constitute the marginal opportunity set of mixed economies. Public enterprise, a particularly important subset, ultimately can be fully understood only in terms of its institutional opportunity costs.

Notes

1 A short definition of public enterprise encompasses organizations owned and/or controlled by governments (central, provincial, and local) and financed largely by selling in a market. For a more elaborate definition and a discussion of alternatives see Leroy P. Jones, *Public Enterprise and Economic Development: The Korean Case* (Seoul: Korean Development Institute, 1975), pp. 22–42.
2 See Patrick O'Brien, *The Revolution in Egypt's Economic System* (New York: Oxford University Press, 1961), p. 214.
3 Peter Evans, "Multinationals, State-Owned Corporations, and the Transformation of Imperialism: A Brazilian Case Study," *Economic Development and Cultural Change* 26, No. 1 (Oct. 1977):43–64.
4 Peter Evans, *Dependent Development: The Alliance of Multinationals, State and Local Capital in Brazil* (Princeton: Princeton University Press, 1979).
5 Rehman Sobhan and Muzaffer Ahmad, *Public Enterprise in an Intermediate Regime: A Study in the Political Economy of Bangladesh* (Dacca: Bangladesh Institute of Development Studies, 1980).
6 Leroy Jones and Il Sakong, *Government, Business and Entrepreneurship: The Korean Case* (Cambridge: Harvard University Press, 1980), pp. 105–6.
7 Talcott Parsons, "Some Reflections on the Institutional Framework of Economic Development," in *The Challenge of Development*, ed. Alfred Bonne (Jerusalem: 1958), p. 123.
8 Except as noted, all data in this subsection come from two sources: N. S. Ramaswamy, V. J. Kesary, P. V. George, G. K. Nayar, V. G. Kamath and P. D. Deenadayalu, *Performance of Indian Public Enterprises* (New Delhi: Standing Conference of Public Enterprises, 1978); and Jones, *Public Enterprise and Economic Development*.
9 "Industrial Policy Resolution of 1956," in Government of India, *Second Five Year Plan* (New Delhi: Central Statistical Organization, 1956), p. 47.
10 Park Chung Hee, *Our Nation's Path* (Seoul: Hollym, 1970), p. 218.
11 Railways were 32% of transport and communications in India in 1972–3 but only 10% in Korea in 1973. Thus, if the Korean rail system had been as important as India's, the public-enterprise share of transport and communications would have risen to 53% in Korea vs. the 61% figure reported for India. Calculated from Jones, *Public Enterprise and Economic Development*, pp. 76 and 236, and Government of India, *Statistical Abstract 1975* (New Delhi: Central Statistical Organization, 1976), p. 409.
12 This cumbersome term is used to refer to both the take-over of existing firms (i.e., nationalization) and the establishment of new ones.
13 Sobhan and Ahmad, *Public Enterprise in an Intermediate Regime*, pp. 7–17.
14 Il Sakong, "Macroeconomic Aspects of Public Enterprise in Asia: A Comparative Study," working paper, (Seoul: Korea Development Institute, 1979), pp. 47–50.
15 Many reports of higher shares are simply incorrect. A common fallacy is to take public-enterprise *sales* as a share of GDP or GNP. Definitional problems generally

46 **Why public enterprise?**

create only small errors, except where there is a failure to distinguish between the public-enterprise sector and the public sector as a whole. Another common source of difficulty is using the much higher asset or investment shares as a proxy for value-added shares.

16 Frederick L. Pryor, "Public Ownership: Some Quantitative Dimensions," in *Public Enterprise: Economic Analysis of Theory and Practice,* ed. William G. Shepherd (Lexington, Mass.: Lexington Books, 1976), pp. 3–22. Measured as a share of employment. Note that the "public sector" includes "public institutions" – which do not market their output (e.g., the military) – as well as public "enterprise."

17 Sakong, "Macroeconomic Aspects of Public Enterprise in Asia," p. 55.

18 The use of a market-failure approach to explaining the size and structure of the public-enterprise sector in LDCs is hardly novel. Predecessors include John B. Sheahan, "Public Enterprise in Developing Countries," in *Public Enterprise: Economic Analysis of Theory and Practice,* ed. William G. Shepherd (Lexington, Mass.: Lexington Books, 1976), pp. 205–33; Deepak Lal, "Public Enterprises," mimeographed (London, 1977), and Jones, *Public Enterprise and Economic Development,* pp. 13–18.

19 Some 2,000 small-scale decentralized units in rice and flour milling and cotton ginning were divested. See Investment Advisory Centre of Pakistan, *Role of Performance of Public Enterprises in the Economic Growth of Pakistan* (Karachi: IACP, 1979).

20 Jan Tinbergen, "Optimal Organization of the Economy," in *Public Expenditure Analysis,* ed. Balbir S. Sahni (Rotterdam: Rotterdam University Press, 1972), pp. 21–35.

21 For introductions to these bodies of literature, see Harvey Leibenstein, *Beyond Economic Man* (Cambridge: Harvard University Press, 1976); Henry Simon, *Administrative Behavior* (New York: Macmillan, 1976); Oliver Williamson, *Markets and Hierarchies* (New York: Free Press, 1975); Eric Furubotn and Scetozar Pejovich, *The Economics of Property Rights* (Cambridge, Mass.: Lippincott, Ballinger, 1974); and A. M. Spence, "The Economics of International Organization: An Introduction," *Bell Journal of Economics,* 6, No. 1 (Spring 1975):163–72.

22 This does not pertain, of course, if a negative value is placed on an increase in the welfare of some individual or group.

23 H. Linnemann, J. P. Pronk, and Jan Tinbergen, "Convergence of Economic Systems in East and West," in *Comparative Economic Systems,* ed. Morris Bornstein (Homewood, Ill.: Irwin, 1974), pp. 493–510. Also see Jan Tinbergen, "The Significance of Welfare Economics for Socialism," in *On Political Economy and Econometrics: Essays in Honor of Oscar Lange,* ed., the Anniversary Committee of the Polish Scientific Publishers (Oxford: Pergamon Press, 1965), pp. 591–9.

24 Examples of second-best interventions in terms of public-enterprise pricing are found in Abram Bergson, "Optimal Pricing for a Public Enterprise," *Quarterly Journal of Economics* 36, (Nov. 1972):519–44, and W. J. Baumol and W. J. Bradford, "Optimal Departures from Marginal Cost Pricing," *American Economic Review* 60, No. 3 (June 1970):265–83.

25 Leroy P. Jones, "Performance Evaluation of Public Enterprises: A Methodology with an Application to Asian Fertilizer Plants," mimeographed (Boston University).

26 William S. Comanor and Harvey Leibenstein, "Allocative Efficiency, *X*-Efficiency and the Measurement of Welfare Losses," *Economica* 36, No. 3 (Aug. 1969):304–9.

27 Sheahan, "Public Enterprise," pp. 206–10.

28 A case can certainly be made that the curves are not linear but "*U*-shaped," reflecting initial scale economies in supervision. We omit this complication as it does not alter the main points of our argument.

29 Figure 2.2, like the one that precedes it, has only heuristic value, because a particular activity need not, and generally will not, be horizontally coincident on the different curves. That is, it may be on the left of the benefits curve but on the right of one of the cost curves. Only benerve that, when positive, depicts a public-enterprise sector.

30 E.g., see Linnemann, Pronk, and Tinbergen, "Convergence of Economic Systems."

31 All data in this subsection are from Jones, *Public Enterprise and Economic Development.*

32 That public enterprises overwhelmingly sell in imperfect output markets also has a major implication on the cost side. To the extent that public operation entails cost inefficiencies, these must be financed somehow. In noncompetitive internal markets these may be passed on in part to the consumer, whereas in competitive internal or export markets they cannot. This fact by no means reduces the real costs of public enterprise but does serve to mask them and reduce pressures for reform.

33 For elaboration on the role of family conglomerates in Korea and the role of public banks in controlling their behavior, see Jones and Sakong, *Government, Business and Entrepreneurship,* pp. 101–10.

34 Direct plus indirect domestic linkages are theoretically superior measures but at this level of generality yield similar results and for present purposes do not warrant the greater expository detail. See Jones, *Public Enterprise and Economic Development,* pp. 98–105.

35 Thomas Trebat, "Public Enterprises in Brazil and Mexico: Comparative Structure, Control and Performance," mimeographed (New York: Bankers Trust, 1980), pp. 15, 18.

36 Leroy Jones, "Public Enterprise in Less-Developed Countries," *Wall Street Journal,* Dec. 7, 1979, p. 15.

37 Documentation Centre for Corporate and Business Policy Research, *The Future of Public Sector in India* (New Delhi: DCCBPR, 1979), pp. S-63–4.

38 Ibid., pp. S-6 to S-13. Figures are largely in quantities, so it is not possible to calculate how large a fraction of public-enterprise output is in highly concentrated industries; however, there can be no question that the figure is very high.

39 See Sobhan and Ahmad, "Public Enterprise in an Intermediate Regime."

40 See Malcolm Gillis and Ralph E. Beals, *Tax and Investment Policy for Hard Minerals: Public and Multinational Enterprise in Indonesia* (Cambridge, Mass.: Ballinger, 1980).

41 The propositions also could be formalized, of course, in a set of equations involving vector and matrix algebra, but for present nonquantitative purposes, the verbal equivalent will suffice.

42 And to a limited extent because optimal technical characteristics vary with factor endowment to the extent that factor substitution is possible.

43 For elaboration on this argument in a wider context, see Charles Wolf, Jr., "Economic Efficiency and Inefficient Economics," *Journal of Post-Keynesian Economics,* No. 3 (Fall 1979):71–82.

[3]

Managing state-owned enterprises

In all countries—developing and developed, market and socialist—governments are showing increasing concern over the performance of their state-owned enterprises (SOEs). One reason is that SOEs make large and growing claims on the budget. In a sample of twenty-seven developing countries in 1976–79, the net budgetary payment to nonfinancial SOEs averaged more than 3 percent of GDP. Current spending alone—subsidies and other transfers—represented 1.4 percent of GDP. State enterprises are also important foreign borrowers; nonfinancial SOEs accounted for 28 percent of all Eurocurrency borrowing by developing countries in 1980.

Governments, intent on curbing SOE borrowing and getting value for the money they spend, are searching for ways to improve SOE efficiency. In theory, efficiency is highest when an enterprise strives to maximize profits in a competitive market, under managers with the autonomy, motivation, and capability to respond to the challenge of competition. Inefficient enterprises would not be able to compete and would go bankrupt. But SOEs seldom face such conditions. Governments may have established SOEs for reasons quite different from—and often incompatible with—profit maximization. SOEs often operate in noncompetitive markets; the absence of competition is one reason for creating them. Their autonomy is often compromised by government intervention in their operating decisions. Managers may not be held accountable for results or given incentives to improve performance. The way they are selected and rewarded often encourages qualities more appropriate to a central bureaucracy than to a competitive enterprise. Even nonviable SOEs are seldom liquidated.

These special constraints on SOEs need not become an excuse for poor performance. Efficiency can be greatly enhanced by setting clear and attainable objectives, reducing undue interference, holding management accountable for results, designing a framework of incentives, and developing a team of managers with appropriate skills. These are the main topics of this chapter, which ends with a review of the issues involved in liquidating and privatizing SOEs.

The growing fiscal burden

Accounting deficiencies and different ways of classifying SOEs make it difficult to generalize about their financial performance or to assess the return to capital. Available data for SOEs in twenty-four developing countries showed a small operating surplus before depreciation in 1977. However, no account was taken of interest payments, subsidized input prices, taxes, or accumulated arrears. Proper provision for these items and depreciation would show SOEs in many of these countries to be in deficit.

Since SOEs often control some of the largest revenue-earning activities (petroleum and mining, for example), their poor aggregate performance is especially disturbing. Evidence from individual countries indicates low and declining profitability. For example, Turkish public enterprises, which were breaking even in the early 1970s, averaged net losses equivalent to 3.9 percent of GDP during 1977–79. Subsequent policy measures resulted in a profit of 0.1 percent of GDP in 1981 and an estimated 0.5 percent in 1982. Mexican SOEs (excluding the state petroleum company), which earned profits equivalent to 0.3 percent of GDP in 1970, showed a net loss of 1.2 percent of GDP in 1980. Senegal's SOEs, which had been in surplus in the mid-1970s, recorded a deficit in 1977–78 and again in 1979–80, and the number of money-losing companies reached forty-two (out of sixty-eight in 1980). The picture is not entirely black; in India, for example, the gross pretax return on capital employed grew from 7.8 percent (before interest payments) in 1980–81 to 12.2 percent in 1981–82. Low profitability limits the ability of SOEs to self-finance their investments, increasing their dependence on central government resources. Figure

FIGURE 8.1

Net claims on the budget of nonfinancial state-owned enterprises

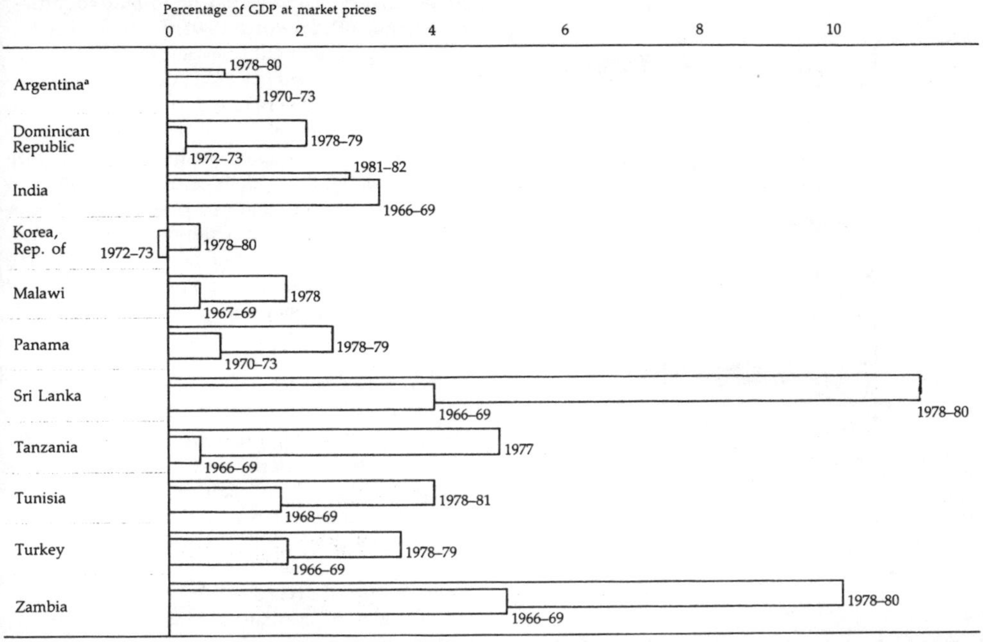

The length of the bars indicates government subsidies, transfers, and net lending to nonfinancial SOEs, less SOE dividends and interest payments to government, as a percentage of GDP at market prices.

a. Major enterprises only.

Sources: World Bank; Peter Short (1983).

8.1 shows how the net claims on the budget have grown for a sample of twelve developing countries. These figures include legitimate and desirable equity investments by government, of course, but they also reflect the limited ability of SOEs to generate internal resources.

In an aggregate analysis it is impossible to determine the extent to which these results reflect general economic conditions or price controls and how much they are caused by a failure to minimize costs or maximize productivity. Evidence from individual enterprises indicates substantial room for efficiency gains. A modest improvement in efficiency could have significant effect. For example, a 5 percent increase in SOE revenues plus a 5 percent drop in costs would generate resources amounting to:

- Almost 2 percent of GDP in Turkey, or 10 percent of tax revenues
- Some 1.5 percent of GDP in Tanzania, enough to finance all its spending on health
- As much as 2.2 percent of GDP in Mali—roughly two-thirds of expenditure on education or twice that on health
- Some 1.4 percent of GDP in Bolivia—14 percent of tax revenue or one and a half times the spending on health.

The nature of SOEs

The term "state-owned enterprise" covers all state-owned industrial and commercial firms, mines, utilities, and transport companies, as well as financial intermediaries. The number of SOEs has been on the rise in most countries. Figure 8.2 shows the increase in a sample of eight countries. SOEs are distinguished from the rest of the government because their revenue comes from the sale of goods and services and because they are self-accounting and have a separate legal identity. Beyond that, their circumstances and characteristics may appear to vary widely. A state enterprise might be op-

FIGURE 8.2

Growth of nonfinancial state-owned enterprises

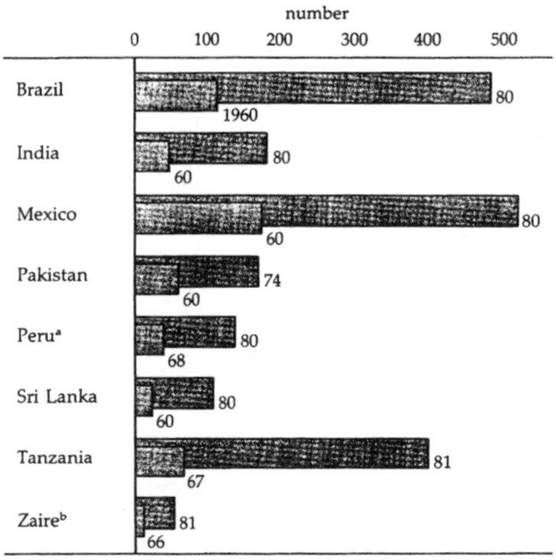

The length of the bars indicates the number of majority state-owned enterprises in selected countries for specific years. Local government SOEs are not included.

a. Includes minority shareholdings.
b. 100 percent state-owned enterprises only.

erating in a command economy surrounded by other SOEs, or it may be one of a handful of state firms in a predominantly free market.

In practice, however, SOEs share many qualities. Most economies are a mixture of markets and central controls, and whatever the mixture, the problems of trying to ensure SOE efficiency are strikingly similar. Conflicting objectives, insufficient SOE autonomy, inadequate measures for judging performance, lack of incentives linked to performance, and bureaucratic rather than commercial management styles—all these have prompted attempts at reform in socialist and market economies alike. When such reforms fail, the consequences are also similar. Every economy finds that financial weaknesses in SOEs are transmitted to other public and private firms. They suffer if SOEs command financial resources to which others might ordinarily be entitled, or if they fail to supply promised goods or services.

Increased SOE efficiency typically requires internal improvements—better financial management, more careful inventory control, and a balanced production line, for example. But these reforms will not solve the wider problems of relations between SOEs and government. This chapter will concentrate on these common problems of SOEs and suggest ways of tackling them. Of course, suggestions have to be tailored to the characteristics of individual firms and countries. A government's approach toward a manufacturing SOE selling in competitive export markets will differ from its treatment of a large, natural monopoly. The former might be required to maximize profits; the latter's prices might be set according to its marginal cost or it might be required to minimize costs. Similarly, the options of countries will vary. In some countries it might be possible to fire poor SOE managers and replace them with better ones. A country with less managerial talent might have no alternative but to try and improve the skills of its less capable managers.

Defining objectives

One of the most important and difficult tasks for governments is to clarify and rank the objectives of their SOEs. Where state enterprises are expected to pursue both commercial and social goals and to answer to many different constituencies, their performance will suffer unless they are given a clear sense of priorities. Without that, their results cannot be measured against expectations, while losses can be too easily attributed to social goals, and poor management thereby concealed.

The cost of noneconomic goals

SOEs are frequently expected to contribute to the broader goals of government policy. The consequences can be perverse, as illustrated by the experience of the Ghana Cocoa Marketing Board (see Box 8.1). For instance, SOE prices may be controlled in order to benefit the poor or to assist counterinflationary policies. But SOE consumers are often large industrial users or wealthy people, so they—not the poor—benefit most. For instance, energy and food subsidies in Egypt in 1979 amounted to more than $4 billion; three-quarters of the subsidies went to the relatively more affluent urban areas and 62 percent of these went to the richer half of the urban population. Furthermore, the costs of subsidies are shifted from the consumer to the taxpayer or, if the deficit is financed through inflationary monetary expansion, to the public at large. Given the regressive nature of taxes in many developing countries and the impact of inflation on the poor, the net result may be to increase income inequalities.

Box 8.1 Conflicting objectives: the Ghana Cocoa Marketing Board

Agricultural marketing boards are often subject to conflicting economic and social objectives. Those principally concerned with the domestic market for basic foodstuffs are expected to shield consumers (mostly urban) from scarcities and high food prices while simultaneously protecting farmers' incomes. Boards that deal mainly with export crops are expected both to raise fiscal revenues and to insulate farmers from fluctuations in world prices. Experience in Ghana illustrates what can happen when one conflicting objective becomes dominant.

The Ghana Cocoa Marketing Board (CMB) was established in 1947, following pressures from farmers to eliminate middlemen and traders. Initially CMB's stated objective was to market and export cocoa and to stimulate the activities of smallholders. After ten years of operation, however, CMB's governing legislation had been amended by two other objectives: to protect farmers from extreme fluctuations in world cocoa prices and to tax export earnings. The revenue objective finally prevailed over the other goals. Producer prices were initially set to cover the board's development and operating costs and to allow it to accumulate reserves. However, the need for government revenues soon predominated: after 1965, the board was no longer permitted to hold reserves. The government's share of sales revenues increased from 3 percent in 1947–48 to almost 30 percent after 1953–54 and reached 60 percent in 1978–79. CMB's share of revenues was set to cover operating costs and rarely exceeded 20 percent; farmers' earnings became a residual.

As a result of this policy and of the overvalued exchange rate, the price received by Ghanaian cocoa farmers has been declining in real terms since the early 1960s. By 1979 producer prices averaged about half their 1963 level, even after taking account of subsidies on seeds and other inputs. Furthermore, the CMB was unable to protect farmers from sharp price fluctuations. The prices they were paid fell by 30 percent in 1949–50, by 17 percent in 1959–60, and by 34 percent in 1965–66.

As cocoa has become less profitable, Ghana's production has plummeted—from a peak of about 540,000 tons in 1965 to about 250,000 tons in 1979. The volume of exports has fallen by almost 80 percent over the same period. An estimated 45,000 tons a year has been smuggled to neighboring countries, a foreign exchange loss equivalent to about 15 percent of the average value of Ghana's exports in 1974–78. By 1979 Ghana had lost its rank as first world producer and exporter of cocoa, which it had held since the early 1960s. Many farmers have switched to other crops, such as maize and rice, which in Ghana yield a net return per hectare about twice that of cocoa. But this switching still involves heavy losses for the country. If farmers were to receive even half the world price for cocoa and no input subsidies, their net return per hectare (at 1979 prices) would be more than seven times that of rice and more than fifty times that of maize.

Similarly, SOEs are often used to expand employment. The excessive wage bills that result can seriously damage an SOE's financial performance while overmanning can be bad for morale. Since SOEs are usually capital-intensive, they can make only a limited contribution to alleviating unemployment. In a survey of seventeen developing countries in 1982, nonfinancial SOEs were responsible for less than 15 percent of modern sector employment, ranging from a low of 5.5 percent in Latin America to a high of 20.4 percent in Africa.

Where noncommercial achievements are expected of SOEs, a government can judge the net gain (or loss) to society only by making these goals explicit and by calculating their costs and benefits. But a strong case can be made for letting an enterprise operate on commercial, profit-seeking lines, and then using its profits to achieve social goals. The profits of an SOE could then be invested to generate new growth and jobs, rather than siphoned into paying the wages of redundant workers. A commercially oriented SOE can be a most effective tool for improving social welfare, as exemplified by the experience of the Kenya Tea Development Authority (KTDA—see Box 8.2).

Setting objectives

In practice it is hard to define targets for SOEs by an assessment of costs and benefits. Often there are strong political motives for keeping objectives fuzzy and not analyzing trade-offs. But since noneconomic goals are frequently given as a reason for poor performance, governments should at least view this excuse with skepticism and require SOE managers to document the financial effects of having to meet such goals.

Some governments have gone further. France and Senegal, for example, have negotiated formal agreements with SOEs to establish a clearer operating framework (see Box 8.3). Under such arrangements, governments pledge to meet their financial obligations and to eschew ad hoc interference; for their part, SOEs accept negotiated performance targets. The agreements help both parties to translate vague intentions into specific tasks. Contracts also make the costs of achieving objectives more transparent, thus allowing a more rational consideration of costs and benefits. Their success rests on substantial political commitment—as well as a readiness of both parties to

Box 8.2 Autonomy, accountability, and incentives: KTDA

The Kenya Tea Development Authority (KTDA) was created as a state-owned enterprise in the early 1960s. It has organized the planting of about 54,000 hectares of tea by some 138,000 smallholders, and has become a major processor and the world's largest exporter of black tea. Thanks to its commercial orientation, KTDA developed an industry that substantially benefits the 1 million members of tea-grower households plus untold numbers of laborers, traders, and others in the economically vibrant tea districts. KTDA achieved these results without operating subsidies, in marked contrast to the generally poor results of smallholder tea schemes in South Asia or elsewhere in East Africa. Its success has had three ingredients:

- Autonomy. KTDA was set up to be a commercial enterprise and was not given many secondary social responsibilities. It has never been financially dependent on the government. Its start-up and development costs were financed largely by external borrowing. Its operating costs are covered by a flat-rate levy deducted from the monthly "first payment" to farmers. (Growers receive a fixed payment per kilogram every month and a second payment based on market prices at the end of each season.) Although the levy has not changed for the past ten years, KTDA has avoided government subsidies by keeping down costs. Good performance and support from growers helped secure independence.

From the outset KTDA had control over all strategic aspects of tea production: credit, extension, propagation, transport, processing, and marketing. With such authority KTDA could tightly control the quality of the tea—often a weakness of smallholder production. KTDA has also moved into factory operations and thus controlled the quality of processed tea.

- Accountability. Since KTDA's objectives were clearly defined, the government was able to develop a set of standards against which its performance could be evaluated. Through its representative on the board, the government holds KTDA responsible for results. Added to this, the tea growers sit on district tea committees and are represented on KTDA's board. Some are also shareholders in KTDA factories or members of factory boards. The growers play an important role since they have strong personal incentives to hold the Authority to high standards. Similarly, KTDA's factory managers, workers, and field staff are held accountable for results by their supervisors; their performance is monitored and evaluated against predetermined standards.

- Incentives. The basic set of incentives for both growers and KTDA is provided by world market prices. KTDA has not tried to insulate itself from that market by building up large reserves (or running deficits). Sustained market pressure is thus used to enhance the drive for premium tea production by demonstrating the direct link between quality and returns.

In recent years KTDA has become vulnerable to the falling trend in world tea prices. Its finances have also been threatened by a drop in output because of drought and some shift by growers to higher-income crops. Furthermore, KTDA is moving from a phase of rapid expansion to one of consolidating its gains, a transition that has been difficult for both public and private enterprises throughout the world.

renegotiate if the contracts are threatened by unforeseen economic developments.

Control without interference

SOE autonomy needs to be counterbalanced by some central control. Unless governments monitor the performance of their SOEs and make the main decisions on investment and debt, their macroeconomic management will be undermined, as Brazil's experience has demonstrated (see Box 8.4). Yet central control can itself be poorly organized. All too often, different official agencies intervene in SOE decisions that should be the prerogative of management, and yet government fails to coordinate their action. Too much interference can be combined with too little control. In addition, policy that swings between autonomy and central control can prevent coherent direction of SOEs. The challenge is to design a system that holds management accountable for results while giving it the power to achieve them.

Institutional links between government and enterprise

To try and reduce arbitrary intervention by government, countries have devised institutional arrangements that place government at arms' length from SOEs. Boards of directors or holding companies have been widely used to create a buffer between SOE management and the central bureaucracy, to provide policy direction, and to report on results. Special bureaus, commissions, and ministries have become a popular way of centralizing information and control of SOEs.

These arrangements have a mixed record, showing that institutional changes alone rarely achieve a satisfactory balance between independence and control. Furthermore, arrangements that work well for one country or enterprise may not do so elsewhere. For example, the successful Ethiopian Telecommunications Authority has a politically oriented board of directors dominated by a minister (see Box 8.5)—an arrangement that has proved disastrous in other countries.

To avoid such direct political control, many countries rely on holding companies. Some have proved a useful way of achieving government aims while giving SOEs greater discretion in day-to-day operational matters; others have become counterproductive, substituting one form of ex-ante bureaucratic intervention for another. An added drawback of introducing an extra layer of bureaucracy is that it also uses scarce managerial resources.

On the positive side, the Istituto per la Ricostruzione Industriale (IRI) in Italy has been credited with cooperating with government to achieve its social goals while freeing the individual enterprises to pursue profits. Nevertheless, IRI has been caught between conflicting government aims—such as the directive to make profits and yet support failing subsidiaries to bolster employment. Holding companies can also provide technical assistance and managerial talent. Portugal's holding

Box 8.3 Contracts between the state and its enterprises: the experience of France and Senegal

France

The concept of contracts for state enterprises was first introduced in France in the late 1960s to increase both the autonomy and accountability of SOE managers. Initially only two contracts between government and SOEs were signed; four more were added in 1979, and in 1981 the new government announced its intention to negotiate more contracts with the expanded state enterprise sector. By early 1983, eight contracts had been signed and more were being negotiated.

The French experience has been mixed. The first two contracts were overtaken by the 1973 oil shock and subsequent stagflation; although they contained procedures for revisions, these were not adequate to cope with the unprecedented conditions of the mid-1970s. A serious deficiency of the agreements was their failure to specify remedies for nonperformance. The contract with the electricity company provided that the state could suspend the contract if the results were not achieved, but adjustment rather than suspension is often the more appropriate response. The plans were also weakened or opposed by the bureaucracy, which disliked the degree of pricing freedom which contracts would have given SOEs.

Despite these shortcomings, the contracts have helped clarify relations between the state and SOEs. They allowed the implications of government's pricing and subsidy policy to be discussed. The medium-term focus of the contracts (most covered three to five years) required the government to be more consistent in its policies, particularly in the annual discussions of the enterprises' investment programs. Furthermore, the contracts made the company's results more transparent, by distinguishing between normal operations and social objectives. For example, the railway's contract specified that the company be compensated for losses on passenger lines that it was not allowed to close. Similarly, Air France was compensated for having to operate the Caravelle IIIs and to split operations between two Paris airports.

Senegal

The Senegalese government has negotiated contract plans with five SOEs since 1980, and is in the process of negotiating five more. Although it is too early to draw any firm conclusions, initial results are promising and suggest some lessons for other developing countries.

The preparation of the three-year plans helped in strategic planning for the SOEs. It forced them to identify the sources of their operating deficits, and to articulate medium-term operating and investment goals. Thus, for the first time Air Senegal and the Dakar bus company (SOTRAC) calculated losses per passenger-kilometer on certain services that the government obliged them to operate.

The contracts allowed the government to compare more systematically the cost of social objectives and investment proposals with their benefits. As a result, loss-making air services to certain remote areas were cut back. The government also reconsidered a costly investment in passenger rail equipment after the railway's plan presented a thorough quantification of its long-term implications for the company's debt service and operating revenues. Ultimately, senior ministers decided to concentrate new investment on freight, rather than passenger, traffic. The government also adopted formulas for regular tariff adjustments linked to increases in the cost of inputs (especially fuel) for most enterprises. It agreed to place limits on staff numbers to protect enterprises from pressures to take on excess or ill-qualified personnel.

Most of the contracts have produced measurable improvements in SOE performance. SOTRAC has been guaranteed regular tariff increases, quarterly payment of a specific subsidy for money-losing suburban lines, and financial support for more buses and a second maintenance terminal. For its part, the company has set strict targets for worker productivity, maintenance, and more efficient fleet utilization targets which, so far, it has met. Improvements in cash flow alone enabled SOTRAC to eliminate its bank overdraft and 30 percent of its arrears to suppliers in the first year of the contract. The one contract that seems to have failed did so because of the magnitude of the restructuring required to reduce the company's substantial operating deficit.

Initially, the effect of the contracts on the budget and investment program was not adequately assessed. Nor was provision made for monitoring performance with agreed sanctions in the case of noncompliance. The Senegalese government is taking steps to remedy this, including six-month joint reviews of contract execution.

Box 8.4 The control of state-owned enterprises in Brazil

Until 1979 the Brazilian government had no consolidated information on earnings, spending, or debt of its SOEs. It therefore had no way of comparing consolidated public investment with financial resources, so public investment often exceeded the amount of money actually available, thus increasing inflation and the country's foreign debt.

In addition to their own revenues earned on the sale of goods and services, the SOEs received substantial transfers from the government. These included earmarked tax revenues, credits from official financial institutions, inter-enterprise transfers, and loan guarantees. With the multiplication of these extrabudgetary funds, control over the economic and financial operations of SOEs was gradually eroded. Projects were started without adequate provision for their financing, and supplementary transfers were often required to prevent large-scale layoffs and defaults to suppliers, contractors, and creditors.

Faced with growing inflationary pressures and a deteriorating balance of payments, in 1979 the government introduced a series of significant reforms. It phased out most of the SOEs' earmarked taxes, and centralized authority over SOE finances in a new agency in the Planning Ministry, the Special Secretariat for Control of the State Enterprises (SEST). SEST is responsible for approving and monitoring the budgets for 382 SOEs and autonomous institutions. These are summarized in an annual SEST budget authorized by the president. All foreign and domestic credit operations by these SOEs require prior SEST approval, as do any proposals to create, expand, or liquidate any state enterprise. So far the Planning Ministry and SEST have been primarily concerned with setting and enforcing firm-by-firm ceilings. They have not become seriously involved in evaluating SOE investment plans, but this may change as a result of the first multiyear consolidation of government investment programs in 1982.

Box 8.5 Ethiopian Telecommunications Authority

The Ethiopian Telecommunications Authority (ETA) has expanded its telecommunication services rapidly, and in the main cities quality is considered good for a developing country. For example, periodic checks show that less than 2 percent of test calls fail due to congestion or faulty equipment. ETA's telephone service is one of the least expensive in Africa, yet it has generated a good financial rate of return on net assets. This allows it to make a reasonable contribution to its investment; 33 percent of the latest program will be financed internally. Labor productivity is high for a developing country: ETA has 50 staff per 1,000 telephone lines, compared with 75 to 150 staff per 1,000 lines in most African countries.

The Authority is run by a policymaking board and a professional manager. Board members are all government officials; the chairman is the minister of transport and communications. Its composition gives the board a political, policymaking orientation. The company's general manager, in contrast, is recruited from the ranks of ETA, and is expected to run the company as a commercial operation within the guidelines set by the board. While board membership has changed frequently, there has been reasonable continuity in ETA's top management, with only six general managers since 1952.

The board conveys the government's general objectives to the firm's management, which then draws up a five-year corporate plan for review and amendment by the board. ETA's current plan responds to the priority the Ethiopian government has assigned to increasing rural services. The company also submits an annual budget with quantitative targets; at the end of the year the board compares results against targets, holding managers accountable and removing them for poor performance.

By channeling its objectives through the board, the government has helped avoid putting conflicting demands on ETA. ETA's board has powers that in many other countries are vested in several different ministries and agencies. It sets tariffs, hires and fires the general manager, and gives final approval to the company's staffing plan, budget, and investment proposals (with the exception of foreign borrowing, which must also be approved by the minister of finance and the planning authorities). The board has not interfered in the daily operations of the company. The general manager can fire incompetent staff, compete for funds in the domestic capital market, and make the necessary decisions to implement the plan.

company, Instituto dos Participacoes do Estado (IPE), for instance, helps subsidiaries negotiate credits if they also agree to undertake reforms. IPE also recruits experts to assist its subsidiaries in improving corporate planning or management information systems. It also provides training and finances outside studies.

Such merits need to be set against less favorable experiences elsewhere. Pakistan, for example, created a Board of Industrial Management (BIM) in 1973 to direct twelve corporations (with about fifty production units) on the model of Italy's IRI. The reports of two government commissions found that BIM had drastically reduced the production units' operating autonomy and weakened managerial authority. It was therefore abolished in 1978.

A different approach to decentralizing has been tried in several Eastern European countries (East Germany, Bulgaria, Poland, and Romania), where a new administrative level has been put between the ministry and the enterprise. Here again, experience shows that structural changes by themselves are not enough to alter the underlying balance of power. The *centrale* in Romania, for example, were created in 1968 and given certain minor powers over enterprise investments, borrowing, input supply, and marketing. But the ministries continued to intervene directly both in the enterprises and in the day-to-day operations of the centrale.

Some countries have centralized control in government bureaus or specialized ministries. India, for example, created the Bureau of Public Enterprises (BPE) as part of the Ministry of Finance in 1965. In 1979 Brazil set up the Secretariat for the Control of State Enterprises, and in Pakistan the Ministry of Production controls all state-owned manufacturing enterprises. These bodies are responsible for setting performance standards (or expenditure limits in the case of Brazil), evaluating results, and approving debt and investments. The BPE collects and analyzes data on India's SOEs and in 1982 set performance targets with the enterprise managers. It also gives technical assistance and training, does special studies, and provides guidelines in such areas as wage settlements. Central bodies thus obtain valuable information on SOEs, a prerequisite for effectively assessing and controlling performance. However, sometimes they become involved in unnecessary detail; one such body has set standards for factory perimeter fencing. Central bodies can play a vital role in monitoring performance or they can become an annoying bottleneck obsessed with trivia. Their role depends largely on whether a government is concerned with short-term goals, such as implementing austerity programs or curbing SOE abuses, or with the long-run process of changing relations between SOEs and government.

Holding managers accountable for results

There are strong arguments for creating conditions in which SOEs can be instructed to maximize profits and then be judged by that standard. Profit is a composite indicator that applies positive weights (prices) to benefits (outputs) and negative weights to costs (inputs). If the weights are correct, a profit-maximizing firm strives to achieve maximum benefits for minimum costs—the definition of efficiency. For SOEs, this criterion needs modifying for four reasons: many SOEs are monopolies; the profit relevant for society is different from private profits; many SOE objectives conflict with profit maximization; and market prices may be distorted.

These qualifications need not negate the use of profits as a guide to performance.

- Monopoly. The best way to end monopoly power is to introduce competition. Where that is not possible, the prices of a monopoly SOE can be set according to its marginal costs (see discussion in Chapter 6); the SOE can then be instructed to maximize profits. If that produces unacceptably high prices, the enterprise can still be required to minimize costs. Although adjusting administered prices typically involves practical and political problems, the long-run benefits can be substantial.
- Accounting for public profits. Some items (such as interest payments) can be excluded from public profits so as not to encourage SOE managers to waste time on, for example, interest arbitrage, which may be deemed irrelevant to their tasks. Targets can also be set for activities such as investment, maintenance, and research, which might not be compatible with short-run profit maximization or cost minimization.
- Conflicting goals. If the SOE is required to perform noncommercial roles that reduce its profits (such as hiring extra staff to increase employment or setting up a plant in a particular area to promote regional development), the government can reimburse it for the extra costs or reduce its profit target accordingly. Careful calculation is needed of the cost of noncommercial goals: if the subsidy is too high, the incentive for the company to improve its efficiency is reduced.
- Distorted prices. These can be rectified by using shadow prices for assessing SOE results. Shadow prices are calculated to reflect the opportunity costs of an enterprise's inputs and outputs. For example, the price of imported fuel may be held down by a government subsidy, but SOE accounting should value it according to its world price to ensure it is used efficiently.

The results derived from shadow-price accounting can differ widely from conventional profits and losses, as one study of SOEs in Egypt demonstrated. In almost all twenty-seven industries sampled, the financial rate of return calculated on the basis of extensively controlled market prices pointed in opposite directions from the economic rates of return based on shadow prices. Industries producing oils, soaps, and detergents showed a 14.4 percent economic rate of return, yet financial profitability was negative; nonferrous metals earned a

Box 8.6 Performance evaluation in Pakistan

Pakistan's performance evaluation system, launched in 1981, uses "public profitability" as an indicator of performance. "Public profits" are private profits adjusted for those elements not deemed relevant to an SOE. For example, taxes and interest, which are private costs but public benefits, are excluded so as not to encourage SOE managers to devote time to minimizing taxes or to interest arbitrage. Rather, public profitability aims to encourage managers to maximize net economic benefits, judged from a national perspective. Costs of noncommercial objectives (such as the extra cost of purchasing from local suppliers to encourage domestic industry) are deducted before profits are calculated and treated as an "in-kind" dividend to the government.

Since many prices are administered and there are problems of monopoly pricing, market prices may not reflect true economic scarcity. Since SOE managers generally cannot affect prices, it would be unfair to reward or penalize them for the effects of changing prices on profitability. The ideal solution would be to eliminate the divergence between market prices and real economic costs. Where that is not feasible, a second-best remedy is to use shadow prices that reflect true economic costs. Shadow prices, however, are complex and controversial to administer. Pakistan is therefore judging its SOE managers, for control purposes only, by trends in public profit at constant prices; that is, constructing a quantum index of profits based on quantum indices of inputs and outputs. This is an acceptable approximation of efficiency in performance evaluation (though not in project evaluation), since it is concerned with the trend rather than the level of performance. All enterprises will be judged on the basis of their return to fixed operating assets, or public profitability in constant terms. The performance of any individual firm will be compared with its record over the past five years, to make allowance for the fact that some enterprises operate under greater handicaps than others.

Used in isolation, public profitability would encourage managers to ignore activities with current costs but future benefits (such as planning, maintenance, training, or innovation). Government and SOEs will therefore negotiate extra targets for these areas, assigning them weights that vary over time and from one company to another. A firm will first have to show that it can use existing resources efficiently; hence, 90 percent of its initial target may be assigned to public profitability.

At the end of the year the performance of each SOE will then be rated according to how close it came to meeting its composite target. The monitoring and evaluation will be done by the Experts Advisory Cell, a semi-autonomous agency responsible to the Ministry of Production but financed by a levy on the SOEs themselves. The Cell has been able to maintain a remarkable degree of independence and, because it is outside the civil service system, to attract a specialist staff. At a review meeting with the Cell, managers will be able to present an explanation of their results. The government proposes to reward good performance with a salary bonus.

15.5 percent financial rate of return, but the economic return was negative. Not only would it be misleading to judge an SOE on the basis of its financial performance, but a manager reacting to financial signals under these circumstances would make the wrong economic decision. Shadow prices can be complex to calculate and administer, so the best solution is to move market prices closer to them by removing distortions wherever feasible.

While these four refinements have been extensively analyzed in theoretical work, their application has proven practically and politically difficult. Some countries are moving to overcome these problems. One system for judging the performance of manufacturing SOEs in Pakistan is described in Box 8.6. The Republic of Korea and Venezuela have also initiated similar projects that will tackle the more complex problem of evaluating enterprises responsible to different ministries.

Information on performance

Assessing SOE performance requires a regular flow of reliable information. But in many developing countries the internal management information systems of SOEs are deficient or nonexistent. SOEs (as well as private companies) are not audited according to uniform standards; more than seventy developing countries have no accounting standards. Trained accountants are scarce, because in many developing countries (outside Latin America) accounting became part of the university curricula only after 1960. Even now there are often no uniform standards of training.

These weaknesses are gradually being rectified. Many francophone West African countries have tried to adapt France's accounting model to their needs. This program—the OCAM *plan comptable*, started almost twenty years ago—has met with mixed success. But its application has been too inflexible, with too much reliance on expatriate experts and too little attention paid to local accounting capabilities. In Senegal the accountancy profession has proposed a two-tiered system, with annual external audits conforming to internationally accepted procedures required for all companies above a certain size and "limited review audits" for all other companies. The latter would be stricter than the current standard but less comprehensive (and cheaper) than full-scale audits.

The development of uniform and credible accounting requires a trained body of practitioners as well as a system to set and review standards and to qualify accountants. This foundation can be built up by designating responsibility within the government for the development of accounting; establishing accounting standards backed by an appropriate legal framework; assessing staff needs and designing training for bookkeepers and accountants; and fostering a professional association that could assume responsibility for enforcing standards.

Formal accountancy procedures are not the only way managers can improve the information on which they base their actions. Improvements can also be obtained through a management audit, which requires the firm to establish and adhere to a basic information system and routine control procedures. As with a financial audit, an outside auditor would check that these procedures function properly and generate reliable data that management and government can compare with targets. Many large accounting firms can now assist enterprises in setting up and using management-auditing systems.

A somewhat similar management tool is the action plan, designed to focus efforts on improving efficiency and monitoring results. The experience of the Bolivian railways illustrates how action plans work in practice. The railway had three action plans between 1973 and 1979, with objectives that ranged from reorganizing workshops and repairing rolling stock to rehabilitating and maintaining track. Monitored targets included the average percentage of total cars and locomotives in operating condition during the year, the number of staff, the turnaround time for maintenance, and the amount of track to be rehabilitated. Action plans specify the measures to be used to achieve the targets (such as training or allocation of foreign exchange for the purchase of spare parts) and the timing.

Pressure from competition, the public, and clients

Governments cannot always arrange for their SOEs to be exposed to competition. Many state firms are monopolies producing goods and services that are not traded internationally or that the government prefers to produce domestically for reasons of national security or public interest. In other cases, the economy may be too small to support another domestic producer. Where it is possible to do so, however, exposing SOEs to competition can be a simple and effective way to promote their efficiency. And if managers are required to pursue noncommercial goals for political or social reasons, competition will help to quantify the costs of those goals. Thus Peru recently reduced tariffs and eliminated import quotas to force industries to compete with imports.

Another possibility is to split large public monopolies into smaller competing units, especially if the monopoly did not benefit from economies of scale. In Hungary, for example, at least 130 new enterprises were established by breaking up horizontal trusts and large state firms. For competition to be fully effective in promoting efficiency, these measures must be accompanied by pricing freedom. Privileged access to subsidized credit and inputs would have to end. Also, managers must be given discretion to respond to competitive pressures, which may mean reducing staff or ending unprofitable services. The enterprise might also have to be reimbursed for the extra costs of meeting social goals.

Organized public pressure is another way of encouraging SOE efficiency. Britain, for example, has consumer councils. Although they have no executive powers, they monitor the service provided by public monopolies and act as a proxy for market forces. The Electricity Consumer Council examines not just tariffs but also power cuts, delays in connections or repairs, and responsiveness of staff to customer inquiries and complaints.

Clients can also induce efficiency; accountability to growers was an important factor in the success of the Kenya Tea Development Authority. SOEs can be required to publish timely annual reports and accounts, to be tabled in Parliament or made publicly available. Chile, for example, recently required state companies to publish their financial balances in the newspapers.

Appropriate managerial incentives and skills

Institutional success is often attributed to the presence of "a good manager." Competent staff are no doubt essential for any efficient enterprise. They do not operate in a vacuum. They need incentives to attract and motivate them, and the power to be effective.

Incentives linked to results. Some of the most effective rewards are nonpecuniary—recognition, greater responsibility, promotion, and national honors. Autonomy can also be a strong incentive for SOE managers. For example, the threat of losing its independence motivated the management of the Kenya Tea Development Authority. By the same token, managers need to know that they face penalties for poor performance, such as losing their jobs.

As for pecuniary incentives, few countries have used performance bonuses or profit sharing to motivate top management. An exception is Mexico, which distributes 7 percent of SOE profits to all employees in proportion to their salaries. In Hungary, ministries judge the size of bonuses to senior SOE managers by reference to such factors as profitability, exports, development of new products, and punctuality of deliveries. Many more countries award performance bonuses to workers, and their experience reveals some of the difficulties involved. Bonuses run the risk of becoming so automatic and large that they are treated as part of everybody's salary; they are not easily related to the actions and decisions of individual managers. To be effective, profit-sharing schemes require that managers affect profits and that profits be a fair guide to performance. Otherwise managers of SOEs in which profits are inherent in their operating conditions—such as many petroleum or electricity companies—would be enriched, while a manager who stems chronic losses might go unrewarded.

Appropriate managerial skills. The skills of a public enterprise manager need to be closer to those of his private sector counterpart than to those of a government bureaucrat. Nevertheless, in some countries managers are part of the civil service, or at least subject to its pay scale. Even where this is not the case, their pay seldom matches private salaries. Although the prestige and challenge of running what are often the largest corporations in the country may sometimes compensate for lower pay, low salaries tend to deter skilled managers and increase staff turnover. To give one of many examples, salaries in a Turkish public utility averaged one-third those of the private sector in 1981 and the company has had seven general managers in the past ten years. In addition, good SOE managers who face frequent unjustified interventions, or whose achievements go unnoticed for want of a system to evaluate them, tend to become disgruntled and leave.

The growing number of SOEs has contributed to a chronic shortage of managers in many sub-Saharan African and South Asian countries, a shortage sometimes exacerbated by programs for rapid indigenization. Many senior posts are left vacant or are filled by unqualified staff. For example, in Tanzania half of the ten large agricultural SOEs had no financial manager in 1980. In the Nigerian Electric Power Authority, thirty-five of eighty-seven higher management posts were vacant in 1981. The lack of competent middle managers often leads general managers to take over lower supervisory functions. In a centralized system they may also be the only point of contact with outsiders. The organization thus becomes too dependent on its chief executive.

The shortage of managers also contributes to a high rate of turnover, as competent people are shifted around to head troubled SOEs. A study of nine countries in sub-Saharan Africa found that the average tenure of SOE general managers in the 1970s was less than two years. Even countries without a managerial shortage change SOE managers with damaging frequency if selection of top managers is based on nepotism or political patronage. To counteract this, some countries (such as India and Brazil) have set up management selection boards to nominate candidates on merit alone. Continuity of top management is especially important in a company's formative years. Furthermore, continuity allows a good chief executive time to attract and retain talented middle managers. For example, the Hindustan Machine Tool Company, one of the most successful Indian SOEs, was also one of the few public corporations in India to have the same chief executive for almost fifteen years.

In certain specialized areas (mining in Zaire, for example), management contracts with expatriate firms have helped alleviate the shortage of managers. Another step is to give priority to managerial development in SOEs. In the past, more attention has been paid to technical expertise for SOEs than to their managerial requirements. Although SOE management training does not lend itself to centralized direction, governments can encourage SOEs to earmark funds for training. Some of the largest have their own management training centers but most rely on business schools, management consultants, expatriate advisers, and foreign suppliers or collaborators.

"Twinning" an SOE with its counterpart in another country has proved an effective way of transferring know-how and training staff. Companies offering technical assistance as twins are not exclusively from North America and Europe. Among many examples from developing countries are the Port of Singapore, the National Irrigation Agency of the Philippines, and the Tunisian Water Au-

Box 8.7 TANESCO: a study in institution building

The Tanzania Electric Supply Company Limited (TANESCO) was founded as a private company in 1931 and acquired by the government of Tanzania in 1964. It now operates as an SOE under the sponsorship of the Ministry of Water and Energy. TANESCO has more than 6,000 employees and produces about 98 percent of the country's electricity consumption.

Management continuity and a firm commitment to staff training have been critical to TANESCO's development. Over the past twenty-eight years, it has had only four general managers, and many of its senior staff have been with the company for at least ten years. The proportion of Tanzanians in senior posts has risen from 20 percent in 1964 to 85 percent in 1980. In 1968, TANESCO established its own technical training institute, which was developed with assistance from the Swedish International Development Agency. European and Indian expatriate staff provided on-the-job training. By 1974, after the first stage of the company's literacy program, all employees were able to read and write. Between 1976 and 1981 TANESCO sent fifty staff overseas to obtain engineering degrees. The first Tanzanian general manager, who was appointed in 1973 and retired in 1981, used foreign management consultants to reorganize the utility on functional lines and expanded the programs for training and staff development.

The "twinning" of TANESCO and the Electricity Supply Board of Ireland (ESB) in 1977 had a decisive influence on the development of the company's managers. During the first year of the scheme, about twenty TANESCO staff members were given from three to twelve months' training in Dublin followed by a brief period of on-the-job training with ESB or in similar utilities in the United Kingdom and the United States. Both "twins" took great care to design a training program that fitted TANESCO's needs. When the trainees returned to Tanzania, their shared experience in Ireland helped them to work better as a team.

thority. The more-developed SOE may temporarily provide its twin with some of its own staff as advisors and trainers, may make periodic visits to give technical assistance, or may employ the staff of its twin at its own facility for on-the-job training (see Box 8.7).

The administrative burden placed on SOE managers may be partly caused by their diversion to extraneous activities. For example, in Peru the management of a public fishing plant also runs a hotel. While diversification can be profitable and logical, it is often done for the wrong reasons and, by straining resources, damages the SOE's mainstream activities.

Liquidation

By saving the economy the burden of nonviable enterprises, liquidations act as a major force for efficiency. Because of the financial and social consequences, however, governments are reluctant to let big firms close, whether they are in the public or the private sector. Even among small firms, SOEs are seldom liquidated. But the costs of keeping nonviable companies alive are considerable—fiscal drain, administrative demands, and waste of potentially productive resources. To take an extreme case, in Peru a freeze-drying plant owned by the state was built without adequate study of the market or its suppliers of raw materials. From the start, the firm's production costs exceeded its revenues. It was shut down and reopened on several occasions. Finally, in 1980 and after fifteen years of losses, it was liquidated.

This case also illustrates the need for a proper legal framework to allow speedy liquidation. Peruvian law makes it almost impossible to dismiss workers (in both the public and private sectors). Although the company offered its staff a bonus over and above required severance pay to leave, for more than six months after the plant was shut down a small group of workers continued to report for work each day to receive their wages. Until all the staff had left, the assets could not be sold.

Liquidation and other forms of divestment give the government the flexibility to put resources to more productive use. Since these gains have to be weighed against short-term costs, vested interests often deny the state the possibility of even considering the option—to the long-run detriment of the economy.

Divestiture

Selling state-owned enterprises is another way of easing their administrative and financial burden on the state. A number of governments, including Bangladesh, Brazil, Chile, Italy, Jamaica, Republic of Korea, Pakistan, Peru, Philippines, United Kingdom, and Zaire, have divested or are planning to divest SOEs. Generally, however, the number and importance of the enterprises sold is not large.

After an initial attempt to promote industrialization through state ownership, the Japanese government in the 1880s sold many state firms, including fifty-two factories, ten mines, and three shipyards. Between 1974 and 1980, Chile sold some 130 state enterprises, with a value of more than $500 million. (In addition, more than 250 enterprises nationalized between 1971 and 1973 were returned to their former owners.) Despite these measures, in 1979 the eight largest Chilean companies (in terms of net worth) were still publicly owned.

Other privatizing programs have been far more limited. Brazil created a commission for divestiture in 1981: by mid-1982 it had sold ten enterprises and was in the process of selling another thirty-six, while ten other SOEs have been legally dissolved. Jamaica has set up a divestiture committee which has sold three enterprises and leased four hotels. Pakistan denationalized some 2,000 rice, flour, and cotton mills, while Bangladesh returned 35 jute and 23 textile mills to the private sector.

Although divestiture can produce important net gains to society when the costs of public operation outweigh the benefits, it has been hard to implement. It is politically sensitive and prompts charges of corruption. In addition, governments often try to sell only their money losers, for which there are few buyers. Even profitable nationalized companies may be hard to sell. An informal survey of the potential market for Peruvian SOEs found that likely buyers were reluctant to purchase even fairly small companies. The reasons given included fear of renationalization and concern about extensive government regulation of formerly public firms. These perceptions may mean governments have to accept a lower price than the market value for a similar private firm. Both Chile and Japan sold most of their state firms on attractive terms.

Another reason divestiture is so difficult in developing countries is the absence of a strong capital market. Public companies are often large and domestic investors may not be able to raise enough capital to buy them. And selling large SOEs to oligopolists who already dominate the private sector might reduce competition. It could also result in unhealthy ties between financial institutions and industry, further reducing the flexibilty of capital markets.

Efforts to develop the stock market, and schemes that appeal to small savers through their pension funds, could make it easier for governments to divest. Spreading ownership more widely and divesting only gradually can improve the chances of privatization; it may even reduce the attendant political controversy. Leasing can also be a promising route to divestiture: a private manager might be brought in to run a potentially profitable enterprise for a share of the profits and an option to buy.

Agenda for reform

This chapter has suggested ways of improving SOE efficiency, concentrating on the problems that are common to most SOEs in most countries. Judging from what is known about the ideal conditions for operating efficiently, it has examined how the reality of SOEs differs from the theoretical ideal. By recognizing the SOEs' special circumstances and constraints, it is possible to develop an agenda for reform that would correct some of their main weaknesses:

- Setting clear-cut and attainable objectives is the inescapable first step toward improved SOE performance. The costs of noncommercial constraints placed on SOEs should be calculated and weighed against the benefits to society.
- Once constraints have been identified and costed, governments can instruct many SOEs to maximize their profits, taking into account other objectives that reduce profits by reimbursing the companies or lowering their profit targets.
- Where there are price distortions, shadow pricing offers a way to assess SOE performance consistent with economic efficiency. The better alternative is to move to market pricing (or marginal cost pricing where market pricing is not feasible). This would encourage greater efficiency by giving the correct market signals to managers and consumers. Although market pricing typically entails short-run political problems and costs, the long-run benefits are substantial.
- Negotiated agreements, such as contracts or corporate plans, can help put relations between SOEs and government on a more constructive plane. In particular, two-way contracts can help win SOE management over to the idea of reform by laying out benefits as well as responsibilities.
- Once government has laid down objectives, managers can be made responsible for choosing the methods of achieving them.
- Systems for monitoring and evaluating performance are needed to transform good intentions into results. By promoting domestic and international competition and encouraging consumers and other customers to make their views known, governments can add to the pressures for good SOE

performance. Some of the most powerful incentives are nonpecuniary (recognition, prestige, awards).

• Managerial ability is a key to the success of SOE reform. Managerial incentives linked to performance are important in motivating top managers. Compensation and training should be geared to create a corps of competent SOE managers with appropriate skills. Efforts should also be directed at encouraging continuity of senior staff.

• The managerial and fiscal burden of SOEs can be reduced by liquidating nonviable enterprises as well as by selective sales. These should not be treated as instant solutions, but rather as integral parts of the process of replacing the burden of central administration by decentralized market forces.

With strong political backing, this agenda is feasible. In any administrative system there are strong vested interests opposed to change. Opposition to reform may come from managers of powerful SOEs or senior government bureaucrats fearing loss of power, labor unions fearing job cuts, SOE clients fearing an end to subsidized outputs, suppliers fearing reduced SOE spending, or even from SOE competitors (some private companies profit nicely when prices or incentives for a sector are geared to allow an inefficient SOE to survive).

Since these elements are interrelated, a piecemeal approach is unlikely to achieve the desired results. Without clear objectives there can be no standards by which to judge performance; without accountability few governments would increase SOE autonomy; autonomy becomes license without performance evaluation; incentives can be linked to performance only if there is a meaningful way to measure results; performance evaluation makes sense only if managers have the autonomy to influence outcomes; without performance evaluation there is no way to distinguish good managers from bad. Developing a framework to guide SOEs toward efficiency is thus a lengthy, complex process that requires commitment, persistence, and flexibility on the part of state authorities and enterprise management.

MANAGEMENT OF PUBLIC INDUSTRIAL ENTERPRISES

Mahmood A. Ayub and Sven O. Hegstad

Why do some state industries do better than others? Those in Brazil, for example, achieve better financial and economic results than their counterparts in Ghana or Pakistan. Yet within Brazil, the national iron ore company (CVRD) and the national petroleum company (PETROBRAS) are much more successful than the copper and railroad companies. In India, Hindustan Machine Tools is a dynamic concern; other public enterprises, even those in the same industry, are far less successful.

The variations have two possible sets of explanations. The first consists of country-specific characteristics—cultural, social, political, macroeconomic, and institutional. These explain differences between countries in the performance of state industries. The other covers differences that are specific to particular companies, such as the degree of autonomy, domestic and foreign competition, and the corporate and managerial culture. This set explains why, within the same country, state firms vary in their performance.

The two sets of factors clearly overlap. This article deals only with those influences on performance that are peculiar to public firms and can be affected by policymakers. It therefore excludes cultural and social factors, even though these can be of critical importance in determining the success of public enterprises. Similarly, the quality of individual chief executives significantly affects the performance of public enterprises, but that is also true for private firms. The article also excludes the macroeconomic and institutional environment, because that matters for public and private firms alike. However, the study does assume that governments intent on improving the performance of state enterprises would adopt appropriate macropolicy measures as well.

This study deals chiefly with public *industrial* enterprises. Since they generally produce tradable goods in markets with varying degrees of competition, they are distinct from enterprises such as utilities and transport companies, which often are natural monopolies. However, most of the organizational and management issues facing state industries are relevant to other public companies, though the remedies for poor performance may differ.

The Role of Public Industrial Enterprises

Of the 500 largest non-U.S. industrial corporations on the *Fortune* list for 1985, some 71 were in the public sector. They accounted for 19 percent of sales, 21 percent of assets, and 26 percent of employment in the 500 firms. Over the past decade the importance of these state companies has increased (see table 1).

There is no indication that the share of public ownership of industrial value added is related to a country's gross domestic product (GDP) per capita.[1] Economic, political, social, and historical factors have determined the size of a country's public sector, regardless of its stage of economic development. Nonetheless, there does seem to be a pattern to the share of public ownership among various subsectors, regardless of whether a country is developed or developing. This pattern (see table 2) can be explained largely by whether certain industries are considered to be strategic or to possess economies of scale.

The share of public industrial enterprises in total value added is generally much smaller than their share in total investment—that is, they are more capital-intensive than private companies are. For the sample countries, the average share of public industrial enterprises in investment was 26 percent, more than twice their 11 percent share in GDP. As Sheahan remarked, "in Brazil and in India it is almost as if industries were divided between private and public enterprise according to their capital intensity" (Sheahan 1976). To a large extent, this

Table 1. ***Share of Public Enterprises in Non-U.S.*** **Fortune** ***500 Companies, 1975 and 1984***

Item	*1975*	*Percentage of total*	*1984*[a]	*Percentage of total*
Number of enterprises	54	10.8	71	14.2
Total sales (US$ billion)	162	19.7	359	19.0
Total assets (US$ billion)	156	20.5	339	21.0
Total employees (million)	3.0	17.5	3.8	21.4

a. A significant portion of the increase in the number of public enterprises, their sales, and assets is explained by the nationalization of many industrial enterprises in France since 1981.
Source: Fortune, August 1976 and August 1985.

Table 2. ***Public Ownership of Selected Industrial Subsectors, 1984***

Country	*Textiles*	*Electronics*	*Petro-chemicals*	*Cement*	*Motor vehicles*	*Mining*	*Fertilizers*[a]	*Steel*	*Telecom-munications*[b]
Austria	○	○	n.a.	○	●	◔	●	●	●
Brazil	○	◔	◑	○	○	◕	◕	◕	◕
France	◔	◑	◑	○	◑	◑	●	◕	●
Ghana	n.a.	○	○	◕	n.a.	●	●	n.a.	●
India[c]	◔	◑	◑	◔	◔	◕	◕	◕	●
Israel[d]	○	◑	◔	○	○	n.a.	●	○	●
Italy	○	◔	◔	○	◔	◑	◕	◕	◑
Pakistan	○	◑	◑	◕	◕	◔	◑	●	●
Portugal	○	◔	◕	●	n.a.	◔	◕	●	●
Sweden	◔	○	○	○	○	◑	◑	◕	●
Tunisia	◑	○	○	●	n.a.	◑	n.a.	n.a.	●
Zambia	◑	n.a.	◑	◑	n.a.	●	●	n.a.	●

○ Nearly all private ◔ 25 percent public ◑ 50 percent public ◕ 75 percent public ● Nearly all public

n.a. Not available or negligible.

Notes: In a number of industrial and developing countries, some public companies have substantial (but less than 50 percent) ownership in private hands. However, for the purpose of this article, these companies are considered fully public.

a. Nitrogenous fertilizers only.

b. Services, not manufacturing.

c. The entry for motor vehicles takes into account the recently established, publicly owned Maruthi plant.

d. The entries for motor vehicles and steel indicate majority ownership not by the private sector but by the General Federation of Labor Trade Unions (Histradut).

bias reflects the fact that some public enterprises were set up precisely because the capital requirements of industries such as steel and oil refining were too heavy for the private sector to finance. However, it may also reflect the way that public enterprises are able to obtain relatively cheap financing from the state and thus are encouraged to favor capital-intensive production.[2]

Performance of Public Industrial Enterprises

Assessing the performance of state enterprises is made difficult by inadequacies in the available data. This study accordingly used a "weight of evidence" approach, of the kind favored by historians and jurists, rather than one of testing hypotheses statistically. Relevant indicators include financial profitability, self-financing ratios, productivity growth, and the contribution of state enterprises to budgetary deficits and external debt.

Financial profitability is far from perfect as an indicator of performance. Big profits may indicate efficiency, but they may also reflect market distortions and monopolistic pricing. For example, some of the more profitable public enterprises in Ghana (including the distillery and cocoa factories in Accra and Takoradi) owe their financial success almost wholly to monopolistic positions and to heavy protection from foreign competition; at international prices, their value added is negative. In Pakistan, some 90 percent of the sales of public industrial enterprises are subject to price controls. However, financial profitability does have the merit of showing whether a public enterprise depends on the national treasury for its operations. As will be argued later, the degree of managerial autonomy in state enterprises (which is an important determinant of performance) depends largely on the degree of independence from treasury financing.

The data for the sample countries show that the financial rates of return for public industrial enterprises have generally been low. For example, the fifteen largest Portuguese public enterprises achieved an average rate of return on capital of about 10 percent in 1977–83, compared with an inflation rate averaging about 21 percent a year. In Ghana, the comparable rate of return was about 18 percent, compared with an average rate of inflation of 96 percent. In Pakistan, the return on capital averaged about 2 percent during the 1970s and slightly over 4 percent during 1980–83, compared with an average rate of inflation over the whole period of about 12 percent.[3] In India, the average pretax return on capital in 140 public companies in 1978–83 was about 11 percent in current terms—but more than 90 percent of the profits came from the petroleum industry.

Among industrial countries, Austrian public industrial enterprises (in the OIAG Group) registered an average return on capital of about 3 percent during 1975–80; since 1980 many of the firms have made losses. In Sweden, the Statsforetag enterprises kept fairly even pace with the rest of Swedish industry during 1970–76 in both sales per employee and profitability, even though their return on capital reached the 10 percent target only once (in 1974). However, the group made losses in all subsequent years until 1983.

In real value added growth, the relative performance of public enterprises has been somewhat better. For example, Brazil's public enterprises expanded their real value added by 3.7 times during 1966–75, compared with 2.4 times in Brazilian industry as a whole (though there are no data to show how far this difference reflects a higher level of investment by public enterprises or a faster increase in total factor productivity). Since 1975, value-added increases have been significantly lower, both for public enterprises and for industry in general. Similarly in Portugal real value added per employee in the thirteen largest state industries increased by 83 percent during 1976–79. In subsequent years the increase was only 2 percent.

Financial performance varies widely among public enterprises in the same country and between the same industries across countries. In Israel, within the Israel Chemicals Limited (ICL) group, the most profitable subsidiary—the Dead Sea Works—had an average annual return on revalued capital of 12 percent in 1980–83 and 18 percent in 1984, rates that are considered high for the heavy chemical industry. But another subsidiary in the same group—Chemicals and Fertilizers—has been barely profitable, to some extent because it has concentrated on the domestic market where fertilizer prices are controlled. In Zambia, some subsidiaries of Indeco (such as Zambia Breweries, Zambia Oxygen, National Breweries, Zamefa, Supa Baking, and Chilanga Cement) are highly profitable, whereas Luangwa Industries, Zambezi Sawmills, Nitrogen Chemicals, and Livingstone Motors have been loss-makers. In Ghana, the best performers have been GIHOC's cocoa-processing factory, a liquor distillery, and a fruit cannery; its two sugar factories have made big losses. In Brazil, PETROBRAS and CVRD have been consistently profitable, as have a few smaller public enterprises (such as Mafersa, Celma, and Tasa), but the iron and steel companies (Siderbras, Acesita, and Siderama) have been substantial loss-makers. In India, the gross profits (before tax and interest charges) of state industries during the early to middle 1970s averaged about 19 percent for the petroleum industry, 11 percent for medium and light engineering, 2 percent for steel, and −3 percent for minerals and metals.

The same variation in performance occurred in the industrial countries in our sample. In Austria, OMV and SGP have been the only consistently profitable public industrial enterprises; the largest loss-makers were the two steel companies, Voest-Alpine and VEW. In France, state industries can be classified into three groups according to their profitability: the heavy loss-makers (the two steel firms, Usinor and Sacilor, and, since 1983, Renault); those firms that break even or have light losses (mainly Thomson, the electronics and telecommunications company, and EMC, the chemical company); and the profitable firms (such as Dassault, Matra, Saint-Gobain, and Roussel).

Across industries, too, variations in profitability have been significant (table 3). The most profitable subsectors in 1984 were mining and petroleum; the least profitable, steel and automobiles. Almost without exception, steel companies have been the largest drain on national treasuries. Surplus capacity and low prices have resulted in huge losses in many countries, including France, Italy, Sweden, Brazil, Austria, India, and Pakistan. The fact that the steel industry is considered strategic and is usually dominated by strong trade unions has made it hard to reduce costs.

Comparing Public and Private Performance

Any comparison of state industries with their private counterparts needs to be made with caution. Public enterprises are often expected to fulfill at least some social objectives, and this can affect their financial performance. Moreover, the public sector in many countries includes loss-making companies that governments acquired for noneconomic reasons. Furthermore, the public sector is often dominated by slow-growing basic industries. Further problems can arise when too static a view is taken—as when, for example, a new inexperienced public enterprise is compared with a well-established private one. In this sense, comparisons of public and private firms' performance in

Table 3. *Profitability of Public Industrial Enterprises, by Subsector, 1984*

Subsector	*Number of firms*	*Number of loss-making firms*	*Gross assets (US$ billions)*	*Net income (US$ billions)*	*Net income as % of gross assets*
Mining[a]	5	1	14,808	1,097	7.4
Petroleum[b]	26	2	183,356	7,029	3.8
Tobacco	2	0	874	16	1.8
Chemicals	5	2	17,895	293	1.6
Aerospace	3	0	7,751	73	0.9
Electronics	2	1	16,657	66	0.4
Steel and metal manufacturing	15	7	49,234	−1,853	−3.8
Motor vehicles	4	2	25,949	−1,467	−5.7
Total	62	14	316,524	5,254	1.7[c]

a. Average profitability was substantially affected by CVRD of Brazil. Without it, the average falls to 2.9 percent.

b. Not included is YPF of Argentina, whose large losses distort the picture considerably. If YPF were included, average profitability would decline to 1.8 percent.

c. Average, not total.

Source: "The Largest Non-U.S. Corporations Ranked by Sales," *Fortune,* August 19, 1985.

this study (and most others) are not rigorous; they should be considered as only indicative and illustrative.

With these caveats, the evidence in this study suggests that within the sample countries, and sometimes within the same industries, public enterprises have generally been less profitable than private ones. In Israel, for example, a sample of twenty-five state industries and thirty-seven private companies (in which fourteen public and twenty-four private ones were in the same industrial subsectors) showed that pretax profits for public enterprises averaged 1.6 percent of sales in 1976–78, compared with 11.6 percent in private companies (Diskin 1980). A comparison of large public and private Brazilian firms for 1974 and 1978 indicates that the rate of return on equity for public enterprises was roughly one-half the return earned by the private sector. In India, which has one of the largest and most diversified public sectors among developing countries, the financial performance of public enterprises has been significantly worse than that of private enterprises in the same industry, though not necessarily in the same product line (Sri Ram and others 1976). A recent study of India's fertilizer industry concluded that, while productivity in the most efficient public enterprises was comparable with that in the best private firms, in the public sector as a whole it was lower than in the private sector (Gupta 1982). The differences in performance were explained partly by the higher input costs of public enterprises—the result of their obligation to use indigenous feedstocks and of their outmoded technology (public fertilizer plants were established as "pioneer" enterprises in the 1950s, whereas the first private firm started in 1968).

In the case of France, the publicly owned Renault Company more than held its own with private French automobile companies until 1983. However, research for this study indicates that French state companies were more severely affected by the recession of 1980–82 than their private counterparts and recovered less rapidly. As public enterprises often borrow at lower rates of interest than private firms can, the difference in performance between public and private firms is even greater than the statistics presented in table 4 suggest.

The relatively poor performance of state industries can largely be explained by their concentration in product lines and basic industries (such as steel, automobiles, and fertilizers) that have experienced little growth in recent years, or in developing new industries (such as aerospace). However, it is still true that these enterprises have contributed significantly to the macroeconomic problems of many countries. For example, in Brazil during 1980–82, the major federal enterprises accounted for almost 50 percent of the overall deficit of the federal government. In India, the net transfers (current and capital) from the central government to public industries increased from about US$890 million in 1978 to US$2.3 billion in 1983. State industries have also

Table 4. *Financial Profitability of Enterprises in Non-U.S.* Fortune *500 Companies, 1984*
(percent)

Subsector	*Public industrial enterprises*	*Private industrial enterprises*
Mining	7.4	15.5
Petroleum	3.8	4.4
Tobacco	1.8	8.5
Chemicals	1.6	3.5
Aerospace	0.9	2.9
Electronics	0.4	3.6
Steel and metal manufacturing	−3.8	0.7
Motor vehicles	−5.7	3.3
Weighted average	1.7	4.0

Note: Profitability is defined as net income as a percentage of gross assets.
Source: "The Largest Non-U.S. Corporations Ranked by Sales," *Fortune,* August 19, 1985.

been responsible for a significant part of the external debt in some countries.[4] Most notably, Brazil's public enterprises account for over two-thirds of the country's external public debt. In Zambia, the foreign debt of ZIMCO alone accounts for over half of the country's total debt. At the end of 1982, public enterprises accounted for about 60 percent of Portugal's external public debt of US$13.5 billion and some 90 percent of its short-term external liabilities of US$4 billion.

The response of several developing countries to mounting economic problems has been to tighten their monetary policies. In the absence of a tighter fiscal policy, there has been some "crowding out" of the private sector even in countries such as Brazil and Turkey that attach great importance to private sector development. It would have been better to reduce the public sector deficit and ease the constraints on credit to private companies.

Key Determinants of Performance

No country, developed or developing, has devised a perfect way to manage its public industrial enterprises. Even if one were found, social and cultural differences would make its blind replication almost meaningless. But of the many ways of managing public enterprises, some are clearly better than others.

To some extent, the reasons why public industrial enterprises generally do less well than their private counterparts are due to the differences inherent in their ownership. These include the fact that the directors of public enterprises (government officials) have no financial stake in the business; the limited threat of bankruptcy and reorganization, because of the easy recourse that state firms have to government finance; political opposition to reducing payrolls, even when financial conditions suggest that is needed; and the circuitous chain of decision-making devised to ensure public accountability. However, these inherent factors are only part of the explanation. Evidence from our study indicates that three other influences are equally important: the competitive environment, financial autonomy and accountability, and the extent and manner in which managerial autonomy and accountability are ensured. These will be examined in turn.

Competition

Although it is impossible to make a rigorous statistical analysis of the correlation between competition and performance, evidence from the sample countries strongly indicates that those state industries subject to a more demanding, competitive environment tend to perform better. For both public and private firms, the biggest constraints on competition are inappropriate macroeconomic, trade, and industrial policies. These include overvalued exchange rates, import quotas and bans, high tariffs, price controls, domestic content legislation (especially in automobiles and electronics), investment licensing, and regulations on entry and exit.

As well as changing these policies, governments can do some specific things to foster competition for state industries. Such competition can occur even among public enterprises that are considered strategic. A good example is the Heavy Mechanical Complex (HMC) at Taxila in Pakistan. The company faces competition in the production of road rollers and sugar mills from the privatized firm Ittefaq Foundry. In the construction of cement plants it has to compete not only with imports (allowed in with a duty of 20 percent), but also with another public enterprise, Karachi Shipyard. In electrical towers, boilers, and overhead traveling cranes, it faces competition not only from private firms but also from the publicly owned Pakistan Engineering Company (PECO). The competition facing the various petrochemical subsidiaries of PETROBRAS in Brazil is even more intense.

There is every reason to believe that Festinger's social comparison theory, which states that "people most strenuously seek to evaluate their performance by comparing themselves to others, not by using absolute standards" (quoted in Peters and Waterman 1982), applies to public enterprises as well. Central monitoring agencies should therefore make information on comparative performance widely available. In countries where such agencies review performance targets, they could make a comparative analysis of performance with all the state industry managers present at the time—and the results could be widely publicized. Many public enterprise managers interviewed in Brazil and Pakistan stressed their fear of unfavorable coverage in the national press.

Another way to subject public enterprises to competitive pressures is to encourage them to export. Of course, no amount of encouragement or cajoling can make them export if the macro framework is biased strongly the other way. But so long as the framework is appropriate, even a small amount of exporting can make a big difference. India's HMT exports only about 8 percent of its sales, but this seems to be enough to give the company access to new management techniques and new technologies.

In industries in which economies of scale are not important, competition can also be enhanced by breaking up monolithic holding companies or even large enterprises. The break-up of Statsforetag in Sweden into smaller sectoral holding companies has definitely increased competition and made public enterprises more conscious of efficiency. The proposal of the new Bolivian government to break up the Bolivian Mining Corporation (COMIBOL) into several competing companies could be a useful experiment. Occasionally, the break-up of large enterprises may be necessary but not sufficient for better performance. For example, the breaking up of FCI in the early 1970s in India made only a limited difference, mainly because the companies were still hampered by tough regulations. This underlines the importance of a favorable regulatory and policy environment within which companies can change their performance.

Financial Autonomy and Accountability

One of the main reasons why public industry runs into financial and economic problems is the lack of a clear separation between management and operations, on the one hand, and political and strategic considerations, on the other. In many cases, this results in diffuse and conflicting objectives, a loss of the managerial autonomy needed for efficient commercial operations, and a civil service culture where chief executives are more administrators than entrepreneurial businessmen. In such an environment, employment, investment, and pricing decisions are often made without due consideration for their financial consequences.

The confusion of operational and political responsibilities is often the starting point of a vicious circle for state industries. Once a firm is driven into loss, staff morale suffers and performance then deteriorates even further. As the financial problems accelerate, the government is forced to centralize decisionmaking even more and impose more controls. It injects more and more capital into the loss-makers and tries to retain staff by paying them higher and higher salaries. For example, in Portugal it was found, among the fifteen largest public enterprises visited, that the loss-making ones on average had increased salaries significantly more than the profit-making ones. But financial support alone gives only temporary relief, unless it is combined with comprehensive restructuring. In many cases that happens only after a series of costly crises. This vicious circle is illustrated in figure 1.

A prerequisite for improving the performance of state industries is to delegate more decisionmaking to their managers. The managers interviewed for this study cherished financial autonomy above all, in the sense of being substantially free of the need to rely on treasury financing. The two French steel companies (Usinor and Sacilor) have been chronic loss-makers; as a result all major decisions require prior approval by their sponsoring ministry. By contrast, Saint-Gobain and Roussel, essentially profitable, have enjoyed the greatest possible managerial autonomy. Similarly, in Sweden the profitable Tobacco Company has had significantly more freedom than the loss-making NJA (steel) company, even though both are subsidiaries of the same holding company, Statsforetag. Profitability also largely explains the greater autonomy of PETROBRAS and CVRD in Brazil as compared with the steel companies and the railroad company (RFFSA). And Israel Chemicals Limited, one of the most autonomous public enterprises, has had no major financial support from the government since it was established in 1967, relying instead on retained profits.

Figure 1

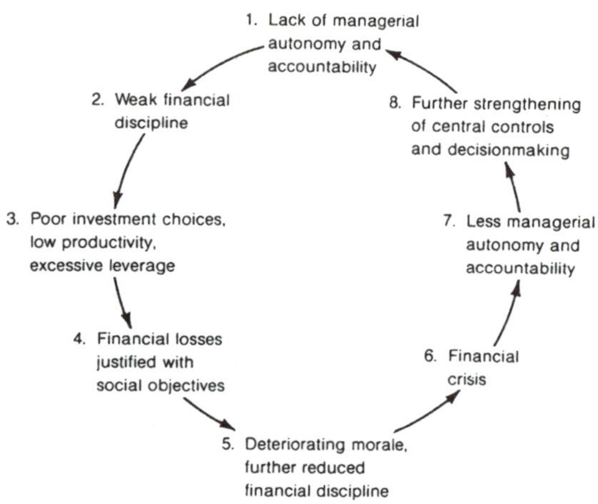

There are several ingredients of financial autonomy: greater market discipline, sound financial objectives, clear social objectives, elimination of subsidies, appropriate capital structure, greater discipline in financial relations, and establishment of performance measurement and incentive systems.

Greater Market Discipline

A combination of more autonomy in financial matters and greater exposure to markets normally creates among public enterprise managers a stronger sense of responsibility and a deeper interest in the financial health of their company. One way of institutionalizing financial discipline is to give state industries access to capital markets. Independent bankers scrutinize investment and financing decisions before they provide any loans. The use of bond markets, equity markets, and joint ventures opens the public enterprise to public scrutiny and to special audits and reporting requirements. Interviews with managers in Israel suggested that in companies whose minority shares are traded on the Tel Aviv Stock Exchange (such as Dead Sea Works, Chemicals and Fertilizers, and Cables of Zion), financial performance and discipline have been improved because of the obligation to publish semiannual financial statements and because of the firms' potential exposure to legal suits by shareholders for nonbusinesslike management.

Whenever possible, public enterprises should be encouraged to raise money from private creditors rather than the government and the central bank. When government provides the finance, it should charge market interest rates, and it should encourage joint ventures and the floating of a minority of the equity of state companies.

Sound Financial Objectives and Dividend Policies

Sound financial management involves specifying a company's financial objectives, monitoring progress toward them, and holding managers accountable for the outcome. The main measures of performance include return on assets or capital employed, return on equity, dividend pay-out ratio, debt equity ratio, and a prespecified level of internal financing of large investment projects. In varying degrees, these ratios are being used by public enterprise managers in the sample countries. One exception is Austria, where financial objectives are not defined explicitly but are couched in terms of "satisfactory" profitability and cash flow. In Sweden, officials of the agency that oversees state industries argued the establishment of broad financial objectives and enforcement of a clear dividend policy are even more essential in state enterprises than in private firms. They stressed that even though the dividends paid by state companies are often small, the principle of paying them matters more than the amount. In most countries in this study, dividend payments were either insignificant or nonexistent. But the enforcement of a dividend policy demonstrates unmistakably that the government gives high priority to financial management. It also forces management to focus on productivity and profitability improvements so as to meet the company's "new" financial obligations.

Clear Social Objectives

Public enterprises are often expected to pursue social objectives as diverse as redistributing income, subsidizing particular regions of a country, and creating or maintaining employment. The problem is not the fulfillment of these objectives, which can often be desirable. The problem is that the multiplicity of objectives and the absence of a sense of priorities allow social goals to become an excuse for poor performance. (In contrast, the maxim of Texas Instruments of the

United States is "more than two objectives is no objectives.") Perhaps the best examples in our sample of countries are the bicycle plant at Chipata in Zambia, the Aboso Glass Factory and the Bolgantanga Meat Factory in Ghana, and the Bolan and Shahdadkot textile mills in Pakistan. Among industrial countries, a good example of conflicting objectives is the state-owned aluminum company (ASV) in Norway, whose operations are substantially constrained by the need to provide employment in a region with few alternative job opportunities. Social objectives have also been extremely onerous for CDF-Chimie (heavy chemicals) and EMC (chemicals) in France. In the case of EMC, it has been estimated that the cost of providing specific social services exceeded its overall deficit in 1984.

When using state industries for social purposes, governments need to consider two questions. Are the social objectives being fulfilled? Are there no better ways of achieving them?

There is evidence that the pursuit of social objectives by public enterprises can produce perverse results. One example is Zambia's publicly owned agro-based industries (largely producing vegetable oil products, detergents, and soap), where stringent price controls on refined oil and fats (only recently lifted) have led not only to large financial losses but also to low morale and a shift in the product mix away from the production of oil and fats. This result was precisely opposite to the government's social priorities. Price controls are intended to benefit the poor, but end up subsidizing large industrial users, wholesalers, or affluent urban dwellers. The State Cement Corporation of Pakistan (SCCP) has sold cement in Lahore at a price that was Rs0.2 a bag below the cost of production plus freight charges (from its Zeal Pak plant at Hyderabad, some 700 miles away); it did so chiefly to appease the urban elite in the city where the head office is located. In other countries, similarly excessive efforts to promote employment have resulted in serious losses of efficiency and low morale (see Shirley 1983).

In many instances, there may be better ways of making social changes. For example, the objective of regionally balanced economic growth is better achieved by encouraging private investment through tax concessions and cash grants. The impressive industrial growth in the economically depressed Northeast region of Brazil over the past two decades was achieved with hardly any public investment. Often it is more effective to allow public enterprises to operate on commercial, profit-seeking lines and then use their profits to achieve such goals as income redistribution and employment creation.

Even in cases where *investment* decisions have been taken on social grounds, the *operational* decisions need not be (Jones 1983). In some of the sample countries, governments have set up large integrated iron and steel plants largely or wholly for strategic and national security reasons. These noncommercial objectives are achieved once the plant is working. Thereafter it can be left to operate along commercial lines. It may well earn a lower financial return as a result of its poor location or absence of comparative advantage, but society stands to gain by allowing the plant to earn as high a return as possible.

In some countries, especially France, Italy, and Sweden, public enterprises are compensated explicitly on a contractual basis for undertaking social objectives.[5] This approach helps to ensure that state companies are not saddled with excessive social burdens and, at the same time, avoids random departures from efficiency criteria. However, such compensatory payments should be viewed as second-best or even third-best solutions, and thus used sparingly. Moreover, if the contracts become too large relative to a public enterprise's normal activities, management may lose sight of its main objective.

Elimination of Government Subsidies

Easy recourse to government subsidies usually reduces the pressure on public managers to close nonviable operations and control costs. When state enterprises are heavily dependent on subsidies, the government and management should agree on a plan for phasing them out over a limited period. This action may have to be matched by a program of physical and financial restructuring.

Appropriate Capital Structure Policies

Several major benefits arise from using a proper mix of debt and equity, as opposed to using mostly or only debt in financing public enterprises. A mixture of debt and equity increases the enterprise's ability to borrow in financial markets, serves as a check against overexpansion, stimulates a keener awareness of profit, and strengthens a company's ability to survive recessions.

Greater Discipline and Transparency in Financial Relations

The accounts of the major public enterprises in our sample contained a complicated maze of transfers between central government and public enterprises. To improve financial discipline and to be able to record "true" financial results, governments should demand tax, duty, interest, dividend, and amortization payments from public enterprises, just as they do from private companies. Losses and negative cash flow would then have to be financed in a more transparent way through new equity, loans, or other means.

If governments are to require financial discipline from public enterprises, they must demonstrate the same quality in their own financial management. They can do so in various ways: (a) a government commitment to pay in new equity capital as part of a large investment project should duly consider the risks involved and the government's own capacity to afford the capital; (b) when government payments to public enterprises have been approved by the appropriate ministries, they should not be questioned and delayed by other ministries; and (c) public enterprises should not be used to finance government deficits. This last point means that viable enterprises should be allowed to decide how to use their surpluses. The rationale is that public enterprise managers who have made profits are normally better placed to decide upon its productive use than are bureaucrats more distant from the market place.

Establishment of Performance Measurement and Incentive Systems

An effective system for measuring and controlling performance will reveal whether, and how far, the directors of state industries are meeting their financial commitments. It underlines the importance placed on financial objectives, performance, and discipline. It is a basis for rewards and punishments. And it gives the government a tool to control the credit it is advancing to state enterprises as a whole.

The amount of detail in an ideal financial system will vary from country to country and firm to firm. In general, the more an enterprise is subject to competitive market forces and the less it depends on government financial support, the less detailed will the centralized data requirements need to be. In countries such as France, Norway, and Sweden, it may be enough to collect the enterprises' annual reports. But in countries such as Ghana and Zambia, governments may have to require quarterly financial statements and production and personnel data and may publish a summary of the performance of all public enterprises at the end of each year.

The monitoring arrangements need to be linked to an incentive system. Incentives are most effective in a relatively competitive environment and where managers have considerable financial and managerial independence. In highly protected economies, bonuses need to be used with caution since they may well increase the incentive for an inefficient expansion of operations.

Managerial Autonomy and Accountability

Two key determinants of the performance of state industries are the extent to which the government decentralizes decisionmaking to their managers, and how it manages its relations with them. This section deals with the issue of *how much* decisionmaking power should be delegated and what managerial environment can help in decentralizing. Once the government has decided how much control it wants, the other issue is *how* it organizes its ministries, specialized agencies, and other bodies to enable it to exercise that control effectively.

Private enterprises are run within three different frameworks: ownership, strategic, and operating. The role of the owners is to define the business charter, set the overall objectives of the enterprise, appoint and dismiss the board of directors, and approve annual accounts and dividend payments. These powers are formally executed through an annual shareholders' meeting. The strategic role is the responsibility of the board of directors. Its major functions are to decide on plans, to monitor performance against targets, and to appoint, advise, and dismiss the chief executive. Typically, the board meets four to eight times a year and is composed of people with stature and relevant professional experience. The operating role is performed by the chief executive and his top management. Their responsibility is to manage and develop the business in accordance with agreed objectives.

How do the organizational structures of state industries differ from this prototype? The short answer is that governments, as owners, invariably encroach on the strategic and operational functions—and this is the cause of much of the poor performance of state companies. A simple example can illustrate what happens. In several sample countries, boards of directors have to seek ministerial approval for relatively small investments, hiring and firing of staff, wage setting, decisions on working capital, procurement policies, foreign travel, and much else. It may sometimes be justified for governments to involve themselves in decisions that private firms would handle at the board level. But involvement in operational matters is time-consuming for an already overstretched bureaucracy; the ministries lack the information and the business perspective to make the correct decisions; and, most important, it absolves the management of its responsibility and accountability for how a company performs.

The countries included in this study provide a rich variety of organizational structures. The most decentralized are those in Sweden and Norway. Intermediate ones are in Austria, Brazil, France, Israel, Italy, and Portugal, while highly centralized structures are found in Ghana, India, Pakistan, and Tunisia. A comparison of the two polar cases—Sweden and Norway, on the one hand, Ghana, on the other—is instructive. In Sweden, the Cabinet, the formal owner of public enterprises, has delegated this responsibility to the Ministry of Industry. Within the ministry, a Unit for State Participations (Unit 5), staffed by eight professionals, actually executes the ownership role for the state industries, which employ some 90,000 people. In Norway, a similar number of staff within the Ministry of Industry perform the ownership role for state industries, which employ 50,000 people. The Unit for State Participations does not intervene in the boards' decisionmaking, does not maintain a data bank of financial or operational data, does not keep a roster of management candidates, and does not perform any management services. Executives of Unit 5 are directors on only a limited number of boards. They stress that, in their role as board members, they take care to act in the best interests of the enterprise and *not* to overpower the board with their ownership role. Only in times of crisis and when state financial support is required does the Unit for State Participations increase its involvement in decisionmaking. Most public enterprises are organized as limited liability stock corporations and are regulated by corporate law. Where a firm also has private shareholders, the board reflects the fact.[6]

For the past fifteen years most of Sweden's state enterprises were organized under one superholding company. This company was recently broken down into one holding company for medium-size enterprises and a number of branch-oriented corporations, each owned directly by the Ministry of Industry. This change was in line with the government's belief in decentralized decisionmaking.

By contrast, public enterprise managers in Ghana have little autonomy. Their companies were responsible for about 60 percent of total industrial production in the country in 1975–81, but their performance has generally been poor. The Ghana Industrial Holding Company (GIHOC) was established in 1967. A central government body named the State Enterprise Commission (SEC), with varying responsibilities for development and control of public enterprises, has been established and reestablished three times, in 1965, 1976, and 1981. In its current incarnation, its roles are to advise the government on issues involving performance, strategy, finance, and personnel and to monitor and evaluate performance. The structure of control places the ownership role with the sectoral minister. Lines of responsibility are then supposed to flow through the holding company's board and management down to the board and management of the operating companies. In practice, most control remains in the ministries, with the sectoral ministers holding the key positions. For example, prices are set by the Prices and Incomes Board, a unit under the Ministry of Finance and Economic Planning. The dismissal of five or more workers must be authorized by the Ministry of Labor (except in cases of proven criminal offenses). Import licenses are allocated by the Ministries of Trade and Finance, while letters of credit for approved import licenses are the responsibility of the Bank of Ghana and the commercial banks. Approval of immigrant quotas for non-Ghanaian staff is handled by the Ghana Investment Center and the Ministry of Interior. Wage contracts need the recommendation of the Prices and Incomes Board and the approval of the Ministry of Finance.

Many government officials involved in public enterprises underestimate the complexities of running a company. An enterprise is not only input, production functions, systems, and output. Its success depends on creativity, flexibility, dedication, perseverance, and hard work, particularly of top managers. Most of the planning officials and civil servants appointed as directors and chief executives of public enterprises lack the knowledge, experience, and motivation to blend together the many ingredients of a successful company. Governments should therefore hire top-quality entrepreneurs and managers and should design the organization in such a way as to shield these people from undue political and bureaucratic interference.

As economies move from industrial infancy through growth and maturity into the postindustrial era, so their state industries tend to change their organizational structures. At the risk of oversimplification, figure 2 and table 5 show five increasingly decentralized stages, which are mirrored in the whole process of industrialization. As industrialization advances, so the complexities and competitiveness of the marketplace and the speed of change all accelerate. Rigid and bureaucratic management models become obsolete; decentralized structures become a necessity for survival.

'igure 2

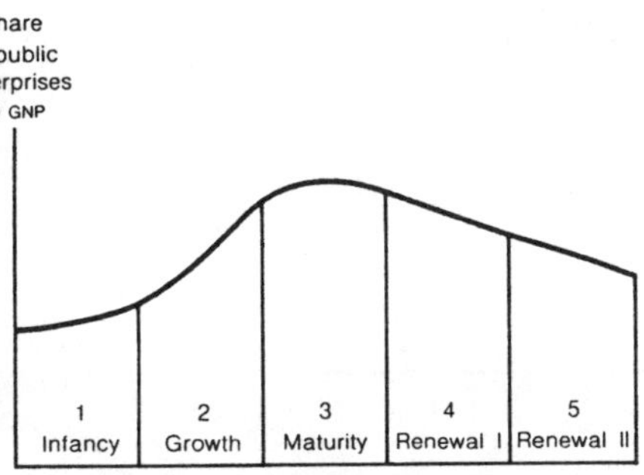

Naturally, not every country will necessarily go through all five types of organization, but most countries go through a process of decentralization. For example, India never used holding companies on a big scale, although its ministries sometimes functioned like holding companies. Some countries may temporarily move toward more centralized structures; this happened in Brazil in the 1980s, as a response to the sprawling growth of state industries in the 1970s. Similarly, public enterprises in Italy enjoyed considerable autonomy in the 1950s and the early 1960s, but this was reduced because of an ideological shift toward central planning. There have been relatively few such periods, and they do not reverse the long-term trend of increasing decentralization. Recently, the Italian super-holding company, IRI, has adopted a divestiture strategy of selling part of the equity of its major subsidiaries to the private sector.

There is no reason for developing countries to wait for the post-industrial era to move into some of the more decentralized forms of organization. Naturally, the types of powers granted and of services provided by central units, and the mix between market and government controls, will vary significantly between countries. But these varying levels of powers, services, and controls could basically apply within the same type of decentralized structure.

It may be that the role of state industries in economic life will

Table 5. *Characteristics of Public Enterprises by Stage of Development*

Stage	*Characteristics*
1. Infancy	Public enterprises are organized as departments of government. • ownership role: government • strategic role: government • operating role: government
2. Growth	Public enterprises are regulated by civil service codes. • ownership role: government • strategic role: government and management • operating role: management and government
3. Maturity	Public enterprises are governed by holding and superholding companies. • ownership role: government • strategic role: holding company • operating role: management
4. Renewal I	Public enterprises are owned by government and regulated by commercial codes. • ownership role: government • strategic role: board of directors • operating role: management
5. Renewal II	Public enterprises are joint public-private ventures; stocks are issued on stock exchanges. • ownership role: government and private • strategic role: boards of directors • operating role: management

shrink from now on. Most of the circumstances that motivated the creation of public enterprises, such as the lack of industrial infrastructure, the nonexistence of equity markets, and a limited private sector, have diminished in importance. The emerging high technology and service-related industries are typically not capital-intensive; and being entrepreneurial in character, they are ill suited to the bureaucratic cultures frequently found in public enterprises. Some longstanding state industries are being wholly or partly privatized in countries as diverse as the United Kingdom, Norway, Sweden, Italy, Spain, the Federal Republic of Germany, Japan, Turkey, Uganda, Togo, Cameroon, Brazil, and Argentina.

The experience of state industries, as well as of large private enterprises, shows that the worst repercussions of a poor organizational structure can be avoided through scrupulous adherence to the following principles: (a) clear demarcation of the roles and responsibilities of the government, the board of directors, and the management of public enterprises; (b) full delegation of authority in line with delegated responsibility; (c) appointment of professional directors and managers with experience directly relevant to their tasks; and (d) introduction of a management philosophy that judges managers on the basis of financial viability and a limited set of other indicators. Adequate decentralization is not, by itself, enough for satisfactory performance. However, its absence can confound even the most meticulously designed organizational structure.

Coordination within the Government

Once the government has decided *how much* decisionmaking power to delegate, the next issue is *how* to organize its own ministries and specialized agencies to ensure that decisionmaking is effective. The multiplicity of government bodies involved in public enterprises has frequently led to confusion, duplication, and excessive control. Superimposed on this diffusion of responsibility is the tendency for public enterprises to suffer the extremes of political interference whenever the government changes.

One way to coordinate decisionmaking and to prevent excessive political interference is by establishing supervisory agencies of some kind. Such bodies can be thought of as "focal points": some perform the full ownership role, others are more limited. The functions of these units and examples are provided in table 6.

Focal points with supervisory functions can be useful in obtaining timely and relevant information on state industries, a prerequisite for

Table 6. *Focal Point Organizations*

Focal points with an ownership role

Responsibilities

- To establish and amend the charter of the enterprise
- To hire and fire the board of directors
- To approve annual accounts and dividend payments
- To hire auditors
- To monitor performance

Examples

Norway: Public Enterprise Unit in Ministry of Industry
Sweden: Unit Five in Ministry of Industry
Austria: Ministry of Public Enterprises
Italy: Ministry of State Participations
Canada: Overseeing Agency for Crown Corporations

Focal points with a supervisory or advisory role

Responsibilities

- To define financial and operational objectives
- To review multiannual plans and budgets
- To monitor performance on a monthly or quarterly basis
- To provide technical assistance and training

Examples

Brazil: Special Secretariat for the Control of State Enterprises (SEST) within Ministry of Planning
India: Bureau of Public Enterprises (BPE)
Pakistan: Experts Advisory Cell (EAC) within the Ministry of Production
Israel: Government Company Authority (GCA) within the Ministry of Finance
Ghana: State Enterprise Commission (SEC)

assessing performance.[7] One such has been SEST in Brazil. By having a clear role and objectives, it has shown how to improve the efficiency of public enterprises. In its six years of existence, SEST has increased their accountability without getting involved in day-to-day operations, even though some of its responsibilities (such as recommending ceilings and targets for certain categories of spending) could have led to excessive interference in the operational side of public enterprises. Through its monitoring of key economic variables, and with political support from the government, it has brought the priorities of all state industries more into line with the needs of the economy as a whole. Yet it has done so by focusing on broad aggregates and ensuring that they were achieved.

SEST's small (fewer than fifty professionals) but competent staff eschewed getting involved in the day-to-day affairs of the enterprises. Their tasks have been to

- recommend targets for all major categories of revenues and expenditures, foreign debt, imports, and fuel consumption of public enterprises
- recommend distribution of state industry profits and dividends
- recommend new equity capital increases for public enterprises
- recommend the creation and acquisition of new companies, as well as the liquidation and divestiture of old ones.

Their recommendations are made directly to the president of the republic for final approval.

The contrast between SEST and SEC of Ghana is instructive. The precise role of SEC has never been clear, and its political support has been patchy. The agency's work is frustrated because the reports from public enterprises come in late, sometimes so late as to be virtually useless. Yet the managers of state industries consider the agency to be an unnecessary bottleneck in their operations.

While one main characteristic of state industry management is excessive government interference, it is equally common to find a lack of effective control, a situation that creates uncertainty, misunderstanding, and sometimes distrust—and that frequently ends up in excessive interference. The dual purpose of supervisory agencies is therefore both to protect the directors and management from undue political maneuvering and also to exercise effective control over a limited number of variables.

Evidence from the sample countries shows that it is desirable to give supervisory agencies some elements of the ownership role as well as their supervisory functions. This is done in Austria, Italy, Norway, and Sweden. In Brazil, the success of SEST depends partly on the fact that it has been granted several powers that normally belong to the ownership role. There are strong reasons for requiring that a supervisory agency report not just to a single ministry. The agency might be responsible to an intersectoral committee, for example, or operate as a quasi-governmental unit, or be attached to the office of the prime minister or president. Such arrangements give the agency greater status and ensure that it does not become beholden to the narrow views of a single ministry.

Establishing an institutional and policy framework that is conducive to good performance by state industries is a challenging task. Arrangements will of course vary among countries depending on factors such as the level of economic development, the availability of free markets, and the political philosophy. In essence, however, this article has proposed a framework that stresses the decentralization of decisionmaking to the directors and management, and the strengthening of their capabilities. It has not attempted to quantify the benefits of this approach. But it has provided compelling examples of how the performance of state industries varies widely, with the variations often being attributable to the way the industries are organized and run.

Abstract

This study identifies the factors that influence the performance of state industries. Based on a review of thirteen countries, the authors isolate three qualities in the business and managerial environment that distinguish successful public enterprises from the others. These are (a) the degree of competition that public enterprises are exposed to; (b) the degree of financial autonomy and accountability under which public enterprises operate; and (c) the extent and manner in which managerial autonomy and accountability are ensured. It is impossible, and perhaps misleading, to assess statistically the importance of each of these factors. Where all three exist, however, the performance of public enterprises is significantly better than in those cases where most or all of these factors are absent.

Notes

This article is a summary of a more detailed study by the authors (Ayub and Hegstad 1986). The background material for that study comprised thirteen country case studies of public enterprise sectors. The countries included were Austria, Brazil, France, Ghana, India, Israel, Italy, Norway, Pakistan, Portugal, Sweden, Tunisia, and Zambia. The authors are grateful to many readers for helpful comments but especially to Kemal Dervis, Leroy Jones, Harinder Kohli, Anne Milne, Mary Shirley, and Anil Sood.

1. The correlation coefficients of per capita GDP with the shares of public industrial enterprises in industrial and total GDP were only 0.05 and 0.03, respectively. Kendall's rank coefficients were, respectively, 0.14 and 0.39 (a zero value signifies a random pattern and 1.00 indicates exactly similar rank orders), results that are only significant at 1 percent and 10 percent levels of confidence, respectively.

2. While high capital intensity is characteristic of the public enterprise sectors in most sample countries, it is particularly marked in Ghana. Two sugar factories and a state footwear factory installed conveyors to undertake tasks that are not even mechanized in the United States (Killick 1983).

3. The data refer to the public industrial enterprises under the jurisdiction of the Ministry of Production, which account for most of public industrial value added and employment.

4. In some cases, of course, the external borrowing of public enterprises was not

voluntary but forced on them by governments that used the creditworthiness of these enterprises to contract external loans.

5. This approach was recommended by the Nora Report in France. See Groupe de Travail de Comite Interministerial des Enterprises Publiques (1969).

6. While it is difficult to observe a causal relationship between private participation in public companies and their performance, many observers believe that the professional competence of the experienced private sector individuals on the board of the Swedish steel holding company, SSAB, has contributed significantly to its successful restructuring to date.

7. For example, prior to the establishment of SEST in Brazil in 1979, even information on the number of public enterprises in existence was not readily available.

References

Ayub, Mahmood A., and Sven O. Hegstad. 1986. "Public Industrial Enterprises: Determinants of Performance." World Bank Industry and Finance Series 17. Washington, D.C.

Diskin, Ehud. 1980. "Attitude toward Risk in Israeli Private and Public Enterprises." Ph.D. dissertation. Jerusalem: Hebrew University.

Groupe de Travail de Comite Interministerial des Enterprises Publiques. 1969. *Rapport sur les Enterprises Publiques*. Paris: Documentation Français.

Gupta, M. 1982. "Productivity Performance of the Public and the Private Sectors in India: A Case Study of the Fertilizer Industry." *Indian Economic Review* 17, no. 2.

Jones, Leroy. 1983. "The Linkage between Objectives and Control Mechanisms in the Public Manufacturing Sector." In United Nations Industrial Development Organization (UNIDO). *The Changing Role of the Public Industrial Sector in Development*. Vienna.

Killick, Tony. 1983. "The Role and Performance of the Public Sector in the Industrialization of Some African Developing Countries: An In-Depth Assessment." In UNIDO. *The Changing Role of the Public Industrial Sector in Development*. Vienna.

Peters, Thomas J., and Robert H. Waterman, Jr. 1982. *In Search of Excellence*. New York: Harper and Row.

Sheahan, John B. 1976. "Public Enterprise in Developing Countries." In William G. Shepherd, ed. *Public Enterprise: Economic Analysis of Theory and Practice*. New York: Lexington Books.

Shirley, Mary. 1983. *Managing State-Owned Enterprises*. World Bank Staff Working Paper 577. Washington, D.C.

Sri Ram, V., and others. 1976. *Performance of Public Sector Undertakings*. New Delhi: Economic and Scientific Research Foundation.

[5]

The Problem of Public Enterprise in Developing Countries: Is Privatization the Solution?

John F. Coburn and Lawrence H. Wortzel

Introduction

Just twenty-five years ago, there were very few state-owned enterprises (SOEs) in either the industrialized or the developing countries of the non-Communist and Socialist worlds. In recent years, however, the state has come to play an increasing role in business ownership. Although this trend was pronounced in many countries of Western Europe, it has been most notable in the developing nations of Asia, Africa, Latin America, and the Middle East.

Table 1 illustrates the number of state companies in selected developing countries and the major position state ownership occupies in their national economies. In Venezuela, for example, 7 of the 10 largest companies are numbered among some four hundred state-owned enterprises. In Brazil, the 10 largest commercial enterprises are SOEs; these companies represent 5 percent of GDP, account for 70 percent of total government investment, employ 1.4 million persons, and are responsible for half of Brazil's $90 billion foreign debt.[1] Egypt's SOEs account for about 80 percent of that country's total industrial output, and Turkey's 150 state-owned companies control an estimated 47 percent of Turkish industry.[2]

Researchers who have studied the growth of SOEs have concluded that the motives for building a state-owned sector have been based primarily on economic policy rather than on political ideology.[3] For example, many SOEs were established to invest in areas that were important to the country's development but were either too costly or too risky for the local private sector to enter or "off limits" to foreign capital for reasons of national interest. Typical of these cases were government investments in steel, mining and minerals processing, petrochemicals, and other "basic industries." In some instances, however, investments were made in high-technology areas, as in the case of Embraer, Brazil's state aircraft company.

A second motive for creating SOEs was to maintain government control over industries thought to be best run as monopolies. State-owned telecommunications, electric power, and commodity-trading companies are common examples.

Rescuing failing private companies to preserve employment and essential services constitutes a third major reason for state intervention in economic enterprises. The Jamaican government's takeover of much of the sugar and hotel industry during the economically troubled 1970s illustrates this phenomenon.

Finally, many state-owned enterprises have come into being through the nationalization of foreign-owned enterprises. This has been particularly prevalent in the mining, telecommunications, and petroleum industries.

The creation of an SOE has, in certain instances, solved the problems it was created to handle. Korea and Brazil, for example, have developed efficient steel industries that are competitive on a worldwide basis. Brazil's Embraer has developed efficient aircraft that are not only in service in Brazil but also in use by airlines in the United States and elsewhere. But these are the exception rather than the rule. Unfortunately, many SOEs seem to have created more problems than they have solved. The World Bank, in its 1983 World Development Report, concludes that the problem with SOEs is economic inefficiency, leading to a financial burden that echoes throughout the economy.[4] Increasingly, the call is for "privatization," the argument being that subjecting the SOE to the discipline of the marketplace will, per se, make it more efficient.

So much has been written recently about privatization of public enterprise that one could easily view it as the solution to the general problem of state-owned enterprise throughout the world. To be sure, privatization is taking place. The privatization initiatives currently under way in Britain and, to a lesser extent, West Germany, are well documented. In the developing world, significant public enterprise divestment has occurred in Chile, and initial privatization steps have been taken in (among others) Panama, Brazil, Jamaica, Sri Lanka, Pakistan, Bangladesh, and Senegal. In addition, plans for privatization exist in a number of countries (e.g., Venezuela, Peru, and Malaysia), although actual divestments have yet to occur.

Against this backdrop several important questions emerge: How successful has privatization been to date, and how extensive will it be in the developing world over the next few years? To what extent will Britain's privatization program be replicated elsewhere? And to what extent will privatization provide a lasting cure for the ills of public enterprise?

In principle, privatization is a highly desirable objective and should be vigorously pursued wherever possible. In practice, however, given economic and political realities in most of the developing world, extensive privatization is unlikely to take place over the next few years. Because of the immense state sector in many developing nations, and because of the economic and political difficulties associated with divestiture, it is likely that--even in the most successful pursuit of privatization--a large number of companies will remain under state control. This will be especially true for the largest enterprises, which often represent the greatest financial deficits and which in many instances dominate the most crucial sectors of the economy.

This means that in most of the developing world, privatization--however desirable--simply will not take place to an extent sufficient to provide a solution to the problem of state enterprises. For this reason, it would be a mistake to view privatization as a panacea.

26

Instead it should be seen as one of a number of strategic actions that, when taken together, would result in the overall reform and improvement of state enterprise. Privatization will have to be pursued selectively, but, in the interim, enthusiasm for privatization must not divert the attention of government leaders and international development policymakers from the equally important task of instituting the necessary structural, policy, and management reforms within existing state companies to ensure that, as soon as possible, they are made to operate with a reasonable degree of efficiency, productivity, and financial gain.

In this chapter we briefly review some of the financial, economic, and operational difficulties experienced by most SOEs and then examine the privatization record to date, focusing on impediments to privatization. Based on this examination, we identify the characteristics of SOEs that make them appropriate candidates for privatization and suggest strategies for carrying this out. Finally, recommendations are offered for achieving more efficient management for those SOEs that, for whatever reason, are likely to remain in state hands.

The "Problem" of State Enterprise

Much has been written in recent years about the varied problems of state enterprises: operating deficits, low productivity, heavy dependence on domestic and foreign credit, poor quality of goods and services, corruption, and suboptimal resource utilization. These ills are by no means universal; efficient and profitable state-owned companies do exist, even in the developing world. Singapore Airlines, Petroleo Brasileiro, the National Commercial Bank of Jamaica, and Korean Steel are notable successes. Unfortunately, these companies form a minority, and the evidence suggests that, on balance, the financial burden of most state enterprises far outweighs whatever social and political benefits they provide.

The burden of poorly performing state enterprises rests on the shoulders of all nations, but most heavily in the developing world, which can least afford it. It is one thing to have an inefficient state sector in the United Kingdom, Germany, or Sweden, where a strong private sector exists and where both consumers and producers have a reasonable degree of choice among domestic and imported goods and services. But in the developing world, state enterprises often substitute for the private sector and in many instances are the only source of the products or services they represent. In some countries, such as Mexico, Egypt, Tanzania, and Indonesia, the public-enterprise sector virtually overwhelms the economy because of the high proportion of GNP, national investment, public borrowing, and employment that it represents. In these countries, when public enterprises are inefficient and costly, the impact is usually felt nationwide.

Much has been written about the causes of poor performance in state enterprise: unclear (and often conflicting) objectives; the imposition of political (and often uneconomic) activities; the control of management process (input) rather than performance (output); the confusing lines of authority and responsibility between SOEs and their supervisory entities; overstaffing for social ends; and many others that need no elaboration here.

Privatization: The Solution?

Given the plethora of problems besetting state enterprise during a time of world recession, international debt crisis, and increasing economic and fiscal conservatism, the privatization of state enterprise is being proposed with increasing frequency as the only lasting solution to the state enterprise dilemma.[5] Despite the publicity in favor of privatization during the past few years, however, the record to date has been modest at best. Table 2 summarizes privatization trends in major developing nations with market economies and sizable state sectors. The values assigned each country are based on our assessment of each country's "net" record in recent years. Actual and professed privatization minus any nationalization of enterprise that may have occurred during this period:

Net Privatization Formula

Actual Privatization + Professed Privatization - Nationalization = Net Privatization

As this table suggests, the record on a worldwide scale is meager. The most successful efforts to privatize have taken place in just a few countries, but even in these countries, a large number of public enterprises still remain. For example:

-- Chile, the first country since Japan in the 1800s to undertake large-scale privatization, has reversed the expropriation (as opposed to selling shares) of 259 companies and has sold off other companies worth $400 million. Despite this very major effort, 66 companies still remain in government hands; these companies account for 18 percent of GNP and have an asset value more than ten times that of the privatized companies.[6]

-- In the past three years, Jamaica has sold three small companies--an airline food service company, and two agricultural companies--and has leased bus company routes and several sugar mills to private operators.

-- In 1982 Brazil sold ten relatively small SOEs and is said to be planning to sell some thirty-six more, yet hundreds of companies remain under government control.

-- Bangladesh and Pakistan have sold off a variety of small rice, flour, cotton, and jute mills, but in each of these countries the major "infrastructural" government companies remain unsold.

In the rest of the developing world, privatization has consisted more of rhetoric than of action. For example, Venezuela, Peru, and Argentina have all vowed for several years to privatize many of their SOEs, but none has yet taken any visible action to this end.

Barriers to Privatization in Developing Nations

Why has the privatization track record not been more impressive, particularly in the developing world, where the problem is most acute? The answer lies in three factors that seem to represent major obstacles to any large-scale privatization effort in developing nations: (1) financial barriers; (2) political barriers; and (3) the lack of a clear plan.

1. Financial barriers: In addition to the sheer number of state-owned enterprises, the market value of these enterprises in most countries far exceeds the availability of private capital to pay for them.

   Capital availability is a problem, even in the industrialized countries. Consider, for example, the case of Great Britain, a country with sophisticated capital markets and a solidly established private sector. To date; the sale of slightly more than half of the government's share in four companies (Britoil, British Aerospace, Cable and Wireless, and the Port Authority), together with complete divestiture of Amersham International, have soaked up some $3.25 billion in private sector capital.[7] Full divestiture of British Airways would require another $1.2 billion.[8] The sale of 51 percent of British Telecom will require private investment capital of $6 billion--a sum more than five times the largest public equity offering ever made in the United States ($1.2 billion by AT&T in 1983). This sum is also 25 percent greater than the value of all public issues in Great Britain last year.[9] Needless to say, adding companies like British Leyland, Rolls-Royce, British Airways, and others to this list within the next few years will place a substantial burden on local capital markets. In fact, as much as a quarter of the shares of British Telecom will have to be offered in the United States, and this divestment may have to be spread over several years to lessen its impact on capital markets.

   If the partial privatization of ten state enterprises in Britain will tax the country's private capital markets to the extent described above, imagine how difficult it would be to execute the sale of large SOEs in countries in the developing world. What sources of domestic private capital could possibly buy out the majority portion of large SOEs in countries like Bolivia, Pakistan, Peru, Turkey, Tanzania, Egypt, or Bangladesh? In Jamaica, where would local private capital come from to buy the government's share of Air Jamaica, the Public Service Company, or the bauxite companies? Even in more developed countries such as Portugal, Venezuela, Argentina, Brazil, and Mexico, where could enough private capital be found to make significant inroads in their hundreds of SOEs, some of which are among their largest enterprises and, in some cases (like PEMEX, Petrobras, and PDVSA), rank among the one hundred largest companies in the world.

The impact of privatization, in at least some instances, will not be limited to the capital required to execute the sale of the enterprise. In some cases, a sizable injection of capital may have to be made to get the company into an operating position to be sold. Britain has managed this successfully with British Airways, Jaguar, and Rolls-Royce. In other cases, SOEs may need to expand to meet demand for their products and services, and, once privatized, these firms may be regular customers of the local capital markets or financial institutions.

Moreover, even if sufficient capital can be found, there is likely to be a large opportunity cost attached to using the capital for privatization. Using capital in this way diverts it from investments that might have considerably greater impact on the country's economic growth. The propensity of business executives to choose the least risky of a group of alternative investments is well known. Given a choice between buying an existing SOE and starting a new enterprise, they are likely to opt for the existing enterprise, particularly if it is being offered at a discounted price, as in Britain and Chile.

To be sure, some of the financial burden could be eased by selling all or part of the SOE to foreign investors. In many cases, however, doing so would compromise one of the major reasons for forming the state enterprise in the first place: to keep what were considered key industries and activities under national control. In these instances, foreign capital might be politically unacceptable.

2. Political barriers: Even if large-scale privatization were financially possible, there is little reason to believe that such a program would be politically feasible in many countries. This is especially true for most of the developing countries, where private-sector ownership of large enterprises is discouraged in many sectors, and where the concentration of economic wealth in a few private hands (whether foreign or domestic) is a politically sensitive issue.

   Table 3, which depicts ownership patterns in key sectors of the economies in nine of the largest Latin American countries and Jamaica, illustrates the degree of state control in sectors that are considered to be of "strategic national importance" or "national sensitivity." As it happens, these sectors contain many of the largest companies, which frequently are entities using enormous amounts of domestic and foreign debt and producing sizable economic losses. Unfortunately, these are also the companies that, for political reasons, are the most difficult to privatize.

   In the case of Venezuela, for example (table 4), state enterprises dominate most of the key productive sectors of the economy. Despite the promises and plans of the new Lusinchi government to launch a large-scale privatization program, it is difficult to see how any of the companies listed in table 4, with the possible exception of Aeropostal airline, could withstand the political backlash that a privatization effort would undoubtedly create. In fact, the net trend may be toward government ownership in Venezuela and not in the opposite direction. A new coal mining company is currently being formed (CarboZulia), a new state-owned bauxite company has recently been established (Bauxiven), and there is talk of a second large-scale steel mill company (SiderZulia). There is also debate in leftist political circles about nationalizing the only remaining private electric company, Electricidad de Caracas.

3. Lack of planning: The third obstacle to privatization programs is the absence of planning and structure for such programs once they are announced. Among the most crucial aspects of this are (a) the absence of clearly established criteria for determining which enterprises are to be privatized, and in what order; (b) the lack of clear "rules of the game" as to what form of privatization to pursue in different situations (divestment, leasing, or management contracts); (c) the lack of clearly established procedures specifying the mechanics of the privatization process; (d) the absence of a clearly established organizational entity within the government for handling the privatization program; and most important, (e) the lack of clearly established goals as to the overall scope, timing, and results of the program. Moreover, because the president or prime minister usually plays an active role in the program's decision making on a day-to-day basis (rather than limiting involvement to policy-making and delegating the detailed implementation to others), the program often becomes highly politicized, and the speed of implementation is drastically reduced as a result.

Therefore, regardless of how desirable privatization may be in principle, in practice there are some important barriers to carrying it out, which must be recognized and overcome. In particular, governments must spend enough time to plan their privatization efforts in advance, and they must be careful in choosing only the best candidates for privatization to ensure success during the early stages of the privatization "learning curve."

Deciding When to Privatize: The "Zero-Base SOE" Model

The decisions surrounding privatization in any country and in any industry depend on many different economic and political variables, and therefore vary from one set of circumstances to another. To say, for example, that, in general, textile mills, hotels, or cement companies should belong to the private sector might be appropriate for Indonesia, Peru, or Venezuela, but might be inappropriate or unrealistic in Tanzania or Mexico. Moreover, the choices depend on the existing mix of enterprises in the country as well as on other national characteristics.

One approach is to adopt a "zero-base" model for determining national industrial ownership. In zero-base budgeting, one begins with a budget of zero, and every expenditure must be carefully justified by organizational unit and by function. In applying a zero-base model to its state-owned enterprises, the nation would begin with the assumption that all industry should be private (e.g., zero state enterprise) unless certain conditions exist making private ownership either undesirable or infeasible. The conditions for exempting an enterprise from private ownership would be carefully spelled out for each country, depending on its own political, social, and economic interests. Under this model, the entire state-enterprise sector would be subjected to this "zero-base SOE test" every few years. In this way, each SOE's existence would have to be justified periodically in terms of the specific benefits it provides against the costs incurred. Those enterprises no longer meeting this criterion would be excluded from the nation's "SOE budget" and would, therefore, become candidates for privatization.

A periodic examination is recommended because economic and political environments change over time. For example, state ownership of steel or electric power companies are usually called for at early stages in a country's economic development. As the country grows, however, such firms may well become capable of conversion to viable private enterprises that provide necessary goods or services without subsidization. Similarly, SOEs created to provide employment become less necessary as alternative employment opportunities open up. Finally, as a country matures politically, its government may be able to substitute regulatory control for direct control and still achieve the desired social and economic results. Even if the periodic zero-base SOE test does not lead to privatization, the recurring process may lead to better SOE performance because of the inevitable questions it will raise about SOE goals, management, and operating methods.

Criteria for including certain enterprises or sectors in the "national SOE budget" under the zero-base approach might include the following:

-- if there is sufficient domestic private capital, or if there is a high opportunity cost of local capital for privatization, coupled with politically or economically unacceptable use of foreign capital

-- if it is impossible to obtain a reasonable sale price for the private offering

-- if social benefits provided by the enterprise are important, and if under private control the enterprise would be likely to pursue a strategy resulting in the elimination of its principal social benefits (e.g., raise prices, eliminate workers, reduce or eliminate service, disinvest in high priority regions)

-- if regulatory control cannot be substituted for ownership control

-- if privatization were to result in an unacceptable concentration of ownership in the hands of oligarchic groups.

Applying the above criteria to politically moderate, middle-income, market economy countries (such as Colombia, Venezuela, Portugal, Mexico, Argentina, Sri Lanka, Korea, or the Ivory Coast), the following industries would probably not qualify for inclusion, and would therefore be candidates for privatization, under the "zero-base" model: hotels, textile mills, sugar mills, food processing companies, commercial banks, cement companies, and small manufacturing companies.

Once the industries or companies to be privatized have been chosen within a given political and economic setting, two further decisions must be made. First, priorities must be set among the candidates because it is likely that there will be more candidates than the economy can handle at any one time. Priorities should be based on some criterion of expected gains in economic efficiency in comparison to the capital required to purchase the enterprise. One way to do this would be to construct pro forma financial statements covering some relevant time horizon under the alternative of both public and private ownership. Where appropriate, a comparison could also be made of the relative social benefits anticipated under each mode of ownership. The enterprises could then be ranked according to the magnitude of the benefits to be gained from privatization.

To minimize strain on capital markets, private investors can be encouraged to use debt rather than equity capital in buying SOEs--in a sense applying the concept of the leveraged buyout to the sale of state enterprise. Since there are not likely to be lending institutions equipped to handle such transactions, a development bank would have to lend private investors the funds to buy the SOE, and the loan would be repaid out of earnings. The leveraged-buyout alternative should be limited, however, to those situations in which the investors in the firm will also be its managers.

Alternatives to 100 Percent Divestment

Privatization can be achieved by various routes: full or partial divestment, leasing to private interests, and management contracts are among the most common. Whereas divestment is generally the preferred form of privatizing state enterprise, it is not possible in cases where the state is not willing or able to sell land or transfer title to mineral rights or transportation routes. In Jamaica, for instance, the Jamaica Omnibus Service was "privatized" by leasing routes to private operators, and the major sugar estates are being removed from national control through the use of management contracts with private operators.

When there are more divestment candidates than the country's capital markets can handle, an alternative to consider is partial privatization--selling some portion of state shares either to the general public, to one or more specific groups or individuals, or to the SOE employees themselves. If, after the sale, the government is willing to limit its role to that of investor and to leave the management to the private-sector partners, a partial sale may accomplish as much as 100 percent divestment.

Another possibility is to establish joint ventures with foreign capital. Such arrangements can be advantageous when managerial or technical expertise is required to make the enterprise more efficient. This alternative is also appropriate when the foreign partner can assist in arranging export opportunities by providing market access or marketing expertise. Examples of successful joint ventures of this type include the government of Colombia and Exxon in coal mining, the Venezuelan government and a consortium of Japanese and North American investors in aluminum, and the government of Liberia and Bethlehem Steel in iron ore mining.

What to Do until (or instead of) Privatization

Although partial privatization, joint ventures, leveraged buyouts, and other techniques may speed the privatization process, there will still be some SOEs that must remain under state ownership either permanently or for a time. Whereas privatization is an important element in solving the problem of state enterprise, it cannot be viewed as the only answer. In some circumstances, privatization may not be feasible from a financial or political vantage point. In other circumstances, it may be feasible but may take many years to effect. In either event, most countries will probably have to live with the majority of their SOEs for some time. It is therefore worthwhile to make efforts to improve the performance of the SOEs that will remain.

What can be done in lieu of privatization to improve the performance of state enterprises? To be sure, much as been published over the past decade about reforming state enterprise. Much of this focuses on clarifying objectives, improving the relationship between enterprises and their sponsoring ministries, establishing elaborate schemes for measuring the cost of social objectives, establishing formal performance contracts between the enterprise and the government, and developing shadow-pricing mechanisms that allow the enterprise's true economic performance to be measured.[10] Most of these measures have been tested, but for the most part, they have been difficult to implement as permanent or even temporary solutions.

There may be some simpler and more practical short-term actions governments and state-owned enterprises might adopt. Taken together, they could have an important long-term impact on the SOEs. These actions would also benefit the privatization effort inasmuch as strengthening an SOE's financial condition will greatly facilitate the sale of its shares to a risk-averse private sector. Such actions would also result in a stronger enterprise--one more capable of sustaining itself when the time for privatization comes. Some of these short-term actions include the following:

1. Minimizing management turnover. The cost of management turnover in any organization is enormous. Unfortunately, rapid management turnover is endemic within the state-enterprise sector of most developing nations. Conversely, it is no coincidence that some of the most efficient and profitable SOEs in the world are those that have enjoyed senior management continuity. Petroleos de Venezuela, Renault, Embraer, and Singapore Airlines are examples. In France, the case of Elf Aquitaine is illustrative. After

building this state-owned petrochemical giant into one of France's most profitable companies, Elf's president, Albin Chalandon, was replaced in 1982 by the new Socialist government for what were largely political motives. Since then, Elf's profits have declined 40 percent, and the company faces a crisis of mounting long-term debt, refining losses, and declining cash flow.

To avoid such unnecessary disruption, SOE chief executives should be allowed at the minimum a three- to five-year renewable term of office. In addition, the chief executive's term should not coincide with terms of those in public office. Most important, SOE chief executives should be appointed by the SOE Board of Directors, rather than by the political ministry, as is frequently the case. Finally, contracts should be drawn up between the board and the chief executive that specify the terms and conditions of dismissal--based on specific performance indicators rather than on vague, subjective, political grounds.

2. <u>Conducting formal annual audits</u>. Just as private sector shareholders expect periodic audits of the company's financial and management practices, so should public enterprise stakeholders expect audits of their companies.[11] Even if the overseeing government ministry does not require it, SOE managers and Boards of Directors themselves should take the initiative to conduct such audits as a way of enhancing managerial self-discipline and preventing the kind of scandalous behavior that has been too often exhibited by SOE management--even in such prestigious companies as PEMEX in Mexico and Pertamina in Indonesia. Independent audits are relatively inexpensive to perform, and in most capital cities there are several domestic and international auditing firms to choose from. From the government's standpoint, audits have the benefit of forcing the company to produce an annual set of consistent financial statements that, if done for all SOEs, greatly facilitates the ministry's job of evaluating performance, approving budgets, and reviewing major expansion proposals on a consistent basis. Conducting audits will also assist the eventual privatization program. In Jamaica, one of the major obstacles to the current privatization effort is the fact that many state enterprises have not been audited for several years and therefore lack reliable financial statements on which to base a corporate valuation.

3. <u>Offering management bonuses</u>. Because SOEs are part of the government, SOE salaries are tempered by the government wage scale, even though the enterprise may be autonomous and fall outside the civil service system. Relatively low management salaries are probably an unavoidable fact of life for these entities. Unfortunately, low salaries may make it impossible for the SOE to attract the good management it needs. This problem is most acute in the developing countries, where management talent is in short supply, anyway.

The use of incentive bonuses may be a way to attract and retain better management. Because many SOEs exist (at least in principle) as profit-making entities, applying a portion of the company's profits to pay management bonuses would seem perfectly appropriate and would help to bridge the perennial gap between SOE and private-sector compensation. Even in cases where SOEs are not profitable because of artificially low prices or government-imposed social costs, management should be allowed to earn a bonus for having achieved or surpassed certain agreed-upon performance targets (such as increasing productivity, developing new markets, enhancing sales). To implement this notion, companies could develop special formulas to accumulate a corporate-wide management bonus pool during the year, to be paid out to key executives at year-end, based on specific, predetermined criteria for management performance. The formal yearly audit could be used to develop the required data.

4. Permitting greater control and autonomy to SOE managers. The literature on state-owned enterprises often depicts SOE managers as helpless pawns of the political system, their hands tied by the many restrictions, contradictions, and political vagaries imposed on them. This may be the case in many situations; however, SOE managers probably have more power and control than they believe they have. They might gain the autonomy that everyone agrees they need simply by taking more calculated risks--by sticking their necks out more in defense of the enterprise and its basic productive objectives. The case of Petroleo Brasileiro (Petrobras) is exemplary. This company has had such strong leadership for so many years that today it is virtually a ministate unto itself.[12] In the case of Ferrominera, the large Venezuelan iron ore company, strong and persistent management has taken many risks in terms of reducing employment and cutting costs. Today the company has stemmed what was a very severe seven-year decline in profitability, despite the continued depression in world iron ore prices. The Turkish state tobacco enterprise provides another example of a dramatic turnaround resulting from strong and independent management. Of course, there are risks associated with independence, and too much autonomy can lead to dismissal, as in the case of Elf's Chalandron. But if governments want real managers to run their SOEs, this is the risk they and their SOE managers will have to take.

Of course, there are numerous other reform measures that could and should be taken to improve SOE effectiveness, including the introduction of competition, the expanded use of SOE-multinational joint ventures (SOEs gain management and technology while multinationals gain markets and raw materials), and the professionalization and depoliticization of SOE boards. If these and other relatively simple measures are adopted, the 1980s could see major SOE improvement throughout the world.

Conclusion

On balance, privatization--however desirable--may not offer the long-awaited solution to the problem of state enterprise, particularly in the developing world, where the problem is most acute and where privatization is most urgently needed. Therefore, while pursuing privatization, government leaders and international development policymakers are encouraged not to lose sight of the possibilities for reforming state enterprises if they are to remain in government hands. Some relatively simple and immediate actions can be taken as initial steps in this process. Taking these steps could even lead to a new paradox: SOEs that would be attractive to private-sector investors but that are too profitable for the government to sell.

Table 1

Size and Importance of State-Enterprise Sector in Selected Developing Countries

Country	Approximate Number of SOEs	Indication of National Economic Importance
Mexico	600 with full or partial government ownership	Over 10% of GDP
Brazil	500 with full government ownership; 200-300 more with partial government ownership	About 5% of GDP
Venezuela	400 with full or partial government ownership	Over 25% of GDP
Peru	150 companies with full or partial government ownership	About 20% of GDP; over 50% of national investment
Argentina	300 companies with full or partial government ownership	N/A
Jamaica	Between 75-100 companies with majority government ownership	N/A
Turkey	150 companies, mostly with full government ownership	N/A
Egypt	N/A	Over 60% of manufacturing value-added
Tanzania	400 companies with full government ownership	About 15% of GDP and nearly 40% of manufacturing value-added
Sri Lanka	125 companies with full or partial government ownership	N/A
Pakistan	175 companies	N/A
Korea	N/A	Nearly 10% of GDP and about 28% of national investment
India	200 companies with full government ownership	Over 10% of GDP

Sources: World Bank; New York Times; Wall Street Journal; The Economist; and other journals.

Note: N/A = no information available.

38

Table 2

Privatization Trends in Major SOE Countries

Europe		Latin America		Other	
U.K.	++	Chile	++	Senegal	++
W. Germany	+	Brazil	+	Bangladesh	+
Portugal	0	Jamaica	+	Pakistan	+
Italy	0	Panama	+	Sri Lanka	+
Austria	0	Venezuela	0	Indonesia	0
Sweden	0	Peru	0	India	0
Norway	0	Colombia	0	Malaysia	0
France	-	Argentina	0	Korea	0
Spain	-	Ecuador	0	Egypt	0
		Costa Rica	0	Nigeria	0
		Bolivia	-		
		Mexico	-		
		Guyana	-		
		Nicaragua	-		
		Trinidad	-		

Key:

++ Privatization program solidly in place with visible results.

\+ Announced government policy or program to privatize major portions of state sector, but tangible results not yet visible.

0 No observable trend toward either private or public ownership.

\- Net decrease in private-sector role over past few years; net increase in government ownership.

Notes

1. New York Times (17 July 1983).

2. Wall Street Journal (17 February 1984).

3. See, for example, Yair Aharoni, Markets, Planning and Development; Renato Mazzolini, "Government Controlled Enterprises: What's the Difference?" Columbia Journal of World Business (Summer 1980), pp. 28-39; Raymond Vernon, "The International Aspects of State-Owned Enterprises," Journal of International Business Studies (Winter 1979), pp. 7-14.

4. World Bank, World Development Report, 1983 (New York: Oxford University Press, 1983).

5. The term "privatization" is used to refer collectively to all of the various means of decreasing state control of business enterprise: full or partial divestment; leasing to private operators; the use of management contracts with private managers; and so forth.

6. Mary M. Shirley, Managing State-Owned Enterprises, World Bank Staff Working Paper no. 577 (1983), p. 59.

7. Fortune (31 October 1983).

8. Wall Street Journal (13 December 1983).

9. Ibid.

10. Many of these remedies are discussed in World Development Report, 1983.

11. See Yair Aharoni, "Performance Evaluation of State-Owned Enterprises: A Process Perspective," Management Science 27, no. 11 (November 1981): 1340-1347, for a lucid discussion of performance measurement in SOEs.

12. Wall Street Journal (17 November 1983).

Other sources:

Kempe R. Hope, "Improving Public Enterprise Management in Developing Countries," Journal of General Management 743 (Spring 1982): 72-85.

Leroy P. Jones and Edward S. Mason. "Role of Economic Factors in Determining the Size and Structure of the Public Enterprise Sector in Less-Developed Countries with Mixed Economies," in Public Enterprise in Less-Developed Countries, ed. Leroy P. Jones, pp. 17-47 (Cambridge: At the University Press, 1982).

[6]

Privatisation in Less Developed Countries: An Overview

Paul Cook and Colin Kirkpatrick

1. INTRODUCTION

Privatisation has attracted much attention in recent years, and reflects a world-wide interest in reducing the role of the state in national economies, while enhancing the scope of private ownership and the private sector. The growing appeal of privatisation embraces both the ideological desire for smaller government and a belief in the superior economic performance of the private sector.

The term 'privatisation' is used to describe a range of different policy initiatives designed to alter the balance between the public and private sectors. Here we distinguish three main approaches to privatisation.

The first and most common usage of the term refers to a change in the ownership of an enterprise (or part of an enterprise) from the public to the private sector. Denationalisation, or divestiture, can proceed in a number of different ways. In the industrial countries where capital markets are well developed, it can be brought about by the sale of all, or part, of the privatised enterprise's equity to the public. But, in most less developed countries (LDCs) where capital markets are rudimentary or non-existent, denationalisation is more likely to involve the sale of the enterprise as a complete entity. Denationalisation may also take the form of joint-ventures, which introduce a private sector involvement into the public enterprise. In extreme cases, divestiture may involve the abandonment or formal liquidation of the state-owned enterprise.

A second mode of privatisation involves the liberalisation, or deregulation, of entry into activities previously restricted to public sector enterprises. The removal of restrictions on market entry is intended to increase the role of competition, and to the extent that private enterprises are successful in entering the hitherto protected markets, a variant of privatisation will have occurred, even though no transfer of ownership of assets has been involved.

The third sense in which the word privatisation has been used is where the provision of a good or service is transferred from public to private sector, while government retains ultimate responsibility for supplying the service. Franchising, or contracting-out, of public services and the leasing of public assets to the private sector are examples of this form of privatisation.

In this survey we concentrate on the first two of these notions of privatisation—the ownership of productive assets and the degree of competition under which they operate.[1] As we shall see, the improvements in economic performance that privatisation is intended to yield are most likely to occur if a transfer of activities from the public to the private sector is accompanied by increased market competition.

The emergence of privatisation as a major issue for policy discussion in the second half of the seventies can be traced to the convergence of several factors. This period saw the election of governments in a number of industrialised countries—most notably the United Kingdom and the United States—that were committed to the greater use of the market as a means of securing economic objectives. At the same time, the structural obstacles encountered by the industrial countries in achieving full employment and satisfactory economic growth were exacerbated during the 1970s, as these economies experienced difficulties in adjusting to the large shifts in relative prices induced by the oil price increases. Deregulation and increased market competition were seen as the means of accelerating the process of structural adjustment. The subsidisation of declining industries, often in public ownership, was also perceived to be a constraint upon the process of industrial restructuring. Privatisation in its various forms was seen, therefore, as a solution to existing structural problems and as a means of achieving the necessary adjustment in the economy.[2]

Interest in privatisation is not confined to the industrial countries. In many LDCs privatisation is being actively considered as a policy option, and a growing number of developing countries have formulated detailed proposals for privatising significant segments of economic activity.[3] This chapter will examine the role of privatisation in LDCs. The next section considers the forces that have led to the current interest in this policy. This is followed by a review of the case for privatisation resulting from a shift in economic thinking about the development process and disenchantment with the performance of state-run activities. The fourth section of the chapter examines more closely the relation between privatisation and performance, in particular focusing on the expected economic, financial and social benefits. The fifth section briefly reviews the extent to which the various forms of privatisation have been implemented in LDCs. The final section presents a number of concluding comments concerning the significance of privatisation as a policy option for LDCs.

2. THE PUBLIC ENTERPRISE SECTOR IN LDCs

The public, or state-owned, enterprise sector lies at the heart of the privatisation debate, and the growing importance of the sector in many LDCs has led to increased concern with its economic performance and contribution to the development process.

The average contribution of public enterprises to GDP in LDCs rose from 7 per cent at the beginning of the 1970s to about 10 per cent at the end of the decade (World Bank, 1983, p. 49). There is considerable variation between countries however, ranging from 3 per cent in Paraguay and Nepal to 38 per cent in Ghana and Zambia. In most LDCs, the share of public enterprise investment in total gross fixed capital formation exceeds 25 per cent, and in some cases accounts for more than 60 per cent of total investment.[4]

Public enterprises are found in almost all types of economic activity in LDCs. They are traditionally concentrated in the public utilities and natural resources sectors, but are also prominent in manufacturing in a large number of countries. For example, 65 per cent of manufacturing value added is generated in public enterprises in Egypt, 60 per cent in Tunisia and 50 per cent in Zambia. On average, the public enterprise sector appears to be more prominent in the manufacturing sector in the LDCs than the industrial countries—in the early 1980s, 34 per cent of LDC public enterprises were engaged in manufacturing as compared to 23 per cent in industrial countries (Pathirane and Blades, 1982)—but again there is considerable variation between countries.

This heterogeneity in the size and composition of the public enterprise sector in the developing countries reflects the range of considerations that have influenced the establishment of public enterprise activities.[5] Economic analysis rationalises direct government participation in productive activities as a response to private market imperfections or failure. Various forms of market failure—indivisibilities, economies of scale, monopoly, externalities—prevent the economy from achieving an efficient resource allocation, and the establishment of public enterprises may be justified as being one way of correcting these specific forms of market imperfection.[6] However, as Hemming and Mansoor (1987) note, while market failure can provide a strong rationale for government intervention, this intervention need not take the form of public ownership. For example, the market failures could be corrected through the use of regulatory controls, legal restraints, and taxes, transfers and subsidies. To explain why public ownership has been the preferred mode of intervention, it is necessary to consider a number of additional factors.

An important set of arguments in LDCs relates to economic growth. Where private sector activity is constrained by high risk aversion, poorly developed financial markets or a paucity of information, 'entrepreneurial substitution' has been a motive for establishing public enterprises. Second, in economies characterised by limited integration between different sectors, public investment can perform the role of ensuring that the conditions necessary for industrial growth are met. Thus, in many LDCs the need to accelerate the process of industrialisation has led to public sector participation in sectors believed to have significant linkage effects. Basic industries such as iron and steel, chemicals, heavy engineering, fertilisers and petrochemicals have often been seen as performing a catalytic function in the early stages of industrialisation by providing essential inputs to other manufacturing activities. Even when these products can be imported at lower resource cost, publicly-owned domestic production in these 'commanding heights' activities may be rationalised in terms of their strategic economic importance. Third, where the growth of the economy is constrained by inadequate savings, the public enterprise sector may be seen as a potential source of investible surplus.

In addition, public enterprises were often established and used as an instrument for the pursuit of distributional goals. The public enterprise may be used to create or preserve employment. It may be used as a counterweight to the concentration of private economic power, or to strengthen the economic position of particular ethnic groups or geographical regions. The public enterprise's output may be supplied at subsidised prices as a means of assisting low-income consumers. This may be achieved either by subsidising the output of public enterprises directly, or by lowering costs through subsidies to input supplies.

Finally, various 'non-economic' considerations have influenced the decision to establish public enterprises in many LDCs. In some cases, public ownership has been pursued for ideological reasons, with public ownership of the means of production being seen as a necessary condition for the establishment of socialism and, therefore, advocated as an end in itself. In other instances, public ownership is perceived as a necessary counterweight to foreign ownership and influence in the economy.

3. THE CASE FOR PRIVATISATION IN LDCs

The current interest in privatisation is a reflection of a fundamental reassessment of the role and contribution of the public enterprise sector in the process of economic growth and development. In part, this has emerged as one element in a more general shift in the dominant development paradigm; in part, it stems from a concern with the perceived weaknesses in the performance of the public enterprise sector.

The new development orthodoxy

In the 1950s and 1960s the dominant view in development economics was that markets frequently failed to work efficiently in LDCs. The stress was on the need for active state intervention and participation to offset these market failures, and as we saw in the preceding section, this led to the expansion of the public enterprise sector and the widespread adoption of economic planning. This interventionist approach was actively supported by the major international and bilateral aid agencies, which encouraged development planning, provided technical assistance to strengthen planning capabilities, and allocated investment funds to public sector projects.[7]

The results of planning in LDCs were disappointing. Measuring performance in relation to the targets set in the plans indicates that the majority of countries failed to achieve the planned objectives (United Nations, 1977; Killick, 1983; Shen, 1977). Public sector investment projects frequently performed poorly (UNIDO, 1979; Baum and Tolbert, 1985). The import substituting industrialisation strategy, which formed an integral part of the interventionist approach to development in the 1950s and 1960s, was associated with widespread inefficiencies and resource misallocation (Kirkpatrick, 1987).

The perception that development planning had 'failed' led to a shift in the dominant paradigm towards a neo-classical, market-oriented view of the development process and policy.[8] Neo-classical economics can be described as:

> ... a paradigm that tells one to investigate markets and prices, perhaps expecting them often to work well, but also to be on the watch for aberrations and ways of correcting them. Perhaps the single best touchstone is a concern for prices and their role. (Little, 1982, pp. 25–6)

The debate therefore, is about the exact role of the price mechanism and the private sector in the mixed economy. Thus, Krueger (1986), in describing the research priorities of the World Bank, argues that:

it must be emphasised that the current reappraisal of the role that governments should play in development does not entail any commitment to *laissez-faire*. Understanding where governments' comparative advantage lie, and the mechanisms that may correct government failure, is therefore the big challenge for research in development economics. (pp. 202–3)[9]

The policy prescriptions which flow from the neo-classical analysis involve an increased role for markets and the price mechanism in LDCs. This requires a strategy of 'economic liberalisation', involving the removal of various forms of government intervention in product and factor markets which are seen as 'distorting' the price signals and 'repressing' the market mechanism. The reduction or elimination of these restrictions in financial, trade and labour markets is expected to lead to an improvement in economy-wide efficiency and growth by allowing markets to operate effectively.[10]

In the context of the privatisation debate, the neo-classical analysis translates into policy prescriptions directed towards a reduction in the size of the public sector, the removal of government regulation and controls, the fostering of competition, and a greater reliance upon the market and price mechanism for the allocation of resources.

It is widely held that the public sector has become too large in many LDCs. The World Bank's 1981 report on economic prospects in sub-Saharan Africa ('Berg Report') concluded that:

It is now widely evident that the public sector is over-extended, given the present scarcities of financial resources, skilled manpower, and organisational capacity. This has resulted in slower growth than might have been achieved with available resources, and accounts for the present crisis. (World Bank, 1981, p. 5)

Although it is frequently made, the argument that the public sector in LDCs is 'over-extended' and requires 'rolling-back', as a general proposition is empirically unproven. Evidence to support the hypothesis of an inverse relationship between macroeconomic performance and the size of the public sector is lacking. Nunnenkamp (1986) was unable to detect any statistically significant cross-country relationship between the relative importance of the public enterprise sector in LDCs (as measured by their output and investment shares) and various indicators of the countries' economic performance (real growth in GDP and gross fixed investment, the level of industrialisation, the growth in employment). Kirkpatrick (1986) found a negative, but statistically insignificant, correlation between the share of public enterprise output in GDP, and growth in income in the 1970s, for a sample of twenty-three LDCs.

A variant of the argument that public sector growth adversely affects economic growth performance is found in the 'crowding-out' hypothesis. Here, it is argued that public sector investment can lower private investment if it utilises scarce resources that would otherwise be available to the private sector, where, for example, public sector investment is financed by taxation or debt issue which is paid for from the private sector's investible surplus. This hypothesis was tested by Blejer and Khan (1984) using pooled cross-section data for twenty-four LDCs over the period 1971–79. They reported that the effect of aggregate public sector investment on private investment was consistent with the crowding-out hypothesis, but the substitution coefficient between public and private investment was very small and not significantly different from zero. When public investment was disaggregated by type, it was found that an increase in the infrastructural component of government capital formation raised private investment, presumably since it enhanced the possibilities for private investment activity. Increases in other kinds of public investment were found to have some crowding-out effect, but the degree of substitution between public and private investment was significantly less than unity.

The size of the public sector *per se* does not have a significant bearing on the performance of the sector or the economy.[11] What matters is the effectiveness with which resources allocated to the public sector are utilised. Growing concern with the apparent inefficiencies in the public enterprise sector's performance has been the second motivation for the current interest in privatisation in LDCs.

Public enterprise performance

It is widely believed that in most developing countries the performance of the public enterprise sector has been disappointing. Originally established to be leaders in the LDCs' industrialisation, to generate public savings for investment and growth, and to achieve social and redistributive goals, are public enterprises now perceived to have performed poorly in fulfilling these various objectives.

The following quotations convey the current sense of disillusionment with the public enterprise sector in LDCs:

Unless there is a change in the operating effectiveness of parastatals, particularly in industry, they will not take their proper place as growth points.' (World Bank, 1981, p. 38)

In many countries the expansion of the public sector has stretched its managerial capacity to the point where serious inefficiencies result.' (World Bank, 1983, p. 46)

Over the years, inefficiency has flourished in many state enterprises, its overt consequences masked by the ready availability of budgetary support.' (IMF, 1986, p. 16)

Actual experience with the operations of state enterprises reveals that many have not effectively served to redistribute income.' (IMF, 1986a, p. 30)

The performance of a public enterprise is difficult to measure. In principle, the process of performance evaluation ought to follow a sequential procedure of identifying the objectives set for the public enterprise, constructing indicators to measure the degree of attainment, and then measuring performance. In practice, there are considerable difficulties in following this procedure—objectives are seldom specified in a clear and unambiguous way, objectives may be mutually inconsistent, there are problems in devising satisfactory single- and multiple-goal performance measures, and the necessary data are often not available.[12] Similar problems arise in attempting to compare the performance of public and private enterprises. It is seldom possible to compare like-with-like, because either the public and private enterprises operate under different market conditions, or the publicly-owned enterprise is required to pursue different operational criteria.

The existing information on public enterprise performance must be interpreted, therefore, with caution, and few firm generalisations can be drawn from it.

Economic performance There is a small but growing body of evidence which compares the performance of public and private enterprises in LDCs, using the criterion of productive (technical) efficiency (i.e. the degree of economy in resource inputs used to produce a given output). This evidence is reviewed in Millward (this volume).

The evidence on productive efficiency performance does not demonstrate that public enterprises in LDCs are always outperformed by private enterprises. Millward's detailed examination of the studies undertaken so far leads to the conclusion that 'there is no evidence of a statistically satisfactory kind to suggest that public enterprises in LDCs have a lower level of technical efficiency than private firms operating at the same scale of operations'.[13] However, there are very few examples of totally comparable public and private sector enterprises, which allow one to isolate the effect of ownership on productive efficiency from other factors such as scale of operation and product mix. Furthermore, within the samples of enterprises studied there is a wide range in performance, with the technical efficiency of public enterprises ranging from worst- to best-practice.

The available evidence on productivity performance in the public enterprise sector in LDCs, therefore, is inconclusive. It is insufficient to support any generalised assumption as to the inferior performance of public enterprises as compared to similar enterprises in the private sector. Nevertheless, poor economic performance does occur in the public enterprise sector, and there are undoubtedly instances where existing enterprises have the potential to achieve significant improvements in efficiency. It is important, therefore, to identify the major sources of inefficiency and to devise appropriate policy initiatives to improve economic performance.

Perhaps the most common cause of inefficiency in the public enterprise sector is political interference. In many LDCs the public enterprise is an important instrument for political patronage. Senior staff are frequently political appointments with little industrial management experience; employment, purchasing and pricing decisions are subject to political intervention; the boundaries of government and enterprise control are ill-defined and continually shifting.[14] The absence of clearly defined objectives and the limited operational autonomy given to public enterprises inevitably have an adverse impact on the efficient internal operations of the public enterprise sector.

A failure to set specific objectives for the public enterprise and to monitor performance in relation to them can lessen the incentives to managerial efficiency. The theory of property rights argues that in the classical small firm where ownership and management coincide, the manager–owner has a direct interest in cost-minimisation since reward is directly related to performance.[15] But, in the large corporate enterprise ownership and management are separated and the owners of the property rights have limited control over management. Managers may have little direct interest in the profitability of the organisation and may be more concerned with the scale of operations of the business or, more generally, 'enjoying a quiet life'. In the private sector, however, these non-profit maximising activities are constrained by the potential sanction of takeover, which is the principal means by which the capital market can exert pressure on the private firm to maximise profit. But, in the case of the public enterprise the threat of takeover or bankruptcy does not exist, and productive efficiency is, therefore, likely to suffer.

The public enterprise may also fail to achieve allocative efficiency if it operates in a monopoly environment. Welfare economics yields the well known marginal equivalence conditions for allocative efficiency, defined as a situation in which consumers' needs are met at prices that reflect the cost of provision. If markets are competitive, the forces of competition ensure that allocative efficiency is achieved, provided that external effects and distributional consequences are unimportant.[16] Therefore, if the public enterprise operates in a monopoly environment, it has little incentive to respond to market demand and is unlikely to achieve allocative efficiency.

Few of the public–private firm studies relating to LDCs give explicit consideration to the influence of competition on the firms' economic performance. There is, however, a certain amount of more general evidence on the relationship between market structure and firm-level performance in LDCs.

Various studies have examined the effect of seller concentration in the manufacturing sector on price–cost margins, and have found that, in most cases, there is a positive and statistically significant association between seller concentration and the profitability measure used.[17] Typically, the relationship is a continuous one, with profit margins being progressively higher in those industries with the higher concentration levels. The evidence from LDCs is consistent, therefore, with the view that the allocative efficiency of firms—public and private—is improved by a competitive market environment.

Financial performance The public enterprise sector in LDCs has frequently failed to generate an investible surplus and instead has created a budgetary burden for the public sector. The overall deficit—defined as the difference between current plus capital expenditure and revenue plus receipts of current transfers and of non-government capital transfers—of public enterprises in LDCs averaged almost 4 per cent of GDP in the mid–1970s, as compared to an average of 1.7 per cent in the industrial countries (Short, 1984). If government current transfers are excluded from receipts, the LDC average rises to 4.6 per cent. Furthermore, the public enterprise overall deficits in LDCs have increased in recent years, by 2.5 per cent of GDP between the late 1960s and mid–1970s. Overall deficits for public enterprises are not undesirable *per se*, and it may be appropriate to run deficits to finance investment needed to expand marketable output. Nevertheless, it is relevant to note that the degree of self-financing appears to be low: comparing current and capital account balances suggests that if receipts of current government transfers are excluded, the self-financing ratio of state enterprises amounted to only 10 per cent in the mid-1970s, in those developing countries for which data were available.

Public enterprise deficits have been financed either by borrowing by the state enterprises in domestic and international financial markets or by central government transfers. In the mid-1970s, for those developing countries for which a breakdown of sources of finance is available, it appears that about 25 per cent of the state enterprises' deficits were met by direct foreign borrowing. In the period 1976–78, state enterprises accounted for one-third of all international borrowing by LDCs (World Bank, 1980). A further 60 per cent of the overall deficit was financed from central government and the banking system, the remaining 15 per cent being covered by other domestic borrowing.

These financing demands have a direct effect on macroeconomic variables and performance. Where the public enterprise sector can borrow from the central bank, there will be an immediate impact on domestic credit and money supply. Where transfers from government are used, the overall public sector deficit is increased. When foreign borrowing occurs, the debt ratio is raised. In some LDCs, in an attempt to relieve the burden on the state budget, public enterprises have been required to raise funds for investment and working capital directly from the domestic commercial bank sector.[18] At the same time, governments have often directed the commercial banks to grant loans to the public enterprise sector on preferential terms.

The precise effect of these financing requirements on macroperformance will vary from country to country, but their magnitude suggests that in many LDCs the public enterprise sector's financial deficit will contribute significantly to inflation and balance of payments difficulties.[19] A concern with the impact of the public enterprise sector financial deficit on macro-stability is reflected in the priority given in the International Monetary Fund's stabilisation programmes to improving public enterprise financial performance. In a survey of ninety-four Fund-supported adjustment programmes in developing countries during the period 1980–84, it was found that sixty-eight of the programmes included policy recommendations relating to non-financial state enterprises, aimed mainly at improving financial performance (IMF, 1986a). Indeed, the current attention given to the financial position of the public enterprise sector in LDCs probably relates more to the macroeconomic consequences of large budget deficits than to a concern with profitability as an indicator of enterprise performance.

Besides examining the financial performance from a macroperspective and drawing inferences about the profitability of the public sector as a whole from the size of the sector's overall deficit, a large number of studies have examined financial performance more directly. These concern individual enterprise studies, and sectors or country studies drawn from samples of public enterprises.

Caution needs to be exercised in interpreting financial profitability data since measurement differences arise both between enterprises and across countries. As Nellis (1986) notes, the definition of a public enterprise varies across countries. Differences also exist in the treatment of depreciation, inflation, subsidies and taxation. Many LDCs produce statistics covering the entire public enterprise sector, making it difficult to separate manufacturing enterprises from the more traditional public utility and natural monopoly enterprises.[20] Individual enterprise data are often concealed in the consolidated figures for a holding company.[21]

Market structure and regulations can also affect the significance of financial profitability as an indicator of performance. A monopoly position, with protection from foreign competition, can allow the public enterprise to make financial profits while its economic performance is poor. Price controls can adversely affect the public enterprises financial performance.[22] In addition, public enterprises are often expected to fulfil certain social objectives which may also affect financial performance.

Again, it may be difficult to get a clear indication of profitability where indirect subsidisation occurs. Input prices may be subsidised, particularly where the supplier is another public enterprise. Bank credit may be offered at subsidised rates. Exemptions from indirect taxes and customs duties on imported inputs, or from general income tax, will further complicate the interpretation of profit and loss statements (Floyd, 1978; Gillis, *et al.*, 1982).[23]

Subject to these caveats, a number of common features can be deduced from individual studies. One significant feature is the wide variation in the financial performance of different public enterprises in the same country. In Zambia, for example, some of the subsidiaries in Indeco, the government's holding company, have been highly profitable (breweries, cement, industrial oxygen), while others including chemicals and saw mills, have made losses (Ayub and Hegstad, 1987, p. 83). Similar variation is reported for Brazil, Sri Lanka (Cook, 1985), and Pakistan (Cook, 1983).

Variations in profitability are also evident across regions and individual sectors. Although the generally poor financial performance of public enterprises in sub-Saharan Africa has been highlighted in various studies, performance at the individual enterprise level has been highly variable (Bovet, 1985; Nellis, 1986). Across industries, the most profitable sectors appear to be mining and petroleum, the least profitable steel and automobiles (Gantt and Dutto, 1968; Ayub and Hegstad, 1987).

Studies that have attempted to compare the financial performance of public and private enterprises appear to show that the publicly-owned firms have recorded lower profitability than their private sector counterparts in the same industry. This is illustrated by Ayub and Hegstad's (1986) study covering Ghana, India, Pakistan, Tunisia and Zambia. Similar conclusions emerge from comparative studies in Senegal (Killick, 1983), Tanzania (Kim, 1981) and Indonesia (Funkhouser and MacAvoy, 1979).

Distributional performance Public enterprises in LDCs are often expected to pursue social objectives, which can range from subsidising particular consumer groups, assisting certain regions, and creating or maintaining employment. Thus, in addition to economic and financial performance, consideration must be given to the public enterprise sector's performance in fulfilling 'non-economic' objectives.

In many LDCs the public enterprise sector is seen as an important instrument to promote income redistribution. While economic theory would suggest that distributional objectives should be pursued through the use of the fiscal system, in practice LDC policy makers typically operate in a 'second-best' environment in which limitations on the use of tax and subsidies measures require them to pursue their re-distributive goals by employing other, less direct instruments. The public enterprise sector is, therefore, frequently used to create employment, to assist employees through the payment of higher wages and benefits, and to benefit consumers by subsidising the price of public enterprise outputs.

Has the public enterprise sector been an effective means for advancing redistributive objectives in LDCs? While acknowledging the difficulties in identifying the distributional impact of the public enterprises, critics would argue that they have not served to redistribute income (IMF, 1986a; Jones, 1985). Employment opportunities have been lessened by the adoption of capital-intensive technology in production, improvements in employees' wages and employment conditions have created a privileged labour elite, subsidies on output have failed to reach the lowest income group, benefiting the better-off, and price controls on foodstuffs have disadvantaged poor rural producers.

The empirical evidence appears to support the view that public enterprises have failed to realise their redistributional goals, and, in some circumstances, have produced perverse results. In Zambia, stringent price controls on refined oils and fats produced by publicly-owned agro-based enterprises ended up subsidising large industrial users, wholesalers, and affluent urban dwellers (Ayub and Hegstad, 1987). In Bangladesh, some 75 per cent of the public enterprise sector's manufactured output was subject to price control. In almost all cases the administered ex-factory price was set at a level significantly below the market clearing price, giving rise to windfall gains at the distribution and retailing stages, where market prices ranged from 80 to 400 per cent above the official price (Sobhan, 1983).

Killick (1983) indicates that in Africa public enterprises have been associated with accelerated Africanisation of industrial employment, and this had distributional consequences since it resulted in a shift in the total wage bill from foreigners towards nationals. However, this process may worsen the interpersonal distribution of income within a country if a high proportion of the occupations formerly undertaken by foreigners were highly paid.

4. PRIVATISATION AND PERFORMANCE

Privatisation is advocated primarily as a means of improving the performance of the public enterprise sector. The main arguments in support of privatisation are examined in this section. In particular, the impact of denationalisation and deregulation on efficiency (productive and allocative) and financial performance are discussed separately.

Denationalisation and performance

Efficiency performance The earlier discussion of the causes of poor economic performance in the public enterprise sector in LDCs suggests a number of reasons why privatisation in the form of a change of ownership may have a significant impact on productive efficiency.

A change to partial or complete private ownership can be expected to lessen the scope for political intervention in the operations of the enterprise. The enterprise's objectives will be simplified, overly complex networks of disfunctional bureaucratic controls will be reduced, and the likelihood of arbitrary 'interference' in operating decisions will be lessened. Each of these changes can be expected to contribute to an improvement in productive efficiency. It may be noted, however, that these changes are not conditional on privatisation: internal reform of the public enterprise is an alternative option for realising the same gains. 'The key factor determining the efficiency of an enterprise is not whether it is publicly or privately owned, but how it is managed. In theory it is possible to create the kinds of incentives that will maximise efficiency under any type of ownership.' (World Bank, 1983, p. 50).

A second argument derives from the property rights theory, and suggests that the change in ownership, by altering the structures of property rights, will improve the incentives for productive efficiency performance. This supposes, however, that the private firm needs to perform efficiently to remain in business. If privatisation merely converts a public monopoly into a private monopoly, the enterprise will not be compelled by competitive pressures to improve its productive efficiency.

A further argument is that the change in ownership will impose the discipline of private capital markets on the enterprise, thereby improving productive efficiency. While this argument may be important in industrial countries, it has limited relevance to LDCs, where the capital market is typically underdeveloped and denationalisation will normally involve the sale of the enterprise to individual purchasers, or the introduction of private capital into joint ventures. Even in industrialised countries where a privatised enterprise has a monopoly, the capital market may only impose an incentive to lower costs solely to improve profits rather than to benefit consumers through lower prices (Peacock, 1984).

It can be concluded, therefore, that privatisation in the form of denationalisation is unlikely to significantly increase productive efficiency.

Will denationalisation lead to an improvement in allocative efficiency? In the preceding section it was argued that allocative efficiency is a function of market structure rather than ownership. Thus, in the absence of competition, privatisation in the form of asset sales is unlikely to result in gains in allocative efficiency.

A more recent literature has argued, however, that competition in the sense of many firms competing in the same market, is not a necessary condition for achieving allocative efficiency. The contestable markets' literature argues that the existence of only a small number of firms in a particular market does not, in itself, imply monopoly power, if barriers to entry and exit are absent (Baumol and Willig, 1986). If barriers to entry are minimal, then whenever a monopolist creates profitable opportunities for new entrants by raising prices above costs, he becomes vulnerable to profitable 'hit and run' strategies by potential entrants. The policy implication is that the removal of artificial entry barriers, thereby making markets more contestable, will prevent monopoly abuse and guarantee allocatively efficient pricing practices by the monopoly. However, the conditions needed to satisfy the contestability model are rarely met in practice.[24] The efficiency results of the theory are dependent upon the assumption that the entrant must be able to exit from the market at no cost when it is no longer profitable to remain. 'Free' exit in this sense means there must be no 'sunk' costs, that is, costs that cannot be eliminated when production ceases. It is difficult to conceive of economic activities where this condition is satisfied. Thus, while the contestable markets' literature rightly draws attention to the influence of entry conditions on market behaviour, it is misleading to suppose that the elimination of artificial barriers to entry will in itself be sufficient to secure allocative efficiency gains.

Financial performance[25] An important motive for denationalisation is the anticipated alleviation of the public enterprise budgetary burden on the government. In considering the impact of privatisation on the public finances it is essential to distinguish between the consequences of ownership transfer *per se*, and the associated effects on the operations of the privatised enterprise.

The immediate effect of asset sales will be a once-and-for-all reduction in the government deficit, equal to the sales revenues. However, if the public enterprise is profitable, its privatisation means that the government forfeits the future stream of income. If the sale has been correctly priced, the sales revenue will be equal to the discounted present value of this future income stream and the change of ownership leaves the public sector's net worth unaltered. If the price is set too low, perhaps deliberately to favour the purchasers, then the public sector's net worth is reduced. Should the government use the sales revenue to reduce taxation or increase expenditure, the deficit in the sale year remains unchanged, but is increased in subsequent years.

The above argument applies in the case of profit-making public enterprises. However, in many instances privatisation is advocated for loss-making public concerns, whose losses are being covered by transfers from government. In theory, if the only change which occurs with privatisation is that of ownership, the 'sale' of loss-making enterprises will involve the payment of a lump sum subsidy to the buyer, or an agreement to maintain existing subsidies.[26] The change of ownership of loss-making enterprises may, therefore, have an insignificant impact on the public finances.

The more important changes in the government's budgetary position will occur if privatisation alters the operations of the enterprise. If privatisation is expected to result in an improvement in the financial performance of the enterprise, it will be possible to sell loss-making enterprises, provided the anticipated gain in profitability is sufficiently large. In this situation the drain on the government's overall budget is reduced. This argument should be qualified, however. As we saw in the preceding section, an improvement in both financial and efficiency performance will only occur if privatisation is associated with competitive market conditions. Where a public enterprise monopoly is privatised, or where the privatised firm is granted protection from market competition, an improvement in financial performance is the result of greater exploitation of market power.

The government is likely to face, therefore, a policy trade-off between efficiency and financial objectives. The sale of public enterprises will be easier, and sales revenue higher, if the privatised firm is offered market protection, but economic efficiency will be adversely affected. Alternatively, exposing the firm to increased competition promotes efficiency but reduces the attractiveness of the firm to the private buyer and, hence, lowers the government's potential sales revenue.

Deregulation, liberalisation and efficiency performance

The main conclusion to emerge from the preceding discussion is that gains in efficiency performance are more likely to result from an increase in market competition than from a change in ownership. It follows that if the principal objective of privatisation is to increase economic efficiency, the policy priority should be to increase competition, not to transfer productive activities to the private sector. However, the liberalisation (i.e. measures to increase competition) of markets is not a simple matter, and policy formulation in the area is confronted by several major complications. Among the factors that constrain market competition in LDCs, the following are of particular importance.

First, where the public enterprise is a natural monopoly with extensive market power, deregulation (the removal of government-imposed restrictions that prevent entry by private sector rivals) is unlikely to produce the desired increase in competition, and hence efficiency performance.[27] The removal of the statutory entry barriers may simply result in the firm erecting its own entry constraints. Indeed, market concentration may increase if deregulation permits the monopoly firm to engage in anti-competition, predatory activities designed to eliminate competing firms by, for example, reducing prices to below cost in markets which rivals are attempting to enter (Vickers, 1984). Paradoxically, therefore, deregulation in the sense of removal of market entry restrictions, will need to be accompanied by new regulatory mechanisms to control anti-competitive behaviour.[28]

A similar process of increased market concentration may occur if protection against competing imports is reduced. The deregulation of imports removes statutory barriers to entry, forces inefficient domestic firms out of the market, and results in a smaller number of domestic producers. The import-discipline hypothesis is a recent variant of the contestable markets argument, and argues that even if deregulation of imports leads to increased concentration, the domestic firms will be constrained by the threat of entry by foreign competitors to adopt entry-forestalling prices that closely approximate competitive prices. Melo and Urata (1986), for example, argue that the removal of import restrictions in Chile increased the level of industrial concentration while at the same time the price–cost margins of producers were significantly reduced.[29] On the other hand, if foreign capital is prominent in the domestic economy, the attributes of the transnational corporation—intra-firm trade and transfer pricing, differentiated products, superior managerial and organisational skills—may act as entry barriers to other firms, and accelerate the process of industrial concentration through the acquisition of local enterprises.[30]

A further complication in devising policies for increasing competition in LDCs relates to market failure in the form of externalities. Standard neo-classical analysis recognises that where an activity's total benefits cannot be 'captured' in market prices, an unregulated market system will result in a suboptimal allocation of resources. The infant industry argument, for example, accepts that a period of protection from imports may be necessary to enable domestic firms to become established, and through time, competitive. A recent version of this argument emphasises the contribution of selective protection and government support in enabling

LDCs to create the technological capacity to acquire and make effective use of technological knowledge.[31] Following in the Schumpeterian tradition, this approach emphasises the role of technological innovation and diffusion in inducing economic growth and structural change. The costs of acquiring a national technological capacity can be high, particularly if a lengthy learning period is involved; costs can be uncertain due to incomplete information; investment may yield substantial externalities and the benefits to the individual enterprise may not be easily appropriated. A degree of market protection or government subsidisation may be a necessary condition, therefore, for the development of the domestic technological capacity which underlies the dynamic growth process.[32]

Government industrial policy that intervenes to foster new, strategically important industries through selectively targeted protection and subsidisation policies has been an important factor in the economic success of the newly industrialising countries of East Asia. Commenting on the rapid growth and structural change achieved by these economies, Bradford (1987, p. 314) notes that:

> ... the evidence here suggests that a supply-push development model with government playing a key role in stimulating capital formation through macropolicies and in accelerating structural change through sectoral strategies affecting the output and export mix may provide a more accurate framework for capturing the causal elements explaining rapid transitional growth.

This argument implies, therefore, that a policy of general and indiscriminate deregulation may not be entirely appropriate for generating rapid industrialisation and economic growth in LDCs.

The third issue relates to deregulatory privatisation measures as part of a more comprehensive liberalisation strategy. As the chapters by Commander and Killick, and Mosley, point out, privatisation often forms one element in the policies of structural adjustment and economic reform recommended by the international development agencies. However, understanding of the optimal integration and timing of the various elements in a liberalisation programme is limited. As Bruno (1985, p. 867) notes:

Economic theory tells us that a fully liberalized economy is most probably Pareto superior to a heavily controlled economy. It can also tell us something about the advantages of certain departures from full liberalization in some markets. However, theory tells us virtually nothing about optimal transition paths from a distorted system to one that is fully liberalized. Unfortunately, this is the most important problem for any successful reform.

Furthermore, according to the well-known theory of the second-best, if existing restrictions are relaxed sequentially, it is not possible to know, *a priori*, if the overall level of welfare will be increased or reduced.

The results of liberalisation programmes in Latin America in the late 1970s and early 1980s have deviated significantly from the theoretical predictions, encouraging a reassessment of the economic liberalisation strategy.[33] Some observers have attributed the 'failure' to the simultaneous deregulation of all markets, with a failure to recognise that the speed of adjustment in various markets differs. For example, the opening of financial, trade and capital accounts at the same time is believed to have caused an inflow of foreign capital, attracted by high domestic interest rates, which led to an appreciation of the real exchange rate, thereby lowering profitability in the tradeable goods sector and discouraging an improvement in the trade account balance. The critical issue is, therefore, the sequencing of the liberalisation of different markets.[34] Other commentators have seen the problem as being that the liberalisation reforms have been implemented when the economy is in serious macroeconomic disequilibrium, with high inflation and severe foreign exchange shortages. Concentration on long-term market liberalisation measures aimed at promoting more efficient resource allocation has resulted in insufficient attention being given to short-run stabilisation policies to reduce inflation and balance of payments difficulties. The liberalisation programme then collapses due to the instability in the macroeconomic environment. Successful liberalisation is conditional therefore, on the adoption of appropriate stabilisation policies.[35] A further explanation has been sought in the political repercussions of liberalisation measures. Deregulation threatens the 'rents' accruing to various groups. If the pressure from the potential losers outweighs the support from those who will subsequently gain from liberalisation, the reform programme is modified or aborted.[36]

Thus, it is generally recognised that a sudden and simultaneous deregulation of markets is non-optimal, but beyond that there is only limited knowledge of the economic and political dynamics of market liberalisation in LDCs.

Privatisation and redistribution

Any attempt to assess the impact of privatisation on distributional objectives is confronted by a variety of conceptual and empirical obstacles. First, one needs to separate the effects of the privatisation measures from other policy changes that occur at the same time. This will be particularly problematic when privatisation forms part of a more general programme of economic liberalisation. Second, it is desirable to consider the effects that emerge over the longer-term. Third, it is necessary to assess the effects of privatisation on different economic groups. Added to these methodological problems, there are major application difficulties. Ideally, one would require a data set that enabled one to assess the importance of the various income and relative price effects associated with privatisation measures for different income groups. The comprehensive data base required for this kind of exercise is seldom available in LDCs. Faced with these problems, one is forced to proceed on a more *ad hoc* basis, attempting, as Killick and Commander (this volume) have done, to identify the areas in which significant distributional effects might be expected to occur.[37]

The difficulties in assessing the distributional effects of privatisation, however, should not be used to justify a neglect of the issue. There can be no presumption that the impact will improve income distribution, and given the importance which is attached to distributional objectives in many LDCs, the effect of privatisation on the distribution of income and wealth requires careful consideration.

Summary

The argument in this section on privatisation and performance can be summarised as follows. Improvements in economic performance are more likely to result from an increase in market competition than from a change from public to private ownership. There are important constraints, however, on increasing competition in LDCs. Where state monopolies dominate the market, the removal of statutory barriers to entry will be insufficient to stimulate competition, and regulatory agencies will have to be established to control the behaviour of the privatised enterprises. But analysis and experience of this type of regulatory policy in the context of LDCs is rudimentary. Second, a policy of selective government intervention can be readily justified in terms of correcting for market failure associated with externalities. A version of the infant industry argument can be used to support the case for government encouragement by protection or subsidisation of strategically important industries, in terms of the long-term dynamic gains accruing from the creation of a domestic technological capacity. Finally, uncertain outcomes arise in relation to the phasing and integration of the different deregulation measures in a comprehensive liberalisation programme.

5. PRIVATISATION IN PRACTICE

Privatisation has been extensively debated as a policy option in many LDCs, and a number of developing countries have already implemented privatisation measures.[38]

In Asia, both Malaysia and Singapore have sold a share of their national airline equity on private markets. As the papers by Low and Craig (this volume) show, both these countries have ambitious plans to extend their privatisation programmes in the fields of communications, manufacturing and various municipal services. Thailand also has plans to privatise its telecommunications system, as well as railways and municipal transport systems. Elsewhere in Asia, in Bangladesh almost 100 publicly-owned enterprises, including the steel and engineering corporation, have been privatised since 1982, and further denationalisation covering the banking sector is planned.

Latin America has a longer history of privatisation. The paper by Marshall and Montt (this volume) documents the checkered experience in Chile which began in 1974, when the new regime initiated a major privatisation programme which reduced the public enterprise sector to a strategic group of fifteen companies. In Mexico, public enterprises in the hotel and automobile sectors have been sold, and it is intended to extend the privatisation programme to include the publicly-owned domestic airline. Brazil has drawn up a list of 520 companies for partial denationalisation, although the government intends to retain a controlling interest.

In Africa, Togo, Ivory Coast, Kenya, Mali and Niger have each announced plans to sell off public sector enterprises, although as the papers by Sandbrook and Stren (this volume) indicate, there are major constraints which will limit the pace of privatisation in African countries.

Despite these examples, the overall picture is that so far only limited divestiture has taken place in LDCs. A recent survey covering the post–1980 period found that partial or total sale of public enterprises had occurred in only fifteen developing countries (excluding Chile and Bangladesh) and covered fewer than 100 enterprises. In most cases the privatised firms were small in terms of asset value and employment, and had previously been in private ownership (Berg, 1985). A recent World Bank report estimated that for low-income African countries, no more than 5 per cent of public enterprises had been privatised or closed down in the 1980s (World Bank, 1986, p. 2).

Rather more progress has been made in the deregulation and liberalisation aspects of privatisation, with measures relating to the reform of the public enterprise sector becoming an increasingly important element in the conditionality attached to World Bank and IMF lending programmes. Of the ninety-four IMF-supported adjustment programmes in LDCs during the 1980–84 period, the majority contained policy recommendations relating to non-financial state enterprises (IMF, 1986a). Sixty-one per cent of programmes contained provisions for reducing subsidies to public enterprises and introducing prices that would cover operating costs while at the same time making a reasonable contribution to capital maintenance and new investment.[39] Twenty-seven programmes curtailed current transfers to state enterprises, and eleven specified subceilings on credit to state enterprises. More than a quarter of the programmes contained intentions for the divestiture of enterprises to the private sector. Twenty-five programmes included measures aimed at improving managerial efficiency and autonomy.

A similar concern with measures aimed at improving public enterprise performance is evident in the World Bank's lending programme. Mosley (this volume) established that of the forty Structural Adjustment Loans introduced in twenty-one LDCs between 1980 and 1986, some 73 per cent did call for some action in the area of 'public enterprise financial performance'. In 62 per cent of the programmes there was a requirement for deregulation of pricing or licensing legislation. A detailed examination of the programmes shows that the emphasis in the Bank's recommendations has been on deregulation and competition, rather than on divestiture.[40]

Why has divestiture in LDCs been limited? The slow pace of privatisation can be attributed to a variety of factors, some relating to practical problems of implementation, others reflecting reservations as to the repercussions that would follow the adoption of a programme of denationalisation.

The experience in industrial countries has shown that, even where there is a sophisticated financial infrastructure, it is difficult to establish the appropriate market value for the enterprise assets. The problems of valuation and public sale are compounded in developing countries where, as Commander and Killick show, the capital market is insufficiently well-developed to handle large equity sales. The absence of a well-developed financial system means that divestiture will have to be made by direct placement with local or foreign interests large enough to handle the transaction. The government may be unwilling, however, to have its assets transferred to certain groups of potential buyers, if it results in a further concentration of wealth. In some countries, it will be politically unacceptable to sell enterprises to wealthy racial minority groups. Similar objections may be raised to increased ownership by foreign interests.

A further constraint on the pace of denationalisation in LDCs may result from uncertainty as to the economic benefits of privatisation. The previous section showed that divestiture may do little to improve the economic performance of the enterprise if it simply transfers the ownership from public to private sector. As Mansoor's paper suggests, the financial benefits may also be limited, if, for example, tax and subsidy concessions are offered as inducements to the sale of loss-making enterprises. If market protection is offered as a further incentive to buyers, the potential economic gains from increased competition are sacrificed for budgetary gains.

Third, the resistance from interest groups that stand to lose from privatisation is likely to form a powerful political constraint. This opposition will come from the labour force employed in the public enterprises who fear job losses, and from government officials whose area of authority and opportunity for patronage will be reduced. Where liberalisation is threatened, further resistance will come from those groups who currently enjoy the protected economic rents created by the system of regulations and controls. The opposition by various sectional interests that are threatened by privatisation may well be more immediate and more vocally expressed than the anticipated longer-term benefits from greater economic efficiency.

This suggests that the espousal of the privatisation objective in many LDCs has been for reasons of expediency as much as from ideological conviction. We have already alluded to the pressure for privatisation that has been exerted by external institutions, particularly the IMF and World Bank and bilateral agencies such as USAID. There may be an understandable reluctance on the part of many LDC policy makers to fully commit themselves to what may appear to them as the latest in a succession of different 'priority areas' for the lending agencies. Priorities alter, and as Heald (1985, p. 57) puts it, 'policy fashions, though useful in overcoming inertia and vested interests, carry their own dangers: today's problem often seems to be unwinding the damaging consequences of yesterday's fashion'. The irony of the international agencies advocating the dismantling of the publicly-owned institutions that they themselves created in the 1960s, has not gone unnoticed. Where privatisation is undertaken, it may simply reflect the policy-maker's judgement as to the token measure needed to secure the continued inflow of foreign assistance. As

Lal (1987, p. 281) observes, 'it is rare for liberalization to follow some intellectual conversion of policy-makers who, having seen the errors of their ways, seek to find a second best welfare maximising transition from a controlled to a market economy'.[41]

6. CONCLUDING COMMENTS

The arguments advanced in this chapter lead to the conclusion that the significance of privatisation as a policy option for all LDCs has been greatly exaggerated. In some countries denationalisation is likely to be difficult to achieve, its budgetary and economic benefits often appear to be limited, and it may involve significant political costs.[42] Furthermore, the public enterprise sector is frequently used to meet distributional and other social objectives that would be sacrificed if the enterprises were transferred to private ownership. These considerations would seem to suggest that the size of the public enterprise sector in LDCs is unlikely to be significantly reduced as the result of extensive privatisation sales.

The interest in privatisation does reflect, however, a widespread concern with the performance of the public enterprise sector in LDCs. We have discussed the problems in assessing performance and the dangers of making generalisations about 'poor' public enterprise performance. Nevertheless, 'despite the inconclusive nature of the evidence, it is difficult to believe that existing public enterprises are not capable of achieving significant improvements in efficiency' (Hemming and Mansoor, 1987, p. 6).

An improvement in the economic performance of the public enterprise sector is more likely to result from an increase in market competition than from a change in ownership. There are major constraints, however, in creating a more competitive market environment in LDCs. The prevalence of market failure means that deregulation may not be a sufficient condition for increased competition. A more general programme of economic liberalisation is confronted by problems of phasing and timing, and experience with this type of programme has revealed the economic adjustment problems that arise in making the transition from a regulated to a deregulated environment.[43]

The most fruitful area for generating improvements in the economic performance of the public enterprise may be in the reform of the relationship that typically exists between government and the public enterprise sector in LDCs.[44] The number of government departments with overlapping responsibilities and control of the public enterprise sector may need to be reduced, and government decision-making exercised by establishing a supervisory agency for the public enterprise sector.

A clear demarcation of the roles and responsibilities of government and enterprise will serve to make political 'interference' in the operations of individual enterprises more overt and thereby less prevalent. The granting of greater operating autonomy to the public enterprises needs to be coupled, however, with clearly specified objectives in terms of which performance can be measured. The chapter by Jackson (this volume) discusses how such performance measures for the public sector might be devised. To encourage improved performance it may be necessary to reform the system of incentives to enterprise management, with rewards being more directly related to performance—'introducing a management philosophy that is less control-oriented and procedure-bound, and more concerned with judging managers on the basis of enterprise viability' (Ayub and Hegstad, 1986, p. 6). Having established a new organisational and managerial framework for the public enterprise, an improvement in economic performance may require a measure of 'rehabilitation', involving investment in the rationalisation and modernisation of the sector.

The prospects of widespread privatisation in LDCs are limited. Denationalisation is difficult to achieve and its potential benefits are uncertain. The opening up of the public enterprise sector to domestic or international competition is often difficult, and in some instances, inappropriate. In these circumstances, it would appear that improvements in the internal management of the public enterprise sector will offer the main means of improving economic efficiency and performance. Public sector reform, rather than privatisation, is likely to be the major focus of public enterprise policy in LDCs in the coming period.

NOTES

1. For further discussion of franchising, see Domberger (1986). Other activities labelled as privatisation have included the introduction, or raising, of user charges for goods and services supplied by public enterprises, and the transfer of public sector activities to the voluntary and charitable component of the private sector. Hulme (1987) has postulated that an expansion in the operations of the private voluntary sector can be anticipated in LDCs pursuing policies of economic liberalisation. For a detailed case study of the non-profit sector in Sri Lanka, see James (1982).
2. For a useful discussion of structural adjustment policies in the industrial countries, see IMF (1985), Supplementary Note 7.
3. Although open to other interpretations, the figures that emerged from a USAID investigation seeking information on the status of privatisation efforts in various LDCs may be taken as indicative of LDC interest in privatisation. All but four of the nearly sixty replies received indicated that divestment and privatisation of state-owned enterprises were of concern to the governments concerned, with the degree of interest ranging from the early stages of discussion to the initiation of steps to divest or liquidate specific industries (Cowan, 1986).
4. Further data on the share of public enterprises in output and investment are given in Short (1984).
5. For a taxonomy of public enterprise objectives, see Choksi (1979), Gray (1984, appendix 1).
6. For a detailed account of the market failure approach to explaining the size and function of the public enterprise sector in LDCs, see Lal (1980). The motives for establishing public enterprises in LDCs are also discussed in Kirkpatrick *et al.* ((1984), Chapter 5; Gillis (1980); Jones and Mason (1982).
7. Toye (1986) contrasts the attitude of the bilateral aid agencies in the 1960s when 'they were engaged in competing with each other to finance public sector steel mills', with their approach in the 1980s when 'they are ultra-private enterprise in orientation' (p. 64).
8. The characterisation of the planning era as a 'failure' can be contested. See, for example, Kirkpatrick *et al.* (1984), pp. 200–5; Killick (1986).
9. Other advocates of the market are prone to present their case in more ideological terms, see Bauer (1981); Lal (1983). The well-established arguments on distortions, externalities and second-best, which demonstrate the fallibility of the free-market analysis, are either ignored or treated as theoretical oddities, and all government policies are regarded as distortionary, likely to impede the harmonious functioning

of markets (Helleiner, 1981). For contrasting critiques of the market-paradigm, see Toye (1985); Hahn (1982).

10. Balassa (1975, 1982) gives concise statements of the case for economic liberalisation in LDCs. For assessments of the arguments, see Kirkpatrick (1987); Cook (1986).
11. Two strands of the concern for the performance of the public sector are not directly covered in this review. The first concerns the relationship between government current and capital expenditure and their effects on macroeconomic variables and growth, which in the literature became known as the 'recurrent cost problem' (Heller, 1974; Anderson and Pinfold, 1979; Pinfold and Anderson, 1981; Lim, 1983; and Gray and Martens, 1983). The second relates to the extent to which both public and private sector enterprise performance in terms of low capacity utilisation is adversely affected by input supply bottlenecks (Bautista, *et al.*, 1981).
12. As Rees (1984, p. 12) points out, the danger is then that performance evaluation is based on the evaluator's value judgement as to what the objective ought to be—typically financial performance or economic efficiency performance are chosen—rather than on the objectives that have actually been set. The selection of performance criteria is also discussed in Jenkins and Lahouel (1983) and Gray (1984).
13. The evidence from industrial country studies is equally inconclusive, see Millward and Parker (1983). Yarrow (1986) and Domberger and Piggott (1986) reach a somewhat different conclusion from surveys of a similar body of literature.
14. It is important in considering reforms to make a distinction between political interference and excessive bureaucratic controls, since the motives for each will differ.
15. For a review of the property rights theory, see Furubotn and Pejovich (1972). Similar arguments are made in distinguishing between principals (government departments) and agents (public enterprises).
16. This is an important proviso, since the inability of the market to achieve allocative efficiency often provides the rationale for establishing public enterprises.
17. These studies are reviewed in Kirkpatrick *et al.* (1984), Chapter 3. This chapter also discusses the theoretical and empirical problems that arise in interpreting the results of market structure–performance studies.
18. For example, Bovet (1985) (cited in Nellis, 1986) reports that in the seven countries in the West African monetary union, public enterprise borrowing on average accounted for 37 per cent of all domestic credit in the 1970s. For a general discussion of public enterprise financing, see Short (1984); Gillis, *et al.* (1982).
19. Nunnenkamp (1986), however, found that the cross-country correlation between state enterprises' deficits and inflation rate was statistically insignificant. The correlations with debt indicators were significant in most cases.
20. Killick (1983) in particular comments on the problem with regard to Senegal.

21. See Low (this volume) on Singapore, and Turok (1981) on Zambia.
22. For example, in Ghana, some of the more profitable public enterprises, including the distilleries and cocoa factories, owe their financial performance to monopolistic positions and heavy protection from foreign competition. In Pakistan, some 90 per cent of the sales of public industrial enterprises were subject to price controls (Ayub and Hegstad, 1987).
23. Difficulties over the interpretation of accounts relate to private sector enterprises as much as to public enterprises. A feature in many LDCs that are liberalising is the attempt to compensate for the bias given to the public sector in the pre-liberalisation period by giving positive incentives (generous tax holidays, subsidised export credit, import duty concessions) to private sector firms.
24. See Vickers and Yarrow (1985) and Shepherd (1984) for critical assessments of contestable markets theory. Recent contributions to the testing of the theory are reviewed in Baumol and Willig (1986).
25. This topic is examined in detail by Mansoor (this volume).
26. The issue of debt write-off prior to a sale is compounded in LDCs since public enterprise deficits have in some countries been partly financed through foreign loans.
27. Many public enterprises are set up in response to the market failures associated with economies of scale and indivisibilities.
28. For a discussion of industrial concentration and competition policy in LDCs, see Kirkpatrick *et al.* (1984), Chapter 6. Killick (1981) points to the potential opposition to anti-monopoly control that comes from politicians, managers and trade unions who may benefit from monopoly power. This tendency is strengthened when governments engage in joint ventures with private investors.
29. As the authors note, however, the period covered in this study relates to the beginning of the liberalisation 'experiment' in Chile. Subsequent developments led to the collapse and renationalisation of many privatised firms. See Marshall and Montt (this volume).
30. For a discussion of the relationship between market structure and transnationals in LDCs, see Lall (1978); Kirkpatrick *et al.* (1984), Chapter 4.
31. See, for example, Westphal (1982); Pack and Westphal (1986); Yarrow (1986a).
32. Schumpeter (1934) argued that monopoly and supernormal profits were necessary to provide incentives for the discovery and application of technological information.
33. For details of the 'failure' of economic liberalisation 'experiments' in Latin America, see World Development (1985); Economic Development and Cultural Change (1986); Choksi and Papageorgiou (1986).
34. The timing and sequencing of liberalisation measures is discussed in Michaely (1986) and Edwards (1987). Others have emphasised the need to supervise liberalisation measures, see Dooley and Mathieson (1987).
35. The links between stabilisation and liberalisation policies are considered in Bruno (1986) and Fischer (1986).

36. For a discussion of the political economy of liberalisation programmes in LDCs, see Nelson (1984) and Lal (1987).
37. The difficulties of assessing the distributional impact of particular policy incentives are discussed in IMF (1986a). Addison and Demery (1986) examine the various dimensions in which the distributional effects of various liberalisation policies might be assessed.
38. For details of privatisation plans in individual LDCs, see *The Economist*, 21 December 1985, pp. 69–84; Asian Development Bank (1985); Berg (1985).
39. Paul (1985) discusses the adoption of user-charges as part of a privatisation programme.
40. This is further evidenced in the small but growing interest in direct lending to the private sector by multilateral aid agencies.
41. Lal (1987) suggests that there is a sort of 'Laffer curve' of government intervention, so that after a certain stage, increased government intervention, instead of increasing the area of government control, diminishes it. Thus a major motivation for liberalisation in many LDCs is, paradoxically an attempt by the state to regain control over the economy.
42. Besides, viable privatisation may itself involve a length preparatory period (Her Majesty's Treasury, 1987). The UK experience has shown that long before the transfer of ownership the prospective enterprise is subjected to a variety of controls aimed at improving performance. In the case of the UK gas industry, these included specified financial targets, performance aims relating to operating costs and external borrowing controls. Similar schemes have admittedly been adopted in some LDCs, most notably with the government-invested enterprises in the Republic of Korea (Park, 1986). But, as the case of Korea shows, although the adoption of performance related measures was not specifically introduced as a pre-privatisation initiative, its successful results were largely achieved by a high degree of political commitment which may be difficult to duplicate in all LDCs.
43. Ayub and Hegstad (1986, pp. 19–20) have argued that in addition to general liberalisation, specific measures such as encouraging public enterprises to seek export market sales can have a significant effect on performance.
44. For the internal reform of the public sector, see Shirley (1983); also Ayub and Hegstad (1987); World Bank (1983), Chapter 8.

REFERENCES

Addison, T. and Demery, L. (1986), 'Liberalisation strategies and income distribution in developing countries', Mimeo, Overseas Development Institute, London.

Anderson, D. and Pinfold, T. (1979), 'The relationship between operating and investment expenditures: a problem of planning and budgeting', *Journal of Economic Development*, December.

Asian Development Bank (1985), *Privatization: Policies, Methods and Procedures*, edited by D. Heald, Manila: Asian Development Bank.

Aylen, J. (1987), 'Privatisation in developing countries', *Lloyds Bank Review*, No. 163, pp. 15–30.

Ayub, M.A. and Hegstad, S.O. (1986), 'Public industrial enterprises: determinants of performance', World Bank Industry and Finance Series, 17, Washington DC.

———(1987), 'Management of public industrial enterprises', *World Bank Research Observer*, Vol. 2, No. 1, pp. 79–101.

Balassa, B. (1975), 'Reforming the system of incentives in developing countries', *World Development*, Vol. 3, No. 6.

———(1982), 'Disequilibrium analysis in developing countries: an overview', *World Development*, Vol. 10, No. 12, pp. 1027–38.

Baum, W.C. and Tolbert, S.M. (1985), *Investing in Development: Lessons of World Bank Experience*, Oxford: Oxford University Press for the World Bank.

Bauer, P.T. (1981), *Equality, The Third World and Economic Delusion*, London: Methuen.

Baumol, W.J. and Willing, R.D. (1986), 'Contestability: developments since the book', *Oxford Economic Papers*, Vol. 38 Supplement, pp. 9–36.

Bautista, R., Hughes, H., Lim, D., Morawetz, D. and Thoumi, J., *Capital Utilisation in Manufacturing*, Oxford: Oxford University Press for the World Bank.

Berg, E. (1982), *Changing the Public-Private Mix: A Survey of Some Recent Experience in LDCs*, DM/83/10, Washington DC, IMF.

———(1985), 'Divestiture of state-owned enterprises in LDCs', report prepared for the World Bank, November, 1985.

———(1987), 'Privatization: developing a pragmatic approach', *Economic Impact*, No. 57, pp. 6–11.

Blejer, M. and Khan, M.S. (1984), 'Government policy and private investment in developing countries', *IMF Staff Papers*, Vol. 31, pp. 379–403.

Bovet, D. (1985), 'Financial impact of public enterprises in sub-Saharan Africa', World Bank, August (cited in Nellis, 1986).

Bradford, C.I. Jr. (1987), 'Trade and structural change: NICs and next tier NICs as transitional economies', *World Development*, Vol. 15, No. 3, pp. 299–316.

Bruno, M. (1985), 'Introduction to "liberalisation with stabilisation in the Southern Cone of Latin America"', *World Development*, Vol. 13, No. 8, pp. 867–70.

———(1986), 'Opening-up: liberalization with stabilization', Mimeo, Economic Development Institute, World Bank, Washington DC.

Choksi, A. (1979), 'State intervention in the industrialization of developing countries: selected issues', *World Bank Staff Working Paper*, No. 341, Washington DC: World Bank.

Choksi, A. M. and Papageorgiou, D. (eds) (1986), *Economic Liberalization in Developing Countries*, Oxford: Basil Blackwell.

Cook, P. (1983), 'Industrial development in Pakistan', Mimeo, Asian Development Bank, Manila.

———(1985), 'Industrial sector study: Sri Lanka', Mimeo, Asian Development Bank, Manila.

———(1986), 'Liberalisation in the context of industrial development in LDCs', *Manchester Discussion Papers in Development Studies*, No. 8602, University of Manchester.

Corbo, V., Melo, J. de, and Tybout, J. (1986), 'What went wrong with recent reforms in the Southern Cone?', *Economic Development and Cultural Change*, Vol. 34, No. 3, pp. 607–40.

Cowan, L.G. (1986), 'An overview of privatisation and the A.I.D. experience', paper presented at US Agency for International Development (A.I.D.) Conference on Privatization in LDCs, Washington DC, February.

Domberger, S. (1986), 'Economic regulation through franchise contracts' in J. Kay, C. Mayer and D. Thompson (eds), *Privatization and Regulation: The UK Experience*, Oxford: Oxford University Press.

Domberger, S. and Piggott, J. (1986), 'Privatization policies and public enterprise: a survey', *Economic Record*, June, pp. 145–62.

Dooley, M. and Mathieson, D. (1987), 'Financial liberalisation and stability in developing countries', *IMF Working Paper*, WP/87/19, March.

Economic Development and Cultural Change (1986), 'Growth, reform and adjustment: Latin America's trade and macroeconomic policies in the 1970s and 1980s', Special Issue edited by S. Edwards and S. Teitel, Vol. 34, No. 3, pp. 423–671.

Edwards, S. (1987), 'Sequencing economic liberalization in developing countries', *Finance and Development*, Vol. 24, No. 1, pp. 26–30.

Fischer, S. (1986), 'Issues in medium-term macroeconomic adjustment', *World Bank Research Observer*, Vol. 1, No. 2, pp. 163–82.

Floyd, R.H. (1978), 'Some aspects of income taxation of public enterprises', *IMF Staff Papers*, Vol. 25, No. 4, pp. 310–42.

Funkhouser, R. and MacAvoy, P.W. (1979), 'A sample of observations on comparative prices in public and private enterprise', *Journal of Public Economics*, Vol. 11, pp. 353–68.

Furubotn, E.G. and Pejovich, S. (1972), 'Property rights and economic theory: a survey of recent literature', *Journal of Economic Literature*, Vol. X, No. 4.

Gantt, A.H. and Dutto, G. (1968), 'Financial performance of government-owned corporations in less developed countries', *IMF Staff Papers*, Vol. 15, pp. 102–42.

Gillis, M. (1980), 'The role of state enterprises in economic development', *Social Research*, Vol. 47, pp. 248–89.

Gillis, M., Jenkins, G.P. and Lessard, D.R. (1982), 'Public enterprise finance: towards a synthesis' in L.P. Jones (ed.), *Public Enterprise in Less Developed Countries*, Cambridge: Cambridge University Press, pp. 257–80.

Glade, W. (ed.) (forthcoming), *State Shrinkage: Comparative Inquiry into Privatisation*, Austin: University of Texas Press.

Gray, C.S. (1984), 'Towards a conceptual framework for macroeconomic evaluation of public enterprise performance in mixed economies', in R.H. Floyd, C.S. Gray and R.P. Short, *Public Enterprise in Mixed Economies*, Washington DC: IMF.

Gray, C. and Martens, A. (1983), 'The political economy of the "recurrent cost problem" in the West African Sahel', *World Development*, Vol. 11, No. 2, pp. 101–18.

Hahn, F. (1982), 'Reflections on the invisible hand', *Lloyds Bank Review*, No. 144, April, pp. 1–21.

Hanke, S.H. (1986), 'The privatisation option: an analysis', *Economic Impact*.

Heald, D. (1985), 'Privatisation policies, methods and procedures' in Asian Development Bank, *Privatization: Policies, Methods and Procedures*, edited by D. Heald, Manila: Asian Development Bank.

Heald, D. and Thomas, D. (1986), 'Privatization as theology', *Public Policy and Administration*, Vol. 1, pp. 49–66.

Helleiner, G.K. (1981), 'The Refsnes Seminar: economic theory and north-south relations', *World Development*, Vol. 9, No. 6, pp. 539–56.

Heller, P.S. (1974), 'Public expenditure in LDCs with recurrent cost constraint: the Kenyan case', *Quarterly Journal of Economics*, Vol. 88, No. 2.

———(1981), 'Diverging trends in the shares of nominal and real government expenditure in GDP: implications for policy', *National Tax Journal*, Vol. 17, pp. 61–74.

Heller, P.S. and Tait, A.A. (1983), 'Government employment and pay: some international comparisons', *IMF Occasional Paper*, No. 24, Washington DC: IMF.

Hemming, R. and Mansoor, A.M. (1987), 'Privatization and public enterprises', *IMF Working Paper*, WP/87/9, 25 February, Fiscal Affairs Department, IMF.

Her Majesty's Treasury (1987), 'Privatisation in the United Kingdom', HM Treasury, London, February.

Hill, H. (1982), 'State enterprises in a competitive industry: an Indonesian case study', *World Development*, Vol. 19, pp. 1015–23.

Hulme, D. (1987), 'The non-governmental sector and privatisation in LDCs', Mimeo, Institute for Development Policy and Management, University of Manchester.

International Monetary Fund (1985), *World Economic Outlook*, Washington DC: IMF.

———(1986), *World Economic Outlook*, Washington DC: IMF.

———(1986a), *Fund-supported Programs, Fiscal Policy, and Income Distribution*, Occasional Paper 46, Washington DC: IMF.

James, E. (1982), 'The non-profit sector in international perspectives: the case of Sri Lanka', *Journal of Comparative Economics*, Vol. 6, pp. 99–129.

Jenkins, G.P. and Lahouel, M.H. (1983), 'Evaluation of performance of industrial public enterprises: criteria and policies', *Industry and Development* (UNIDO), No. 7.

Jones, L.P. (1985), 'Public enterprise for whom? Perverse distributional consequences of public operational decisions', *Economic Development and Cultural Change*, Vol. 33, No. 2, pp. 333–47.

Jones, L.P. and Mason, E.S. (1982), 'Why public enterprise' in Jones, L.P. (ed.), *Public Enterprise in Less Developed Countries*, Cambridge: Cambridge University Press.

Kay, J.A. and Thompson, D.J. (1986), 'Privatisation: a policy in search of a rationale', *Economic Journal*, Vol. 96, No. 381, March, pp. 18–32.

Kay, J.A., Mayer, C. and Thompson, D. (1986), *Privatization and Deregulation—The UK Experience*, Oxford: Oxford University Press.

Killick, T. (1981), *Policy Economics*, London: Heinemann Educational Books Ltd.

———(1983), 'The role of the public sector in the industrialisation of African developing countries', *Industry and Development* (UNIDO), No. 7, pp. 57–88.

———(1983), 'Development planning in Africa: experiences, weaknesses and prescriptions', *Development Policy Review*, Vol. 1, No. 1, pp. 47–76.

———(1986), 'Twenty-five years of development: the rise and

impending decline of market solutions', *Development Policy Review*, Vol. 4, No. 2, pp. 99–116.

Kim, K. (1981), 'Enterprise performance in the public and private sectors: Tanzanian experience, 1970–75', *Journal of Developing Areas*, Vol. 15, No. 3, pp. 471–84.

Kirkpatrick, C. (1986), 'The World Bank's views on state-owned enterprises in less developed countries: a critical comment', *Rivista Internazionale di Scienze Economiche e Commerciali*, Vol. 33, No. 6–7, pp. 685–96.

———(1987), 'Trade policy and industrialisation in developing countries' in N. Gemmell (ed.), *Surveys in Development Economics*, Oxford: Basil Blackwell.

Kirkpatrick, C., Lee, N. and Nixson, F. (1984), *Industrial Structure and Policy in Less Developed Countries*, London: George Allen and Unwin.

Krueger, A. (1986), 'Changing perspectives on development economics and World Bank research', *Development Policy Review*, Vol. 14, pp. 195–210.

Lal, D. (1980), 'Public enterprises' in J. Cody, H. Hughes and D. Wall (eds), *Policies for Industrial Progress in Developing Countries*, Oxford: Oxford University Press for the World Bank.

———(1983), *The Poverty of Development Economics*, London, Institute of Economic Affairs, Hobart Paper No. 16.

———(1987), 'The political economy of economic liberalization', *The World Bank Economic Review*, Vol. 1, No. 2, pp. 273–99.

Lall, S. (1978), 'Transnationals, domestic enterprises and industrial structure in host LDCs: a survey', *Oxford Economic Papers*, Vol. 30, No. 2, pp. 217–48; reprinted in I. Livingstone (ed.) (1981), *Development Economics and Policy: Readings*, London: Allen and Unwin, pp. 148–63.

Lim, D. (1983), 'Government recurrent expenditure and economic growth in less developed countries', *World Development*, Vol. 11, No. 4, pp. 377–80.

Little, I.M.D. (1982), *Economic Development: Theory, Policy and International Relations*, New York: Basic Books.

Melo, J. de and Urata, S. (1986), 'The influence of increased foreign competition on industrial concentration and profitability', *International Journal of Industrial Organization*, Vol. 4, pp. 287–04.

Michaely, M. (1986), 'The timing and sequencing of a trade liberalization policy' in A.M. Choksi and D. Papageorgiou (eds), *Economic Liberalization in Developing Countries*, Oxford: Basil Blackwell.

Millward, R. and Parker, D.M. (1983), 'Public and private enterprise: comparative behaviour and relative efficiency' in R. Millward *et al.*, *Public Sector Economics*, London: Longman.

Nellis, J. (1986), 'Public enterprises in sub-Saharan Africa', Mimeo, Public Sector Management Unit, World Bank, Washington DC.

Nelson, J. (1984), 'The political economy of stabilisation: commitment, capacity and public response', *World Development*, Vol. 12, No. 10, pp. 983–1006.

Nunnenkamp, P. (1986), 'State enterprises in developing countries', *Intereconomics*, July/August, pp. 186–193.

Pack, H. and Westphal, L. (1986), 'Industrial strategy and technological change', *Journal of Development Economics*, Vol. 22, pp. 87–128.

Park, Y. (1986), 'A system for evaluating the performance of government-invested enterprises in the Republic of Korea', *World Bank Discussion Papers*, 3, November.

Pathirane, L. and Blades, D. (1982), 'Defining and measuring the public sector: some international comparisons', *Review of Income and Wealth*, Vol. 28, No. 3, pp. 261–289.

Paul, S. (1985), 'Privatization and the public sector', *Finance and Development*, Vol. 22, No. 4, December, pp. 42–45.

Peacock, A. (1984), 'Privatisation in perspective', *The Three Banks Review*, No. 144, December.

Perkins, F.C. (1983), 'Technology choice, industrialisation and development experiences in Tanzania', *Journal of Development Studies*, Vol. 19, pp. 213–43.

Pinfold, T. and Anderson, D. (1981), 'Co-ordinating operating and investment expenditures: the need for balance in planning and budgeting' in Norcliffe, G. and Pinfold, T. (eds), *Planning African Development*, London: Croom Helm.

Rees, R. (1984), *Public Enterprise Economics*, 2nd edition, London: Weidenfeld and Nicolson.

Schumpeter, J. (1934), *The Theory of Economic Development*, Cambridge Mass: Harvard University Press.

Shackleton, J.R. (1986), 'Privatising the Third World', *Banca Nazionale del Lavoro Quarterly Review*, No. 159, December, pp. 429–439.

Shen, T.Y. (1977), 'Macro development planning in tropical Africa', *Journal of Development Studies*, Vol. 13, No. 4.

Shepherd, W. (1984), 'Contestibility vs. competition', *American Economic Review*, Vol. 74, pp. 572–87.

Shirley, M. (1983), 'Managing state-owned enterprises', *World Bank Staff Working Papers*, No. 577, Washington DC.

Short, R.P. (1984), 'The role of public enterprises: an international statistical comparison' in R.H. Floyd, C.S. Gray and R.P. Short, *Public Enterprise in Mixed Economies*, Washington DC: IMF.

Sobhan, R. (1983), 'Distributive regimes under public enterprise: a case study of the Bangladesh experience' in F. Stewart (ed.), *Work, Income and Inequality: Payments Systems in the Third World*, London: Macmillan, pp. 138–67.

Taylor, L. (1983), *Structuralist Macroeconomics*, New York: Basic Books.

Timmer, C.P. (1973), 'Choice of technique in rice milling in Java', *Bulletin of Indonesian Economic Studies*, Vol. 9, No. 2, pp. 57–76.

Toye, J. (1985), 'Dirigisme and development economics', *Cambridge Journal of Economics*, Vol. 9, pp. 1–14.

———(1986), 'Promoting the private sector: should the World Bank do more or less?', in World Bank, *Recovery in the Developing World*, Washington DC: The World Bank.

Turok, B. (1981), 'Control in the parastatal sector of Zambia', *Journal of Modern African Studies*, Vol. 19, No. 3, pp. 421–446.

Tyler, W.G. (1979), 'Technical efficiency in production in a developing country: an empirical examination of the Brazilian plastics and steel industries, *Oxford Economic Papers*, Vol. 31, pp. 477–95.

UNIDO (1979), *Industrial Priorities in Developing Countries*, New York: United Nations.

United Nations (1977), 'Implementation of development plans: the experience of developing countries in the first half of the 1970s', *Journal of Development Planning*, Centre for Development Planning, Projections and Policies, No. 12, pp. 1–65.

Vickers, J. (1984), 'The economics of predatory practices', *Fiscal Studies*, Vol. 6.

Vickers, J.S. and Yarrow, G.K. (1985), *Privatization and the Natural Monopolies*, Public Policy Centre, London.

Westphal, L.E. (1982), 'Fostering technological mastery by means of selective infant-industry protection' in M. Syrquin and S. Teitel (eds), *Trade, Stability, Technology and Equity in Latin America*, New York: Academic Press.

World Bank (1980), *Borrowing in International Capital Markets, 1979*, Washington DC: World Bank.

———(1981), *Accelerated Development in Sub-Saharan Africa: An Agenda for Action*, Washington DC: World Bank.

———(1983), *World Development Report*, Washington DC: World Bank.

———(1986), *Financing Adjustment with Growth in Sub-Saharan Africa, 1986–90.*

———(1986a), 'Divestiture in developing countries', Public Sector Management Unit, Mimeo, July.

World Development (1985), 'Liberalization with stabilisation in the Southern Cone of Latin America' Special Issue, edited by V. Corbo and J. de Melo, Vol. 13, No. 8, pp. 863–1015.

Yarrow, G. (1986), 'Privatisation in theory and practice', *Economic Policy*, April, pp. 323–78.

———(1986a), 'Strategic issues in industrial policy', *Oxford Review of Economic Policy*, Vol. 1, No. 3, pp. 95–109.

[7]

World Development, Vol. 17, No. 5, pp. 601–615, 1989.
Printed in Great Britain.

0305–750X/89 $3.00 + 0.00

Privatization in Developing Countries: A Review of the Issues

NICOLAS VAN DE WALLE*
Princeton University, New Jersey

Summary. — The theory and early experience of privatization in developing countries are reviewed. Privatization has been spurred by widespread dissatisfaction with the performance of public enterprises and the need to cut government expenditures. Unless it is accompanied by liberalization measures, privatization of public enterprises is unlikely to result in significant gains in economic efficiency. The sequencing of privatization and liberalization reforms will often determine their impact on efficiency, but the correct order of implementation is not clear. Political opposition to privatization is likely to be limited to the state bureaucracy, which will often be able to mobilize in order to limit the impact of reforms. Early implementation experiences suggest technical difficulties are as constraining as political factors.

1. INTRODUCTION

Just as the 1960s and 1970s were characterized by the rapid expansion of the public sector in the developing world, the 1980s have seen widespread attempts by policy makers to curtail the state's economic role. The divestiture, or privatization, of public enterprises has featured prominently in these attempts, just as an earlier generation of policy makers had emphasized direct state intervention to redress perceived failures in the operation of private markets. Privatization first gained prominence in Great Britain under the leadership of Margaret Thatcher's government. It quickly spread to the developing world, under the impetus of strong support by the international donor community, the need to cut government expenditures in the face of fiscal crises after the oil shocks of the 1970s, and an intellectual and ideological climate increasingly hostile to state intervention in the economy. A recent study estimates at some 1,400 the number of privatization efforts underway at the end of 1987. Over 80 developing countries are involved in these efforts, including countries like China, Tanzania and Algeria, which have traditionally favored a prominent role for the state in the economy.[1] Moreover, these experiences have spawned a voluminous and growing scholarly literature, as the references listed at the end of this essay make clear.

It is perhaps an appropriate time to take stock of and assess the issues which have emerged in relation to the theory and experience of privatization in the developing world. This paper will undertake that task. We define privatization as "a transfer of ownership and control from the public to the private sector, with particular reference to asset sales."[2] Equity sales, as well as management, leasing and franchising arrangements between a public enterprise and the private sector are considered examples of partial privatization. We define public enterprises as revenue-generating entities owned or controlled by the state, and our analysis focuses on proposals concerning their reform. These fairly narrow definitions seem most analytically useful, given limitations of space. In particular, it is appropriate to draw a clear distinction between privatization thus narrowly defined as a class of institutional reform, and liberalization, defined as a change in the relative prices operating in the economy. Thus, we do not follow the lead of those who define privatization as any reform that increases the unhindered play of market forces in the economy. A process of agricultural marketing reform that reduces input and output price distortions is a case of liberalization; privatization does not necessarily imply any changes in

*The author wishes to thank Bob Christiansen, Mary Shirley, Ashok Subramanian and John Waterbury for helpful comments on an earlier draft. Support from the Ford Foundation and from the Princeton University Center of International Studies is gratefully acknowledged. The usual disclaimers apply.

relative prices. Liberalization and privatization reforms have been linked in the economic policy *Zeitgeist* in recent years, but their impact and the constraints to their implementation are likely to be quite different. It is analytically useful to distinguish their respective effects, as this will allow us to determine the circumstances in which privatization or liberalization reforms alone are likely to be effective, as well as the circumstances in which they should be combined. Many of the benefits ascribed to privatization are, in fact, the result of liberalization.

A major theme of this essay is that ownership changes are rarely appropriate instruments with which to improve economic regulation in developing countries, whether they come in the form of nationalization as they did for the first 30 years after World War II, or of privatization as in recent years. In economic terms, privatization is unlikely to generate major gains in efficiency, unless it is accompanied by other reforms which alter the relative prices prevailing in the economy. The privatization of public enterprises in developing countries may well be justified under certain circumstances, however, and we will examine the relationship between privatization and liberalization policies in order to determine the ways in which these two kinds of reform can be combined to maximize efficiency gains.

The political impact of privatization is more difficult to predict. In most developing countries, the economic distinction between public and private is blurred, and the extent of regulatory failure is little correlated with patterns of ownership. The incentives to engage in rent seeking, corruption and patronage do not depend on the number of public enterprises in the economy, but rather on the extent to which prevailing prices do not reflect the scarcity value of goods and services. Moreover, the distributional impact of privatization reforms on different social groups is unlikely to be significant, although some employees may lose their jobs and specific groups of the population may be hard hit. On the other hand, the ideological and symbolic impacts of privatization may be significant in reshaping perceptions about the state's rightful place in the economy.

The analysis begins with a brief review of the reasons for which public enterprises have become a privileged target of economic reformers in recent years. Section 3 analyzes the theoretical justifications for privatization which have been developed in the literature. In the absence of accompanying liberalization measures, the potential impact of divestiture is shown to depend on the extent to which the public enterprise has demonstrated productive inefficiencies. Section 4 evaluates the constraints on the implementation of privatization reforms; it is argued that administrative and managerial difficulties are likely to be as constraining as political opposition. Establishing effective regulation of the privatized firms may prove more demanding of the state's administrative capabilities than outright ownership. Throughout the text, references will be made to the burgeoning literature on privatization implementation experiences in developing countries.

2. PUBLIC ENTERPRISES AND THE NEED FOR REFORM

A pervasive dissatisfaction with the performance of public enterprises (PEs) is at the heart of the appeal of privatization to policy makers in developing countries. It is thus useful to briefly examine the record of public enterprises there. We skip over their characteristics and number, which have been well described elsewhere.[3]

PEs were created for complex and varied reasons. First, it was widely thought that nationalization and PEs in general would provide governments access to much needed revenues. Governments mistakenly believed that PEs would generate large profits with which they would be able to finance investments in priority sectors of the economy. Second, public production corresponded closely to an ideological climate in which the private sector was held in low esteem and a large public role in the economy was seen as necessary for rapid and sustained development.[4] Control over a few strategic industries was justified as needed to help steer the economy and overcome critical bottlenecks. National security reasons were sometimes added to these justifications, particularly regarding heavy industry.

Third, local private entrepreneurs were in short supply, did not have access to adequate levels of capital, or were linked to unpopular minorities and foreign powers. In part because of political restrictions, as well as the anti-business climate that government policy created and that constituted disincentives for investment, there was sometimes no alternative to public production. In many countries of sub-Saharan Africa, for example, accusations of hoarding, speculation and unfair trading practices by foreign-born businessmen and middlemen led governments to nationalize marketing and distribution operations, or to tax them so heavily that the private sector disinvested from these areas.

Fourth, in political terms, PEs constituted important resources for state elites to be developed and harnessed in the form of potential rents, jobs and the servicing of constituencies. Patronage and technocratic considerations combined to make public production a popular policy outcome. In some instances, distributional considerations played a role; for example, states justified investments to lesson regional inequities or to enhance employment creation. They invested in social services and housing, and in capital-intensive agricultural schemes to modernize poor regions.

In sum, regulating or controlling certain markets was an objective of many nationalization measures. Improving market efficiency was not a major preoccupation, however, and PEs were rarely created to handle market failures, as is sometimes implicitly argued on their behalf today. There may well be efficiency arguments for PEs,[5] but there is little evidence that these weighed heavily on decision-making in developing countries.

Thousands of PEs were created in the developing countries between the mid-1960s and the early 1980s. On average, they accounted for over a quarter of gross fixed capital formation in developing countries in the early 1980s.[6] Their performance is generally considered to be unsatisfactory, albeit with important exceptions. PEs lose money, or do not make as much money as they should, given that they often benefit from privileged access to capital, various subsidies, and protection from domestic and foreign competition.[7] One author has summarized common weaknesses of PEs: unclear, multiple or contradictory objectives, bureaucratic meddling, overly centralized decision making, inadequate capitalization, managerial ineptitude, excessive personnel costs and high labor turnover.[8]

Governments' patience with PEs has worn thin in recent years, as economic conditions have worsened and fiscal crises have become endemic in the developing world. In addition, the ideological climate has changed and turned against the public sector in favor of the private sector, in the kind of policy cycle described by Hirschman.[9] Faced with burgeoning deficits, governments are less tolerant of financial losses and economic inefficiency, even though the PEs continue to pay political dividends. Moreover, the distributional justifications for PEs have rarely been borne out in practice. Many of the normative rationales for PEs have become less convincing to policy makers, who are now more likely to see the disadvantages of the public sector than its advantages or available alternatives.

3. THE IMPACT OF PRIVATIZATION

Unhappiness with PEs is not, by itself, sufficient reason for their privatization. The litmus test for any economic reform must be that it will result in improvements which would not have occurred in its absence or because of an alternative reform. It is not enough that improvements occur, a causal relationship between the policy and the outcome has to be established. This condition makes evaluations of policy reform often ambiguous and should be remembered throughout the discussion.

In practice, several justifications have been formulated on behalf of privatization. For developing country policy makers, the major impetus for the divestiture of public enterprises to the private sector has been its potential impact on public finances. In addition, however, it has been justified in economic efficiency terms, mostly within the donor community but also within academic circles, albeit more ambivalently. Critics of privatization have, in addition, pointed to its negative impact on the poor. We discuss each of these issues in turn.

(a) *Fiscal impact*

For governments in the throes of economic stabilization efforts, tangible increases in revenues or decreases in expenditures weigh much more heavily than the less tangible prospect of greater economic efficiency some time in the future. Divestiture will cut government expenditures and help restore budgetary balance. Cutting back is not only linked to the current stabilization plans, it is perceived as a long-term structural requirement. This fiscal justification for divestiture is certainly plausible, particularly for the poorer developing countries. In sub-Saharan Africa, for example, it is increasingly believed that the revenues available to the state in low-income countries are structurally inadequate for developmental needs in infrastructure, social services, and basic public goods such as research and agricultural extension.[10] As external sources of finance have dried up and deficits are no longer sustainable, the state has to establish tighter priorities and cut back in areas where its presence is not essential. Rather than do a lot of things badly, it is better for the state to do a small number of things well. The argument is convincing, but perhaps more so in the long run. In the immediate future, savings in government expenditures in most developing countries often will go to servicing debt. The proceeds from privatization programs cannot be expected to result in increased expenditure for high priority areas anytime soon.

In any event, the impact of privatization on public finances is ambiguous. In the simplest, ideal-world theoretical case, a PE's sale price should be exactly equivalent to the discounted stream of expected profit remittances the state would have received if the PE had remained in the public sector, as long as it assumed that the private and public sectors face the same tax liabilities, and perform at the same productivity levels. If this is the case, then only the composition of state assets changes, but their level does not; the fiscal impact of the privatization, strictly speaking, is nil.[11] The ideal-world theoretical case applies whether or not the PE is profitable; in the more interesting case, the PE loses money and the state then has to pay the buyer the discounted value of the PE's foreseeable losses. This is not so far fetched; in practice, governments often rehabilitate a PE prior to putting it up for sale, or they provide privileges to the buyer in the form of subsidies, tariff protection and statutory protection from competition.[12] Such concessions suggest that there may well be a tradeoff between budgetary and efficiency gains from privatization. To maximize the sale price, the government may be induced into legislating more protection for the newly private firm than the PE had enjoyed. Indeed, in several instances, the generous conditions granted to private investors have been the source of considerable controversy, notably in Chile, Togo and Bangladesh.[13]

In practice, different assets are not perfect substitutes and liquid assets may be more useful to the government than equity in a PE. If so, privatization has a real fiscal impact. Moreover, if the private sector is expected to run the firm more efficiently, that expectation will be reflected in a higher sale price, which will then further exceed the PE's discounted income stream. The theoretical case assumes perfect information and foresight. In fact, the extent to which the private sector is able to run the firm more efficiently than the public sector will be a matter of conjecture and debate during the course of the negotiations between government and buyer. These factors suggest that privatization will have a real fiscal impact, but the simple theoretical case is useful in pointing out that many of the alleged gains are illusory, and reflect the substitution of present for future government consumption. It is the short time horizon of hard-pressed state officials which has made the fiscal impact of privatization seem so appealing.

(b) *Efficiency gains*

The fiscal gains from privatization have probably weighed most heavily on developing country governments attempting to balance public accounts. International Monetary Fund (IMF) stabilization plans have systematically included PE reform with the explicit aim of short-run public expenditure reduction.[14] In addition, proponents of privatization have argued that it can have an important impact on economic efficiency. Early advocates of privatization assumed the general gains in economic efficiency to be important, based on the alleged superiority of private production, but did not attempt to clearly identify the gains. Grand claims were made on the basis of ideology and conjecture that privatization could greatly enhance overall economic efficiency and thus have a strong impact on national output.[15] This view has not resisted scrutiny. A more tempered view has emerged in the mainstream literature, which suggests that efficiency gains from privatization will in fact be modest and limited to reductions in productive and regulatory inefficiencies.[16]

Three kinds of efficiency gains have been identified as potentially arising from privatization. First gains in allocative efficiency can result if relative output prices in the economy more closely reflect scarcity values because of the reforms. Second, gains in productive efficiency can arise from a more optimal use of inputs within the enterprise after divestiture. Finally, if we accept Stigler's model of regulatory failure or Wolf's of nonmarket failure, inefficiencies arise specifically from public intervention in the economy and it is argued that privatization will reduce them.[17]

(c) *Gains in allocative efficiency*

How well markets function will determine privatization's impact on allocative efficiency. PEs operating in competitive markets should be privatized, since there is no first or second best rationale for public intervention of any sort. In these cases, gains in efficiency will be minor, since the PEs will have already been exposed to a competitive environment. These PEs will typically be found in the service or manufacturing sectors in areas where there are no scale economies, and where the market can support several firms.

It would appear that the potential for important efficiency gains is to be found in imperfect markets, or in potentially competitive markets where public ownership is the result of unwarranted intervention. In either case, however, gains in allocative efficiency from privatization are unclear. In competitive markets, public ownership is sometimes associated with inefficient intervention: a statutory public monopoly established in a market that could support several firms; a PE granted protection from competition; or perhaps public ownership subsidized to support state distributional objectives. In such cases, greater efficiency gains can be expected from regulatory reform than from privatization itself, even though in practice the two often come together.

The likely gains in imperfect markets are similarly modest. As Mansoor and Hemming argue, "allocative efficiency is a function of market structure rather than ownership."[18] In the absence of other reforms that affect the pattern of relative prices in the economy and increase competition, the privatized enterprise still faces the same prices as the PE before it. Privatization by itself will not change the nature of the market in which the firm operates, and the environment which shapes its pricing decisions. A public monopoly makes way for a private monopoly, for example, but monopoly pricing will remain in effect.

(d) *Gains in productive efficiency*

With some important exceptions, the gains in allocative efficiency from divestiture are likely to be modest. The case for privatization then rests with the gains in productive efficiency it will bring about within the firm. Privatization advocates argue that PEs are more likely to exhibit greater internal inefficiencies than private firms for several reasons. First, PEs tend to misuse production inputs because they are protected from competition and thus allow considerable slack or "x inefficiencies" to develop in their production processes.[19] PEs in many countries have easy access to capital, often at subsidized levels, and can thus be expected to undervalue capital in their investment decisions. Subsequent to privatization, an enterprise would compete with other firms for access to capital, and use it more efficiently.

Second, the property rights school argues that managerial incentives to maximize profits and minimize costs are undermined by public ownership and regulations;[20] public managers are given numerous and inconsistent objectives by government overseers. Unwieldy bureaucratic controls and the absence of shareholders with a direct interest in profits lessen the pressure on managers to maximize company performance, and may indeed put a premium on "not rocking the boat."[21]

How important are these inefficiencies in production? There are few estimates. While x inefficiencies are assumed to be important in some cases, it is not clear in what proportion they result specifically from public ownership rather than from protection from competition more generally. In addition, because PEs are saddled with noncommercial functions, criteria for performance are more ambiguous and difficult to monitor effectively. In many countries, PEs have been burdened with employment creation or overt redistributive functions; in such situations it is difficult to distinguish technology-induced inefficiencies from those brought on by government social welfare objectives.

(e) *"Nonmarket" efficiency gains*

Almost 50 years ago, Oskar Lange argued on behalf of public production that there are numerous ways in which the state can mimic the workings of the market and send signals to economic agents to ensure their efficient behavior.[22] Reforms of PEs in the past typically emphasized streamlining procedures, and establishing new lines of authority and sophisticated information processing systems that were supposed to help the state better mimic the market. The principle of divestiture was long resisted because of a widespread belief that PEs were not inherently less efficient than private firms. In recent years, however, it has been argued that certain problems result specifically from state intervention; these are referred to as "non market" or regulatory failures. The central argument is that the state can never adequately replicate the market's ability to process information in a decentralized fashion; government intervention will overlook certain crucial aspects of the market, will fail to adjust to new and changing circumstances, or will bring about unforeseen side effects. Thus, nonmarket failures after state intervention will be worse than the market failure the government set out to correct.[23] Moreover, public intervention in the economy typically involves assigning various social and political objectives to the PE and meddling with its daily management on behalf of these diverse objectives.

The nonmarket failure argument was first developed with reference to developed countries. A slightly different justification for privatization has extended the argument to take into account the special weaknesses of state capacity in developing countries. This is the view that governments in developing countries have overstretched their limited managerial and administrative capacities with too many peripheral activities, and that as a consequence performance in the most important areas is being undermined. Privatization of PEs will lessen these managerial burdens and allow the state to focus on its essential functions with increased human as well as financial resources.[24] There is some truth in this view. In many developing countries, the most serious constraints on policy are not to be found in its design, but rather in its implementation by extremely thin administrative hierarchies with limited means and capabilities. Policy objectives are undermined and altered during implementation.[25] States in the developing world are increasingly hampered by the budget cuts which austerity has imposed in recent years, but they have always been characterized by inadequate managerial capacity. The impact of divestiture on government capacities should not be exaggerated, however. Some managerial capacity will be privatized along with the PE, as public managers will move to the better-paid private sector. More importantly, the regulation of the privatized PEs, notably those operating in imperfectly competitive markets, will require the development of public bodies and generate new administrative burdens. Once again, limited state capacity is more an argument for liberalization and greater reliance on the market than it is for divestiture.

(f) *The distributional impact*

Some critics of privatization have argued that its impact is likely to weigh disproportionately on certain groups of the population, and that these groups will typically be the relatively underprivileged in society.[26] The potential distributional impact of privatization is twofold. First, it may have an impact on the employees of the PE if, subsequent to the privatization, the firm goes bankrupt, government operating subsidies decrease, or there are layoffs by the new owner. The evidence suggests that PE employees are not typically among the poorest in most of these countries, however, and privatization is unlikely to make them so, even if it may bring about real hardship for certain laid off employees.[27]

Second, privatization may affect the poor if the goods and services provided by the PE becomes less accessible to them. Here, the evidence is more compelling; PEs providing social services of a public good nature such as public transportation, health and education may service groups which a private sector provider may not find sufficiently profitable. Some transportation routes to remote regions may no longer be serviced. Prices for services may increase dramatically after privatization, notably if cross-subsidization practices common to PEs are abandoned. In the agricultural sector, private input distribution and marketing agents may pay less attention to smallholders than did public institutions, and concentrate instead on the bigger commercial farmers. Provision of such public goods as research and extension may falter — these services tend to benefit the smaller farmers more.[28]

These effects should not be exaggerated. In many countries, PEs have not had a very good record of reaching the poor. Agricultural institutions in many countries have long been beholden to large farmer interests.[29] PEs often reflect an urban bias and inadequately serve rural populations, where there may be larger pockets of poverty.[30] A case study of the privatization of public transport in Rabat, Morocco argues that privatization dramatically improved the quality of service, without decreasing the number of routes serviced by the different companies.[31]

In some cases, privatization may have a negative effect on the poor. This, however, is an argument against reform only if it can be shown that public provision is the most effective and efficient manner of reaching the poor. If not, poverty alleviation measures that target the poor directly are likely to be more cost effective than maintaining the PE. Rather than subsidize an entire transport system, for example, the government can subsidize only the lines that cover the poorer regions. Moreover, subsidies and tax breaks can induce private agents to service the poor.

There are few *a priori* reasons to believe that privatization will necessarily result in greater inequities or increases in poverty; when it does, other cheaper policy instruments can usually be found to compensate adequately. An empirical question, as yet unresolved, concerns whether policy makers engaged in privatization campaigns have in fact used these instruments to compensate the poor when the need arises. In the ideological climate in which privatization is carried out, there may be a tendency to underestimate negative distributional consequences.

4. PRIVATIZATION AND LIBERALIZATION

It is rarely denied that privatization will help

reduce productive and regulatory inefficiencies. The debate in the literature concerns how large the reductions will be, and the extent to which they will occur without concomitant increases in competition through various liberalization measures. In terms of our original litmus test, the debate concerns whether other reforms are more likely than privatization to bring about the desired improvements. We have argued that many inefficiencies are less a function of ownership than of government regulation and market structure. Private monopolies may well be more efficient than public ones, but how much more will depend largely on the effectiveness of the regulatory environment. If the public monopoly was statutory, but did not reflect market structure, then the possibility of competition may keep the enterprise honest, and output prices close to marginal cost even if new firms do not enter the market. The state may have to regulate the industry, however, in order to prevent anti-competitive or predatory behavior.[32] If the industry is a natural monopoly and entry is unlikely, the government must regulate it or accept monopoly pricing. Similarly, the government must decide whether to allow foreign imports into the country to compete with the privatized firm.

Privatization should thus be seen as an instrument of competition policy, to be accompanied by other measures which promote efficient markets. The proper sequencing of privatization and liberalization is emerging as a critical issue for policy makers, as is the extent to which one can substitute for the other. The evidence on these matters is varied and ambiguous, as we shall see.

Proponents of PE reform argue that public ownership obstructs liberalization reforms, and that a return to private ownership will help facilitate their implementation. They argue that governments support PEs for socio-political ends, and that this leads to various subsidies, tariffs, and taxes. The success of privatization efforts may well create support for more fundamental reforms and make them politically more palatable.[33] The evidence from Western Europe suggests, however, that privatization may not be a prelude to deregulation. As Kay and Thompson have demonstrated with relation to Great Britain, managers of PEs being privatized can successfully lobby for an anti-competitive regulatory environment to protect their privileged positions after the reform.[34] It can be argued, however, that the privatized firm will have less political influence than the PE before it and that it will be more difficult for bureaucrats to meddle in a firm that is not formally under their jurisdiction. In the short run, the regulatory environment would limit the gains in allocative efficiency; in the long run, however, various advantages would wither away and the private firm would not be able to lobby as effectively as the PE for their resumption.

The American context shows the extent to which various private sector dominated industries have been able to "capture" the regulatory process, and extract rents from the state. An information asymmetry between the firm and the state's regulators regarding production technology and costs will always favor the former. This has in practice led to abuses and inefficiency. Indeed, some scholars argue that adequate regulation of an industry requires so much information about that industry's costs and technology that outright ownership is likely to be more efficient.[35] Information costs are likely to be higher for state regulation than for state ownership. These precedents are particularly inauspicious for developing countries, where administrative capabilities and standards of probity are lower and the safeguards of a free press and active consumer groups are often nonexistent.[36]

In certain instances, divestiture serves as a political palliative for liberalization. Brittan explains that the Thatcher government's privatization program is at least partly the direct consequence of the government's inability to make good on its electoral promise to reduce public spending and levels of taxation; privatization, in this view, was promoted as an "ideological substitute" for liberalization policies.[37] In developing countries, donor pressure to reduce the state's role in the economy has led some recalcitrant governments to promote privatization rather than directly attack various economic privileges. Commitment to privatization has been at times halfhearted. Still, in Chile, the two types of reforms were implemented concurrently by a reform-minded government.[38] Similarly in the communist countries which have experimented with economic reforms, divestiture of PEs has been seen as an instrument of liberalization.[39]

One lesson from this discussion is that it is useful to evaluate the two kinds of policy reforms together. The government's true intent in privatizing a PE can probably by gauged by examining its recent record, or probable actions in the near future, with regard to deregulation. It may well be true that governments that are committed to liberalization and competition need privatization much less than those which are not, while those least committed to privatization are unlikely to feel a need to improve the prospects for competition.

5. OBSTACLES TO PRIVATIZATION

Answers to some of these hypotheses and theoretical disputes can be expected from the privatization experiences currently underway. The most thoroughly researched experiences are those of Great Britain, perhaps because of the importance of privatization efforts there since the end of the 1970s.[40] More recently, privatization experiences in developing countries have been the subject of research as well.

Several scholars have noted that implementation has lagged well behind stated intentions, and that privatization programs have been slow, uneven, and plagued by unforeseen obstacles. A few countries, like Bangladesh or Chile, have gone ahead with ambitious and comprehensive programs. In most countries, however, privatization has been limited to small PEs of the manufacturing and services sector which were previously under private ownership. Admittedly, privatization is a novel and complicated process that would take time in the best of circumstances, but a review of the country experiences reveals that two kinds of constraints have consistently undermined privatization efforts: first, a number of implementation issues have proven salient; and, second, political constraints on reform-minded governments have helped slow down the rate at which they can bring about privatization. In many instances, these two sets of constraints are not only undermining the process of privatization, they are also lessening its impact on economic efficiency.

(a) *Implementation constraints*

Technical constraints on implementation are related to both managerial deficiencies within the state and weaknesses within the economy. Privatization requires a level of administrative capacity possessed by few developing countries. Problems have emerged in some cases because of the absence of well-established, competent management consulting groups, accounting firms, and investment banks to provide technical advice and arbitrate between competing claims regarding the value of the PE being privatized. As a consequence, foreign experts often have been summoned. The valuation of the PE's assets is subject to lengthy delays, often exacerbated by the poor records kept by the PE. Governments are sensitive about the results of the valuation exercise not only because they want to get the highest sale price, but also because it may raise questions about past public management and investment decisions.[41] The process is thus prone to political controversy, bringing about further delays. Once the PE's assets have been evaluated, administrative capacity is needed to assess buyers' bids, arrange finance and insurance, as well as to deal with the complex legal issues raised by the divestiture. In many cases, a comprehensive rehabilitation plan for the PE has to be designed, evaluated and financed before divestiture is possible. Moreover, governments will want to set up the appropriate regulatory structures around the newly privatized firm, particularly when it retains monopoly power or is meant to carry out specific social functions. Several case studies suggest these issues can paralyze privatization programs for long periods of time, or undermine their smooth implementation, given the state's limited administrative and planning capacity.[42]

Capital markets in developing countries are typically weak and unable to assist in the transfer of PEs to the private sector. Because stock markets are small and poorly regulated, or simply nonexistent, large investments in equity are unusual and privatization has to take place through outright sale of assets. The private sector and local banks may not be able to finance purchases of PEs, often among the biggest enterprises in the country,[43] and governments may be unwilling to sell assets to potential foreign investors. High savings ratios in many countries and vibrant activity in certain speculations suggest that the private sector should not be underestimated. Several case studies indicate that investors can be found quickly for certain businesses, particularly when they are of modest sizes.[44] One should not forget, however, that public ownership of the large natural monopolies was originally resorted to, at least in part, because the private sector would not or could not undertake such large investments. Many governments have maintained a policy mix that has contributed to the backwardness of capital markets and the weakness of private entrepreneurs.[45] Moreover, private investors may initially look upon privatization programs with considerable suspicion, given unfulfilled government promises of reform in the past, or they may decide to wait for policy changes in the regulatory environment, without which investments in PEs may not be considered sufficiently lucrative.

(b) *Political constraints*

There are several political constraints to privatization. We should distinguish those which are common to all types of economic policy reform from those that are specific to privatization. Like all economic reforms, privatization has distributional consequences and favors certain groups within society at the expense of others. The losers can be expected to organize against privatization, particularly if the negative impact of the reform is spread over a relatively small group.[46] If privatization itself has little effect on the pattern of relative prices, then its macroeconomic and distributional consequences are likely to be less tangible and less important in scope than, for example, the termination of certain consumer subsidies or import tariffs.

Privatization can be distinguished from other classes of economic reform in that its costs will be borne intensely by a small number of people and its benefits will be spread out over a large number. Public choice theory suggests that in such situations collective action will be easier to organize against the reform than for it.[47] This has typically been the case for privatization. It has enjoyed increasing ideological support among the technocratic elite in many countries, but has so far failed to mobilize popular support. Business groups might have been expected to be among its leading supporters, even when they were not likely to benefit materially from the reform, because privatization holds out the possibility that the private sector's position will advance. In fact, there are few countries in which the business establishment has actively promoted privatization. This may change as the benefits of reform become clearer, but it shows that privatization programs have not yet enjoyed much popular support.

Opposition to privatization has been much more concerted. In some cases, privatization has been expected to lead to cutbacks in personnel costs, and labor groups have organized against it. Of course, governments can resort to a full arsenal of techniques to overcome such opposition. Berg and Shirley are probably correct to argue that "mothballing" of PEs, where they are allowed to sit idle and waste away over long periods of time, is used as a viable strategy to diffuse labor unrest over privatization.[48] In any event, short of liquidation, privatization will usually not include dramatic labor compression insofar as the new owners of the firm can be expected to keep a large proportion of the work force; the government can compensate the proportion of the labor force concerned, or can extract an agreement concerning layoffs from the new owners. In some cases, of course, rehabilitation prior to divestiture has included important reductions in labor, without which the firm would not have been profitable. In general, there have been few parallels in developing country privatization experiences with the massive restructuring of highly-unionized mining concerns in Western Europe, which laid off tens of thousands of employees and depressed the economies of entire provinces. Major layoffs in the course of structural adjustment programs have been more common in the state bureaucracy itself, or in non-commercial parastatals. In Brazil, only one of the 17 PEs privatized as of 1985 had more than 1000 employees, and the 18 firms being considered for privatization in Costa Rica employs less than 1% of the labor force.[49]

So far, we have implied that the political impact of privatization will be unimportant. Quite the opposite may be true, however, for several reasons. Privatization may have a powerful effect on the balance of economic power between the public and private sector, at least symbolically. In some sense, it may be seen as changing the "rules of the game."

Corporatist patterns may be upset by such rule changes. Privatization is likely to undermine trade union power, as it is typically concentrated in the public sector. Unions may react strongly against the reform, not only because of its direct impact on employment, but also because of a fear that the union's political power will decrease in the private sector, and a sense that a longstanding *modus vivendi* with the government is being upset.

In many countries with ethnic, religious or regional tensions, political stability has rested on a delicate social contract, in which certain groups are implicitly granted economic power as long as they do not compete for political power, or vice versa. Privatization disturbs such arrangements by altering the balance of economic and political power. The groups to which the PE might be sold if privatized have posed serious problems in many countries. In Kenya, it is well known that the scope of privatization policies is limited by the fact that the most likely purchasers would be Kikuyu or Asian business groups, an eventuality which is considered politically unacceptable. Ethnic considerations are also important in Cameroon, where fear of Bamileke dominance recently led the president to block the privatization of a major bank.[50] In other countries, fear of foreign business groups has slowed down privatization programs. This is the case with Syro-Lebanese and South Asian businessmen in much of sub-Saharan Africa, and with ethnic Chinese in many countries of East Asia.

The political impact of privatization will depend in part on the state's ideological investment in public production in the past. Countries like Algeria, Mexico, or Tanzania which have promoted a large social, redistributive and economic role for the state under the flag of socialism or nationalism are likely to find such reforms more politically sensitive. Similarly, regime discontinuities, such as coups d'etat or elections, are likely to provide governments windows of opportunity in which to promote privatization programs. 'This clearly happened in Chile in the mid-1970s, for example, and in Jamaica with Seaga's electoral victory in 1980.[51]

Much of the political opposition to divestiture will be generated within the state apparatus, and will revolve around the prerogatives of the bureaucracy. A number of case studies have shown that opposition to privatization has crystallized among the management of the concerned PE and has extended to the line ministry overseeing it. In some cases, they have been able to block privatization. In other cases, as we discussed above, these groups have been able to coopt the privatization process and limit its impact on competition and economic efficiency. For example, they have exerted influence on the regulatory environment, making sure they will continue to play a managerial or regulatory role over the private firm.[52]

Within the state elite, privatization has engendered bitter conflict. Such conflicts are related to the benefits and power that accrue to particular elements of the bureaucracy, which oversee the PEs and are thus envied by other, rival elements. They are also related to sincere ideological differences within the state elite over the role the state should play in economic development. The interplay between individual interests, ideological conflicts and bureaucratic politics in the Philippines has been well illustrated by Haggard.[53] The Aquino government's privatization efforts have been led by technocrats with a sincere desire to cut government expenditures and expand the role of the private sector. At the same time, the large PE sector is dominated by interests closely linked to the Marcos regime, and remains a vexing irritant to the new regime. Privatization efforts thus combine the partly inconsistent motives of restoring fiscal balance and increasing economic efficiency with those of wrestling control over vast political resources away from hostile groups. Economic liberalism has been undermined by the exigencies of regime consolidation, and bureaucratic conflicts over ministerial jurisdiction appear to have added to the confusion. As a result, implementation has slowed to a crawl, and the original momentum for reform has abated.

Even if some of the PEs being privatized are running losses, many are potentially quite lucrative because of their physical assets, or because the state has granted various anti-competitive advantages, such as a statutory monopoly or protection from foreign imports. Thus, the sale of the PE can generate extensive influence peddling, rent seeking, and graft by business groups.[54] To some state elites, the PE being privatized represents a valuable political resource to be dispensed with care. Case studies from Zaire and the Ivory Coast indicate that the presidents of these countries personally intervened to make sure that PEs were sold at advantageous terms to political allies.[55] In other instances, state elites have been loathe to disturb the PE sector, because their political support base runs through its labor force. This appears to be the case in Tanzania and Turkey,[56] countries in which PEs account for a large proportion of the formal economy's labor force. Those elites will contemplate reform only when the present political economy is no longer sustainable and political survival is contingent upon reform.

6. CONCLUDING REMARKS

We have reviewed a number of issues relating to the privatization of PEs in developing countries. Policy makers in developing countries invested PEs with many ambitious objectives in the decades that followed World War II; many of them were not reached and PE performance has been considered disappointing in recent years. Today there are widespread calls for privatization, and equally ambitious reasons are given for returning these institutions to the private sector.

Privatization is unlikely, however, to overcome the kinds of economic and political forces that undermined public production. Unless it is accompanied by a liberalization program, the effects of privatization on both economic efficiency and government expenditures are likely to be modest. Its psychological impact is conceivably more important, as a way of preparing the way for more fundamental liberalization measures, but in many cases we see that governments undertake privatization to prevent further reforms. Large-scale privatization may have an effect on an intangible balance of power between the private and public sectors. As such, it can arouse much more popular opposition than its modest distributional consequences might lead one to expect. The most likely opponents to privatization will probably be found in the state apparatus itself, wary of losing valued rents and prerogatives.

Of course, the analytical distinction made here between liberalization and privatization may be largely academic for countries undergoing ambitious structural adjustment programs that incorporate a host of economic policy reforms in a short time. Indeed, if economists cannot readily distinguish them, it is understandable that the relative impacts of privatization and liberalization efforts are confused by the countries undergoing austere stabilization measures. In these cases, privatization, a policy with more tangible results than liberalization, may bear the brunt of the people's discontent. Governments have helped the privatization cause in such circumstances with information campaigns, or by labeling what are effectively privatization efforts with some more neutral term.[57]

In any event, the most important obstacles to divestiture so far have been implementation difficulties, which largely explain the slow progress of most programs. The pace of implementation will presumably accelerate with the development of precedents and experience.

Ultimately, it is difficult to reach definitive conclusions regarding the relative impacts of liberalization and privatization. Since the two reforms have been promoted together in practice, it is hard to distinguish their relative effects. Because the political circumstances under which policy is implemented can vary so much, and because it is impossible to determine outcomes in the absence of the policy change, the evaluation of specific policies is fundamentally ambiguous. Claims made on behalf of privatization can rarely be proven or disproven. What can be suggested is that, in at least some cases, liberalization or regulatory reform is better able than privatization to bring about gains in economic efficiency. In other cases, such reforms must accompany privatization if it is to have any impact. There can be no general presumption that privatization is a *sine qua non* for a successful liberalization campaign, or vice versa. In certain circumstances, privatization may turn out to be the prerequisite for other reforms; in others, liberalization alone will make subsequent privatization redundant. In yet other cases, privatization will not be effective until after liberalization measures have been implemented. In the absence of other policy reforms which increase competition in the economy, the impact of privatization on economic efficiency is likely to be modest.

NOTES

1. See Vuylsteke (1988), p. 41. This study, along with its companion volumes, Nankani (1988) and Candoy-Sekse (1988), provides a wealth of information on the progress of privatization implementation efforts.

2. The definition is quoted from Hemming and Mansoor (1988b), p. 1.

3. See Short (1984), Nellis (1986) and Jones (1982) for such discussions.

4. See Killick (1981) for a discussion relating to Africa.

5. See, for example, Rees (1984), pp. 1–9.

6. See Short (1984), pp. 117–120.

7. See Borcherding *et al.* (1982), Millward (1982), and Yarrow (1986) for discussions and somewhat ambiguous evidence that public sector firms tend to be less efficient than their private sector counterparts.

8. See Shirley (1983).

9. See Hirschman (1982).

10. See Anderson (1987).

11. This discussion draws on Heller and Schiller (1988) and Hemming and Mansoor (1988b).

12. See Vuylsteke (1988) and Nankani (1988).

13. See Yotopoulos (1988), D'Almeida (1986) and Lorch (1987), respectively.

14. Thus, for example, a recent IMF evaluation of its stabilization plans justified the PE reform included in 25 different programs between 1980–84 only in terms of the resulting savings in expenditure. See Fiscal Affairs Department (1986), pp. 29–31.

15. See, for example, Goodman (1985), Hanke (1987) and Butler (1985).

16. See, for example, Kay and Thompson (1986), Rees (1986), and Hemming and Mansoor (1988b).

17. See Stigler (1975) and Wolf (1979). Their work is of course more a critique of government regulation than of public ownership.

18. Hemming and Mansoor (1988b), p. 13.

19. The term was coined by Leibenstein (1966).

20. See Demsetz (1968), and Furubotn and Pejovich (1972).

21. See Aharoni (1982).

22. See Lange (1964).

23. See Savas (1982) and Wolf (1979).

24. See Hyden (1983) for example.

25. See Grindle (1980).

26. Though there are few analyses of the distributional impact of privatization specifically, a large literature exists on the distributional consequences of structural adjustment in developing countries, including privatization; see for example UNICEF (1987), Helleiner (1987), Addison and Demery (1985), and Green (1987).

27. Heller and Tait (1984) provide statistical evidence and comparisons of public sector salaries in developing countries.

28. On privatization issues in agricultural marketing, see Christiansen and Stackhouse (1987), Abbot (1987), and Maddock (1987).

29. See Bates (1981) on sub-Saharan Africa; Grindle (1986) on Latin America.

30. See among many others Lipton (1977) for a discussion of urban bias.

31. Damis (1987).

32. See Vickers (1985).

33. Brittan makes this argument to suggest that privatization amounts to "slightly better than nothing" rather than "slightly worse than nothing" (1986), p. 38.

34. See Kay and Thompson (1986).

35. Sappington and Stiglitz (1987) make this argument.

36. It is ironic that the literature on regulatory failure cited above in defense of privatization has largely been inspired by the perceived weaknesses of the regulatory environment in the United States, a country which has traditionally eschewed public ownership.

37. Brittan (1986), p. 35. See also Brittan (1984).

38. See Yotopoulos (1988).

39. On the Chinese reforms, for example, see Kelliher (1986).

40. On the British experience, see Ascher (1987), Beesley and Littleshild (1983), Brittan (1984), Hastings and Levie (1983), Kay (1987), Kay and Thompson (1986), Klein (1984), and Vickers and Yarrow (1985).

41. See Berg and Shirley (1987).

42. Lorch (1987), and Leeds (1987) provide two interesting case studies; see also Vuylsteke, pp. 97–101 and passim.

43. See Aylen (1987).

44. See the case studies of Jamaica, Morocco, and the Ivory Coast by Leeds (1987), Damis (1987), and Wilson (1987) respectively.

45. See, for example, Elkan (1988).

46. The political constraints to all forms of economic reform in the developing countries are well analyzed in Bienen and Gersovitz (1985, 1986), Nelson (1984), and Lal (1987).

47. Bates (1988) provides several interesting essays on political economy issues in developing countries using a public choice approach.

48. See Berg and Shirley (1987).

49. See Berg and Shirley (1987), pp. 4–5.

50. Personal communication, Yaounde 1988.

51. The Chilean case is well documented in Foxley (1983). On Jamaica, see Leeds (1987).

52. Kay and Thompson (1986) describe this process for Great Britain.

53. See Haggard (1988).

54. On rent seeking, see Krueger (1974).

55. See Wilson (1987) and Callaghy and Wilson (1988). In the early 1970s, large sectors of the Zairian economy were similarly nationalized, and handed over to be managed by barons of the regime, indicating if nothing else that the distinction between the public and private sectors can be a fine line.

56. See Leeds (1988) on Turkey. On this general point, see Bienen and Gersovitz (1985).

57. See Berg and Shirley (1987).

REFERENCES

Abbot, J., "Institutional reform of marketing and related services to agriculture, with special reference to Africa," *Agricultural Economics*, Vol. 1, No. 1 (1987), pp. 143–157.

Abernethy, David B. "Bureaucratic growth and economic decline in sub-Saharan Africa," Paper presented at the 26th Annual Meeting of the African Studies Association (Boston, MA: December 7–10, 1983).

Addison, Tony, and Lionel Demery, "Macro-economic stabilization, income distribution and poverty: A preliminary survey," Overseas Development Institute Working Papers, No. 15 (London: Overseas Development Institute, 1985).

Aharoni, Yair, "State-owned enterprise: An agent

without a principle," in L. P. Jones (Ed.), *Public Enterprise in Less Developed Countries* (New York: Cambridge University Press, 1982).

Alchian, A. A., "Some economics of property rights," *Il Politico*, Vol. 30 (1965).

Anderson, Dennis, *The Public Revenue and Economic Policy in African Countries*, World Bank Discussion Paper No. 19. (Washington, DC: The World Bank, 1987).

Ascher, Kate, *The Politics of Privatization; Contracting out Public Services* (London: Macmillan Education 1987).

Aylen, J. J., "Privatization in developing countries," *Lloyds Bank Review*, No. 163 (January 1987).

Balassa, Bela, "Public enterprise in developing countries: Issues of privatization," Development Research Department, Economics and Research Staff Report No. DRD292. (Washington, DC: World Bank, 1987).

Barbier, Jean-Pierre, and Gilles Peltier, "La Rehabilitation des entreprises publiques du secteur industriel en Afrique au sud du Sahara," *Revue Tiers Monde*, Vol. 27, No. 107 (1986), pp. 616–626.

Bardhan, Pranab, *The Political Economy of Development in India* (New York: Basil Blackwell, 1984).

Bates, Robert (Ed.), *Towards a Political Economy of Development* (Berkeley, CA: University of California Press, 1988).

Bates, Robert, *Markets and States in Tropical Africa: the Political Basis of Agricultural Policies* (Berkeley, CA: University of California Press, 1981).

Baumol, W. (Ed.), *Public and Private Enterprise in a Mixed Economy* (New York: St Martin's Press, 1980).

Baumol, William J., John C. Panzar, and Robert D. Willig, *Contestable Markets and the Theory of Industry Structure* (San Diego, CA: Harcourt Brace Jovanovich, 1982).

Beesley, Michael, and Stephen Littleshild, "Privatization: Principles, problems and priorities," *Lloyds Bank Review*, No. 149 (July 1983), pp. 1–20.

Berg, Elliot, and Mary Shirley, *Divestiture in Developing Countries*, World Bank Discussion Paper No. 11 (Washington, DC: The World Bank, 1987).

Bienen, Henry S., and Mark Gersovitz, "Consumer subsidy cuts, violence, and political stability," *Comparative Politics*, Vol. 19, No. 1 (October 1986), pp. 25–44.

Bienen, Henry S., and Mark Gersovitz, "Economic stabilization, conditionality and political stability," *International Organization*, Vol. 39, No. 4 (1985), pp. 729–754.

Borcherding, T. E., W. W. Pommerehne, and F. Schneider, "Comparing the efficiency of private and public production: The evidence from five countries," *Zeitschrift für Nationalökonomie: Journal of Economics*, Supplement 2 (1982).

Brittan, Samuel, "Privatization: A comment on Kay and Thompson," *The Economic Journal*, Vol. 96 (March 1986), pp. 33–38.

Brittan, Samuel, "The politics and economics of privatization," *The Political Quarterly*, Vol. 55, No. 2 (1984), pp. 109–128.

Butler, Stuart, *Privatization Federal Spending: A Strategy to Eliminate the Budget Deficit* (New York: Universe Books, 1985).

Callaghy, Thomas M., and Ernest James Wilson III, "Africa: Policy, reality or ritual?" in Raymond Vernon (Ed.), *The Promise of Privatization* (New York: Council on Foreign Relations, 1988).

Cameron, David, "On the limits of the public economy," *The Annals of the American Academy of Political and Social Science* (January 1982), pp. 46–62.

Candoy-Sekse, Rebecca, and Anne Ruiz Palmer, *Techniques of Privatization of State-Owned Enterprises — Vol. III: Inventory of Country Experience and Reference Materials* (Washington, DC: World Bank Technical Paper No. 90, 1988).

Christiansen, Robert E., and Lee Ann Stackhouse, "The privatization of agricultural trading in Malawi" (Cambridge, Harvard University, Kennedy School of Government, Center For Business and Government, December 1987).

Corbo, Vittorio, and Jaime de Melo (Eds.), *Scrambling for Survival: How Firms Adjusted to the Recent Reforms in Argentina, Chile and Uruguay*, World Bank Staff Working Papers, No. 764 (Washington, DC: The World Bank, 1985).

Courchene, Thomas J., "Privatization: Palliative or panacea; an interpretive literature survey," in Thomas E. Kierans, and W. T. Stanbury (Eds.), *Papers on Privatization* (Montreal: The Institute for Research on Public Policy, 1985), pp. 1–37.

Cowan, L. G., "Divestment, privatization and development," *The Washington Quarterly*, Vol. 8 (Fall 1985), pp. 47–56.

D'Almeida, Ayite-Fily, "La privatization des entreprises publiques en Afrique au sud du Sahara," *Le Mois en Afrique*, No. 245–246 and No. 247–248 (1986).

Damis, John, "The privatization of the transport sector in Morocco: A case study" (Cambridge, MA: Harvard University, Kennedy School of Government Center For Business and Government, December 1987).

Demsetz, H., "Why regulate utilities," *The Journal of Law and Economics*, Vol. 11 (1968), pp. 55–65.

The Economist, "Selling the silver," October 19, 1985.

Elkan, Walter, "Entrepreneurs and entrepreneurship in Africa," *World Bank Research Observer*, Vol. 3, No. 2 (July 1988), pp. 171–188.

Feigenbaum, Harvey B., "Public enterprise in comparative perspective," *Comparative Politics*, Vol. 15, No. 1 (October 1982), pp. 101–122.

Fiscal Affairs Department, International Monetary Fund, "Fund-supported programs, fiscal policy, and income distribution," Occasional Paper No. 46 (Washington, DC: International Monetary Fund, 1986).

Foxley, A., *Latin American Experiments in Neoconservative Economics* (Berkeley, CA: University of California Press, 1983).

Furubotn, E. G., and S. Pejovich "Property rights and economic theory: A survey of the recent literature," *The Journal of Economic Literature*, Vol. 10 (December 1972).

Goodman, John C. (Ed.), *Privatization: The Proceed-*

ings of A Conference (Dallas, TX: The National Center for Policy Analysis, 1985).

Green, Reginald Herbold, "Articulating IMF stabilization programmes with structural adjustment in SSA agriculture," Paper prepared for the ODI conference "The Design and Impact of Adjustment Programmes on Agriculture and Agricultural Institutions" (London: Overseas Development Institute, 1987).

Grindle, Merilee S., *State and Countryside: Development Policy and Agrarian Politics in Latin America* (Baltimore, MD: Johns Hopkins University Press, 1986).

Grindle, Merilee S. (Ed.), *Politics and Policy Implementation in the Third World* (Princeton, NJ: Princeton University Press, 1980).

Gulhati, Ravi, *Recent Economic Reforms in Africa: a Preliminary Political Economy Perspective*, EDI Policy Seminar Report Series (Washington, DC: The World Bank, 1987).

Haggard, Stephan, "The Philippines: Picking up after Marcos," in Raymond Vernon (Ed.), *The Promise of Privatization* (New York: Council on Foreign Relations, 1988), pp. 91–122.

Hanke, Steve H. (Ed.), *Privatization and Development* (San Francisco, CA: International Center for International Growth, 1987).

Hastings, Sue, and Hugo Levie (Eds.), *Privatization?* (Nottingham: Spokesman, 1983).

Heald, David, "Privatization: Analyzing its appeals and limitations," *Fiscal Studies*, Vol. 5, No. 1 (1984), pp. 36–46.

Helleiner, Gerald K., "Stabilization, adjustment and the poor," *World Development*, Vol. 15, No. 12 (1987), pp. 1499–1513.

Heller, Peter S., and Christian Schiller, "The fiscal impact of privatization, with some examples from Arab countries," mimeo (Washington, DC: International Monetary Fund, 1988).

Heller, Peter S., and Alan A. Tait, "Government employment and pay: Some international comparisons," Occasional paper No. 24 (Washington, DC: International Monetary Fund, 1984).

Hemming, Richard, and Ali Mansoor, "Is privatization the answer?" *Finance and Development*, Vol. 25, No. 3 (September 1988a), pp. 31–33.

Hemming, Richard, and Ali M. Mansoor, "Privatization and public enterprises," Occasional Paper No. 56 (Washington, DC: International Monetary Fund, 1988b).

Hirschman, A. O., *Shifting Involvements: Private Interests and Public Action* (Princeton, NJ: Princeton University Press, 1982).

Hyden, Goran, *No Shortcuts to Progress* (Berkeley, CA: University of California Press, 1983).

Jones, L. P. (Ed.), *Public Enterprise in Less Developed Countries* (New York: Cambridge University Press, 1982).

Kay, J. A., *The State and the Market: the UK Experience with Privatization* (New York: Group of 30 Occasional Paper No. 213, 1987).

Kay, John, Colin Mayer, and David Thompson (Eds.), *Privatization and Regulation: The UK Experience* (Oxford: Clarendon Press, 1986).

Kay, J. A., and D. J. Thompson, "Privatization: A policy in search of a rationale," *The Economic Journal*, Vol. 96 (March 1986), pp. 18–32.

Kelliher, Daniel, "The political consequences of China's reforms," *Comparative Politics*, Vol. 18, No. 4 (1986), pp. 479–494.

Kent, Calvin A., *Entrepreneurship and the Privatizing of Government* (New York: Quorum Books, 1987).

Kierans, Thomas E., and W. T. Stanbury (Eds.), *Papers on Privatization* (Montreal: The Institute for Research on Public Policy, 1985).

Killick, Tony, *Policy Economics* (London: Heineman, 1981).

Klein, Rudolf, "Privatization and the welfare state," *Lloyds Bank Review*, No. 151 (January 1984), pp. 12–29.

Krueger, Ann, "The political economy of the rent seeking society," *The American Economic Review*, Vol. 64 (June 1974), pp. 291–303.

Lal, Deepak, "Political economy of economic liberalization," *World Bank Economic Review*, Vol. 1, No. 2 (January 1987), pp. 273–300.

Lamb, Geoffrey, *Managing Economic Policy Change; Institutional Dimensions*, World Bank Discussion Paper No. 14 (Washington, DC: The World Bank, 1987).

Lange, O. (Ed.), *On the Economic Theory of Socialism* (New York: McGraw-Hill Book Company, Inc. Paperbacks, 1964).

Leeds, Roger S., "Turkey: Rhetoric and reality," in Raymond Vernon (Ed.), *The Promise of Privatization* (New York: The Council on Foreign Relations, 1988), pp. 149–78.

Leeds, Roger S., "Privatization in Jamaica: Two case studies" (Cambridge, MA: Harvard University, Kennedy School of Government, Center For Business and Government, December 1987).

Leibenstein, Harvey, "Allocative efficiency vs. 'X-efficiency'," *American Economic Review* Vol. 56, No. 3 (June 1966), pp. 393–415.

Leonard, David K., "The political realities of African management," *World Development*, Vol. 15, No. 7 (1987), pp. 899–910.

Lipton, Michael, *Why Poor People Stay Poor: A Study of Urban Bias in World Development* (London: Temple Smith, 1977).

Lorch, Klaus, "The privatization transaction and its longer-term effects: A case study of the textile industry in Bangladesh" (Cambridge, MA: Harvard University, Kennedy School of Government, Center For Business and Government, December 1987).

Maddock, Nicholas, "Privatizing agriculture: Policy options in developing countries," Vol. 12, No. 4. *Food Policy* (November 1987), pp. 295–298.

Mayer, Colin, and Shirley Meadowcroft, "Selling public assets: Techniques and financial implications," *Fiscal Studies*, Vol. 6, No. 4 (1986), pp. 42–56.

Millward, R., "The comparative performance of public and private ownership," in E. Roll (Ed.), *The Mixed Economy* (London: Macmillan, 1982).

Moe, Ronald C., "Exploring the limits of privatization," *Public Administration Review*, Vol. 47, No. 6 (1987), pp. 453–460.

Nankani, Helen, *Techniques of Privatization of State*

Owned Enterprises. Volume II; Selected Country Case Studies (Washington, DC: World Bank Technical Paper Number 89, 1988).

Nellis, John R., *Public Enterprises in Sub-Saharan Africa* (Washington, DC: The World Bank, 1986).

Nelson, Joan, "The political economy of stabilization: Commitment, capacity, and public response," *World Development*, Vol. 12, No. 10 (1984), pp. 983–1006.

Neuberger, Julia (Ed.), *Privatization . . . Fair Shares for All or Selling the Family Silver?* (London: Papermac, 1987).

Otobo, Dafe, "Bureaucratic elites and public sector wage bargaining in Nigeria," *The Journal of Modern African Studies*, Vol. 24, No. 1 (1986), pp. 101–26.

Paul, Samuel, "Privatization and the public sector," *Finance and Development*, Vol. 22 (December 1985), pp. 42–45.

Pirie, Masden, *Dismantling the State: the Theory and Practice of Privatization* (Dallas, TX: National Center for Policy Analysis, 1985).

Posner, Michael, "Privatization: The frontier between public and private," *Policy studies*, Vol. 5 (July 1984), pp. 22–32.

Pryke, Richard, "The comparative performance of public and private enterprise," in John Kay, Colin Mayer, and David Thompson (Eds.), *Privatization and Regulation: The UK Experience* (Oxford: Clarendon Press, 1986), pp. 101–118.

Ramanadham, V. V., *Studies in Public Enterprise: From Evaluation to Privatization* (London: Frank Cass, 1987).

Rees, Ray, "Is there an economic case for privatization?" *Public Money*, Vol. 5 (March 1986), pp. 19–26.

Rees, Ray, *Public Enterprise Economics*, second edition (London: Weidenfeld and Nicolson, 1984).

Reusse, E., "Liberalization and agricultural marketing," *Food Policy*, Vol. 12, No. 4 (1987), pp. 37–46.

Roth, Gabriel, *The Private Provision of Public Services in Developing Countries* (New York: Oxford University Press for the World Bank, 1987).

Sappington, David E. M., and Joseph E. Stiglitz, "Privatization, information and incentives," *Journal of Policy Analysis and Management*, Vol. 6, No. 4, (1987), pp. 567–582.

Savas, E. S., *Privatizing the Public Sector* (Chatham, NJ: Chatham House Publishers Inc., 1982).

Savas, E. S., *Alternatives for Delivering Public Services: Towards Improved Performance* (Boulder, CO: Westview Press, 1977).

Shirley, Mary, "The experience with privatization," *Finance and Development*, Vol. 25, No. 3 (1988), pp. 34–35.

Shirley, Mary M., *Managing State Owned Enterprises*, World Bank Staff Working Paper 577 (Washington, DC: The World Bank, 1983).

Short, R. P., "The role of public enterprises: An international statistical comparison," in Robert H. Floyd, Clive S. Gray and R. P. Short (Eds.), *Public Enterprise in Mixed Economies: Some Macroeconomic Aspects* (Washington, DC: International Monetary Fund, 1984).

Starr, Paul, "The limits of privatization," *Proceedings of the Academy of Political Science*, Vol. 36, No. 3 (1987), pp. 124–137.

Starr, Paul, "The meaning of privatization," mimeo (Princeton, NJ: Princeton University, 1985).

Stigler, George, *The Citizen and the State* (Chicago: University of Chicago Press, 1975).

Taylor, C., *Why Governments Grow* (Beverly Hills, CA: Sage, 1983).

Trebat, Thomas J., *Brazil's State Owned Enterprises: A Case Study of the State as Entrepreneur* (New York: Cambridge Univeristy Press, 1983).

Tyler, William G., "Technical efficiency in production in a developing country: An empirical examination of the Brazilian plastics and steel industries," *Oxford Economic Papers*, Vol. 31 (November 1979), pp. 477–495.

UNICEF, *Adjustment with a Human Face*, Giovanni Cornia, Richard Jolley, and Frances Stewart (Eds.) (Oxford: Clarendon Press, 1987).

Vernon, Raymond (Ed.), *The Promise of Privatization* (New York: Council on Foreign Relations, 1988).

Vernon, Raymond, and Y. Aharoni, *State-Owned enterprises in the Western Economies* (New York: St. Martin's Press, 1981).

Vickers, John, "Economics of predatory practices," *Fiscal Studies*, Vol. 6 (1985), pp. 24–36.

Vickers, John, and George K. Yarrow, *Privatization and the Natural Monopolies* (London: Public Policy Center, 1985).

Vuylsteke, Charles, *Techniques of Privatization of State-Owned Enterprises; Volume I: Methods and Implementation*, World Bank Technical Paper, No. 88 (Washington, DC: The World Bank, 1988).

Waterbury, John, "The soft state and the open door: Egypt's experience with economic liberalization," *Comparative Politics*, Vol. 18, No. 1 (October 1985).

West Africa, "Ghana's Divestiture," June 27, 1988, pp. 1152–1153.

Wilson, Ernest, "Privatization in Cote D'Ivoire: Three case studies" (Cambridge, MA: Harvard University, Kennedy School of Government, Center For Business and Government, December 1987).

Winpenny, J., "Divestiture of public enterprises in developing countries," *Development Policy Review* (forthcoming).

Wolf, C. Jr., "A theory of non market failure," *The Public Interest*, Vol. 55 (1979), pp. 114–133.

Yarrow, George, "Privatization in theory and practice," *Economic Policy* Vol. 1 (April 1986), pp. 323–364.

Yotopoulos, Pan A., "The (rip)tide of privatization: Lessons from Chile," mimeo (Stanford, CA: Stanford University Press, 1988).

Zulu, Justin, and Saleh Nsouli, "Adjustment programs in Africa: The recent experience," Occasional Paper No. 34 (Washington, DC: International Monetary Fund, 1985).

[8]

World Development, Vol. 17, No. 5, pp. 673–682, 1989.
Printed in Great Britain.

0305–750X/89 $3.00 + 0.00

Privatization in Rent-Seeking Societies

WILLIAM GLADE*
The University of Texas, Austin, and The Wilson Center, Washington, DC

Summary. — Four Latin American countries have devoted particular attention, though not equal action, to privatization policies, the implementation of which has shed considerable light on the dynamics of rent-seeking societies. The fact that democratization, in some form, is also underway in each of the four has intensified the interplay of forces that shape the implementation of privatization programs. The experiences of Mexico and Chile, in particular, demonstrate how important it may be to "privatize" the private sector by reforming macroeconomic policies and opening the economy to external competition before, or at least concurrently with, tackling the privatization of the public sector. The obstructive force of rent-seeking behavior is shown most clearly in the Argentine case, while the Brazilian experience is useful, along with that of Mexico, as a reminder that rent-seeking dynamics are not necessarily incompatible with structural transformation and high rates of growth.

1. INTRODUCTION

A great deal of insight into efficiency conditions in Latin America's newly industrialized countries (NICs) can be obtained from looking at their experience with privatization policies. Three of the countries we shall examine — Argentina, Brazil, and Mexico — are generally recognized as having made it into the NIC category. The fourth, Chile, is industrially less advanced, but its policy history up to 1970 was similar in major respects to that of the other three cases, and by a number of social indicators (degree of urbanization, literacy levels, and such) it would rank behind Argentina but ahead of the other two countries. Hence, Chilean experience, too, helps clarify the structure and functioning of systems that now face the problem of regaining economic momentum amid world conditions quite different from those that prevailed during the heyday of their post-World War II industrial expansion.

It is not entirely beside the point that all four countries are, in different ways, also coping with difficult challenges in another aspect of national existence: namely, the democratization of political processes. The connection between problems in the two areas of social organization, economic and political, is more than coincidental, as we shall see.

In these four countries, as elsewhere in Latin America, privatization, like economic planning in the 1950s and 1960s, has been both widely debated and formally incorporated into the public policy agenda. But, also as in the case of economic planning, it has more often been discussed and enacted than actually carried out in a degree sufficient to have significant impact on national economic processes. Save in Chile, actual implementation of privatization has lagged well behind what might have been expected, given the magnitude of the public sector crisis that surfaced in the early 1980s with the collapse of foreign voluntary lending. Even the conditionality stipulations associated with the lending under duress that has occurred since the onset of the crisis have failed to produce a great deal of movement, at least until recently, in the larger countries of our set.

For Mexico in particular, a caveat is in order. By some official estimates it would appear that a substantial amount of privatization has taken place, but this may well be one of those instances in which there is less here than meets the eye. For

*Thanks for support of the project from which these findings were taken go to the Institute of the Americas and the Center for US–Mexican Studies of the University of California at San Diego, the Wilson Center, the Tinker Foundation, the Program on US–Mexico Studies of the LBJ School of Public Affairs at the University of Texas, the Hewlett Foundation, the Commission for the Study of International Migration and Cooperative Economic Development, and the Howard Heinz Endowment. The grants made possible the author's field research in the summer of 1988, country studies by the research collaborators, and the analysis conducted during 1988.

one thing, beginning with the aggressive Echeverrian spree of interventionism, during which hundreds of parastatals were established (almost impulsively), the tally of state enterprises has varied from source to source even within the government. By some counts, the total eventually reached between 800 and 900; by others the aggregate was more on the order of 1,100–1,200. An independent survey by the Office for Public Sector Studies of the University of Texas Institute of Latin American Studies enumerated upward of 1,400 parastals. Many, however, were small operations, either trust funds/endowments (*fideicomisos*) set up to finance particular undertakings, or quasi-governmental bodies established to do what in other settings would typically be handled by a federal agency. Besides this, the number of entities was constantly shifting. Thus, the total size of the parastatal sector was never clear to begin with, and its configuration has for years been ambiguous.

Under the circumstances, there is obviously room for different assessments of how much the parastatal sector has actually contracted, particularly since the Mexican government has counted as privatization the merging of some official entities with others, as well as their transfer to state and local governments. In some instances, the transfer of enterprises to the so-called social sector (mainly labor unions closely linked with the ruling party) has also been counted as privatization. Indeed, different branches of the Mexican government have, even when reporting for the same period, given different figures for the number of state-owned companies sold to others. That a definitive list of privatized and "privatizable" firms, with their exact disposition, is not to be had from any official source may, of course, have more than a little to do with the unusual acrimony surrounding the policy, a point to which we shall need to return later.

2. PRIVATIZATION OBJECTIVES

The term privatization has been employed in a variety of ways in the Latin American cases covered here, not simply to designate a transfer of asset ownership. Even leaving aside the obfuscating amplitude of current Mexican usage, the referent of the term has usually been broader than merely the removal of assets from the public sector and their placement under private control. Such a static view of the process is unnecessarily restrictive and misses what, as a practical matter, is the legitimating logic of the policy on instrumental, as opposed to ideological, grounds: namely, the effects of different regimes of asset control on the quality of asset management. Just as the case for private ownership has been argued, ever since the days of Adam Smith, as much on instrumental grounds (the general results for society) as on Lockean and other notions of natural right, an expanded view of privatization has quite properly looked to the bearing of a related set of policy changes on the efficiency of asset management.

In this deideologized recasting of the concept, a variety of measures have sailed under the privatization flag in the four countries under review. This includes, for example, the transfer of assets from one type of public ownership to another when this leads to significantly enhanced operations from an economic point of view, which is to say management in accordance with the directives of the market. Also included are cases in which the judgment of the market leads to extinction of an uneconomic enterprise. In Mexico, where, as noted, some parastatals have been given to state and local authorities (without discernible improvement in their management), Vehiculos Automotores Mexicanos (VAM) and Renault de Mexico were both sold to Renault of France — itself, of course, a state-owned enterprise. In the case of VAM, Renault was actually paid by the government to take on the firm and its debt. Following this transfer, the company was shut down. A year or so later, Renault de Mexico was likewise closed, thereby implementing the verdict of the market on both operations. In Argentina, too, privatization has been applied to two parastatals in which ownership would be shared with foreign public enterprises, one national (the Spanish telephone company) and the other multinational (the Scandinavian Airlines System). A competing bid for the latter even involved Argentine national private investors acting in association with a foreign public enterprise, Alitalia. Unlike Mexican transfers that gave ownership to trade unions or local or state governments, but left management essentially unchanged in quality, the clear intent in these cases has been to upgrade the operating efficiency of asset use. To be sure, noneconomic considerations have intruded in the Argentine situation as well, but not in quite the unalloyed way that they came into the picture in the case of some Mexican "social property" transfers.

All the cases that can reasonably be included under the privatization rubric involve changes in asset management that produce a closer approximation of the kind of asset use obtained in a competitive market context. Though it might be argued that, in this sense, the recent Chilean policies that have used privatization to promote a broader distribution of ownership depart from an unmodified action of the market, as the capital market is structured at present, it seems justifiable to include these instances in that they look to more competitive conditions of capital supply in the long run, Chilean experience in the late 1970s having pointed up the dangers of undue concentrations of economic power. What is at issue, *au fond*, is the degree to which rent-seeking behavior is encouraged or discouraged in the course of changes in asset management.

The point may, in fact, be taken as the very touchstone of privatization. Not much is gained, for example, if a public monopoly is simply converted, other things remaining equal, into a private monopoly in which management is otherwise undisturbed in its conduct of business affairs. From a social perspective, the organizational changes that may be meaningfully described as privatization are only of benefit if they lead to such ends as technological improvement, lower production costs, better products, a broader distribution of the fruits of efficiency, and so on — an alteration, in other words, of a system that has long tended to privatize profits while socializing costs. Though in many instances privatization may involve deregulation to allow the market to work its way, in other cases it may, paradoxically, necessitate increased regulation to accomplish its aims. This may be true in the case of the public utility type of monopoly or other instances of market failure. Chile discovered as much when it began to privatize local electric power companies and confronted the need to enact regulatory legislation to guide the conduct of the privatized companies. Either way, the rent-seeking society framework, as developed by Buchanan, Tullock, and others, provides a useful platform from which to interpret what has been happening — and what are the prospects for privatization over the years ahead.[1]

3. RENT-SEEKING PRIVATIZATION

The earliest privatization in recent times took place in Argentina, in the 1960s, when the municipal surface transport system was turned over to competing private bus companies. By all accounts, this led to a marked improvement in the efficiency and effectiveness of the system. Yet it did not lead very soon to an extension of privatization to other fields, despite the coming to power in 1976 of a military government of neoliberal orientation.[2] Instead, it was in Chile that privatization began in earnest and really took hold. Considering the context in which this program began, however, it is appropriate to interpret the initial Chilean efforts, as well as subsequent efforts in Argentina, Brazil, and Mexico, as cases of rent-seeking privatization.

To call the policies thus is not in any sense intended to imply that they were deliberately misleading. On the contrary, in the view of the public authorities of all four countries, they were carrying out authentic programs of privatization as best they then understood the term. In all four cases, moreover, the early program involved cases of reprivatization — the return to the private sector of enterprises previously lodged there — so there was extra reason for the governments involved to think of these as genuine instances of privatization.

In Chile, where the first wave of reprivatizations began soon after Allende was ousted from office, circumstances rather than ideological preferences drove the new policies.[3] During the years of the Unidad Popular government, the parastatal sector had been rapidly inflated, far beyond the capacity of the system of public administration to absorb new functions. This came about by an expansion of the operations of the Chilean Development Corporation (CORFO), by a wave of nationalizations, and through the seizure of many firms by workers under the instigation of party militants associated with the government. By 1973, the state was managing 60% of the irrigated land, a great deal of which had been expropriated not long before Allende was elected, and more than 85% of financial services and the mining industry were run by public enterprises.

The challenge was too formidable, especially in a minority coalition administration in which rival factions were jockeying for advantage and to some extent pursuing their separate agendas. Efficient administration essentially collapsed, and thanks to the pervasive disorder the production system was in shambles. It is instructive to note that by the end of the Unidad Popular regime, the management of even some of the major public enterprises was no longer in a position to prepare the annual reports on company operations. What is more, most of the fiscal deficit, which reached some 25% of GDP, was attributable to the mishandling of such a huge portion of the country's resources by increasingly politicized management.

Just as in the Soviet Union the New Economic Policy (NEP) was a necessary corrective to the period of wartime communism, so, too, in Chile those who succeeded to power with the fall of Allende had to implement quickly the practical measures necessary to get the economy functioning again. Consequently, during 1974–75, approximately 250 enterprises were returned to their former owners, including those that had been "intervened" by the workers. Resumption of private ownership was, in all likelihood, facilitated by the fact that the new military regime had not yet fully clarified, or perhaps evolved, its general policy stance and there was an initial expectation that, with Unidad Popular out of the way, the policy framework might not be too different from that which prevailed up to the time of the Allende administration: i.e., an environment in which rent-seeking behavior was supported, even stimulated, by a whole panoply of direct and indirect interventionist measures.

By the time that the second wave of Chilean privatizations occurred (roughly from 1976 to 1985), a new policy orientation was being installed, which, had it been anticipated, might well have dampened the enthusiasm of some of the erstwhile owners for recovering their factories during the first phase. In addition to the monetarist measures of the initial period of military rule — decontrol of prices, demobilization of labor unions, drastic exchange rate devaluation (which offset some of the lower tariffs), stringent control of monetary expansion, and reduction of government spending — the economy was opened further to import competition by a combination of measures that placed substantial tariff reduction in tandem with a decelerated process of devaluation. To break inflationary expectations, the government even allowed the currency to become overvalued for a significant period.

Although the ensuing readjustment squeezed out a good many sources of economic rent and drove many firms under, there remained another source of rent, the institutional structure itself, that had been disregarded while attention was concentrated on installing a laissez-faire policy framework. The structural feature in question was the highly unequal access of firms to bank credit and the strong differential advantage consequently held by firms with ownership links to financial institutions and, through them, to foreign borrowing. With domestic interest rates soaring and, after mid-1976, the currency showing increasing overvaluation, banks, operating in a context of minimalist regulation, found it advantageous to borrow cheaply abroad to finance a wave of highly leveraged acquisitions by the firms connected with bank ownership. Thus, during the time that CORFO was selling its interest in some 150 companies it had picked up during the Allende period, along with another 47 companies from its portfolio of holdings, rent seeking continued, based on gross inequality in the distribution of private economic power, and the privileged access this afforded to what was, in effect, subsidized borrowing. This allowed speculative conglomerate empires to be assembled on a scale previously unknown in Chile, an exercise of *Finanzkapital* straight out of Hilferding. The episode ended with the onset of a crisis in mid-1981, after which the government took over eight of the most important banks to stave off the collapse of an overextended financial system. In the process, the government was forced to assume responsibility for a considerable portion of the foreign credits that had been secured by private borrowers before the debacle, thereby repeating the historic habit of socializing losses.

In Mexico, approximately a decade after the first reprivatizations in Chile, the policy of "destatization" was introduced.[4] The first step was the return to full private ownership of around 200 enterprises in which the state had acquired a stake with the banking nationalization of 1982, the shares having been previously part of the banks' investment portfolios. As in the Chilean case, there appears to have been an expectation that the denationalized firms would return to the *status quo ante* so far as concerns the Mexican business environment, except for the new situation of the financial intermediaries and exchange controls. The government having rejected membership in the GATT in the Lopez Portillo administration, there was relatively little inkling, at the time of the reprivatization, of what lay ahead, particularly in the area of trade policy. It was, in other words, a reasonable expectation that reprivatized firms would continue to operate amid the customary tariffs, import licenses, fiscal inducements, and so on that had for years composed the incentive system for manufacturing. Only later did management have to confront the unprecedented opening of the Mexican economy that brought tariffs to remarkably low levels, abolished most import licensing, and ushered the country into the GATT.

By 1986, however, the macro-environment began to change. The customary efforts to use the power of the state to transfer wealth from one group to another by taxes and regulation ran up against the government's new determination to open the economy by eliminating most import licenses, radically lowering tariffs, and curbing though not altogether eliminating the redistributive ventures that had long been the stock in trade of the state. The decision to enter the GATT, reversing the official policy of the Lopez Portillo administration, appeared to confirm the new policy orientation. By exposing more sectors of the economy to international competition, it took Mexico along the course to substantive privatization that Chile was already pioneering in Latin America. Rent-seeking opportunities remain abundant, especially for those holding sinecures in the public and parastatal sector, much of which has yet to feel the pinch of reform, and among certain labor bosses. More and more, however, the companies reverting to private ownership and management have to deal with an operating environment that has been more comprehensively constrained by market forces. Apart from the public/parastatal sector and the residual tariff protection (the latter modified in some periods by foreign exchange policies), there remains one presently indeterminate but potentially pervasive redoubt of rent-seeking behavior: the nationalized banking system. Indeed, it is quite possible that with the contraction of space available for rent seeking elsewhere in the economic structure, the pressures may have intensified to use credit allocation as a means of preferment, though not, of course, on quite the same basis as before the takeover of the financial intermediaries.

In Brazil and Argentina, reprivatization has likewise figured in the early steps to restructure the economy, but generally on a much smaller scale, at least thus far, and without the liberalization of foreign trade that has marked the Chilean and Mexican experiences. Brazilian privatization, for example, has moved at a snail's pace thus far.[5] Mendes, for one, has found that the total sales proceeds from the 1980–86 drive were, at approximately US$190 million, equivalent to less than 0.6% of the overall net worth of the federally-owned public enterprises at the end of 1985 — or roughly 1.5% of the market value at that time of the shares of the subset of these firms that was listed on stock exchanges.[6] Returns from the four other parastatals sold to private investors in 1987, and from the sale of the assets of a fifth parastatal that had been shut down, added only another US$27 million to the total. Of the 17 firms transferred, at least seven were companies that had started off in the private sector but that had passed into government ownership through receivership. At the same time, the business environment that absorbed these privatizations (and reprivatizations) was one little modified from the pervasive intervention that has surrounded and guided Brazil's modern industrial development for decades. It is revealing that when the state siderurgical holding company reviewed several joint ventures in which Japanese capital had been invested for possible privatization, the foreign partners are said to have objected on the grounds that privatization would have constituted, from their point of view, an undesirable change of status in their holdings.

Almost exactly the same objection was raised in Argentina when the Ministry of Defense set in motion plans to dispose of its holdings in a number of manufacturing joint ventures. There, however, the private partners in the firms were national and threatened court action to block the sale on the grounds that privatization would forfeit some of the main inducements that had attracted their capital in the first place, including tax and tariff advantages and the intimate link with the firms' major customer, the state. The proposed partial privatization of Aerolineas Argentinas ran up against a not altogether different situation, when the government proposed the sale of 40% of its shares to Scandinavian Airlines System (SAS), which would thereafter have a major role in management of the firm. Owners of a previously reprivatized parastatal, Cielos del Sur (formerly Austral Airlines), attempted to put together a counteroffer, with the participation of Alitalia and, at one point, Swissair. The basis for the strong contending bid for Aerolineas operations, it is believed, came from the privatized rival's dismay at finding that its competitor on domestic flights might become the efficient SAS management rather than the notoriously inept Aerolineas administration. Meanwhile, knowledgeable observers report that organized worker protest, in July of 1988, to a proposal to break up the huge Gas del Estado monopoly had been instigated not only by union leaders anxious to avoid a challenge to their monopoly hold on the company's work force, but also by established suppliers who were loath to see their market take on a more competitive character — and further, according to some, by Gas directors with links to the established web of interests.

In Argentina as in Brazil, the few state companies actually sold to the private sector have been mostly reprivatizations of firms that had been taken by the state in bankruptcy.[7] The five years ending in mid-1988, for example, saw only four reprivatizations, from a government portfolio of some 305 parastatals. The value of the privatized assets reached only US$32 million, in an economy with a GNP of several billion US dollars. The commitment of the government to privatization may be gauged not only by the foregoing but also by strategies used by the state elsewhere in the program. At first, for example, there was discussion of allowing towns and cities, or other geographical entities, to form telephone companies for local service, the national monopoly having deteriorated to the extent that it seemed to illustrate all the jokes anyone had ever made about telephone service. Firms in the financial district of Buenos Aires were also authorized to explore the establishment of a new user-operated exchange that could modernize technology and, through improved service capabilities, enable the institutions of the district to make effective use of the new data storage, retrieval, processing, and transfer systems. Before this last initiative had got very far, however, the government, in a procedure of questionable legality (since it did not rely on competitive tenders), began negotiating with the Spanish national telephone company to take a 40% interest in and provide managerial services to the Argentine firm, with part of the arrangement being to allow the Argentine enterprise to retain its national near-monopoly position. The factors that prompted this unusual pairing were, apparently, the political support the Spanish government had lent the Alfonsin administration during the difficult period in which Argentine democracy was being restored, and a belief that a Spanish government-owned company, while not a technology leader in telecommunications, would not be perceived as an imperialist threat to Argentine national interests. To date, therefore, only a few peripheral telephone services in outlying areas have been privatized.

Opposition to privatization has been joined by powerful labor organizations linked with the Peronist camp and there appears to be only mild sympathy, at best, for it within the government, apart from the two agencies that are charged with developing and implementing a privatization program. Thus far, too, support from the private sector has been somewhat muted, except for a few of the bolder organizations, so that although there appears to be a general public receptivity that springs from exasperation with the present quality of public services, the program has failed to achieve any real momentum. Further, the amount of opening and restructuring of the national economy that has been effected is, to date, quite limited. As much as in Brazil, if not more so, the observation seems to fit that before the public sector is privatized it might be well to try to privatize the private sector.

4. SUBSTANTIVE PRIVATIZATION

In all four cases, subject to the varying degrees to which national structures have been exposed to market direction, there have also been privatizations that have taken enterprises set up by state initiative and either sold them to private investors or closed them down as unsalvageable. In Chile, which has done by far the most, and Mexico, which would come in second on this score, these transactions have for the most part taken place in a context of environmental privatization, which is to say privatization of the decisional environment through a relaxation of political constraints on the operation of market forces. Inasmuch as such decisional privatization reinforces the social aims of micro-level privatization by reducing economic rent, it would seem to merit the label "substantive privatization" to indicate that it touches the very substance of the economic process. In Brazil and Argentina, there has been, as noted, much less dismantling of the apparatus of intervention, so there the privatized firms have continued to function in a politicized market economy in which preferred investors owe possibly significant portions of their returns to state action in one guise or another.

Chile has gone the farthest down this road, having also done the most to strengthen the market at the expense of the state.[8] Not very many firms have been actually closed by government authorities, but this reflects the generally good management, except for the early 1970s, that has historically characterized Chilean parastatals, especially those managed under the aegis of the Corporación de Fomento (CORFO). It has also been testimony to the ability of CORFO technicians, and others in public employment, to rehabilitate firms in need of such efforts to prepare them for privatization. Of the other government entities involved in privatization, perhaps only Brazil's Banco de Desenvolvimento Economico e Social (BNDES) would be equally knowledgeable and experienced, as an organization, in the efficient conduct of business operations, in all phases of investment planning and analysis, in diagnosing the sources of business difficulty and providing appropriate remediation, and, in general, handling a great many of the other functions associated with both investment banking and the management of industrial holding companies. The experience of both Chile and Brazil, for that matter, argues strongly for placing the privatization program in the hands of an agency of this type, one that by the nature of its past operations has good connections with private sector managers, technical specialists, and the institutions of the capital market.

In Chile, this stage of the privatization process came on the heels of the experiences mentioned earlier, after the shortcomings of the older approach had been highlighted by the 1982–84 recession. It was at this point, too, that serious attention began to be given the possibilities of a major expansion of stock ownership. To this end, packages of shares were sold to small investors, assorted employee stock ownership plans were devised, and the privately managed worker pension funds began to appear as important purchasers of corporate securities in the newly privatized concerns. Especially favorable, which is to say subsidized, purchase schemes were put together to produce the new popular capitalism. In addition, limits were often placed on the size of the larger single ownership blocks, and debt-equity swaps were used to place the ownership and management of some companies in the hands of foreign investors. During 1985–88, some of the larger public enterprises, including the steel company, public utilities, and some mining firms were increasingly incorporated into the privatization process.

Mexico's efforts have been much less sweeping, but in addition to the liquidated companies mentioned above, the state, after considerable procrastination in actually implementing the decision, moved to shut down a number of money-losing sugar mills, urban development companies, and fishing companies. It let one of the unprofitable airlines slide into liquidation. Perhaps most dramatically of all, the state halted production at the giant, but hopelessly obsolete, steel mill in Monterrey — a company that had been established around the turn of the century as the first integrated iron and steel works in all of Latin America. Over the years, the Fundidora Monterrey had fallen on hard times. In the 1970s, it was taken over by the government, in what was ultimately an unsuccessful rescue operation. Among the parastatals actually sold to private investors were a major luxury hotel chain, several individual hotel properties at various resorts, six soft drink bottlers, a famed luxury restaurant in Mexico City's *Zona Rosa*, sundry equipment manufacturers, a large paper producer and a number of smaller manufacturers of paper products, plastics manufacturers, eight of the sugar mills, 13 fishing companies, film companies, and automotive parts manufacturers. The large Cananea copper mining company, an historic property and one particularly rich in symbolism for the Mexican Revolution, was also put on the block, though at last report problems had developed in financing its sale. Another large copper company, Mexicana de Cobre, has, however, apparently been sold. So far as can be determined, there is no authenticated master list of privatized properties, but the foregoing at least gives a good indication of the assortment of companies covered by the program.

Once again, however, one must use caution in interpreting Mexican results. The much-trumpeted closure of AeroMexico, for instance, went hand in hand with the creation of a new airline company owned partly by large private investors and an AeroMexico union. The central bank, however, is reported in some sources to have retained a substantial share. In some lists of privatized concerns, trade unions are recorded as purchasers of a miscellany of enterprises, in which the state may or may not also be a partner. In an undetermined number of cases, enterprises reported closed appear to have existed only on paper from the beginning. Nevertheless, such ambiguities aside, there can be little doubt that a fair amount of real progress has been made — and that the largest state-owned firms remain untouched, and in most cases untouchable, by privatization.

Brazilian sales of parastatals, prompted by a need to keep the fiscal deficit down, have not contributed greatly to this end, as we noted earlier. Besides the reprivatized firms, a few state-initiated companies, or in some instances their fixed assets, have also been sold to the private sector through procedures that have been changed over time. The range of firms so affected has been far narrower than in either Chile or Mexico, but nonetheless the assortment has been varied, including firms in such lines as chemicals, paper and paper pulp, cement, synthetic rubber, magnetic alloys, and copper smelting. As in Chile, some companies have been transferred through negotiated direct sales, while others have been sold through the stock exchange. A very few enterprises have been closed. The government's wage policy, which, to combat inflation, has involved holding wage increases in the public sector below those in the private sector, has seemingly eliminated some of the bureaucratic opposition to privatization. In one notable recent case, that of a government-initiated computer software concern, the recognition that the company was increasingly noncompetitive in the labor market for highly-skilled professionals led the state to relinquish its ownership of what had been conceived as a pioneering venture. Some of the enterprises sold have not been large, but in one instance, that of the Aracruz firm, the company was the country's largest paper and pulp producer.

Argentina has likewise sold off a small number of concerns that had their origin in the state's entrepreneurial efforts, and divested itself of minority shareholdings in a rather large number of small to medium-sized companies, in some of which the government's interest was held by the Banco Industrial and in others of which it was held by Fabricaciones Militares, a holding company of the armed forces.

5. OTHER FORMS OF PRIVATIZATION

In all four countries, privatization has also

taken other guises. In a fair number of instances, it has involved semi-privatization or partial privatization: i.e., the sale of some of the shares to private investors with the state holding the balance. Through this means, for example, some of the nationalized banks in Mexico have been converted into mixed enterprises. This technique has been more often applied to the industrial field, especially in Brazil, where the motivation has been that of upgrading the management and technology of the converted firms. The expectation has been that the market value of the privately held shares would serve as an indirect register of the efficiency of asset management in these mixed companies. In Chile, on the other hand, semi-privatization has most often been simply a way station on the road to complete privatization, a reflection, as it were, of the limited absorptive capacity of the local capital market at any given time.

The statistics about the total number of partial or semi-privatization cases the four countries have carried out are not clear for several reasons. For one thing, it is by no means uncommon for the state to retain an interest in companies announced to have been privatized, though this is not always made clear at the time. For another, all four governments have long held either majority or minority shareholding positions in a large number of mixed enterprises, including joint ventures with multinational or foreign corporations, usually through industrial development agencies or investment banks that are operated by the state. In Mexico, where the oversight of parastatal entities is scattered among a number of government ministries, a number of these firms are also, in fact, mixed enterprises. Partial or semi-privatization could, further, be extended to cover state firms operated under contract by private management. This technique is not widely employed, but it nevertheless is sometimes used as preparatory to outright privatization where, as in some of the BNDES firms, the intermediate step is judged necessary to rehabilitate run-down companies and ready them for sale on the market.

Still another variant has been called simulated privatization, which occurs when monitoring and control systems, and appropriate performance criteria, are installed to compel publicly-owned and managed firms to conform to private sector operating standards. CODELCO, the huge Chilean state enterprise in the copper industry, is a prime case in point, for it displays all the dynamism of a privately managed company and makes its way, operationally speaking, in a competitive international market. There are a good many other examples, however, among the firms held by Nacional Financiera (the Mexican government's industrial investment bank), most of CORFO's holdings, and several of the Brazilian government's enterprises, in industry as well as in finance.

A final variation, peripheral privatization, occurs when sundry operations of a public sector organization are contracted out, generally under competitive building, to private sector operators. The idea is not exactly new — the tax farmer was, after all, a loathsome figure in Biblical times and mercenary armies have been used down through the ages. It has frequently been fraught with risk on account of the same kinds of administrative problems that are associated with ensuring the integrity of government procurement programs. These difficulties aside, peripheral privatization has been employed on occasion, perhaps more in the Southern Cone than elsewhere, though not nearly so often as one might have expected. It is reported to have been used in Argentina to test the waters, as it were, for privatization in a more complete sense, but just how extensive this has been is impossible to say. Neither of the privatization offices in the government has compiled systematic information on the practice.

6. CONCLUDING OBSERVATIONS

The firmest conclusion to come from this review is that consistency between macroeconomic and microeconomic policies helps considerably in accomplishing the purposes of privatization and, if anything, it is at the macroeconomic level that the more important impact is to be had: through changes in the environment within which private decisions are taken. The experiences of both Chile and, in lesser measure, Mexico seem to indicate that significant gains come about when the two levels of policy operate in tandem.

At the same time, all four cases serve to illustrate the linkage between economic and political rewards in producing an equilibrium in national systems as a whole. For decades, rent has been distributed lavishly to buy political support. Constituency building, in turn, has been used to yield a kind of political rent to the governments in charge of this extensive system of differential reward. Chile, for example, appears to have been able to make the most headway because of its special political circumstances: namely, the ability of the government to put normal politics on hold while the economic rewards were being re-sorted and rent was being suppressed. Neither could have been done so readily had government leaders been operating in a competitive political "market."

In Mexico, where the political system has been opening up and where it was more open than the Chilean system to begin with, the bi-level effort to eradicate rent-seeking behavior has, along with macroeconomic conditions, apparently fed social discontent and upset the old political equilibrium. No longer does the government possess such a plentiful arsenal of means for conciliating the multiple contending interests, though already there are signs that some in both government and the ruling party think that liberalization has gone too far and that conditions may warrant restoring some of the means of rent-conferring intervention.

Brazil and Argentina, in turn, represent instances in which there has been no real systematic effort to do away with opportunities for rent seeking and in which micro-level privatization has been more sporadic than in the other cases. The delicacy of the political situation in each country would seem to militate against resolute efforts to bring more substantive privatization into the picture and to implement the structural reforms at the macro-level that would be necessary to join micro-level privatization more securely with economic efficiency and the absence of rent seeking. Political circumstances, moreover, make such changes even less likely in Argentina than Brazil, at least at present.

Lastly, however, it must be conceded that the efficiency gains associated with privatization at all levels are only part of the picture when it comes to explaining national economic performance. Both Brazil and Mexico, the latter for much longer than the former, have enjoyed periods of high growth; both did so in a context shot through with rent-seeking behavior. Chile, in a similar context, fared much less well over the years, while Argentina, at least equally interventionist, was also, clearly, an economic underachiever in terms of its resources as well as in terms of the growth path it had attained before the 1930s. (The cases of Japan and South Korea, of course, demonstrate even more clearly that a guided, regulated economy is not, in and of itself, incompatible with outstanding performance.) All four cases together, then, suggest the wisdom of moderating expectations: about how easily privatization might be implemented and how well economies will actually perform once it is.

NOTES

1. For a useful compendium of thinking about this concept, see Buchanan, Tollison, and Tullock (1980).

2. Ramos (1986) provides reliable background information on policy changes effected in Argentina and Chile.

3. Material on Chile developed from field interviews and documentary research (henceforth mentioned as field notes) and the work of co-researcher José Piñera Echenique (1988).

4. Field notes and the work of co-researcher Oscar Vera (1988).

5. Field notes and the work of Rogerio L. F. Werneck (1988).

6. Mendes (1987).

7. Field notes and the work of co-researcher Javier Gonzalez Fraga (1988).

8. Aside from the sources of information acknowledged above, this draws on Marshall and Montt (1986).

REFERENCES

Buchanan, James M., R. D. Tollison, and Gordon Tullock (Eds.), *Toward a Theory of the Rent-Seeking Society* (College Station, TX: Texas A&M University Press, 1980).

Gonzalez Fraga, Javier, "Privatization in Argentina," mimeo (La Jolla, CA: Institute of the Americas, May 1988).

Marshall, Jorge, and Felipe Montt, "Evaluation of Privatization," mimeo (Santiago: Corporación de Investigaciones en Economia Aplicada, August 1986).

Mendes, J. C., "Uma análise do programa Brasileiro de privatizaçao," *Conjuntura Econômica* (September 1987).

Piñera Echenique, José, "Privatization in Chile," mimeo prepared for a conference on Privatization of Public Enterprises in Latin America (La Jolla, CA: Institute of the Americas, May 1988).

Ramos, Joseph, *Neoconservative Economics in the Southern Cone of Latin America, 1973–1983* (Baltimore, MD: The Johns Hopkins University Press, 1986).

Vera, Oscar, "The political economy of privatization in Mexico," mimeo (La Jolla, CA: Institute of the Americas, May 1988).

Werneck, Rogerio L. F., "The uneasy steps of privatization in Brazil," mimeo (La Jolla, CA: Institute of the Americas, May 1988).

[9]

World Development, Vol. 17, No. 5, pp. 633–641, 1989.
Printed in Great Britain.

0305–750X/89 $3.00 + 0.00

Privatization: Not the Only Answer

HEIDI VERNON-WORTZEL
Northeastern University, Boston, Massachusetts

and

LAWRENCE H. WORTZEL
Boston University

Summary. — Governments in many developing countries created state-owned enterprises (SOEs) to produce goods or provide services the private sector seemed unwilling or unable to offer. In many cases, SOEs have turned out to be problem children — at best, inefficient and, at worst, unable to fulfill their original functions. Now the recommended solution to the problem of state-owned enterprises is privatization. But privatization is no more a solution to the problems of SOEs than SOEs were a solution to the problems they were created to solve. The problem of SOEs is not ownership, but rather a lack of explicit goals and objectives, and an absence of organization cultures and systems that support and encourage fulfillment of those goals and objectives. In some circumstances, privatization may aid in fulfillment of an enterprise's goals and objectives because of the culture and systems it fosters; in other cases not.

1. INTRODUCTION

Developing countries turned to state ownership of certain enterprises for reasons that were primarily pragmatic, rather than ideological; they created state-owned enterprises (SOEs) to provide goods and services or to serve social goals the private sector appeared unwilling or incapable of addressing. Country governments used SOEs as instruments of social or industrial policy. They created SOEs to provide specific goods or services at a particular level to a population. In some countries, SOEs have also come into being when governments bailed out failed private sector firms.

Many SOEs have addressed their economic purposes, and a substantial number have even managed to satisfy the needs of the people for whom they were created. The costs of using SOEs, however, have been monumental. The literature abounds with well-documented stories of inefficiency, losses, and corruption among SOEs across a wide spectrum of developing countries. In addition to performing very poorly, some SOEs are evidently now pursuing goals other than those for which they were created and, by so doing, are not fulfilling their original purposes. All too often it seems, SOEs once created seem to take on a life of their own.

In cases where the state took over failed private sector firms, it simply compounded these firms' existing problems, institutionalizing the existing inefficiencies, compounding the losses, and possibly also adding corruption to the list of the enterprise's problems. The net result is that in many developing countries, SOEs have become a substantial drain rather than a contributor to their countries' economies. Faced with mounting SOE costs, beset by burgeoning needs for funds to be used for other purposes, many governments have sought to dispose of SOEs that have become a burden rather than a help.

The obvious solution seems to be privatization. Some proponents of privatization see it as an end or goal in itself. They operate from an ideological premise that as many functions and activities as possible should be in private rather than government hands. Their arguments are based on deep-seated convictions about the efficiency of free markets and the importance of ownership in guiding enterprise behavior. They assume, implicitly, that the primary function of any enterprise is to operate as efficiently as possible and argue that privatization is the only solution to SOE problems. Their goal is efficiency, and they see privatization as the only way to achieve it.[1] Others see privatization simply as a means for correcting the deficiencies of SOEs. In their view, privatization is a pragmatic rather than an ideological solution to the problem of SOEs.

Their goal is constructive change through privatization.[2]

To be sure, state ownership does not necessarily cause enterprises to perform poorly. There are, in fact, examples of state-owned enterprises, such as those in Brazil and South Korea, that perform quite well. Certainly, private sector ownership is no guarantee of good performance. Private sector firms in every corner of the world go bankrupt every day. The determinants of a firm's success or failure are not who owns it. Rather, the firm's success or failure is a function of to what extent, and in what direction, its owners exercise the authority that comes with ownership and its managers carry out their jobs. Simply stated, enterprise success, regardless of ownership, is a matter of developing a strong, appropriate culture within the firm, of hiring the right managers and seeing that there are appropriate control and motivation mechanisms in place to properly guide their behavior. Unfortunately, in all too many cases, SOEs have not fostered the right culture or hired the right managers. Nor have they used control and motivation mechanisms that would lead to good performance.

Both ideologists and pragmatists, however, can point to a great deal of evidence showing that, in a wide range of situations, firms with private sector ownership perform more efficiently than firms that are state owned. The argument for efficiency gains has been simply that privately-owned firms are subject to the discipline of market forces and must earn profits to survive, but state-owned firms can be subsidized and supported in a number of ways by governments. Also assumed in the privatization argument is that efficiency and not equity considerations are paramount goals or objectives of SOEs.

In this article, we take the pragmatists' position. We will look at a range of potential solutions of SOE problems. As many researchers have noted, privatization has psychic, opportunity, and economic costs that are so high that it may not be feasible in all cases. In some cases, actions other than privatization might provide the desired benefit — constructive change — at significantly lower cost.

2. PRIVATIZATION PROGRAMS: THE RESULTS TO DATE

Many developing countries instituted privatization programs because they were spurred by the need to improve SOE performance, or to stop the cash drain. In some cases, these countries were pressured by organizations such as the World Bank. In the 1960s and 1970s they thought SOEs could solve the economic and social problems the private sector could not or would not tackle. Now privatization, they thought, would solve the problems the SOEs had created.

Over the last several years, privatization has been the subject of numerous articles, books, and anthologies. Researchers have presented chronicles of particular countries' privatization programs, have identified both benefits and problems associated with privatization, and have identified some successes and failures.

Table 1 is a selective survey of some privatization programs initiated by a range of developing countries. This table is not meant to be a systematic survey of privatization programs. Its purpose is only illustrative. The data are taken from papers presented at three international conferences on privatization.

As Table 1 shows, there seems to be little consistency across countries in the nature of enterprises chosen as targets for privatization. There is more consistency in the reasons reported for choosing these particular targets. Overwhelmingly, the countries wanted to improve performance of the enterprises chosen. In a few cases, the reported results of the programs are clear, but in most cases not. An analysis of these programs suggests that, regardless of the worthiness of the privatization goal and the extent to which countries may embrace it, privatization is proceeding slowly, at best. Specifically, analysis indicates that:

- (i) For the most part, countries have chosen privatization candidates opportunistically. Rather than formulating and implementing a cohesive privatization strategy for the country, they have selected candidates on some other basis.
- (ii) Those few countries, such as Jamaica, that have tried to develop privatization strategies, and to tie these to country-wide economic goods, have had great difficulty successfully implementing such strategies.
- (iii) Where privatization has been accomplished, the privatized enterprise may be more efficient than its state-owned predecessors. But where there have been goals for the enterprise other than efficiency, it is unclear whether the privatized enterprise is meeting those other goals.
- (iv) As economic development proceeds, the need for and role of SOEs in the economy changes.

Clearly, barriers to privatization are substantial. Political, social and economic barriers occur at the government policy making level. There are

Table 1. *Survey of privatization programs*

Author(s)	Region or country	Institution(s) privatized	Reasons for privatization; Criteria	Results
Koo	South Korea	Commercial banks	Efficiency of market sector control over interest rates	Unsuccessful. Government still regulates rates, directs credit.
Al-haj *et al.*	Malaysia	General comments	Still provide equity	Possibly too much monopoly position. Take up capital
Pakkasem	Thailand	Urban transport	(subsidized sector) Efficiency	Much better service
Chishty	Bangladesh	Jute textile mills	Create favorable investment climate; instill confidence in prospective entrepreneurs	Competition. Better performance from mills still state owned
Iqbal	Pakistan	Flour, rice, milling, cotton ginning	General popularity; administrative nightmare of restructuring and operating	? not clear
Jayasinghe	Sri Lanka	Variety	Poor performance	Textiles now concerned with profits rather than social goals
Kelly de Escobar	Venezuela	Variety	Poor performance; effects of development (stronger private sector)	Restructuring; private sector partners' inefficiency
Haggard	Philippines	?	Dispose of nonperforming assets acquired from state banks; improve efficiency	Very little privatization has actually occurred
Kapstein	Brazil	Formerly private firm taken over by government when bankrupt	Concern with government influence over the economy	Nova America — a successful, but little movement in traditionally state-owned sector
Leeds	Turkey	The "easiest to sell"	Increase efficiency; obtain economic growth	No privatization, but ground work completed
Callaghy and Wilson	Africa	Idiosyncratically *ad hoc* choices	Budgetary drains; foreign exchange scarcity; economic decline; inefficiency; collapse of the colonial political economy	Asset divestiture small and peripheral enterprises; some contractual management; most common: withering away of dying SOEs
Marshall	Chile	Banks; manufacturing firms; agricultural firms	Concern with government intervention; protectionism	Rapid privatization made system more vulnerable to financial difficulty
Kennedy	Jamaica	Catering company; local transportation	Restart economic growth; part of deregulation effort	Limited "simulated privatization" by making SOEs more responsive to market forces
Ortiz de Zavallos	Peru	Variety	Economic growth; efficiency	In planning stage

also formidable administrative obstacles a privatization program must overcome, such as finding willing and capable buyers, and developing mechanisms for valuation and transfer of ownership. In addition, governments have other agenda items that interfere with privatization programs.[3]

It is too easy to forget that privatization carries with it costs as well as benefits. Privatization programs incur considerable administrative time and effort which might be used better elsewhere. They also incur very significant opportunity costs as well, because the private sector may divert money and managerial effort from other endeavors in order to purchase and manage the ex-SOEs. In developing countries, competent government executives, competent entrepreneurial managers, and capital are all in short supply.

Realistically, developing countries simply cannot and will not be able to privatize as many

SOEs as they would like. Nor will they be able to accomplish extensive privatization programs within the time period they have targeted. The rule will be that SOEs will be privatized more slowly. Reality is also that government will usually want to dispose first of those SOEs that are draining resources. These enterprises can, of course, be the most difficult to privatize because no one wants to accept the risks inherent in taking them over.

Faced with such realities, countries must choose their privatization candidates carefully. They must actively seek alternatives to privatization as well, alternatives that will provide at least some of the benefits expected from privatization, but that are more easily accomplished, and at a lower cost. Researchers and policy makers have proposed alternatives to accomplish the same purposes as privatization. These include techniques such as partial divestment, management contracts, and leasing of production facilities.

This is not to suggest that privatization is wrong, but instead to point out that, since the process is difficult, there may be lower-cost, equally feasible methods for achieving the same goals. Countries should think not just about achieving privatization, but instead about achieving constructive change. SOEs and private sector enterprises are different, and privatizing an SOE may not always lead to constructive change.

(a) *SOEs versus private sector organizations — the essential difference: ends versus means*

With the exception of state takeovers of failed private sector enterprises, as we have noted, most SOEs were formed for the express purpose or objective of providing a specific good or service at a particular, defined level of quality to a particular population. Providing the good or service was the enterprise's end; capital and labor were simply means to achieve that goal.

To be sure, some governments formed SOEs with other, or additional, socio-political goals in mind. A list of such goals might include promoting industrialization, creating jobs, defending national interests, reducing regional differences and saving declining firms or industries (Vernon, 1984). Even when an SOE was formed with specific product or service provision goals in mind, government pressures all too often imposed additional socio-political goals on the enterprise. In the case of firms that were formed specifically to produce goods or services, imposition of these additional goals were often incompatible with efficient delivery of the required goods and services. Inevitably, these additional goals made the enterprises less efficient. The key problem with SOEs was, first, that they became inefficient or wasteful in their use of capital and labor. This led, in turn, to inefficient performance (overly expense, or poor quality goods and services) or even failure to deliver the ends. Converting such SOEs to private sector enterprises will not automatically focus them on their ends — the goods and services they were formed to deliver.

Private sector firms see means and ends differently from SOEs. Private sector firms do not focus directly on providing a particular, defined level of goods or services. Most often their primary objectives are financial. Their aim is to earn profits, or at least to provide a livelihood or security for their owners.

In the private sector, an enterprise meets its objectives by offering a product or a service; but offering that product or service is not the enterprise's objective. The aggressive private sector firm will change its product or service offerings as quickly as possible to better meet its objectives. So, for different reasons, the private sector firm may not provide the product or service package the government had in mind when it created a specific SOE.

SOEs that were created primarily to serve socio-political goals and objectives such as job creation or reducing regional disparities clearly had efficiency as a secondary goal; like the private sector enterprise, the products or services such firms produced became the means, rather than the end. Unlike the private sector firm, however, there were no mechanisms or incentives for the SOE to operate efficiently. In economist's terms, in both cases the government injected x-inefficiency into its SOEs.

3. WHY X-INEFFICIENCY: AN ORGANIZATION CULTURE EXPLANATION

The problems of SOEs are not caused by their state ownership, but they may be a consequence of how their owners have exercised the rights and privileges of ownership. We are by no means alone in arguing that the problems of SOEs are not purely a function of their state ownership. Ramamurti (1987), for example, makes a persuasive argument that the poor performance of SOEs is due to their control systems, which he says are excessive in quantity but deficient in quality. They over-monitor day-to-day activities while providing too little strategic direction.

The results any organization obtains are a function of how the people in that organization behave. People in organizations behave in ways they perceive to be in their own best or self-interest. Typically, the self-interests of people in organizations focus on first job security, then on power and status, and finally on financial rewards and perquisites. They will take those actions that enhance their self-interest and avoid those that are detrimental to it.

Organizations, like countries, develop cultures. Organization culture is the vehicle that transmits the message of what enhances self-interest and what does not. An organization's culture consists of patterns of beliefs and expectations that, in turn, produce norms that influence the behavior of people in the organization (Schwartz and Davis, 1981). An organization culture both influences and is influenced by the kind of people it attracts, its formal structure and the systems that are in place for managing, controlling, evaluating, and rewarding its people.

Norms can be reinforced by evaluation, control, and incentive systems that reward behavior strongly consonant with the norms and punish behavior that deviates from them. Organization culture emerges and develops from within as people in the organization learn what they must do to survive and prosper. A strong organization culture is vital if an organization is to meet its goals and objectives, but it cannot emerge unless those goals and objectives are clear and unambiguous.

(a) *The pull of two constituencies: competing cultures*

At first, SOE cultures, formed around providing specific products or services, may have developed norms that encouraged customer-satisfying behavior, and even economically-efficient behavior. As a result, a customer-oriented culture could develop. When governments imposed objectives on SOEs that inhibited or more often conflicted with their product or service objectives, the enterprise's cultural norms changed, and a government-oriented organization culture developed. This culture conflicted with the customer-oriented culture.

The government-oriented culture introduced new norms: norms that encouraged behavior aimed at satisfying government objectives. Several writers (Vernon, 1984; Zif, 1981; Aharoni, 1981) have recognized the conflicting goals SOE managers face. Where these conflicts have been resolved, they have typically been resolved in favor of the government agenda rather than the customer agenda. This is because the government owners had much greater power than customers to control SOE managers' behavior, to reward and punish them. Where conflict was not resolved, the tug-of-war between a government-focused culture and a customer-focused culture produced a schizophrenic organization, unable to serve either government policy or its customers well.

There is a good bit of evidence that organization cultures can be strengthened, unified, even changed. The requirements for change are reasonably clear. These include: (i) first developing and then promulgating a clear, explicit set of goals and objectives; (ii) developing and implementing a specific plan for introducing behavior change into the organization; and (iii) providing motivation for behavior change by supporting it with appropriate control and reward systems.[4]

4. TURNING SOEs AROUND: A PROGRAM FOR ACHIEVING CONSTRUCTIVE CHANGE

Turning an SOE around is a three-step process, which may or may not require a change in ownership. The steps are:

Step 1. Explicitly deciding on the enterprise's goals and objectives.

Step 2. Identifying the required changes in the organization's culture.

Step 3. Implementing the changes, including, if necessary, changes in the organization's ownership structure.

We next examine each step in the process.

The tasks and processes we will describe may seem, at first inspection, to be exceedingly complex and difficult to accomplish. They may be, except when compared against the time, energy, and effort required to design and implement a privatization program. In fact, what we propose may be considerably less complex and time consuming to manage than a privatization program. Moreover, our recommended procedures will collect information that can be extremely useful in valuing a firm and in identifying the right kind of buyer should privatization be required.

(a) *Step 1: Deciding on goals and objectives for the enterprise*

The purpose of this exercise is to identify as explicitly as possible the goals and objectives the enterprise should pursue. Ideally, enterprises should have a single set of compatible goals and objectives. The multiple goals and objectives of the organization should not conflict. Unfortunately, there are many situations in which SOEs may have legitimate goals and objectives that are in conflict.

For example, banks in developing countries might be expected to serve two roles: to channel capital to particular sectors of the economy that should be developed; and to handle all transactions as efficiently and free of risk as possible. Local transportation services are simultaneously expected to run efficiently and provide services to and from locations equitably. They may be expected to do so, even when such activities result in inefficient use of assets, or recoup only a part of the costs involved in providing the services. Where the inevitable conflicts exist, they must either be eliminated, or explicit trade-offs among them must be identified and made.

A useful place to start the process is to identify the enterprise's present goals and objectives. Most likely, a realistic statement of goals and objectives will not exist and these will have to be deduced. The enterprise's present behavior, when carefully analyzed, can provide good clues from which its existing goals and objectives can be inferred. By carefully observing an organization's behavior, one can usually deduce its strategy, and from its strategy its goals and objectives.[5] This identification procedure is important in order to provide a baseline for the changes required in Step 2.

The next task is to determine what the enterprise's goals and objectives should be. This is a more feasible undertaking than it might seem on the surface. Discussion with the enterprise's major stakeholder groups can establish what the enterprise should be doing, and at the same time can aid in determining what the enterprise is actually doing. Customers are an excellent source of information about what the enterprise's product service goals and objectives should be. Discussions with government officials and related stakeholders can identify the socio-political goals and objectives they think the enterprise should pursue.

In recommending that stakeholders other than customers be considered when formulating an enterprise's goals and objectives, we are recognizing that a country, especially a developing country, can legitimately set socio-political as well as economic goals and objectives for its enterprises. Regional development and employment may be important in the long term, but economically inefficient for the present.

This part of the procedure will highlight any conflicts among desired goals and objectives. Having identified conflicts, the enterprise should make choices that will minimize the conflict, or failing that, take steps that will offer the culture the best chance of accomodating the conflict. In any event, comparing existing goals and objectives with desired goals and objectives provides a gap analysis, measuring the changes the enterprise must undertake. Superimposing on this gap analysis a study of the enterprise's culture, it is possible to identify requirements for change.

(b) *Step 2: Identifying required changes in organization culture*

The first task in this step is descriptive. It is to identify the salient elements in the present culture, and the systems that support the culture. Schein (1983) identifies five such elements which we modify for our purposes here. The elements are:

(i) Goals and objectives: What people believe is the enterprise's core mission. What it is there to accomplish.

(ii) Strategy: What people in the organization believe are the primary tasks and functions of the group or groups in which they work.

(iii) Means for accomplishing the strategy: How the organization is structured. What its reward system is.

(iv) Performance measures: How performance is measured against strategy, e.g., what information and control systems are in place.

(v) Correction mechanisms: What is done when and if the enterprise goes off course.

Both present and desired goals and objectives are defined in Step 1. Both descriptive (cultural elements as they exist now) and normative (cultural elements as they should exist given the desired goals and objectives) statements of the culture should be developed. By comparing the normative and the descriptive, a second gap analysis can be performed. The two gap analyses, one of goals and objectives, the other of culture, systems, and structure provide a basis for identifying the specific changes that must be made in the enterprise. Having identified the needed changes, one can then look at how to implement them.

(c) *Step 3: Implementing the changes*

Productive cultures, those that further an enterprise's goals and objectives, thrive best when they are supported by external as well as internal motivation and control mechanisms. We look first at external mechanisms. There are at least four types of culture supporting external control mechanisms: market control; legislation; subcontracting, performance contracting, and asset leasing; and direction by ownership. Each has somewhat different cultural and ownership requirements.[6]

Market control is possible where the enterprise must compete for business, where the customer has the power to choose among alternatives or not to buy at all. Coupling a market control situation with an explicit reward system based on economic performance and backed by good control and information systems will, in time, almost guarantee a culture with beliefs and norms, and thus behavior focused on economic performance. Where strong market control is possible, ownership should not matter at all. Such enterprises can be owned either by the state or by the private sector, and can perform equally well, providing the owners let the market exert its discipline on the enterprise.

Legislation, subcontracting, performance contracting, asset leasing, and ownership direction are alternatives where market control is not feasible. Legislation is an alternative for indivisible natural monopolies such as telephone services, but a rather unsatisfactory one when used alone. Typically, legislation might try to regulate both rates (economic) and availability of service (socio-political). The result in the telephone company might be a schizophrenic culture and a conflicting or very unclear set of control and reward systems.

In such situations, coupling legislation with strong ownership direction could well be a way of forcing a single culture to develop. Depending on the owner, however, the culture is likely to develop in concert with different owners' objectives. In state hands, the objectives and goals are likely to focus primarily on the socio-political. In private hands, economic goals are, of course, likely to come to the fore. It may be easier to force legislated socio-political goals on a private sector enterprise than to get a state-owned enterprise to perform efficiently without market control. On balance, then, private ownership may be a better choice.

Divisible monopolies, such as local transport and refuse collection, are very amenable to subcontracting, performance contracting, or asset leasing, especially if the contractors or lessees are individuals or small groups rather than large enterprises. Roth (1987), for example, reports on the success of small buses called *gbakas* in Abidjan, private buses in Buenos Aires and Calcutta, and taxis and jitneys in Cairo. In each case, the privately-owned vehicles substantially outperformed their state-owned counterparts. The vehicles were owned by individuals, and the principle of individual ownership can be more broadly applied to leasing routes or contracting for specific services. The principle should apply to garbage trucks as well as to buses, for example. Treating divisible monopolies in this manner gets around the problem of changing the culture, since there is no large organization with which to deal.

Ownership direction is the mirror image of market control. It is a mechanism that might be employed where there is no strong possibility of market control, but where strong direction in the use of resources or choice of customers is required. It is especially useful where legislation or contracting cannot offer sufficient direction. Examples might include banks, where allocation of capital is a governmental concern, and heavy construction firms where projects include socio-political as well as economic dimensions. Such enterprises are amenable to state ownership, and with strong direction from their state owners can develop a culture that focuses on satisfying the government's socio-political agenda. But in doing so, the enterprise may be likely to forego efficiency in performing its mission; the culture that will emerge is likely to mitigate against it.

If efficiency is a goal of such enterprises, it is very important to develop an efficiency-focused culture as well as a socio-politically-focused one. But the two cultures must work in such a way as to minimize cultural conflict. One solution is to combine ownership direction with some form of performance contracting. In this case, performance contracting does not mean contracting with an external group, but rather with people inside the enterprise.

In a bank, for example, it is possible to distinguish between people who make decisions to grant a certain loan, and those who perform other banking functions such as handling deposits. Similarly, in a construction company, it is possible to distinguish between those who decide which jobs to accept and those who carry out the work. In both cases, one can set up performance contracts that motivate and reward the doers for doing their jobs without compromising the enterprise's socio-political objectives. At the same time, this combination should increase the chances that they will meet these objectives while running their enterprises efficiently.

5. CONCLUSIONS

In summary, the problem of SOEs is not one of ownership but one arising from a lack of clear goals and objectives, coupled with inappropriate control, motivation and reward systems. This situation has led to the development of organization cultures within SOEs that are either dysfunctional or that are made up of conflicting subcultures.

The remedy is not primarily a matter of simply changing the enterprise's ownership. What must be done is to first explicitly identify what the enterprise's goals and objectives should be, and then to identify the cultural norms and behavior required to meet the goals and objectives. Having taken these steps, one can then decide what form of external direction will best encourage the formation and maintenance of the appropriate culture. Only then can one decide what form of ownership best provides that direction.

NOTES

1. See Waters (1985) for a lucid presentation of this point of view.

2. Boneo (1986) expands considerably on these points.

3. For a discussion of obstacles to privatization, see Austin, Wortzel, and Coburn (1986).

4. For extensive discussions of mechanisms for achieving organization culture change, see, for example, Kilmann *et al.* (1985) and (1988).

5. See Andrews (1980) for a discussion of this topic.

6. Jones (1975) *inter alia* suggests relationships between control possibilities and enterprise types.

REFERENCES

Aharoni, Yair, "Performance evaluation of state-owned enterprises: A process perspective," *Management Science*, Vol. 27, No. 11 (November 1981), pp. 1340–1347.

Al-Haj, Data'Seri, Radia Soenarno, and Zainal Aznam Yusof, "The experience of Malaysia," in Asian Development Bank (Eds.), *Privatization — Policy, Methods, and Procedures* (Manila: Asian Development Bank, 1985), pp. 215–236.

Andrews, Kenneth R., *The Concept of Corporate Strategy*, revised edition (Homewood, IL: Richard D. Irwin, Inc., 1980).

Austin, James E., Lawrence H. Wortzel, and John F. Coburn, "Privatizing state-owned enterprises: Hopes and realities," *Columbia Journal of World Business*, Vol. 21, No. 3 (Fall 1986), pp. 57–67.

Boneo, Horacio, "Privatization: Ideology and praxis," in William P. Glade (Ed.), *State Shrinking: A Comparative Inquiry into Privatization* (Austin, TX: Institute of Latin American Studies, University of Texas, 1986).

Callaghy, Thomas M., and Ernest James Wilson III, "Africa: Policy, reality, or ritual," in Raymond Vernon (Ed.), *The Promise of Privatization* (Washington, DC: Council on Foreign Relations, 1988), pp. 179–230.

Chishty, Md. Shamsul Haque, "The experience of Bangladesh," in Asian Development Bank (Eds.) *Privatization — Policy, Methods and Procedures* (Manila: Asian Development Bank, 1985), pp. 261–292.

Hafsi, Taieb, Moses N. Kiggundu, and Jan J. Jorgensen, "Strategic apex configurations in state-owned enterprises," *Academy of Management Review*, Vol. 12, No. 4 (1987), pp. 714–730.

Haggard, Stephan, "The Philippines: Picking up after Marcos," in Raymond Vernon (Ed.), *The Promise of Privatization* (Washington, DC: Council on Foreign Relations, 1988), pp. 91–121.

Iqbal, Zafar, "The experience of Pakistan," in Asian Development Bank (Eds.), *Privatization — Policy, Methods, and Procedures* (Manila: Asian Development Bank, 1985), pp. 293–318.

Jayasinghe, Imdrance, "The experience of Sri Lanka," in Asian Development Bank, (Eds.), *Privatization — Policy, Methods, and Procedures* (Manila: Asian Development Bank, 1985), pp. 319–338.

Jones, Leroy, *Public Enterprise and Economic Development: The Korea Case* (Seoul: Korea Development Institute, 1975).

Kapstein, Ethan V., "Brazil: Continued state dominance," in Raymond Vernon (Ed.), *The Promise of Privatization* (Washington, DC: Council on Foreign Relations, 1988), pp. 122–148.

Kelly de Escobar, Janet, "Venezuela: Letting in the market," in Raymond Vernon (Ed.), *The Promise of Privatization* (Washington, DC: Council on Foreign Relations, 1988), pp. 57–90.

Kennedy, Peter J. Jr., "State shrinkage: The Jamaican experience," in William B. Glade (Ed.), *State Shrinking: A Comparative Inquiry into Privatization* (Austin, TX: Institute of Latin American Studies, University of Texas, 1986), pp. 177–202.

Kilmann, Ralph H. *et al.* (Eds.), *Corporate Transformation* (San Francisco, CA: Jossey-Bass, Inc., 1988).

Kilmann, Ralph H. *et al.* (Eds.), *Gaining Control of the Corporate Culture* (San Francisco, CA: Jossey-Bass, Inc., 1986).

Koo, Bon-Ho, "The experience of the Republic of Korea," in Asian Development Bank (Eds.), *Privatization — Policy, Methods, and Procedures* (Manila: Asian Development Bank, 1985), pp. 193–214.

Leeds, Roger S., "Turkey: Rhetoric and reality," in Raymond Vernon (Ed.), *The Promise of Privatization* (Washington, DC: Council on Foreign Relations, 1988), pp. 149–178.

Lewis, Meryl Reis, "Sourcing workplace cultures:

Why, when, and how," in Kilmann, Ralph H. *et al.* (Eds.), *Gaining Control of the Corporate Culture* (San Francisco, CA: Jossey-Bass Publishers, 1986), pp. 126–136.

Marshall, Jorge, "Economic privatization: Lessons from the Chilean experience," in William B. Glade (Ed.), *State Shrinking: A Comparative Inquiry into Privatization* (Austin, TX: Institute of Latin American Studies, University of Texas, 1986), pp. 101–129.

Ortiz de Zavallos, Felipe, "Peru: An insider's view," in William B. Glade (Ed.), *State Shrinking: A Comparative Inquiry into Privatization* (Austin, TX: Institute of Latin American Studies, University of Texas, 1986), pp. 129–169.

Pakkasem, Phisit, "The experience of Thailand," in Asian Development Bank (Eds.), *Privatization — Policy, Methods, and Procedures* (Manila: Asian Development Bank, 1985), pp. 215–236.

Ramamurti, Ravi, "Controlling state-owned enterprises," *Public Enterprise*, Vol. 7, No. 2 (March 1987), pp. 99–117.

Roth, Gabriel, *The Private Provision of Public Services in Developing Countries* (Washington, DC: Oxford University Press, 1987).

Schein, Edgar H., "Coming to a new awareness of organization culture," *Sloan Management Review*, Vol. 25, No. 2 (Winter 1984), pp. 3–16.

Schein, Edgar H., "The role of the founder in creating organizational culture," *Organizational Dynamics*, Vol. 12, No. 1 (Summer 1983), pp. 21–36.

Schwartz, Howard, and Stanley M. Davis, "Matching corporate culture and business strategy," *Organizational Dynamics*, Vol. 10, No. 1 (Summer 1981), pp. 30–48.

Vernon, Raymond, "Linking managers with ministers," *Journal of Policy Analysis and Management*, Vol. 4, No. 1 (January 1984), pp. 35–55.

Waters, Alan Rufus, "Privatization: A viable policy option?" in Asian Development Bank (Eds.), *Privatization — Policy, Methods and Procedures* (Manila: Asian Development Bank, 1985), pp. 17–56.

Zif, Jehiel, "Managerial strategic behavior in state-owned enterprises: Business and political orientations," *Management Science*, Vol. 27, No. 11 (November 1981), pp. 1326–1339.

[10]

PUBLIC ADMINISTRATION AND DEVELOPMENT, Vol. 10, 3–18 (1990)

The relevance of privatization to developing economies

DAVID HEALD

University of Aberdeen

SUMMARY

Policy design is important for both public enterprise reform and privatization. The obstacles to privatization and the incentives to carry out 'inappropriate' privatization are considered. Discussions of privatization as divestiture need to be integrated into a wider policy framework. Privatization also needs to be considered in relation to specific sectors, and not as a blanket panacea. Policy reform should be built on a proper analysis of the weaknesses of the public enterprise sector. Real commitment to public enterprise reform has been lacking in many developing countries. Three dilemmas experienced in the privatization programmes of developed economies are considered for their relevance to developing countries: budgetary stress, competition versus denationalization, and 'people's capitalism'. The distinctive characteristics of developing economies are considered including the availability of policy instruments, social costs, and the ability to negotiate with multinationals. Two matters in particular require urgent attention: the sponsoring arrangements for public enterprises; and arrangements concerning subsidiaries. The relevance of privatization lies in the promotion of competition and divestiture of enterprises in industrial sectors which can be made competitive, not in the invitation of large-scale privatizations which raise complex monopoly and regulatory problems.

INTRODUCTION

Primarily because of events in the developed world, predominantly in the United Kingdom, the issue of privatization is gaining much attention in developing countries. Motives in the developed countries have varied significantly, ranging from highly ideological commitments to private enterprise to much more pragmatic responses to undoubted policy and financial difficulties. The purpose of this article is to assess the potential relevance of privatization to Third World economies. There has been considerable discussion of the differences in context between developed and developing countries, but rather less focus upon the lack of homogeneity within the Third World itself. For example, Thailand is dramatically different from Pakistan and the newly industrializing countries of South East Asia bear little relationship to sub-Saharan Africa.

This article shows that policy design is a crucially important stage of the process of either public enterprise reform or of privatization. The proper approach to discussing the future of the public sectors in particular countries is to adopt a tough and

---

Professor David Heald holds a chair in the Department of Accountancy, University of Aberdeen, Aberdeen AB9 2TY, Scotland. He has consulted extensively on privatization for international organizations including the Asian Development Bank, the (United Kingdom) Overseas Development Administration and the United Nations Development Programme. Responsibility for the views expressed rests entirely with him, and they should not be attributed either to these organizations or to the governments of the developing countries for which he has worked.

0271–2075/90/010003–16$08.00

questioning attitude towards the performance of existing public sector organizations (why do they exist, what are they achieving, how might they be improved, should they be abolished?), whilst rejecting the views of those (for example, Waters, 1985; Letwin, 1988) who wish to export/import privatization as their contribution to an international crusade.

Contrasting images and interpretations can be drawn from the rapid emergence of privatization as a significant policy issue in many countries, whether or not much has yet happened there. The problem can be formulated as either:

a. the *obstacles* to privatization, often presented in terms of the 'vested interests' which seek to defend the *status quo*; or
b. the *dangers* of 'inappropriate' privatization once the ball has started rolling and the advantages for particular interests become evident: privatization will benefit some interests just as surely as it damages others.

Berg and Shirley (1987) concentrate exclusively upon the 'obstacles' to privatization generated by bureaucratic and political processes in developing countries. In contrast, this article considers both the obstacles to privatization and the incentives to 'inappropriate' privatization (Dunleavy, 1986).

If the purpose is to redefine the nature and boundaries of the public and private sectors, it is possible that some privatization measures will contribute towards greater efficiency, whereas other measures will be damaging even on the measure of efficiency (i.e. without considering other goals of public policy). Privatization might at times seem a difficult game to start but the ball, once rolling, may violate the line between 'appropriate' and 'inappropriate' privatization. How seriously one takes this dilemma will depend upon judgements about the optimal public/private mix; the starting point in a particular country; and assessments of the likely process of adjustment.

Terminology has predictably become a problem. Sometimes, privatization is taken to mean only denationalization (divestiture) by which there is ownership transfer from the public sector to the private sector. At other times, it covers a much wider range of initiatives (Heald, 1983), such as the substitution of user charges for tax finance; contractorization whereby public employees are replaced by contractors' employees, or the letting of management contracts whilst retaining ownership; and liberalization measures which promote competition in markets previously reserved for statutory monopolies. It is misleading to conduct discussion of divestiture in isolation from wider questions. However, my experience as a consultant indicates that it is astonishingly difficult to persuade the relevant policy-makers and politicians to discuss privatization within the context of an integrated policy framework.

Moreover, it is essential to specify carefully the particular sectors of the economy to which the discussion and/or policy proposals relate (Heald, 1985b). Just as the developing countries have gone through stages when state direction and ownership were seen as the dominant requirement for economic development, privatization seems to have recently emerged as a panacea. If an unqualified case for privatization is embraced ('public bad, private good'), it is then almost impossible to generate a debate which acknowledges that different sectors may raise very different issues of economic organization and of salience to 'public purposes'. Textiles, telecommunications and health care raise profoundly different questions: it is therefore unlikely that uniform 'solutions' can be found, let alone that they would be desirable.

The most important prerequisites for a sensible discussion are therefore a sophistication about the issues of public policy (whether national security, national control over economic development, control of monopoly, or interpersonal or territorial equity) raised by different sectors, and an accompanying willingness to differentiate the policy response according to the circumstances of the case. Critical questions about priorities should then emerge, which reflect both technical analysis and value judgements about the trade-offs between objectives. Accordingly, the role which privatization, as one of a range of policy instruments, might play in improving economic performance can then be specified. Practical judgements will clearly inform decisions. For instance, there is a high opportunity cost in terms of other government expenditure imposed by tolerating inefficient and patronage-ridden public industrial enterprises.

The swinging of the pendulum strongly in favour of the role of the private sector and of the acceptance of foreign investment should not obscure the fact that there are political considerations, in the non-pejorative sense, which may figure prominently in particular cases. In countries which have acquired independence from colonial rule within living memory, there may be symbols of the independence movements which are untouchable because of fears of a neocolonial dependence: large-scale foreign ownership of plantation sectors might not be acceptable in some countries. Moreover, governments may be faced with delicate political situations where problems of ethnic relations or civil disorder might be aggravated by job losses or shifts in patterns of ownership.

The starting point for policy reform should be a proper analysis of the weaknesses of the present public enterprise sector, and of the associated control system (Ayub and Hegstad, 1986). The extensive literature on the problems of public enterprise control reveals many common themes: issues concerning the relationship of public enterprises to the government budget; the respective roles of management, and of the sponsoring minister and his department; the conflicting timescales relevant to forward planning of enterprises and to ministerial horizons; the problem of specifying and then holding in place a system of economic and financial control which recognizes the opportunity cost of capital and encourages efficiency-promoting pricing structures; the establishing of mechanisms for performance appraisal; and the role which exposure to competitive pressures might play in the overall control system. Such a list seems to be fairly international, applying to developed as well as developing countries. In countries which were formerly part of the British Empire and which have maintained cultural links with the United Kingdom, there has been a large amount of straightforward imitation of Morrisonian-type structures for public enterprises (i.e. public corporations) across manufacturing industry as well as public utilities, in contexts lacking the cultural supports which might make these work successfully. If developed countries such as the United Kingdom have found it almost impossible to sustain stable answers to the questions above, there must be doubts about whether solutions can be found in developing countries. There are thus grounds for pessimism about public enterprise revitalization strategies.

In some developing countries, the nature of the political system generates additional features which are not only undesirable in themselves but also obstruct policy reform. Public enterprises can become the vehicle for corruption of various forms: straightforward embezzlement and bribery for personal aggrandisement, often at the expense of aid-financed projects; the development of 'croneyism' through patronage at high levels; the siphoning off of money and resources for party political or factional purposes; and the packing of public enterprises at lower levels with supporters of the ruling political party, however unqualified, and without regard for genuine manpower requirements. Possibly the worst example was the Philippines under Marcos (Briones, 1986), but there are imitations and echoes elsewhere. Such activities can, in extreme cases, pervert development priorities and inflict severe damage upon both the economy and the society as a whole. If public enterprises are to play a constructive role in economic development, pathological features such as the widespread tolerance of inefficiency and corruption clearly have to be tackled. Otherwise, there will have to be significant rethinking about the role which actual, rather than idealized, public enterprises can play. I would regard this as an exceptionally important point; judgements about it would strongly influence my attitude as to the desirable policy mix in particular developing countries.

A real commitment to improved public enterprise performance often seems to have been lacking, seemingly for two reasons. First, there has been a widespread loss of confidence in 'public' solutions, and the civil servants and managers charged with the implementation of reform packages often believe that reform is an inferior substitute for (some ill-specified form of) privatization. Without enthusiasm and belief on the part of key actors in the process, it is difficult to be optimistic about the chances of success. In contrast, privatization is seen as a 'clean break'.

Second, it is sad to watch countries repeat very similar mistakes to those which have already proved disastrous elsewhere: a particularly striking example is the inordinately centralized and bureaucratic system established for the textile industry in Bangladesh after it broke away from Pakistan (Chishty, 1985). There has been a striking failure to spread 'good practice', so that countries might learn from the successes and failures of others. One commendable example was Shirley (1983) which was given extensive coverage in the World Development Report for 1983 (World Bank, 1983). Such work is not necessarily disseminated well, nor digested on the ground by operational staff: compare, for example, the penetration of cost-benefit manuals such as Little and Mirrlees (1974). Moreover, academic commentators on the political left sometimes fail to distinguish between the crude privatizers of the ideological right and the much more sophisticated concerns of World Bank policy staff such as Shirley: a good example of this blurring is Ghai (1985), writing about the future of public enterprises in Africa. Unfortunately, however, the World Bank's interest in management reforms probably came rather late to have much effect, as attention swung towards the privatization option. Although the overall picture is depressing, there are examples of constructive innovation and good practice as in South Korea and Pakistan (Jones, 1975, 1982; Shirley, 1983; Hartmann and Nawab, 1985; Park, 1987).

Whether or not particular countries are able to run their public enterprise sectors effectively might in part depend upon the nature and style of the system of government: closed and authoritarian systems might find it easier to resist 'clientelist' pressures. Aylen (1987) has demonstrated that there are significant differences between groups of countries in how public enterprise sectors are controlled and managed, reflecting in part what might be described as a 'hard'/'soft' state dichotomy. Similarly, the practical effects of privatization may themselves be conditioned by such factors. In summary, therefore, there are grounds for resisting over-generalizations about whether policy improvements within the public sector are feasible, and whether privatization measures can be appropriately and effectively executed.

The international dissemination of privatization is sometimes characterized by a combination of aggressive ideology and of naive managerialism. The large merchant banks have obvious financial interests in promoting particular kinds of privatization, almost exclusively divestiture. Such organizations have no direct interest in appropriate policy design as opposed to the implementation of particular policies. Unsubtle approaches by international organizations might well prove counter-productive, both in terms of how much privatization actually takes place and the forms which it takes.

THE PRIORITY ATTACHED TO CONFLICTING POLICY OBJECTIVES

Practical experience in developed countries has demonstrated that public enterprises can be privatized. The extent of ownership transfer has far exceeded the expectations held when the UK privatization programme began diffidently in 1979. However, the process of implementation (Steel and Heald, 1984, Heald, 1988a) has highlighted three dilemmas in terms of the relative priority to be attached to the underlying policy objectives which are sometimes mutually reinforcing but sometimes conflicting:

1. the extent to which a privatization programme is driven by (a) problems caused by the inclusion of public enterprise external financing within public sector borrowing totals; or (b) a desire to finance existing expenditure/tax cuts through mechanisms which disguise the true government fiscal deficit and reduce the public sector's net worth;
2. the trade-off between denationalization and liberalization; and
3. the symbolic importance currently attached in some developed countries to the extension of individual share ownership by means of privatization issues, with the declared motive of 'making everyone a capitalist'.

Given the pressures encouraging policy emulation, it is highly relevant to ask which aspects of developed country experience it would be appropriate to follow. Accordingly, the numbered points above each lead to a short section.

Budgetary stress

In many developing countries, the financing of public enterprises constitutes a much more significant claim upon government finances than in developed countries (Short, 1984). One of the strongest drives for reform and/or privatization will be unpleasant budget realities. However, a number of careful distinctions have to be made and kept in view during the consideration of policy options. The claims of public enterprises upon the budget can, in principle, be separated into revenue subsidies and capital injections (though sometimes items described as the latter are in reality disguised subsidies). An important distinction should be drawn between planned subsidies (for example, for the support of public transport operators) and subventions to offset unplanned losses (as when steel or other manufacturing companies are kept afloat). Decisions have to be taken about the extent to which public enterprises should rely upon the budget for capital injections, or should have separate access to the banking system or the capital market. Given the extent to which the government is assumed to stand behind them (whether or not the guarantees are formal or merely implicit), there are obviously difficult judgements about whether such financing should be regarded as an integral part of government financial operations.

Privatization is thus relevant to the budget in a number of different ways. First, if privatization led to greater efficiency and/or lower financial losses, there might be a reduced call on the budget for subventions. Second, privatization of industrial enterprises might lead to faster elimination of uneconomic capacity and, by distancing the government from the adjustment process, eliminate its legal obligation to make up losses and otherwise limit its exposure. Third, by privatizing an enterprise like telecommunications, the business would no longer look to the government for its financing needs and thus eliminate a claim upon the budget. Unfortunately, however, nothing is as clear cut. Counter possibilities can be cited in each of these three cases: the claims upon the budget might remain unchanged or become larger, because the government is financing an activity over which it has relinquished operational control; the industrial enterprises might successfully lobby for government subsidies or for increased protection, the latter saving public funds but raising a host of other issues; and questions ought to be asked about whether the economic effects of the privatized telecommunications company raising capital (whether debt or equity) are likely to be different from similar amounts being raised either by the public enterprise itself or by the government for onward transmission.

Careful empirical work on individual countries is therefore essential. In Thailand, for example, much of the discussion about the possible (partial) divestiture of Thai International (the highly-regarded national carrier) and the Electricity Generating Authority of Thailand focuses upon their requirements for external finance, often raised abroad and large enough to affect Thailand's overall foreign debt position (Pakkasem, 1985). However, this is exactly the kind of situation in which the warning given by two economists at the IMF (Hemming and Mansoor, 1988; Mansoor, 1988) should be taken on board. In terms of impact on the budget, gains from such divestiture are likely to be negligible, as future cash flows to the budget are being converted into a lump sum now. In addition, asset sales can involve significant transactions costs and uncompensated wealth transfers when public assets are sold at a discount on market value. The weaker the domestic capital markets, the greater will be such costs unless foreign ownership of the enterprise is judged acceptable, thus opening up the possibility of flotation abroad. Problems will arise if governments under dire fiscal stress resort to extensive fund-raising by means of selling enterprises: large discounts might reinforce the positions of privileged political and business élites, thus routing the notion that privatization is in part about the promotion of competition. The UK practice of treating the proceeds of asset sales as negative expenditure, in order to massage the fiscal deficit, has been much criticized. The 1986-88 Chirac Government in France isolated (at least part of) privatization proceeds from general revenue and expenditure. Such a precedent is worthy of serious consideration by developing countries, and the international agencies should ensure that their own activities, such as IMF packages and loan conditionality, do not discourage transparency.

Competition versus denationalization

It is possible to take two views about the relationship between denationalization and increased competition. Denationalization might be seen as a necessary step towards securing greater competition, on the argument that governments would never tolerate 'fair competition' against their own enterprises. Alternatively, it can be argued that a preoccupation with denationalization will mean sacrificing opportunities for introducing more competition. There is, of course, a vital distinction between logical connections (in principle, denationalization could precede liberalization) and practical assessments of likelihoods (Heald, 1985a). A pivotal question concerns which view will be proved correct in the circumstances prevailing in developing countries.

The relevant differences in context are not difficult to specify. First, unlike developed countries, where public enterprises in manufacturing or other internationally traded goods are comparatively unimportant, public enterprises often figure prominently in such sectors in developing countries. Accordingly, there will be a substantial number of enterprises located in sectors in which there are no technical barriers to competition and which do not impinge upon 'public purposes'. However, decisions about such divestitures cannot properly be separated from those about the trade policy régime. In countries which currently combine inefficient public industrial enterprises with high levels of effective protection, prior decisions ought to be taken about the future of tariff policy before divestiture is even contemplated. Enterprises which have negative value added at border prices ought to be closed down rather than privatized. The line between liquidation and privatization might sometimes be rather fine, but there are advantages in keeping such a distinction in mind. The profitability of enterprises post-privatization will crucially depend upon the tariff policy under which they have to operate. Many of the private enterprise enthusiasts who welcome the prospect of privatization are far less enthusiastic about exposing private industry to market tests in the form of international competition. The concessions, current or prospective, which are extracted by the purchasers of privatized enterprises should be monitored carefully.

The Togo steel mill, leased to an American entrepreneur, has been lavishly praised as an example to follow (Robbs, 1987). In contrast, Berg and Shirley (1987), who strongly urge that concessions to the purchasers of privatized assets should be resisted, observe that the steel mill is financially profitable only because of concessions such as a 41 per cent duty on imports. From the perspective of the acquirer, the privatization was highly attractive, yielding a payback period of about six months: the 10-year lease will cover less than five per cent of the enterprise's annual debt service. The problem is that such monitoring is likely to be inherently difficult because any undertakings which are given are likely to be shrouded in commercial and governmental confidentiality. Moreover, decision makers are frequently reluctant to acknowledge the symmetry between explicit budget subsidies and implicit subsidies from tax expenditures or tariff concessions. Propagandist advocacy of the private sector often deliberately blurs or denies this equivalence. If not handled with extreme care and polish, divestitures could prove a serious obstacle to subsequent tariff reform. Consequently, wherever possible, the desired tariff framework for a particular sector should be put in place (or, at the very least, clearly specified and announced, as when a series of tariff reduction steps is contemplated) before divestiture is effected.

Second, a series of questions has to be asked about the effectiveness of public regulation over the economy. It is possible to take the view that divestiture should be accompanied by a parallel sweeping away of government regulation. In one sense, as when licensing controls on market entry or on foreign trade are abolished, this might indeed be the case. However, the process of deregulation might more usefully be interpreted as a process whereby the instruments of regulation are changed, often to less direct mechanisms, rather than one by which government forswears responsibility. In other words, it is far more complicated than just 'getting government off the backs of the people'. There are fundamental questions to be resolved concerning market structure and public regulation; notably whether a particular developing country can establish effective regulatory institutions and sustain their credibility against manifold pressures. Such issues will prove particularly important when the privatization of utilities is being contemplated, such as telecommunications in Malaysia and Sri Lanka, and electricity supply in Turkey. In such sectors, denationalization explicitly involves the substitution of regulation for ownership.

Third, and paradoxically, reform of the institutional framework for the private sector is a prerequisite for a successful privatization programme, defined as one which improves efficiency and not simply in terms of clocking up enterprises privatized. The crucial areas concern competition policy (where institutions are undeveloped and frequently lack operational credibility); corporate disclosure (where limited provisions are not policed); and corporate ownership patterns (where there are family or 'business house' concentrations of economic power, sometimes closely plugged into political élites). It is very easy to see how an extensive programme of divestitures on concessionary terms could reinforce existing patterns of power and control. On the 'worst case' scenario, this could lead to aggravated (or indeed new) problems of 'croney capitalism', fed by corruption and black money. Procedures to ensure transparency when public assets are transferred to the private sector are easier to recommend than to enforce. However, much can be learned in terms of legal and administrative procedures from the experience of other countries. There are cultural differences in what is regarded as acceptable behaviour and even well-designed procedures can be overruled at the highest political level (for example, the sale of Noorani Tiles in Sri Lanka). Developed countries have experienced analogous problems with regard to insider trading in capital markets: these practices have proved difficult to regulate because they are perceived to be 'crimes without victims'.

Decisions ought to be taken about the desirable balance between denationalization and liberalization. It seems likely that many of the pressures will give priority to denationalization: the ideological crusade for private enterprise; the budgetary exigencies facing finance ministries; the short-term spoils to be distributed; the anti-competitive instincts and interests of management; the fears of employees and their unions that conditions and collective bargaining arrangements would be undermined by liberalization; and the fact that far more concrete 'achievements' (i.e. the count of enterprises sold) can be recorded. If such a prospect is unattractive, there remains the outside possibility that there might be some form of counter-alliance between tough-minded reformers who wish to see greater efficiency within the public sector and those market-oriented economists who are more concerned with competition than ownership. For that to be translated into effective action, however, there would have to be a calmer climate within which the performance of public sector organizations could be assessed on a systematic basis, and which casts aside the automatic rubbishing which must ultimately damage performance.

People's capitalism

The efforts of the UK Government to structure privatization equity issues in such a way as to secure a massive extension of individual share ownership have attracted worldwide attention. Because the British Telecom flotation captured the imagination of so many opinion-formers and policy-makers in developing countries, there is likely to be a desire to imitate this process in the context of large-scale privatizations. This raises two questions: the role which wider share ownership played in the UK privatization programme; and the possibilities of replication in a developing country.

The notion of 'people's capitalism' represented a presentational triumph in terms of the legitimation of the transfer of public assets to private hands. The 'success' of flotations is popularly measured by the media and by governments in terms of the number of founding shareholders. In France and the United Kingdom (but not in Japan), the shareholder 'count' is a heavily-publicized criterion of success. The long-term implications of wider share ownership are, in any case, quite difficult to assess: notably, whether individual share ownership will lead to the internaljeization of beliefs in the capitalist system, and be transformed into votes against renationalization and for the parties committed to private enterprise. However, there are serious grounds for doubts about such policy encouragement to individual share ownership. Because of the long-running bull market and deliberate underpricing, individuals have been encouraged to buy shares on an implicit assumption that prices always go up and never down. Moreover, individual share ownership for many of these first-time investors runs strongly counter to elementary ideas of portfolio theory, and the economic (rather than tax-induced) move towards institutional investment. In the context of developing countries, these doubts acquire even greater force. A policy which simultaneously legitimizes the transfer of assets to the private sector and provides large windfall gains to affluent groups is open to severe criticism, given the extent of income and wealth inequalities.

Existing capital markets are not only thin and underdeveloped (Asian Development Bank, 1986), but often also rife with insider trading and other dubious practices. The privatization of profitable enterprises might play a constructive role in developing the formal capital market, but this development is much more likely to take place in the context of less glamorous flotations priced at as near market value as judgement permits with the aim of attracting financial institutions and specialist investors. Generally, however, flotations will play a smaller role in privatization programmes than in developed economies such as the United Kingdom, France and Japan, with equity placements or direct sales of enterprises or assets being much more frequent. Nevertheless, the opportunities to establish or to revitalize capital markets in Third World countries are substantially greater than has often been appreciated. An interesting example is the reprivatization by public offering in December 1986 of the National Commercial Bank of Jamaica, itself nationalized in 1977 (Leeds, 1987). Organized by a British merchant bank, this flotation mirrored almost exactly the British precedents in terms of oversubscription, discount on market value, employee subscription and widespread individual applications. Virtues and vices were thus very similar. Improving capital markets involves rechannelling existing private savings through formal capital markets. Amongst the pre-conditions to be met for successful development are the necessity for confidence that there will not be uncompensated nationalizations and that there will be effective regulation of the capital market so as to limit financial abuses.

A counter argument

It is important to recognize that a counter argument can be mobilized, denying the importance of the policy trade-offs studied in this section. It might be contended that desperation for cash is the only reason why governments would relinquish control over enterprises through divestiture, but that this self-interest drives policy in a direction which is judged appropriate on other grounds. Similarly, concessions, such as in the case of the Togo steel mill, have enabled privatization to be effected and thus overcome the inertia and lethargy which have paralysed reform in Africa. Once the programme has acquired momentum, it will be possible to avoid making the same mistakes in future privatizations, even where remedial action is not possible in the particular case. In any event, the reputational benefits for Togo, as evidenced by a story in *Time* magazine (28 September, 1987), are worth much more than the resource costs of this particular contract. 'Bad' privatizations will make possible 'good' privatizations.

Periods of transition from one set of institutional arrangements to a different set are undoubtedly difficult to manage and to analyse. Theoretical arguments can become elastic when utilized for purposes of advocacy and it is not always easy to detect advocacy. It seems paradoxical that those who urge privatization as a cure for state failure should appeal to an invisible hand within government which guides policy in appropriate directions. Appeal to wider social benefits was exactly the line of argument which led to state intervention in the first place, whereas now it is being used to defend particular paths of state withdrawal. Moreover, elaborate arguments in terms of social benefits have been constructed, to the effect, for example, that uneconomic coal mines in developed countries should not be closed. Because such arguments can be used opportunistically, judgements have to be made as to whether to accept the counter argument about the privatization transition process and whether to believe that the resulting policy distortions can themselves be rectified or will proliferate.

DEVISING AND IMPLEMENTING POLICY REFORM

Privatization or revitalization

A more searching test for public policy objectives and for measurement of policy outcomes is, of itself, desirable. However, continuous abuse of the public sector may destroy the credibility of public institutions and undermine their capability to act, whether in a service-provision or regulatory mode.

A cautious approach is not the same as paralysis. Policy reform in the public enterprise sector is desperately urgent in many developing countries. Although the mix of policy will depend upon the circumstances of the particular case, that does not remove the urgency. Privatization should not be seen as a free-standing policy, but rather as one set of instruments within a package of policy reform. It is a question of a process of adjustment towards economies being more open to the world economy and characterized internally by a reasonable degree of competition. Although this will involve encouraging the private sector, it also means that the public sector should carry out effectively its own assigned tasks (Marsden and Belot, 1987). There needs to be a degree of pragmatism about instruments, with the key question being whether existing institutions deliver the desired policy outputs. In particular, the governments of developing countries lack the full range of policy instruments available to their counterparts in the developed world, particularly in the tax/transfer field and with regard to credible instruments of regulation. This consideration will be relevant to decisions about public production versus regulation, and those about public enterprise pricing versus use of the tax/transfer system for particular redistributive objectives.

There should be no illusions about the social costs of adjustment whether or not these are imposed through retrenchment in the public sector or through privatization. Significant employment losses will cause more personal hardship in a developing country, lacking the income maintenance systems of an industrialized country. Tensions concerning the balance of economic activity between regions, and in some countries between ethnic groups, are likely to be prominent on the political agenda, and raise difficult issues of policy design, implementation and transition.

Privatization is, of course, delicate territory. The international agencies are vulnerable to being portrayed as facilitators of a new colonialism based upon foreign capital rather than foreign administration. Yet they undoubtedly could play a constructive role. There is scope for the collection and exchange of information on the experience with various kinds of reform and privatization initiatives. Careful attention must be paid to ensuring accurate feedback of actual developments in particular countries so that reliance does not have to be placed upon inaccurate media reporting, hurried visits, or what are essentially propaganda sources. It is equally important that such material is then collated and interpreted by reliable analysts. Developing countries face a steep learning curve when discussing either divestiture or management contracts with multinational companies with experience of operating similar plant throughout the world. Pooled knowledge, perhaps through the international agencies, would afford some protection to governments of developing countries. Otherwise, implementation will be slow and uneven, and political bitterness against acquirers, especially if foreign, might accumulate.

For that reason, the pioneering work of Elliot Berg and Mary Shirley for the World Bank has been extremely important (Berg, 1982; Berg and Shirley, 1987). Nevertheless, there are limits to what can be achieved from what are predominantly desk studies, because it quickly becomes difficult to select between conflicting accounts. Definitive case studies, conducted along broadly comparable lines, are required. However, such exercises are costly and predictably difficult to undertake.

In 1988, the World Bank published a three-volume study on privatization techniques and experience (Vuylsteke, 1988; Nankani, 1988; Candoy-Sekse, 1988). This is an essential reference work which should help decision-makers to view their own technical and political problems in the light of experience elsewhere in the world. Although such work is derivative and can only be as good as its sources, it provides 'points of entry' to experience in particular countries, the relevant detail of which can be verified and up-dated.

There does not seem to be any developing country which could be highlighted as representing 'best practice'. Although praised in the propagandist literature, the ambitious Chilean denationalization programme has attracted criticism for the way divestiture restored historic patterns of ownership concentration and interconnected family control (Marshall, 1986; Overseas Development Institute, 1986). Large divestiture programmes have been undertaken in Bangladesh and Jamaica, whereas the ambitious programme in Turkey appears to have stalled. World Bank pressure on

Ghana to divest enterprises against a strict time schedule may have proved counter-productive. The experience of Argentina and the Philippines will be worth watching closely, not least because they are (albeit fragile) democracies. One of the clear policy lessons which has been learned is to avoid over-ambition and to recognize that time-consuming preparations are necessary.

Establishing a privatization programme

Privatization, in its various forms, should play a role in packages of economic reform in those developing countries whose economies are presently highly state-dominated, and where there are clear failures of policy design (for example, on the public/private mix) and of implementation (inefficiency and/or corruption). To acknowledge that there is a need for tougher questioning of both the public/private mix in ownership and of the respective reliance placed upon administrative procedures/market mechanisms is, however, a far cry from an enthusiastic advocacy of privatization as panacea.

Accordingly, this article has attempted to instil some kind of order into the conceptual issues which should in principle be resolved before embarking upon a privatization programme. In practice, policy-makers in finance ministries tend to be looking for tool kits, rather than for exhortations to address fundamental prior questions. One of the main objectives here has therefore been to point to the potential consequences of jumping straight to implementation. A great deal obviously depends upon the perceived objectives of policy. If the goal is to transfer as many enterprises as possible into the private sector as quickly as possible, the obvious first step is to establish a 'dedicated' privatization unit and then buy in financial expertise from an experienced merchant bank. However, if the objective of the reform/privatization package is greater efficiency, such an approach brings serious pitfalls because merchant banks are singularly unconcerned with competition, trade policy or foreign ownership issues. The privatization unit itself might see its task narrowly in terms of numbers processed, and might find it difficult to avoid its key personnel being poached. A related question is whether there should be a master plan or whether, because this approach might enable opposition to coalesce, a more informal and gradualist style of policy development is more appropriate. It seems quite possible that an essentially pragmatic government might effect more efficiency-improving privatization than one ideologically committed to privatization.

It is often difficult to predict the likely course of developments. The more information which is secured about the policies and achievements of particular governments, the more scepticism is generated about how seriously professed enthusiasm for privatization should in reality be taken. Quite often, governments seem to be saying things for the benefit of the external audience, according to what the listener is thought to want to hear. The domestic policies and preferences of influential countries in the international institutions (such as the United States, France (under Chirac), Japan, the United Kingdom and West Germany) have been well publicized. Governments of developing countries often tell rather different stories to domestic audiences. It then becomes very difficult to know what governments actually think, or to diagnose the tensions within governments which reflect the conflicting ideological, political and economic pressures upon them. A key factor in determining whether public enterprise reform or privatization can be effected will be the beliefs about the government's ultimate intentions which are held by interested parties. 'Positioning' on particular measures often depends as much upon expectations as to where the policy will ultimately lead, as upon the detailed measure itself. Two scenarios seem plausible: either, very little will actually happen in terms of reform or privatization; or, privatization will be pursued on a mindless 'counting the numbers and proceeds' basis, with scant regard for the fundamental political and economic issues involved.

Proper control of those enterprises which are to stay in the public sector depends upon improving the capabilities of the Ministry of Finance, partly by system improvement and partly by reducing overload. Accordingly, the overloading of the monitoring capabilities of the central machinery is the most convincing argument for the divestiture of small, irrelevant and peripheral public enterprises. Therefore, a significant clear out of such enterprises would of itself be beneficial. Such divestitures would contribute to the development of local capital markets; it seems odd that there should be so much discussion about public utilities for which weak capital markets make foreign ownership inevitable. Similarly, development finance corporations and banks have often acquired 'accidental' shareholdings, for example through foreclosures. Such enterprises are far more appropriate candidates for divestiture than public utilities or large enterprises raising monopoly questions. There is substantial danger of inappropriate 'institutional transfer'.

At a more detailed level, it seems appropriate to be very wary of large rehabilitation schemes undertaken prior to divestiture; it is possible that the incremental discounted cash flows on subsequent divestiture will be significantly less than the discounted costs (even if the project costs are partially aid-financed). Especially if the purchaser is a foreign company, it is by no means certain that the rehabilitation expenditure will be regarded as useful. World Bank policy staff have made this point in the context of both Peru and Mali, but it is far from clear that it is always taken into account by the operational staff of international agencies.

Public enterprise reform strategies

Irrespective of the mix between reform and privatization which is adopted in any particular country, there are two sets of issues which require urgent attention. First, the sponsoring arrangements for public enterprises are often in dire need of restructuring: this is, in part, a technical exercise but one which must be conducted within constraints imposed by the political and bureaucratic context. Without such steps, the information base available to the Ministry of Finance is likely to be inadequate, both with regard to enterprise performance and to financial flows. There is, of course, a worry which ought to be articulated: that the increased 'power through knowledge' thereby accruing to the Ministry of Finance can be used for 'ill' as well as 'good'. There are in any case dangers accruing from exaggerated belief in centralized wisdom. Consequently, resistance to such 'reforms' on the part of public enterprises and sponsoring ministries do raise substantive concerns as well as defend vested interests.

Second, the present arrangements concerning subsidiaries in certain countries give rise to dangers in terms of public accountability, efficiency and financial rectitude. Subsidiaries are created, partly as a means of circumventing rigid Ministry of Finance controls over public enterprises, partly as a vehicle for privatization in the form of joint ventures, sometimes with foreign partners. However, the way in which this is done may put the budget sorely at risk, especially where there is close interaction between the operations and finances of the public enterprise (subject to Ministry of Finance supervision) and of a wholly-owned or partly-owned subsidiary (outside this net). If such arrangements are allowed to develop haphazardly, the public enterprise can be bled by the subsidiary, thus exposing the budget (such as Sri Lanka's Cement and Ceramics Corporations). Consequently, there ought to be clarification of the extent to which a public corporation is liable for its subsidiaries, and also whether the government stands behind its public corporations or whether they really do have limited liability (as the Sri Lankan legislation proclaims). Such arrangements are crucially important for the control of public enterprises (for example, concerning the bankruptcy threat); the protection of the budget; and for the integrity of the banking system, especially in countries where the commercial banks are state-owned and there is heavy public enterprise borrowing from them.

In terms of policy example, the large-scale privatizations of the United Kingdom are of limited relevance. More could be learned from the public sector reforms in New Zealand. The Labour Government has implemented a massive restructuring of its public sector, partly in response to a dramatic deterioration in the country's trading position. The 'corporatization' programme has been designed to clarify the objectives of public sector organizations, with one important feature being the transfer of functions out of departments into agencies and enterprises (Boston, 1987). It should be a question of learning rather than of direct transplanting: differences in political culture, levels of economic development, country size and bureaucratic capabilities will determine which reforms are feasible.

POSTSCRIPT

The final typescript of this article was completed in March 1989. These brief comments have been added at proof stage in December 1989.

The remarkable events in Eastern Europe have made privatization an exceptionally topical issue. For example, the Polish Government formed by the trade union organization Solidarity has espoused private enterprise and has appointed a minister for privatization. The Adam Smith Institute, a free-market think tank closely associated with 'new right' Conservative Members of the UK Parliament, has been advising Solidarity and organizing seminars on British-style privatization.

There is only space for two brief comments. First, the British Government's privatization programme, as it affects public utilities, has been vigorously criticized by academic economists (Vickers and Yarrow, 1988), for emphasizing denationalization rather than competition. There is opinion poll evidence of strong public opposition to current measures of privatization (such as water and electricity) and suspicion that health sector reforms are the precursor of privatization. Thus, overseas and domestic views of UK privatization have diverged sharply. Second, whatever views are taken of UK privatization, it must be remembered that the programme has evolved over a 10-year period in which the Conservative Party—in particular, Mrs Thatcher—has dominated British politics. It has been within such a political context (Heald, 1988b) that the necessary legislative programme, administrative arrangements and financial mechanisms have been effected. The tasks facing Eastern European countries are formidably more complicated.

Developing countries lack the administrative and financial infrastructure of industrialized countries. The enthusiastic advocacy of a policy of privatization and people's capitalism by Pakistan's Prime Minister Benazir Bhutto (Bhutto, 1989; Lamb, 1989) is noteworthy for two reasons. First, the Pakistan Peoples' Party Government of 1971–77 implemented an extensive nationalization programme. The political climate has changed remarkably. Rather than international agencies pressing privatization upon unwilling governments, they may now have to caution against the infeasible and inappropriate. Second, such an imitation of UK policy with regard to major enterprises and monopolies would surely exceed the administrative capabilities of a country with high illiteracy rates. More fundamentally, it would distract attention from the task of making the economy more market-oriented, by promoting competition and using divestiture as an *instrument* in support of that objective.

Pakistan is also of interest because of the World-Bank sponsored signalling system for public enterprises which has been recommended as the model for adoption in other countries such as Egypt. A comprehensive assessment is provided by Shirley (1989). In brief, the system has enjoyed some success, though it has become much less ambitious: for example, measuring performance in terms of financial rather than 'public' profitability. It has also depended heavily upon the highly-trained manpower available in Pakistan.

REFERENCES

Asian Development Bank (1986). *Capital Market Development in Selected Developing Member Countries of the Asian Development Bank*, Asian Development Bank, Manila.

Aylen, J. (1987). 'Privatization in developing countries', *Lloyds Bank Review, No.* **163,** January, pp. 15–30.

Ayub, M. A. and Hegstad, S. O. (1986). *Public Industrial Enterprises: Determinants of Performance*, Industry and Finance Series Volume 17, World Bank, Washington DC.

Berg, E. (1982). *Changing the Public–Private Mix: A Survey of Some Recent Experiences in LDCs*, DM/83/10, International Monetary Fund, Washington DC.

Berg, E. and Shirley, M. M. (1987). *Divestiture in Developing Countries*, World Bank Discussion Paper 11, World Bank, Washington DC.

Bhutto, B. (1989). Opening speech to national seminar on 'Privatization and Investment', Islamabad, 2–3 August 1989.

Boston, J. (1987). 'Transforming the public sector in New Zealand: Labour's quest for improved efficiency and accountability', *Public Administration*, Vol. **65**, pp. 423–442.

Briones, L. M. (1986). 'The role of government-owned or controlled corporations in development', *Public Enterprise* (Ljubljana), Vol. **6**, pp. 227–237.

Candoy-Sekse, R. (1988). *Techniques of Privatization of State-owned Enterprises, Volume III: Inventory of Country Experience and Reference Materials*, World Bank Technical Paper No. 90, World Bank, Washington DC.

Chishty, Md. S. H. (1985). 'The experience of Bangladesh', in Asian Development Bank, *Privatization: Policies, Methods and Procedures*, Asian Development Bank, Manila, pp. 261–292.

Dunleavy, P. (1986). 'Explaining the privatization boom: public choice versus radical approaches', *Public Administration*, **64,** pp. 13–34.

Ghai, Y. (1985). 'The state and the market in the management of public enterprises in Africa: ideology and false comparisons', *Public Enterprise* (Ljubljana), Vol. **6**, pp. 15–26.

Hartmann, A. and Nawab S. A. (1985). 'Evaluating public manufacturing enterprises in Pakistan', *Finance & Development*, Vol. **22**, No. (3), September, pp. 27–30.

Heald, D. A. (1983). *Public Expenditure: Its Defence and Reform*, Basil Blackwell, Oxford.

Heald, D. A. (1985a). 'Will the privatization of public enterprises solve the problem of control?', *Public Administration*, Vol. **63**, pp. 7–22.

Heald, D. A. (1985b). 'Privatization: policies, methods and procedures', in Asian Development Bank, *Privatization: Policies, Methods and Procedures*, Asian Development Bank, Manila, pp. 57–95.

Heald, D. A. (1988a). 'The relevance of UK privatisation for LDCs', in Cook, P. and Kirkpatrick, C. (eds), *Privatisation in LDCs*, Wheatsheaf, Brighton, pp. 68–90.

Heald, D. A. (1988b). 'The United Kingdom: privatization and its political context', *West European Politics*, **11**, 31–48.

Hemming, R. and Mansoor, A. (1988). *Privatization and Public Enterprises*, International Monetary Fund Occasional Paper 56, Washington DC.

Jones, L. P. (1975). *Public Enterprise and Economic Development: the Korean Case*, Korean Development Institute, Seoul.

Jones, L. P. (ed) (1982). *Public Enterprise in Less Developed Countries*, Cambridge University Press, Cambridge.

Lamb, C. (1989). 'Pakistan prepares to embark on the privatisation trail', *Financial Times*, 19 July 1989.

Leeds, R. (1987). *The Privatization of the National Commercial Bank of Jamaica: A Case Study*, John F. Kennedy School of Government, Harvard University, Cambridge, Massachusetts.

Letwin, O. (1988). *Privatising the World*, Cassell, London.

Little, I. M. D. and Mirrlees, J. A. (1974). *Project Appraisal and Planning for Developing Countries*, Heinemann, London.

Mansoor, A. (1988). 'The fiscal impact of privatization', in Cook, P. and Kirkpatrick, C. (eds), *Privatisation in LDCs*, Wheatsheaf, Brighton, pp. 180–194.

Marsden, K. and Belot, T. (1987). *Private Enterprise in Africa: Creating a Better Environment*, World Bank Discussion Paper 17, World Bank, Washington DC.

Marshall, J. (1986). 'Economic privatization: lessons from the Chilean experience', in Glade, W. (ed), *State Shrinking: A Comparative Inquiry into Privatization*, Austin, Institute of Latin American Studies, University of Texas at Austin, pp. 101–128.

Nankani, H. (1988). *Techniques of Privatization of State-owned Enterprises, Volume II: Selected Country Case Studies*, World Bank Technical Paper No. 89, World Bank, Washington DC.

Overseas Development Institute (1986). *Privatisation: the Developing Country Experience*, ODI Briefing Paper, London.

Pakkasem, P. (1985). 'The experience of Thailand', in Asian Development Bank, *Privatization: Policies, Methods and Procedures*, Asian Development Bank, Manila, pp. 237–253.

Park, Y. C. (1987). 'Evaluating the performance of Korea's government-invested enterprises', *Finance & Development*, Vol. **24**, No. (2), June, pp. 25–27.

Robbs, P. (1987). 'Togo's steel mill: a white elephant turns bullish', *Development International*, Vol. **1**, pp. 50–51.

Shirley, M. M. (1983). *Managing State-owned Enterprises*, World Bank Staff Working Paper No. 577, Washington DC.

Shirley, M. M. (1989). *Evaluating the Performance of Public Enterprises in Pakistan*, Working Papers WPS 160, World Bank, Washington DC.

Short, R. P. (1984). 'The role of public enterprises: an international statistical comparison', in Floyd, R. H. (ed), *Public Enterprise in Mixed Economies: Some Macroeconomic Aspects*, International Monetary Fund, Washington DC, pp. 110–194.

Steel, D. R. and Heald, D. A. (eds) (1984). *Privatizing Public Enterprises: Options and Dilemmas*, Royal Institute of Public Administration, London.

Time (1987). 'Wheeling and dealing in Togo', p. 42, European edition, 28 September.

Vickers, J. and Yarrow, G. (1988). *Privatization: An Economic Analysis*, MIT Press, London.

Vuylsteke, C. (1988). *Techniques of Privatization of State-owned Enterprises, Volume I: Methods and Implementation*, World Bank Technical Paper No. 88, World Bank, Washington DC.

Waters, A. R. (1985). 'Privatization: a viable policy option?', in Asian Development Bank, *Privatization: Policies, Methods and Procedures*, Asian Development Bank, Manila, pp. 17–55.

World Bank (1983). *World Development Report 1983*, Oxford University Press for the World Bank, New York.

THE WORLD BANK ECONOMIC REVIEW, VOL. 10, NO. 3: 451-85

Why and When Do Governments Initiate Public Enterprise Reform?

Jose Edgardo Campos and Hadi Salehi Esfahani

Initiating public enterprise reform is a complex decision influenced by economic factors as well as the ideological biases and personalities of political leaders. Nevertheless, the use of a contracting framework yields important generalizations about what drives the decision. This article argues that the decision depends fundamentally on the potential efficiency gains from the reform and its associated transactions costs. Costs arise because of asymmetries in information and opportunism, problems that usually plague contract negotiations. The article identifies observable variables that may affect either the potential gains or the transactions costs, uses them to construct a simple probit decision-making model, and tests the model using data from fifteen developing countries over a twenty-year period.

In the last ten years considerable attention has been cast on public enterprises, much of it centering on their poor performance and the burden they impose on national treasuries. Yet in many countries, reform of such enterprises has proceeded at a slow and uneven pace. Many governments have been reluctant to alter incentives within the public enterprise sector that would improve efficiency, and are even more reluctant to privatize. Even under intense pressure from external agencies, some governments have muted necessary large-scale reforms. Clearly, factors other than economic efficiency influence the possibility, nature, pace, and extent of public enterprise reform. The objective of this article is to identify some of those factors.

We adopt the view that economic policies represent a set of contracts between the government and various socioeconomic groups that addresses problems of market failure and demands for redistribution. There is no shortage of frameworks for analyzing the determinants of economic policy, but most rely on concepts that are difficult to operationalize and test. For example, models of economic policy based on the notion of the degree of state autonomy (for example, Evans 1992) are not falsifiable. Also, models of

Jose Edgardo Campos is with the Economic Development Institute at the World Bank, and Hadi Salehi Esfahani is with the Department of Economics at the University of Illinois at Urbana-Champaign. The authors would like to thank the regional economists in the World Bank and colleagues in the Policy Research Department who have commented on earlier drafts, Rebecca Hife for research assistance, and Tyler Cowen for comments. They are also grateful to three anonymous referees who provided invaluable comments and suggestions.

policy reform focused on the role of "insulated change teams" (for example, Waterbury 1993) are incomplete. Since such teams are themselves a creation of the government, they cannot serve as explanatory variables. The existence of the team is an endogenous variable that must be explained as part of the overall policy determination. Finally, there is a whole gamut of interest-group or class-based theories. Our framework is in part interest-group based, but it differs from the others in that it treats the government (or the state) as an independent actor, not simply as a passive agent of interest-group demands. Our approach is most closely related to North's (1981) "predatory state," although in our approach the state might be termed pragmatic rather than predatory. The idea of economic policy as a contract can be dated from at least Goldberg's (1976) proposal to analyze regulation as an administered contract.

According to our framework, policy reform can be interpreted as a renegotiation of contracts that entail direct government involvement in production toward more efficient, market-oriented ones. But to consent to a reform package, interest groups that currently support or could support the ruling coalition must know what they will gain from the reform, how the gains will be distributed, and whether the distribution of rewards will indeed be honored by the government. Thus the reform decision is hampered by the usual contracting problems—that is, problems of information and opportunism.

Imperfect and asymmetric information between interest groups and the government can lead to prolonged bargaining, to resource expenditure on signaling and screening, and to fewer options for recontracting. Opportunism also reduces recontracting options and calls for costly arrangements to convince interest groups that they will receive the rewards promised to them. Opportunism is a potentially serious problem in government-interest group contracts because many terms of such contracts are implicit, given the government's role as the enforcer of its own responsibilities. Lack of well-defined property rights also makes it difficult to determine when the government is acting in an expropriatory manner. These problems can be partially mitigated by institutions and rules that constrain the government, but such a solution is often incomplete. In particular, the need to ensure procedural fairness impedes flexibility and efficiency (Owen and Braeutigam 1978). Furthermore, because property rights are at least partly implicit, it is difficult for the government to obtain commitment from, or compensate, agents affected by policy changes.

Both opportunism and information problems involve transactions costs, whose magnitude depends (positively) on the volume of redistribution entailed by the reform; that is, a reform entails both benefits and costs. Benefits stem from the efficiency gains that would accrue from the reform of the public enterprise sector. Costs arise from the risks that the reform poses to the government and its constituency and from the need to establish mechanisms to reduce such risks.

A government's decision to reform public enterprises depends on whether the potential efficiency gains exceed the associated costs.[1] The government can use the gains to compensate losers and to reward new supporters; however, because it has to shoulder some costs to produce those gains, it would do so only if net gains accrue. This approach is a close cousin of Rodrik's (1994), which uses the concept of "efficiency gains-redistribution cost ratio" as the main determinant of trade reform. We take the analysis further: we derive the relationship between the decision to reform the public enterprise sector and a number of structural and institutional variables that influence the related costs and benefits.

On the basis of this framework, we derive several operational hypotheses relating the reform decision to the broad characteristics of the economy and the public sector that can have a significant impact on the costs and benefits of public enterprise reform. We compile a data set to carry out preliminary tests of the hypotheses and to show how the methodology can be used for predicting whether or not countries attempt reform. In particular, we present evidence relating reform attempts to macroeconomic downturns, the extent of public ownership in the economy, the sectoral structure of the economy (specifically, the relative size of the nonagricultural sector), per capita income, and the degree of openness to international trade. The relationship between some of these variables and macroeconomic and trade reforms has been discussed in the literature, but empirical evidence is scarce. (See, however, Rodrik 1994, Alesina 1994, Drazen and Grilli 1993, and Edwards 1993.) Similar investigations in the case of public enterprise reform are, to the best of our knowledge, rare.

We focus on the attempt to reform, not on the success or failure of such attempts. We deal with the latter issue in Campos and Esfahani (1995). Our concept of reform attempt includes actions by the government, such as privatization, commercialization, and so on, to enhance efficiency through changes in the incentives facing public enterprise managers. To qualify as a reform attempt, these changes must affect more than just a few small public enterprises. Section I of this article describes our analytical framework; section II analyzes the influence that economic downturns and a country's economic structure and trade orientation have on public enterprise reform; and section III concludes. Our choice of variables is explained in the appendix.

I. The Analytical Framework

That political leaders strive to remain in power is a basic fact of politics. In industrial democracies as well as in strong-arm dictatorships, politicians constantly seek to keep their power. In the United States in particular, incumbents use their position to increase their chances of being reelected (Erikson 1971; Mayhew 1975), and, as a consequence, reelection rates have increased tremen-

1. Galal and others (1994) extensively document the gains from selling public enterprises. Although their work covers only privatization, it suggests that, in many circumstances, public enterprise reform can yield substantial gains.

dously over time (Fiorina 1989). In many developing economies, political leaders have all employed various means to stay in power; see, for example, the Kuomintang in Taiwan (China) (Amsden 1979; Wade 1990), the military regimes in the Republic of Korea (Amsden 1989; Haggard 1990), the post-independence governments in Zambia and Ghana (Bates 1981; Bates and Krueger 1993), and the populist and conservative parties in Argentina (O'Donnell 1978). It is therefore reasonable to assume that the dominant political objective of any regime is to remain in power and that a regime formulates policies and strategies around this objective.

Retaining power requires establishing sufficient political support from the polity. Without such support governments fall, coalitions collapse, dictators are deposed, parties are defeated, and presidents are unseated. Political support is obtained in part through quid pro quo arrangements—income transfers exchanged for support, such as votes or campaign funds. Governments "sign" social contracts with various socioeconomic groups. For example, in industrial countries, regulation is often used to direct transfers to politically influential groups. Farmers in Canada, Japan, the United States, and Western European countries have long benefited from regulations that raise their incomes above what they would be under free market conditions (Gardner 1981; Rausser 1982; Michelmann, Stabler, and Storey 1990). In developing countries, protection of domestic oligopolistic industries from import competition has been extensive (Little, Scitovsky, and Scott 1970). More generally, empirical work has shown that government intervention has often been used for redistribution (Stigler 1971; Anderson and Tollison 1984; Rowley, Tollison, and Tullock 1988; Michelmann, Stabler, and Storey 1990; Krueger 1974; Bates 1981; Bardhan 1984; Ake and Mohammed 1986). And theoretical work has shown this to be a logical outcome of a "tenure-maximizing" regime—one that stays in power for as long as possible (Brock and Magee 1978; Becker 1983; Findlay and Wellisz 1984). Government interventions cannot be divorced from issues of redistribution, because it is partly through redistribution that a regime sustains itself.

Redistribution in this context does not necessarily mean a transfer of wealth from rich to poor—in the real world of politics it often means transfers from the less influential to the more influential. The more influential groups are typically better organized and thus more capable of providing support for, or withdrawing support from, the incumbent regime (Olson 1965). Such groups might be firms in large, highly concentrated industries; labor unions; urban groups; the military; ethnic groups; landlords; or even individuals capable of influencing less organized groups. In addition, the threat of participation in spontaneous riots and revolutions could help channel benefits to unorganized groups as well. The large consumption subsidies in the form of cheap staples maintained in many countries may reflect such concerns. Whatever the case, regimes must pay close attention to the demands of at least a subset of interest groups, and more often than not, these demands include some form of transfer.

Several implications for public enterprise reform follow from this framework. Redistribution can be accomplished directly or indirectly. Regulation is an indirect instrument for redistribution; the operation and control of public enterprises is a more direct instrument. Public enterprises are a convenient vehicle through which regime leaders can redistribute wealth. State ownership and control over employment, wages, input purchases, and so on give the regime easier access to resources with which to reward supporters and punish detractors. Thus, although these enterprises may genuinely address some market failure or social objective, they are temptations for a regime, which can use them to build and maintain political support. They are particularly tempting to regimes in developing countries, where political institutions are much less developed—mechanisms for establishing and enhancing accountability, transparency, and competition take generations to mature. We would thus expect these enterprises to be used to promote politically motivated redistributive arrangements, as Campos and Esfahani (1994) prove with evidence from a wide range of countries indicating the extensive use of public enterprises for politically motivated redistribution.

Given the importance of public enterprises in securing political support, regimes would likely resist reform. But when rent redistribution and centralized control significantly distort production incentives and cause large efficiency losses, political leaders may search for ways of exploiting the gains from increased market orientation to buy further support from their existing or potential constituency. The larger the expected efficiency gains are, relative to the political and economic costs involved in providing alternative means of rent allocation or changing the existing allocation, the more attractive the reform option is.

Expected efficiency gains depend on two factors: the extent of inefficiency and the extent of the reform's credibility (that is, the likelihood that the reform measures will be sustained in the future). The costs of redistribution, on the other hand, depend on the volume of redistribution and the information imperfections regarding the distribution of gains and losses across interest groups. Information asymmetry, in particular, increases the costs of policy renegotiations, because it can give rise to a war of attrition in which each interest group delays reform by refusing to concede, claiming that its gains from reform are small—and thus that the reform costs must be shifted toward other groups (Alesina and Drazen 1991).

The costs of public enterprise reform are likely to be commensurate with the amount of rent that is redistributed through public enterprises. The reason is that at the time such rents come into existence, the recipients either attempt to erect political and legal means to protect those rents or condition future political support on implicit or explicit guarantees of continued rent flow. This point has long been made in the literature on rent seeking (see, for example, Krueger 1974) and is to some extent inherent in any arrangement for creating incentives (whether for production or for political support). Incentives do not take effect without some institutional mechanism ensuring that the arrangement is difficult to change unilaterally and, therefore, promises of future rewards are likely to be honored. The costs that such rent and incentive-protection mechanisms impose on policy change can be exacerbated by informational problems. These provide an additional explanation for the persistence of inefficient policies and can also help explain why reform of public enterprise policies often takes the form of abrupt change rather than gradual adjustment to new information and unfolding events. Renegotiation costs are likely to be fixed, and every time the government modifies its policies, the agenda for redistributing rents opens up. Then the regime has to deal with rent-protection mechanisms.

Innumerable variables may influence the size of potential efficiency gains, rents, reform credibility, and informational imperfections. Shifts in these underlying variables alter the economic and political calculus of policy change and may trigger reform. Later we focus on a number of important variables that can be measured more easily and can be used to predict a given country's readiness for reform. Naturally, this procedure leaves out many other important but less quantifiable variables. In particular, many of the variables that influence a reform program's credibility are difficult to document and analyze. Other sets of relevant but hard-to-measure variables are the structure of rent distribution through public enterprises, the nature of beneficiary and loser groups, and the structure of the country's politics. For example, the costs of reforming a public enterprise are likely to differ if the public enterprise is used for passing on rents to consumers rather than to input suppliers. Similarly, the political influence of the recipient groups with respect to others and their ability to claim part of the gains from reform are also relevant factors. Given the limited scope of available data, we have little choice but to rely heavily on key aggregate variables that can be more easily documented.

In the case of credibility we assume that past actions of the government and the consequences of those actions can serve as the main variables. Specifically, we use the degree of outward orientation of the economy as a measure of commitment to liberal economic policies. However, institutional structures that make policy change difficult also lend credibility to reform policies, unless the policies are inherently unsustainable. We do not incorporate institutional structures in our present analysis, mainly because we do not have a comparable measure of the cost of such policy change across countries. But we do not see this as a major bias in our results, because the same barriers also add to the costs of adopting the reform, although institutional barriers to policy change increase the probability that the gains from a reform will be realized. In this sense the net impact of institutional structure on reform attempts may be small, although, as we show in Campos and Esfahani (1995), the impact on the success of reforms, once the reforms have been adopted, is significant.

In the following pages we focus on a limited number of variables and argue why these variables are important for public enterprise reform and what theoretical influences they might have on the reform decision. Since our arguments are mostly heuristic, the readers may disagree with some of the theoretical links we establish. When the readers do disagree, they may simply view our empirical work as an attempt to identify a number of important predictors of public enterprise reform (see the appendix).

Because many variables are involved in the economic and political calculus of reform, no single variable can be pinpointed as the sole cause. Each variable influences only the probability of the initiation of reform, given other variables. For example, although we identify economic downturns as a catalyst for reform, they are neither necessary nor sufficient for reform. If other underlying variables raise the expected efficiency gains relative to the costs of redistribution sufficiently, a reform could materialize, absent an economic downturn. Likewise, a downturn may not necessarily induce a reform attempt if other conditions are not met.

Economic Downturns

The literature on macroeconomic and trade reform recognizes the relationship between economic crises and policy change.[2] (For recent discussions of the relationship between economic crises and macroeconomic and trade reform, see Rodrik 1994, Alesina 1994, and Drazen and Grilli 1993.) Our framework suggests that this relationship may also apply to public enterprise reform. To be sure, there may be a trivial relationship between economic downturn and privatization if economic crises cause extensive failure in the private sector and the government is forced to adopt and rehabilitate them. In such cases, privatization may simply reflect returning the economy to its long-term growth path. Such episodes are relatively rare, however. The more common case of reform, which we discuss in more detail in the next section, involves changing the incentives for firms that have long operated as public enterprises. We also argue that macroeconomic downturns are the forms of economic crisis most likely to lead to public enterprise reform.

In our analysis we ignore the possibility that sectoral- or industry-level crises may also trigger reform for three reasons. First, in developing countries, public enterprises are present in many sectors, and substantial reforms in the public enterprise system often require relatively widespread adverse shocks. (In our definition of "reform attempt" in section II, we exclude cases in which policy changes have been minor or have affected an insignificant portion of the public enterprise system.) Second, when crises are limited to a sector or an industry, the government can use resources from public enterprises in other parts of the economy to mitigate the consequences for groups that support the government. This possibility curtails the impetus for reform, compared with situations in which the shrinkage of resources is more widespread. Third, significant sectoral-

2. Political crises are also sometimes mentioned as factors behind reform attempts. Our contracting framework suggests that, if anything, political crises should delay reform because they shorten the regime's horizon and reduce the survival probability of any reform program. But testing these hypotheses is not easy, because it is difficult to identify episodes of political downturn. Our experiments with a few indicators were inconclusive.

and industry-level crises are likely to be reflected in macroeconomic performance.

Why should we expect a strong adverse economic shock to induce a regime to reform public enterprises? Given a regime's desire to maintain power, a regime should not wait to act until things deteriorate badly. One explanation lies in the impact that shocks have on both the potential gains from costs of reforms and redistribution of these costs. The explanation that follows is along the lines argued by Rodrik (1994). In the context of trade reform he argues that, for every dollar of efficiency gain, some amount of income is effectively transferred from those that were beneficiaries under the status quo to other groups. During a downturn, this amount is much smaller. This, suggests Rodrik, explains why trade reform is politically so difficult in normal times and why times of downturn provide an opportune moment for undertaking structural reforms. Similarly, Drazen and Grilli (1993) argue that, in the context of Alesina and Drazen's (1991) war-of-attrition model, reform is accepted sooner if an economic downturn increases the costs of the status quo relative to the postreform situation. However, they go further and demonstrate theoretically that introducing distortionary policies to induce a downturn may be welfare enhancing for economies caught in a low-level political equilibrium. Bradburd (1993) and Waterbury (1993) make somewhat different arguments. Bradburd's argument is based on asset specificity. He argues that groups will continue to block efforts to change the existing arrangements only if the assets whose values depend heavily on the continuance of these arrangements fall below lobbying costs. Waterbury maintains that a free-rider problem keeps groups from opposing reforms during a downturn. Maintaining the status quo is a public good for those groups who benefit from it. During a downturn, the benefits to each group shrink, and thus no single group has the incentive to absorb the cost of lobbying. Each group would rather concentrate on striking individual deals with the regime in order to cut its losses. The result is that none of the beneficiary groups do anything to preclude reforms.

As we have argued above, the costs of renegotiating the implicit or explicit contracts that are part of the existing public enterprise policy impede attempts to remove inefficiencies. But movements in the underlying determinants of costs and benefits can tip the balance and trigger reform. Adverse shocks to domestic production can play such a role, because they tend to reduce the rents available through public enterprises, and thus diminish the amount of redistribution required to achieve market-oriented reform. For example, when public enterprise production falls because of a shortage of imports, the government will have fewer resources available to transfer to public enterprise workers or customers. Thus lower amounts of rent will be taken away from the beneficiaries when the reform takes effect: the current beneficiaries will lose less.

The potential gains from reform, however, are unlikely to decline and may increase when the economy experiences a long-term adverse shock. The reason is that, in the absence of market orientation, public enterprises respond sluggishly to shocks. As a result, sectors dominated by public enterprises will be much slower to rebound, making it more difficult for resources to flow toward their optimal uses and for growth to resume. There is an issue regarding the potential gain from the privatization of a specific firm: a negative demand shock may in fact reduce the gain. But for a large-scale reform in developing countries, this effect is unlikely to arise. In contrast to the situation in industrial economies, where demand shocks are generally caused by a fall in consumption or investment demand, in developing countries such shocks are more often caused by the government. The government is typically predisposed to overspending, so that weak aggregate demand (without prior runaway inflation) is rarely a problem: generally the government constricts demand in order to control inflation. Part of this intervention includes reducing the deficits of public enterprises, which in turn induces a fall in the rents that are distributed through public enterprises. This drop reduces the opportunity cost of the beneficiaries of those rents and thus the potential opposition to large-scale public enterprise reforms. Instituting reforms then creates the potential for efficiency gains, since privatized public enterprises will have more flexibility (than traditional, bureaucratically controlled public enterprises) for exploiting new possibilities once demand returns to normal.

Regimes may also delay reform until an economic downturn occurs because of underlying uncertainties about the distribution of gains and losses. Before economic conditions deteriorate, interest groups are likely to be uncertain about who will lose if no action is taken to prevent economic decline. They are also likely to be uncertain about which policy would prevail once attempts to dismantle the status quo begin and about what the outcome of a given reform program would be. Such uncertainties can discourage political actors from attempting to initiate reform, because expected costs may outweigh gains for decisive groups (Howitt and Wintrobe 1995; Fernandez and Rodrik 1991). But once a downturn occurs, part of this uncertainty will be resolved, because certain groups will find themselves on the losing side. Although the uncertainty about the outcome of various reform options may remain, the implicit social contracts become easier to renegotiate. In short, an economic downturn raises the ratio of potential gains to redistribution costs and thus encourages reform. We posit that *economic downturns create conditions that make regimes more likely to introduce public enterprise reforms.*

A related explanation is that even if the government does foresee the crisis, it may not have the political support to launch a reform, since the general population may not recognize the onslaught of a crisis. Only when the crisis materializes does the general population come to recognize it, and only then will the population be willing to take sides.[3]

But a downturn is not always sufficient to jerk a political regime into action. Many countries have experienced major downturns, and their governments did

3. We are grateful to one of the referees for pointing this out.

not attempt to introduce public enterprise reforms; nor is it necessary—countries have embarked on reforms even when no shock had occurred. Other factors influence the likelihood that a regime will undertake a reform.

The Structure of the Economy

Potential net benefits of public enterprise reform will likely depend on the activities undertaken in the economy and on how they are divided between the public and private sectors. Because countries with a variety of structures undertake reform, the relationship cannot be a simple one; it needs to be dissected so that it can be specified and measured. In particular, as we argue later, the share of the public sector in the economy has two opposite effects on the probability of reform: a positive effect that arises from the inefficiencies of public enterprises and a negative effect that depends on the complexity of the economy, as reflected by the range of production activities and the linkages among them.

The degree of inefficiency caused by the incentives imposed on the public sector is difficult to measure, though we do know that inefficiencies depend on the type of production. Some activities allow the government to redistribute a great deal of rent at low inefficiency cost, while redistribution through other channels may entail significant production disincentives. For example, in the context of countries that lack the capacity to regulate (owing perhaps to institutional weaknesses), public enterprises may not perform much worse than private enterprises in sectors in which sunk costs are large and the quality of the product is relatively easy to assess. In these countries, however, public enterprises can be highly inefficient in the provision of products that are sensitive to quality (for example, fashion clothing or fresh vegetables and other perishable goods). In these activities, market failure is less likely to occur and, even if it does, it is likely to be of much smaller magnitude. Certainly, government ownership cannot improve performance in markets in which producers must be responsive to the demand for detailed characteristics. As a result, effecting the same redistribution through public ownership in these types of activities is much more costly than in activities in which quality is easily determined. Indeed, in developing countries public ownership has been and remains common in public utilities and heavy industry, but is quite uncommon in fashion clothing and fresh vegetable production. Public ownership of some lines of retail trade was given up even in orthodox, centrally planned economies.

The implicit ranking of economic activities in terms of their efficiency loss per unit of redistribution under public ownership implies that, as the range of activities covered by public enterprises increases, the marginal efficiency gain from reform should increase relative to the costs of redistribution necessary to achieve those efficiency gains (for evidence, see World Bank 1994a). Thus, all things being equal, the net benefits of reform should increase with the relative size of the public sector in the economy.

On the negative side, a larger public sector implies greater renegotiation costs because more information is needed to design and implement the reform, but less information is available because of curtailed competition. Informational imperfections tend to be smaller when most economic activity is carried out in the private sector, because information about the performance of individual public enterprises and the size and distribution of gains from reform are more readily available when public enterprises interact with private firms as suppliers or competitors. For example, competition from private firms can reveal which manufacturing public enterprises are the worst performers. Or, demands of private firms can expose which public enterprises are the worst providers. This information, in turn, indicates which public enterprises are more likely to be targeted for reform. Such factors help all those affected by reform to better understand what the outcome of reform might be, which groups will gain, and which groups might have to bear most of the burden. Hence interest groups would have less incentive to engage in what Alesina and Drazen (1991) call a "war of attrition." Reformers would also be in a better position to devise more effective incentive and redistribution schemes and thus attract wider support for policy change. In contrast, the wider the range of activities dominated by public enterprises, the greater will be the informational burden of a reform program, and the more costly it will be to undertake a reform.

We can empirically distinguish the two effects, because the negative effect depends on the complexity of the economy, but the positive effect does not. Complexity reflects the underlying informational characteristics of an economy: the more interlinkages there are between different sectors in the economy, the more difficult it is to extract information. As the degree of complexity (set of informational attributes) rises, an increase in the size of the public enterprise sector imposes a higher cost of retrieving the information needed to design a reform program. Therefore, juxtaposing the size of the public sector with a measure of complexity should isolate this effect from other effects of public sector size on the net gains from public enterprise reform.

The complexity of the economy itself has an independent effect. When the activities in the economy are highly interlinked, inefficiency in one part can strongly propagate to other parts. In contrast, when large parts of the economy use few inputs from the rest of the economy, inefficiency in the rest of the economy has a limited impact on the economy as a whole. As a result, the efficiency gain from (and the demand for) reform in a given part of the economy increases as the other parts of the economy become less self-contained. (For a discussion of the concept of self-containment and its application to the role of institutions in determining a country's comparative advantage in international trade, see Clague 1991.)

A variable that is easy to measure and captures the above notion of complexity is the relative size of the nonagricultural sector of the economy. This variable reflects the decline of traditional activities—especially those in agriculture—which are more self-contained, and the rise of specialized activities—especially those in industry and services—which depend on inputs from the rest of the economy. Using this measure of complexity, we can summarize the results of the above arguments as follows: *All things being equal, the probability of public enterprise reform is negatively related to the size of the interaction between the public sector and the nonagricultural sector of the economy, but each of these two variables has a positive residual effect on that probability.*

The structural characteristics of the economy may also influence the probability of reform through their impact on credibility. To the extent that these variables increase the potential gains from market orientation, they make reversals more costly and increase the probability of adherence to the new policies. In addition, the government's success in developing nonagricultural sectors under private ownership can indicate the regime's commitment to market-oriented policies and lend credibility to its public enterprise reform program. But all of these effects tend to reinforce the relationships delineated above and are difficult to distinguish from them.

Trade Orientation

Outward orientation of a government's economic policy and a government's involvement in international free trade agreements are important indicators of a regime's commitment to market-oriented policies. Thus a public enterprise reform proposed by such a government is more likely to be perceived as a credible extension of previous actions. But in addition, outward orientation influences the efficiency gain-redistribution cost ratio of public enterprise reform and thus at the margin may induce regimes to undertake public enterprise reform. To see this, although many producers and consumers may receive rents from public enterprises, their inefficiencies ultimately increase the cost of production for the economy as a whole. In inward-oriented economies, final demand is relatively inelastic, and higher costs can be largely passed on to consumers. As a result, the benefits of public enterprise reform are diffuse and difficult to assess. In contrast, in outward-oriented economies a large proportion of producers face relatively elastic demands, and domestic inefficiencies affect their level of competitiveness in world markets. These producers can directly gain from increased public enterprise efficiency through cheaper domestic inputs and, to the extent that this effect is mitigated by real exchange-rate appreciation, they can indirectly benefit from cheaper imported capital and intermediate inputs. Therefore, in outward-oriented economies, enterprise reforms produce more visible gains. For this reason we expect that, *given other factors, the probability of public enterprise reform increases with the increased outward orientation of the economy*. This hypothesis also implies that a successful trade reform can induce a public enterprise reform by making the potential gains visible and creating a clear group of beneficiaries.

II. The Influence of Economic Downturns, Economic Structure, and Trade Orientation

As we show in this section, most attempts at public enterprise reform follow an economic downturn, but the likelihood that a reform is undertaken after a given downturn depends on a country's economic structure and trade orientation. We begin by specifying our indicators for a reform attempt and economic downturn and showing that they are correlated. We then develop a probit model of the reform decision. The model tests whether each of the variables specified earlier has the predicted influence on the probability that a regime will attempt a reform. We end the section with the presentation and discussion of the statistical results.

Our data are based on the experience of a diversified group of fifteen developing countries: Argentina, Chile, Egypt, Ghana, India, Indonesia, the Republic of Korea, Malaysia, Mexico, Nigeria, Pakistan, the Philippines, Senegal, Turkey, and Venezuela. We restrict our analysis to the period from 1972 to 1993 in order to control for the effect of the international environment. The emphasis on private sector-led development in developing countries grew stronger in the 1970s, and, in particular, international lending institutions began to emphasize such policies later that decade. To ensure greater homogeneity in this respect and test the sensitivity of our findings to the selected sample, we also experimented with a smaller sample based on the period from 1978 to 1993. This switch did not significantly change the results.

Downturns and Reform Attempts

By "reform attempt" we mean a proclamation of new policies and guidelines to enhance market incentives of public enterprises, followed by an initiation of some of the proposed policy changes (for example, changes in prices, regulation, layoffs, divestiture, and opening of public enterprise markets). Therefore, changes such as the sale of minority shares in a few public enterprises to raise revenue, or reorganizations of the public sector that shift the responsibility of public enterprises from one government organization to another without giving the enterprises stronger incentives to improve efficiency, do not qualify as reform episodes. Further, it is not enough for policy changes to be announced or to be embodied in new laws and regulations. The proclamation must be followed immediately by the implementation of one or more of the proposed changes.

Of course, there is an element of judgment in labeling some policy changes, especially those in which the scope of change is limited, formal measures are weakened by informal countermeasures, or implementation is marginal and gradual. But as noted later, our results do not appear to be sensitive to possible judgment errors. In general, public enterprise reforms are embodied in the larger context of macroeconomic reforms and are often preceded by such reforms. To assess the sensitivity of our assessment and dating of reform attempts, we also made an alternative count of reform attempts in which we identified a policy change as a reform regardless of whether it was a macroeconomic, trade, or public enterprise reform (or any combination). This indicator is expected to capture public enterprise reforms that start with a macroeconomic or trade reform, which may or may not materialize (see appendix figure A-1 and table 1). In contrast with the public enterprise indicator, which may undercount public

Table 1. *Public Enterprise Macroeconomic Reform Variables and Conditions in Sample Countries*

Country	Years	Public enterprise macroeconomic reform (y_i)	Magnitude of downturn (MD)	Ratio of public to total investment (RPI)[a]	Share of nonagriculture in GDP (SNA)[a]	Interaction term (RPIxSNA)	Trade orientation (TO)[b]	GDP per capita (thousands of 1987 U.S. dollars) (GDPPC)
Downturn episodes								
Argentina	1975–76	0	-4.58	0.3762	0.9195	0.3459	0	3.648
	1978	0	-5.33	0.3958	0.9181	0.3634	0	3.747
	1981–82	0	-12.09	0.3914	0.9184	0.3595	1	3.782
	1985	0	-7.97	0.2460	0.9129	0.2246	1	3.604
	1988–90	1	-11.65	0.2698	0.9132	0.2464	2	3.455
Chile	1972–73	1	-9.11	0.4865	0.9218	0.4485	1	1.447
	1975	1	-13.18	0.6214	0.9259	0.5754	2	1.420
	1982–83	1	-17.51	0.3226	0.9183	0.2962	2	1.477
Egypt	1992	1	-1.77	0.6030	0.7987	0.4816	1	0.739
Ghana	1972	0	-5.94	0.4576	0.4611	0.2110	0	0.523
	1975–76	0	-21.04	0.5645	0.4490	0.2535	0	0.514
	1979–83	1	-28.01	0.7742	0.4795	0.3712	0	0.453
India	1971–72	0	-3.61	0.3820	0.5561	0.2124	0	0.245
	1974	0	-1.09	0.4180	0.5731	0.2396	0	0.241
	1976	0	-0.61	0.4208	0.5804	0.2442	1	0.241
	1979	0	-7.60	0.4338	0.5946	0.2579	2	0.255
	1991	1	-0.70	0.4560	0.6801	0.3101	2	0.342
Indonesia	1982	0	-2.24	0.4350	0.7309	0.3179	2	0.345
Korea, Rep. of	1980	0	-4.87	0.2186	0.7856	0.1717	3	1.660
Malaysia	1975	0	-1.57	0.3146	0.7061	0.2221	3	1.116
	1985–86	1	-5.31	0.4606	0.7818	0.3601	3	1.812
Mexico	1982–83	1	-9.34	0.4240	0.9110	0.3863	3	1.833
	1986	1	-5.79	0.3984	0.9155	0.3647	3	1.948
	1988	1	-0.47	0.3456	0.9133	0.3156	3	1.860
Nigeria	1972	0	-1.81	0.3330	0.4996	0.1664	0	0.376
	1975	0	-6.13	0.4680	0.5346	0.2502	0	0.394

	1978	0	-8.75	0.6168	0.5961	0.3677	0	0.425
	1981–84	0	-33.70	0.6726	0.6510	0.4379	0	0.427
	1986–87	1	-4.51	0.7320	0.6779	0.4962	0	0.337
Pakistan	1971–72	0	-5.20	0.4950	0.6301	0.3119	2	0.223
	1993	1	-0.10	0.4870	0.7446	0.3626	3	0.354
Philippines	1983–85	1	-20.29	0.3048	0.7675	0.2339	2	0.671
	1991–92	1	-5.27	0.1792	0.7677	0.1376	2	0.600
Senegal	1971	0	-1.51	0.5524	0.7169	0.3960	0	0.723
	1973	0	-8.25	0.4554	0.7369	0.3356	0	0.723
	1977–78	0	-13.16	0.4943	0.7264	0.3591	0	0.710
	1980–81	0	-9.38	0.5087	0.7343	0.3735	0	0.708
	1983–84	1	-7.79	0.3708	0.7720	0.2863	1	0.673
	1989	0	-3.47	0.3284	0.7859	0.2581	2	0.674
	1991	0	-1.77	0.3222	0.7840	0.2526	1	0.679
Turkey	1979–80	1	-6.09	0.4622	0.7941	0.3670	1	1.040
	1989	0	-0.54	0.5410	0.8135	0.4401	2	1.226
	1991	1	-0.09	0.4938	0.8221	0.4060	2	1.306
Venezuela	1971–72	0	-4.25	0.2390	0.9500	0.2271	0	3.297
	1974–75	0	-2.46	0.3236	0.9509	0.3077	0	3.240
	1978–85	0	-29.18	0.3660	0.9516	0.3483	1	3.282
	1989	1	-11.34	0.4164	0.9404	0.3916	1	2.648
Reform episodes without downturn								
Indonesia	1986	1	0	0.4648	0.7470	0.3472	3	0.397
Korea, Rep. of	1984	1	0	0.2436	0.8391	0.2044	3	1.996
Malaysia	1991	1	0	0.3882	0.7937	0.3081	3	2.059
Pakistan	1977	1	0	0.5970	0.6615	0.3949	2	0.220
	1990	1	0	0.5274	0.7374	0.3889	3	0.327

a. Values represent the five-year average.
b. Values follow Dollar's (1992) index which assigns a ranking of 0 through 3 to each observation, with 0 indicating the most inward-oriented set of policies and 3 the most outward-oriented set.

Source: Values for the reform variable (y_i) are based on the authors' evaluations from a variety of sources, including country economic reports of the World Bank, Sundaran (1993), Bates and Krueger (1993), Bruton (1992), Gyimah-Boadi (1993), Means (1991), Haggard and Webb (1994), Waterbury (1993), and Williamson (1994). Values for the other variables come from the World Bank data base.

enterprise reforms and responses, the public enterprise-macroeconomic indicator tends to overcount them. The results we report in the text are not very sensitive to the measure employed.

We define "economic downturns" as declines in real gross domestic product (GDP) per capita, and we refer to the consecutive years in which per capita GDP growth is negative as a "downturn episode." This is of course one of many countless concrete definitions we can give to economic downturn. For example, a certain level of decline in the growth rate might be considered a downturn. Alternatively, we could define a threshold for each country's growth rate below which the country would be in a downturn. Or, we could establish a threshold for an increase in the rate of inflation. Our basic rationale for choosing negative per capita GDP growth is that it reflects a shrinkage in resources available to maintain the political-economic system. By running a deficit, the government can temporarily forestall a fall in GDP. But if it tries to do this indefinitely without correcting structural imbalances, the economy will eventually collapse. Our measure of downturn captures these types of situations—those that embody severe economic deterioration. It also captures the costly aspects of other variables commonly used for indicating economic crises, such as accelerating inflation and trade and budget deficits. Another advantage of this measure is that it is independent of a country's level of development.

To examine the link between economic downturns and reform attempts, we first identified all reform attempts and downturn episodes for fifteen developing countries from 1972 to 1991. We plotted per capita GDP growth rates over time for the fifteen countries and identified the downturn episodes. For example, the years 1982 and 1983 represent a downturn episode for Chile (figure 1). Having identified and listed all episodes, we then determined whether each reform attempt could be classified as a response to a downturn. For a reform attempt to qualify as a response to a downturn, we imposed the condition that it had to occur reasonably close to the beginning of a downturn. More specifically, the declaration of the attempt and at least preliminary actions had to have taken place either during a downturn period or within a year from the end of the downturn period.

Examples of downturns and reforms identified in Malaysia and Ghana demonstrate how we identified reform attempts and classified them as responses or nonresponses to downturns.[4] The examples also show the difficulties inherent in deciding which incidents constitute separate reform episodes and whether they are responses to particular downturns.

MALAYSIA. During the 1970s and early 1980s Malaysia's public enterprise sector grew rapidly under the New Economic Policy, which had been adopted in 1970 to expand the wealth and earning opportunities of the country's politically dominant but economically weak Bumiputra population. The number of public

4. Basic information about the other countries in our sample is available from the authors upon request. It can be examined in greater detail to assess the appropriateness of labels assigned to the episodes.

Figure 1. *Growth Rate of Gross Domestic Product per Capita, Chile, 1971–92*

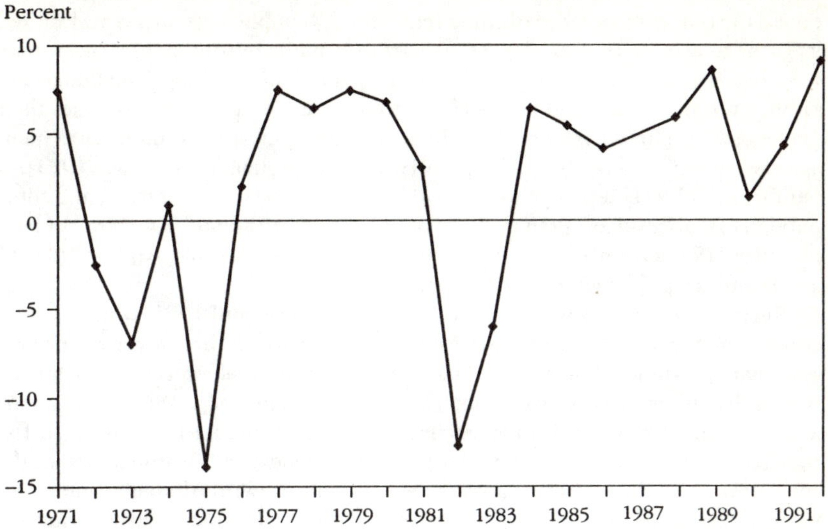

Source: World Bank (1994b).

enterprises grew from 109 in 1970 to 1,014 in 1985. Government investment in them grew from 32 percent of the development budget during the period from 1966 to 1970 to 56 percent during the period from 1981 to 1985. Meanwhile, the Malaysian economy was growing rapidly, except for 1975 and 1985–86, when the per capita growth rate turned negative. These downturn periods were associated with declines in the terms of trade that reduced export earnings and government revenues. The first downturn came when the public enterprise sector was still relatively small. At the time, the New Economic Policy relied mostly on imposing weak employment and ownership quotas on private firms to achieve its objectives. Shortly after the downturn the government tried to strengthen the quota enforcement, but backed off when the business community objected to the pressures. Instead, the government decided to rely more on the expansion of public enterprises to further the goals of the New Economic Policy (Bowie 1991). In our data set we counted this incidence as an episode of downturn without reform.

After 1976 the government quickened the pace of establishing companies in which the Bumiputra were given privileged positions as workers, managers, and institutional or individual equity owners. When the costs of this strategy began to mount in the early 1980s, the controversies about the role of public enterprises grew stronger. But no action was taken until 1985–86, when a terms-of-trade shock combined with the growing inefficiency of the public enterprises gave rise to another economic downturn. In 1986 the government largely abandoned the objective of redistributing rents through public enterprises and shifted its focus to growth (Bruton 1992). As part of a major reform, public enterprises were made more autonomous by decentralizing decisionmaking. The budgets of public enterprises that did not perform well were cut, and in many cases their managers were fired (Means 1991). In many major enterprises, Bumiputra managers were replaced by domestic minority or foreign managers (Bowie 1991). A number of public enterprises were placed under management contract, and some public enterprises were prepared for privatization, although few were actually privatized (Sundaram 1993). We qualified this as a downturn episode that led to an attempt at public enterprise reform.

The post-1986 policy process followed a steady pace until 1991, when the government announced a Privatization Masterplan along with three other major programmatic documents outlining Malaysian economic development policy for the foreseeable future. Soon privatization gained momentum, and within two years the market value of privatized firms reached 29 percent of Kuala Lumpur Stock Exchange capitalization (Sundaram 1993). The new policy was instituted even as the country continued to experience vigorous economic growth. Although from 1986 to 1991 many steps were undertaken to prepare the ground for increased privatization, the Masterplan reflected a major shift in Malaysia's economic policy to remove government ownership as a means of directing the economy. We counted this episode as a case of reform attempt without downturn.

Finally, it should be noted that the expansion of the public enterprise sector and later reforms in Malaysia were carried out under very stable political conditions. The same party has been in power since independence, and since 1970 the premiership has changed hands only twice, in 1976 and in 1981, with the deputy prime minister moving to the position of power in both cases.

GHANA. During the late 1960s and early 1970s the Ghanaian government limited public ownership to approximately fifty public enterprises that had been formed during the 1950s and early 1960s. In 1972 the economy experienced a major decline following a terms-of-trade shock and a military coup. The junta shifted the government's policy toward rapid expansion of the public enterprise sector. Even when another terms-of-trade shock precipitated a 15 percent decline in per capita GDP in 1975 and an additional 5 percent decline in 1976, the government continued to extend the role of public enterprises and follow other expansionary policies (Gyimah-Boadi 1993). We classified both incidents as downturns without reform.

In the second half of the 1970s, extensive rent extraction and redistribution by the government seriously damaged the Ghanaian economy such that even the sources of rent dried up (Leith and Lofchie 1993). The economy was so weak that it could not deal with the decline in the secular terms of trade, which began in 1978—per capita GDP fell precipitously from1979 to 1983. In 1979 a coup by junior military officers, led by Jerry Rawlings, helped transfer power to an elected civilian government. But neither the coup makers nor the civilian government did much to reform public enterprises except for mounting an anticorruption campaign and shuffling some public enterprises from one supervisory organization to another (Gyimah-Boadi 1993). This approach also persisted for about a year after Rawlings regained power with a second coup in December 1981. But as exports and government revenues continued to fall precipitously, political leaders began to shift their position in favor of market-oriented policies.

In 1983 the government adopted an Economic Recovery Program to rehabilitate the economy through extensive liberalization, which consisted of macroeconomic, trade, and public expenditure reforms. After an initial emphasis on stabilization and trade liberalization, the government attended to the problems of the public sector. In 1984 public enterprises were allowed to raise their product prices, while hiring of new workers in the sector was frozen, and a job retrenchment plan was introduced. The government also ordered a study of 100 public enterprises that were to be prepared for privatization.

In 1985, performance contracts were set up for the managers in a number of public enterprises, and a task force was formed to compile a package of deeper public enterprise reforms. The program developed by the task force finally resulted in the advertisement of thirty-two public enterprises for sale in mid-1988. By 1993, eighty-six public enterprises had been or were being divested, thirty-two of which were cases of liquidation (World Bank 1993). Meanwhile the political situation has remained stable, and the economy has responded well to the reform measures, maintaining a positive growth rate (averaging 1.76 percent from 1984 to 1992) despite a continued terms-of-trade decline.

We considered the economic decline of the early 1980s and the policy changes in the mid-1980s to be an episode of downturn with a reform response. The reform was slow to materialize, and its implementation has been problematic; but there is little doubt that a reform attempt did begin around 1983–84. We could have counted the divestiture program in the second half of the 1980s as a separate reform attempt, but an examination of the history of Ghana's Economic Recovery Program suggested to us that divestiture was part of the original plan, each stage of which was carried out slowly.

Empirical Analysis

Examining all of the downturn episodes identified in the sample, we see that almost 80 percent of reform attempts (nineteen out of twenty-four) were preceded by economic downturns. Moreover, the five reforms that took place without downturns occurred in situations in which the country strongly met the structural and trade-orientation criteria for reform readiness (see table 1 and the following discussion). Therefore, although this evidence is limited to fifteen countries, it suggests that for most developing countries, economic downturn may be an almost necessary condition for public enterprise reform. But it is clear from figure 2 that downturns are by no means a sufficient condition: only

Figure 2. *Public Enterprise Reform Responses to Economic Crisis*

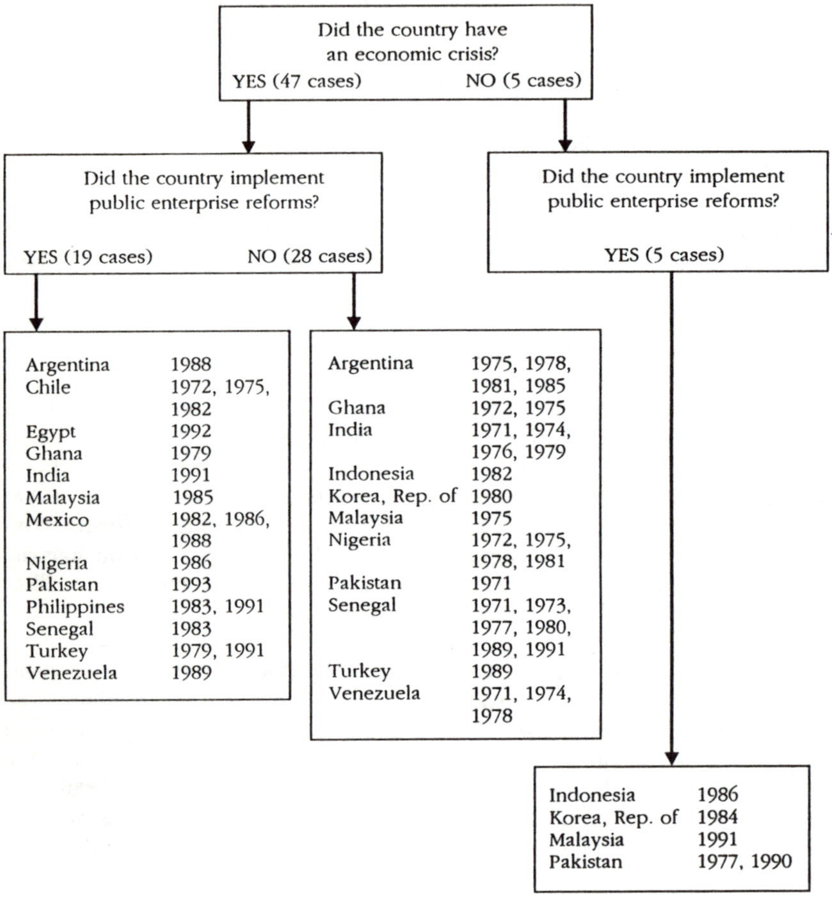

Source: World Bank data; Bruton (1992); Gyimah-Boadi (1993); Haggard and Webb (1994); Leith and Lofchie (1993); Means (1991); Sundaram (1993); Wade (1990); Waterbury (1993); Williamson (1994).

40 percent of downturns were followed by public enterprise reforms. Note that our observations do not change significantly if attention is restricted to the post-1978 period, when market-oriented policies gained wider acceptance: there were thirty-one downturn episodes, seventeen of which were associated with one of the twenty-one reform attempts (table 1).

Can characteristics of downturns or structural and trade orientation variables explain why some downturns led to attempts at reform but others did not? To answer this question, we undertake a probit analysis of reform attempts conditional on the occurrence of an economic downturn. To operationalize this analysis, we assign numbers (1 through 47) to the downturn episodes that we have identified and then define a dummy dependent variable, y_i:

$$y_i = 1, \text{ if downturn } i \text{ resulted in a reform attempt}$$
$$0, \text{ otherwise.}$$

We relate y_i to six variables listed in table 1. The first three right-hand-side variables (in the fourth, fifth, and sixth columns) reflect the role of the economy's structure: respectively, the five-year average ratio of public investment to total investment (*RPI*) prior to each downturn episode, the five-year average share of nonagricultural sectors in GDP (*SNA*) prior to each episode, and an interaction term between *RPI* and *SNA* (*RPI*×*SNA*). *We expect an increase in SNA or RPI to raise the likelihood that a regime will attempt a public enterprise reform and an increase in their interaction to reduce the likelihood.* That is, we expect positive coefficients for *RPI* and *SNA* but a negative coefficient for *RPI*×*SNA*.

The fourth explanatory variable (in the seventh column in table 1) is an index of the outward orientation of trade policy (*TO*) prior to each downturn episode. It is based on Dollar's (1992) cross-country real exchange rate comparisons. This index assigns a ranking of 0 through 3 to each observation, with 0 indicating the most inward-oriented set of policies and 3 the most outward-oriented set. Since Dollar provides only average ranking for the period from 1976 to 1985, we adjusted the ranking up or down over time according to changes in trade policy whenever a significant policy change could be detected. *We expect the coefficient of TO to be positive since outward orientation increases the likelihood of a reform attempt.*

The fifth variable (in the third column of table 1) is the magnitude of downturn (*MD*), which we define as the cumulative decline in GDP over the length of the downturn. For instance, suppose a country's per capita GDP falls by 5 percent in year *t*, then by 7 percent in year *t* + 1, and then 3 percent in year *t* + 2. The magnitude of this downturn would be 15 percent. To the extent that the decline in GDP per capita tends to reduce available rents for redistribution through public enterprises, this variable should measure the strength of incentives to initiate reform. Therefore, *we hypothesize that the probability that a regime will attempt a reform increases with the magnitude of the downturn.*

Finally, in the last column (table 1) we introduce the level of GDP per capita in constant 1987 U.S. dollars (*GDPPC*) to control for the level of development. This variable is an example of many country characteristics that may be correlated with the first five variables and may influence the reform decision in ways that cannot be determined a priori. We limited our experimentation with such variables to keep enough degrees of freedom for the probit model. As far as the impact of *GDPPC* on the probability of reform is concerned, higher GDP per capita can facilitate reform (because the general level of development may reflect institutional capacity and commitment capability) or render reform unnecessary (because the ability to produce a high income may indicate the country's success in reducing public enterprise inefficiencies).

The model that we test is the following:

$$y_i = 1 \text{ if } z_i + e_i > 0 \text{ and } y_i = 0 \text{ if } z_i + e_i \leq 0 \text{, where}$$

$$z_i = a_0 + a_1 SNA_i + a_2 RPI_i + a_3 RPI_i \times SNA_i + a_4 TO_i + a_5 GDPPC_i + a_6 MD_i + e_i$$

and e_i is a random term with a mean of zero. The function z_i is the reform-readiness function. Note that $\text{Prob}(y_i = 1) = \text{Prob}(z_i + e_i > 0)$, that is, the higher the value of z_i, the more reform ready country *i* is and, thus, the greater is the likelihood that country *i* will attempt a public enterprise reform when a downturn occurs.

Because there are repeated observations from each country, the e_i's cannot be assumed to be identically and independently distributed. But it is also difficult to disentangle the complex correlation matrix of this term for the sample. To examine the seriousness of this problem, we repeated the exercise with the sample of thirty-one episodes during the period from 1978 to 1993. Since this sample has fewer observations per country, a major difference in the estimates obtained from the two samples could be taken as an indication that the results are unreliable. We also experimented with a sample that excluded three episodes (Chile 1972–73, Chile 1982–83, and the Philippines 1983–85) in which the economic downturn was itself a partial cause of expansion in the number of enterprises under government ownership. In these cases privatization may be seen as a return to normal conditions, and the reform decision may have a different motivation than in other episodes. But the statistical results proved robust to these and similar changes in the sample (compare tables 2 and 3 with tables 4 and 5).

We also investigated the effects of defining our episodes somewhat differently. We divided the time period 1978–93 into two equal subperiods, 1978–85 and 1986–93. We selected all the subperiods in which a downturn occurred and formed our dependent variable, y_i, on the basis of whether the subperiod contained a public enterprise reform episode or not. For the downturn-reform episodes, we used the average over the five-year period preceding the beginning of the downturn for each of the independent variables. For the downturn with no reform episodes, we used the average for the subperiod. No fundamental changes resulted from this perturbation.

The frequency distribution of predicted, compared with actual, outcomes for the full and post-1978 samples is similar, suggesting that the estimates are not very sensitive to the correlation matrix of the error term (tables 2 and 3). The model has a decent fit since 85 percent of the outcomes can be predicted on the basis of the right-hand-side variables. Moreover, the coefficient estimates gen-

Table 2. *Probit Estimation Results for the Full and Post-1978 Samples*

Equation	*Constant*	*Ratio of public to total investment (RPI)*[a]	*Share of nonagriculture in GDP (SNA)*[a]	*Interaction term (RPIxSNA)*	*Trade orientation (TO)*[b]	*GDP per capita (thousands of 1987 U.S. dollars) (GDPPC)*	*Magnitude of downturn (MD)*	*Log-likelihood*
Full sample								
1	–42.026	56.777	51.674	–67.560	1.1084	–1.8361	1.1119	–15.28326
	(–2.589)	(2.327)	(2.466)	(–2.169)	(–2.386)	(2.617)	(0.322)	
2	–42.363	57.982	52.187	–69.041	1.0924	–1.8105		–15.33486
	(–2.641)	(2.426)	(2.522)	(–2.261)	(2.626)	(–2.394)		
3	–24.101	29.231	31.773	–35.185		–1.4649		–20.92167
	(–2.720)	(2.199)	(2.673)	(–2.013)		(–2.930)		
4	–14.282	19.640	13.207	–18.057	0.94625			–20.08399
	(–2.282)	(1.719)	(1.787)	(–1.238)	(3.194)			
Post-1978 sample								
5	–37.311	53.696	46.671	–65.271	0.85159	–1.4714	–1.226	–13.84862
	(–2.175)	(2.046)	(2.080)	(–1.925)	(1.960)	(–1.937)	(–0.313)	
6	–36.642	51.828	45.607	–62.744	0.89165	–1.4937		–13.89815
	(–2.143)	(2.023)	(2.047)	(–1.901)	(2.119)	(–1.948)		
7	–26.335	34.798	35.338	–43.914		–1.3694		–16.94097
	(–2.262)	(2.020)	(2.271)	(–1.930)		(–2.422)		
8	–11.757	18.430	11.202	–18.626	0.87505			–16.77872
	(–1.669)	(1.416)	(1.326)	(–1.103)	(2.520)			

Note: The dependent variable is the public enterprise reform dummy, y_i. *t*-ratios are in parentheses. The full sample (1972–93) has forty-seven observations, and the post-1978 sample (1978–93) has thirty-one observations.

a. Values represent the five-year average.

b. Values follow Dollar's (1992) index, which assigns a ranking of 0 through 3 to each observation, with 0 indicating the most inward-oriented set of policies and 3 the most outward-oriented set.

Source: Authors' calculations.

Table 3. *Frequencies of Actual and Predicted Outcomes for the Full and Post-1978 Samples*

	Full sample			*Post-1978 sample*		
	Predicted			*Predicted*		
Actual	*0*	*1*	*Total*	*0*	*1*	*Total*
0	25	3	28	11	3	14
1	5	14	19	4	13	17
Total	30	17	47	15	16	31

Note: Results are from equation 2 for the full sample and from equation 6 for the post-1978 sample (see table 2). The predicted outcome has maximum probability. The full sample (1972–93) has forty-seven observations, and the post-1978 sample (1978–93) has thirty-one observations.

Source: Authors' calculations.

erally have the expected signs and display high statistical significance. The predicted probabilities of reform (reported in the last column of table 6) also show that the model identifies reform-ready conditions with reasonable accuracy. The only unexpected result is the insignificant coefficient of *MD*. The reason for this may be that *MD* does not reflect the relevant characteristics of downturns, which are important in triggering reform. We made some attempts to examine this possibility by including in the model changes in the rate of inflation and budget and trade deficits during the downturns. But neither variable was significant. The negative coefficient of GDP per capita could not be predicted a priori. The finding suggests that higher-income countries are less likely to engage in public enterprise reform, either because there are more resources to be redistributed as rents or because there are fewer gains to be made from reform.

To test the robustness of our probit model, we tried to predict the reform readiness of countries that attempted a reform without a downturn. These reform episodes were not included in the estimation sample because that estimation was conditional on the occurrence of a downturn. But our framework would suggest that to attempt reform without experiencing a downturn, a country must be ready for reform so that no additional impetus is needed. Therefore the data from these episodes should generate high positive values for the reform-readiness function and, thus, high predicted reform probabilities. Of the five cases of reform without downturn that we investigated, four have a positive z_i and predicted reform probabilities greater than 0.85 (table 6). Moreover, in those four cases the values of z_i are all higher than 1.10, which is the average z_i for all reforms associated with downturns. In fact, only 38 percent of the reforms associated with downturns had a z_i higher than 1.1 (table 6). Thus it seems that the model predicts reform readiness reasonably well in these cases, and in this sense does identify important preconditions for reform.

Dissecting the measure of reform readiness into its components can provide information as to why in one situation a country attempts to reform while in a different situation the same country or another does not. In order to simplify

Table 4. *Probit Estimation Results for the Reduced Full Sample*

Equation	*Constant*	*Ratio of public to total investment (RPI)*[a]	*Share of nonagriculture in GDP (SNA)*[a]	*Interaction term (RPIxSNA)*	*Trade orientation (TO)*[b]	*GDP per capita (thousands of 1978 U.S. dollars) (GDPPC)*	*Magnitude of downturn (MD)*	*Log-likelihood*
1	−39.897	55.253	48.58	−65.071	1.043	−1.5945	−0.59938	−14.61944
	(−2.518)	(2.324)	(2.368)	(−2.145)	(2.554)	(−2.060)	(−0.152)	
2	−39.805	54.732	48.47	−64.48	1.0524	−1.6171		−14.63109
	(−2.499)	(2.314	(2.350)	(−2.132)	(2.589)	(−2.114)		
3	−23.204	28.143	30.08	−33.137		−1.3403		−20.34340
	(−2.532)	(2.065)	(2.446)	(−1.851)		(−2.597)		
4	−14.497	20.534	13.27	−19.008	0.92175			−17.98100
	(−2.226)	(1.717)	(1.718)	(−1.242)	(3.107)			

Note: The dependent variable is the public enterprise reform dummy, y_i. The reduced full sample has forty-four observations. Three episodes are excluded from the full sample: Chile 1972–73 and 1982–83 and the Philippines 1983–85. *t*-ratios are in parentheses.

a. Values represent the five-year average.

b. Values follow Dollar's (1992) index, which assigns a ranking of 0 through 3 to each observation, with 0 indicating the most inward-oriented set of policies and 3 the most outward-oriented set.

Source: Authors' calculations.

Table 5. *Frequencies of Actual and Predicted Outcomes for the Reduced Full Sample*

	Predicted		
Actual	*0*	*1*	*Total*
0	25	3	28
1	5	11	16
Total	30	14	44

Note: Results are from equation 2 (see table 2). The predicted outcome has maximum probability. The reduced full sample has forty-four observations. As explained in the text, the observations for Chile (1972–73 and 1982–83) and for the Philippines (1983–85) are excluded.

Source: Authors' calculations.

this analysis, for each episode in table 6 we present the product of the right-hand-side variables of the probit model and their estimated coefficients (from equation 2 of table 2). In the sixth column of table 6 we also show the value of $a_0 + a_1SNA_i + a_2RPI_i + a_3RPI_i{\times}SNA_i$, which measures the net impact of structural variables on the reform-readiness function. We call this component structural reform readiness to distinguish it from the effect of trade orientation and per capita income. The higher the value of this measure, the more predisposed a country is toward attempting a reform, given the level of GDP per capita and trade orientation.

Structurally, reform-ready countries are those that by virtue of their relatively large nonagricultural or public sectors can gain significantly from public enterprise reform. These countries may delay reform if their incomes are high and their economies are inward oriented, for example, Argentina and Venezuela, or if they do not experience a downturn to trigger reform, for example, Egypt. Interestingly, Argentina, Venezuela, and Egypt have initiated reforms as their circumstances have changed. Egypt experienced a downturn in the early 1990s. Argentina and Venezuela, after repeated incidents of downturn, ended up with much lower per capita incomes. They have also reoriented their trade policies. Comparing the experiences of these two countries with those of Chile and Mexico, which have been more active reformers, is interesting because the four countries were structurally similar, but Chile and Mexico had lower initial incomes and greater outward orientation.

Most countries that did not reform despite repeated economic downturns were those that lacked structural reform readiness. For example, Nigeria in the 1970s had relatively small nonagricultural and public sectors compared with the rest of the sample. Its relatively closed economy also reduced the impetus for public enterprise reform. But in the 1980s when the size of Nigeria's public sector increased sharply and its nonagricultural sector expanded, a downturn led to a reform attempt. Ghana, India, and Senegal have had similar experiences. But India's and Senegal's increased openness to international trade contributed to reform readiness, and in Ghana a major expansion in the relative size of the public sector was the main contributory factor. It is interesting to observe that the inclusion of trade orientation and GDP per capita substantially affects the coefficients of the structural variables. The reason is that *RPI* and *SNA* are correlated with trade orientation and GDP per capita. Indeed, regressions of explanatory variables on each other based on our sample show that *RPI* is negatively (and significantly) related to both trade orientation and GDP per capita, while *SNA* is positively (and significantly) related to both variables. This confirms the common view that to reach higher levels of income, economies must become increasingly nonagricultural and open and must reduce their reliance on the public sector. It also supports our arguments that outward orientation is complementary to a large nonagricultural private sector and helps trigger reform when structural reform readiness is high.

The above discussions are not meant to give the impression that the results of our model are definitive. Certainly, the model can be refined by incorporating more explanatory variables, especially institutional characteristics and disaggregated structural measures. There is also a need to develop appropriate tests to deal with possible alternative hypotheses explaining the relationships we found in our empirical analysis. Nevertheless, the exercise shows that the model helps explain why reform did or did not occur in each situation, and establishes a practical way of assessing a country's readiness for reform. Moreover, when a country does not meet the preconditions for reform, the model shows how that may change as a result of changes in country characteristics.

III. Conclusions

Initiating reform in a country's public sector is a complex decision. It may be influenced by economic and political conditions, as well as other circumstances, such as the ideological biases and personalities of political leaders. Nonetheless, our theoretical and empirical analyses suggest that important generalizations based on a contracting framework could be made. By tracing the impact of a number of variables reflecting the conditions of the economy on the costs and benefits of renegotiating public enterprise policies, we presented evidence that reform is more likely under the following circumstances:

- *When the economy experiences an adverse shock.* Public enterprise rents decline, redistribution is less costly, and gains from reform may in fact increase.
- *The larger the size of the nonagricultural sector.* Public enterprises and the rest of the economy are more interlinked so that potential gains from reform are higher.
- *The larger the size of the public sector relative to the size of the economy.* The public sector is more likely to include activities for which the efficiency gains swamp the costs of redistribution.

Table 6. *Reform-Readiness Assessments in Sample Countries: Contributions of Each Variable to Reform-Readiness Function, z*

Country	Years	Constant	Ratio of public to total investment (RPI)[a]	Interaction term (RPI×SNA)	Share of nonagriculture in GDP (SNA)[a]	Structural reform readiness[b]	GDP per capita (thousands of 1978 U.S. dollars) (GDPPC)	Trade orientation (TO)	Reform readiness	$Prob(y_i = 1)$
Downturn episodes without reform										
Argentina	1975–76	–42.36	21.81	–23.88	47.99	3.55	–6.60	0.00	–3.05	0.00
	1978	–42.36	22.95	–25.09	47.91	3.41	–6.78	0.00	–3.37	0.00
	1981–82	–42.36	22.69	–24.82	47.93	3.44	–6.85	1.09	–2.31	0.01
	1985	–42.36	14.26	–15.50	47.64	4.04	–6.53	1.09	–1.40	0.08
Ghana	1972	–42.36	26.53	–14.57	24.06	–6.33	–0.95	0.00	–7.28	0.00
	1975–76	–42.36	32.73	–17.50	23.43	–3.70	–0.93	0.00	–4.63	0.00
India	1971–72	–42.36	22.15	–14.67	29.02	–5.86	–0.44	0.00	–6.30	0.00
	1974	–42.36	24.24	–16.54	29.91	–4.76	–0.44	0.00	–5.19	0.00
	1976	–42.36	24.40	–16.86	30.29	–4.54	–0.44	1.09	–3.88	0.00
	1979	–42.36	25.15	–17.81	31.03	–3.99	–0.46	2.18	–2.27	0.01
Indonesia	1982	–42.36	25.22	–21.95	38.14	–0.95	–0.62	2.18	0.61	0.73
Korea, Rep. of	1980	–42.36	12.67	–11.86	41.00	–0.55	–3.01	3.28	–0.27	0.39
Malaysia	1975	–42.36	18.24	–15.34	36.85	–2.61	–2.02	3.28	–1.35	0.09
Nigeria	1972	–42.36	19.31	–11.49	26.07	–8.47	–0.68	0.00	–9.15	0.00
	1975	–42.36	27.14	–17.27	27.90	–4.60	–0.71	0.00	–5.32	0.00
	1978	–42.36	35.76	–25.38	31.11	–0.88	–0.77	0.00	–1.65	0.05
	1981–84	–42.36	39.00	–30.23	33.97	0.38	–0.77	0.00	–0.39	0.35
Pakistan	1971–72	–42.36	28.70	–21.53	32.88	–2.31	–0.40	2.18	–0.53	0.30
Senegal	1971	–42.36	32.03	–27.34	37.41	–0.26	–1.31	0.00	–1.57	0.06
	1973	–42.36	26.41	–23.17	38.46	–0.67	–1.31	0.00	–1.98	0.02
	1977–78	–42.36	28.66	–24.79	37.91	–0.58	–1.29	0.00	–1.87	0.03
	1980–81	–42.36	29.50	–25.79	38.32	–0.34	–1.28	0.00	–1.62	0.05
	1989	–42.36	19.04	–17.82	41.01	–0.13	–1.22	2.18	0.84	0.80
	1991	–42.36	18.68	–17.44	40.91	–0.21	–1.23	1.09	–0.34	0.37
Turkey	1989	–42.36	31.37	–30.39	42.45	1.07	–2.22	2.18	1.04	0.85

Venezuela	1971–72	–42.36	13.86	–15.68	49.58	5.40	–5.97	0.00	–0.57	0.28
	1974–75	–42.36	18.76	–21.24	49.62	4.78	–5.87	0.00	–1.09	0.14
	1978–85	–42.36	21.22	–24.05	49.66	4.47	–5.94	1.09	–0.38	0.35
Downturn episodes with reform										
Argentina	1988–90	–42.36	15.64	–17.01	47.66	3.93	–6.26	2.18	–0.14	0.44
Chile	1972–73	–42.36	28.21	–30.96	48.11	2.99	–2.62	1.09	1.46	0.93
	1975	–42.36	36.03	–39.72	48.32	2.26	–2.57	2.18	1.88	0.97
	1982–83	–42.36	18.71	–20.45	47.92	3.81	–2.67	2.18	3.32	1.00
Egypt	1992	–42.36	34.96	–33.25	41.68	1.03	–1.34	1.09	0.79	0.78
Ghana	1979–83	–42.36	44.89	–25.63	25.02	1.92	–0.82	0.00	1.10	0.86
India	1991	–42.36	26.44	–21.41	35.49	–1.84	–0.62	2.18	–0.28	0.39
Malaysia	1985–86	–42.36	26.71	–24.86	40.80	0.28	–3.28	3.28	0.28	0.61
Mexico	1982–83	–42.36	24.58	–26.67	47.54	3.10	–3.32	3.28	3.05	1.00
	1986	–42.36	23.10	–25.18	47.78	3.33	–3.53	3.28	3.08	1.00
	1988	–42.36	20.04	–21.79	47.66	3.55	–3.37	3.28	3.46	1.00
Nigeria	1986–87	–42.36	42.44	–34.26	35.38	1.20	–0.61	0.00	0.59	0.72
Pakistan	1993	–42.36	28.24	–25.04	38.86	–0.30	–0.64	3.28	2.33	0.99
Philippines	1983–85	–42.36	17.67	–16.15	40.05	–0.79	–1.21	2.18	0.18	0.57
	1991–92	–42.36	10.39	–9.50	40.06	–1.41	–1.09	2.18	–0.31	0.38
Senegal	1983–84	–42.36	21.50	–19.76	40.29	–0.34	–1.22	1.09	–0.46	0.32
Turkey	1979–80	–42.36	26.80	–25.34	41.44	0.54	–1.88	1.09	–0.25	0.40
	1991	–42.36	28.63	–28.03	42.90	1.14	–2.36	2.18	0.96	0.83
Venezuela	1989	–42.36	24.14	–27.04	49.08	3.82	–4.79	1.09	0.12	0.55
Reform episodes without downturn										
Indonesia	1986	–42.36	26.95	–23.97	38.98	–0.40	–0.72	3.28	2.16	0.98
Korea, Rep. of	1984	–42.36	14.12	–14.11	43.79	1.44	–3.61	3.28	1.10	0.86
Malaysia	1991	–42.36	22.51	–21.27	41.42	0.29	–3.73	3.28	–0.16	0.44
Pakistan	1977	–42.36	34.62	–27.27	34.52	–0.49	–0.40	2.18	1.30	0.90
	1990	–42.36	30.58	–26.85	38.48	–0.15	–0.59	3.28	2.53	0.99

a. Values represent the five-year average.
b. This is the value of $a_0 + a_1SNA_i + a_2EPI_i + a_3RPI_i \times SNA_i$, which measures the net impact of structural variables on reform readiness, that is, the value of z_i.
Source: Authors' calculations.

- *The smaller the (multiplicative) product of the relative size of the nonagricultural sector and the public sector.* In a nonagricultural economy, redistribution is more complex, and the informational obstacles to reform tend to be greater when most of the economy is under public ownership.
- *If the economy is more outward oriented.* Efficiency gains are likely to be larger when producers face more elastic demands in international markets and there is a larger constituency demanding reduction in the costs of public enterprise inefficiency.
- *If the per capita income is lower.* Controlling for other factors, high-income countries are likely to have either larger resources for redistribution or reduced public enterprise inefficiency as a result of implementing appropriate solutions in the past.

Despite its inevitable shortcomings, our analytical and empirical framework for analyzing the determinants of public enterprise reform yields a reasonably robust model with strong predictive powers. It also has some important policy implications. In particular, it suggests that foreign aid may dampen the impetus for reform. Foreign aid affects the reform decision in two ways. First, it alleviates the impact of an economic downturn, and second, it acts as a brake on the fall in per capita income. Consequently, even countries that might be structurally reform-ready may opt to postpone introducing reforms. But the model also suggests that trade liberalization may strengthen the impetus for reform. This implies that making trade liberalization a condition for receiving aid may neutralize the dampening effect of aid. Aid can also be directly conditioned on public enterprise reform measures. This of course requires that the imposition of conditionality be credible. The advantage of conditionality on trade liberalization rather than on public enterprise reform is that donors are more likely to have a direct interest in the maintenance of liberal trade and, thus, respond to violations of the conditions.

Appendix: Selection of Variables

We began this research with an extensive literature review. Perhaps the predominant theme that came up was that economic crises drove economic reforms. Hence we decided to follow the logic of the argument through the logic of our model and test the hypothesis. We needed a variable that represented a crisis—and chose to use a downturn in the growth rate. From a long list of variables that could conceivably affect the costs and benefits of undertaking public enterprise reform, we focused first on the division of activities between the public and private sectors. We argued that if a country has already reformed its public enterprise sector and cut it down in size, the country should have less to gain from further reform. When public enterprises are confined to a few enterprises with significant public good and natural monopoly elements, the economy is unlikely to gain a great deal from their reform since the size of the sector is small and, moreover, these characteristics are likely to cause problems for any form of sectoral organization, public or private. To capture this effect, we chose the ratio of public to total investment (*RPI*). The larger the public enterprise sector, the larger would be the ratio, and the larger the potential gains from reform.

But we recognized that the relationship may not be simple. From the privatization literature we knew that a developed domestic private sector can facilitate privatization through its financial resources, entrepreneurship, and ability to collect information and assess public enterprises that are sold. As the experience of Eastern European countries suggests, if the entire economy operates under public enterprises, knowledge and experience about how a market-oriented system (especially private firms) operates and information about who might benefit are scarce, and this scarcity makes reform difficult and costly. Therefore, we needed a measure of the part of the private sector that could be helpful for public enterprise reform. We thought an appropriate indicator was the relative size of the nonagricultural private sector, $(1 - RPI)SNA$, where *SNA* is the share of the nonagricultural sector in GDP. Our initial regressions indicated that both variables were significant and had positive coefficients.

Next, we focused on the informational attributes of the economy, which, as implied by our theoretical framework, could be an important determinant of the cost of undertaking a reform. We understood that privatization is only one type of public enterprise reform and concluded that the nonagricultural private sector may be particularly important for its informational role. We also needed a measure of informational requirements. Here we thought that an indicator of the economy's complexity, such as diversity of production, would be appropriate. *SNA* seemed to capture this notion and was included in the regression as a separate independent variable. We then saw that the three terms could be rewritten as *RPI* and *SNA* with an interaction between the two signifying the role of information, hence the final form in which they are presented in the model. To these terms, we added the trade orientation variable to capture the need to enhance the competitiveness of the economy, as well as the government's commitment to market-oriented reforms. GDP per capita was introduced to control for whatever influence other country characteristics associated with the level of development might have. Finally, we toyed around with different measures of economic crisis, such as changes in the inflation rate and budget deficit, but our experimentation suggested that these were not very useful.

Figure A-1. *Public Enterprise/Macroeconomic Reform Responses to Economic Crisis*

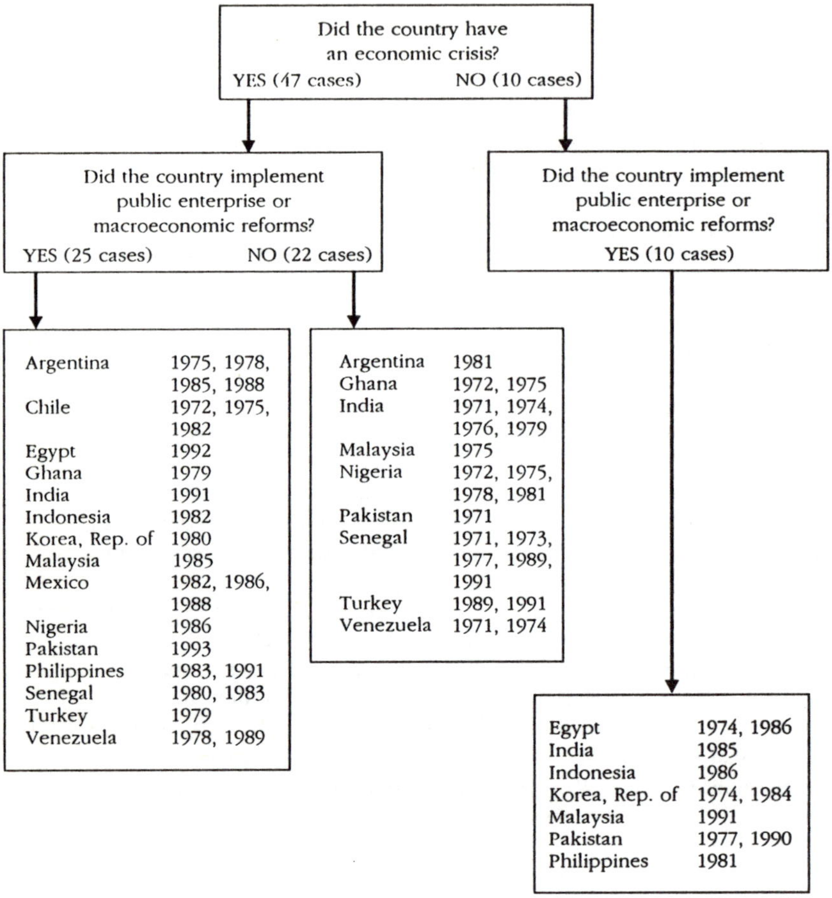

Source: World Bank data; Bruton (1992); Gyimah-Boadi (1993); Haggard and Webb (1994); Leith and Lofchie (1993); Means (1991); Sundaram (1993); Wade (1990); Waterbury (1993); Williamson (1994).

References

The word "processed" describes informally reproduced works that may not be commonly available through library systems.

Ake, Blomqvist, and Sharif Mohammad. 1986. "Controls, Corruption, and Competitive Rent-Seeking in LDCs." *Journal of Development Economics* 21(1):161–80.

Alesina, Alberto. 1994. "Political Models of Macroeconomic Policy and Fiscal Reforms." In Stephan Haggard and Steven B. Webb, eds., *Voting for Reform: Democracy, Political Liberalization, and Economic Adjustment*. New York: Oxford University Press.

Alesina, Alberto, and Allan Drazen. 1991. "Why Are Stabilizations Delayed?" *American Economic Review* 81(5):1170–88.

Amsden, Alice. 1979. "Taiwan's Economic History: A Case of Etatisme and a Challenge to Dependency Theory." *Modern China* 5(3):341–80.

———. 1989. *Asia's Next Giant: South Korea and Late Industrialization*. New York: Oxford University Press.

Anderson, Gary, and Robert Tollison. 1984. "A Rent-Seeking Explanation of the British Factory Acts." In David Collander, ed., *Neoclassical Political Economy: The Analysis of Rent-Seeking and DUP Activities*. Cambridge, Mass.: Ballinger Publishing Company.

Bardhan, Pranab. 1984. *The Political Economy of Development in India*. Oxford, U.K.: Basil Blackwell.

Bates, Robert. 1981. *Markets and States in Tropical Africa*. Los Angeles: University of California Press.

Bates, Robert, and Anne O. Krueger. 1993. *Political and Economic Interaction in Economic Policy Reform*. Oxford, U.K.: Basil Blackwell.

Becker, Gary. 1983. "A Theory of Competition among Pressure Groups for Political Influence." *Quarterly Journal of Economics* 98(3):371–400.

Bradburd, Ralph. 1993. "Why Things Have to Get a Lot Worse before They Get Better: Institutions, Investments, Downturn, and Reform." World Bank, Policy Research Department, Washington, D.C. Processed.

Bowie, Alasdair. 1991. *Crossing the Industrial Divide*. New York: Columbia University Press.

Brock, William, and Stephen Magee. 1978. "The Economics of Special Interest Politics: The Case of the Tariff." *American Economic Review* 68(2):246–50.

Bruton, Henry J. 1992. *The Political Economy of Poverty, Equity, and Growth: Sri Lanka and Malaysia*. New York: Oxford University Press.

Campos, Jose Edgardo, and Hadi Salehi Esfahani. 1994. "Public Enterprises as Political Instruments." World Bank, Policy Research Department, Washington, D.C. Processed.

———. 1995. "Credible Commitment and Success with Public Enterprise Reform." World Bank, Finance and Private Sector Development Division, Washington, D.C. Processed.

Clague, Christopher. 1991. "Relative Efficiency, Self-Containment, and Comparative Costs of Developed Countries." *Economic Development and Cultural Change* 39(3):507–30.

Dollar, David. 1992. "Outward-Oriented Developing Economies Really Do Grow More Rapidly: Evidence from 95 LDCs, 1976–1985." *Economic Development and Cultural Change* 40(3, April):523–44.

Drazen, Allan, and Vittorio Grilli. 1993. "The Benefit of Crises for Economic Reform." *American Economic Review* 83(3):598–607.

Edwards, Sebastian. 1993. "The Political Economy of Inflation and Stabilization in Developing Countries." NBER Working Paper 4319. National Bureau of Economic Research, Cambridge, Mass. Processed.

Erikson, Robert. 1971. "The Advantage of Incumbency in Congressional Elections." *Polity* 3(3):395–405.

Evans, Peter. 1992. "The State as Problem and Solution: Predation, Embedded Autonomy, and Structural Change." In Stephan Haggard and Robert Kaufman, eds., *The Politics of Economic Adjustment*. Princeton, N.J.: Princeton University Press.

Fernandez, Raquel, and Dani Rodrik. 1991. "Resistance to Reform: Status Quo Bias in the Presence of Individual-Specific Uncertainty." *American Economic Review* 81(5):1146–55.

Findlay, Ronald, and Stan Wellisz. 1984. "Toward a Model of Endogenous Rent-Seeking." In David Collander, ed., *Neoclassical Political Economy: The Analysis of Rent-Seeking and DUP Activities*. Cambridge, Mass.: Ballinger Publishing Company.

Fiorina, Morris. 1989. *Congress: Keystone of Washington Establishment*. New Haven, Conn.: Yale University Press.

Galal, Ahmed, Leroy Jones, Pankaj Tandon, and Ingo Vogelsang. 1994. *Welfare Consequences of Selling Public Enterprises: An Empirical Analysis*. New York: Oxford University Press.

Gardner, Bruce. 1981. *The Governing of Agriculture*. Lawrence, Kans.: Regents Press of Kansas.

Goldberg, Victor P. 1976. "Regulation and Administered Contracts." *Bell Journal of Economics* 7(2):426–48.

Gyimah-Boadi, Emmanuel. 1993. "The Political Economy of Public Enterprise Reforms in Ghana." World Bank, Finance and Private Sector Development Division, Washington, D.C. Processed.

Haggard, Stephan. 1990. *Pathways from the Periphery*. Ithaca, N.Y.: Cornell University Press.

Haggard, Stephan, and Steven B. Webb, eds. 1994. *Voting for Reform: Democracy, Political Liberalization, and Economic Adjustment*. New York: Oxford University Press.

Howitt, Peter, and Ronald Wintrobe. 1995. "The Political Economy of Inaction." *Journal of Public Economics* 56(3):329–53.

Krueger, Anne O. 1974. "The Political Economy of the Rent-Seeking Society." *American Economic Review* 64(3):291–303.

Leith, Clark J., and Michael Lofchie. 1993. "The Political Economy of Structural Adjustment in Ghana." In Robert Bates and Anne O. Krueger, eds., *Political and Economic Interactions in Economic Policy Reform*. Oxford, U.K.: Basil Blackwell.

Little, Ian, Tibor Scitovsky, and Maurice Scott. 1970. *Industry and Trade in Some Developing Countries: A Comparative Study*. London: Oxford University Press.

Mayhew, David. 1975. *Congress: The Electoral Connection*. New Haven, Conn.: Yale University Press.

Means, G. P. 1991. *Malaysian Politics, The Second Generation*. Oxford, U.K.: Oxford University Press.

Michelmann, Hans, Jack Stabler, and Gary Storey, eds., 1990. *The Political Economy of Agricultural Trade and Policy*. Boulder, Colo.: Westview Press.

North, Douglas. 1981. *Structure and Change in Economic History*. New York: Norton.

O'Donnell, Guillermo. 1978. "State and Alliances in Argentina, 1956–1976." *Journal of Development Studies* 15(1):3–33.

Olson, Mancur. 1965. *The Logic of Collective Action*. Cambridge, U.K.: Cambridge University Press.

Owen, Bruce M., and Ronald Braeutigam. 1978. *The Regulation Game*. Cambridge, Mass.: Ballinger Publishing Company.

Rausser, Gordon. 1982. "Political Economic Markets: PERTS and PESTS in Food and Agriculture." *American Journal of Agricultural Economics* 64(5):821–33.

Rodrik, Dani. 1994. "The Rush to Free Trade. Why So Late? Why Now? Will It Last?" In Stephan Haggard and Steven B. Webb, eds., *Voting for Reform: Democracy, Political Liberalization, and Economic Adjustment*. New York: Oxford University Press.

Rowley, Charles, Robert Tollison, and Gordon Tullock. 1988. *The Political Economy of Rent-Seeking*. Boston: Kluwer Academic Publishers.

Sundaram, Jomo. 1993. "Public Enterprise Reform in Malaysia." World Bank, Policy Research Department, Washington, D.C. Processed.

Stigler, George. 1971. "The Theory of Economic Regulation." *Bell Journal of Economics* 2:3–21.

Wade, Robert. 1990. *Governing the Market: Economic Theory and the Role of Government in East Asian Industrialization*. Princeton, N.J.: Princeton University Press.

Waterbury, John. 1993. *Exposed to Innumerable Delusions: Public Enterprise and State Power in Egypt, India, Mexico, and Turkey*. Cambridge, U.K.: Cambridge University Press.

Williamson, John. 1994. *The Political Economy of Policy Reform*. Washington, D.C.: Institute for International Economics.

World Bank. 1993. "Ghana 2000 and Beyond: Setting the Stage for Accelerated Growth and Poverty Reduction." World Bank, Africa Regional Office, Western Africa Department, Washington, D.C. Processed.

———. 1994a. *Adjustment in Africa: Reforms, Results, and the Road Ahead*. New York: Oxford University Press.

———. 1994b. *World Tables 1994*. Baltimore: Johns Hopkins University Press.

Part II
Theoretical Perspectives on Privatisation

[12]

State-owned enterprise: an agent without a principal

Yair Aharoni

State-owned enterprises (SOEs) comprise a large and rapidly growing sector of the economy in the majority of countries in the world today. They have been established to achieve a broad array of public policy purposes in very diverse political and economic systems. Typically, they account for half or more of total government investment, and in 1978 the international borrowings alone of public-sector enterprises amounted to more than $30 billion, equal to the total foreign borrowings by central governments in the past year.[1] As international exporters, importers, and investors, SOEs are helping to shape the emerging structure of trade and payments relations in the 1980s. Their presence outside their traditional domain of public utilities is being felt especially in natural-resource–based and modern high-technology industries with high barriers to entry, in which private multinational firms have heretofore taken the lead. They are moving into a dominating position also in senescent industries such as textiles, shipbuilding, and steel, where the government moved in to save present firms from going under.

Yet despite the proliferation of SOEs since World War II, we actually know very little about the way they are managed. One reason for this lack of knowledge may be the tendency of economic theory to assume a perfect-market economy, in which firms passively transfer inputs procured in a perfect market into output sold in similar markets. Until recently, little attention has been paid to the problems and cost involved in managing an enterprise. By the same token, early socialist theoreticians saw the nationalization of production facilities as a way to achieve some equity and reduce "exploitation." They, too, however, did not pay much attention to the problem of managing the enterprises once nationalized. Rather they assumed – naïvely as it turned out – that "society will be transformed into a huge organization for cooperative production" in which everyone will work in accordance with the national plan.[2]

In the real world, firms do not operate in a neoclassical competitive environment. Rather, they have certain size and are managed hierarchically; the managers operate under uncertainty, and the information collected is costly.

The help of Ravi Ramamurti, my research assistant at the Harvard Graduate School of Business Administration, and that of anonymous reviewers is gratefully acknowledged.

68 Principal-agent relationships

Uncertainty cannot be fully eliminated by the use of contingency contracts. Under these conditions, the management of the firm has discretion in the choice of strategies, product lines, organizational forms, and policies. They are guided not by an internalized need to achieve a prescribed plan but by other motivations. Thus, managers may use their discretion to expand their staff or to achieve slack or on-the-job leisure.[3] One cannot assume that all decision makers in the economy are working together to achieve identical goals. Therefore, the relationships between managers and the state officials controlling them, as well as the negative and positive incentives to managers, are of crucial importance.

One way to look at the relationships between managers and owners of firms is in the terms of the principal–agent theory. An agency relationship exists when one party (the agent) acts on behalf of another (the principal). The two parties have unequal interests but may have an incentive to cooperate. Contractual arrangements are sought that will induce an agent to behave as if he was maximizing the welfare of the principal. Most analyses of agency relationships assume that the agent can choose a line of action that, together with exogenous events, determines the payoff. The principal is assumed to be unable to change the payoff.

The relationships between owners and managers of business firms are examples of agency relationships. Managers are contracted to act on behalf of (private or public) shareholders. However, as in all agency relationships, the manager is assumed to act to maximize his own interests. Therefore, a ''perfect'' contract would structure the manager's incentives to correspond exactly to those of the shareholders. In real life situations, no contract is expected to meet this standard, and agency costs are more than the costs specified in the contract.

What are these additional costs? First, there are certain costs of detecting decisions incongruent with the shareholders' interests. The higher the costs of monitoring managers' behavior, the larger their discretion. In real life, monitoring costs are high because the principal (shareholder) does not have an independent source of information. In addition, under uncertainty, optimal decision making depends on the risk preferences of managers and shareholders, which may not be identical. Moreover, to avoid replacement costs, shareholders may allow managers a certain amount of discretion.[4]

All these types of agency costs – distinct managers' interests, monitoring and detection costs, replacement costs – as well as such environmental variables as uncertainty about strategy, are likely to apply to SOEs. However, the agency costs cannot be conceptually defined in SOEs because the principal is not identifiable. The notion that the government or the minister is the principal and that the enterprise is the agent is misleading. Rather, the populace as a whole is the principal, with a variety of agents acting on its behalf. These agents include various government ministers, members of parliament, managers of firms, and so on. All these agents are in fact a coalition – a group working together who share *some*, but not all, goals. SOE shares are not traded in the market, and the populace does not have an effective voice in their direction and control. As state ownership does not necessarily imply social ownership, the mechanism of goal formulation is an important one. A case can be made that SOE management has as legitimate a claim to the participation in the goal formulation on behalf of the principal as do the other agents. The multiple and often ill-defined objectives make performance measurement almost impossible. As a result, the market may police SOE managers much less than in the case of private enterprise.

These problems of social ownership are developed in Sections 4.1 and 4.2. In Section 4.3, an independent of multiple legitimate claimants to the goal-specification function.

4.1 Shareholders without shares

Private firms are owned by individuals who may buy or sell ownership rights at some price. SOEs are ultimately owned by all citizens of a country and are financed from the general pool of funds mobilized by the government through taxes or other means. However, the SOE "shareholders" do not hold any shares that can be traded in the market, and no market mechanism allows them to signal their views on the performance of the enterprise, nor can they take part in a proxy fight for a take-over bid. Therefore, the citizens of the country do not have even the minimal influence enjoyed by shareholders of a modern corporation.

The state is not a person, not even a single organization. It acts through a variety of ministers, legislators, and civil servants, who are themselves agents of the general public. These different agents invariably see their mission as different from one another. Thus, different objectives are sought by different government ministries, and interorganizational conflicts are normal phenomena. These conflicts affect the process of SOE goal specifications. A government official concerned with foreign affairs may see the reduction of the state's dependence on imported technology as a prime goal and therefore seek an increase in the SOE research and development budget. The minister of labor may see the state's role as maximizing employment and thus favor more labor-intensive procedures for the SOE. The finance minister, viewing himself as "the shareholder," may want the firm to pay higher dividends. Yet another minister, whose agency buys the firm's output, may seek to reduce its prices. These competing representatives cannot be considered *the* principal of the firm whose interests are well defined. Consequently, no "perfect" contract can structure managers' incentives so that their interests will match the principal's goals. These goals are rarely, if ever, stated explicitly and trade-offs among them are not agreed. Thus, different agents give the enterprise conflicting, parallel commands, which turn SOEs into hybrids, expected to achieve both traditional economic goals in the marketplace and all sorts of social goals: help for the poor, increased employment, a redistribution of income, development of laggard regions, and so on. They are also expected to achieve political goals such as the avoidance of perceived domination by foreign multinationals, developing of new technologies, and enhancement of the glory of the state. Several agents seek to resolve the ambiguity of goals in ways that suit them best. Goal conflicts among state agents are sometimes "solved" by formally assigning two or more of these objectives to an SOE. At other times, conflicting commands are faced by SOEs because several external agents of society, rightly or wrongly, view SOEs as legitimate tools for achieving overall national goals. Thus, the principal (the populace) is represented by a loose coalition of agents: sponsoring minister, the treasury, the civil servants, other ministers, and the parliament. Their decisions are influenced by all sorts of interest groups – consumers, labor unions, and others – all of which claim at least some right to participate in the process of goal formulation. Even in countries with a decentralized framework of control, there is a continuous flow of ex ante intervention in various decisions.

Can the principal be assumed to be a collective term for a coalition of ministers, interest groups, civil servants, trade unions, and parliament members? Even such an assumption does not seem to hold, as SOE managers often try to influence the process of goal specification, resist the imposition of certain goals in many different ways, and claim the right to participate in the formulation of goals.

4.2 Legitimacy of goals and strategies

There are three major explanations for the ability of SOE managers to resist certain goals imposed on them by various government agencies. The first is the difference between managers' self-interest and that of other state agents. This is by now a well-theorized phenomenon in both large diffused ownership corporations and SOEs. The notion that professional managers single-mindedly operate the firm to maximize profits has long been rejected. It was replaced by "behavioral" or "managerial" theories.[5] This difference in self-interests is also at the root of the agent – principal problem and the view of the firm as a set of contracts.[6]

Second, SOE managers can afford to resist certain goals because it is difficult to measure their performance. In a private firm, managerial performance is scrutinized by the board of directors, which in turn is viewed as a market-induced institution. In an SOE, managerial performance cannot be gauged, because of the many conflicting and ill-defined objectives. Moreover, in many countries, the control structure is not clearly defined, and the board cannot discipline or replace a manager, at least not without a lengthy negotiation with a sponsoring minister and other agents. Therefore, although a market for the services of managers does exist,[7] and although managers might be dismissed, the policing of managers is much more difficult. In such a situation, ambitious managers may be able to achieve more discretion than private-sector managers. Less ambitious managers, faced with conflicting goals and restrictions, may simply choose to defer to governmental constraints. In extreme cases, managers may develop what Phatak called the "don't rock the boat syndrome."[8] With this approach, managers avoid changes that may alienate any powerful groups: Redundant workers are not dismissed, erring staff are not disciplined, no obsolete plant is closed, and no organizational changes are made. In short, managers simply develop apathy.

Third and most important, managers consider themselves to be the trustees of the "real" interest of the state at least as much as the government employees. Managers sometimes bring to their job the same set of values and ideologies that belong to the rest of the business world. As they see it, the intervention of various government ministries to achieve non-economic goals is an encroachment on their prerogatives as the trustees of the economic interests of the firm. SOE managers would probably argue that if the government, for social reasons, wants an enterprise to deviate from its economic mission, it should compensate it for the economic losses incurred. Such a point of view has been presented independently by public committees on SOEs in different countries.[9]

Managers of large corporations accept the legitimacy of the shareholders' interests, although they may not always actually pursue those interests. SOE managers may question the legitimacy of demands from government, not only because they try to maximize their own utility but because they perceive the "real" goals of the amorphous principal – the state – to be different. Further, many of them maintain that operational efficiency requires that decisions on objectives and strategy be made within the enterprise itself. In here lies the major difference between SOEs and large private corporations with diffused ownership. SOE management feels it has as legitimate a claim to goal specification as other agents. The government may require the SOE to avoid price increases to combat inflation, to procure locally made and more expensive goods or to maintain the size of its labor force to secure employment, or to pursue certain objectives perceived as important in achieving a short-term political gain. In all these cases, managers may have different perceptions of the legitimate role of the enterprise. They see it as their legitimate right – even their duty to the "real" interest of the state – to try to evade the issue or even fight openly against such a request. They would thus attempt to avoid the order, get around it, or procrastinate. In certain cases, managers may even bring "their" cases before the public by leaking information to the press or by applying to the president or prime minister to appeal a sponsoring minister's decision.

In summary, the behavior of an SOE cannot be explained within the principal-agent theory. Rather, an SOE should be viewed not only as a set of contracts among factors of production but as a coalition of the managers, the board of directors, government ministers, civil servants, parliament members, and others. The principal of the property-rights theory and the classical theory of the firm does not exist. Instead, there are different members of a coalition who share the belief that its survival should be maintained by the continuation of the enterprise.

The actual outcome and degree of discretion managers enjoy in their operations seem to be the result of a fight for power among the various agents of the state. Managers of SOEs seem to spend more time than their private-sector counterparts in managing the environment and aiming at co-opting the controlling agencies or assuring their allegiance. The outcome of this fight for power, that is, the actual strategic choices made, can be predicted only in terms of contingency theory. Although it is beyond the scope of this chapter to propose such a contingency theory, a few examples may be helpful.

The ability of an SOE manager to choose the strategy he prefers and the objectives he sees as most relevant is a joint function of his personality, the legal and institutional environment in which he operates, and the time and expertise of those monitoring him. In general, experience shows that the bigger the firm is, the more independent it is of the government (by generating its own funds), the more technical the information needed to operate the enterprise, and the more expertise concentrated in management at the firm level, the more management can dictate goals. In addition, management enjoys more discretion in its strategic choices when it operates internationally (by being at least partially outside the domain of government control), has a large number of customers and product lines, has a greater freedom to choose its customers, product lines, and suppliers. Finally, the degree of goal congruency is a crucial variable. The more legitimate are the demands of government agencies in the eyes of the manager, the more he will abide by them. I have discussed these points extensively in another publication.[10] Here it is enough to note that the real problem is to define the legitimate role of different state organs and the dimensions of social controls. In practice, these dimensions are ill defined, and conflicts on goals constantly occur.

Even in the rare case in which goals are explicitly stated, they eventually are modified in the daily operations of the enterprise through numerous managerial decisions once the enterprise is established. The lack of performance measurement makes it difficult to monitor these changes. In addition, actual monitoring systems used by different government controllers often lead to distortion.

The complex relationships between the SOE and its environment cannot be solved by an "optimal contract," because the optimality characteristics are ill defined. Different agents of the state, including the managers of the enterprise and their controllers as well as other constituents, look for ways to reach some quasi resolution of conflicts, often by ill-defining the objectives of the enterprise or by official requirements to achieve multiple and conflicting goals.

Lack of agreement on goals seems to be at the root of many difficulties pointed out by studies of SOEs. In the public-administration literature, the problem is referred to as "the accountability vs. autonomy" issue: SOEs are said to need "enough" autonomy to run their business operations without having to face the rigid difficulties inherent in the bureaucratic structure of government. At the same time, it is felt that an SOE should be accountable to government and parliament, and the latter should dictate its goals. Yet, the balance between "autonomy" and "accountability" has never been satisfactorily struck. The preceding analysis shows that this is no accident. The way the coalition of forces is structured bars the definition of precise goals. Even in less complex situations, as pointed out by Cyert and March, a quasi resolution of conflicts is a way of life.[11] However, even though conflicts cannot always be solved, they can be brought into the open to force decision makers to be confronted with several concrete choices. As there is no one principal but several tiers of agents, these agents can be forced to argue on choices to be made - and therefore implicitly on the goals - if independent "goal audit" is introduced, embodied in a broader comprehensive audit, as an integral part of the institutional design. Note that because goals are formulated as a result of interaction in a coalition, different institutional designs may change membership in the coalition and the relative power of different coalition members.

4.3 Comprehensive audit

The term *comprehensive audit* is used here in the sense suggested by Churchill and Cooper.[12] In compreshensive audit, the process of objective appraisal is extended to all aspects of management. The auditor is not necessarily a CPA, nor does he stop at the accounting attest function. Comprehensive audits are not restricted to financial transaction: They are extended to an examination and appraisal of the propriety of the objectives pursued and the methods used, effectiveness in stating objectives and in attaining them, and finally, the efficiency of performance as measured by the benefits received and the resources utilized.

Comprehensive auditing is done by a third party - someone whose interests are not identical with those who are audited or with the government ministry sponsoring the enterprise. The auditors are also agents who may have their own views about the "proper" objectives to be pursued. Also, the development of a comprehensive, audit scheme requires a considerable amount of skill. However, comprehensive audit is a major step in assuring that SOEs are accountable along socially relevant dimensions. In doing so, questions of goals pursued and the "right" objectives are put on the agenda of a public debate once the results of the audit are published.

Comprehensive audits have been tried by different state auditing organs - the General Accounting Office in the United States, the Cour des Comptes in France, the Auditor General in Canada, and the State Controller in Israel are some examples. In all these cases, it seems that such an audit helps to alleviate the lack of a principal. The audits by themselves, of course, cannot create agreed objectives. Different individuals continue to hold different points of view about the propriety of the objectives pursued, but the publication of comprehensive reports brings the conflict to the surface. It also helps in discussing the propriety of objectives actually pursued. This is an important development in an area where agreement on objectives is difficult to obtain and their achievement difficult to control. Needless to say, the impact of the report is largely a result of its general availability to the public. A report presented to management, and to it alone, will not have such an impact.

It might be noted that the existence of the audit creates an audit-anticipation effect.[13] Objectives that management, or the government, feels are improper in the eyes of the public will not be pursued in the first place. The very anticipation of an audit changes the behavior of those that expect to be audited.

To be sure, the institutional mechanism of comprehensive audit is not free of side effects: It costs money and requires managers to divert their energies from managing the enterprise to answering requests for audit. In addition, SOEs may be reluctant to reveal commercial information, as full disclosure puts them in a position of comparative disadvantage by allowing them less commercial secrecy than their private counterparts. Finally, in a parliamentary regime, as the government controls the parliament, state comprehensive audits may be less effective than one might wish. For that matter, state comprehensive auditing may be even less effective in regimes where democratic institutions are less powerful and less diffused, and where checks and balances in the political systems are not adhered to. In fact, in some such regimes, the government may not allow such audit to be carried out in the first place.

A variation of a ''goal audit'' may be one in which the government decides on the objectives of each enterprise at the time of creation and on an internal governmental body that reports directly to the board of directors and the government as a whole rather than to a specific sponsoring ministry without publishing the results. This may result in a redefinition or clarification of goals as the avoidance of publicity may reduce the resistance of the ruling coalition to such an audit. However, it may also reduce its effectiveness, as publicity is important in deciding on SOE objectives and priorities while keeping some modicum of freedom.

4.4 Conclusions

The agency-costs theory cannot be applied directly to the measurement of the costs of managing SOEs. By the same token, Williamson's definition of discretion does not apply.[14] Both the agent–principal theory and the Williamson hypothesis about discretion assume a clear objective and an identifiable principal. Therefore, Williamson can measure the size of discretion, at least conceptually, as the difference between the maximizing of the welfare of the principal and the actual behavior of the agent plus the cost of the contract. The major problem faced by organizational designers in planning the institutional relationships between SOE management and its constituents is that they somehow have to face the issue of a precise definition of the goals of the state in the establishment and operation of the firm.

The problem of setting goals for SOEs is to a large extent insoluble. As long as we do not have a theory of the state, as long as we do not know what the legitimate objectives of such enterprises are, how they are decided, and who decides on both objectives and trade-offs, there is no way to give a normative answer to whether or not the performance of a certain enterprise is ''socially desirable.'' Yet individuals have a feeling of what is legitimate and what seems to be in the public interest. Therefore, an independent audit of goals and objectives, at least under some conditions, may make the problem recognizable and thus partially solvable. At the very least, the decisions of management and other state agents may be subjected periodically to public scrutiny and subsequent adjustment. Without an open system of goals statement and auditing, state ownership may degenerate into a shift of power to a new managerial or bureaucratic class instead of achieving socially desirable objectives.

Notes

1 "Public Sector Enterprise: A State in the Market," *The Economist,* Dec. 30, 1978, p. 41.

2 N. L. Burkharin and E. Preobrazhensky, *The ABC of Communism* (London: Penguin, 1969), p. 114. English translation of 1920 Russan original.

3 O. E. Williamson, *The Economics of Discretionary Behavior: Management Objectives in a Theory of the Firm* (Englewood Cliffs, N.J.: Prentice-Hall, 1964), pp. 49–52.

4 For examples of optimal literature, see M. Harris and A. Raviv, "Some Results on Incentive Contracts," *American Economic Review* 68 (Mar. 1978):20–30; M. Harris and A. Raviv, "Optimal Incentive Contracts with Imperfect Information," *Journal of Economic Theory* 20 (Apr. 1979):231–59; B. Holmström, "Moral Hazard and Observability," *Bell Journal of Economics* 10 (Spring 1979):74–91; and S. Shavell, "Risk Sharing and Incentives in the Principal and Agent Relationship," *Bell Journal of Economics* 10 (Spring 1979):55–73.

5 For a discussion of these theories, see W. Baumol, *Business Behavior: Value and Growth* (New York: Macmillan, 1959); H. Simon, "Theories of Decision Making in Economics and Behavioral Science," *American Economic Review* 49 (June 1959):253–88; R. Cyert and J. March, *A Behavioral Theory of the Firm* (Englewood Cliffs, N.J.: Prentice-Hall, 1963); R. Marris, *The Economic Theory of Managerial Capitalism* (New York: Free Press, 1964); and Williamson, *Economics of Discretionary Behavior.*

6 Two well-known examples are A. Alchian and H. Demsetz, "Production, Information Costs, and Economic Organization," *American Economic Review* 62 (Dec. 1971):777–95; and M. Jensen and W. Meckling, "Theory of the Firm: Managerial Behavior, Agency Costs and Ownership Structure," *Journal of Financial Economics* 3 (Oct. 1976):305–60.

7 E. Fama, "Agency Problems and the Theory of the Firm," *Journal of Political Economics* 88 (Apr. 1980):288–307.

8 A. Phatak, "Governmental Interference and Management Problems of Public Sector Firms," *Annals of Public and Cooperative Economy* 40 (July-Sept. 1969).

9 Some well-known examples are the Nora Committee report in France (*Rapport sur les entreprises publique* [Paris: La Documentation française, Apr. 1967]); the white paper on nationalized industries in the United Kingdom (*Nationalized Industries: A Review of Economic and Financial Objectives* [London: HMSO, 1967], Commnd. 3437); the Israeli Government Companies Law 5737-1978 (*Sefer Ho Chukkim* 770 [1978]:163); the Statsföretag law in Sweden; and Canada's privy council report on crown corporations (*Crown Corporations: Direction, Control, Accountability: Government of Canada's Proposals* [Ottawa: Privy Council Office, 1977]).

10 See Y. Aharoni, "Managerial Discretion," in *State-Owned Enterprise in the Western Economies,* ed. Y. Aharoni and R. Vernon (London: Croom Helm, 1981), pp. 184–93.

11 Cyert and March, *Behavioral Theory of the Firm.*

76 **Principal–agent relationships**

12 N. Churchill and W. Cooper, ''Comprehensive Auditing'' (paper presented at meeting of Institute of Chartered Accountants of Ontario, Ottawa, June 12, 1978).
13 See N. Churchill, ''The Effects of an Audit'' (Ph.D diss., University of Michigan, 1962). A summary of the relevant material is available in N. C. Churchill and W. W. Cooper, ''Effects of Auditing Records,'' in *New Perspectives in Organizational Research,* ed. W. W. Cooper, H. J. Leavitt, and M. W. Shelley (New York: Wiley, 1964), pp. 250–75.
14 Williamson, *Economics of Discretionary Behavior.*

[13]

Ownership and Incentives

2.1 Introduction

Transfer from the public to the private sector (or vice versa) of entitlements to the residual profits from operating an enterprise necessarily implies a change in the relationships between those responsible for the firm's decisions and the beneficiaries of its profit flows. In general, the change in the allocation of property rights leads to a different structure of incentives for management and hence to changes in both managerial behavior and company performance. This chapter therefore analyzes some of these immediate incentive effects of privatization in the context of U.K. market arrangements and political institutions.

The relationships between managements and the proximate or ultimate recipients of residual profit flows can be viewed as giving rise to a particular set of agency problems. The general agency problem can be characterized as a situation in which a principal (or group of principals) seeks to establish incentives for an agent (or group of agents), who takes decisions that affect the principal, to act in ways that contribute maximally to the principal's own objectives. The difficulties in establishing such an incentive structure arise from two factors: (a) the objectives of principals and agents will typically diverge, and (b) the information available to principals and agents will generally be different (for example, the former might not be able to observe some of the decisions of the latter).

Within this framework managements of firms can be regarded as agents acting (in the case of private ownership) for shareholders or (in the case of U.K. public ownership) for the department of government to which they are responsible. Alternatively, in the latter case, government departments may themselves be considered to be agents acting for the ultimate principals, the voting public. Either way, an immediate consequence of privatization will be some shift in the objectives of principals. In addition, it is also to be expected that the transfer of ownership will be associated with some change in the types of incentive systems that can be offered to managements. Thus, under private ownership, rewards can be linked to the company's share price via share ownership or options schemes, while poor financial performance might be penalized by the threat of a takeover by another firm.

The implications of these differences in principal–agent relationships will be considered in sections 2.2 and 2.3 below. Of particular interest are the possible effects of ownership on economic efficiency, and, in examining this issue, it is useful to distinguish between allocative efficiency in the market, which depends upon the output levels of firms with given cost structures, and internal efficiency, which depends upon the total costs to the firms of producing given bundles of outputs.

In public policy debate in Britain, it has often been claimed that the privatization of firms with market power tends to improve internal efficiency, but at the risk of worsening allocative efficiency unless some of the effects of profit-seeking behavior are held in check by sufficiently rigorous competitive and/or regulatory constraints. As will be seen in sections 2.2 and 2.3, this view, while not necessarily incorrect as an empirical summary of final outcomes, rests upon a number of specific assumptions about the incentive structures associated respectively with private and public ownership. Thus, to explore further the nature of the trade-off between allocative and internal efficiency that exists when a firm is transferred from public to private ownership, section 2.4 of the chapter sets out a simple formal model that incorporates changes both in objectives and in the effectiveness of the system for monitoring managerial performance. In this example it turns out that unit costs are lower under private ownership if and only if the private monitoring and incentive system is significantly better than the public system.

Section 2.4 also serves to highlight a very important point in the economics of privatization. Ownership arrangements are only one of a variety of factors that influence managerial incentive structures and economic performance, and, in particular, the competitive structure of the industry in which the firm is operating and the regulatory constraints that it faces will each have significant effects on incentives (and hence on both allocative efficiency and internal efficiency). Moreover, the impact of changes in any one of these three sets of influences (ownership, competition, and regulation) on efficiency will, in general, be contingent upon the other two.

Competitive forces and regulatory policies will be examined in detail in chapters 3 and 4 and, for the moment, it need only be noted that the theoretical analysis indicates that the effects of privatization cannot properly be assessed in isolation from these additional influences on incentives. This conclusion is also supported by empirical studies of the relative performance of public and private industry in the U.K. and elsewhere, some of which are summarized and discussed in section 2.5.

Although somewhat uneven in quality and scope, the empirical literature does at least serve to counter the simplistic view that the effects of ownership on performance are uniform and independent of other economic conditions.

2.2 Private Ownership

2.2.1 Principal–Agent Theory

Economic analysis of the behavior of privately owned firms most frequently rests upon the assumption that the aim of decision makers is the maximization of profit, where the latter is defined to encompass both current and future financial flows. However, while it is likely that privatization will indeed lead managers to place greater weight on profit goals, the changes involved are rather more complex than a straightforward shift to profit maximization. It will therefore be useful first to consider some general features of the underlying principal–agent problem, together with their implications for the behavior of a "typical" company that has been transferred to the private sector.

A general description of the agency problem runs as follows. There exists a principal and an agent—the owner and the manager of a firm, for example—who do not share the same objectives. The principal wants to induce the agent to act in his (the principal's) interests, but he does not have full information about the circumstances and behavior of the agent, and so he has a monitoring problem. This prevents the principal from successfully telling the agent what to do, for he cannot fully observe what is happening. In any event, he would usually want the agent's behavior to depend on circumstances that perhaps only the agent can observe. Principal–agent theory is concerned precisely with this problem of information and incentives. It addresses the central question: what is the optimal incentive scheme for the principal to lay down for the agent?

There are two versions of the basic principal–agent model. Let W and π be the utility functions of the principal and agent respectively, let a be the agent's action (which might be his level of effort), and let θ represent the state of the world. The principal cannot observe a or θ individually, but he can observe the outcome $x(a, \theta)$ of the agent's action given θ, and he makes his own action (e.g. a payment to the agent), denoted y, a function of that observed outcome. Thus the principal's problem is to choose $y(x)$, the *incentive scheme* for the agent. In doing so he must recognize two constraints. First, the agent will behave in a self-interested way given the incentive scheme. Second, the incentive scheme must be attractive enough for the agent to be willing to participate in the venture with the principal.

The two versions of the basic model differ according to whether the agent can or cannot observe θ at the time when he chooses his action. If he cannot, the agent chooses a to maximize his expected utility given $y(x)$. Much now depends upon the agent's attitude to risk. If he is risk-neutral, the optimum incentive scheme takes a simple form: the principal receives a flat amount from the agent whatever happens. That is, the agent bears all the risk (but being risk-neutral he does not mind that), incentives are "perfect," and there is no monitoring problem. However, if the agent is averse to risk, optimality requires the principal to offer the agent some insurance in bad states of the world. This dulls the agent's incentives, because he gains only part of the benefit resulting from extra effort on his part. The asymmetry of information can therefore give rise to "slack."

In the second version of the model the agent *can* observe θ before deciding on his action. His strategy in the face of incentive scheme $y(x)$ will then be a function $a(\theta)$, since the best action will depend upon circumstances (i.e. on θ). As before, the principal must also ensure that the incentive arrangement is sufficiently attractive for the agent to want to take part in it. (This "participation constraint" can take a variety of forms depending on whether it needs to hold for all θ, on average, or whatever.)

There are numerous applications of principal–agent theory in economics, including relationships between regulators and managers (see section 4.3), employers and workers, lenders and borrowers, landlords and tenants, insurers and the insured, and tax authorities and households. A fuller exposition of the theory and some of its uses is given by Rees (1985), whose bibliography contains detailed references. In what follows, however, we will initially be concerned only with the relationships between the shareholders and managers of a privately owned company.

The decisions in such a company will be taken by professional managers whose payoffs will not exclusively be dependent upon profit flows. At the simplest level, it can be assumed that managerial utility is a function of income and effort levels, although several other relevant variables have been suggested in the literature, including the sales revenue of the firm, its growth rate, and the level of discretionary managerial expenditures. The inclusion of one or more of these additional variables is usually motivated by a desire to capture the implications of managerial preferences for greater power and increased prestige.

The typical large company will have many shareholders, each of whom possesses a relatively small fraction of the total equity of the firm. In addition the shares in the company will be marketable. Hence, at any time, a shareholder can transfer his property rights to another investor and thereby terminate his direct relationship with the company. As a consequence, substantial changes in the number of principals and in the distribution of shareholdings can occur quite rapidly (see Alchian and Demsetz, 1972).

In these circumstances the pursuit of its own objectives by the management of the firm will be constrained by three groups of participants in capital markets:

(i) the firm's shareholders, seeking contractual arrangements with management that maximize their own payoffs;

(ii) other investors or their agents (e.g. managers of other companies), who might purchase the firm's shares as a prelude to attempting to alter existing contractual arrangements;

(iii) the firm's creditors (including lenders at fixed interest), who could seek managerial changes in the event of threatened or actual default.

The impact of these three groups on managerial incentives will be analyzed under the headings of shareholder monitoring, takeovers, and bankruptcy.

2.2.2 Shareholder Monitoring

Before examining the problems faced by principals in specifying and enforcing managerial contracts, it is necessary first to consider shareholders' objectives. The working assumption that will be made is that shareholders seek to maximize their expected financial return (profit) from the company. One justification for this approach is that, if shareholders hold diversified asset portfolios, it is reasonable to suppose that in respect of their returns from any one individual firm they will be approximately risk-neutral. There are, however, a number of possible objections to the assumption, and since some of them may be significant in the context of the U.K. privatization program they should be noted explicitly.

First, in a world of uncertainty, asymmetric information, differential taxation, and incomplete markets, the interests of different shareholders will not coincide. Even if it were true that each sought to maximize his expected financial return from the firm, in general there would be a lack of unanimity in shareholders' rankings of alternative managerial policies. For example, an institution such as a pension fund might prefer a higher dividend payout ratio than an individual investor faced with a somewhat different tax position. This is, of course, a general problem in the theory of the firm that can only be dealt with at the cost of a substantial increase in the complexity of the analysis (see Ekern and Wilson, 1974).

Second, if shareholders are also consumers of the firm's products, their interests in decisions will not be confined to the effects of managerial actions on financial returns. To illustrate, while a higher price might contribute positively to shareholder welfare through an accompanying increase in company profits, it would have the additional effect of reducing welfare derived from the shareholder's consumption of the final output. The point is particularly relevant where consumers of a monopolist's products hold a substantial fraction of its share capital (e.g. a newly privatized utility company such as British Telecom or British Gas).

Third, for a variety of reasons, many of the shareholders of a company transferred to the private sector may not in fact have diversified asset portfolios. Thus, by encouraging wider share ownership in general, and employee share ownership in particular, the U.K. privatization program has created a large class of small shareholders with interests in only a very limited number of companies. In such circumstances the risk-neutrality assumption may well be inappropriate.

We will return to some of these points later when we come to analyze the detail of privatization policies in Britain. Initially, however, our focus will be on other aspects of the agency problem surrounding privately owned firms, and, for the moment, the assumptions that shareholders are expected-profit maximizers and are unanimous in their rankings of managerial actions will suffice.

Given this assumption, then, the first issue to be considered concerns the implications of dispersed share ownership for the effectiveness of shareholder monitoring of management. If there existed only one, risk-neutral, shareholder, we could hypothesize a benchmark optimal contract between the firm's owner and its management. The terms and conditions of such a contract would depend upon factors such as the relevant production function, managerial preferences, and the information structure of the problem (who knows what and when, and the methods and costs of acquiring more information). At this stage the precise details of the optimal contract are not important; all that needs to be assumed is that there are nonzero specification and enforcement costs. A single owner would bear all these costs but, in return, would receive all the residual profit flow from the firm.

When the ordinary share capital of a firm is divided amongst many investors, the activity of specifying and enforcing managerial contracts confers external benefits on others. If one of the shareholders engages in this task, he bears the full cost of the activity but receives only a fraction of the total gain. For example, if the increase in expected profit resulting from an incremental increase in monitoring by i, assumed to cost c_i, is equal to $\Delta\pi$, the individual shareholder will only receive a benefit of $\mu_i\Delta\pi$, where μ_i is the fraction of the shares held by i. In such circumstances there is a danger that, from the perspective of shareholders as a whole, the intensity with which managers are monitored will be suboptimally low. If that is the case managers can be said to have discretion to pursue their own objectives and it may not be appropriate to base analysis of company behavior on the expected-profit-maximization assumption.

A second reason why dispersed shareholdings might lead to suboptimal monitoring of managements emerges from possible characteristics of the monitoring technology. As a result of factors such as economies of scale in the acquisition of information, it could be more cost effective to have monitoring activities concentrated in a single pair of hands, thereby avoiding the possible duplication of effort associated with multiple shareholdings. In other words, cost conditions might be such as to make monitoring of management a natural monopoly.

The problems associated with dispersed shareholdings, and in particular their implications for assumptions about the objectives of the firm, have long been recognized in the economics literature. Nevertheless, profit maximization, together with its variants that allow for risky profit flows, has continued to maintain a dominant position in the formal analysis of company behavior. One defense of this standard position rests upon the takeover threat which will be discussed in section 2.2.3. Other arguments include the following.

First, company law establishes a framework in which monitoring activities can be centralized via a board of directors for the firm. Directors are elected by shareholders, and serve as agents for the latter in specifying and enforcing managerial contracts. For example, the directors can establish incentive structures that link managerial remuneration to financial performance through such mechanisms as profit-related bonuses and share option schemes. While this arrangement introduces a further layer of principal–agent relationships (with attendant monitoring problems), it is at least arguable that the existence of nonexecutive directors partially attenuates the discretion of managements.

Second, it is sometimes claimed that, for many firms, the degree of dispersion of shareholdings has been exaggerated. Thus, when the holdings of various members of the same family are consolidated it frequently turns out that, for medium-sized firms at least, there exists a group that accounts for a significant fraction of the share capital. Again the point is not that external effects in monitoring activities are absent, but rather that such effects are smaller than is sometimes supposed.

Third, to reduce risk, the typical investor will hold a diversified portfolio of shares. For large institutional investors such as pension funds and insurance companies, the holdings may be spread over hundreds of companies and in total may amount to billions of pounds. The principal–agent relationship between a given investor and a given management should not therefore be viewed in isolation from other similar relationships elsewhere. In deciding upon the appropriate level of monitoring activity in respect of one company, the shareholder will take account of any secondary effects that such an activity will have upon the value of his holdings in other firms, since, in conditions of imperfect information, actions will send information signals to other managements that tend to affect the latter's behavior (cf. Kreps and Wilson, 1982). Thus, active monitoring of one management may help to create or maintain a reputation for toughness that in turn serves to restrict the discretion of the managers of other firms in which the investor has an interest. Put more formally, the incremental benefit of an increase in monitoring of one management can be expressed as $\Delta\bar{\pi} + \mu_i\Delta\pi$, where $\Delta\bar{\pi}$ is the increase in expected profit from other companies in the portfolio. Hence, even if μ_i is relatively small, there might still be substantial incremental payoffs from monitoring, and hence the suboptimalities implied by the earlier analysis could be relatively small.

Finally, even accepting the existence of managerial discretion at the senior management level, the implications of this phenomenon for profit performance may not be clear cut. The existence of larger rewards at the top of the hierarchy serves as a prize that intensifies internal competition for the acquisition of senior management positions, with associated benefits for company performance. That is, when the managerial function is viewed as a whole, the existence of large prizes at the top may serve as a relatively satisfactory incentive structure for shareholders. Moreover, in conditions of oligopolistic competition it will not generally be optimal for shareholders to have profit-maximizing managers acting as their agents. Thus, if managers derive utility from higher sales or market shares, the existence of discretion arising from dispersed shareholdings will influence the decisions of rivals and will thereby have an indirect effect on the profits of the firm in question. It is therefore possible to envision circumstances in which, via its effects on the behavior of rivals, more dispersed share ownership is associated with *higher* realized profit flows (cf. Vickers,1985c).

In conclusion, it can be seen that, because the principal–agent relationships between managements and shareholders exhibit a number of subtleties, it would be premature to conclude that models of company behavior embodying one or other variant of the profit-maximization hypothesis should be abandoned when shareholdings are dispersed. However, uncritical acceptance of the notion that the managers of privately owned firms will *always* be constrained to act in the best interests of their shareholders is an equally unacceptable position. What is indicated is a more case-specific approach to the incentive problem that allows for some quantification of the various factors that are relevant to the principal–agent relationships.

2.2.3 Takeovers

Thus far we have been considering situations in which the management of a newly privatized firm is confronted by a large number of shareholders who seek to introduce incentive structures aimed at maximizing expected profit. Since shares are marketable, however, the size distribution of shareholdings can change quickly as a result of investors' buying and selling decisions. In particular, at any time, one individual or institution can seek to purchase *all* of the shares by making a takeover bid for the company. If successful, the bid would concentrate ownership and eliminate the externalities associated with multiple holdings. It can therefore be argued that, as a consequence of marketability, dispersion of shareholdings is not a factor of great significance for managerial incentives.

Consider, for example, a management that was not maximizing expected profit. A takeover raider could purchase all the shares of the company and then proceed to specify and enforce the optimal contract appropriate to the new single-shareholder situation. Suppose that the shares of the target company can be acquired at a price p, and that the value of each share following the introduction of the optimal contract is p^*. Suppose further that there are n shares in the target company on the market and that the transactions cost of the acquisition is f. Then the capital gain available to a successful raider is equal to $n(p^* - p) - f$ and, assuming that potential acquirors are profit maximizers, a takeover will occur when this expression is positive. Alternatively, the condition for a profitable takeover can be rewritten as $p < p^* - f/n$.

The argument is now straightforward. If the management of a firm fails to act in ways consistent with the optimal contract, the share price of the company will fall and the cost of purchasing shares will decline relative to np^*, the value of the firm contingent upon the existence of the optimal contract. As the deviation between p^* and p increases, the management will at some point become vulnerable to a takeover raid. The existence of this perceived threat of takeover in turn acts as an incentive mechanism that deters management from the pursuit of policies that are substantially at variance with the interests of its shareholders.

The effectiveness of the takeover mechanism in establishing incentives for good financial performance is a matter of some importance for the analysis of privatization policies. When a firm is transferred from the public sector the introduction of shares creates a market for corporate control, and if this market functions in the way described in the preceding paragraphs it can be argued that, whatever the implications of privatization for allocative efficiency, the transfer of ownership will produce powerful incentives toward internal efficiency. Thus, if the firm's internal efficiency is poor, its share price will be relatively low and management will be vulnerable to a hostile bid. The argument does not, of course, imply that *any* deviation from maximum internal efficiency will be punished in this way: some degree of managerial discretion will exist, if only because the transactions costs of takeovers are finite. If, however, the latter are low, management's performance will be heavily constrained by the threatened loss of control.

Detailed economic research on takeovers has revealed several reasons, some theoretical and some empirical, why the above line of argument might lead to a misleading perspective on the efficiency of the market for corporate control. Following Grossman and Hart (1980), consider first the decision faced by a shareholder who receives an offer to buy from a raider intent on increasing the market value of the target company. Let the value of the offer be p per share and assume that, because shares are widely held, each investor believes that his own sell/hold decision has a trivially small effect on the outcome of the bid. If the offer is expected to succeed, the value of the shares will rise to p^*, and it will be better for the shareholder to decline the offer and free-ride on the performance improvement that it is anticipated the raider will generate. In such circumstances all shareholders will decline the offer and the bid will fail. Hence, in equilibrium (where expected outcomes coincide with actual outcomes), there can be no successful takeovers at an offer price less than p^*. However, transactions costs imply that raids are unprofitable at offer prices greater than or equal to p^*. It follows that there is no equilibrium price at which successful takeovers will occur.

The stark simplicity of the free-rider argument's implications are contradicted by the historical record of takeover activity in the U.K. Between 1964 and 1970, for example, approximately one in three of all companies quoted on the London Stock Exchange disappeared as a result of acquisition, and a "mistake" theory of takeovers is clearly incapable of providing a satisfactory account of this and similar episodes. There are a number of possible explanations of the discrepancy between theory and evidence, including the following:

(i) strategic behavior by holders of diversified portfolios who accept offers in order to establish reputations as willing sellers and thereby put greater pressure on the managements of other companies in their portfolios;
(ii) the lack of protection afforded to minority shareholders under U.K. company law, which leaves them vulnerable to oppression by the controlling interest (e.g. via profit transfers out of the target company) in the event that they do not sell and the bid succeeds;
(iii) the compulsory acquisition provisions of U.K. company law—once an acquiror has obtained acceptances in respect of 90 percent of the ordinary share capital the remaining 10 percent (or less) can be compulsorily purchased at the offer price accepted by the majority—which can be used by the raider to eliminate the payoffs from free-riding strategies.

The first of these points is another version of the reputation argument outlined in section 2.2.2 above. The second has been developed by Grossman and Hart, who treat the post-raid level of oppression of minority interests as a control variable that can be set *ex ante* by the shareholders of the target company. Suppose, for example, that an acquiring company can transfer an amount $\gamma\,(>0)$ per share from minority shareholders to itself. If a raid is expected to succeed, the maximum post-acquisition value of a share to a minority holder then becomes $p^* - \gamma$. Thus, if $\bar{p}$ is the value of each share if the raid fails, selling is the optimal decision (irrespective of expectations of success and failure) if the offer price satisfies the two "acceptance" conditions: $p > p^* - \gamma$ and $p > \bar{p}$. However, the "profitability" condition for a successful bid is, as before, $p < p^* - f/n$. The three acceptance and profitability conditions can therefore simultaneously be satisfied, and hence equilibrium takeover bids can occur, if $\gamma > f/n$ and $p < p^* - f/n$. That is, provided the per-share level of oppression exceeds f/n, the effectiveness of the takeover constraint on the behavior of incumbent managements is restored.

There are considerable obstacles, however, to the precise specification of the level of oppression of minority interests, and there is little evidence that the instrument has been widely used by individual groups of shareholders as a mechanism of managerial control in Britain. Rather, protection of minority interests has been determined by the general provisions of company law and the regulations of bodies such as the City of London Panel on Takeovers and Mergers. In practice, U.K. company law offers only extremely limited protection for minority holders, and, although this eliminates the payoffs from free-riding strategies, it does so at the risk of creating incentives for socially excessive rates of takeover activity: partial takeovers become attractive as a result of the prospective returns from oppression of minority interests, and, if a bid is expected to succeed, there is the possibility that shares could be acquired at a price *below* the pre-bid market level because of the threat of partial expropriation. The provisions of company law have therefore been buttressed by regulations set out in the City Code on Takeovers and Mergers, several of which are designed to protect shareholders against these two outcomes (see Yarrow, 1985). However, as its name implies, the City Code is a form of self-regulation and the associated Takeover Panel has only limited powers of control. Hence, the question of whether or not the existing regulatory framework does in fact provide a level of shareholder protection commensurate with effective functioning of the takeover mechanism continues to be vigorously debated.

The compulsory acquisition provisions of section 209 of the Companies Act 1948 represent a more direct policy response to free-rider problems associated with takeover bids. If an offer is contingent upon acceptances in respect of at least 90 percent of the shares of the target company, the incentives to hold shares in the hope of participating in post-acquisition performance improvements are removed, since, if the acceptance level is attained, the successful raider has a right to purchase all the remaining shares. The vast majority of mergers and acquisitions in Britain are, in fact, characterized by offers that are contingent upon a 90 percent acceptance rate (see Franks and Harris, 1986a).

The compulsory acquisition solution to the free-rider problem is not entirely straightforward, however. Unless accompanied by a sufficiently damaging threat of oppression, the cost of declining an initial offer, even if it is expected eventually to succeed, may be relatively small. Then, if shareholders anticipate that, if the bid is not initially successful, an improved offer will be made (possibly as a result of competition from a second bidder), incentives to hold shares may be restored. Nevertheless, we believe that, taken as a whole, the British regulatory and legal framework does successfully overcome many of the adverse consequences of free-rider strategies, and therefore permits the threat of takeover to act as a potentially important constraint on managerial behavior. Although the solution is not perfect, and many residual problems remain, any major deficiencies in the market for corporate control are more likely to be the result of other influences that are at work in the market, to some of which we now turn.

Thus far it has been assumed that the objective of the acquiring firm is expected-profit maximization and that takeovers are triggered by deviations in the target management's behavior from that implied by its optimal incentive contract. Both assumptions are open to question. In the first place, raids may be motivated by a desire to increase managerial utility rather than to increase shareholder welfare. Thus, takeovers should be viewed as a potential *instrument of* managerial-utility maximization as well as a *control on* such behavior. Given this point, it is by no means clear that high levels of takeover activity will always be in the interests of shareholders. Second, even if raiders *are* profit seekers, takeovers may be motivated by factors such as the gains from increased market power or from reductions in tax liabilities. King (1986), for example, has argued that British merger activity has historically been correlated with stock market prices as a result of a tax-induced distortion in the pricing of financial assets. The implications of these factors are that even an efficient management may be vulnerable to takeover bids and, more generally, that the link between internal efficiency and the takeover threat may be weakened.

One consequence of this last point is illustrated by the following model of the incentive effects of takeover threats. Suppose that managerial utility is given by $U(x)$, where $U_x < 0$, $U_{xx} < 0$, and x can be interpreted as either the level of managerial effort or a measure of the internal inefficiency of the firm. Let x^* be the effort level associated with the optimal contract. Without loss of generality, $U(x^*)$ can be set equal to zero, and for simplicity we assume this also to be the utility of management in the event that the firm becomes a takeover victim. It is further assumed that the market value of the firm is an increasing function of effort, and that higher effort therefore reduces the perceived probability of takeover. In particular, suppose that the probability of takeover in the period $(t, t+\mathrm{d}t)$, conditional upon the firm having survived until time t, is equal to $h(x; \theta)\,\mathrm{d}t$, where $h_x < 0$ and θ is some parameter affecting the relationship between effort and the likelihood of takeover. (In reliability theory, the function $h(.)$ is called the hazard rate.)

In these circumstances the discounted present value of expected managerial utility is given by

$$\int_0^{\infty} U(x) \exp[-(r + h)t]\,\mathrm{d}t = \frac{U(x)}{r + h(x; \theta)}, \tag{2.1}$$

where r is the discount rate. Maximizing this expression with respect to x yields the first-order condition

$$\frac{U_x}{U} = \frac{h_x}{r + h} \,. \tag{2.2}$$

The equilibrium level of effort is therefore determined by the condition that the marginal proportionate increase in utility consequent upon a reduction in effort is equal to the present value of the marginal increase in the probability of takeover, where the latter is calculated at a discount rate equal to $r + h$. Thus, as can be seen more directly from (2.1), one effect of the takeover threat is to increase the discount rate that managers apply to future utility (from r to $r + h$). Determination of the equilibrium effort level, denoted $\bar{x}$, is illustrated graphically in figure 2.1.

Consider next the effect of a change in the parameter θ which leads to an increase in the conditional probability of takeover at effort level x (θ can be interpreted as reflecting conditions in the market for corporate control). As can be seen from figure 2.1, the implications of the change for the equilibrium effort level depend upon whether the function $h_x/(r + h)$ is shifted upwards (effort decreases) or downwards (effort increases). In general the effect is ambiguous, depending upon the relative magnitudes of two counteracting forces. First, the increase in the conditional probability of takeover raises the denominator in the expression on the right-hand side of (2.2), leading, other things being equal, to an upward shift of the function. Intuitively, managerial discount rates are raised, producing

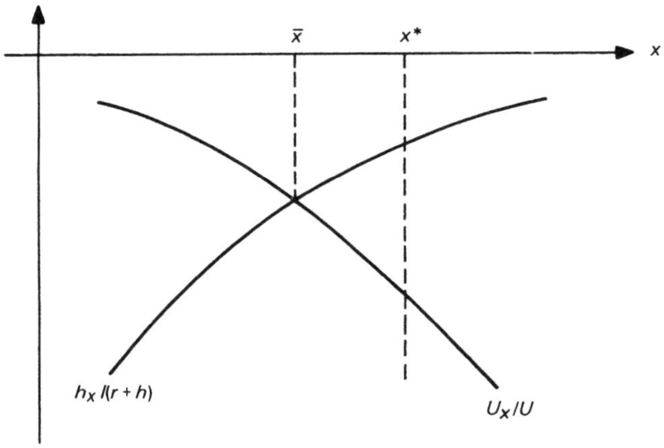

Figure 2.1 Takeover threats and managerial effort

greater incentives for shirking while the incumbent management is still in control of the firm ("making hay while the sun shines"). Second, greater takeover activity can be expected to increase the sensitivity of the probability of takeover to changes in effort or internal efficiency. That is, the absolute value of the derivative h_x can be expected to increase. Other things being equal, this shifts the function $h_x/(r + h)$ downwards, leading to greater effort being applied. In this case the intuition is that increased shirking is punished more heavily by a greater increase in the probability of takeover.

The model therefore demonstrates the possibility that a more active market in corporate control may be associated with lower internal efficiency. The effectiveness of the takeover threat depends upon the strength of the link between managerial effort and the probability of takeover. However, since raids may be motivated by factors other than the potential capital gains resulting from the correction of poor managerial performance, the creation of freely transferable property rights associated with privatization does not have uniformly benign implications for internal efficiency. One potentially adverse effect is an increase in managerial discount rates. In the model above this feeds through into an incentive to reduce effort levels, but it is easy to see how an increased emphasis on shorter-term payoffs could also have adverse implications for other decision variables (e.g. investment) in more elaborate analyses.

It can also be noted that, since acquisition of other firms may be one of the favored methods of increasing managerial welfare, an increase in the threat of takeover could produce a positive feedback effect by encouraging potential target companies to become raiders themselves, thus exacerbating the control problem. This is one example of a more general class of problem connected with the incentives for incumbent managements to engage in defensive actions to counteract the takeover threat, which actions may themselves have undesirable effects on shareholders' interests. Particularly in countries such as the U.K., where shareholders have very little direct influence on acquisition decisions, an unconstrained market in corporate control could easily generate an excessive level of takeover activity.

We conclude, therefore, that theoretical analysis of takeovers indicates a number of possible limitations to the effectiveness of this form of capital market constraint on the performance of managements. That is not to say, however, that takeover threats have no role to play in promoting internal efficiency. Indeed, in general we believe that raiders can, and often do, perform a useful function in this regard, particularly where they have better information about the performance of incumbent managements than the latter's own shareholders (see Scharfstein, 1986). The point is simply that the impact of the takeover threat depends heavily upon the precise characteristics of the relevant capital market, including factors such as the extent of shareholder protection afforded by the regulatory and legal frameworks, the constraints imposed by competition law, and the relevant fiscal system. Since these vary from country to country, we should not be surprised to find that the role played by the takeover constraint also shows marked international variations. Given our concern with privatization in Britain, it will therefore be useful to examine briefly some of the available U.K. evidence on the effectiveness of the market for corporate control.

The most extensive empirical work on U.K. acquisitions has been conducted by Singh (1971, 1975) who has sought, among other things, to estimate the empirical relationship between company performance and the likelihood of takeover (which relationship is the cornerstone of the argument that takeovers generate incentives for managers to act in the interests of owners). Singh found only small differences in profitability and other measures of financial performance between companies that became takeover victims and companies that did not, casting doubt on the notion that relatively poor performance leads to a sharp increase in the threat of takeover. In contrast, the data did suggest that the likelihood of takeover diminished significantly for firms above a certain size, suggesting that the most effective defense against unwanted bids is for potential targets themselves to seek rapid growth by means of acquisitions. Although later experience indicates that very large companies have now become more vulnerable to unsolicited takeover bids than in the periods studied by Singh, it remains true that the sizes of newly privatized firms such as British Telecom and British Gas provide incumbent managements with substantial protection against takeover threats. In these cases, therefore, there must be considerable doubt as to the efficacy of the takeover constraint on managerial performance.

Meeks (1977) examined the other side of the capital market discipline argument: if raids are motivated by the capital gains that can be realized from improving the performance of an inefficient company, it is to be expected that the financial performance of successful acquirors will itself improve following the takeover. In his sample, however, he could find no evidence of general post-raid increases in the profitability of acquirors, and, if anything, there was a slight, though not statistically significant, deterioration in profitability relative to industry averages.

Unfortunately, the findings of Singh and Meeks cannot be regarded as decisive evidence against the hypothesis that the probability of takeover is strongly linked to company financial performance. Suppose, for example, that such a relationship exists, but that the management of each firm chooses to act in a way that leads to a probability of takeover that is constant across firms. In equilibrium there would then be no observed differences in the average profitabilities of firms that were and were not takeover victims in a given period. Moreover, competition among potential acquirors might ensure that, where takeover bargains were accidentally available, the gains were appropriated by the targets' shareholders. That is, competition in the market for corporate control might drive the returns from acquisition down to approximately normal levels, implying that no significant net gains could be expected to accrue to successful raiders.

The results of later studies by Firth (1979, 1980) are less ambiguous. Firth found that, although on average the combined market values of acquirors and acquirees in his sample were not materially affected by the takeovers, the average share prices of acquirors fell significantly upon the announcement of the bid while the share prices of acquirees increased substantially. In other words, on average the takeovers led to supernormal losses for the acquirors' shareholders, in line with the hypothesis that takeovers tend to be used as an instrument for improving managerial welfare. Although these results are quite consistent with the view that managers are also constrained by a link between performance and the threat of takeover, taken in conjunction with the theoretical model outlined above they do illustrate the point that shareholder interests may not always be well served by a highly active market for corporate control.

Firth's results have recently been challenged by Franks and Harris (1986a, 1986b) who, using a larger sample and a longer sample period, concluded that acquisitions *did* increase the aggregate market value of the companies involved, and that on average there was no evidence of supernormal losses to acquirors' shareholders. The Franks and Harris results are in line with those of the majority of U.S. studies of the issue (e.g. Halpern, 1973; Mandelker, 1974; Asquith, 1983), although it should be noted that there are dissenting voices (e.g. Malatesta, 1983). Since a large fraction of U.K. takeovers have been of a broadly horizontal nature, to the extent that they do actually exist, such gains may, of course, simply reflect increases in market power rather than improvements in internal efficiency. Where researchers have specifically tried to uncover efficiency improvements attributable to takeovers, the results have not been very encouraging for the capital market incentives argument. Thus, Cowling *et al.* (1980) found no evidence for the proposition that mergers had led to significant improvements in the internal efficiencies of the companies in their sample, while Newbould (1970) concluded that both *ex ante* appraisals of acquisitions and *ex post* plans to realize potential efficiency gains were, in a high proportion of the cases he studied, extremely limited in scope.

To summarize, although theoretical analysis and empirical evidence do not yield unambiguous conclusions about the strength of the managerial incentives generated by the existence of a market for corporate control, they do indicate certain imperfections in the market that may limit the impact of capital market disciplines on internal efficiency. One problem is the relative lack of shareholder influence on acquisition decisions, over which managers continue to have considerable discretion. Acquisitions therefore appear frequently to have been used to promote managerial interests at the expense of shareholders, and the consequent high level of takeover activity may, by raising managerial discount rates, have had negative consequences for both internal and allocative efficiency. Another potential limitation, which is of some importance for the policy evaluations contained in chapters 8 through 11, is that the takeover constraint may be relatively weak in cases where the target firm is very large.

2.2.4 Bankruptcy

Bankruptcy can be viewed as another means by which managers may lose control of the company, and can therefore be regarded as leading to an alternative version of the takeover constraint. In discussing the implications of bankruptcy, however, the analysis of the previous section has to be modified to take account of a number of special features of control loss that occurs via this mechanism, including (a) the circumstances in which bankruptcy is likely to occur, (b) the fact that proceedings may be initiated by a different group of economic agents (creditors, for example), and (c) the legal and regulatory framework governing the process.

At the simplest level, bankruptcy can be assumed to occur when the market value of the firm's assets falls below the value of its outstanding liabilities. It therefore sets a floor value for the market capitalization of the firm. If it is assumed that managerial utility is a decreasing function of effort, that there is no uncertainty, and that bankruptcy is the only operative constraint, utility-maximizing managers would choose an effort level such that the total market value of the firm is exactly equal to the value of its debt. In these circumstances, while the value of the firm might be increased by raising its debt level, shareholders would derive no benefits from the change: the value of equity would always be zero.

Once uncertainty is introduced, however, it is easy to see how the threat of bankruptcy affords some protection to ordinary shareholders. To illustrate, let the market value of a firm with debt level D be $\pi(x) + \theta$, where θ is now a random variable with zero mean. The probability of bankruptcy is then the probability that $\pi + \theta < D$, which can be rewritten as $\theta < D - \pi$. It is therefore equal to $F(D - \pi)$, where $F(.)$ is the cumulative distribution function of θ and $F'(.) > 0$.

If $F(.)$ is reinterpreted as a hazard rate, a straightforward adaptation of the model in section 2.2.3 leads to the assumption that managers will seek to maximize

$$\int_0^{\infty} U(x) \exp\{-[r + F(.)]t\} \, dt = \frac{U(x)}{r + F(.)}$$

where managerial utility in the event of bankruptcy has again been normalized to zero. The first-order condition for the optimal effort level is

$$\frac{U_x}{U} = -\frac{F'\pi_x}{r + F(.)}. \tag{2.3}$$

If θ^m is the maximum value of θ, the market value of the ordinary shares of the company will be positive provided that the solution of equation (2.3) is such that $0 < \pi(x) + \theta^m - D$ since there will then be states of nature in which the total value of the firm exceeds D and in which shareholders will therefore receive positive returns.

Condition (2.3) is similar in form to equation (2.2) in section 2.2.3. The numerator of the expression on the right-hand side of (2.3) is the marginal reduction in the probability of bankruptcy resulting from increased effort, while the denominator is the effective managerial discount rate. As before, it can be seen that a finite probability of bankruptcy raises this discount rate and that, in general, the overall impact of an increase in the probability of bankruptcy on the effort level is ambiguous in sign.

It can be expected that the tightness of the bankruptcy constraint will largely be dependent upon the difference between the maximum expected value of the firm, denoted π^*, and the firm's debt level. The impact of the constraint on managerial decisions is likely to be greater where market conditions are such as to reduce the value of this spread. Thus, when the relevant industry is experiencing a period of recession or of more intense product market competition, the role of the bankruptcy threat as a control mechanism is likely to be enhanced. However, in boom conditions its role, relative to the other constraints on managerial behavior, will tend to be more limited.

If shareholders are able to control the level of debt of the firm they will be able to use this instrument to influence managerial behavior by varying the incentive structure that faces the management. This can be seen by noting that, since the level of debt is a parameter of the managerial-utility maximization problem set out above, the equilibrium effort level will be a function of D, denoted $x(D)$. Hence, via changes in D, shareholders can, in principle, influence the internal efficiency of the firm.

There are at least two limitations, however, on the strength of the incentives that can be established in this way. The first emerges as a consequence of the effects of increased debt on the managerial discount rate. Thus, particularly when probabilities of bankruptcy are relatively high, increasing debt may have a relatively greater impact on the denominator of the right-hand side of (2.3) than on the numerator, in which case the effort level becomes a *decreasing* function of D. In effect, if managers believe that the firm has a good chance of going out of business whatever decisions they take, this will lead them to the conclusion that they should enjoy more managerial discretion in the short run. If this occurs, on the criterion of promoting internal efficiency there will usually be a finite optimum debt-to-equity ratio. At this point the usefulness of the bankruptcy constraint as a control mechanism will have been exploited to the fullest possible extent, and further improvements in efficiency will not be feasible via reliance on this mechanism alone.

The second limitation of the bankruptcy constraint is that, in practice, determination of the firm's level of debt is a decision that is most frequently delegated to managements. Hence, managers can ease the constraint, and thereby simultaneously weaken the incentives for internal efficiency and increase their own utility, by choosing lower debt levels than shareholders would wish to see. It is, of course, true that managers will have regard to the consequent negative effects on the market value of the firm's equity. The extent of the concern with valuation effects, however, will be governed by the constraints on managers arising from the threats of shareholder intervention or takeover. Hence, in very many circumstances it is the latter that will be the effective control mechanisms. Only when market values are low as a result of factors such as depressed demand or intense product market competition is it likely that the threat of bankruptcy will play a substantial role. Thus, for example, it is unlikely that this particular control mechanism will have much effect on the incentives for internal efficiency in privately owned monopoly utilities.

2.3 Public Ownership

For publicly owned firms the task of monitoring managerial performance is entrusted to government. Compared with private ownership, the most obvious differences in the relationships between managers and their immediate principals arise from the facts that (a) the principals do not typically seek to maximize profits, (b) there are no marketable ordinary shares in the firm, and hence no *market* for corporate control, and (c) there is no direct equivalent to the bankruptcy constraint on financial performance.

Even more than in the case of private ownership, the precise detail of the principal–agent relationships surrounding public industry is heavily influenced by the institutional structures of the relevant economy. Since chapter 5 will be devoted to an examination of the nature and record of public ownership in Britain, the discussion in the current section will be restricted to the broader economic issues and problems associated with the specification of objectives and with the framework of control.

2.3.1 Public Interest Theories

Public interest theories are based upon the assumption that, in their dealings with industry, government departments seek to maximize economic welfare. The rationale for this approach is that such bodies are themselves agents for, and therefore properly should act in the best interests of, the wider public. Put another way, public interest theories abstract from the incentive problems associated with this agency problem by implicitly assuming that a first-best solution to it can be attained. We will return to this issue in section 2.3.2.

The usual approach is to assume that the objectives of government departments are defined by some form of social welfare function—thereby also begging questions connected with the aggregation of individual preferences—and the most frequently adopted specification is that social welfare is equal to the sum of consumers' and producers' surpluses, denoted S and π respectively. In other words, it is assumed that government departments seek to maximize a partial equilibrium measure of economic efficiency. There are, however, two "public interest" reasons why, in practice, governments might want to attach differential weights to consumers' and producers' surpluses in their objectives.

The first arises from *distributional* objectives. In the case of a privately owned firm, if shareholders are typically more wealthy than the average taxpayer a government concerned with redistribution might wish to reduce transfer payments from taxpayers to shareholders. Moreover, irrespective of the type of ownership, low income households often account for a substantial fraction of the sales of some utility industries (because income elasticities of demand for the goods are low), in which case the government might attach extra weight to consumer interests for distributional reasons. In addition to these possible "egalitarian" motives for distributional objectives, a government concerned only with domestic welfare would discount the proportion of a (wholly or partially) privately owned firm's profits accruing to overseas shareholders (a factor that is relevant in the telecommunications and gas privatizations discussed in chapters 8 and 9).

A second reason why a government would not be indifferent to transfer payments to the firm arises from the costs of raising public funds. For example, the payment of a subsidy to the firm requires raising tax revenue from elsewhere in the economy or extra government borrowing or money creation. But higher taxes will add to the distortion of economic decisions in other markets (for example, higher income tax would affect the trade-off between work and leisure). Similarly, borrowing or money creation would cause costs to be incurred elsewhere. In short, the payment of an additional £1 subsidy to the firm would impose upon the rest of the economy a cost that is in excess of £1.

The simplest way to incorporate distributional considerations is to write the government's objective as $W = S + \alpha\pi$, where $0 < \alpha < 1$. The cost of public funds can be represented by stating the objective as $W = S + \alpha\pi - \lambda T$, where $\lambda > 0$, T is the transfer paid to the firm, and λT captures the cost of the extra distortions created elsewhere in the economy. Although these versions of a government's objective function have the virtue of simplicity, it must be remembered that they are very crude when viewed in the light of the complex general equilibrium effects that should ideally be taken into account. The shortcomings of the partial equilibrium approach are well known, but it does at least provide a useful starting point from which the analysis can proceed.

Given a welfare-maximizing government, and assuming for the moment that monitoring of management is equally effective under both types of ownership, it is immediately obvious that public ownership has some potential advantages over the private alternative. In particular, it provides government with additional policy instruments to correct any deviations between social and private returns that arise from failures in goods and factor markets. To give just one example, profit-maximizing monopolists may engage in a variety of business practices that run counter to the public interest, and, while it may be feasible to limit such behavior via the provisions of competition or regulatory policies, the complexities of this type of exercise in conditions of asymmetric information may render public ownership the preferred framework in which to tackle the problems.

The market failure argument can also be applied to the market for corporate control: government monitoring does not encounter the public good problems associated with dispersed shareholdings and avoids the transactions costs of share purchases that are incurred by takeover raiders seeking to gain control of a firm. In contrast with a shareholder who owns only a small fraction of the outstanding shares, government departments can directly intervene in managerial decision making or can set appropriate incentive structures for the managers of publicly owned firms. Thus, for example, government can, *in principle*, provide profit-related bonuses and/or fire personnel when performance is poor.

The loss of some instruments of control (e.g. takeover and bankruptcy threats) that results from public ownership does not necessarily imply, therefore, that monitoring is thereby made less effective. For privately owned firms, Williamson (1975) has argued that hierarchical arrangements can, in appropriate circumstances, produce more efficient monitoring than capital markets. Indeed, it is difficult to understand why firms of any size should exist at all if hierarchical solutions to the control problem were not more efficient than market solutions in a wide range of economic conditions.

Determination of the balance of advantage between hierarchical and market control systems, however, is a complex exercise. One of the major aspects of performance monitoring is the acquisition of relevant information about the firm. Under public ownership this information-gathering role is effectively entrusted to a single body, whereas private ownership typically involves the participation of many individuals and institutions that are frequently specialists in the given task. While there may be scale economies in the acquisition of information, it is also likely that competition among independent monitors will lead to the discovery of a greater volume of relevant information. The possibility remains, therefore, that, even from the idealized perspective of public interest theories of governmental policy, private monitoring may provide the more effective method of control.

2.3.2 Government Incentives

The assumption that the public interest can be represented by a well-defined function which governments seek to maximize is clearly rather heroic. In one sense it can be regarded as the obvious counterpart of the assumption that privately owned firms are profit maximizers, since the latter is based upon the notions that shareholders' interests are well defined and that managers act in the best interests of their shareholders.

Nevertheless, just as in the case of private ownership, an examination of the relevant principal–agent relationships is required to assess whether or not the assumption is likely to provide a sound basis for analysis of the behavior of publicly owned enterprises.

The position is complicated by the fact that two distinct groups of public officials are involved in monitoring activities: politicians and civil servants. The full monitoring hierarchy is therefore made up of the general public, its elected political representatives, nonelected civil servants, and the managers of the publicly owned firms. Hence, it is necessary to analyze a number of separate principal–agent problems.

Consider first the relationships between the general public and its elected representatives. As in the case of managers, it is unlikely that preferences of politicians can accurately be captured by a simple and general objective function. The variables upon which utility might be assumed to depend are numerous and include factors such as monetary rewards, effort levels, and power. One feature of the problem does stand out, however, and that is the relative insecurity of tenure enjoyed by politicians: the period spent by one individual as head of a department responsible for the control of a particular public enterprise is frequently rather brief, and may be ended by electoral failure or by promotion or demotion. Since the politicians of a given party have a common interest in electoral success, it is likely that promotion and demotion within the period of office of a given administration will in turn depend heavily upon the individual's contribution to the electoral prospects of his own party. If it is assumed (a) that the utility of politicians is much higher in office than out of office and (b) that the effects on utility of changes in other variables are substantially smaller in magnitude, this suggests that a useful starting point for the analysis of political behavior is the hypothesis that decisions are taken with a view to maximizing the probability of electoral success.

Given this hypothesis, it might still be maintained that, with respect to the behavior of publicly owned firms, politicians will seek to achieve economic efficiency. For, if resources were not allocated in an efficient manner, there would be scope for improving the welfare of some sections of the public without making others worse off, which should have a positive, or at least nonnegative, effect on the electoral prospects of the political party in power.

The argument does depend, however, upon voters being well informed about both the decisions made on their behalf and the eventual consequences of those decisions, and in practice there will be very considerable informational asymmetries between politicians and voters. Consider, for example, the position of a typical member of the public. He or she will have an opportunity to vote once every four or five years and will face an almost zero probability of influencing the outcome of the election. Further, the election will be concerned with a wide range of issues, not just with the question of the stewardship of any one publicly owned firm. In these circumstances, the average voter has very little incentive to acquire costly information about the performance of elected representatives in monitoring particular firms.

Furthermore, the benefits and costs of political decisions are often not evenly spread throughout the population. Those groups that are substantially affected by monitoring activities (the workers in a publicly owned firm, for example) will therefore have greater incentives to acquire information than the average voter, with the result that informational asymmetries between different groups of voters will also emerge.

The latter asymmetries imply that politicians responsible for the monitoring of public industries may no longer derive electoral benefits from improvements in economic efficiency. To illustrate, suppose that improvements in the internal efficiency of an enterprise are possible but that, in the absence of compensatory transfer payments, they would lead to a fall in the welfare of workers in the industry. Political action to encourage managers to reduce unit costs would be observed by workers who suffer materially as a consequence, but the benefits from lower taxes and/or lower prices, if widely spread throughout the population, might not be visible to the recipients. On the other hand, if workers in the industry *were* compensated for their losses, this would draw the attention of taxpayers to the magnitude of the benefits from efficiency improvements that they (the taxpayers) would be required to forego so that workers can continue to enjoy the fruits of the earlier inefficiency. Thus, whether or not compensation is actually paid, informational asymmetries indicate that an efficiency improvement could sometimes lead to a worsening of electoral prospects. In a similar vein, there could be electoral benefits in setting politically sensitive prices (e.g. domestic telephone rates, electricity and gas prices) at levels below marginal cost, since the direct positive impact on consumers is more visible than the indirect negative effects arising from the accompanying changes in fiscal policy.

To summarize, in addition to suggesting that consumers' and producers' surpluses will be accorded differential weights in government objectives, the asymmetric information arguments imply that payoffs to workers in publicly owned firms will also be a factor that affects the utility of elected officials. Thus, an appropriate specification of the *political* objective function might be

$$GW = S + \alpha\pi - \beta x - \lambda T$$

where x is some measure of the effort applied to cost reduction in the industry. The negative weight attached to x in this equation captures the electoral payoffs from easing the pressures on the wage rates and effort levels of workers in the industry.

In the context of public ownership in Britain there is one further point about the role of politicians in the monitoring hierarchy that is worth making at this stage. Until recently, the option of linking managerial rewards to performance in relation to underlying political objectives has been eschewed. This may have been due in part to the difficulties of measuring some of the components of the underlying objective function (consumers' surplus and workers' rents, for example) but also probably reflects an unwillingness explicitly to reveal those objectives. Whatever the cause, the result has been that control of public enterprises has frequently involved political intervention in the detail of the managerial decision process itself, rather than the "arm's length" relationship between departments and managers that was envisioned when many of the enterprises were first nationalized (see chapter 5). The consequent confusion of roles is therefore an additional source of potential inefficiencies in the control of nationalized industries.

Turning to the civil servants who, in support of their ministers, undertake much of the detailed monitoring work, it can be expected that insecurity of tenure will play a less central role in explaining behavior than in the case of elected politicians. The two most commonly cited variables that are likely to affect utility in this case are the size of the relevant government department or subdepartment and the rents accruing to the officials (see Niskanen, 1971). Thus, if y is a variable measuring the output of the department, z is the actual unit cost level (assumed to be a decision variable), and c^* is the efficient unit cost level, the utility of officials might be assumed to be given by a function $U[y, (z - c^*)y]$ which has positive first-partial derivatives. An economic model of bureaucratic behavior could then be constructed by assuming that this function is maximized subject to a fixed budget constraint of the form $yz = B$.

Suppose, for example, that $U(.) = y^2(z - c^*)$. In that case it can easily be shown that equilibrium activity and unit cost levels will be equal to $B/2c^*$ and $2c^*$ respectively. The activity of the department is therefore an increasing linear function of the budget, while unit costs are always equal to twice their optimal level. Substituting back into the utility function we find that maximized utility is equal to $B/4c^*$, so that, as is to be expected in general, the payoffs to officials are an increasing function of their departmental budget. (Some models of bureaucratic behavior, which are more concerned with the process of budget determination than with output/efficiency choices, simply assume that officials aim to maximize an indirect utility function $U(B)$.)

The activities of civil servants are, of course, monitored by the politicians who are in charge of their departments. As the above example shows, however, if the size of budget is the only instrument of control, the resulting outcomes may be far from satisfactory: unit costs in the model are twice their optimal levels. More direct monitoring of bureaucratic activity will therefore be required if effective performance is to be achieved, but there are a number of reasons for believing that the results will not be entirely satisfactory. First, there is the problem of asymmetric information between civil servants and departmental ministers which, in countries such as the U.K., is exacerbated by the relatively brief periods of tenure of particular ministerial offices by given politicians. Lacking good information about departmental performance, and in particular lacking suitable benchmarks against which such performance can be evaluated, ministers may find it extremely difficult to improve efficiency. Second, the incentives for ministers to search for performance improvements are generally fairly weak since the resulting payoffs are unlikely to have much of an impact on electoral prospects. Third, the factors that increase the welfare of civil servants are likely, other things being equal, to have positive effects on ministerial welfare: ministers can also be assumed to favor increases in the size of their departments and to derive some benefits from higher rents to the civil servants who surround them. Indeed, U.K. departmental ministers are frequently notorious for the tenacity with which they seek to increase or defend their own budgets.

Although it can be expected that a given level of bureaucratic activity will be conducted at greater than minimum unit cost, it is not clear whether the level of activity itself is likely to be suboptimally high or low in relation to either political or social objectives. The key factor is the size of the budget: whichever of the two objectives is used as the benchmark, the higher the budget expenditure the more likely it is that the departmental activity level will be excessive, as can be seen from figure 2.2.

In the diagram, the line MB shows the marginal benefit of departmental activity, and it is assumed that the budget is set at a level where the total benefit of the activity is equal to its total budgetary cost (i.e. that

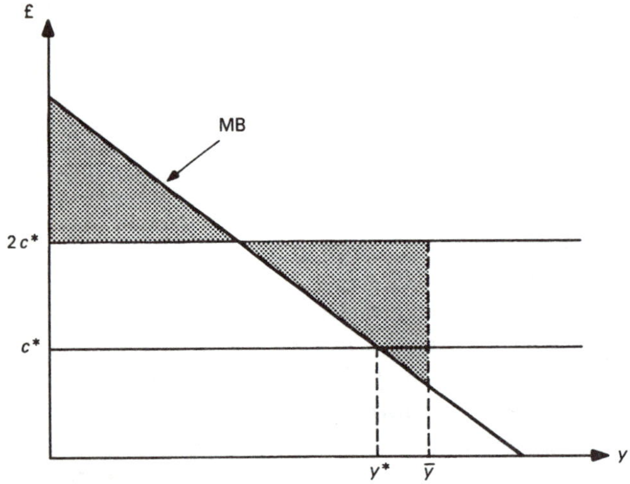

Figure 2.2 Determination of bureaucratic activity level

bureaucratic activity absorbs all the potential surplus that is available). The equilibrium activity level is therefore $\bar{y}$, which is determined by the condition that the two shaded triangles are equal in area. The optimal activity level, given by the condition that marginal benefits are equal to (efficient) marginal costs, is y^*, which is less than $\bar{y}$. Equilibrium output $\bar{y}$, however, is directly proportional to the size of the budget so that, if the latter were reduced, it could easily turn out to be the case that bureaucratic activity is suboptimally low ($\bar{y} < y^*$).

To conclude, judged in terms of public interest criteria, we have identified four potential sources of suboptimality in the framework of control for publicly owned industries: displacement of social objectives by political objectives; a preference for direct political intervention in managerial decisions over an "arm's length" relationship that would restrict government departments to the task of setting appropriate managerial incentive structures; internal inefficiencies in bureaucracies; and inefficient levels of bureaucratic activity. The implications of these factors for the performance of publicly owned firms will vary with the precise institutional details of differing frameworks of control, and we will have more to say on this issue in chapter 5. However, as a matter of general principle, it can safely be concluded that incentive structures for public enterprises will tend to exhibit significant imperfections at each level of the monitoring hierarchy and, in particular, that public interest theories of political decisions are unlikely to provide an adequate conceptual basis for the analysis of behavior in nationalized sectors of the economy.

2.4* Ownership and Economic Efficiency: A Benchmark Model

As noted in the introduction to this chapter, it is possible to argue that the privatization of a firm that enjoys substantial market power will tend to improve internal efficiency, but at the risk of worsening allocative efficiency unless profit-seeking behavior is held in check by an appropriate framework of competition and regulation. The purpose of this section, therefore, is to examine this possible trade-off between internal and allocative efficiency in the context of a very simple model in which a monopoly firm is privatized. The assumptions underlying the analysis are intended to capture (albeit in a highly stylized way) a number of the features of private and public ownership that have been discussed in sections 2.2 and 2.3. A more extensive treatment of the issue has been provided in a recent paper by Bös and Peters (1986).

Consider therefore the situation of a private monopolist supplying a homogeneous good, and suppose that, by virtue of the principal–agent problems outlined in section 2.2, managerial incentives to engage in cost-reducing activity are imperfect. That is to say, the manager is rewarded only partially for the benefit that the owners receive from cost reduction. To reflect this assumption it is postulated that the manager maximizes

$$\begin{aligned} A(q,x) &= \pi(q,x) - (a-1)x \\ &= [p - c(x)]q - ax, \end{aligned}$$

where q is the output level, x is expenditure on cost-reducing activities, p is price, $c(x)$ is unit cost, and a measures the cost of effort to the private manager relative to the benefit to him of greater profit. If $a = 1$ he would have the "right" incentives for effort (i.e. he would be a profit maximizer), but in general we shall assume imperfect incentives, in which case $a > 1$.

Under public ownership the manager of the firm is assumed to maximize

$$\begin{aligned} B(q,x) &= S(q,x) + \pi(q,x) - (b-1)x \\ &= V(q) - cq - bx, \end{aligned}$$

where $V(q)$ is consumer utility from output q. For simplicity, in this specification consumers' surplus and producers' surplus have been assumed to have equal weights in the political objective function, and the resource costs of any transfers to or from the firm have been assumed to be zero. The parameter b measures the cost of effort to the public manager relative to the benefit to him of greater social welfare ($= S + \pi$). Imperfections in the public monitoring system, including any weight given to the rents of workers in political objective functions, are reflected in the assumption that $b > 1$ (workers' rents can be taken to be negatively related to managerial effort). If public and private monitoring systems were equally effective, we would have $a = b$, but if incentives are keener under private ownership, as many would contend, then we have $a < b$.

In summary, the effects of privatization in this simplified setting are to change the (ultimate) principal's objective from welfare maximization to profit maximization and to alter monitoring and incentive arrangements (as represented by the change from b to a in the managerial objective function). The resulting trade-off is clear. Public managers choose the socially optimal level of output for a given cost level, whereas private managers do not, since they seek monopoly profits. Thus allocative efficiency under public ownership is better than that under (unregulated) private ownership. However, if $a < b$, then, for given output, private managers achieve greater internal efficiency than public managers. The overall balance of advantage will therefore depend upon the relative magnitudes of these two effects.

In what follows we denote outcomes under private ownership by a circumflex and those under public ownership by an asterisk. When public monitoring arrangements are no less efficient than private mechanisms we have the following result:

$$\text{if } a \geqslant b, \text{ then} \quad \begin{aligned} q^* &> \hat{q} \\ p^* &< \hat{p} \\ x^* &> \hat{x} \\ c^* &< \hat{c} \\ W^* &> \hat{W}. \end{aligned} \tag{2.4}$$

That is, public ownership is superior in terms of both internal and allocative efficiency. The (straightforward) proof of the proposition is omitted, but the intuition is as follows. Public managers produce more output and set a lower price than private managers with similar cost levels because they set price equal to marginal cost rather than marginal revenue equal to marginal cost. Since they produce more, public managers also have a greater incentive to reduce costs because the resulting savings are enjoyed across a larger volume of output. Therefore public managers both produce more *and* make more cost-reducing effort, and social welfare is unambiguously higher.

It follows from considerations of continuity that public ownership is also superior when $a < b$ in a neighborhood of b. Hence, a necessary condition for the superiority of private ownership is that a should be distinctly less than b. In other words, private incentive systems must be significantly better.

Matters can be taken a little further by postulating isoelastic functional forms for $p(q)$ and $c(x)$:

$$p = \sigma q^{-\varepsilon}, \quad \sigma, \varepsilon > 0;$$
$$c = \beta x^{-\alpha}, \quad \beta, \alpha > 0.$$

Thus, ε is the inverse elasticity of demand and α is the elasticity of unit cost with respect to the relevant expenditures. Under the given demand conditions $V(q)$, which is the integral of the inverse demand curve from 0 to q, is $\sigma q^{1-\varepsilon}/(1-\varepsilon)$, and is therefore equal to the revenue of the firm multiplied by $1/(1-\varepsilon)$. We require $1 > \varepsilon$ for this to be well defined, in which case the effect of the change in objectives is equivalent to a proportionate outward shift in the firm's demand curve.

The resulting maximization problems are now fairly straightforward. For example, in the private ownership case the first-order conditions yield

$$\sigma(1-\varepsilon)\hat{q}^{-\varepsilon} - \beta\hat{x}^{-\alpha} = 0$$
$$\alpha\beta\hat{x}^{-\alpha-1} - a = 0.$$

For the publicly owned firm, the output term in the first equation becomes $\sigma q^{-\varepsilon}$ and b replaces a in the second equation; otherwise the expressions are similar. It can be shown that the second-order conditions are satisfied in both cases if, as we will assume, $\varepsilon > \alpha/(1+\alpha)$.

Solving the two models and comparing the equilibria, we find that

$$\hat{q} \gtrless q^* \text{ according as } (1-\varepsilon)^{(1+\alpha)/\alpha} \gtrless a/b. \tag{2.5}$$

This shows how outputs (and hence prices) under the two regimes depend upon the demand elasticity and the sensitivity of cost to effort, as well as the relative effectiveness of the monitoring schemes. As demand becomes more elastic (i.e. ε becomes smaller), the monopoly mark-up of the private firm is reduced, quantity increases, and price becomes lower. This enhances the incentive for cost reduction, and it may be the case that costs are reduced so much that, even with the monopoly mark-up, the price is lower under private ownership. Condition (2.5) also brings out the importance of α, which measures the scope for cost reduction. If α is small enough, public ownership certainly implies lower prices.

With respect to the comparison between cost-reducing activities we have that

$$\hat{x} \gtrless x^* \text{ according as } (1-\varepsilon)^{1/\varepsilon} \gtrless a/b. \tag{2.6}$$

Again, the elasticity of demand is found to be of central importance. For any a and b, if the elasticity is sufficiently low (ε close to 1), then $x^* > \hat{x}$ and costs are lower under public ownership. The limit of $(1 - \varepsilon)^{1/\varepsilon}$ as ε approaches zero is $1/e = 0.3679$, and therefore a must be *much* smaller than b for it to be true that $\hat{x} > x^*$, no matter how elastic demand may be.

Conditions (2.5) and (2.6), together with the assumptions that $a < b$ and $\varepsilon > \alpha/(1 + \alpha)$, imply that

$$\hat{q} \geqslant q^* \text{ implies } \hat{x} > x^*.$$

This is entirely natural. If the private firm produces more than the public firm, then it achieves more cost reduction because the private incentive system is keener. Conversely, if $x^* > \hat{x}$, then $q^* > \hat{q}$: if the public producer has lower costs, then it produces more than the private firm.

A detailed comparison of aggregate welfare under public and private ownership involves messy expressions, but some relatively simple results can be derived from the above propositions. For example, if $a/b \geqslant (1-\varepsilon)^{1/\varepsilon}$, condition (2.6) implies that $x^* > \hat{x}$. Hence, $q^* > \hat{q}$, and it follows that $W^* > \hat{W}$. Thus, $a/b \geqslant (1-\varepsilon)^{1/\varepsilon}$ is a sufficient condition for social welfare to be higher under public ownership. By similar reasoning it can also be shown that $a/b \leqslant (1-\varepsilon)^{(1+\alpha)/\alpha}$ is a sufficient condition for social welfare to be higher under private ownership.

The cases involving intermediate values of a/b lead to much more cumbersome expressions, but the above analysis of sufficient conditions at least indicates some of the principal features of the problem, and in particular the importance of α and ε, the fundamental parameters of technology and demand. Thus, for example, if ε is interpreted as a measure of the degree of competition faced by the firm and if α is interpreted as a measure of the the rate of technical progress in the industry, the analysis tends to support the notion that the merits of privatization are greater in technologically progressive industries where competition is effective. However, given both the static nature of the analysis and the assumption of only one firm, it would be wrong to stretch the interpretations too far.

It should also be stressed that only unregulated private enterprise has been considered. The incorporation of regulation would introduce a new policy instrument into the model, involving a further trade-off between internal and allocative efficiency (see chapter 4), and can generally be expected to lead to results that are more favorable to private ownership than are those derived above. Nevertheless, the possibility of regulation is unlikely to affect the central implication of the analysis, which is that privatization is likely to improve social welfare only if it provides significantly keener managerial incentives than does the control system for public enterprise.

2.5 Performance under Public and Private Ownership: The Evidence

Given that the relative performance of publicly and privately owned firms in respect of allocative and internal efficiency will depend upon a range of factors that includes the effectiveness of the respective monitoring systems, the degree of competition in the market, regulatory policy, and the technological progressiveness of the industry, evaluation of the welfare implications of privatization necessarily depends upon empirical assessment of the role and significance of each of these various factors. Much of the second part of the book will be devoted to this task for cases that have arisen in the context of the U.K. privatization program. At this stage, however, it will be useful to take a preliminary look at the findings of the more general literature that has been concerned with empirical comparisons of the performance of public and private firms.

Unfortunately, despite the large number of studies that have been conducted, the results of this empirical literature are less informative than might be anticipated. In the first place, many studies focus almost exclusively upon the ownership variable and fail to take proper account of the effects on performance of differences in market structure, regulation, and other relevant economic factors. In part, this is simply a consequence of data problems: the limited number of observations available renders it difficult to conduct complex multifactor analyses. It is also attributable, however, to theoretical failures: even where sufficient data are available, statistical tests have rarely been sophisticated enough to take account of the interacting (nonseparable) effects of ownership, competition, and regulation on incentive structures, and hence on the performance of firms.

Second, in measuring performance there has been a tendency in the empirical literature towards reliance upon variables that are easily observable. Thus, rather than attempting to estimate the sum of producers' and consumers' surpluses, the more usual approach is to examine factors such as profitability, factor productivity, and unit cost levels. As a consequence, in some studies the methodology leads to a bias in favor of private ownership. Given some degree of market power, it might be expected that private firms will tend to be the more profitable, but this in itself has no direct bearing on the question of economic efficiency.

Similarly, a finding that private firms have lower unit costs than their public counterparts does not necessarily imply that their contributions to social welfare are greater; questions relating to allocative efficiency and to the quality of goods or services provided also need to be taken into account.

In the light of this second set of comments it is perhaps surprising that, in surveying the empirical literature up to around 1980, Millward (1982) concluded that there appeared to be no general ground for believing that managerial (i.e. internal) efficiency was lower in public firms. However, a closer examination of the material on which Millward based his article, taken in conjunction with the results of later work, suggests a slightly different conclusion, namely, that privately owned firms tend, on average, to be the more internally efficient when competition in product markets is effective. Thus, subject to the latter condition about competition and provided that other allocative inefficiencies associated with market failures are not substantial, we would argue that the available evidence supports a presumption in favor of private enterprise. However, when market power is significant, and particularly when company behavior is subject to detailed regulation, there is little empirical justification for a general presumption in favor of either type of ownership, and case-by-case evaluation of the various trade-offs is therefore in order.

Investigation of the relative performance of public and private enterprises has been most active in the United States, where the two types of ownership frequently coexist in similar market conditions. The industries that have been most extensively covered include electricity generation and distribution, water, and refuse collection; see Millward (1982), Yarrow (1986), and Boardman and Vining (1987) for bibliographies. With respect to electricity supply, a number of economists (Meyer, 1975; Pescatrice and Trapani, 1980; Fare *et al.*, 1985) have concluded that, after allowing for differences in output mixes and input prices, public sector utilities typically have lower unit costs than privately owned utilities. However, the results are not entirely convincing. As in Europe, public electric utilities have access to cheap capital and, given the capital intensity of the industry, their relative unit costs are highly sensitive to the adjustments made to allow for this factor. Thus, one recent study (Edison Electric Institute, 1985) has argued that earlier papers failed to make adequate allowances for the lower input prices facing public utilities and that, once the appropriate corrections are made, the evidence indicates that ownership has little effect on internal efficiency. Nevertheless, it can safely be concluded that the evidence does not establish the clear-cut superiority of private ownership in respect of cost efficiency.

Analysis of the pricing behavior of public and private electric utilities in the United States also serves as a warning against the presumption that allocative efficiency is necessarily improved by public ownership. Both Peltzman (1971) and De Alessi (1977) found that time-of-day pricing (which, in electricity supply, can be expected to lead to higher allocative efficiency) was more common in private utilities. Tariff structures, however, are heavily influenced by the regulatory environment, and there is evidence suggesting that this is the more important determining factor: jurisdictions in which the quality of regulation is generally regarded as high have been pioneers in the introduction of time-of-day pricing. Moreover, the publicly owned electricity industries in both Britain and France were early proponents of sophisticated peak-load pricing structures.

Work on the U.S. water industry suggests similar conclusions. For example, Crain and Zardkoohi (1978) found that, although regulated private water utilities exhibited over-capitalization (see section 4.2.1), their higher labor productivity implied that, on balance, their unit costs were lower than in public utilities. In contrast, a later paper by Bruggink (1982) found in favor of public enterprise on unit cost criteria. Taken in conjunction with the research on U.S. electric utilities, we are therefore led to the conclusion that, where firms face little product market competition and are extensively regulated, there is no generally decisive evidence in favor of one or other type of ownership.

Research on refuse collection in the United States highlights a different point. Here the findings are much more supportive of the proposition that private firms exhibit greater internal efficiency (see Kitchen, 1976; Savas, 1977; Stevens, 1978), but the more important factor in determining performance may be competition rather than the type of ownership *per se*. The incidence of private firms will tend to be correlated with the existence of competitive tendering for contracts, and the effects of the latter may incorrectly be ascribed to the ownership variable. Thus Savas (1977) found that the gap between the unit cost levels of public and private firms was closed by competitive tendering arrangements.

This last result is not altogether surprising. Competition acts as a selection mechanism that weeds out the less efficient firms: enterprises that survive are those that have passed the selection test and, provided that the competition between the different types of enterprises is fair (which is, of course, a major proviso), substantial differences in the internal efficiencies of the survivors are not to be expected. Confirming evidence of the importance of competition can be found in the study by Caves and Christensen (1980) of the relative performance of the two Canadian railroad companies, one privately owned and the other publicly owned. On the basis of their findings, Caves and Christensen argue that "public ownership is not inherently less efficient than private ownership," and that the "oft noted inefficiency of government enterprises stems from the isolation from *effective* competition rather than public ownership *per se*." It should be stressed, however, that in this context effective competition presupposes equitable treatment of publicly and privately owned enterprises and that in practice this condition will not always be satisfied. Thus, the tendency of governments to subsidize public firms may account for the rather different findings of Boardman and Vining (1987), who conclude that private companies exhibit significantly better performance in competitive environments.

It would also be wrong to interpret the results of Savas and of Caves and Christensen as implying that, even when markets are effectively competitive in the full sense, there is absolutely *no* link between internal efficiency performance and the type of ownership of the firm (i.e. that ownership does not matter). Supposing, for example, that private firms generally *are* the more efficient, it is to be expected that this will show up in the frequency with which they win contracts. That is, although the unit costs of surviving public firms may, on average, be as low as the costs of their private rivals, we would expect to see far fewer of them in competitive markets. Since this is exactly what we do observe, the evidence, although not conclusive, is at least consistent with a general presumption in favor of private ownership in these conditions. Moreover, in practice, it is often difficult to envision the practical development of greater competition in product markets, and of more effective franchise bidding systems, without allowing actual or potential entry of private firms. Ownership and competition may conceptually be distinct, but that is not to say that changes in the pattern of ownership have no implications for competitive behavior. Thus, in industries where public ownership predominates and where one of the goals of public policy is to promote greater competition (see chapter 3), the available evidence offers some support for certain types of privatization policies.

Evaluation of the relative performance of private and public firms in the U.K. has been much less systematic than in the United States. The existence of state monopolies in utility industries such as electricity, gas, telecommunications, and water has meant that there are no immediate domestic benchmarks against which the performance of the public enterprises can be assessed. As a consequence, most empirical work has focused upon more competitive market structures where the two types of ownership have coexisted.

A good example of this type of study is the paper by Pryke (1982), which compares economic performance in three industries: airlines, ferries and hovercraft, and the sale of gas and electricity appliances. Pryke analyzed a range of productivity, profitability, and output variables, and concluded that, in each case, the private firms tended both to be more profitable and to exhibit greater internal efficiency than their public sector rivals. These findings have been reinforced by later work on airlines (Forsyth *et al.*, 1986) and ferries (Bruce, 1986). Similarly, Rowley and Yarrow (1981) found a slight deterioration in the productivity performance of the British steel industry following nationalization in 1966, coupled with more significant declines in market share and in the rate of diffusion of new steelmaking processes. With respect to refuse collection, a U.K. study by Hartley and Huby (1985) supports the earlier conclusions of U.S. research: the introduction of competitive tendering appears to have promoted reductions in unit costs.

However, each of the U.K. papers is open to objections of one form or another. For example, in the Pryke studies it is not clear that like is always compared with like: in respect of the sales of electricity and gas appliances, the public firms are compared with the more efficient of the private companies operating in the market, thereby biasing the results against the former. In the steel industry paper, the sample period ended in 1975, before the dramatic improvements in productivity that occurred (under public ownership) from the late 1970s onwards (see section 5.7.3). Finally, an Audit Commission study (1984) of refuse collection costs discovered wide variations in public sector performance, with the better public enterprises exhibiting lower unit costs than many of the private firms in the sample.

Nevertheless, U.K. research does provide additional backing for our earlier conclusion that, where competition is effective, the available evidence suggests that private enterprise is generally to be preferred on both internal efficiency grounds and, subject to the qualification that other substantive market failures are absent, social welfare grounds. To repeat, this does not mean that, in competitive markets, we believe that public enterprise is always and everywhere the less efficient type of ownership. Relatively efficient public enterprises can and do survive, but, on average, we would expect the frequency of this occurrence to be lower than for private enterprises.

2.6 Concluding Remarks

In this chapter we have examined some of the implications of different types of ownership for managerial incentive structures and enterprise performance. Broadly speaking, it can be concluded that "ownership matters" in the sense that changes in the structure of property rights are likely to have significant effects upon firm behavior. At this level of abstraction, however, it is hard to be very precise about the detailed implications of changes in the ownership of a firm, since the latter depend upon factors such as the relevant institutional environment, including the framework of regulation for firms with market power, and the market structures of the industries in which the firms operate. The main message, therefore, is simply that managerial incentive structures are determined via a complex set of interactions among factors that include the type of ownership, the degree of product market competition, and the effectiveness of regulation.

Given the incentive problems associated with the control of publicly owned firms, it is likely that public monitoring systems are generally less effective than their private counterparts. It has been shown, however, that this in itself does not imply that, judged against social welfare criteria, the performance of public industry will be inferior, since allowance also has to be made for the effects of the shift in the objective functions of principals. Where product markets are competitive, it is more likely that the benefits of private monitoring systems (e.g. improved internal efficiency) will exceed any accompanying detriments (e.g. worsened allocative efficiency), a view that is generally confirmed by empirical studies of the comparative performance of public and private firms. In the absence of vigorous product market competition, however, the balance of advantage is less clear cut and much will depend upon the effectiveness of regulatory policy.

References

Alchian, A. and H. Demsetz (1972). Production, Information Costs and Economic Organization. *American Economic Review* 62: 777–795.

Asquith, P. (1983). Merger Bids, Uncertainty, and Stockholder Returns. *Journal of Financial Economics* 11: 51–83.

Audit Commission (1984). *Securing Further Improvements in Refuse Collection.* London: HMSO.

Boardman, A.E. and A.R. Vining (1987). *A Comparison of the Performance of Private, Mixed and State Owned Enterprises in Competitive Environments.* Working Paper 1206, Faculty of Commerce, Columbia University, New York.

Bös, D. and W. Peters (1986). *Privatization, Efficiency, and Market Structure.* Discussion Paper A-79, Institute of Economics, Bonn University.

Bruce, A. (1986). State to Private Sector Divestment: The Case of Sealink. In Coyne, J. and M. Wright (eds), *Divestment and Strategic Change.* Oxford: Phillip Allan.

Bruggink, T.M. (1982). Public versus Regulated Private Enterprise in the Municipal Water Industry: a Comparison of Water Costs. *Quarterly Review of Economics and Business* 22:111–125.

Caves, D.W. and L.R. Christensen (1980). The Relative Efficiency of Public and Private Firms in a Competitive Environment: the Case of Canadian Railroads. *Journal of Political Economy* 88: 958–976.

Cowling, K. *et al.* (1980). *Mergers and Economic Performance.* Cambridge: Cambridge University Press.

Crain, W.M. and A. Zardkoohi (1978). A Test of the Property Rights Theory of the Firm: Water Utilities in the United States. *Journal of Law and Economics* 21: 395–408.

De Alessi, L. (1977). Ownership and Peak Load Pricing in the Electric Power Industry. *Quarterly Review of Economics and Business* 17.

Edison Electric Institute (1985). *Analysis of the Differences among Alternative Forms of Utility Ownership in the U.S.A.* Washington, DC: Edison Electric Institute.

Ekern, S. and R. Wilson (1974). On the Theory of the Firm in an Economy with Incomplete Markets. *Bell Journal of Economics* 5: 171–180.

Fare, R., S. Grosskopf and J. Logan (1985). The Relative Performance of Publicly Owned and Privately Owned Electric Utilities. *Journal of Public Economics* 26: 89–106.

Firth, M. (1979). The Profitability of Takeovers and Mergers. *Economic Journal* 89: 316–328.

Firth, M. (1980). Takeovers, Shareholders Returns and the Theory of the Firm. *Quarterly Journal of Economics* 94: 235–260.

Franks, J.R. and R.S. Harris (1986a). *Shareholder Wealth Effects of Corporate Takeovers: The U.K. Experience 1955–85.* Working Paper, London Business School and University of North Carolina at Chapel Hill.

Franks, J.R. and R.S. Harris (1986b). The Role of the Mergers and Monopolies Commission in Merger Policy: Costs and Alternatives. *Oxford Review of Economic Policy* 2(4): 58–76.

Grossman, S. and O.D. Hart (1980). Takeover Bids, the Free-Rider Problem and the Theory of the Corporation. *Bell Journal of Economics* 11: 42–64.

Halpern, P.J. (1973). Empirical Estimates of the Amount and Distribution of Gains to Companies in Mergers. *Journal of Business* 46: 554–573.

Hartley, K. and M. Huby (1985). Contracting-out in Health and Local Authorities: Prospects, Progress and Pitfalls. *Public Money*, September 1985.

King, M. 1986. *Takeovers, Taxes, and the Stock Market*. Mimeograph, London School of Economics.

Kitchen, H.M. (1976). A Statistical Estimation of an Operating Cost Function for Municipal Refuse Collection. *Public Finance Quarterly* 4(1): 56–76.

Kreps, D. and R. Wilson (1982). Reputation and Imperfect Information. *Journal of Economic Theory* 27: 253–279.

Malatesta, P.H. (1983). The Wealth Effect of Merger Activity and the Objective Functions of Merging Firms. *Journal of Financial Economics* 11: 155–181.

Mandelker, G. (1974). Risk and Return: The Case of Merging Firms. *Journal of Financial Economics* 1: 303–335.

Meyer, R.A. (1975). Publicly Owned versus Privately Owned Utilities: a Policy Choice. *Review of Economics and Statistics* 57: 391–399.

Millward, R. (1982). The Comparative Performance of Public and Private Ownership. In Roll, E. (ed.), *The Mixed Economy*. London, Macmillan.

Newbould, G.D. (1970). *Management and Merger Activity*. Liverpool: Guttistead.

Niskanen, W.A. (1971). *Bureaucracy and Representative Government*. Chicago: Aldine-Atherton.

Peltzman, S. (1971). Pricing in Public and Private Enterprises and Electric Utilities in the United States. *Journal of Law and Economics* 14: 109–147.

Pescatrice, D.R. and J.M. Trapani (1980). The Performance and Objectives of Public and Private Utilities Operating in the United States. *Journal of Public Economics* 13: 259–276.

Pryke, R. (1982). The Comparative Performance of Public and Private Enterprise. *Fiscal Studies* 3(2): 68–81.

Rees, R. (1985). The Theory of Principal and Agent. *Bulletin of Economic Research* 37: 3–26, 75–95.

Rowley, C.K. and G.K. Yarrow (1981). Property Rights, Regulation and Public Enterprise: the Case of the British Steel Industry 1957–75. *International Review of Law and Economics* 1: 63–96.

Savas, E.S. (1977). Policy Analysis for Local Government: Public Versus Private Refuse Collection. *Policy Analysis* 3: 49–74.

Scharfstein, D. (1986). *The Disciplinary Role of Takeovers*. Mimeograph, MIT, Cambridge, MA.

Singh, A. (1971). *Takeovers: Their Relevance to the Stock Market and the Theory of the Firm*. Cambridge: Cambridge University Press.

Singh, A. (1975). Takeovers, Economic Natural Selection and the Theory of the Firm. *Economic Journal* 85: 497–515.

Stevens, B.J. (1978). Scale, Market Structure and the Cost of Refuse Collection. *Review of Economics and Statistics* 60: 438–448.

Vickers, J.S. (1985c). Delegation and the Theory of the Firm. *Economic Journal* (Conference Papers) 95: 138–147.

Williamson, O.E. (1975). *Markets and Hierarchies: Analysis and Antitrust Implications*. New York: Free Press.

Yarrow, G.K. (1986). Privatization in Theory and Practice. *Economic Policy* 2: 324–377.

[14]

Competitive Forces

3.1 Introduction

The next step in our analysis of the economic effects of privatization is to consider how competitive and regulatory constraints influence company behavior under public and private ownership. In the previous chapter we examined the discipline on managers of private firms that is sometimes provided by competition in the market for corporate control, and now we turn to the role of competitive forces in product markets. Regulatory constraints will be the subject of chapter 4.

It is important at the outset to underline the obvious fact that *privatization*—the transfer of ownership—and *liberalization*—the opening up of competitive forces—are logically quite distinct concepts. Public ownership does not imply state monopoly, and private ownership does not entail competition. Nevertheless privatization and liberalization are frequently intertwined in policy debate and public perception. The political presentation of privatization policies has emphasized the stimulation of competitive forces, and the privatization of companies such as British Telecom (BT) was indeed accompanied by some important liberalizing measures. Although there is no logical connection between public enterprise and the absence of competition, there are several practical reasons why the two have often gone together.

First, public ownership is one of the main solutions to the problems of market failure that arise in industries where competition is impossible or undesirable, or where major externalities exist. Much of the postwar nationalization in Britain was motivated, at least in part, by the belief that competitive solutions were unsuitable in the markets in question, and there were particular concerns about natural monopoly in industries such as gas, electricity, railways, water, and telecommunications. Although many of these concerns were—and still are—well founded, the danger exists that competitive forces become too neglected, and are assumed to be irrelevant, when perhaps they have a useful role to play. Conditions of demand and technology may change so that yesterday's natural monopoly no longer persists, and the difficulties of efficiently controlling public enterprise may turn out to be such that competitive forces have significant advantages despite being imperfect.

A second possible link between public enterprise and monopoly has to do with the interests and influence of public sector managers and related civil servants. In the spirit of the "capture" theories of American-style regulation (see section 4.5 below) some would contend that managers of Britain's nationalized industries have successfully resisted the advent of effective competition by their influence on political decision making, institutional inertia, and the support of employees. In contrast, consumers and potential competitors have a relatively ineffective voice. On this view privatization is connected with liberalization insofar as it breaks the anticompetitive institutional blockage. However, as we shall see later, it can equally be argued that managers of companies being privatized—such as BT and British Gas—have been quite successful in limiting the competitive threats that they subsequently face in the private sector.

In any event, it is important to try to understand the costs and benefits of attempted competitive solutions to the market failure problems in the industries in the privatization program, and the aim of this chapter is to present some of the pertinent theories of competition. The recent economics literature on industrial organization has made several important (and sometimes controversial) contributions, and we shall emphasize three themes in particular.

First, and most important, is the role of *potential competition*, which we discuss in section 3.3. The main question here is whether liberalizing conditions of entry into an industry creates entry threats of sufficient power to impel the incumbent firm or firms to behave efficiently and in accordance with consumer preferences. In their theory of contestable markets, Baumol and others examine free entry in its purest form—in which case the answer is in the affirmative. But the economics of strategic entry deterrence and predatory behavior shows that in many circumstances incumbent firms may be able to thwart potential competitors by anticompetitive tactics. The economics of potential competition is therefore highly pertinent to the problems of regulating privatized industries. Do the forces of potential competition operate with such effectiveness as to remove or diminish the need for regulation? Or do policies of liberalization actually require public intervention to ensure that potential competition is effective?

Our second theme is competition as an *incentive mechanism*, which we consider in section 3.4. The problems of monitoring and rewarding managers' effort and efficiency arise under both public and private ownership. The asymmetry of information that exists between the managers of the firm and the government ministry or regulatory agency is at the heart of the matter. The competitive process and the results it delivers (especially in the form of comparisons between rivals' performances) can reveal information in a most economical fashion, and it therefore acts as a natural and useful incentive mechanism. Thus the competitive process provides a spur to *internal* efficiency and the elimination of X-inefficiency, as well as serving as a mechanism conducive to *allocative* efficiency.

Thirdly, in section 3.5, we look specifically at competition issues that arise in connection with *networks* and *vertical relationships*. These have been important in several of the industries where privatization has occurred, of which telecommunications is a good example. If a subscriber in town A wishes to call another in town B, he must use three elements of the telecommunication system—the local networks in A and B, and the long-distance link between the towns. In effect he demands a composite commodity consisting of local and long-distance links. The local networks are monopolized by BT, the dominant firm, but there is scope for competition in the supply of the long-distance link, which BT also offers. Unless constrained from doing so, BT will thwart competition in the long-distance market. This is the crucial *interconnection* issue. It has parallels in the gas and electricity industries, where rival producers rely on the transmission networks of the dominant firms. The economics of vertical relationships therefore bears on U.K. regulatory policy and the wider question of whether vertical separation of a privatized company is appropriate.

Before proceeding to these questions, however, we first outline some relevant welfare economics of actual and potential competition, with particular reference to industries with economies of scale.

3.2 Some Relationships between Competition and Welfare

There is of course a vast literature on the welfare properties of industrial competition, and this is not the place to attempt a survey. Instead we shall briefly discuss two issues of particular relevance to the privatization program. The first is the trade-off between allocative efficiency and scale economies, and the related question of whether free entry can lead to undesirable losses of cost efficiency. The second issue concerns the role of public enterprises in markets where they compete with private firms. We consider how public firms should behave, and what objectives their managers should be given, in those circumstances.

3.2.1 The Trade-Off between Allocative Efficiency and Scale Economies

An argument often advanced for restricting entry into industries with economies of scale is that entry leads to undesirable duplication of fixed costs, and that it is better to have a few (or even just one) large firms than to have more smaller ones. However, the problem is that market power is greater when there are fewer firms, and monopolistic behavior worsens allocative efficiency. The trade-off between allocative efficiency and scale economies is central to many problems in competition policy (e.g. mergers), and precisely the same question—albeit in a much more complex form—arises for example in relation to the licensing of network operators to compete with BT. Two questions can be asked about the trade-off. First, what number of firms maximizes social welfare? Second, does free entry lead to the existence of too few or too many firms at the market equilibrium?

As to the ideal number of firms, the *first-best* outcome when there are economies of scale is to have a single firm operating where price equals marginal cost. This is optimal because the cost of an extra unit of output is equal to consumers' willingness to pay for it. The first-best outcome attains allocative efficiency *and* productive efficiency (no duplication of fixed costs).

However, there are two difficulties with this outcome. First, the firm makes a loss. If lump-sum transfers were feasible, the government could costlessly make good the loss, but otherwise it could not. If such transfers were costly enough, the problem would be to maximize W subject to $\pi \geqslant 0$. The solution to this *second-best* problem would be to have a single firm producing where price equals average cost. The second difficulty is that the firm is unlikely to want to operate where price is equal to marginal (or average) cost, especially if it is privately owned. Regulatory constraint might somehow compel that outcome, but our present concern is with competitive forces unfettered by regulation.

The following simple model illuminates the trade-off between scale economies and allocative efficiency. (For more detailed treatments the reader is referred to Williamson (1968), von Weizsäcker (1980), Perry (1984), Mankiw and Whinston (1986), and Suzumura and Kiyono (1987).)

Suppose that we have an industry consisting of n similar firms each supplying the same homogeneous good. Let $V(Q)$ be consumer utility and $P(Q) = V'(Q)$ be the inverse demand curve for the good, where Q is the sum of the firms' outputs.

Let $q(n)$ be output per firm when there are n firms in the industry, and let $C(q)$ be the cost function of each firm. We shall suppose for simplicity that social welfare is equal to the sum of consumer and producer surplus. As a function of the number of firms, social welfare can then be written as

$$W(n) = V[nq(n)] - nC[q(n)]. \tag{3.1}$$

We must now specify how the market equilibrium depends on the number of firms, i.e. how q depends on n. For example, we could assume that there is Cournot behavior at market equilibrium. That is to say, firms operate at an equilibrium in which none has any incentive to alter its behavior given the output decisions of its rivals. But rather than specifying any particular oligopoly solution concept, we shall simply assume that $\mathrm{d}q/\mathrm{d}n < 0$, i.e. output per firm falls as the number of firms increases. This assumption holds true in a wide range of circumstances, including Cournot behavior in normal cost and demand conditions. In the model the assumption implies that the market equilibrium number of firms will not be too small, and tends to be excessive (see Mankiw and Whinston, 1986; Suzumura and Kiyono, 1987). The reason is as follows.

If we were allowed to treat the number of firms n as a continuous variable, then the socially optimal number of firms n^*, given market equilibrium behavior, would be such that

$$\frac{\mathrm{d}W(n^*)}{\mathrm{d}n} = 0. \tag{3.2}$$

In fact the number of firms must be an integer, and there is little chance that n^* is an integer. But if $W(n)$ is single-peaked (when n is regarded as a continuous variable) then the optimal number of firms is one of the two integers closest to n^* as defined by (3.2).

The market equilibrium number of firms when there is free entry is given by the condition that further entry would be unprofitable. Let $\pi(n)$ be profit per firm as a function of n. If n was a continuous variable, the equilibrium number of firms $\hat{n}$ would be given by

$$\pi(\hat{n}) = 0. \tag{3.3}$$

If we take the equilibrium number to be one of the integers neighboring $\hat{n}$, we can now compare n^* and $\hat{n}$ to see whether there will be too much or too little entry at the market equilibrium. Differentiating W with respect to n in (3.1) we obtain

$$\frac{\mathrm{d}W}{\mathrm{d}n} = \left(q + n\frac{\mathrm{d}q}{\mathrm{d}n}\right)V' - C - n\frac{\mathrm{d}C}{\mathrm{d}q}\frac{\mathrm{d}q}{\mathrm{d}n}. \tag{3.4}$$

Recalling that $V' = P$ and rearranging terms we obtain

$$\frac{dW}{dn} = n\left(P - \frac{dC}{dq}\right)\frac{dq}{dn} + (Pq - C). \tag{3.5}$$

The second term on the right-hand side of (3.5) is profit per firm, which is zero at free-entry equilibrium. As regards the first term, imperfect competition implies that $P > dC/dq$ (i.e. price exceeds marginal cost), and the assumption that $dq/dn < 0$ therefore implies that $dW/dn < 0$ at $\hat{n}$. It follows that social welfare (as defined) would be increased at the margin by reducing the number of firms below the free-entry equilibrium level. If n is treated as a continuous variable, the optimal number n^* is less than the equilibrium number $\hat{n}$. Thus there is a tendency for excessive entry in the context of the model.

In other words, if output per firm falls with n, then the entry of a new firm is good for consumers, bad for existing firms, and approximately neutral at equilibrium for the new firm, but the benefit to consumers is outweighed by the detriment to existing firms. The result might be different if social welfare gave more weight to consumer surplus than to producer surplus. For example, if no weight is given to producer interests, all that matters is the sign of dQ/dn, which is the response of industry output to changes in n. Under plausible assumptions this is positive, and there is too little entry at the market equilibrium.

Of course it would be foolish to draw any policy conclusions from preliminary analysis of the kind described above. For one thing, policy measures designed to influence the number of firms in the industry (e.g. licensing of entry) must be considered alongside policies (such as regulation) that are intended to affect firm behavior more directly. Secondly, the *threat* of entry can itself have a major influence on industry conduct—n firms surrounded by unsurmountable entry barriers are likely to behave very differently from n firms facing entry threats from potential competitors. It is partly for this reason that the liberalization of entry conditions has been so central to the debate on privatization in Britain. We will return to the important theme of entry threats and potential competition in section 3.3 below, where we consider a number of nonprice aspects of company behavior, including product differentiation, investment, advertising, and research and development (R&D). Thirdly, there are major informational advantages from having more competitors, and incentives for internal efficiency can be enhanced. These important effects are omitted from analysis above, but we discuss them further in section 3.4 below.

3.2.2 Public Enterprise in Competition

We began this chapter by saying that public ownership and competition are perfectly compatible with each other. Indeed, we believe that it would often be advantageous to confront public enterprises with competitive forces even where privatization is not taking place. Legislation in Britain in 1981–1983 opened up the (legal) possibility of some competition with public enterprises in the telecommunications, gas, and electricity industries, and although privatization has since occurred in two of those three sectors, it did not necessarily have to follow liberalization.

There are several reasons why competitive forces might improve industry performance when public enterprise exists. First, internal efficiency might be enhanced by the disciplining effect of competitive threats upon the managers of public firms. It has been said that the greatest of all monopoly profits is the quiet life, and if that is so, there is a case against public monopoly. This case is all the stronger if mechanisms for regulating public enterprise—whether they are explicit or implicit—have serious weaknesses, as both empirical and theoretical evidence suggests. In particular, competitive forces break the "monopoly of information" about industry conditions that may otherwise exist, and which tends to hamper the effectiveness of the regulatory regime. Note that competition need not be an alternative to regulation—it can instead be a useful supplement to it.

A second advantage of opening up the possibility of competition with a dominant public firm is that it creates opportunities for innovation. Rival firms might have the incentive to introduce new products or processes into parts of the public firm's market which the public firm had little incentive to introduce or perhaps had not even thought of. This in turn acts as a spur to the public firm to be more innovative itself, which takes us back to the point in the previous paragraph.

These points will be amplified when we come to consider entry threats and the role of competition as an incentive mechanism. But first we briefly consider some of the questions addressed in the (relatively small) literature on competition in "mixed markets"—i.e. markets in which private and public firms compete.

The simplest case to study is a homogeneous goods duopoly with a welfare-maximizing public firm and a profit-maximizing private firm. If it is assumed that marginal cost is an increasing function of output, the Nash equilibrium in quantities involves the public firm's operating where its marginal cost equals the market price and the private firm's operating where its marginal revenue equals marginal cost. However, if the public firm is a Stackelberg leader (i.e. has first move), it can obtain a better outcome because it can choose any point on the private firm's reaction function (instead of just the Nash outcome). Welfare is enhanced by the public firm's producing less than its Nash output in order to induce a beneficial expansion in the output of the private firm (given that it has a downward-sloping reaction function).

Beato and Mas-Colell (1984) reverse this move order by giving the public firm the second move. Since the public firm will choose to operate where price equals marginal cost, this is equivalent to the public firm's being committed in advance to a marginal cost (MC) pricing rule. The private firm is then the Stackelberg leader and will optimize given the reaction function (i.e. the MC pricing rule) of its public competitor. Beato and Mas-Colell find that the outcome implied by the MC pricing rule compares favorably with the result obtained when the public firm is the Stackelberg leader. Harris and Wiens (1980) also give second move to the public firm but allow it to commit itself to any strategy in advance. With such powers of commitment, it is best for the public firm to promise to behave in such a way that the competitive price comes about. Then the private firm is induced to act so that price equals marginal cost. However, unlike the MC pricing rule, this commitment by the public firm lacks credibility.

De Fraja and Delbono (1986) consider what objective should be given to the managers of a public firm faced by a number of profit-maximizing competitors. They find that, if the number of firms is large enough, it may be better for the public firm to have profit maximization, rather than welfare maximization, as its objective. Even if there is only one private competitor, Nash equilibrium social welfare is increased if the public firm's managers give some weight to profit in their calculations. The reason is that the Nash equilibrium is then shifted towards the outcome that results when the public firm is the Stackelberg leader (see above).

Finally, Cremer *et al.* (1987) ask whether social welfare would be improved by changing the ownership—or, more precisely, the objective—of some firms in an industry of n firms producing a homogeneous good under increasing returns to scale. They show in their framework that it is often optimal to nationalize a single firm, but that complete nationalization may be desirable.

The literature on competition in mixed markets is not extensive, although we believe that the topic is important. The approaches reported above do not consider the effects of competition upon incentives for internal efficiency (see section 3.4), but they do show how public enterprise can have a positive role in improving allocative efficiency in imperfectly competitive markets. The results of the analysis are sensitive to assumptions about move order and objectives, but the simple MC pricing rule emerged as an attractive guideline in markets where competitors are few. However, it can be desirable for public enterprises to attach more weight to profits where competition is stronger.

3.3 Potential Competition and Entry Threats

Privatization of firms in competitive markets raises few problems for industrial policy because competition between firms in the market effectively regulates company behavior and provides reasonably good incentives for internal and allocative efficiency. But the mechanism of competition between existing firms cannot be relied upon if the incumbent firm being privatized has a preponderant market share and if it is not being split into units that will subsequently compete with each other. It is then only the entry and growth of new rivals—or at any rate the threat of it—that can provide competitive disciplines for the incumbent firm. If these do not exist, regulation of the incumbent's pricing behavior will be needed to check monopolistic abuse. Regulation in the form of policies to prevent anticompetitive behavior may be needed to make entry threats properly effective.

In this section we examine the theory of contestable markets and recent theories of strategic entry deterrence and predatory behavior. Two of the main questions that we have in mind were stated in the introduction to this chapter. Do the forces of potential competition operate with such effectiveness as to remove or diminish the need for regulation? Or do policies of liberalization actually require regulation to ensure that potential competition is effective?

3.3.1 The Theory of Contestable Markets

In a contestable market the threat of potential competition is at its most potent. The incumbent firm or firms are compelled to meet consumers' wishes with maximum efficiency, for otherwise new entrants will simply take their business away. The theory of contestable markets proposed by Baumol and his colleagues was developed in a series of articles beginning in the late 1970s and was expounded in the book by Baumol *et al.* (1982) and in Baumol's (1982) presidential address to the American Economic Association. The theory has provoked great academic controversy and has featured prominently in public debate on regulation and antitrust. An evaluation of the theory is essential for an understanding of the role of competitive forces in constraining the behavior of apparently dominant firms, and hence it is at the heart of much debate on privatization policy.

One of the main contributions of contestability theory has been to illuminate the economics of multiproduct industries and to introduce important cost concepts (such as economies of scope and trans-ray convexity). However, we shall begin by focusing on its contribution to the theory of potential competition in the context of an industry supplying a single product. Our plan is first to define what is meant by "contestability," then to infer what properties must hold in a contestable market, and finally to discuss the implications of the theory for practical policy making in the light of the criticisms that have been made of it. More extensive discussions of contestability theory are provided by Baumol and Willig (1986), Brock (1983), Schwartz (1986), Sharkey (1982), Shepherd (1984), and Spence (1983).

A contestable market is one in which existing firms are vulnerable to hit-and-run entry. All firms—actual and potential—have access to the same production methods, and hence their *cost functions are identical.* Moreover, entry involves *no sunk costs*: a firm can enter the market without making irrecoverable expenditures, and so there are no barriers to exit. Therefore

> "Even a very transient profit opportunity need not be neglected by a potential entrant, for he can go in, and, before prices change, collect his gains and then depart without cost, should the climate grow hostile." (Baumol, 1982, p. 4.)

The distinction here between sunk costs and fixed costs should be noted. Fixed costs are costs that do not vary with the level of output; they are not always sunk. For example, a firm that leases a photocopier for a short period of time incurs a fixed cost but not sunk costs. It is perfectly possible to have a contestable market with high fixed costs, so long as there are no sunk costs, and indeed a natural monopoly market can in principle be contestable and vulnerable to hit-and-run entry.

If equilibrium exists in a contestable market, the following properties hold.

(i) Price P equals average cost AC. That is to say, all firms make zero profits. If $P >$ AC there would be an incentive for a new firm to enter the market and displace an incumbent firm by slightly shading its price. If $P <$ AC a firm would do better to leave the market, which can be done costlessly in view of the assumption that sunk costs are absent. It follows that $P =$ AC at equilibrium.

(ii) There is no inefficiency in production. If an existing firm was producing its output at more than minimum cost, rivals would find it profitable to enter the market, take the other firm's business, and produce more efficiently.

(iii) Price is at least as great as marginal cost. If some firm was operating where $P <$ MC, a new firm could profitably enter the market producing slightly less than the other firm and take that firm's business by shading price infinitesimally. This strategy would be profitable because the marginal revenue lost by reducing output, which is approximately equal to P, is less than the saving of MC.

(iv) If there are two or more firms at equilibrium in the market, then price is no greater than MC. If one of the existing firms was operating where $P >$ MC, a new firm could come in and produce slightly more than that firm. The entrant's marginal revenue MR ($= P$) would exceed his MC, and so he would make more profit than the firm displaced. The entrant could (and would) also take some of the business of other incumbent firms by an arbitrarily small price reduction. This argument does not go through if initially there is only one firm in the market, because then the only way for a firm to increase sales volume is to lower price. Figure 3.1 shows how $P >$ MC is possible at equilibrium in a market characterized by natural monopoly cost conditions. (Note that (iii) and (iv) together imply that $P =$ MC if there are two or more firms at equilibrium.)

(v) The number and configuration of firms at equilibrium is such that industry output is produced at minimum cost. Therefore there is productive efficiency at the industry level as well as the level of the firm (see

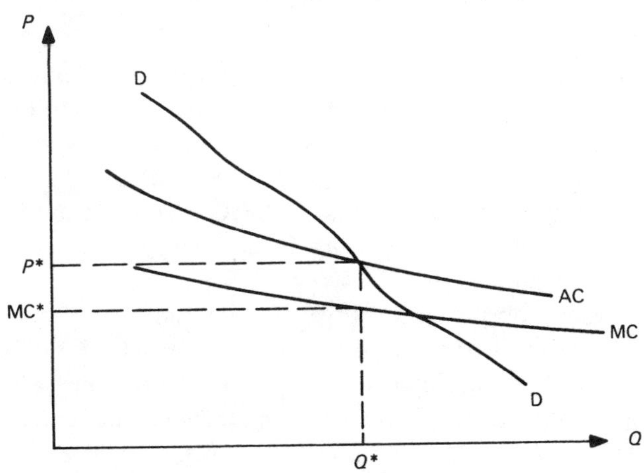

Figure 3.1 Equilibrium with price greater than marginal cost

(ii)). If this property did not hold, a new entrant producing at minimum average cost could profitably enter the industry by taking business from firms producing at higher cost levels. This result about productive efficiency at the industry level implies that market structure is endogenous in a contestable market.

Results (i) through (v) above were stated in the context of a single-product industry in order to show as clearly as possible why they hold. The arguments generalize naturally to multiproduct industries, where (i) through (v) also hold. We shall state two more results about equilibrium in contestable multiproduct industries.

(vi) There will be no cross-subsidies between products. This follows from the fact that price must be at least as great as marginal cost for all products in the industry. Otherwise a new firm could profitably enter producing slightly less of the product in question than some existing firm. This profit opportunity is ruled out only if cross-subsidy is absent.

(vii) Under certain assumptions about cost conditions (trans-ray convexity and declining ray average costs), a natural monopolist deters entry by charging Ramsey prices. Ramsey prices maximize welfare subject to a minimum profit constraint. (The basic reason for this result can be outlined as follows. If firm B wants to take the business of firm A, it will seek to maximize its profits subject to the constraint of offering consumers a more attractive deal than firm A. The dual of this constrained optimization problem is to maximize consumer wellbeing subject to a minimum profit constraint. That is essentially the same as the Ramsey optimization problem.)

By now it will be evident that the properties that hold at equilibrium in a contestable market are highly desirable by the yardsticks of traditional welfare economics. There is internal efficiency, because firms—individually and collectively—are compelled by the entry threat to produce at minimum cost, and there is allocative efficiency because $P = \text{MC}$, except possibly in a natural monopoly (in which case pricing is optimal subject to the nonnegative profit constraint).

The theory has been proposed as a competitive benchmark that is in a sense more general than the traditional textbook model of perfect competition. Instead of a huge number of very small firms being the hallmark of competition, it is entry threats that make for competition in a contestable market, even though only one or two firms might exist at equilibrium. Indeed market structure is determined endogenously by the

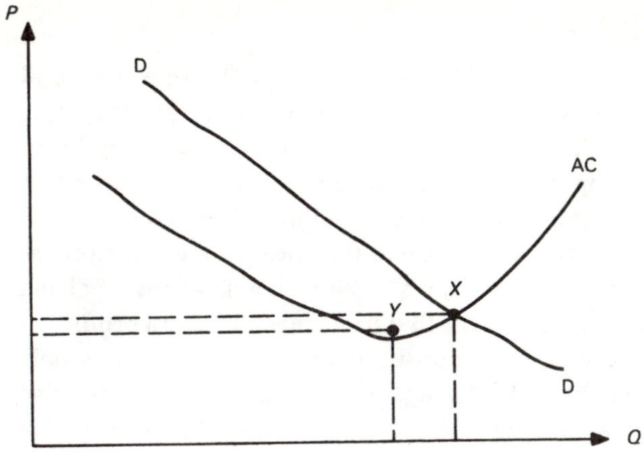

Figure 3.2 An example of nonsustainable natural monopoly

fundamental parameters of technology and demand. It is sunk costs (as opposed to fixed costs) that are of central importance—a point which has implications for policy.

The desirable properties stated above rest on the assumption that equilibrium in a contestable market exists. Unfortunately it need not do so, as the following examples show. Figure 3.2 depicts a natural monopoly industry—cost and demand conditions are such that single-firm production is most efficient. However, the price–output combination X is not an equilibrium, because it is vulnerable to entry by a firm operating at point Y. The entrant can undercut the firm and still make a profit. This is an example of the *nonsustainability* of natural monopoly. A generalization of this example is an industry with textbook U-shaped average cost curves. If P^* is the minimum average cost and if q^* is the associated level of output, equilibrium exists in the contestable market only if demand at price P^*, denoted by $D(P^*)$, is an integer multiple of q^*. The chance of this happening is effectively zero. This problem can be avoided by supposing that cost curves are flat-bottomed, but that is perhaps a rather artificial step to take.

A second important reason for nonexistence can arise in multiproduct industries (see Faulhaber, 1975). Suppose that there are three products in the industry and that there is demand for one unit of each product. Let $C(k)$ be the cost of producing k of the products ($k = 1, 2,$ or 3). It is quite possible that

$$\frac{3}{2}C(2) < C(3) < C(2) + C(1), \tag{3.6}$$

for example if $C(1) = 6$, $C(2) = 8$, and $C(3) = 13$. There is a natural monopoly because the most efficient way to produce the three products is for one firm to produce all of them. But that state of affairs is vulnerable to entry by a firm producing two out of the three products. A three-product firm could cover its costs provided that the sum of the prices of the products was no less than 13. In that case the sum of the prices of the two most expensive products could not be less than $8\frac{2}{3}$. But then a new firm supplying only two products could undercut the first firm and still make a profit.

This multiproduct example of the nonsustainability of natural monopoly is sometimes associated with "cream skimming" and "destructive competition." Cream skimming occurs when a rival takes a profitable component of the incumbent's business, leaving the incumbent with a loss on the rest. The (alleged) undesirability of cream skimming is sometimes offered as a justification for restrictions on entry.

Although the nonsustainability of natural monopoly is a theoretical possibility, we would urge that arguments for restrictions on entry based on grounds of cream skimming or destructive competition should be treated with the greatest caution. First, there is a broad class of natural monopoly cost conditions that imply sustainability (see Sharkey (1982) for a full discussion). Secondly, natural monopoly conditions are not as widespread as is often claimed. Thirdly, the vested interests of incumbent firms are such that they should bear a heavy burden of proof when arguing for restrictions on entry. Fourthly, the sustainability problem—and existence problems in general—are of little or no consequence in industries that are not contestable.

At this point it is appropriate to address some of the main criticisms (apart from the existence problems just discussed) that have been leveled against the theory. We shall focus on claims that the theory has minimal relevance to real-world industries and that it is therefore devoid of practical policy implications. If the theory can withstand such criticisms, it has very important consequences, for it suggests that opening industries to potential competition (even industries that are highly concentrated in terms of current market shares) does away with the need for regulatory policies, because the force of potential competition itself produces desirable results.

The first major criticism is that the theory assumes an unnatural sequence of events when entry occurs. In particular, it assumes that the entrant can establish itself, undercut the existing firm(s) on price, and take as much of their business as it likes, all before the existing firms respond

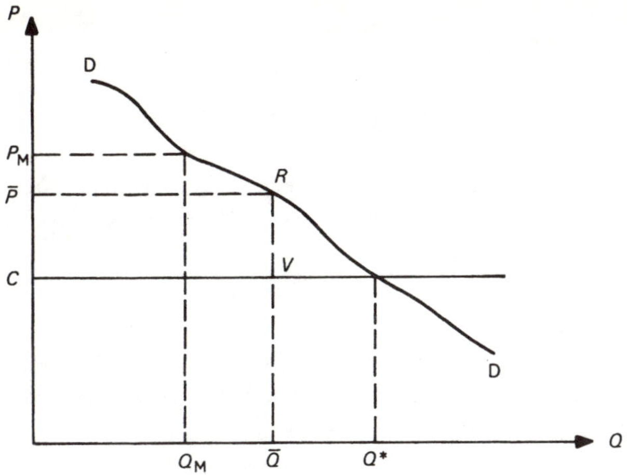

Figure 3.3 Nonrobustness: illustrative market conditions

by lowering their own prices. The criticism is that this implicit assumption—that entry can occur more quickly than price changes by existing firms—is precisely the *reverse* of what it is realistic to suppose.

The second criticism is that the assumption of zero sunk costs is *nonrobust* (see Schwartz and Reynolds, 1983; Dasgupta and Stiglitz, 1985). Proponents of contestability theory can reply to the objection that the assumption of zero sunk costs is never strictly *true* by saying that no theory can be more than an approximation to the truth. But the claim of nonrobustness is more damaging, because it implies that the theory is not useful even as an approximation to reality.

Both criticisms can be illustrated with the aid of figure 3.3. The diagram concerns a market for a homogeneous product. The demand curve is labeled DD, and the constant level of unit costs is denoted by C. Social welfare would be maximized when price $P = C$ and output is Q^*. Suppose the entry into the industry involves sunk cost S, which can be regarded as an entry fee. Suppose that firm A is currently in the market and that firm B is contemplating entry. Let T_A be the time that it would take for firm A to respond to B's decision to enter, and let T_B be the time that it would take B to set up at full scale. Thus, if $T_A > T_B$, then B can set up before A responds to B's entry. But if $T_A < T_B$, then A responds to B's entry before B has set up at full scale. Suppose that, once A has responded to B's entry, competition between them rapidly drives price down to the cost level C. Note that this does not involve firm A's reducing its price below the level of costs. Define T as follows:

$$T = \begin{cases} T_A - T_B \text{ if } T_A > T_B \\ 0 \text{ otherwise.} \end{cases} \tag{3.7}$$

Thus, T is the amount of time that B would have at full scale before A's response drove prices down to level C.

Suppose that A is currently charging price $\bar{P}$. Should B enter the market? If he entered and charged a price just below $\bar{P}$, he would earn a profit flow of almost

$$\pi(\bar{P}) = (\bar{P} - C)D(\bar{P}), \tag{3.8}$$

i.e. the rectangle $\bar{P}RVC$. This profit flow would last for T units of time, at which point profits would be driven down to zero. Entry is worthwhile if this profit flow covers the sunk cost S, i.e. if and only if

$$T\pi(\bar{P}) > S. \tag{3.9}$$

Now, if sunk costs are zero ($S = 0$) and the entrant can set up before the incumbent firm responds ($T > 0$), then any price P in excess of C is vulnerable to entry. This is the case of a contestable market.

If, however, the incumbent can react faster than (or just as fast as) the entrant can establish himself at full scale, then $T = 0$. This is usually the realistic case. Now, if sunk costs are positive—no matter how tiny—then $S > 0$, and from (3.9) it follows that no price would attract the entry of firm B. Therefore A could charge the monopoly price P_M without inducing entry. In this case, even though sunk costs might be miniscule, the threat of entry is nonexistent, and the incumbent can behave as a monopolist with impunity.

The remaining case is that in which $T > 0$ and $S > 0$. The incumbent will deter entry if he charges a price P such that

$$\pi(P) \leqslant S/T. \tag{3.10}$$

Even if S is rather small, this constraint on the behavior of the incumbent firm will be very weak if T is small. It may well be that the monopoly price P_M satisfies (3.10). S must be infinitesimal if the entry threat is to promote anything remotely like competitive behavior in this model.

In short, any departure from the strict assumptions of contestability theory ($S = 0$, $T > 0$) leads to an outcome that may be radically different from the outcome predicted by the theory.

Contestability theory is important insofar as it provides a valuable framework for thinking about a number of problems of industrial organization: it has led to several important lines of research on multiproduct industries; it has introduced important concepts and analytical tools; it allows for the endogenous determination of market structure; it highlights the importance of sunk costs; and it underlines the beneficial role that potential competition can play in improving industrial performance.

However, we have grave doubts about the empirical applicability of contestability theory, especially to major industries of the kind being privatized in Britain. The entrenched dominant positions of companies like BT and British Gas, and the inevitably sunk nature of many costs, are such that entry threats *on their own* cannot remotely be expected to compel the dominant firm to behave benignly. Entry threats are usually very desirable, but they will be impotent unless supplemented by effective competition policies that strike at anticompetitive behavior against potential entrants by incumbent firms. Moreover, there are a number of markets and submarkets where the threat of entry simply does not exist and cannot be made to exist. Direct regulation of the dominant firm is then required.

3.3.2 Strategic Entry Deterrence

In this section we consider in more detail how an incumbent firm with market power might act so as to stifle potential competition. This is a central question for privatization policies in the U.K., because major enterprises such as BT and British Gas have entered the private sector with positions of great dominance, and it is not clear to what extent measures to liberalize entry into their industries will promote truly effective competition. This depends partly upon the nature of policies to guard against anticompetitive behavior designed to thwart potential entrants. A theoretical perspective on this issue is provided by the recent literature on *strategic entry deterrence* (see Vickers (1985a) for a survey). In this section we outline some of the main elements of that literature, and we consider the problem of designing policies against predatory behavior. We postpone until later in the chapter our discussion of competition and entry deterrence in networks and vertically related markets.

The key to strategic entry deterrence by an incumbent dominant firm is to make credible the threat of responding to entry—for example by very aggressive pricing—in such a way that the rival would regret having entered the market. The threat is credible if and only if it is believed to be in the interests of the incumbent to carry it out when entry actually occurs. In order to assess the danger of strategic entry deterrence thwarting potential competition and to consider appropriate policy measures, we must focus precisely on this question of credibility. One school of thought (often associated with the University of Chicago) has it that predatory pricing is irrational, and therefore unlikely to occur, because it hurts the incumbent as much as the entrant. In that case threats of predatory pricing are not credible. But others have recently contended that predatory and entry-deterring behavior of various kinds is entirely possible, and that policy measures are vital if dominant firms are not to choke off the threat of potential competition.

For simplicity, we shall focus on the case where one incumbent firm is seeking to deter the entry of one potential rival. The entry decision of the rival depends upon his beliefs as to the likely profitability of being in the market. Entry will occur if and only if the expected profits exceed the expected costs of entry. How can the incumbent influence those beliefs in such a way as to deter entry? We shall address this question in two steps. First, we shall suppose that each firm is fully informed about the behavior, opportunities, and motivation of the other. Secondly, we shall relax these assumptions about the information available to the firms, and examine the roles of signaling and reputation in entry deterrence.

The best known traditional analysis of entry deterrence is the Bain–Sylos limit pricing model (see Hay and Morris, 1979, pp. 185–190). In that analysis it is assumed to be common belief that the incumbent would not change its pre-entry output level in the event of entry. Although it makes for tractability, that assumption is not credible, because the incumbent almost certainly would wish to change its behavior when faced with a rival. More generally, as Friedman (1979) has observed, in a game of complete and perfect information, and with no intertemporal interdependences of cost or demand conditions, the incumbent's output level before the entry decision ought to make no difference to the rival's assessment of the profitability of entry. Once entry occurs, a new game begins, and the parameters of that game are independent of previous behavior. This suggests that flexible instruments such as price or quantity are less likely to be the means of entry deterrence than instruments that have a more lasting effect upon cost or demand conditions. The key is for the incumbent to *commit* himself to a course of conduct that would be detrimental to an entrant. A large amount of literature, from which but a few items will be mentioned, is devoted to this theme. Figure 3.4 sketches a simple schema.

First, the incumbent chooses the level of some strategic variable K. Numerous interpretations can be given to K, but for the moment regard it as the incumbent's capacity level. If the rival chooses not to enter, he gets zero and the incumbent gets $I^0(K)$, as shown at the foot of the right-hand branch. Note that the incumbent's payoff depends on K even if entry does

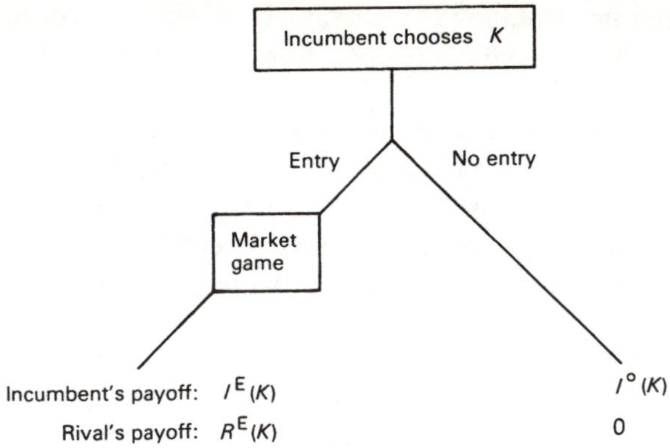

Figure 3.4 Strategic entry deterrence

not occur. If entry does take place, a duopoly exists. Without examining the details of the duopolist's interactions, let us assume that the upshot of the "market game" between them is that the incumbent gets $I^E(K)$ and the rival gets $R^E(K)$ in the event of entry. The schema is broad enough to allow for the rival also to choose some strategic variable after the incumbent's choice of K. This would be included in the black box of the market game.

The incumbent's choice of K deters entry if $R^E(K) < 0$. It may be that entry is deterred even by the level of K that would have been chosen by a pure monopolist facing no threat of entry. Then entry is said to be blockaded. Or it may be that the incumbent does better to permit entry than to deter it. But here our concern is with the remaining case, in which strategic entry deterrence is optimal for the incumbent.

What are the likely instruments of entry deterrence? It is useful to distinguish between those that affect costs (the incumbent's and/or the rival's) and those that affect demand. As to the former, Dixit (1980) showed how the incumbent's choice of *capacity* could deter entry, but in Dixit's model excess (in the sense of idle) capacity is not observed. More generally, K can be interpreted as the incumbent's level of *capital input*. Strategic entry deterrence commonly implies overcapitalization, in the sense that the output eventually produced by the incumbent could have been produced more efficiently with a lower level of capital and a correspondingly higher level of variable factors of production (see Spence, 1977). The same holds when K is interpreted as the incumbent's cost-reducing R&D expenditure. In all these examples, the incumbent's commitment of high K promises that he will supply a high output level, or charge a low price, in the market game.

The choice of K is therefore offputting to the rival, not because of its direct effects, but because of its indirect influence upon the outcome of the market game.

In criticism of the Bain–Sylos analysis, it was stated above that the incumbent's pre-entry output would not affect the rival's entry decision if there were no intertemporal interdependences of cost or demand. But such interdependences do hold if the *experience curve* effect operates—i.e. if a firm's cost level is a declining function of its cumulative output. In that case it is possible for the incumbent's choice of output to deter entry strategically (see Spence, 1981; Fudenberg and Tirole, 1983).

As well as the incumbent lowering his own costs, there may be ways for him to *raise the rival's cost* (see Salop and Scheffman, 1983). For example, by setting high wage rates in the industry, the incumbent increases his own costs and those of an entrant. The direct effect of this upon the incumbent is unfavorable, but if the indirect effect is to deter the rival's entry then the ploy may well be beneficial to him in overall terms.

Another way in which entry might be deterred is for the incumbent to deny the rival access to technology that would allow him to compete. Gilbert and Newbery (1982) examine *pre-emptive patenting*—the acquisition of a patent by an incumbent firm with the purpose of denying the patent, and hence an entry opportunity, to a potential rival. An important factor here is that the incumbent's incentive to win the patent is likely to exceed the rival's incentive, even if the patent is for a technology inferior to that already enjoyed by the incumbent. This is because the incumbent's monopoly persists if he denies entry to the rival, whereas competition, which is less profitable than monopoly, occurs in the event of entry. This result has an important bearing on the question of the persistence of monopoly, for the advantage of the incumbent arises from his *strategic position*; intrinsically the incumbent may be no different from the rival. The result also offers an explanation of the phenomenon of sleeping (i.e. unused) patents, because the pre-emption result does not depend upon the patent's being for a technology that is superior to the incumbent's existing technology.

Turning from the cost side to the demand side, there are further ways in which an incumbent firm can make the prospect of entry unattractive for a rival firm. In some circumstances, strategic *advertising* deters entry, although in Schmalensee's (1983) exploration of advertising and entry deterrence it emerged that low advertising was the way to deter entry. The reason was that high advertising would cause the incumbent to have a higher price in the market game. For the rival, the favorable latter effect would outweigh the disadvantage of high advertising and make entry more attractive. *Brand proliferation*—the introduction of numerous new products—can also serve to deter entry (see Schmalensee, 1978). To use the locational analogy common in the analysis of product differentiation, brand proliferation fills up product space in such a way that there are no remaining slots or niches for profitable entry.

Product differentiation was one of Bain's three sources of barriers to entry. Although advertising is often regarded as a measure of product differentiation, Bain did not see it as the heart of the problem. Schmalensee (1982) shows how buyers' uncertainty about the quality of new brands can give established (or pioneering) brands an advantage in a differentiated market. The new brand would have to be priced substantially below the existing brand to induce consumers to experiment with it; part of the cost of the experiment is the loss of surplus currently being enjoyed on the existing brand. (Farrell (1986) develops this point in his analysis of moral hazard as a barrier to entry.) This is again an example where the incumbent has strategic advantage solely because of already being in the market.

To summarize so far, there are numerous ways in which an incumbent firm can influence cost and/or demand conditions by strategic investments in such a way as to discourage entry into his market. Bulow *et al.* (1985) and Fudenberg and Tirole (1984) have examined in general terms various types of entry deterrence. Returning to the schema above, we can ask whether overinvestment or underinvestment in the strategic variable K deters entry. The answer depends of course upon the specification of the market game. In some instances (such as excess capacity deterring entry), the incumbent deters entry by being "large." Fudenberg and Tirole call this the "top dog effect." In other instances, the incumbent deters entry by being "small," and thereby promises an aggressive response in the event of entry. This is the "lean and hungry look." It may be better for the incumbent to accommodate rather than deter entry. Then he will act strategically to influence the nature of entry, by being either "large" (a "fat cat") or "small" (the "puppy dog ploy"). The aim of all these strategic moves is to cause the rival to choose to act more favorably for the incumbent than he would otherwise do.

So far we have supposed that firms are fully informed about each other's opportunities and motivation, but we now turn to the second step in the analysis of strategic entry deterrence by relaxing this assumption. Milgrom and Roberts (1982a) have shown how limit pricing can be used to deter entry when the potential entrant is uncertain as to the cost level of the incumbent firm. The rival's expectations concerning that cost level—and hence his entry decision—are influenced by the price charged by the incumbent before the entry decision is made. Therefore the pre-entry price can act as a *signal* of the incumbent's efficiency. An incumbent with low costs would like to signal that fact, because the potential rival would then be more reluctant to enter his market. By the same token, an inefficient incumbent would like to masquerade as a low-cost firm in order to make entry less likely. This incentive to signal in an uncertain environment means that the incumbent's pricing can be used as an instrument of entry deterrence. Note that consumers benefit from this kind of limit pricing insofar as it tends to lower price. Other interesting issues arise when there is uncertainty about demand as well as the incumbent's cost level. Then a low pre-entry price might signal either low demand or low costs (see Matthews and Mirman, 1983).

Milgrom and Roberts (1982b) and Kreps and Wilson (1982) have explored another context in which uncertainty about the incumbent plays a role in entry deterrence, namely in connection with *predatory pricing* (see Vickers (1985b) for a survey). They examine a game due to Selten (1978) in which an incumbent firm—a chain store—is threatened by entry in each of a number of towns. Intuitively, we would expect that the incumbent would fight entry if challenged in a town early in the sequence, in order to deter later entrants. However, this is not so if the entrants have complete information about the opportunities and motivation of the incumbent, because in that case he would never fight entry. This is because it is common knowledge that he would not fight in the last town, and so he would have no reason to fight in the last but one and so on. But if the assumption of complete information is very slightly relaxed—so that there is a possibility that the incumbent is somehow committed to fighting—then even an uncommitted incumbent would (rationally) fight entry in early towns to keep up the *reputation* of possibly being a committed fighter. This reputation effect is very powerful, in the sense that a very small amount of incomplete information can make it rational to fight on a large number of occasions.

Another, quite different, context in which predatory pricing is rational has been examined by Benoit (1985) in a paper which also covers the case of imperfect information. He supposes that the entrant's financial resources are such that it would go into bankruptcy after a predatory pricing war of some finite length (say T periods). In other words, its "war chest" is not unlimited. The incumbent's war chest is assumed to be larger than that of the entrant. Assume now that the incumbent would prefer (i) *one* period of predatory fighting followed by perpetual dominance thereafter to (ii) duopolistic coexistence forever. It now follows that it would be rational for the incumbent to engage in predatory pricing rather than to accommodate entry, no matter how large is T. Given the incumbent's preference for (i) over (ii), it would clearly fight to drive out the entrant if $T = 1$. Now, if $T = 2$, both firms know that the entrant would leave the market voluntarily if it were forced into a position where it could survive only one more period before going bankrupt, because it has already been established that the incumbent would force the entrant out otherwise. So the incumbent would find it rational to fight if $T = 2$. The argument can be extended inductively for all T. If the entrant would exit voluntarily at $T = t$, then the incumbent would rationally fight at $T = t+1$, in which case the entrant would exit voluntarily at $T = t+1$ and so on. Here the logic of credible threats works powerfully against entry.

It is now time to draw together some conclusions on strategic entry deterrence. First, there are many circumstances in which a dominant incumbent can act so as to make entry appear an unattractive prospect. Secondly, nonprice behavior is important in this regard, particularly as it affects future cost and demand conditions. Thirdly, it is far too hopeful to suppose that predatory pricing is irrational and that threats of it would therefore be disregarded. In short, there is often ample scope for a dominant firm to undermine "freedom" of entry, and it follows that policies are required to make that freedom effective. In this section we have suggested some of the problems which those policies must address, but it would be foolish to advance general policy prescriptions without taking account of the individual circumstances of particular industries. We will therefore return to the application of the economic principles of strategic entry deterrence and predatory behavior, outlined in this section, later in the book.

3.4 Competition as an Incentive Mechanism

One of the main virtues of competition emphasized by proponents of privatization and liberalization is its role as a mechanism that stimulates *internal* efficiency. Indeed, despite the emphasis of textbook competition theory on *allocative* efficiency in a static environment, it has long been recognized that much of the effect of competition on welfare is due to its role as an incentive system and discovery mechanism in a world of imperfect information (see for example the work of Hayek (1945) and Leibenstein (1966) on X-inefficiency). If competition promotes internal as well as allocative efficiency, then it is doubly beneficial in terms of social welfare.

We considered in the previous chapter whether or not competition in the market for corporate control stimulates internal efficiency by reducing managerial slack, and now we turn to product market competition. Recent work, notably that of Hart (1983), shows how product market competition can influence the nature of incentive contracts between the shareholders and managers of a firm. Suppose that the unit costs of a firm depend on managerial effort and upon some exogenous cost characteristic of the firm. If there is a high degree of correlation between the exogenous cost characteristics of firms in the industry, then competition between them reveals information about managers' effort rates. Being better informed about managerial effort, shareholders can make managerial reward more sensitive to effort, and slack and X-inefficiency can therefore be diminished. Reward can be based, a least in part, upon *relative* performance, and so managers are effectively in competition with each other.

Willig (1985) has performed comparative statics analysis of a principal–agent model to illuminate the effect of product market structure on managerial incentives and behavior. As above shareholders can observe the level of unit costs c, but cannot infer managerial effort from their knowledge of c. The asymmetry of information means that shareholders must reckon with an incentive compatibility constraint when designing an incentive mechanism for managers. That is to say, they must allow for the fact that the managers will behave in a self-interested manner given the incentives that they face. This constraint prevents the attainment of the first-best outcome, and X-inefficiency (in a precise sense) results. Managers gain from this situation, relative to the first-best outcome. Willig does not explicitly examine competition between firms. Instead he introduces a parameter b that is intended to capture the nature of product market competition in a "reduced-form" way. Thus gross profit $V(c, b)$ depends on the parameter b as well as on the level of unit costs. In the comparative statics analysis, the effect of b upon effort and welfare depends on $\partial V/\partial b$, which measures how profit varies with b, and on the cross-partial derivative $\partial^2 V/\partial c \partial b$, which measures how the sensitivity of V to c varies with b. If competition increases that sensitivity without greatly reducing profit, then competition does improve internal efficiency, because managerial reward can be linked more closely to effort.

The effect of competition upon incentives and efficiency has only recently been the subject of precise theoretical analysis, and much remains to be done. There are close parallels between this work and the recent literature on regulation under asymmetric information (see sections 4.3 and

4.6.2 below and the references cited therein). Both are branches of the principal–agent literature that examines the optimal design of incentive contracts. Although this literature on incentive theory is technically quite complex, it succeeds in illuminating some basic points. Imperfect information constrains the design of incentive contracts, and inefficiencies result. Information therefore has value insofar as it makes possible incentive schemes that are more sensitive to effort. Competition can act as a source of this kind of information, because rewards can be based on performance comparisons. Thus there is a theoretical underpinning to the idea that competition promotes efficiency within the firm, as well as efficient behavior in product markets.

3.5 Interconnection, Networks, and Vertical Integration

Having looked at some general aspects of competition theory pertinent to the privatization program, we now address the specific question of competition in networks and vertically related markets. In many industries involved in the U.K. privatization program, several distinct economic activities are required to supply the final product to consumers. Gas must be discovered, extracted, and distributed to the user's appliance. Electricity must be generated and transmitted through the grid. A long-distance phone call in effect consists of a trunk link and local links. The supply of a private branch exchange (PBX) telephone exchange involves both manufacture and distribution. A long-distance coach journey can be thought of as consisting of facilities to embark and disembark as well as the conveyance of the passenger from one town to another.

In such industries it is often the case that effective competition is more feasible in some activities than it is in others. For example, in the current state of technology, competition in long-distance telecommunications is possible, whereas in local networks typically there is natural monopoly and inevitable market power. In the energy industries the prospect of effective competition in the distribution and transmission of energy is remote, but there is no reason in principle why it should not exist in the production of gas or in the generation of electricity.

The question for policy in these circumstances is how to promote and maintain effective competition in activities where it is feasible in the face of monopoly in the related activities. In other words, can the problems of dominance be confined to those activities in which competition cannot exist, or can the dominant firm thwart competition throughout the industry? We shall pursue this question by examining an industry in which output is produced by combining two inputs, A and B. The inputs could be thought of as long-distance and local telecommunications links respectively, or as gas production and distribution. We shall suppose that competition is infeasible in relation to input B, perhaps because natural monopoly conditions of supply prevail, but that competition can be effective in relation to input A.

We shall attempt to answer two questions.

(i) Will the dominant firm in activity B (the "B-firm") find it profitable to thwart competition in activity A?

(ii) If so, what can public policy do to safeguard competition in activity A?

In regard to (ii) we shall focus on two policy measures in particular—*vertical separation* (i.e. banning the B-firm from the A-sector), and rulings on *interconnection* (i.e. stipulating aspects of the relationship between the B-firm and the A-sector).

3.5.1 The Dominant Firm's Incentive to Thwart Competition

To answer question (i) let us begin by supposing that the B-firm can exclude competitors from the A-sector, for example by charging huge prices for the B input. This would happen if BT were allowed to charge Mercury excessive amounts for the local elements of the long-distance calls of Mercury's subscribers, or if British Gas could charge enormous fees for distributing gas produced by rival firms. Suppose that the B-firm is allowed to operate also in the A-sector. Would it wish to exercise its power to exclude rivals there?

If the B-firm's rivals in the A-sector had no cost advantage and if there were nondecreasing returns to scale, then the answer would certainly be positive. Whatever the level of total industry profits without exclusion, the B-firm could achieve at least that level of profit all for itself by excluding rivals in the A-sector and replicating their behavior. Moreover, the B-firm would probably want to change industry behavior, perhaps by restricting industry output, in order to boost industry profits yet further. Excluding rivals in these circumstances therefore allows a double gain—industry profits increase, and the B-firm obtains all of them rather than just part.

We have been speaking as though the inequalities in the previous paragraph were strict, as in general they are, but there is a famous special case in which they are not. This case, in which the B-firm is indifferent between excluding rivals in the A-sector and not doing so, is as follows. Inputs A and B are combined in fixed proportions, there are constant unit costs, and competition in the A-sector is so severe that price is driven down to the level of cost. It then turns out that the B-firm can extract all the monopoly profit that is to be had—for example by buying the A input (by assumption at cost) from the competitive A-sector and combining it with the B input, or by selling the B input to the A-sector with the full monopoly mark-up.

However, as soon as we relax the assumptions of the special case, there is a strictly positive incentive for the B-firm to exclude rivals from the A-sector. If the A and B inputs are combined in *variable* (as opposed to fixed) proportions, then the B-firm's market power is diminished by the ability of rivals in the A-sector to substitute away from the B input, at least to some extent. Alternatively, if *imperfect competition* exists in the A-sector, so that rivals there obtain positive profits, then the B-firm can appropriate those profits (and perhaps more besides) by excluding those rivals.

These rather straightforward arguments do not go through if the B-firm is at a cost disadvantage in the A-sector, or if returns to scale there are decreasing. The reason is that the average cost of producing the industry's output might increase if competitors were excluded from the A-sector, and industry profit might fall as a result. But this will not necessarily happen, because the B-firm will be able to exert greater market power which will tend to increase industry profits. In addition, the B-firm obtains all—rather than part—of industry profit in the event of exclusion. There is therefore a wide range of circumstances in which exclusion is profitable for the B-firm even if cost conditions do not satisfy the assumptions initially made. The example below concerning interconnection will illustrate this point.

3.5.2 Policy Measures to Safeguard Competition

So far we have shown that the B-firm generally has an incentive to thwart competitors in the A-sector by refusing to supply them the B input at reasonable prices. The possible exception is when the B-firm's rivals in the A-sector have a great efficiency advantage there. We now ask whether policy measures exist that can safeguard competition and improve social welfare. We focus on two such measures:

(i) vertical separation—not allowing the B-firm to own any firm that operates in the A-sector;

(ii) interconnect rulings—to stipulate terms of the relationship between the B-firm and the A-sector.

Telecommunications policies in the United States and in Britain illustrate (i) and (ii) respectively. In America when AT&T was broken up after 1982 the long-distance division was separate from the local operating companies. Therefore the local operating companies, being under separate ownership, had less incentive to thwart competition to AT&T in the long-distance market (although some interconnection questions still arose). In contrast, the U.K. Government kept BT intact when privatization occurred. The ability of Mercury—BT's long-distance rival—to compete in the long-distance sector depends on a ruling by Oftel on interconnection which stipulates the terms on which BT must allow Mercury access to its local network.

Although a policy of vertical separation allows competition in the A-sector, it does not necessarily enhance social welfare by itself. The reason is the "double wedge problem" (see Waterson (1984, chapter 5) for a fuller discussion of this and other problems in vertically related markets). Suppose that A and B are combined in fixed proportions to produce the final product. Unless there is *perfect* competition in the A-sector, so that price is driven down to the level of costs, vertical separation has the effect of *raising* the price charged to the final consumer. If the B firm is "downstream," this happens because the B-firm will operate where marginal revenue is equal to marginal cost plus the mark-up of firms in the A-sector. The latter mark-up is absent if the rivals to the B-firm are excluded. Then marginal revenue is equal to the B-firm's overall marginal cost of supplying the final product and, unless the B-firm is relatively inefficient in the A-sector, price is lower with vertical integration. A similar argument operates if the B-firm is "upstream." Unless the A-sector is perfectly competitive, its demand for the B input will be described by a condition that implies that net price exceeds their unit costs. The demand for B is therefore reduced, and it follows that overall output is lower, and the price faced by consumers is higher, than if B were a vertically integrated firm.

In sum, under fixed proportions, with exogenous common unit costs in the A-sector and with no constraint on the market power of the B-firm, vertical separation has undesirable consequences because it exacerbates the harmful effects of the B-firm's monopoly power. This result can be reversed if we relax any of the stated assumptions. First, the assumption of fixed proportions is important, because under variable proportions the market power of the B-firm is weakened by virtue of the ability of rivals in the A-sector to substitute away from input B so as to cut costs. Secondly, if the B-firm has higher costs than other firms in activity A then vertical integration has an obvious drawback. Thirdly, the same is true if competition in activity A has the effect of stimulating internal efficiency in that activity, since costs are then endogenous (see section 3.4). Finally, this entire analysis has supposed that the B-firm is unregulated. If, however, its market power is constrained by regulation, the merits of vertical separation are much stronger. Market power is held in check where it exists, and the advantages of competition are gained where possible. This issue will be taken further in relation to the industries discussed in later chapters, and with the aid of the theoretical perspective on regulation offered in chapter 4.

We now consider rulings on terms of *interconnection* as a second policy measure to combat the B-firm's desire to exclude competitors from the A-sector. More generally we refer to governmental regulation of the terms, notably the price, on which the A-sector can obtain input B from the dominant firm. We use the term "interconnection" because that is the word used in telecommunications economics, where this is central (see section 8.4.1 below). The same issue arises for example in relation to the licensing of innovations, a subject of antitrust cases (for an outline of the theory of licensing see Shapiro (1985)).

The question is to choose the optimal price at which the dominant firm must make input B available to the A-sector. We have already established that the B-firm would set that price at a prohibitively high level to exclude rivals if it had the discretion to do so. We shall use the following simple model to show the determinants of the optimal interconnection price. For simplicity we suppose that the B-firm has only one rival in the A-sector. This corresponds to the situation in the U.K. telecommunications industry: Mercury is BT's only rival in long-distance networks, and BT dominates local networks. Let a and b respectively be the unit costs of producing the A and B inputs, which we assume to be combined in a fixed one-to-one proportion. We will suppose that the cost of combining the inputs to produce the final product is negligible, so that $c = a+b$ is the marginal cost of supplying that product. (Alternatively, we could interpret either a or b as including the cost of combining the inputs.) Let i denote the "interconnection" charge, i.e. the amount paid to the B-firm by its rival for each unit of input B. Therefore the unit cost of supplying the final product is c for the B-firm and $a+i$ for its rival. Let X and Y respectively be the amounts supplied by those two firms, let $Q = X+Y$ be the industry output, and let $P(Q)$ be the inverse demand function. The profit of the dominant firm is then given by

$$\begin{aligned} \pi^D &= XP(Q) + iY - bQ - aX \\ &= [P(Q) - c]X + (i - b)Y, \end{aligned} \tag{3.11}$$

and the profit of the rival is

$$\pi^R = [P(Q) - (a+i)]Y. \tag{3.12}$$

If there is no government intervention, the dominant firm will set i at a prohibitively high level to exclude the rival and will produce where the marginal revenue equals c. In order to say what happens when i does not deter the rival, we need to specify the nature of the duopolistic interaction between the two firms. To this end we introduce a "conjectural variation" term λ as a summary statistic of the degree of rivalry. This term is often interpreted as each firm's expectation of how the other firm's output will change as a result of a change in its own level of output. (However, we are not committed to this interpretation: λ can simply be regarded as a device that saves repeating algebra, because $\lambda = 0$ corresponds to Cournot behavior, $\lambda = -1$ corresponds to Bertrand behavior, and so on).

From (3.11) and (3.12) we now have the first-order conditions

$$(1+\lambda)XP' + P - c + \lambda(i-b) = 0 \tag{3.13}$$

and

$$(1+\lambda)YP' + P - (a+i) = 0. \tag{3.14}$$

Adding (3.13) and (3.14) we obtain

$$(1+\lambda)QP' + 2P = (1+\lambda)c + (1-\lambda)(a+i) \tag{3.15}$$

Now let

$$\eta(Q) = -P/QP' \tag{3.16}$$

be the elasticity of demand. Then (3.15) can be written

$$P[2 - (1+\lambda)/\eta] = (1+\lambda)c + (1-\lambda)(a+i). \tag{3.17}$$

Optimality requires that price P equals marginal cost c. Substituting $P = c$ into (3.17) implies that the optimal interconnection charge is

$$i^* = b - \frac{(1+\lambda)c}{(1-\lambda)\eta}. \tag{3.18}$$

The terms on the right-hand side of (3.18) are b, the unit cost of the B input, and an adjustment term involving λ and η. For $-1 < \lambda < 1$, optimality requires i^* to be *lower than b*. This is in order to offset the duopoly mark-up arising from the imperfect competition between the two firms. This adjustment factor is greater when competition between firms is less intense (i.e. λ is larger) and when the elasticity of demand is lower. Therefore marginal cost pricing ($i = b$) is *sub*optimal unless there is Bertrand, or price-taking, behavior in activity A. In this simple model, an interconnection charge below the level of cost is better. The dominant firm loses and the rival gains from such a policy.

The basic model is very rudimentary, and it can be extended in several directions, for example to the cases of several rivals, cost differences, nonconstant returns to scale, nonlinear pricing, or other social welfare objectives. As it stands the model does not include investment behavior, but it is important for interconnection policy to specify who pays what for investment, since there are externalities between the dominant firm and its rivals. This issue was part of Oftel's ruling on interconnection, which we shall consider in chapter 8.

A simple way of developing the model, which is relevant to the telecommunications industry, is to add a separate market for B. This is appropriate if A and B are long-distance and local links respectively, because there is a demand for local calls (B only) as well as for long-distance calls (which require A plus B). If price discrimination is disallowed, so that the dominant firm is constrained to charge the rival no more for B than it charges consumers in the separate B market, and if the dominant firm is otherwise unregulated, then it has an incentive to raise its price in the B market above the pure monopoly level. This injures the rival in the A-plus-B market and benefits the dominant firm there. This gain outweighs the loss from diverging from pure monopoly behavior in the B market, at any rate for small changes. A ban on price discrimination is therefore liable to introduce distortions elsewhere, and a ruling on interconnection is a superior policy to adopt.

The analysis becomes somewhat more complex if the dominant firm is also subject to regulatory constraint. BT must keep the price of a basket of its services below a given limit. If that constraint binds, the price of its local calls (B only) is inversely related to the price of its long-distance calls (A plus B). It follows that the dominant firm's incentive to price aggressively in the market where there is some competition is stronger, because revenues can be recouped in the other market. The profit function for the dominant firm stated in (3.11) needs extending to cover the other completely monopolized market, with the price in that market inversely related to P. Thus the regulatory mechanism may have the curious effect of making the dominant firm behave more aggressively towards rivals, because the pricing formula allows it to restore revenues elsewhere. We shall discuss further this possible disadvantage of constraining the price level of a wide *basket* of services in chapter 8 on the telecommunications industry.

Another important feature of that industry (among others) is the presence of *network externalities*. The demand for telecommunications services by any one customer depends upon who else is a customer of the same network, since he can call—and be called by—only those people. Network externalities are important for the nature of competition and welfare (see Katz and Shapiro, 1985, 1986; Farrell and Saloner, 1985). In regard to competition, it is clear that a rival would be at a grave disadvantage with respect to the dominant firm if it were denied access to its network of established subscribers. The interconnection question therefore has a further dimension. As to the welfare implications of network externalities, there is possibly a case for some subsidy to new subscribers to the network, since they provide a positive externality to existing subscribers. Space does not permit a fuller treatment of network economics here, but the issue will recur in later chapters.

3.6 Concluding Remarks

Theories about competitive forces of course account for a large portion of microeconomics, and it is therefore impossible in one chapter to say a great deal about them. Nevertheless it was essential for us to outline some selected aspects of those theories in view of the importance attached to competition in the British debate on privatization. To conclude, and to point forward to later chapters, we shall briefly recap on why we selected the topics described in this chapter. Section 3.2.1 looked at the trade-off that sometimes exists between competition and scale economies. This trade-off is at the heart of the question of how many rivals should be licensed to compete with a dominant enterprise such as BT. It also bears on the issue of desirability of unrestricted free entry. Section 3.2.2 discussed public enterprises as competitors, an important topic given that there is no necessary link between private ownership and competition.

Section 3.3 concerned the forces of potential competition, whose virtues have been widely acclaimed by proponents of deregulation and liberalization. Although we too would generally advocate freedom of entry, we argued that contestability theory was not suitable for the analysis of the major industries considered in this book, and we urged the need for policy measures to contain the danger that a powerful incumbent firm could render freedom of entry ineffective by predatory tactics. Section 3.4 briefly described some ways in which the competitive process can act as a mechanism with good incentives for internal efficiency. Such considerations have featured prominently in the debate on privatization and liberalization. Finally, in section 3.5 we examined some aspects of competition in vertically related markets, including the question of interconnection which arises not only in telecommunications but also in such industries as gas and electricity. In the following chapters we shall often have cause to refer back to the analysis of competitive forces described above. But first we must look at the economics of regulatory mechanisms for constraining market power.

References

Baumol, W.J. (1982). Contestable Markets: An Uprising in the Theory of Industrial Structure. *American Economic Review* 72: 1–15.

Baumol, W.J., J. Panzar and R.D. Willig (1982). *Contestable Markets and the Theory of Industry Structure*. New York: Harcourt Brace Jovanovich.

Baumol, W.J. and R.D. Willig (1986). Contestability: Developments Since the Book. *Oxford Economic Papers (Supplement)* 38: 9–36.

Beato, P. and A. Mas-Colell (1984). The Marginal Cost Pricing as a Regulation Mechanism in Mixed Markets. In Marchand, M., P. Pestieau and H. Tulkens (eds), *The Performance of Public Enterprises*. Amsterdam: North-Holland.

Benoit, J.-P. (1985). Financially Constrained Entry in a Game with Incomplete Information. *Rand Journal of Economics* 15: 490–499.

Brock, W.A. (1983). Contestable Markets and the Theory of Industry Structure: A Review Article. *Journal of Political Economy* 91: 1055–1066.

Bulow, J., J. Geanakopolos and P. Klemperer (1985). Multimarket Oligopoly. *Journal of Political Economy* 93: 488–511.

Cremer, H., M. Marchand and J.-F. Thisse (1987). The Public Firm as an Instrument for Regulating an Oligopolistic Market. Paper presented at the 2nd Congress of the European Economic Association, Copenhagen, August 1987.

Dasgupta, P. and J.E. Stiglitz (1985). *Sunk Costs, Competition and Welfare*. Mimeograph, St John's College, Cambridge.

De Fraja, G. and F. Delbono (1986). Alternative Strategies of a Public Enterprise in Oligopoly. Paper presented at the 1st Congress of the European Economic Association, Vienna, August 1986.

Dixit, A. (1980). The Role of Investment in Entry Deterrence. *Economic Journal* 90: 95–106.

Farrell, J. (1986). Moral Hazard as an Entry Barrier. *Rand Journal of Economics* 17: 440–449.

Farrell, J. and G. Saloner (1985). Standardization, Compatibility and Innovation. *Rand Journal of Economics* 16: 70–83.

Faulhaber, B.C. (1975). Cross-subsidization: Pricing in Public Enterprises. *American Economic Review* 65: 966–977.

Friedman, J. (1979). On Entry Preventing Behaviour and Limit Price Models of Entry. In Brams, S.J. *et al.* (eds), *Applied Game Theory*. Vienna: Physica.

Fudenberg, D. and J. Tirole (1983). Learning by Doing and Market Performance. *Bell Journal of Economics* 14: 522–530.

Fudenberg, D. and J. Tirole (1984). The Fat-Cat Effect, the Puppy-Dog Ploy, and the Lean and Hungry Look. *American Economic Review Papers and Proceedings* 74: 361–366.
Gilbert, R.J. and D. Newbery (1982). Pre-emptive Patenting and the Persistence of Monopoly. *American Economic Review* 72: 514–526.
Harris, R.G. and E.G.Wiens (1980) Government Enterprise: An Instrument for the Internal Regulation of Industry. *Canadian Journal of Economics* 13: 125–132.
Hart, O.D. (1983). The Market Mechanism as an Incentive Scheme. *Bell Journal of Economics* 14: 366–382.
Hay, D.A. and D.J. Morris (1979). *Industrial Economics*. Oxford: Oxford University Press.
Hayek, F.A. (1945). The Use of Knowledge in Society. *American Economic Review* 35: 519–530.
Katz, M. and C. Shapiro (1985). Network Externalities, Competition and Compatibility. *American Economic Review* 75: 424–440.
Katz, M.L. and C. Shapiro (1986). Product Compatibility Choice in a Market with Technological Progress. *Oxford Economic Papers* (Supplement) 38: 146–165.
Kreps, D. and R. Wilson (1982). Reputation and Imperfect Information. *Journal of Economic Theory* 27: 253–279.
Leibenstein, H. (1966). Allocative Efficiency versus *X*-Efficiency. *American Economic Review* 56: 392–415.
Mankiw, N.G. and M.D. Whinston (1986). Free Entry and Social Inefficiency. *Rand Journal of Economics* 17: 48–58.
Matthews, S. and L. Mirman (1983). Equilibrium Limit Pricing: the Effects of Private Information and Stochastic Demand. *Econometrica* 51: 981–996.
Milgrom, P. and J. Roberts (1982a). Predation, Reputation and Entry Deterrence. *Journal of Economic Theory* 27: 280–312.
Milgrom, P. and J. Roberts (1982b). Limit Pricing and Entry Under Incomplete Information: An Equilibrium Analysis. *Econometrica* 50: 443–459.
Perry, M.K. (1984). Scale Economies, Imperfect Competition and Public Policy. *Journal of Industrial Economics* 32: 313–333.
Salop, S. and D. Scheffman (1983). Raising Rivals' Costs. *American Economic Review Papers and Proceedings* 73: 267–271.
Schmalensee, R. (1978). Entry Deterrence in the Ready To Eat Breakfast Cereal Industry. *Bell Journal of Economics* 9: 305–327.
Schmalensee, R. (1982). Product Differentiation Advantages of Pioneering Brands. *American Economic Review* 82: 349–365.
Schmalensee, R. (1983). Advertising and Entry Deterrence: an Exploratory Model. *Journal of Political Economy* 90: 636–653.
Schwartz, M. (1986). The Nature and Scope of Contestability Theory. *Oxford Economic Papers (Supplement)* 38: 37–57.
Schwartz, M. and R.J. Reynolds (1983). Contestable Markets: An Uprising in the Theory of Industry Structure: Comment. *American Economic Review* 73: 488–490.
Selten, R. (1978). The Chain Store Paradox. *Theory and Decision* 9: 127–159.
Shapiro, C. (1985). Patent Licensing and R&D Rivalry. *American Economic Review Papers and Proceedings* 75: 25–30.
Sharkey, W.W. (1982). *The Theory of Natural Monopoly*. Cambridge: Cambridge University Press.
Shepherd, W. (1984). 'Contestability' vs. Competition. *American Economic Review* 74: 572–587.

Spence, M. (1977). Entry, Capacity, Investment and Oligopolistic Pricing. *Bell Journal of Economics* 8: 534–544.
Spence, M. (1981). The Learning Curve and Competition. *Bell Journal of Economics* 12: 49–70.
Spence, M. (1983). Contestable Markets and the Theory of Industry Structure: A Review Article. *Journal of Economic Literature* 21: 981–990.
Suzumura, K. and K. Kiyono (1987). Entry Barriers and Economic Welfare. *Review of Economic Studies* 54: 157–167.
Vickers, J.S. (1985a). Strategic Competition among the Few—Some Recent Developments in Oligopoly Theory. *Oxford Review of Economic Policy* 1(3): 39–62.
Vickers, J.S. (1985b). The Economics of Predatory Practices. *Fiscal Studies* 6(3): 24–36.
Waterson, M. (1984). *Economic Theory of the Industry*. Cambridge: Cambridge University Press.
von Weizsäcker, C.C. (1980). A Welfare Analysis of Barriers to Entry. *Bell Journal of Economics* 11: 399–420.
Williamson, O.E. (1968). Economies as an Antitrust Defense: Welfare Tradeoffs. *American Economic Review* 58: 18–36.
Willig, R.D. (1985). *Corporate Governance and Product Market Structure*. Mimeograph, Princeton University.

[15]

Economic Rationales for the Scope of Privatization

Carl Shapiro and Robert D. Willig

In this chapter we seek to identify, at a fundamental theoretical level, the impacts of privatization on the operations of an enterprise. We conduct our analysis in an abstract framework that is rich enough to represent considerations of both efficiency in performance and ability to meet broader public objectives. Our goal is the delineation of various characteristics of an activity's structure and environment that point to either public or private forms of control as the most effective in accomplishing society's aims.[1]

Our approach focuses on informational and incentive differences between public and private enterprise. In particular, we suppose that in a public enterprise government officials possess intimate knowledge of the workings of the enterprise, while such information is controlled by private parties if the activity is privatized. Public enterprise is motivated to satisfy the goals of public management, while private enterprise is motivated to maximize profits, subject to whatever government regulation is imposed on it, and regulation is constrained by the need to attract private capital.

Our focus on information might appear peculiar and quite narrow to some readers. We shall argue, however, that at a fundamental level the intrinsic differences between public and private enterprise must ultimately be based on incentives, and these in turn are based on the available information. This information-theoretic perspective fits our work squarely into the recent and fast-growing economics literature on organizational design and performance, which focuses on the problems and opportunities posed by different patterns of control in settings distinguished by their structures of information and incentives.[2]

Our study of privatization thus asks how a shift from public to private ownership alters the structure of information, incentives, and controls facing the individuals operating the enterprise. These elements in turn determine the enterprise's operating decisions and hence its economic and social performance. Neither public nor private sector enterprises operate perfectly, and our organizational models of the two forms are designed to shed light on the conditions under which one can be predicted to perform better than the other.

In the following section we present the canonical models of private and public enterprise that we subsequently subject to comparative analysis. These models are designed to reflect a common technological and informational environment into which different governance structures can be imposed. We use our models of public and private enterprise in the third section to demonstrate a series of "neutrality results," that is, to identify informational environments in which there is no intrinsic difference in the performance of public and private enterprise. There we justify our focus on private information by showing that the presence of such information is necessary for privatization to have a genuine effect. We then focus on environments in which neutrality between public and private enterprise does not obtain, seeking to derive from our two models some qualitative results concerning the tradeoff between public and private enterprise. In particular, we identify those factors that would lead a public-spirited party to select private or public enterprise. In the fifth section we illustrate our theoretical findings by applying them to several stylized examples of public enterprise: a basic manufacturing operation, a hotel or tourist facility, the production of military equipment, prison management, and the operation of the postal or telecommunications system. There we take a step toward applying our framework to inform an inquiry into the relative merits of public versus private enterprise in practice.

Public Enterprise, Private Enterprise, and Regulation

The labels "public ownership" and "private enterprise" suggest two discrete and very different ways of structuring economic activity and utilizing productive assets. The corresponding simple view of privatization is that it inevitably and significantly alters the way in which resources are allocated. Certainly reading the country studies contained in this volume would not lead one to doubt that privatization "matters." Indeed, one might think it obvious that privatization has a significant influence on an enterprise's operating decisions and hence on the allocation of resources.

The conclusion that privatization typically has a major impact on the allocation of resources is probably correct. We seek, however, some general guidelines indicating the *nature* of the impact of privatization and how it varies with the underlying economic and political environment. Developing such guidelines requires a coherent comparative model of decisionmaking in public sector enterprises and in privately owned companies, the latter possibly subject to government control through taxes, subsidies, and direct regulation.

As one begins to think seriously about and to construct models of public and private sector enterprises, it soon becomes clear that the distinction between these two forms is not nearly so stark or so inevitable as it might appear upon casual consideration.[3] In particular, private enterprises that are subjected to carefully crafted taxes, subsidies, and regulatory oversight may be almost indistinguishable from public ones. Superficially, there might seem to be a stark difference between public and private enterprises because the former can be directed to serve entirely public goals, while the latter are entirely profit-oriented. In cases where there is no market failure, profit maximization coincides with public goals. But even where there is sharp deviation between public goals and profit maximization, private enterprise can be subjected to various forms of regulation to make it better serve public goals.

For example, consider an oft-cited motivation for privatization, namely, to achieve a reduction in the public sector borrowing requirement. Supposedly, privatizing a money-losing public operation will relieve the treasury of the ongoing drain of funds required to cover the enterprise's losses. Why privatization is necessary to achieve this goal is rarely articulated, however. If low prices are the source of the deficit, prices charged by the public enterprise could in principle be raised to generate more revenues. If inefficient operations are the cause, additional oversight or improved incentive mechanisms may be the solution. And if the enterprise's capital requirements are placing a strain on public sector borrowing, shifting these loans to the private sector may be a mere accounting change, not a genuine improvement in efficiency.[4]

Similar arguments can be applied to other common justifications for privatization. For example, if restrictive civil service rules hamper the operations of a public enterprise, relaxing these rules, perhaps on a selective basis, may serve the same goals for which privatization is touted. If trade unions are thought to be overly powerful in a public enterprise, why will they not be equally powerful in affecting the taxes and regulations imposed on the private enterprise? If an industry is thought to be vital for national security purposes or for general economic development, why is an arm's-length subsidy designed to promote domestic production not equally as effective as subsidized public sector enterprise?

We recognize that several of these arguments for privatization are likely to be valid, indeed overwhelming, in particular economic circumstances and especially when the political circumstances unique to each country are taken into account.[5] Our goal, however, is to look beyond these case-by-case considerations to elucidate some general principles regarding those activities most appropriate for privatization.

One way to analyze privatization would be to compare the operations of a public sector enterprise with those of an unregulated private company. Simply privatizing a public enterprise, without establishing any structure of regulatory oversight, taxes, or subsidies, will typically have a substantial effect on the allocation of resources, for the simple reason that an unfettered private company will seek to maximize shareholder profits, whereas a public enterprise is likely to be operated to serve social goals apart from the maximization of its profits. If market failures—externalities, monopoly power, and the like—are severe, then privatization without regulation may well be inferior to public enterprise.

We wish to pose a different question, however: What effect will privatization have if the private company is subjected to sophisticated *regulation,* as well as tax and subsidy policies, designed to account for public-interest goals? In posing the question this way, we can reject arguments such as the one that pursuit of national security goals alone mandates public ownership of an industry; rather, we ask whether national security goals can be better met by public enterprise or by private enterprise facing special tax treatment or regulation designed to promote those goals. Likewise, we do not accept the argument that an industry must be public merely because it is a natural monopoly; we ask whether a private company facing regulatory oversight could perform better than public enterprise.

When the effects of privatization are studied in this way, a surprising answer emerges: Under a remarkably general set of conditions, there is *no difference* between the performance of a public enterprise and that of a private company subject to an optimally designed regulatory and tax scheme.[6] We shall describe and comment below on these "neutrality theorems," which provide conditions under which public sector enterprise and regulated private enterprise are equivalent in terms of resource allocation. These neutrality theorems, which we have adapted from the economics literature on regulation and mechanism design, will be easier to describe after we present the components of our formal models.

In noting these neutrality results, we do not mean to suggest that any objective of privatization can in fact be achieved equally well with carefully chosen policies within the context of the public sector enterprise. Rather we take these neutrality theorems as our starting point in developing models rich enough so that privatization is *not* neutral. Such models are capable of revealing the intrinsic differences between public and private enterprise. The required richness is the presence of *private information* about both the costs and the benefits of the enterprise's operations. We turn now to the development of these models.

Comparative Models of Public and Private Sector Enterprise

We present here our models of public and private sector enterprise. The models are designed to facilitate a comparison of these two forms of ownership and control of productive assets. Figure 1 presents a schematic diagram of our two models, which will become clearer as we describe them in the text.

Our analysis emphasizes private information, that is, information observed by one party that cannot be observed or verified by others. In contrast, public or *contractible* information is either commonly observed or can be verified by a neutral third party such as a court. To illustrate this distinction between public and private information, consider information about employment conditions. The published national unemployment rate contains some information about employment conditions, and we will allow for instructions of the form "increase employment during periods of high employment" to be given to the public official with responsibility for the enterprise. But government officials may have more detailed information about employment conditions that cannot be verified, such as qualitative information regarding unemployment rates in different regions, the extent of underemployment, the alternative opportunities of those who might be hired in the enterprise, skills and unemployment rates among different groups in the population, and so on. Our models are designed to allow for the possibility that hiring decisions at the enterprise more accurately reflect such qualitative, private information if the enterprise is operated in the public sector under the direct control of the public official with the private information about employment conditions.

We include three types of private information: information about the external social benefits of the enterprise's activities, which we call ψ; information about the divergence between the public interest and the interests of the public official who oversees the enterprise, which we call ε; and information about the profitability of the enterprise's operations, which we call θ. Each of these will be described in further detail below.

As we shall see, the form of ownership matters only if there is some private, noncontractible information. Yet our analysis is perfectly capable of including public, contractible information. In fact, our entire analysis could be made *contingent* on such public information.[7] For that very reason, and without affecting any of our comparisons between public and private enterprise, we suppress such public information in all that follows.

We postulate the presence of a public-spirited agent, the *framer*, who originally makes the choice between public and private enterprise and sets up the governance structure for the enterprise chosen. This choice is

FIGURE 1
Schematic Diagram of Public and Private Enterprise

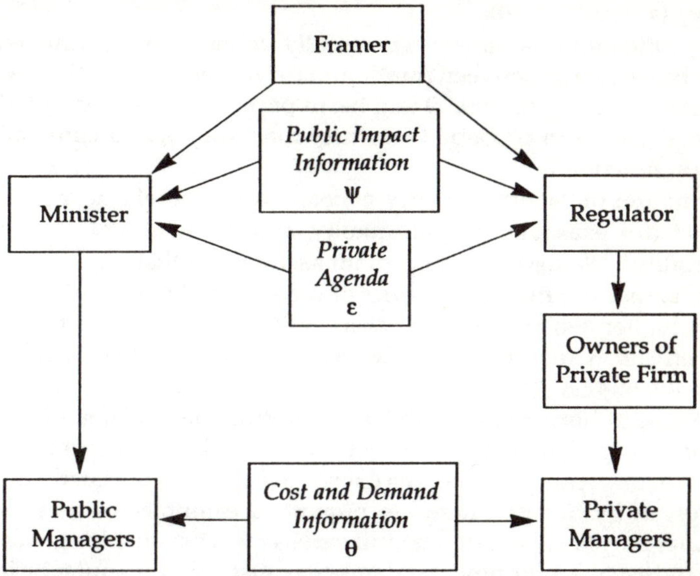

represented in Figure 1 by the two branches emanating from the box labeled "Framer." Our normative analysis is thus cast in the following terms: What is the optimal form of ownership and control for the framer to adopt, and how does this choice depend upon various features of the economic environment? The framer recognizes that political forces will influence subsequent public sector decisions, but he himself is above these forces, acting purely in the public interest.[8]

Public Enterprise

If the enterprise is public, it is controlled and operated by a public official, whom we call the *minister*. The minister may operate under restrictions put in place by the framer. If there are no such restrictions, we call the method of governance *discretionary public enterprise*. With restrictions, we have *nondiscretionary public enterprise*.

By virtue of his role in managing the enterprise, the minister receives private information, θ, regarding the technology of production and the state of demand.[9] We need not distinguish between demand and cost information; both are encompassed in the profit function. The profitability of taking action x is given by $\pi(x,\theta)$. We define θ so that profits are increasing in θ; $\pi_\theta > 0$, where subscripts denote partial derivatives. High values of θ correspond to conditions of high productivity or elevated demand. With the enterprise being run in the public sector, its contribution to the treasury is simply $\pi(x,\theta)$.

The profitability parameter θ is initially unknown at the time when the framer must choose between public and private enterprise. But the framer has prior beliefs about what θ will be; in particular, θ is distributed on the interval $[\theta_0,\theta_1]$ with probability density function $f(\theta)$ and cumulative distribution function $F(\theta)$.

Our notion of "action" is very general. We shall refer to x as "level of activity" (for example, output, quality, and the like) and θ as "level of profitability." We make the important assumption that $\pi_{x\theta} > 0$ at all x and θ, that is, that the marginal return to increasing the activity level is uniformly higher when the total return is higher. All other things being equal, efficiency requires higher levels of activity when costs are lower or demand is higher.

By virtue of his position in the public sector, the minister also observes information, ψ, that bears on the external social benefits generated by the enterprise's operations. The external social benefits associated with action x are given by $S(x,\psi)$. There are numerous examples of these benefits: consumer surplus generated by rail service; worker surplus generated by heavy industry; environmental damages caused by a manufacturing facility; spillover effects of a major factory on related industries or on overall regional development; national security benefits associated with the operation a defense facility; or the effect of the telephone system on national cohesion. $S(x,\psi)$ captures anything that affects the public interest but does not appear in the enterprise's profits.

We need not specify whether the enterprise receives revenues from the sale of its product. Any such revenue is included in the profit function; if there are no revenues, then the external benefits are correspondingly higher, since these include any surplus enjoyed by the enterprise's customers.

Our key substantive assumption is that the public-impact information that inherently resides in the public sector, ψ, does not appear in the profit function. In other words, ψ includes information not on the profitability of the enterprise but only on the external social effects of the enterprise's operations.

The minister makes two decisions. First, he must decide whether to authorize the investments required to operate the enterprise. For simplicity, we model this as a discrete, yes/no investment choice. If investment is not made, no further decisions in this domain are needed. We normalize all agents' payoffs to zero in this event. If investment is made, the minister makes the enterprise's operating decisions, that is, chooses x. Throughout this chapter, for the sake of simplicity, we assume that the investment is always warranted under the objectives of the framer and the public official.

The overall social welfare function that the framer seeks to maximize is given by

$$W = S(x,\psi) + k\pi(x,\theta).$$

This objective is simply external benefits plus enterprise profits, with a magnification factor applied to the net contribution made by the enterprise to the public treasury. This magnification factor, $k > 1$, equals the unit cost of raising public funds, including any distortions caused by the taxes required to finance public sector operations.[10]

The minister has objectives similar but not identical to those of the framer. In particular, the minister's objective is

$$V^M = W + \alpha J(x,\varepsilon).$$

We refer to J as the *private agenda of the minister*, but it could equally well represent divergences between the objectives of a public official, who is subject to short-run political pressure, and the genuine long-run public interest.

The variable α measures the extent of the divergence between the minister's objectives and those of the framer. Under the private-agenda interpretation of J, α measures the extent to which the minister is able to pursue his private agenda, as opposed to W. In this case, α could represent the effectiveness of the political system: a well-functioning political system limits the ability of public officials to pursue their personal interests, leading to a low value of α. Alternatively, ministers are more or less motivated by their personal agendas as α is large or small. Under the "short-run political pressure" interpretation of J, α measures the extent to which public officials are subject to political forces that in fact diverge from the long-run public interest.

The variable ε is observable only to the public official. It captures the idiosyncratic nature of his private agenda, which cannot be foreseen by the framer or observed by others while the minister is in power. The key point is that the framer cannot know just who the public official will be, or what his private aims will be, so it is difficult for the framer systematically to counteract such private agendas. Likewise, the minister's private goals will not be publicly observable, and hence the framer cannot charge a third party, such as the court, with the responsibility of penalizing the minister for pursuing his private agenda.[11]

Note that we are emphasizing certain control and governance problems and totally ignoring others. In particular, by assuming that the minister acts unilaterally to achieve a well-defined objective function, we ignore all of the internal control problems within the public sector bureaucracy. In terms of Figure 1, we are assuming away any agency problems between the minister and his public sector managers. We shall make an analogous assumption when analyzing private enterprise, namely, that no agency problems occur between the owners of the private firm and its managers.

Regulated Private Enterprise

Our model of regulated private enterprise is carefully constructed to capture the same underlying economic and informational environment as that just described for the public enterprise. As in that model, the public official, now playing the role of a *regulator*, observes the public-interest impact variable, ψ, and the private agenda variable, ε. We denote by $\rho = (\psi,\varepsilon)$ the private information of the regulator. And again, the party who will be operating the enterprise—in this case a private firm—observes the profitability parameter θ.

The private investment decision is necessarily more complex than was the public investment decision described above. But it is still a simple yes/no decision, and we assume that its outcome is commonly observable. The added complexity arises from the fact that, in order to attract private investment, the regulator must put into place a regulatory scheme that offers the expectation of at least a competitive rate of return on the private firm's sunk capital, be it physical investment or the purchase of assets previously owned by the public sector. So, in the case of private enterprise, a regulatory "contract" must be specified prior to the investment decision.

We model regulatory schemes as follows (see Caillaud, Guesnerie, and Tirole 1988 for a discussion of the generality of such schemes). The regulator offers a function $T(x)$ specifying that if the firm chooses action x it will receive a transfer $T(x)$ from the public sector.[12] If T is positive, this will constitute a payment; if T is negative it will be a tax or a franchise fee.[13] At this point, we focus on the case in which the regulator has complete freedom to select the regulatory scheme, $T(x)$. We denote this case by *discretionary regulation*. If the framer restricts the regulator's ability to choose $T(x)$, we have *nondiscretionary regulation*.

In response to the regulatory incentive scheme $T(x)$, the private firm first chooses whether to invest in the enterprise. The standard analysis postulates at this point that the private firm will in fact invest in the enterprise if and only if the regulatory contract $T(x)$ offers (expected) non-negative profits.[14] If investment does not occur, there are no further decisions to be taken and all parties earn the payoff of zero. If investment does occur, the private firm ultimately will choose an action x. Giving the firm the final choice of x allows that choice to be sensitive to the realized level of profitability, θ.[15]

This description of regulation has proven to be very powerful. One limitation is its focus on only a single period of production (see Caillaud, Guesnerie, and Tirole 1988 for extensions of this description to multiperiod contexts). It applies without alteration over time, however, if each period of production activity entails independent realizations of the informational random variables. Under this assumption, which we adopt here, the analytic approach is quite general if the regulator already is aware of the firm's public-interest impacts at the time the regulatory scheme is put into place.

The standard treatment is not suitable, however, if the regulator will receive further private information subsequent to investment by the firm. We seek an analysis that is general enough to include the possibility that the regulator will be better informed about public-interest impacts subsequent to investment than he is prior to the firm's investment. If the regulator can exert some discretion subsequent to the firm's investment, those components of $\rho \equiv (\psi,\varepsilon)$ that the regulator does not observe until after the firm's investment also can influence the choice of x by the private firm.

The regulator can give himself postinvestment discretion by using a generalized version of the regulatory scheme just described. In particular, the regulator can offer a *menu* of different regulatory schemes, $\{T(x)\}$, with the understanding that he will be allowed to pick any $T(x)$ from this menu subsequent to investment by the firm and the learning of ρ by the regulator. In fact, we can describe the menu as a single function, $T(x,\rho)$, with the interpretation that if the regulator announces ρ and then the firm chooses x, it will receive a transfer of $T(x,\rho)$.[16]

With this generalized scheme, the firm still must be given a non-negative expected return in order to induce it to make its initial investment. But now the firm must estimate the likelihood of various regulatory schemes being imposed, as well as figure out its own best response to each scheme for each realization of its own profitability.

Assuming that investment does take place, the regulator announces a value of ρ, that is, chooses a regulatory incentive scheme. Finally, the firm, observing its own profitability, chooses the profit-maximizing action in response to the regulatory scheme in force. The private firm's profits are defined as

$$\pi^P = \pi(x,\theta) + T(x,\rho).$$

The framer's objective, social welfare, is

$$W = S(x,\psi) + \pi(x,\theta) - (k-1)T(x,\rho),$$

again reflecting the cost of raising any public funds that must be used to pay the private company (or the benefit of collecting tax revenues from that company).[17] The regulator's objective function is again $V^R = W + \alpha J$.

What Constitutes Privatization?

The essential difference between public and private enterprises, as we are modeling them, is the location of private information about cost and demand conditions. We have postulated that the manager of the enterprise possesses the most detailed information about costs and demand, an assumption that strikes us as quite appropriate, and one that is common in the literature on regulation. Under public enterprise, the detailed cost and demand information resides public managers who report to a public official. Under privatization, this information resides with private managers who report to the owners of a private firm (see Figure 1).

The informational barrier that privatization erects between the public official and the mangers of the enterprise may not be totally impenetrable, however. If the government could audit the private firm sufficiently well to capture all of its managers' private information, then privatization would lose its uniqueness from public enterprise. We argue, therefore, that if privatization is to be meaningful, the government may need to make a commitment to respect private property rights to information by limiting its own ability to extract information from the private firm through an audit.[18] This commitment is above and beyond the well-known one that the government must make to respect private property rights to tangible assets by assuring private parties that their investments will not be expropriated.

The key distinction between public and private sector enterprise, in our view, is that privatization gives informational autonomy to a party who is not under direct public sector control. To put this another way, we have modeled privatization as the *deliberate* introduction of an informational barrier between the public sector official with responsibility for the enterprise—that is, the regulator—and the owners and managers of the enterprise. This barrier is reflected in the additional layer on the right-hand side of Figure 1.

Economists have given much attention to the inefficiencies associated with such informational barriers, which are more commonly called agency problems. In our model, the usual inefficiency is reflected in a reduced payoff *to the public official* if that official must motivate the private firm through regulation rather than control the public enterprise directly. What is novel about our approach is that we consider the *benefits* of introducing an agency problem from the perspective of a higher-level principal, namely, the framer. Since the public official does not precisely share the objectives of the framer—namely, social welfare—the framer sees some benefits to limiting the discretion of that official. Our analysis below compares these benefits with the inevitable costs of separating public-impact information, ψ, from profitability information θ.

When Discretionary Public Enterprise and Discretionary Regulation Are Equivalent

We now describe a number of cases in which the performance of public and regulated private enterprises are equivalent, given that the framer affords discretion to the public official.[19] These are cases in which the regulator can exert sufficient indirect regulatory control to achieve the same results he could obtain as minister with direct control of a public enterprise. If the regulator merely induces the private firm to duplicate the actions that he as minister would choose, the framer is indifferent between public and private enterprise.

First, consider the operation of an enterprise in an environment without any private information whatsoever. Suppose that all information about the external benefits of the enterprise, and all information about its profitability, is contractible. In such circumstances, the regulator could put in place a set of taxes or subsidies, contingent on what will become the commonly known realizations of the public costs and benefits of the enterprise's operations. These taxes and subsidies could be designed to induce the owners to operate the enterprise to serve precisely the regulator's objectives in every contingency.

Perhaps it is not surprising that one can obtain a neutrality result in the complete absence of noncontractible private information, for in such a case there is no truly active role for the managers of the enterprise. They need only carry out the detailed instructions left by the minister or the regulator, and he cannot claim that any new information or extenuating circumstances justify departures from that mechanical mandate. Of course, this description of the case only serves to underscore its lack of realism. In fact, the details of the operation of the enterprise are never commonly known, and thus the nature and identity of the party operating the enterprise can be expected to make a material difference.

Public enterprise and regulated private enterprise also may be equivalent in the presence of private information. There are three distinct cases of interest.

Private Information about Profitability Is Revealed after Investment

In the first case, the private information about profitability is not known before the private investment decision must be made; perhaps this information is revealed only through the physical process of investment or once the private owners have taken possession of the newly privatized public assets. In contrast, in this case, the private information concerning public impacts and private agenda, ρ, is known to the regulator when he must commit himself to the regulatory mechanism, before the time of the investment decision.

Under these conditions, the regulator can exert sufficient indirect control over the private firm to obtain the same outcome and payoff as under public ownership, so the framer is indifferent between public and private enterprise. The regulator's control is secured by paying the firm according to the following schedule:

$$(1) \qquad T^*(x,\rho) = \frac{1}{k}(S(x,\psi) + \alpha J(x,\varepsilon)) + G(\rho).$$

Here $G(\rho)$ is independent of the activity level x and is set as small as possible consistent with inducing the firm to make the required investment.[20]

With this schedule, the regulator induces the same actions and achieves the same payoff as does the minister under public enterprise. The mechanism operates by forcing the firm to *internalize* the objectives of the regulator. The optimality of the $T^*(x,\rho)$ schedule is clearest if k is taken to be equal to 1. Then, the transfer of T^* adds $S(x,\psi) + \alpha J(x,\varepsilon) + G(\rho)$ to the firm's payoff, thereby internalizing the benefits enjoyed by the regulator but otherwise ignored by the firm. For $k > 1$ these transfers are scaled back to account for the extra cost of public funds.

All Private Information Revealed after Investment

The second distinct case in which a surprisingly powerful neutrality result holds occurs when private information concerning both costs and public impacts is revealed only after the investment commitment must be made. Only the prior probability distributions of ρ and θ are known at the time the investment decision must be effected. By contrast, after the investment has been made, but before the activity level must be chosen, the value of ρ will be revealed to the regulator, and the value of θ will be revealed to the manager of the enterprise. Again, the regulator's optimal $T(x)$ results in the same choices of activity levels and the same expected drain on the treasury that would be the result of public enterprise.

The logic behind this result is a straightforward extension of the analysis of the first case. Here, the regulator commits himself to the menu of payment schedules given by $T^*(x,\rho)$, as in equation (1), with the understanding that he will choose a particular schedule from this menu by selecting a value of ρ after investment is made and the true value of ρ becomes known to him, but still before the activity level must be chosen by the firm. The firm is indifferent, ex ante, about which particular schedule will be chosen from the menu by the regulator, because each of them offers the same zero level of expected profits, that is, just enough to induce the firm to make the investment.[21]

Once the true value of ρ is revealed to the regulator, he will be motivated to select the payment schedule $T^*(x,\rho)$ corresponding to that value, because that schedule is optimal for his objective function. In the face of that payment schedule, the firm will be motivated to choose the same activity levels as in the first case above, and here too that is the optimum from the perspective of either the regulator or the public minister.[22]

No Cost of Raising Government Funds

In the third case of neutrality, unlike the first and second cases, the private firm may have private information about its costs before the investment commitment must be made. However, $k = 1$, so that transfers from the treasury are not a matter of concern to the framer, the regulator, or the public minister.

Because the firm knows its value of θ and the regulator is aware of that fact but does not know the pertinent value of θ, the regulator, to assure that the investment will be made, must commit to a payment schedule or to a menu of schedules that provides non-negative profit for all possible levels of θ.[23] Here, because of the stipulation that $k = 1$, this requirement poses no problem for the regulator: he is perfectly willing to add enough funds to any payment schedule to assure its profitability in the light of his indifference to transfers from the treasury. Consequently, it is optimal for the objectives of the regulator to offer the firm the internalization schedules $T^*(x,\rho)$ of equation (1), but with a different portion $G(\rho)$ that is here sufficiently large to guarantee the firm non-negative profit even if its profitability level θ is the worst possible.

In the end, the regulated private firm chooses the same activity levels that the public enterprise would choose, but the drain on the treasury caused by regulation is greater than that caused by public enterprise. Since in this case, however, that drain is not a matter of concern, the framer would find no difference between the performance of public and private forms of organization.

Summary of Neutrality Results

Our neutrality results indicate those elements of the environment that must be considered to develop insights into the fundamental differences between public and regulated private enterprises.[24] We can summarize our neutrality findings as follows:

Proposition 1. The framer is indifferent between permitting the public minister to control the enterprise and permitting the regulator to select a regulatory scheme under any of the following conditions: (1) all eventualities are contractible; (2) all private information about profitability is revealed only after the investment decision is made; or (3) the framer is unconcerned about transfers of funds from the treasury.

It follows from this result that to escape the neutrality between discretionary public enterprise and discretionary regulation we must consider an environment in which noncontractible private information about profitability is available prior to the investment decision and in which there is concern about the drain on the treasury ($k > 1$).[25] We turn now to a detailed analysis of this environment, with the aim of uncovering several dimensions of basic tradeoffs between public and private forms of organization.

Discretionary Public Enterprise versus Discretionary Regulation

Throughout this section we work in the context of the model in which all private information about profitability is revealed before the investment decision must be made.

Discretionary Public Enterprise

We begin by studying the behavior of the minister who exerts direct control over the public enterprise. Characterization of the outcome of such discretionary public management of the enterprise is straightforward. The objective function of the minister is

$$V^M = E_\theta[S(x,\psi) + \alpha J(x,\varepsilon) + k\pi(x,\theta)],$$

where the expectation is taken over the possible values of θ. The minister simply chooses the activity level x as a function of ρ and θ without any constraints. The first-order condition for the optimal choice of x, conditional on the values of ρ and θ, is

$$S_x(x,\psi) + \alpha J_x(x,\varepsilon) + k\pi_x(x,\theta) = 0. \tag{2}$$

Discretionary Regulation

We now turn to the much more complex problem of the regulator who, with knowledge of ψ and ε but in ignorance of θ, selects $T(x)$ to maximize his objective function,

$$V^R = E_\theta[S(x,\psi) + \alpha J(x,\varepsilon) + \pi(x,\theta) - (k-1)T(x)].$$

Below we shall extend this analysis to the case in which the regulator does not observe ρ until after $T(x)$ has been chosen and investment has occurred.

Facing the regulatory incentive schedule $T(x)$, and upon observing θ, the firm chooses its level of x so as to maximize its profits, $\pi^P = \pi(x,\theta) + T(x)$. The regulator chooses $T(x)$ in the fashion that is optimal for his objective function V^R, given this connection between the payment schedule, the actual value of θ, and the firm's choice of x. The constraint on the regulator's choice of $T(x)$ is that it must yield non-negative profits for the firm at all possible levels of θ; otherwise the firm would be unwilling to make the investment at some levels of θ, and we are assuming that the regulator finds it optimal to stimulate the investment at all levels of θ.

The following equation characterizes the actions x that the discretionary regulator optimally induces the private firm to take as a function of the firm's costs, θ:[26]

$$\text{(3)} \qquad S_x(x,\psi) + \alpha J_x(x,\varepsilon) + k\pi_x(x,\theta) - (k-1)h(\theta)\pi_{x\theta}(x,\theta) = 0.$$

Here $h(\theta)$ is the inverse of the hazard rate for θ, that is, $h(\theta) \equiv (1 - F(\theta))/f(\theta)$. Note that equation (3) is identical to equation (2) except for the addition of the final term on the right-hand side of (3).

We denote by $T^{**}(x,\rho)$ the regulator's optimal payment schedule that induces the actions given in equation (3). Under this regulatory scheme, the firm earns expected profits inclusive of transfer payments, which are given by

$$E_\theta[\pi(x,\theta) + T^{**}(x,\rho)] = E_\theta[\pi_\theta(x(\theta),\theta)h(\theta)] > 0.$$

These positive expected profits constitute a drain on the treasury; with $k > 1$ they impose a genuine welfare cost on the framer and the regulator. Nevertheless, as is well known, these *information rents* are a necessary feature of the optimal regulatory mechanism when the firm has superior information about its profitability before the time of the investment decision. Since the firm must be given enough payment to cover its costs when the firm knows that its profitability is minimal, the payments will necessarily yield the firm more than it needs to cover its costs when demand is high or costs are at a lower level.

Information rents are central for understanding the properties of optimal regulation. The larger the activity level sought by the regulator, the greater will be the concomitant level of information rent paid to the firm. As a consequence, the information rents not only deduct from the regulator's payoff, they also induce him to choose lower levels of activity for each value of θ.

So far in this subsection we have discussed the case where the regulator commits to a payment schedule when he already knows the pertinent value of ρ. It is more interesting and realistic to consider the case in which the value of ρ will not be revealed to the regulator until after the investment decision must be made, and a fortiori after the regulatory mechanism has been put into place.

Whether the regulator learns about public impacts before or after the investment decision must be made, discretionary regulation will result in the payment schedule $T^{**}(x,\rho)$. In either case, the activity levels will be characterized by equation (3), and the expected drain on the treasury will be identical.[27] As a consequence, we need not distinguish analytically between the cases in which the regulator learns about public impacts before and after the investment decision must be made.

Public versus Private Enterprise: Activity Levels

We are now prepared to compare the activity levels under public and private forms of ownership. As we noted above, condition (2) describing activity levels under public enterprise is the same as that in equation (3) characterizing the activity levels resulting from optimal discretionary regulation, with the exception that equation (3) has the extra negative term $-(k-1)h(\theta)\pi_{x\theta}(x,\theta)$. Consequently, for any values of ψ, ε, and θ, the value of x that solves equation (2) is greater than the value of x that solves equation (3).[28] Quite simply, under regulation the public official faces an added cost of increasing the activity level, namely the extra rents that must be paid to firms who will operate at that activity level or higher.

> **Proposition 2.** In equivalent circumstances, activity levels are lower under discretionary regulation than under discretionary public management.

Intuitively, under regulation the regulator must give the firm greater informational rents to induce higher activity levels. Such rents are not necessary under public management, so activity levels are uniformly higher under that form of ownership and control. Remember that "activity level" here refers to anything that is more profitable at the margin when overall profitability is high.

We also are interested in determining how changes in the underlying economic environment differentially affect public vs. private enterprise. To answer such questions requires placing additional structure on some of the functions that comprise the model.

Definition. In the *normal case*, (i) $\pi_{xx\theta} \geq 0$, and (ii) the second partial derivative with respect to x of the left hand side of equation (2) is non-negative.

Stipulation (i) of the normal case follows, for example, if θ is a cost parameter and $C(x,\theta) = c + m(\theta)n(x)$ with $m' < 0$ and $n'' \geq 0$. Stipulation (ii) holds in a conventional quadratic model, or, if x were output, with convex inverse demand, convex marginal revenue, and concave marginal cost functions.

Proposition 3. In the normal case, the activity level under discretionary public management is more responsive to changes in its marginal value than under discretionary regulation.

Proposition 3 captures the notion that public enterprise responds more fully than does regulated private enterprise to changes in the objectives of public officials, whether these changes reflect the public interest or merely the private agenda of the public official.

Bounding the Advantage of Public Enterprise

What are the implications of these different activity levels for the relative performance of discretionary regulation and discretionary public management from the perspective of the framer? We have just shown that it is more costly for the regulator to influence the private firm's actions than it is for the minister to alter the actions of the public enterprise. To the extent that the public official's objectives coincide with those of the framer, this reduced flexibility lowers performance. To the extent that the public official is pursuing his or her own private agenda, however, this reduced flexibility raises performance.

In this section and the next we identify those factors that tip the balance, from the framer's perspective, in favor of private or public enterprise. Figure 2 offers a preview of our normative findings in these sections. It compares the framer's expected payoff under discretionary public enterprise, $E[W^P]$, with that under discretionary regulation, $E[W^R]$. As drawn, Figure 2 shows that public enterprise is preferred if the public official's private agenda is sufficiently muted, that is, if α is sufficiently small. At the same time, Figure 2 shows that privatization is welfare-enhancing if the public official's private agenda is sufficiently influential. Our aim in this section and the next is to establish conditions under which Figure 2 is accurate as drawn.

To this end, we begin by comparing the payoff to the *public official*, as distinct from the framer, under the two forms. Clearly the public official

FIGURE 2
The Effect of the Public Official's Private Agenda on the Framer's Payoff

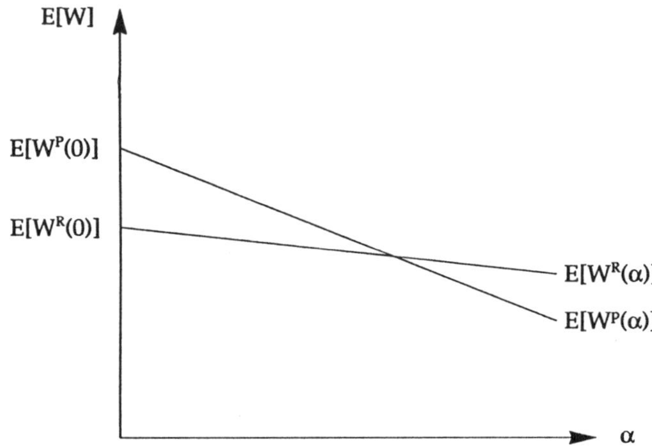

prefers public enterprise, since this gives him an entirely free hand in choosing the activities of the enterprise. We now derive a set of bounds on the increased payoff available to the public official under public enterprise.

Let $E[V^{M*}]$ and $E[V^{R*}]$ be the optimized levels of the expected values (taken over θ) of the objective functions of the minister and regulator that are obtained under discretionary public management and discretionary regulation, respectively. Denote by $\bar{\theta}$ the expected value of θ. Finally, denote the maximal and minimal values of (π_θ) over the support of θ and over the corresponding relevant set of activity levels by $\max(\pi_\theta)$ and $\min(\pi_\theta)$, respectively.

Proposition 4. The public official prefers discretionary public management over discretionary regulation to an extent that depends on the harm associated with treasury drain and the variability in the enterprise's profitability. Analytically,

$$(k-1)(\bar{\theta}-\theta_0)\max_{\theta}(\pi_\theta) > E[V^{M*}] - E[V^{R*}] > (k-1)(\bar{\theta}-\theta_0)\min_{\theta}(\pi_\theta).$$

Proposition 4 reflects the information rents that must be paid from the treasury under regulation. These rents are a drain on the treasury that lowers the objective function of the public official and the framer at the rate of $(k-1)$ per unit.

To prove Proposition 4, we observe that the regulator could always induce the same actions as does the minister if he is willing to pay additional rents to the firm. Conversely, we observe that the minister could always choose the same actions as does the regulator and save on the information rents that the regulator is forced to offer. These two observations lead to the two-sided bound in Proposition 4.

Now recall that when $\alpha = 0$ the objectives of the framer and the public official coincide. Clearly, in this case the framer cannot do better than under discretionary public management. After all, if $\alpha = 0$ the framer need not fear that the public official will pursue his private agenda, so it is best not to raise the costs to that official of redirecting the activities of the enterprise. Simply put, in this extreme case there is no reason to impose an agency problem on the minister so as to limit his pursuit of his private agenda. Combining this observation with Proposition 4 we have

Corollary 1. If $\alpha = 0$, so there is no salient private agenda, then the advantage of public enterprise over regulated private enterprise from the framer's perspective satisfies the same bounds as given in Proposition 4.

Corollary 1 tells us that the bounds in Proposition 4 apply to the distance $E[W^P(0)] - E[W^R(0)]$ in Figure 2.

More Pronounced Private Agendas Favor Privatization

We next ask how an increase in the relative importance of the public official's private agenda affects the framer's choice between public and private enterprise. Our aim is to show that an increase in α, that is, an increase in the salience of the public official's private agenda, makes privatization more attractive from the framer's perspective. In terms of figure 2, we seek to show that the $E[W^P]$ curve falls more steeply than the $E[W^R]$ curve. Let $E[W^P(\alpha)]$ and $E[W^R(\alpha)]$ represent the expected values of the framer's objective function under discretionary public management and regulation respectively, when the salience of the private agenda is measured by α.

Proposition 5. Suppose that the conditions of the normal case apply and the public official's private agenda places a constant marginal value on increased activity, that is, $J(x,\varepsilon) = \varepsilon x$. As the salience of the private agenda grows, the expected value of the framer's objective function falls faster under discretionary public management than it does under discretionary regulation. Analytically,

$$E[W^P(0)] - E[W^P(\alpha] > E[W^R(0)] - E[W^R(\alpha)] > 0.$$

Summary

We now have painted a complete picture of the comparison between discretionary public management and discretionary regulation of private enterprise. Absent a salient private agenda, the information rents that must be paid from the treasury mean that the public form of organization is superior and yields greater levels of desirable activity. On the other hand, activity levels typically are less responsive under regulation than under public management to the vicissitudes of the private agenda, due to the costliness of regulatory control. As a consequence, and as shown in Figure 2, the private agenda diminishes the objective function of the framer less under regulation than under public management.

In sum, we have found that discretionary regulation of private enterprise is more desirable in comparison with discretionary public control, the more salient the private agenda of the public official and the less significant the private information concerning profitability. A poorly functioning political system, or the absence of substantial information at the operating level of the enterprise, imply that privatization is superior to public enterprise.

Nondiscretionary Governance Systems

We now consider governance systems in which the framer gives *no* discretion to the public official. Such nondiscretionary governance systems are the opposite extreme from the completely discretionary systems studied above. Analysis of systems in which the public official is given partial discretion—for example, in which the framer imposes rewards and penalties on the public official that depend on the official's action, or in which the public official is allowed to pick from a restricted set of actions—is beyond the scope of this chapter.

If the framer mandates the actions to be taken by the minister, then the minister is effectively removed as a decisionmaker. Likewise, if the framer mandates the regulatory mechanism to be employed by the regulator, the regulator's role is passive and mechanical. He observes the contractible state of nature and follows the instructions left by the framer, perhaps in the enabling legislation, for the corresponding regulatory mechanism.

The choice between discretionary and nondiscretionary systems presents the framer with a tradeoff. If the public official will receive private information that is pertinent to the public interest, then the framer's objectives might be better served if that official were given some discretion. This same discretion, however, would also allow the public official to influence the enterprise in accordance with his private agenda, to the harm of the framer's objectives. Despite the complexity of the tradeoff between discretionary and nondiscretionary systems, and that between public and private enterprise, we can identify an informational environment in which nondiscretionary regulation is unambiguously the most preferred governance form:

> **Proposition 6.** Private enterprise subject to nondiscretionary regulation is the best organizational form if there is no private information about public impacts and all private information about profitability is revealed only after the investment decision must be made.

The key to Proposition 6 is that nondiscretionary regulation allows the framer to limit sharply the discretion of the public official, who has no socially valuable private information, while still giving discretion to the managers of the enterprise, who possess socially valuable private information about the enterprise's profitability. The only way for the framer to give discretion to the managers of the enterprise but not to the public official is to remove the operation of the enterprise from the public official's control, that is, through privatization.

The argument behind Proposition 6 runs as follows. Observe first that with private profitability information revealed only after investment, there are no information rents paid under regulation. As we showed above, without such rents, discretionary regulation and discretionary public enterprise are equivalent. But with no private information about public impacts, the framer has no reason to give any discretion to the public official, so nondiscretionary regulation is clearly superior to discretionary regulation. Finally, the inability of nondiscretionary public management to yield activity levels responsive to cost and demand conditions renders it too inferior to nondiscretionary regulation in the eyes of the framer. Under the conditions of Proposition 6, nondiscretionary regulation induces choices of activity levels that respond to private information about cost and demand conditions in fashions that are optimal for the objectives of the framer, while avoiding any influence of the private agenda and while requiring the minimal possible expected drain on the treasury.

A general lesson emerges in stark form from the analysis of this case. A regulator of private enterprise can be more effectively monitored and thus more effectively constrained by the framer than can a public minister because the regulator does not have access to the private information on costs and demand that is possessed by the public minister. With less private information, the regulator is less able to disguise his pursuit of his private agenda. Under the privatized form of organization, it is the firm that possesses the private information about profitability, and the firm is motivated to use this information for the pursuit of its profits and not for the pursuit of the private agenda of the public official. In contrast, under public management, the minister is the party with both the private agenda and the private information about profitability; any discretion accorded him to use the cost and demand information beneficially also permits the influence of the private agenda to be exercised banefully.

In short, one general effect favoring privatization arises from its intrinsic separation of cost and demand information from the power to influence activities for the sake of public impacts and private agendas. As a result of this separation, the framer can better restrain the influence of the private agenda on the interventions of the regulator of the private enterprise.

In the most dramatic form of this effect, optimal nondiscretionary regulation is no regulation at all. Then, private enterprise with a commitment of laissez-faire from the framer yields optimal results from the framer's perspective. In this case, discretionary public management would yield lower net social benefits due to the influence of the private agenda on the activities of the enterprise, and nondiscretionary public management would yield lower net social benefits due to the unresponsiveness of the enterprise's activities to cost and demand conditions.

Analytically, this case arises when the revenues provided by the market to the firm are an accurate measure of the gross social benefits of the firm's activities. A very special instance of this arises, for example, if x represents the firm's output of a good or service sold in a perfectly competitive market. More generally, without external benefits, $S(x,\psi) = 0$ for all pertinent values of ψ, and equation (3) shows that with α set equal to 0, T^* is just a lump-sum tax (possibly zero) that does not interfere with the profit-maximizing market incentives of the firm. In summary of this discussion, we have:

> **Corollary 2.** Where market revenues equal the gross social benefits of the enterprise's activities, as under perfect competition, private enterprise with a commitment of laissez-faire is the best organizational form.

More generally, suppose that $S(x,\psi) = -ex$, as would be the case, for example, if x were the firm's output of a good sold in a perfectly competitive market and each unit of the good caused external harm of e to the environment. Then optimal nondiscretionary regulation would impose a Pigouvian (externality-correcting) tax on the firm's output but otherwise permit the firm to maximize its profits. The framer would explicitly deny to the regulator any additional powers of intervention but could stipulate that the size of the Pigouvian tax be determined on the basis of contractible information on the magnitude of the externality effect e. Here, again, public enterprise would perform worse from the framer's viewpoint due to the intrusion of the private agenda or to the unresponsiveness of output resulting from the restrictions designed to chill the influence of the private agenda. Hence we have:

> **Corollary 3.** Under perfect competition with output externalities, private enterprise with a commitment to laissez-faire and externality-correcting taxes is the best organizational form.

Examples

We now briefly illustrate how the reasoning of our general model can be used to inform the choice between public and private enterprise in several different contexts. All of the examples here concern the possible privatization of existing public facilities. In some cases, the private parties bidding to take over public assets have no special information regarding the cost or demand conditions that are likely to face the enterprise. In other cases involving the sale of public assets, particular private firms with experience in related areas will have superior information about cost or demand conditions. In terms of our model, this important distinction is between cases in which θ is known prior to investment and cases in which θ is observed only subsequent to investment.

A Basic Manufacturing Operation

Consider a basic manufacturing operation in a small country. Suppose the output of the manufacturing facility competes with imports that are supplied at a constant world price. If all externalities caused by the operation will be commonly observable, then ψ is absent and there is no reason for the framer to give discretion to the public official. The relevant choice is between nondiscretionary public enterprise and nondiscretionary regulation.

If those bidding for the public assets have no private information concerning the technology of production, then Corollary 3 applies and privatization along with nondiscretionary regulation is called for. Even if those bidding for the public assets do have private information about cost and demand conditions, nondiscretionary regulation is still the preferred form if more than one bidder has this information, for no informational rents need be forfeited if the manufacturing facilities are auctioned off and the bidders cannot collude.

If a single party bidding for the assets enjoys superior cost and demand information, then privatization will surrender profits to that party and increase the drain on the treasury. If this is of little concern, privatization again is the preferred choice. Even if drain on the treasury is a genuine concern ($k > 1$), privatization will still be desirable if the political system is ineffective at controlling the public official's private agenda or will force the public official to serve short-term goals at the expense of the long-term public interest.

A stronger case can be made for retaining the manufacturing operation in the public sector if the externalities caused by the operation will be observable only to future public officials. For example, the true environmental costs of running the operation may be difficult to prove in court, or the benefits to workers of increased employment may be difficult to measure objectively and thus difficult to use as a basis for rewards paid to a private firm. If these externalities will be measured much more accurately by future public officials than by neutral third parties, then privatization may worsen performance. But privatization may be desirable even under these circumstances if the political system functions badly.

A Hotel or Tourist Facility

The analysis of whether to privatize a government hotel or other tourist facility is much like that above for the basic manufacturing operation. The major difference concerns the nature of the externalities generated by the hotel in contrast to the factory.

Many of the externalities generated by a tourist facility are likely to be positive ones, as when a hotel serves the public-good function of attracting tourists into the country. If government officials are likely to have valuable private information about the size of these positive external benefits, then keeping the hotel in the public sector may be the best course of action. On the other hand, if the minister will locate new hotel facilities in regions of the country where he has friends and relatives, rather than regions where demand is greatest or unemployment highest, then this intrusion of his private agenda argues for privatization.

Postal and Telecommunications Services

Postal and telecommunications services are important elements of the economic infrastructure. They tend to generate significant externalities: an improved telecommunications system benefits a broad range of industries, even after accounting for the charges levied on those industries for the services. Additionally, national growth and national cohesion are promoted by improved communications capabilities. Some of these externalities can be measured, but many cannot; external benefits that are difficult to measure objectively but that are known to public officials are captured in our variable ψ. Costs associated with providing these services that are not commonly known are captured in our variable θ.

The decision of whether to privatize the postal service, for example, can be analyzed using the same logical structure as sketched above for a basic industry. One difference is the likely magnitude of market power that a postal and telecommunications monopoly would have.[29] Another difference is the nature of the informational variables ψ and θ. The externalities generated by the telephone system are much more widespread than those generated by a steel factory, and the public official's informational advantage in measuring these externalities, ψ, may be all the more significant. The greater significance of market power argues for the importance of regulatory oversight if privatization is selected. The greater importance of information that resides in the public sector argues against privatization altogether.

Production of Military Equipment

The production of military equipment is different from the examples above in that the entire output of the enterprise is to be used in the public sector. It is quite likely that public officials will have superior information about the national security benefits of producing better or more military equipment. Even if these benefits could be demonstrated in court to enforce contracts with private parties, there may well be national security reasons not to reveal such information. In terms of our notation, ψ is likely to have significant information content.

Given the important informational role played by public officials, it is crucial that the framer allow these officials discretion. Consider, then, the choice between discretionary regulation and discretionary public enterprise. If private companies have superior information about costs, discretionary regulation will require the surrender of informational rents; this drain on the treasury may be a significant factor if $k > 1$. As against this, the importance of the public official's private agenda, α, must be considered. In some countries, concern about such private agendas is very grave in the military context, and production is contracted out to private companies. In other countries, the unwillingness to yield profits to the private sector and the concern about losing control over military secrets and technology keep military production within the public sector.[30] In such countries, our analysis suggests, political structures such as civilian oversight, which are designed to limit the intrusion of the public official's private agenda, are a necessary part of the efficient production of military equipment.

Prison Management

As our final example, consider the management of a prison facility and the choice of whether to hire a private prison management company.

Now we can interpret our public-impact variable ψ as reflecting the importance of protecting the civil rights of prisoners.[31] The framer and the public official are concerned about prisoners' rights, but these rights may be of little matter to a private, profit-oriented prison management company, except insofar as that company is motivated through fines or rewards to respect those rights.

In this example, x represents the choice of how to treat prisoners. Higher levels of x correspond to more lenient treatment of prisoners, with less likelihood of infringing on their rights or less severity of such infringements. Finally, θ measures the severity of a given potential riot situation. Higher levels of θ correspond to situations that are *less* threatening (and thus more profitable for the prison operator).[32]

The ultimate decision to be made is how favorably to treat the prisoners: better treatment is preferred by the prisoners and also by the framer and the public official because it makes violations of their rights less likely and less severe when they do occur. But more favorable treatment may be more expensive and can increase the likelihood that the prison officials lose control and face a riot.[33] Privatization runs the risk of placing officials in charge who will undervalue prisoners' rights as they seek merely to maximize their profits. And prison regulators may not want to the treatment of prisoners, because in some circumstances harsh treatment will in fact be desirable to retain control.

Discretion for the public official is important if the framer does not know what value will be placed on prisoners' civil rights in the future.[34] At the same time, sensitivity to θ, the specific conditions at the prison, is important, since such conditions can and do vary greatly across prisons and across time.

If the intrusion of public officials' private agenda is small, because the officials' private benefit varies little with the different levels of prisoner treatment ($\alpha \ni 0$), then public prison management is superior to privatization. Public management of prisons also is called for if the protection of prisoners' rights is viewed as very important and if any variations in the explosiveness of prison conditions is either small or easily observed. If, however, public officials will tend to depart from the long-term public interest—so as to avoid unfavorable publicity in the immediate term, for example—then the framer may choose to tie the hands of public officials, at least partially, by privatizing the prison.[35]

Conclusions

In this chapter we have developed models of public enterprise and of regulated private enterprise and subjected them to comparative analysis to identify the effects of privatization. Privatization in our models means that the government commits itself to a particular regulatory scheme (or possibly no regulation at all) and limits its own ability to extract information from the private company that is being regulated.

The public-spirited framer who initially chooses between public and private enterprise recognizes that subsequent public officials will not be acting totally in the public interest, either because they will pursue their private agendas or because they will be subjected to short-term political pressures that diverge from the long-term public interest. Under these circumstances, the framer will see some advantages to limiting the discretion afforded to public officials or to making it more costly for officials to redirect an enterprise's activities.

We have shown how privatization naturally raises the cost to the public official of redirecting an enterprise's activities. These increased costs stem from the informational rents that the regulator must surrender to the private firm if he wishes to encourage investment by firms that have private information about profitability prior to making their investment decisions.

There is thus a tradeoff involved in choosing whether to privatize. Privatization has the undesirable effect of raising the cost to the public official of inducing an enterprise, via regulation, to serve legitimate public-interest goals. These increased costs are an obstacle to coordinating the public official's information and the owners' information to achieve the socially preferred outcome. On the other hand, privatization, by eliminating the minister's direct control over the enterprise, limits the minister's ability to redirect the enterprise's activities in ways that promote his personal agenda or succumb to short-run political pressure at the expense of market efficiency.

We have explored the factors that influence this tradeoff. For example, a pronounced private agenda on the part of the public official or a poorly functioning political system favor privatization. On the other hand, if public officials are likely to have significant private information regarding the public impact of the enterprise's activities, then public ownership is the preferred form, even though we permit the privatized firm to be regulated in complex and sophisticated ways by the public-sector official. Likewise, if those who operate the enterprise are likely to have significant private information about the cost and demand conditions under which the enterprise will operate, and if there is a deadweight-loss burden associated with raising funds in the public sector, then public enterprise is the preferred form of ownership and control.

Our analysis is novel in that it identifies the effects of *deliberately introducing* an information problem through privatization. Privatization creates an agency problem between the public official as regulator and the private firm. Standard analyses identify the costs associated with such agency problems. What may be a cost from the viewpoint of the principal, the public official, can be a benefit when viewed by another party with a different objective, namely, the public-spirited framer. Thus our results have a distinct second-best flavor: Given an imperfect political system in which public officials do not purely serve the public interest, it may be desirable to limit their discretion by deliberately introducing an agency problem between them and the owners of a privatized firm. We see the tradeoff between the costs of such an agency problem and the benefits of restricting the discretion of public officials as fundamental to privatization.

Notes

We thank Henry Bienen and John Waterbury for valuable comments on an earlier draft, Mark Dutz for cheerful and competent research assistance, and seminar participants at Carnegie-Mellon, Bell Communications Research, Princeton, and the University of California, Berkeley, for valuable comments. The formal claims in this paper are proven in our technical companion paper, "Privatization to Limit Public-Sector Discretion." Both authors acknowledge the financial support of the John M. Olin Foundation and the Pew Foundation. This paper was completed while Shapiro was a Fellow at the Center for Advanced Study in the Behavorial Sciences.

1. Our analysis is complementary to the existing economics literature on privatization, as exemplified by Kay and Thompson (1986), Yarrow (1986), and Vickers and Yarrow (1988).

2. For excellent surveys and descriptions of this burgeoning literature, see Hart and Holmstrom (1987), Holmstrom and Tirole (1989), and Sappington (1989).

3. Paul Starr (1987, 1988) also argues that the distinction between "public" and "private" is not necessarily so great or so stark as it might appear. He points out, for example, that a government agency can contract out to private companies for many of its services.

4. Of course, in some situations shifting loans from the public to the private sector is more than an accounting change. For example, in countries facing severe debt crisis, a private company may have more credibility as a borrower than does its own government.

5. In terms of realpolitik, needed reforms of public sector control may be infeasible, and the drama, shock, and coalition-creation of privatization may be the only effective route to real change. See our colleagues' case studies for elaboration of these political themes.

6. This statement assumes that the same party who would operate the public enterprise would administer the regulations and set the tax rates.

7. For example, under either public or private enterprise the managers of the enterprise could be instructed to increase employment in times when the

overall unemployment rate is high, to make additional investments when interest rates are low, or to base their capital-labor mix on the statutory minimum wage, which is commonly known.

8. This fiction is simply our way of conducting a normative analysis within a decision-theoretic and game-theoretic framework.

9. For example, the state of the enterprise's capital equipment is likely to affect costs but may be difficult for those not working for the enterprise to observe. Likewise for the state of technological expertise at the enterprise. Alternatively, the managers of the enterprise may have superior private information about the demand facing the enterprise.

10. If the enterprise operates at a loss, then its drain on public funds will lower social welfare and increase the excess burden associated with taxation, just as net proceeds will raise welfare and reduce the excess burden.

11. Alternatively, if the minister is subject to short-run political pressures, we assume that the divergence between these forces and the long-run public interest is unpredictable and, if observable, would not be controllable by a neutral third party such as a court. Under either interpretation of J, we assume that the direction of the minister's bias cannot be anticipated. Formally, we assume $E[\partial J/\partial x] = 0$, where $E[\cdot]$ is the expectations operator, in this case conditioned on the framer's information. This assumption is unrestrictive, since any anticipated bias can readily be counteracted by the framer.

12. We are assuming throughout that the action taken by the private firm is commonly observable.

13. These transfers are defined to include any applicable franchise fees or payments for newly privatized public assets.

14. Here we make the implicit assumption that the government is able to make a commitment to a regulatory arrangement. Without any commitment or an effective reputation mechanism, privatization would be impossible, as potential investors would expect their investments to be expropriated.

15. The regulator *could* directly control the private firm by imposing a large penalty for any action other than the one specified by the regulator. Such rigid regulatory control will not typically be desirable, however.

16. Since only the regulator observes ρ, there is nothing forcing the regulator to announce the true ρ.

17. To see that our specification of social welfare here is indeed consistent with the one used under public enterprise, suppose that the regulator could perfectly capture the firm's profits for each realization of θ. Then the firm could be charged a franchise fee equal to its profits, making $T = -\pi(x,\theta)$. Substituting this value of T into W above returns the framer's objective function under public enterprise, namely $S(x,\psi) + k\pi(x,\theta)$.

18. It is our understanding that the British government finds it much more difficult to obtain detailed information about the operations of British Telecom now that the company is privately owned.

19. We shall return below to a comparison between discretionary and non-

discretionary forms from the framer's viewpoint. At this point we simply note that the framer will likely want to give discretion to the public official if that official's private information is highly pertinent to the efficient operation of the enterprise from a public-interest perspective, that is, if ψ is significant.

20. This internalization procedure was inspired by the work of Loeb and Magat (1979), who were the first to show that a firm with private information about costs could be motivated with a schedule of transfer payments to produce optimally for social welfare, and by Sappington and Stiglitz (1987), who argued that other features of the environment must underlie choices between private and public enterprise, since the Loeb-Magat mechanism could make the two equivalent where it is applicable.

21. Here we need to assume that θ and ρ are independently distributed, and we are relying on the assumption that the regulator and the firm share common priors on the distribution of ρ.

22. This proposition is an adaptation of the results derived in a somewhat different context by d'Aspremont and Gerard-Varet (1979), and explicated and applied by Pratt and Zeckhauser (1986).

23. Recall that for the sake of simplicity we assume that the investment is desirable in all possible environments.

24. This is the same approach taken by Sappington and Stiglitz (1987) in an analytic setting without private information about public impacts and without a private agenda for the public official.

25. Even under these conditions, neutrality still emerges in two environments that are beyond the scope of this chapter. First, if the regulator can partially observe the firm's private information (that is, can observe a variable that is correlated with the firm's information), if there is no limit to the penalties that the regulator can impose on the firm, and if the firm is risk neutral, then Baron and Besanko (1984) show that the information problem between the regulator and the firm is inessential. Second, if two identical firms with knowledge of θ compete to win a government franchise, then, as Sappington and Stiglitz (1987) point out, the regulator need surrender no profits, and neutrality again applies.

26. Baron and Myerson (1982) derived the original version of this equation, which has been much utilized in the recent literature on regulation and mechanism design. See Baron (1989) for a discussion of this literature. Derivation of this equation in our particular model is contained in our companion piece, Shapiro and Willig (1990). The characterizing equation is valid so long as the resulting solution for x is increasing in θ.

27. This claim is proven using an argument similar to that on pp. 69–71. See Shapiro and Willig (1990) for the technical details.

28. Of course, if k were equal to 1, the first-order conditions in equations (3) and (2) would be the same and the optimal activity levels would be the same, as already established in Proposition 1.

29. We assume a monopoly here because telecommunications services may be provided according to economies of scale: there may well be a natural monopoly, at least for some components.

30. The concerns over military secrecy may be overwhelming in practice. It may be more difficult for the government to keep military information secret if private parties are privy to it and indeed if the crucial know-how resides in private organizations.

31. The importance attached to such rights, both for the prisoners themselves and for broader social perceptions of justice, may not be known in advance by the framer and certainly cannot be quantified and used to reward or penalize private prison operators.

32. Our assumption that $\pi_{\theta x} > 0$ now has the interpretation that the costs to the prison operator of treating the prisoners more leniently are less when the situation is less threatening. In a more threatening situation, such treatment increases the likelihood of a riot that may be very costly (both in terms of facilities and personnel and in terms of possible loss of life).

33. If in fact more favorable treatment is no more expensive and eases tensions in the prison, then it is clearly superior. The interesting questions arise in the range of behavior where more lenient treatment is costly or poses certain dangers to prison control.

34. Discretion is less valuable if strategic behavior by prisoners is important. With such behavior, it may be valuable for the framer to commit subsequent officials to certain actions (via a nondiscretionary governance form) so as to deter certain uprisings or riots by prisoners. For example, if regulators were required to fire wardens of prisons where riots occurred, and if wardens were given extensive authority, prisoners might accept as unavoidable a harsh response by the warden to any uprising.

35. In terms of our model, the public official would have to pay the private prison company more for operating the prison if more lenient treatment of prisoners were demanded.

References

Baron, David. 1989. "Design of Regulatory Mechanisms and Institutions." In *Handbook of Industrial Organization*, ed. Richard Schmalensee and Robert Willig. Amsterdam: North-Holland.

Baron, David, and David Besanko. 1984. "Regulation, Asymmetric Information and Auditing." *Rand Journal of Economics* 15: 447–470.

Baron, David, and Roger Myerson. 1982. "Regulating a Monopolist with Unknown Costs." *Econometrica* 50: 911–930.

Caillaud, B., R. Guesnerie, and J. Tirole. 1988. "Government Intervention in Production and Incentives Theory: A Review of Recent Contributions." *Rand Journal of Economics* 19: 1–26.

d'Aspremont, C., and Gerard-Varet, L. 1979. "Incentives and Incomplete Information." *Journal of Public Economics* 11: 25–45.

Hart, Oliver, and Bengt Holmstrom. 1987. "The Theory of Contracts." In *Advances in Economic Theory, Fifth World Congress*, ed. Truman F. Bewley. New York: Cambridge University Press.

Holmstrom, Bengt, and Jean Tirole. 1989. "The Theory of the Firm." In *Handbook of Industrial Organization*, ed. Richard Schmalensee and Robert Willig. Amsterdam: North-Holland.

Kay, J. A., and D. J. Thompson. 1986. "Privatization: A Policy in Search of a Rationale." *Economic Journal* 96: 18–32.

Loeb, M., and W. Magat. 1979. "A Decentralized Method for Utility Regulation." *Journal of Law and Economics* 22: 399–404.

Pratt, J., and R. Zeckhauser. 1986. "Incentive-Based Decentralization: Expected Externality Payments Induce Efficient Behavior in Groups." In *Kenneth Arrow and the Ascent of Modern Economic Theory*. New York: New York University Press.

Sappington, David. 1989. "Incentives." Bell Communications Research, June.

Sappington, David, and Joseph Stiglitz. 1987. "Privatization, Information and Incentives." *Journal of Policy Analysis and Management* 6: 567–582.

Shapiro, Carl, and Robert Willig. 1990. "Privatization to Limit Public-Sector Discretion. Princeton University, January.

Starr, Paul. 1987. "The Limits of Privatization." In *Prospects for Privatization*, ed. Steve H. Hanke. New York: Academy of Political Science.

———. 1988. "The Meaning of Privatization." *Yale Law and Policy Review* 6: 1120–1136.

Vickers, John, and George Yarrow. 1988. *Privatization: An Economic Analysis*. Cambridge, Mass.: M.I.T. Press.

Yarrow, George. 1986. "Privatization in Theory and Practice." *Economic Policy* 2: 324–377.

[16]

A Principal-Agent Approach on Manager Effort and Control in Privatized and Public Firms

Dieter Bös and Wolfgang Peters

1 INTRODUCTION

In Chapter 2, a three-dimensional framework for the treatment of privatized versus public firms was suggested:

1. multiple goals versus one goal;
2. total control versus minimal control;
3. competition versus monopoly.

This Chapter addresses the first two questions, comparing a price-setting public and a privatized firm in a principal-agent approach with observable costs.[1] A price-setting public firm and a price-setting private firm are perceived as the starting point and the end point of a privatization activity: the government has sold the firm to the public. Privatization of price-setting firms is the most interesting case for theoretical studies. Privatization of a competitive firm, say a hotel which was formerly owned by the public sector (for example, British Rail), is of minor interest for a theoretician. Welfare and profit maximization lead to the same result and the competition in the theoretical model leads to fully efficient production regardless of ownership. Privatization of price-setting firms, however, implies a transition from some sort of welfare maximization (low prices) to profit maximization (high prices). To achieve a clear modelling we disregard potential competition and assume that the privatized firm is not regulated. More sophisticated models could allow for both market entry and regulation.

Prices and production decisions of any firm result from the interaction between the owners and the management. In a public firm the government operates as principal, in a private firm the owners take the lead.

Principal-agent approaches are characterized by asymmetric information. When attempting to achieve its goals, the principal is handicapped by lack of certain information which only the management knows precisely. There may be particular parameters affecting efficiency which only the managers know, the principal's knowledge being restricted to the knowledge of the distribution of the parameters. Efforts of the managers may be unobservable and therefore impossible to monitor. Since the principal cannot directly observe the activities of the management, he cannot directly influence the behaviour of the manager. The management has its own objectives, hence it may choose an effort level which is not efficient. This particular situation must be taken into account by the principal when he defines the reward of the management.

In our comparison, the public and the privatized firm are assumed to face the same economic environment: the same demand function, the same technology. This is explained by the fact that the privatized firm is the same as the public firm after it has been sold to private owners. The private owners are perceived to be clever investors who are quite well informed about economic reality. Their informational status compares favourably with that of the bureaucrats who are supposed to audit the public enterprise. Privatization therefore means that the management faces a better informed principal than before.

As already mentioned, in this chapter we deal with changes in the objectives of the firm and the extent of control which are brought about by privatization. In a principal-agent approach, the objective of the firm is articulated by the principal, in our comparison by the private owners of the privatized firm and by the government for the public firm.

The *owners* of a private firm are interested in profit. Thus they have only one goal. The manager of the private firm knows this goal; there is no uncertainty about weights which should be given to various other objectives.

The *government*, on the other hand, is interested in attaining two goals: high consumer welfare and not too high a deficit of the enterprise, possibly including the distortionary costs of financing the deficit of the enterprise. Other government objectives, for instance the maximization of votes, can be thought of as being related to the above-mentioned objectives. After all, the higher the consumer welfare the lower are the prices and this can well be considered as a policy of capturing votes. Similarly, the inclusion of distortionary effects of financing a deficit (Caillaud *et al.*, 1988) can be seen as a policy designed to avoid vote loss as a consequence of distortionary taxation. Accordingly, we define the government's objective as

$$G = \lambda S(p) + (1 - \lambda)\pi \text{ with } \lambda \in [0;1/2], \tag{1}$$

where $S(p)$ is consumer surplus and π is the deficit or profit of the firm. S and π are two objectives which are combined by the weights λ and $(1 - \lambda)$, whereby $\lambda = 1/2$ implies the usual government objective of the sum of consumer and producer surplus, $\lambda < 1/2$ means a stronger accentuation of the distortionary effects of financing a possible deficit. However, $\lambda < 1/2$ could also mean that the government is less interested in consumer welfare and more in getting some profit from the firm. Equation (1) is the simplest possible description of a multiple goal objective of government. The optimization approach boils down to optimizing a weighted average of various goals. In our case λ determines the weighting.

Let us now turn to the extent of control which may be changed by privatization. We define control as activities which reduce marginal costs. These activities can be carried out by the principal and by the agent. In the first case we speak of external control, in the second of internal control. Examples of external control include

- in the case of a private firm: activities of consultation firms like McKinsey if the activity has been required by the owners or respective activities of special members of the board which have been appointed by request of particular private owners,
- in the case of a public firm: examinations by special government commissions or by government representatives which have been appointed to check the performance of the public management.

Internal control includes those activities of the management which aim at reducing marginal costs. This internal control is part of the overall activities of the management. It is that part of the manager's effort which reduces marginal costs.

The chapter is organized as follows. In section 2 we deal with the informational setting in principal-agent models with observable costs. Two special cases of such principal-agent models are investigated. In section 3 we treat the case of a privatized firm whose principal is very well informed and whose goal is maximum profits. In section 4 a public firm is treated whose principal is the government which is less well informed and aims at multiple objectives. We compare the relevant decisions of both the privatized and public firm with respect to price, control by the principal, reward and effort of the manager. Section 5 presents extensions. In particular we deal with the question of a public manager's imperfect information about the government's objectives. In section 6 some illustrative simulations are presented which intend to give more insight into the quantitative relations between control, effort and manager's reward. Section 7 is the conclusion. An appendix presents some necessary, but a little tedious, mathematical details.

2 PRINCIPAL-AGENT RELATIONSHIPS WITH OBSERVABLE COSTS – THE INFORMATIONAL SETTING

2.1 Common Knowledge

We deal with a one-product enterprise which covers demand q at price p. Since the focus is on the interaction between the firm and its owner, we do not explicitly model how the individual consumers behave. Rather we assume that the firm faces a market demand function whose precise functional shape is known by both principal and agent:

$$q = q(p), \quad q' < 0. \tag{2}$$

Much more specific are our assumptions about cost. The cost function is linear, the variable costs are represented by $mc \cdot q$, where mc are the marginal costs. Marginal costs are specified as follows:

$$mc = k - \alpha c - e. \tag{3}$$

The basic marginal costs k can be reduced by the principal's external control c and by the agent's effort e. The principal's control c is effective up to an efficiency parameter α. This efficiency parameter is a random variable. For ease of the mathematical presentation we assume that this variable is uniformly distributed between the lowest value, $\underline{\alpha}$, and the highest value $\overline{\alpha}$. The assumption of a uniformly distributed α could easily be given up without changing the qualitative results.

Overhead costs accrue for two reasons. First, the manager is paid a reward t which is a remuneration for his effort e. Second, costs of $h(c)$ must be spent in order to finance the external control c. The function $h(c)$ is assumed to be convex, i.e. we deal with increasing average costs of external control. The total costs of the firm which accrue to the principal are specified by:

$$C = [k - \alpha c - e]q + t + h(c). \tag{4}$$

The precise functional shape of C is known by both principal and agent. Both also know that α is a random variable which is uniformly distributed between $\overline{\alpha}$ and $\underline{\alpha}$.

2.2 Observability

Let us distinguish two points of time which we call 'ex ante' and 'ex post'. The first, 'ex ante', is the moment where the contract between the principal and the agent is signed. The second 'ex post' is the moment where the contract is fulfilled, that is, the reward to the manager is paid.

In both the public and the privatized firm the principal is able ex post to observe the price, the quantity produced, and the total costs (cf. Laffont and Tirole, 1986). The ex post observability of price and quantity is a very plausible assumption. It is clear that the price can be observed. Also, ex post the quantity can be observed from the annual reports of firms. It requires a little more sophistication to establish the ex post observability of total costs. There are two possible approaches. First, inside information: a representative sent to the board of the firm by the principal may have gained direct knowledge of the amount of C. Second, the principal may calculate the total costs indirectly: if price and quantity are observable, revenue is observable. In the case of a public firm information about total costs is revealed if the firm were to run a deficit. The difference between revenues and total costs is observed and hence total costs. An analogous implicit information about total costs is given to the private principal if the profit of a private firm is distributed to the owners.

Let us now introduce the decisive difference in informational status of the private principal and the public principal. This difference refers to the efficiency parameter. We assume that the private principal has ex ante knowledge of the actual value of the parameter, α. This means that the private principal is able to draw correct information about α from some outside source, not from the agent. The public principal does not know α when signing the contract and the only information about α he can receive comes from the agent.

Hence the private principal can separate the marginal costs without needing informational help from the agent. He knows the linear functional form of mc, knows k, α and c and, accordingly, can calculate the actual value of the manager's effort e. This enables him to condition the contract with the agent on the agent's effort.

The public principal cannot proceed like this. Ex ante, he only knows the distribution of α, but not the actual value. His knowledge can only be improved by signing a contract with the agent. The agent has an informational advantage because of his ex ante knowledge of the actual α. Hence the contract implies a sort of know-how transfer from the agent to the principal. The principal faces the danger of being cheated by the agent. If it is in the interest of the agent to report a false efficiency parameter, he will do so. The principal knows that and therefore can only condition the reward on the marginal costs.

Of course, the public principal will try to induce the manager's optimal choice of effort. This can be achieved by stipulating a contract which induces the manager to inform the principal about the actual value of the efficiency parameter. Thus, ex post, the public principal also comes to learn α. However, this ex post knowledge does not help him. He can only get it on the basis of an incentive compatible contract which has to be signed at a moment where he is uninformed. If the principal does not enter into the contract ex ante, he risks failing to obtain correct information about the efficiency parameter. Ex post the contract must be fulfilled. Renegotiation is excluded. Therefore, the principal is stuck with the dilemma that ex post he knows the actual value of α but has to fulfil a contract which is based on his not knowing α ex ante.

3 THE PRIVATIZED FIRM

Here we assume that the principal is fully informed. However, the principal needs the management to organize production and sale. Resignation by the manager must be avoided. Therefore, the principal cannot dictate any arbitrary level of managerial effort, in spite of his ability to observe and monitor this effort directly. The manager will stay at his job only if his utility does not fall below his reservation utility $\bar{U}$ which he might obtain at some alternative job. The principal has to consider the participation constraint of the manager

$$U(t,e) \geq \bar{U}, \tag{5}$$

where t is the reward paid to the manager and e is his effort. $U_1 > 0$ is the marginal utility of income and $U_2 < 0$ the marginal disutility of effort. $U(t,e)$ is a direct utility function. It depends, first, on the manager's consumption which is represented by his income t, and secondly, on his labour supply which is represented by his effort e. We assume $U(0,0) < \bar{U}$. This implies that work pays. The participation constraint holds only for positive effort and consequently for positive managerial reward.

The principal wants to maximize profits. This requires optimal external control by the principal and optimal effort of the manager. The manager's participation is achieved by paying him a reward for his effort. Since the principal cannot directly observe the manager's effort, he cannot *directly* monitor it. However, the ex post knowledge of total costs C implies the ex post knowledge of marginal costs mc. Hence, the principal can calculate the effort on the basis of his information about mc, k, α and c. Therefore, he can (*indirectly*) induce the manager to choose the optimal e^*, by stipulating a contract which contains the following reward scheme:

$$T = \begin{cases} t & \text{if } e = e^* \\ 0 & \text{otherwise.} \end{cases} \tag{6}$$

The above formulation assumed that the principal sets the price p which he could do because of his full information. Alternatively, he could instruct the agent to set the price and stipulate a reward scheme:

$$T = \begin{cases} t & \text{if } e = e^* \text{ and } p = p^* \\ 0 & \text{otherwise.} \end{cases} \tag{6'}$$

The principal calculates the optimal values of the price p, the external control c, the reward t and the effort level e. Although the actual level of effort is set by the management, the principal calculates e, in order to monitor the manager's behaviour. Since the principal knows the actual value of the random efficiency parameter, he can directly maximize profit conditioned on α. Hence, he faces the following optimization approach:

$$\max_{c,e,p,t} \; pq(p) - [k - \alpha c - e]q(p) - t - h(c) \quad \text{subject to} \quad U(t,e) \geq \bar{U} \quad (\mu). \tag{7}$$

For the following we only deal with $c > 0$. The case of $c = 0$ is explicitly treated in section 5.2 below. We assume that h' and $\bar{U}$ are large enough to guarantee positive marginal costs.

The principal obtains the following marginal conditions:

$$L_p: \quad \frac{p - mc}{p} = -\frac{1}{\epsilon} \tag{8}$$

$$L_e: \quad q - \mu U_2 = 0 \tag{9}$$

$$L_t: \quad -1 - \mu U_1 = 0 \tag{10}$$

$$L_c: \quad \alpha q - h' = 0 \tag{11}$$

$$L_\mu: \quad U \geq \bar{U};\ \mu \leq 0. \tag{12}$$

First, the conditions imply monopoly pricing. The price–cost margin is equated to the inverse price elasticity of demand ϵ. Regulation of the privatized firm could easily be introduced in the model. Consider for instance, an *RPI–X* regulation of the form which has been applied to British Telecom. The price will then be set according to a sort of Ramsey rule. Since both the retail price index and the variable X are exogenous, the price regulation is independent of costs. Hence, the qualitative results on effort and on external control are not influenced by the regulation, although the level of effort and control typically will change because demand changes in response to the regulated price.

Second, the participation constraint in binding ($\mu < 0$ follows from (10) and the assumption $U_1 > 0$). The reward is chosen in such a way that the manager only gets his reservation utility. This is the consequence of the full information hypothesis. The principal is well informed and is able to monitor fully the manager's effort to guarantee an optimum at the manager's reservation utility.

Third, the factor allocation (c, e) is cost-minimizing, taking account of the manager's participation constraint. It can directly be seen that $\alpha q - h' = 0$ is the condition for cost-minimizing control[2]. A similar reasoning holds for the effort level taking account of the participation constraint. Some straightforward transformations yield:

$$-U_2/U_1 = h'/\alpha. \tag{13}$$

The manager's marginal rate of substitution between reward and effort is equated to the marginal rate of transformation between control and effort. This elucidates the way in which the reward is chosen so as to implement the optimal effort.

4 THE PUBLIC FIRM

4.1 Finding a Truthtelling Mechanism

Here the principal is only imperfectly informed. He only knows that α is uniformly distributed and he cannot observe the effort level e. However, the principal can ask the management to announce the value of α and then base the reward on the ex post costs. Note that this reward indirectly influences the agent's effort.

Although the public principal is only partially interested in profit, he is interested in minimizing costs. However, his imperfect information makes it impossible to condition the manager's reward on effort. Ex post the principal is only able to observe the marginal costs. Therefore he conditions the reward on $mc(\alpha)$. Since the principal only ex post learns the actual value of α, he is unable to set the desired price $p(\alpha)$, which task must be shifted to the manager. Hence, the reward must also be conditioned on $p(\alpha)$ to guarantee that the manager sets this price.

The content of the contract is as follows: for any α, as signalled by the agent, the principal is willing to engage in control $c(\alpha)$ and to pay the following reward:

$$T = \begin{cases} t(\alpha) & \text{if } mc = mc(\alpha) \text{ and } p = p(\alpha) \\ 0 & \text{otherwise.} \end{cases} \quad (14)$$

Given this offer, the manager decides to announce a particular value of α. The management would not have any degree of freedom if the principal knew the actual value of α and could monitor the management's behaviour according to this knowledge. But since this is not the case, the management could announce a false $\hat{\alpha}$, if that value implies higher utility. However, when telling lies, the management must be cautious. Since the principal knows ex post the total marginal costs, the effects of control and effort must always add up to that value of marginal cost which the principal will be able to observe ex post, given an announced $\hat{\alpha}$ and an actual α.

Assume that the management announces a particular $\hat{\alpha}$ which may be true or false. Since the reward is conditioned on the marginal costs, the manager calculates the various components of *mc*. He anticipates external control $c(\hat{\alpha})$ depending on the announced $\hat{\alpha}$. This control reduces the basic marginal costs by $\alpha c(\hat{\alpha})$. The manager then calculates the effort he should choose given an actual value α and an announced value $\hat{\alpha}$ of the efficiency parameter. The manager realizes that an identical value of marginal costs can be attained either by a false or a true announcement:

$$mc = \begin{cases} k - \alpha c(\hat{\alpha}) - e(\alpha,\hat{\alpha}) & \text{for } \hat{\alpha} \neq \alpha \\ k - \hat{\alpha} c(\hat{\alpha}) - e(\hat{\alpha}) & \text{for } \hat{\alpha} = \alpha. \end{cases} \quad (15)$$

Since the principal cannot observe α and e, but only calculate equations (15) and observe the numerical value of *mc*, he cannot detect that the management has lied. A consistent lie of the management, therefore, consists in choosing $e(\alpha,\hat{\alpha})$ in such a way that equations (15) are fulfilled for the announced $\hat{\alpha}$, and *mc* is the same in both equations; this means

$$e(\alpha,\hat{\alpha}) = e(\hat{\alpha}) + (\hat{\alpha} - \alpha)c(\hat{\alpha}). \quad (16)$$

The principal knows that the management may be inclined to lie according to (16). Other lies can be excluded from the analysis because they can be detected.

The reward scheme in (14) is chosen in such a way that the management has an incentive to announce the correct value of α. Such a mechanism is called 'truthtelling' and implies $\hat{\alpha} = \alpha$ as an optimal strategy of the manager. This is achieved if the management's utility is maximized by announcing $\hat{\alpha} = \alpha$: the best lie is the truth. The technical details are shown in Appendix 1. To avoid clumsy notation, for a truthtelling mechanism we simplify $t(mc(\alpha),p(\alpha)) := t(\alpha)$.

The management's problem is as follows. It wants to maximize its personal utility

$$V(\alpha) = U(t(\alpha),e(\alpha)). \tag{17}$$

If it is always optimal for the management to tell the truth, its utility is strictly increasing in the actual value, α.

$$V'(\alpha) = -U_2 c > 0 \tag{18}$$

where $V' = dV/d\alpha$. Equation (18) can be interpreted as follows. The left-hand side describes the marginal change in utility which is caused by an increase in the efficiency of control (α). The right-hand side shows that this increase is more relevant, the higher the control. If the efficiency of control increases, the manager can reduce his effort by c units. Therefore, his utility improvement is equal to his utility gain $-U_2$ per unit times c.

4.2 The Optimal Contract

We are now ready for the treatment of the government's optimization. Since α is unobservable, the management must be induced to tell the truth. This 'incentive compatibility' can be guaranteed by explicitly considering the first- and second-order conditions under which the management achieves highest personal utility if it announces α. The first-order condition can be represented by equation (18). The second-order condition will not be explicitly included in what follows to make the model more tractable. We assume this condition holds and, accordingly, bunching is excluded. The participation constraint, of course, must be treated explicitly. However, it can be simplified. Since $V'(\alpha) > 0$, it suffices to postulate $V(\underline{\alpha}) \geq \bar{U}$. At the optimum, this constraint is always binding.

For a more convenient presentation, we invert the manager's utility $U(t.e)$, to obtain:

$$e = E(t,V); \quad E_t = -U_1/U_2 > 0,\ E_V = 1/U_2 < 0. \tag{19}$$

Hence, we deal with the following optimization approach where $c,t,$ and p are control variables and V is state variable:

$$\begin{aligned} &max \int_{\underline{\alpha}}^{\bar{\alpha}} \{\lambda S(\alpha) + (1-\lambda)\pi(\alpha)\}d\alpha \\ &\text{subject to} \\ &V'(\alpha) = -U_2(t(\alpha),E(V(\alpha),t(\alpha)))\cdot c(\alpha), \\ &V(\underline{\alpha}) = \bar{U}. \end{aligned} \tag{20}$$

The principal obtains the optimality conditions on the basis of the following Hamiltonian[3]

$$H(\alpha) = \lambda S(p) + (1 - \lambda)[pq(p) - (k - \alpha c - E(t,V))q(p) - t - h(c)] - \mu U_2(t,E(t,V))\cdot c. \tag{21}$$

$$H_p = 0; H_c = 0; H_t = 0; H_V = -\mu'. \tag{22}$$

The transversality condition is $\mu(\bar{\alpha}) = 0$. Moreover, $\mu(\alpha) < 0$ for $\alpha < \bar{\alpha}$ as explicitly proved in Appendix 2.

4.3 Economic Consequences

4.3.1 Pricing, control and effort

For the economic interpretation let us begin with *pricing*. The $H_p = 0$ condition can be transformed into:

$$\frac{p - mc}{p} = -\frac{1 - 2\lambda}{1 - \lambda} \cdot \frac{1}{\epsilon}. \tag{23}$$

Contrast this price structure with the monopoly price structure (equation 8). As long as $\lambda < 1/2$, the public firm behaves like a profit maximizing monopolist who overestimates the demand elasticity by $(1-\lambda)/(1-2\lambda) > 1$. The extent of overestimation is greater the higher the value of λ, i.e. the greater the government interest in welfare. This overestimation of the elasticity means that the welfare-oriented government treats the customers very cautiously, i.e. a low price. The lowest price, the marginal-cost price, is achieved at the highest λ, namely $\lambda = 1/2$. If, on the other hand, λ is reduced until finally we reach $\lambda = 0$, we approach the profit-maximizing monopoly price.

Next, we turn to *external control*. Since the transversality condition implies $\mu(\bar{\alpha}) = 0$, we obtain from $H_c = 0$

$$\alpha q - h' = \frac{\mu}{1 - \lambda} U_2 \begin{cases} > 0 \text{ for } \alpha < \bar{\alpha} \\ = 0 \text{ for } \alpha = \bar{\alpha}. \end{cases} \tag{24}$$

To evaluate the chosen extent of control recall that a direct differentiation of the cost function C yields:

$$C_c = -\alpha q + h'. \tag{25}$$

At the public firm optimum we have $C_c < 0$ for all $\alpha < \bar{\alpha}$. Further control would reduce costs. The government spends less on control than efficient except in the best of all possible worlds ($\alpha = \bar{\alpha}$). Recall that the principal of the privatized firm always controls efficiently. In the privatized firm the manager could not cheat the principal. In the public firm, the possibility of lies allows the management to reduce effort. As can be seen from equation (16), the higher the external control, the greater the reduction of effort. Hence the incentive to lie is greater the higher the principal's control. Therefore, a truthtelling mechanism is easier to implement the lower the external control.

A similar result is obtained for the *effort of the manager*. From $H_t = 0$ we learn

$$E_t q - 1 = \frac{\mu[U_{21} - U_{22}U_1/U_2]c}{1 - \lambda} \begin{cases} > 0 \text{ for } \alpha < \bar{\alpha} \\ = 0 \text{ for } \alpha = \bar{\alpha} \end{cases} \tag{26}$$

under the assumption that consumption is a normal good and therefore [·] < 0 on the right-hand side.[4] We divide equation (26) by $U_1/U_2 = -E_t < 0$ and obtain:

$$- q - \frac{U_2}{U_1} \begin{cases} < 0 \text{ for } \alpha < \bar{\alpha} \\ = 0 \text{ for } \alpha = \bar{\alpha}. \end{cases} \tag{27}$$

Now recall that a direct differentiation of the cost function C yields:

$$C_e = - q - \frac{U_2}{U_1}. \tag{28}$$

At the public firm's optimum the management applies less effort than is efficient. The reward is not high enough to induce the management to supply efficient effort. Only at $\alpha = \bar{\alpha}$ both control and effort are chosen efficiently. Recall that the manager in the privatized firm always chose efficient effort. In the public firm, however, higher effort requires higher reward to the manager. Hence with a truthtelling mechanism a particular effort level is more costly to achieve than in the case of complete information.

4.3.2 Efficiency at the top

Efficiency is defined as the equality of the marginal rates of substitution and of transformation, as already shown in equation (13) for the case of full information. If the information is incomplete, efficient control and efficient effort are only achieved at the top, i.e. when $\alpha = \bar{\alpha}$. This has been shown in equations (24) and (27). Since the models of the privatized and

Figure 3.1

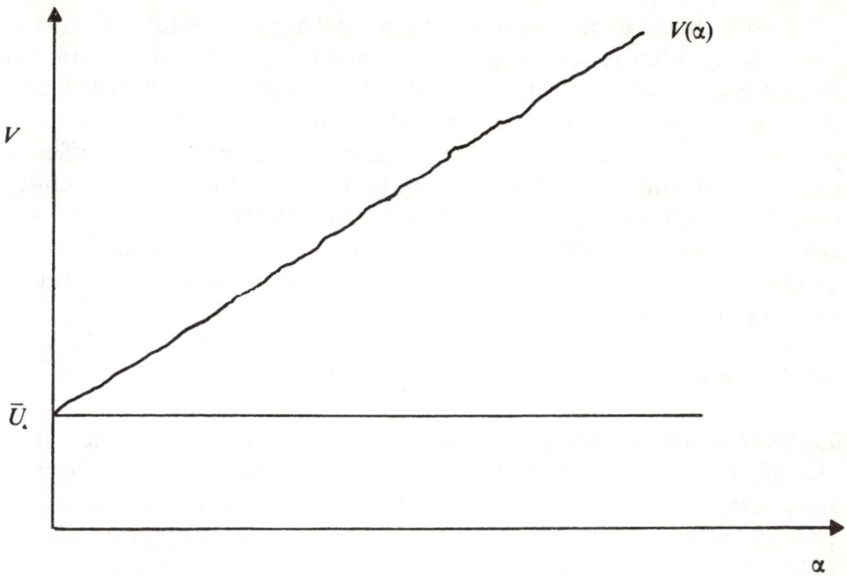

the public firm differ with respect to the informational status of the principal, the above differences in efficiency must be due to differences in information. Complete information allows the principal to pay compensation which keeps the manager at his reservation utility $\bar{U}$ regardless of α, which implies $V'(\alpha) = 0$. Incomplete information, however, requires compensation which is incentive-compatible: the manager's utility must be increasing in α, i.e. $V'(\alpha) > 0$. The two cases are illustrated in Figure 3.1.

If $V'(\alpha) = 0$, the compensation the principal has to pay in the case of low α, has no influence whatsoever on the compensation he has to pay in the case of high α. This is different if $V'(\alpha) > 0$. The decisions on compensation and effort at some level $\tilde{\alpha}$ influence the decisions on compensation and effort at all levels of $\alpha > \tilde{\alpha}$. Otherwise incentive-compatibility, $V'(\alpha) > 0$, cannot be guaranteed. The fact that a decision at $\tilde{\alpha}$ has an influence on decisions at $\alpha > \tilde{\alpha}$ can be seen as a sort of external effect.

External effects are caused by the requirement of incentive-compatibility. Hence, ultimately they go back to the differences in the informational status of the principal. In the case of perfect information, there are no external effects and the marginal rates of substitution and of transformation are equal to each other. The existence of the external effects drives a wedge between the marginal rate of substitution and of transformation. External effects occur as long as there are further α's in excess of $\tilde{\alpha}$. This is not the case at the top. Consequently, at the top, efficient control and effort are chosen.

It may be noted in passing that the principal accepts too low an effort *at the bottom*, although at this point he knows that the manager has no incentive to lie: lies pay only if an $\tilde{\alpha}$ can be announced which falls below the actual value, as can be seen from (16). Hence at the bottom there is no strategic space for lies. Although the principal can enforce an efficient effort level by stipulating a contract (6) for $\alpha = \underline{\alpha}$, in such a case incentive compatibility would require higher manager's utility $V(\alpha)$ for all $\alpha > \underline{\alpha}$ than in the case of acceptance of too low an effort level at the bottom. Considering the external effects induces the principal to accept inefficient effort at the bottom.

4.3.3 The manager's reward

Let us compare the manager's reward in the privatized and in the public enterprise. In the privatized firm, the manager renders only one service to the principal, namely his effort. Information is not transferred since the principal is fully informed. Consider the total differential of the manager's utility

$$V' = U_1 t' + U_2 e' = 0 \tag{29}$$

to obtain

$$t' = -\frac{U_2}{U_1}e'. \tag{30}$$

Equation (30) shows how the change in the manager's services, e', is transformed into a change in the manager's remuneration. The transformation factor is the marginal rate of substitution between effort and income, $-U_2/U_1$, which can be interpreted as the shadow price of effort.

In the public enterprise, however, the manager is rewarded for two services which he renders to the principal: information and effort. This can be seen directly from the incentive-compatibility constraint:

$$V' = U_1t' + U_2e' = -U_2c. \tag{31}$$

A simple transformation yields:

$$t' = -\frac{U_2}{U_1}(c + e'). \tag{32}$$

If α increases, the manager's services change in a twofold way. First, the value of information about α increases by c. Second, the effort increases or decreases by e'. As can be seen in equation (32), the manager's reward changes both in effort and in information.

In the privatized firm the manager's reward increases if his effort increases and vice versa. In the public enterprise, however, the following paradoxical case is not excluded by equation (32): increasing α may lead to a reduction in effort if the manager takes advantage of the better state of the world by working less hard. If the information about the increasing α is valued highly and the effort reduction is not too important, i.e. if $c > |e'|$, then the manager's reward increases in α although he reduces his effort when the state of the world becomes better. This paradoxical case clearly reveals the importance of the transfer of information as one of the two services carried out by the manager. For an example see our simulation analyses in section 6 below.

When comparing the manager reward in the privatized and in the public enterprise, it is also interesting to look at effort and compensation at the lowest and at the highest value of α.

At $\underline{\alpha}$, we have less effort than efficient:

$$e(\underline{\alpha}) < e^*. \tag{33}$$

We know that at $\underline{\alpha}$ both in the full information and in the imperfect information cases the participation constraint is binding

$$\bar{U} = U(t^*(\underline{\alpha}),e^*(\underline{\alpha})) = U(t(\underline{\alpha}),e(\underline{\alpha})). \tag{34}$$

This implies:

$$t(\underline{\alpha}) < t^*(\underline{\alpha}). \tag{35}$$

At the lower end of the efficiency parameters α, the reward is less than efficient.

At $\bar{\alpha}$, on the other hand, we have efficient effort:

$$e(\bar{\alpha}) = e^*. \tag{36}$$

At a full information optimum, the participation constraint is always binding, even for $\bar{\alpha}$. At the second-best optimum utility increases in α. Hence we obtain:

$$\bar{U} = U(t^*(\bar{\alpha}),e^*(\bar{\alpha})) < U(t(\bar{\alpha}),e^*(\bar{\alpha})), \tag{37}$$

where we have substituted $e = e^*$ in the far right term. However, this implies:

$$t(\bar{\alpha}) > t^*. \tag{38}$$

At the upper end of the efficiency parameter α, the manager's reward is

Figure 3.2

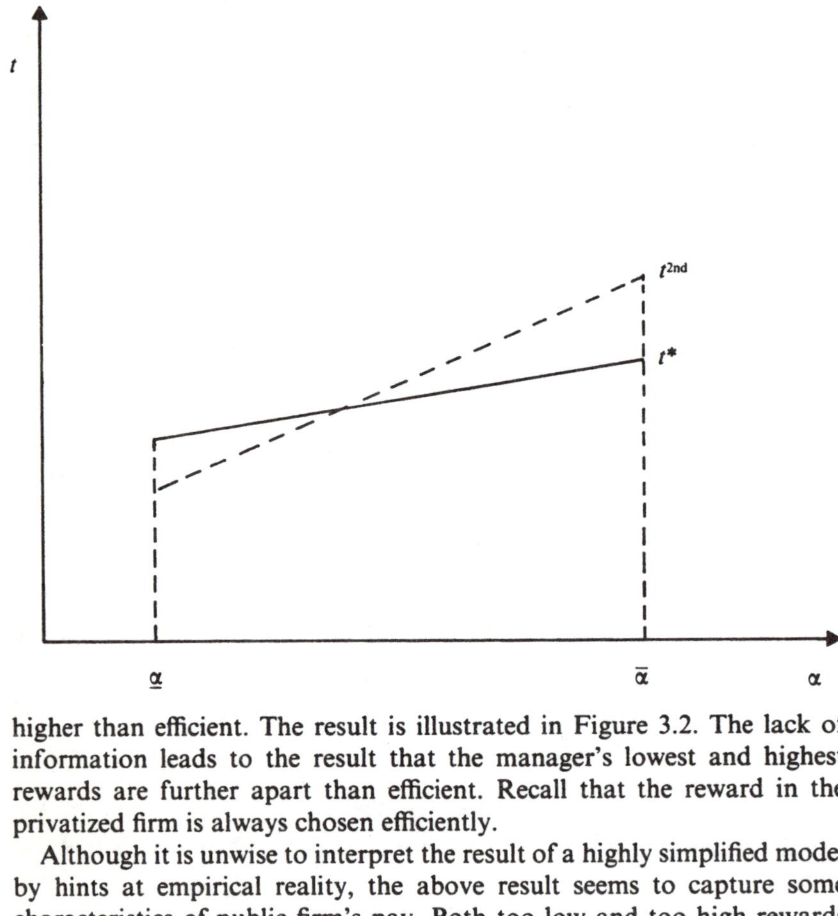

higher than efficient. The result is illustrated in Figure 3.2. The lack of information leads to the result that the manager's lowest and highest rewards are further apart than efficient. Recall that the reward in the privatized firm is always chosen efficiently.

Although it is unwise to interpret the result of a highly simplified model by hints at empirical reality, the above result seems to capture some characteristics of public firm's pay. Both too low and too high rewards have been observed in public firms. Our model shows that such differences could result from the public firm's national adjustment to their imperfect information in worlds of good and bad luck.

5 SOME EXTENSIONS OF THE PUBLIC FIRM MODEL

5.1 Incomplete Information About Multiple Goals

Managers of public enterprises often have complained that they are only incompletely informed about the government objectives. Privatization improves this information because it is straightforward to impute to the private owners the objective of profit maximization.

In our model, let us consider two types of incompletely informed managers: the first does not know the principal's objective function, the second does not know whether the principal has optimized any objective function[5]. In both cases the manager has entered into a contract which gives him a reward $t(\alpha)$ if marginal costs are $mc(\alpha)$ and if the price is set according to $p(\alpha)$. Note that on the basis of this contract the manager is able to maximize his utility $U(t(\alpha),e(\alpha))$ regardless of his lack of knowledge. In the principal-agent approach, the only relevant problem is the determination of the manager's reward. This reward must be chosen in such a way that the manager tells the truth about the economic situation of the firm and applies the optimal effort in adjustment to the actual economic situation. If the government gives the optimal reward, there is no need for the manager to bother about information. The application of the optimal reward scheme, therefore, fully solves the problem of the incompletely informed manager.

5.2 Endogenous Informational Setting

The informational setting in this paper has been given exogenously. We assumed that the principal of a privatized firm is better informed than the principal of a public firm and modelled this assumption by comparing a fully informed privatized and an imperfectly informed public principal.

Let us now look at a more general framework. Assume both privatized and public principal are imperfectly informed. No one is fully informed. Is it possible, in this framework, that full information results from the model? Under particular circumstances this is in fact the case. Let us assume that both privatized and public principal optimize an approach similar to (20) above, i.e. similar to the second-best approach of the public firm. Only the objective function varies. The owners of the privatized firm maximize profit, the government maximizes its multiple objective G. Now consider a corner solution of such an optimization approach which implies $c = 0, \forall\alpha$. If this is optimal, then the efficiency parameter α does not matter. Given the information of the value of total marginal costs, and of k, the principal can directly calculate the unobservable effort of the manager. Hence, in that case the principal is fully informed and able to implement the first best.

Under which circumstances can such a corner solution occur? Let us assume that control is increasing in α, hence $c' \geq 0$.[6] Then $c = 0, \forall\alpha$, whenever $c(\overline{\alpha}) = 0$. A sufficient condition for a corner is as follows

$$H_c < 0 \tag{39}$$

or, equivalently:

$$(\alpha q - h')(1 - \lambda) < \mu U_2. \tag{40}$$

For $\alpha = \bar{\alpha}$, this condition simplifies to:[7]

$$h'(c = 0) > \bar{\alpha} q. \tag{41}$$

If we assume that $h'(c = 0)$ is the same in the privatized and in the public firm, because q will be smaller in the profit-orientated privatized firm than in the welfare-oriented public firm, this condition is more likely to hold in a privatized than in a public firm.

In short, the informational setting we have chosen may also occur as an endogenous result of modelling.

6 ILLUSTRATIVE SIMULATIONS

In the preceding sections we analysed an optimal incentive scheme for managers in privatized and public firms. We obtained qualitative results. Insight into quantitative relations between control, effort and managers' reward can only be found by simulation analyses. Accordingly, in what follows we present a simple example for the solution of an optimal control problem concerned with our principal-agent relation.

For this purpose, we have to specify the functional forms of demand, of manager's utility and of cost of control. As in the theoretical part of the paper, the variable α, which cannot be observed by the principal, is assumed to be uniformly distributed. Hence, we only have to specify the lower and upper bounds for α. Let us first describe the functional forms of demand, utility and cost of control:

$$\begin{aligned} q &= A - Bp \\ U &= t - \frac{e^C}{C} \\ h &= \frac{c^D}{D} \\ &A, B, C, D > 0. \end{aligned} \tag{42}$$

The above specifications are used for the reduction of the complex first-order conditions for the optimum of the public firm. Since the utility function is quasi-linear in effort and reward, the differential equation for the adjoint variable μ can be simplified by combining the necessary conditions for the manager's reward ($H_t = 0$) and utility ($H_V = -\mu'$). Hence, the differential equation reads:

$$\mu' = 1 - \lambda, \tag{43}$$

which can easily be solved by integration. Considering the transversality condition, we obtain:

$$\mu(\alpha) = -(1 - \lambda)(\bar{\alpha} - \alpha). \tag{44}$$

As a result of the specifications chosen, the relevant maximization problems reduce to systems of non-linear equations combining the variables e, c, and p. Moreover, if we assume that both C and D are fixed at 2.0, we obtain linear equations which can easily be solved by the Gaussian algorithm.

The values of the public firm's manager's reward and utility are determined by the optimal quantities of effort and control:

$$\begin{aligned} V(\alpha) &= \bar{U} + \int_{\underline{\alpha}}^{\alpha} e \cdot c \quad \text{and} \\ t(\alpha) &= V + .5\, e^2. \end{aligned} \tag{45}$$

If we normalize $\bar{U}$ to zero, the reward paid to the manager is a monetary equivalent for the effort done. In the privatized firm $V'(\alpha) = 0$ and therefore we have $V = \bar{U} = 0$. The equation for $t(\alpha)$ is the same as for the public firm.

Let us first look at the maximization problem of a privatized firm. The optimal pricing scheme is an inverse elasticity rule, control and effort are chosen so as to minimize cost of production. The demand function completes the system. Hence, we obtain:

(i) Simulation of a privatized firm

$$\begin{aligned} \alpha q - c &= 0 \text{ optimal control} \\ q - e &= 0 \text{ optimal effort} \\ p - [k - \alpha c - e] &= \frac{q}{B} \text{ optimal price} \\ A - Bp &= q \text{ demand} \\ t &= 0.5\, e^2 \text{ optimal reward} \\ V &= 0 \text{ optimal utility.} \end{aligned} \tag{46}$$

In a similar way we can calculate the optimal solution for a public enterprise which has to pay regard to the informational asymmetry. In our special case we investigate a welfare optimum, i.e. the objective function is the sum of consumer and producer surplus. Hence, $\lambda = 0.5$. An optimal incentive scheme, control, effort and marginal cost prices are obtained by solving the following equations:

(ii) Simulation of a public enterprise

$$\begin{aligned} \alpha q - c &= e[\bar{\alpha} - \alpha] && \text{optimal control} \\ q - e &= c[\bar{\alpha} - \alpha] && \text{optimal effort} \\ p - [k - \alpha c - e] &= 0 && \text{optimal price} \\ A - Bp &= q && \text{demand} \\ t &= V + .5\, e^2 && \text{optimal reward.} \\ V &= \int_{\underline{\alpha}}^{\alpha} e \cdot c && \text{optimal utility.} \end{aligned} \tag{47}$$

We are now prepared for the simulation analyses. All parameters are chosen in such a way that sufficient second-order conditions are fulfilled, in order to guarantee a maximum of the objective function. For this purpose we assume: $A = 2.4$, $B = 0.1$, $k = 5.0$. The interval for the efficiency variable α is fixed as $\alpha \in [0.5;1.0]$. This excludes corner solutions for the optimal choice of the principal's control.

In the privatized firm, control, effort and manager's reward increase monotonically in α (Figure 3.3a). The increase in control leads to a reduction in marginal costs and hence in price. The resulting increase in the quantity demanded and supplied requires higher effort of the manager. Now recall that in the privatized firm higher effort always implies higher manager reward:

$$t' = -\frac{U_2}{U_1} e'. \tag{48}$$

The effort increase must be compensated by an increase in the manager's reward to keep his utility at the reservation level.

In the public firm, both effort and manager's reward follow a U-shaped curve if α increases (Figure 3.3b). The minimum of the t-curve is reached at a lower α than the minimum of the e-curve. This implies that there is a range of α's where the reward increases in spite of decreasing manager's effort. Recall that in the public firm the manager renders two services to the principal, namely information and effort, and is rewarded accordingly:

$$t' = -\frac{U_2}{U_1}(c + e'). \tag{49}$$

Figure 3.3a

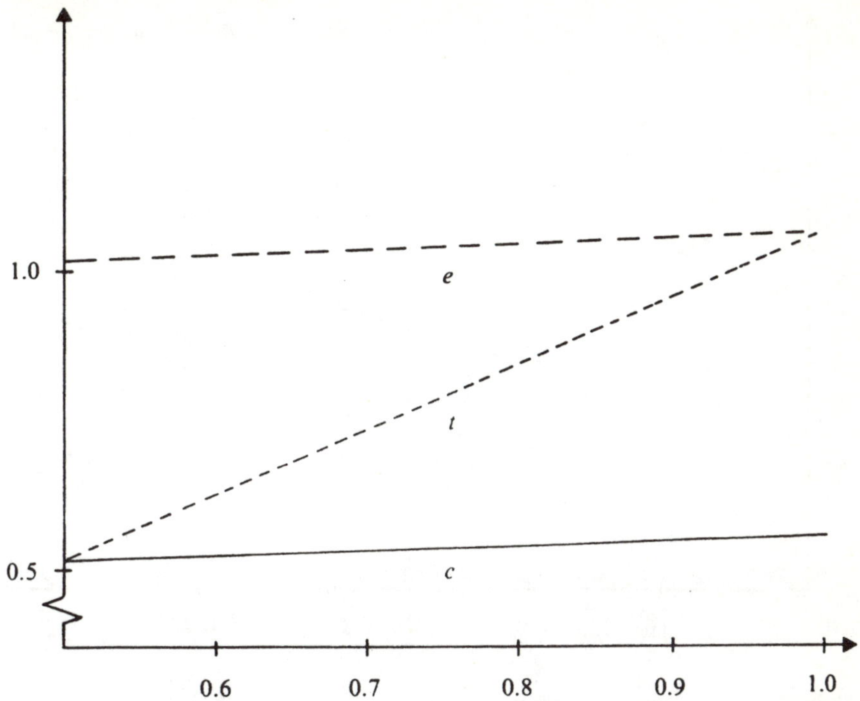

This explains why reward and effort may move into opposite directions. For the principal the value of the information overcompensates the losses which result from the reduced effort. (This is the 'paradoxical case' mentioned in section 4.3.3 above.)

The control expenditures c increase monotonically in α. The reason is simple. Control expenditures reduce the marginal costs by αc. If α is low, control is relatively inefficient. For low α, therefore, effort is the better instrument to reduce marginal cost: optimal effort is high, optimal control is low. However, control becomes more efficient if α increases and therefore is substituted for effort. Effort is even reduced to such an extent that at first the manager's reward is also reduced. Afterwards the above-mentioned paradoxical case occurs. Then, however, effort starts rising. The substitution between control and effort is stopped, both increase in α. This increase in effort can be explained by the 'external effects' argument mentioned in section 4.3.2 above: incentive-compatibility requires that a decision at a particular $\tilde{\alpha}$ has an influence on all decisions at $\alpha > \tilde{\alpha}$. These external effects are more important the lower the value of $\tilde{\alpha}$ because then there are many higher α's which have to be taken into account when

Figure 3.3b

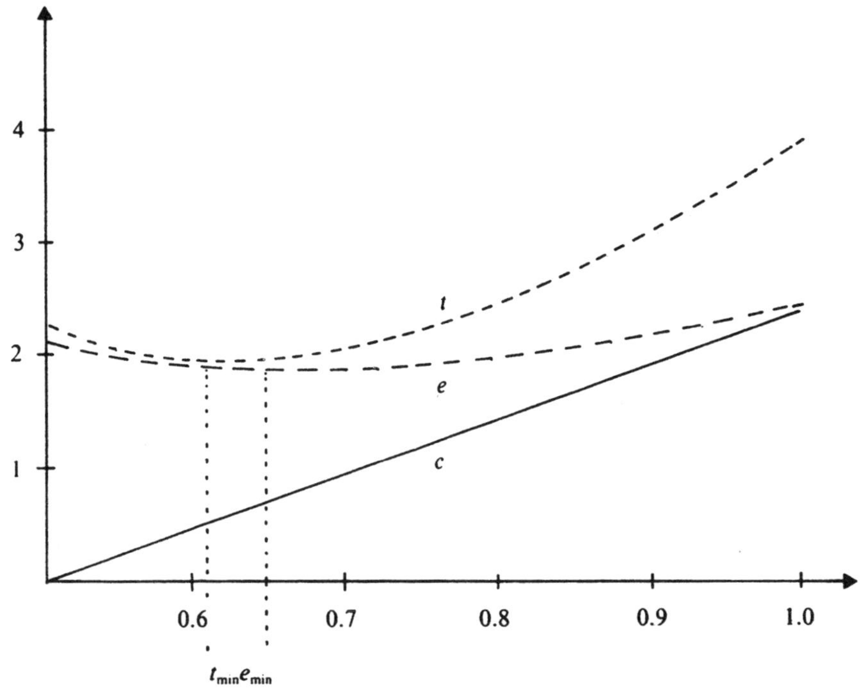

deciding at $\tilde{\alpha}$. The higher the value of α, the less important the external effects. Hence at some intermediate level of α, effort becomes cheap enough to make it worthwhile for the principal to reduce marginal costs by increasing both control and effort.

7 CONCLUSION

We obtain the following results of a transition from public to private ownership:

1. The public firm sets prices according to an inverse elasticity rule, where the chosen price-cost margin also depends on the particular mix of the multiple goals. Marginal-cost pricing is only chosen if the simple sum of consumer and producer surplus is maximized. Privatization implies a move to monopoly pricing.
2. Government's control of a public firm is lower than efficient; the control of private owners is efficient.

3. The manager of a public firm engages in less effort than is efficient; in a privatized firm the manager's effort is chosen efficiently.
4. The reward to the manager of a public firm is more differentiated than efficient. In the case of an unfavourable economic environment the reward is lower than efficient. In the case of a favourable environment the reward is higher than efficient. On the other hand, the manager in a privatized firm is always rewarded efficiently.
5. It is irrelevant whether the public manager is incompletely informed about the particular mix of the government's multiple objectives as long as the government chooses the incentive-compatible reward for the manager.

A. APPENDIX

A.1 Incentive-Compatibility in the Public Firm

The government as principal chooses a compensation payment t so as to induce truthtelling behaviour in the management, i.e. the agent of the problem. This implies:

$$D(\hat{\alpha}) = V(\alpha) - U(t(\hat{\alpha}),\tilde{e}(\alpha,\hat{\alpha})) \geq 0 \quad \forall\alpha,\hat{\alpha}.$$

We assume the distance function $D(\hat{\alpha})$ is twice continuously differentiable. Hence, the above condition can be transformed into a first- and a second-order condition. The government, moreover, chooses t in such a way that the minimum of the distance function is achieved at $\hat{\alpha} = \alpha$ (Figure A.1).

Now minimize $D(\hat{\alpha})$ with respect to $\hat{\alpha}$:

$$\min_{\hat{\alpha}} D(\hat{\alpha}) = V(\alpha) - U(t(\hat{\alpha}),e(\hat{\alpha}) + (\hat{\alpha} - \alpha)c(\hat{\alpha})),$$

$$D'(\hat{\alpha}) = -U_1t' - U_2(e' + c + (\hat{\alpha} - \alpha)c') = 0.$$

If t has been chosen adequately, the minimum occurs at $\hat{\alpha} = \alpha$ and we have:

$$D'(\hat{\alpha}) = -U_1t' - U_2(e' + c) = 0.$$

At an optimum $\hat{\alpha} = \alpha$, moreover, the second-order condition equals:

$$D''(\hat{\alpha}) = -U_1t'' - U_{11}t'^2 - 2U_{12}t'(e' + c) - U_2(e'' + 2c') - \\ - U_{22}(e' + c)^2 \geq 0.$$

Figure A.1

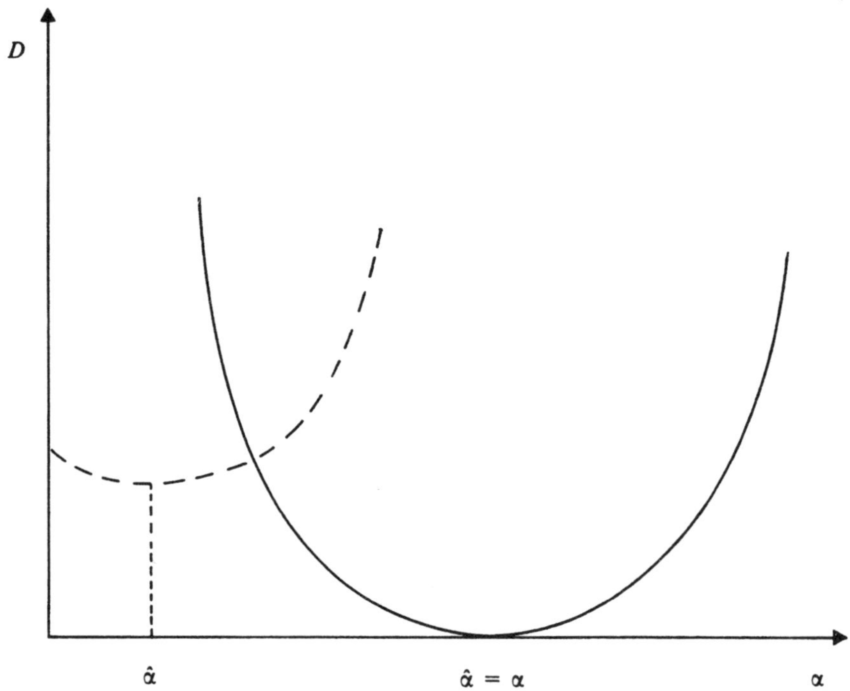

For simplification recall that $D'(\hat{\alpha}) = 0$ for any $\hat{\alpha} = \alpha$. Hence we must have

$$dD'(\hat{\alpha} = \alpha) = 0$$

or, equivalently

$$-U_1t'' - U_{11}t'^2 - U_{12}t'e' - U_2(e'' + c') - U_{12}t'(e' + c) - U_{22}e'(e' + c) = 0.$$

Substitution into $D''(\hat{\alpha})$ yields

$$-[U_{12}t' + U_{22}(e' + c)]c - U_2c' \geq 0.$$

Now insert $D'(\hat{\alpha}) = 0$ to obtain

$$D''(\hat{\alpha}) = -[U_{12} - U_{22}U_1/U_2]t'c - U_2c' \geq 0.$$

Hence, if the following three conditions are met, this is sufficient, although not necessary for a local minimum of the distance function $D(\hat{\alpha})$:

1) $U_{12} - U_{22}U_1/U_2 < 0$, i.e. consumption is a normal good,
2) $t' \geq 0$,
3) $c' \geq 0$.

The first-order condition $D'(\hat{\alpha} = \alpha)$ is equivalent to:

$$V'(\hat{\alpha} = \alpha) = -U_2 c \geq 0.$$

This can easily be shown. Recall the first-order condition

$$D'(\hat{\alpha} = \alpha) = 0 = -U_1 t' - U_2(e' + c). \qquad (+)$$

For any α, total differentiation of $V(\alpha)$ gives

$$V'(\alpha) = U_1 t' + U_2 e'. \qquad (++)$$

$(++)$ is substituted into $(+)$.

A.2 Sign of the Multiplier μ in the Hamiltonian (23)

We start from the H_V condition

$$\mu'(\alpha) = \mu(\alpha)A(\alpha) + B(\alpha) > 0$$

where

$$A = U_{22} c E_V > 0 \quad \forall \alpha$$

$$B = -(1 - \lambda)E_V q > 0 \quad \forall \alpha.$$

Solving the above differential equation we obtain

$$\mu(\alpha) = \mu(\underline{\alpha})e^{\int_{\underline{\alpha}}^{\alpha} A(\alpha')d\alpha'} + \int_{\underline{\alpha}}^{\alpha} B(\alpha')e^{\int_{\underline{\alpha}}^{\alpha'} A(\overline{\alpha})d\overline{\alpha}'} d\alpha'$$

where e is the basis of the natural logarithm (not effort). This equation can be transformed by using the transversality condition $\mu(\overline{\alpha}) = 0$. We obtain

$$\mu(\underline{\alpha}) = -\frac{\int_{\underline{\alpha}}^{\overline{\alpha}} B(\alpha')e^{\int_{\underline{\alpha}}^{\alpha'} A(\overline{\alpha})d\overline{\alpha}} d\alpha'}{e^{\int_{\underline{\alpha}}^{\overline{\alpha}} A(\alpha')d\alpha'}} < 0.$$

After these preparatory steps we can proof the following lemma.

Lemma: $\mu(\alpha) < 0, \forall\alpha < \bar{\alpha}$.

Proof:
$\mu(\underline{\alpha}) < 0$ as shown above. $\mu(\bar{\alpha}) = 0$ from the transversality condition. The following proof is by contradiction. Assume $\mu(\alpha') \geq 0$ for $\alpha' < \bar{\alpha}$. Then $\mu' = \mu A + B > 0$ because $A,B > 0$. Hence $\mu(\alpha) > 0$ for all $\alpha > \alpha'$, which implies $\mu(\bar{\alpha}) > 0$, which is a contradiction to the transversality condition.

ACKNOWLEDGEMENTS

We gratefully acknowledge financial support by Sfb 303 and the German-Israeli Fund, and helpful discussions with Lorenz Nett, Attiat Ott and David Wildasin on an earlier draft of this paper. Dorothea Madsen calculated the simulation analyses in section 6 of the paper.

NOTES

1. With respect to cost-side information of the principal, recent papers deal either with unobservable costs, like Baron and Myerson (1982) or with observable costs. Well-known papers on the second approach include Freixas and Laffont (1985) and Laffont and Tirole (1986).
2. Minimize $C = (k - \alpha c - e)\, q + t + h(c)$ with respect to c.
3. We assume that the Hamilton conditions lead to a maximum. For details see Kamien and Schwartz (1981) or Seierstad and Sydsæter (1986).
4. This assumption was already used to fulfil the second-order condition.
5. As a contrasting informational setting consider the following case: the manager knows that the principal optimizes some objective function and he knows the precise functional shape of this function. However, he does not know the actual value of λ, which determines the weights given to the multiple goals in the government objective function. In this case, the manager need not be informed about λ to solve his personal optimization problem. However, he could calculate λ on the basis of his knowledge of the government's optimization approach.
6. This holds under fairly weak assumptions.
7. Recall the transversality condition $\mu(\bar{\alpha}) = 0$.

REFERENCES

Baron, D.P. and Myerson, R.B. (1982), 'Regulating a monopolist with unknown costs', *Econometrica*, **50**, 911–30.

Caillaud, B., Guesnerie, R., Rey, P. and Tirole, J. (1988), 'Government intervention in production and incentives theory: a review of recent contributions', *Rand Journal of Economics*, **19**, 1–26.

Freixas, X. and Laffont, J.-J. (1985), 'Average cost pricing versus marginal cost pricing under moral hazard', *Journal of Public Economics*, **26**, 135–146.

Kamien, M.I. and Schwartz, N.L. (1981), *Dynamic Optimisation: The Calculus of Variations and Optimal Control in Economics and Management*, Amsterdam, North Holland.

Laffont, J.-J. and Tirole, J. (1986), Using cost observation to regulate firms, *Journal of Political Economy,* **94**, 614–41.

Seierstad, A. and Sydsæter, K. (1986), *Optimal Control Theory with Applications*, Amsterdam, North Holland.

[17]

THE ECONOMIC JOURNAL

MARCH 1996

The Economic Journal, **106** (*March*), 309–319. Published by Blackwell Publishers, 108 Cowley Road, Oxford OX4 1JF, UK and 238 Main Street, Cambridge, MA 02142, USA.

A THEORY OF PRIVATISATION

Maxim Boycko, Andrei Shleifer and Robert W. Vishny[1]

Public enterprises around the world have proved to be highly inefficient, primarily because they pursue strategies, such as excess employment, that satisfy the political objectives of politicians who control them. Privatisation of public enterprises can raise the cost to politicians of influencing them, since subsidies to private firms necessary to force them to remain inefficient are politically harder to sustain than wasted profits of the state firms. In this way, privatisation leads to efficient restructuring of firms. Moreover, privatisation is more effective when combined with a tight monetary policy, and when the new owners of firms are profit maximising investors, rather than their employees or even managers.

In the last decade, privatisation of state enterprises has swept the world. Thousands of state firms from Africa, Asia, Latin America, Western and Eastern Europe have gone private (Kikeri *et al.* 1992). A critical factor behind this move to privatisation is the well-documented poor performance of public enterprises. Donahue (1989) surveys multiple studies showing the significantly higher cost of public relative to private provision of municipal services in the United States. Lopez de Silanes (1993) documents the inferior profitability of state relative to private firms in Mexico in the 1980s. Mueller (1989) and Vining and Boardman (1992) survey dozens of studies of public and private firms around the world, most of which show that private firms are more efficient. More recent studies have actually shown that efficiency improves after privatisation (World Bank, 1992; Megginson *et al.*, 1994). In this paper, we develop a model of privatisation that explains the relative inefficiency of public firms and the improvements of efficiency after privatisation, as well as several other empirical findings concerning privatisation.

The starting point of our analysis is the commonplace observation that public enterprises are inefficient because they address the objectives of politicians rather than maximise efficiency. One key objective of politicians is employment: they care about votes of the people whose jobs are in danger and, in many cases, unions have significant influence on political parties. For example, Donahue (1989) describes evidence showing higher employment per unit of output in publicly provided municipal services. The British government for a long time refused to close grossly inefficient coal mines to preserve mining jobs. While excess employment is not the only politically demanded inefficiency of state firms (for example, Credit Lyonnais, the money losing French state

[1] This paper was presented by Shleifer as the Paish Lecture at the Royal Economic Society 1995 meeting. The authors are grateful to the Bradley, Sage and National Science Foundations for the support of this research, to Eric Maskin for very helpful comments, and to Ilya Segal for excellent research assistance.

bank, made its worst loans to the friends of the governing socialist party),[2] it is surely the most commonly noted one. Below, we focus on the implications of the political demand for excess employment by public enterprises.

In Section II, we present a simple model in which a spending politician, such as an industrial minister, who controls the decisions of a public enterprise, forces it, for political reasons, to spend too much on labour. This politician does not fully internalise the cost of the profits foregone by the Treasury and by private shareholders that the firm might have. The manager can bribe this politician to agree to lower employment, and in some cases corruption improves efficiency. However, corruption contracts are usually neither legal nor enforceable, so inefficiency is not necessarily cured by corruption.

This analysis raises a question: can a reformer make it more difficult for spending politicians to benefit from excess employment of public enterprises? A reformer in this model is a newly elected leader, such as Margaret Thatcher in Britain, Carlos Salinas in Mexico, or Vaclav Klaus in the Czech Republic, who derives political benefits not from excess employment in public enterprises, but from low spending and taxes. It is not that reformers are benevolent, but rather that their political constituents are taxpayers rather than the beneficiaries of public largesse. These reformers want to constrain the actions of their own spending ministries, or alternatively, to tie the hands of future governments (such as future Labour governments in Britain) that might be more inclined to spend money on public enterprise employment. In effect, these reformers represent the interests of the Treasury against those of the spending ministries.

Our paper discusses privatisation as a strategy available to the reformers to reduce inefficiency of public enterprises. By privatisation we mean a combination of the reallocation of control rights over employment from politicians to managers and the increase in cash flow ownership of managers and private investors.[3] At first glance, it seems that privatisation should reduce employment if managers maximise profits and have no interest in excess employment. However, a spending politician still wants to influence firms and can use government subsidies to convince their managers to keep up employment. In principle, there is nothing magic about privatisation: just as the spending politician was willing to give up profits of a public firm on excess labour spending, he is willing to subsidise a privatised firm to 'buy' excess labour spending. How, then, does privatisation serve the reformer's interests and separate the firm from the spending politician?

This question has been addressed by several authors. Schmidt (1990) argues that privatisation reduces the amount of information that politicians have, which may lead to the reduction of subsidies and restructuring. Shapiro and Willig (1990) make a clear case that privatisation must draw a line between politicians and firms, and like Schmidt, use an information argument to show how it works. We agree with the general approach of these papers, although we are not sure why privatisation necessarily changes the information of politicians.

[2] *The Economist*, April 9, 1994.

[3] Grossman and Hart (1986) stress the distinction between control and cash flow rights.

In this paper, we argue that it may be politically less costly for the politician to spend the profits of the firm on labour without remitting them to the Treasury than to generate new subsidies for the privatised firm. The public and the reformers may not be aware of the potential profits that a state firm is wasting, but they are keenly aware of the alternative uses of tax revenues, and would not wish to spend public money to subsidise private firms not to restructure. This difference between the political costs of foregone profits of state firms and of subsidies to private firms is the channel through which privatisation works in this paper. One important conclusion of this analysis is that a tough monetary policy makes privatisation much more effective.

In Sections I and II, we discuss a very simple model in which the only active players are the spending politician and the manager. In Section III, we consider the role of other potentially active players, such as the employees and the core investors. We discuss the effect of worker ownership and outside investor ownership on the likelihood of restructuring. In our model, different types of privatisation have different implications for efficiency.

Section IV concludes.

I. POLITICAL CONTROL OF FIRMS

A simple model

We consider a firm that only chooses its level of spending on labour E. It can spend an efficient amount L or a higher amount $H > L$. The higher spending comes from excess wages and employment. The restriction of only two levels of spending is introduced for simplicity.

There are two players in this model who have preferences over E: the politician and the manager. The manager here is assumed to represent private shareholders. We begin by assuming that the manager and shareholders own a fraction α of the firm's profits, while the Treasury owns a fraction $(1-\alpha)$. The politician himself owns no equity. In a public firm, α is close to zero, whereas in a private firm, α is close to 1.

To begin, we assume that the objective function of the politician (in dollars) is given by:

$$Up = qE - m(1-\alpha)E. \tag{1}$$

The politician prefers higher labour spending since it is a source of political benefits, such as voting support from the employees and labour unions. The marginal benefit to him of an extra dollar of such spending is $q < 1$. But spending more on labour reduces the value of the Treasury's share of profits of the firm. The politician cares about these profits because the Treasury can impose sanctions on him if the firm loses (or fails to make) money. Importantly, the politician does not care directly about the share of the profits foregone by the manager and private shareholders, which matter only to the extent that angering shareholders reduces the net potential political benefit of excess employment q. The cost to the politician of a dollar of profits foregone by the Treasury as a result of spending on labour is m. We assume $m < 1$ because the politician cares less about the Treasury's income than he does about his own money. This, too, creates a bias for too much employment. The politician's objective function thus trades off the political benefits of higher employment against the political costs of the profits foregone by the Treasury.

The objective function of the manager (shareholders) is simply given by his share of profits:

$$Um = -\alpha E. \tag{2}$$

We can extend the model to allow the manager to care about employment directly; the results are very similar as long as the manager cares relatively more about profits than the politician does.

The critical parameter in this model is who controls labour spending. Initially, we assume that the firm is publicly controlled, meaning that E is chosen by the politician. This assumption accurately represents the situation with most public enterprises, where the government exerts substantial influence over their key decisions, particularly when political issues such as employment are involved. For example, the French government refused to back the management of Air France in its attempt to reduce labour costs, with the result that the management left and the employees stayed.

When the politician controls E, we assume he chooses $E = H$. Denote by $\Delta E = H - L$ the incremental gain in labour spending from switching from L to H. Then the assumption that the politician uses his control rights to choose $E = H$ can be rewritten as:

$$m(1-\alpha) < q. \tag{3}$$

This condition says that political benefits per dollar of extra spending on labour exceed political costs per dollar of profits foregone by the Treasury from such spending. In this way, we illustrate the idea that political control leads to inefficiencies that benefit politicians at the expense of the Treasury and other shareholders.

Corruption

Even if the politician controls labour spending and (3) holds, it might be in the interest of the manager (and shareholders) to bribe the politician to cut the firm's labour spending. There are two ways of thinking about this bribe. First, it could be a payoff to change E (or some other decision that the politician imposes on the firm) from H to L. Second, it could be a payment to transfer the control rights over E from the politician to the manager. Since in this model the manager chooses $E = L$ once he gets control rights, the bribe necessary to buy control from the politician is the same as the bribe needed to get the politician to change his decision. We show below that corruption reduces the set of parameter values for which labour spending is excessive.

Denote the necessary bribe by b. With bribes, the politician's utility is given by:

$$Up = -m(1-\alpha)E + qE + b, \tag{4}$$

and the manager's utility is given by:

$$Um = -\alpha E - b. \tag{5}$$

Since utility is transferable, the manager succeeds in bribing the politician to choose $E = L$ if their combined utility is higher at L than at H, i.e., if

$$m(1-\alpha) + \alpha > q. \tag{6}$$

Both (3) and (6) can be satisfied simultaneously: the politician chooses H without corruption but is willing to be bribed and choose efficient labour spending. The bribe divides the surplus between the manager and the politician according to the Nash or some other bargaining solution.

This result illustrates the Coase theorem for our model. When side-payments in the form of bribes are allowed, the manager and the politician choose the outcome that, from their joint viewpoint, is the most efficient. If (6) holds, the 'jointly efficient' outcome coincides with the socially efficient one $E = L$, but if (6) fails, the two may differ. Condition (6) is different from social efficiency in two ways. First, when $m < 1$, the politician does not fully internalise the foregone profits from excessive labour spending. The Treasury is too soft to make him act as a full shareholder. Second, excess labour spending benefits the politician since it enables him to get votes away from other politicians, but it should not enter the social welfare function. Thus corruption generally raises efficiency, in that it allows private investors to buy their way out of some of the inefficiencies demanded by politicians, but it does not always lead to first best.[4]

There are, however, some problems with using corruption to renegotiate to a more efficient resource allocation, even if (6) holds. First, corruption in most societies is illegal, so both the giver and the receiver of a bribe risk going to jail. The illegality of corruption is a particular problem when the bribe-supported outcome leads to substantial losses by the workers, who have an incentive to expose the politician. For the same reason of illegality, the corruption contract is unenforceable in courts. After collecting a bribe, the politician can renew his demand that labour spending be kept at a high level, or ask for another bribe. Since the manager has no recourse to enforce the initial agreement, he might never offer a bribe in the first place. Of course, there are other mechanisms of contract enforcement, such as reputations, but in transition economies the horizons of politicians are often too short to develop a reputation for efficient bribe taking.[5] In this case, we are back to the case of the politician choosing the inefficient outcome as long as condition (3) holds.

II. PRIVATISATION

By privatisation we mean a combination of two changes undertaken by a reformer. The first is turnover of control from spending politicians to managers, often referred to as corporatisation. Such turnover can be implemented by a strong reform government that effectively suppresses the ministries and the bureaucracy, as happened in Czechoslovakia. Alternatively, such turnover can happen more spontaneously, as the power of bureaucracy to protect its control rights diminishes. Such slow turnover of control from politicians to managers occurred in Russia in the early 1990s.

The second change that is usually part of most privatisations is the reduction of the cash flow ownership by the Treasury and the increase of cash flow ownership of managers and outside shareholders. The Treasury can sell its

[4] See Leff (1964), Rose-Ackerman (1978), Shleifer and Vishny (1993, 1994).
[5] For a further discussion of this issue, see Shleifer (1994).

shares for cash, or it can give them away through vouchers or some other allocation scheme. Our model shows how both the reallocation of control rights and the increase in private cash flow rights contribute to restructuring.[6]

When the managers and shareholders interested in maximising profits get control over labour spending, they obviously choose $E = L$. This, however, is not the end of the story. For just as before a manager paid a politician with control rights to agree to $E = L$, the politician can now try to pay shareholders not to restructure. The mechanism that politicians use is typically not bribes, but subsidies from the Treasury to the firms, also known as soft budget constraints.[7] Indeed, this is the main question about privatisation: why would a politician fail to buy his way to high labour spending through subsidies? To show how privatisation leads to restructuring, we must establish conditions under which managers with control rights choose to restructure even when they must forego subsidies from the Treasury.

Denote the subsidy from the Treasury to the firm by t. Since the Treasury owns $(1-\alpha)$ of the cash flows, it gets the fraction $(1-\alpha)$ of this subsidy back, so the effective subsidy is αt. If the politician could ask the Treasury to subsidise the firm at no cost to himself, he would pay the firm infinite subsidies not to restructure and no restructuring will ever take place. But the Treasury has to raise the money for the subsidies through either taxes or inflation, both of which are unpopular. We denote the cost to the politician of making a (net) subsidy αt by $k\alpha t$. In the plausible case, $k < 1$, since subsidies are less expensive to the politician than bribes out of his own pocket, which correspond to $k = 1$.

This model has two parameters that reflect the cost to the politician of foregone Treasury revenue: m and k. The first measures the cost to the politician of profits foregone by the Treasury, the second measures his political cost of subsidies. If the Treasury suffers no illusions from the corporate veil, then $m = k$. However, it is more reasonable to suppose that it is easier for the politician to squander a firm's profits on inefficiencies than to get additional subsidies for it, in which case $m < k$. When a firm squanders its profits, most members of the government do not known that it is potentially profitable and hence do not claim a piece of its profits for the Treasury and indirectly for their own pet projects. As a result, the minister who oversees this firm can spend the profits on political benefits, such as employment at a relatively low political cost. In contrast, when a firm receives a subsidy, the minister must compete for the resources of the Treasury with all the other politicians who argue for their favourite projects. As a result, buying political benefits with the money that is already in the Treasury is more expensive than just spending the profits of the firm. We keep the two parameters k and m separate to be able to evaluate the effect of each on the likelihood of restructuring.

[6] An alternative model of privatisation is to keep control in the hands of politicians but also to give them personal cash flow rights. Such 'nomenklatura privatisation' is easy to analyse in our model, and can be shown to increase efficiency relative to political control with no cash flow rights. Although nomenklatura privatisation has sometimes been advocated for Eastern Europe, it is politically too unpopular to make it a viable privatisation strategy.

[7] Kornai (1979) is the classical study of soft budget constraints. More recent models include Dewatripont and Maskin (1990), Li (1992), and Schmidt (1990).

We assume that corruption is infeasible (bribes are equivalent to the case of $k = 1$), since we have already noted some problems with bribes, and we want to focus on new issues. The objective function of the politician is given by:

$$Up = -m(1-\alpha)E + qE - k\alpha t, \tag{7}$$

and the objective function of the manager is given by:

$$Um = -\alpha E + \alpha t. \tag{8}$$

We can compute the Nash bargaining solution to this problem. Without subsidies, the manager chooses efficient labour spending L. He and the politician then bargain and he chooses labour spending H if he is better off with H and a transfer than he is with L. The politician's incremental utility from switching to H is given by:

$$-m(1-\alpha)\Delta E + q\Delta E - k\alpha t \tag{9}$$

and the manager's incremental utility from switching to H is given by:

$$-\alpha\Delta E + \alpha t. \tag{10}$$

The Nash Bargaining solution is given by maximising the product of (9) and (10) over t, which yields the equilibrium transfer:

$$t = \Delta E[-m(1-\alpha) + q + k\alpha]/(2k\alpha). \tag{11}$$

This bargain fails to be struck if the manager (or the politician) is worse off with $E = H$ and transfer t than he is with $E = L$ and no transfer. The condition for neither of them benefitting from the switch [i.e. both (9) and (10) are negative with t given by (11)] is:

$$k\alpha + m(1-\alpha) > q. \tag{12}$$

When (12) holds, privatisation leads to restructuring in that the politician cannot successfully use subsidies to convince the manager to choose $E = H$.

The left hand side of (12) measures the cost to the politician of getting the firm not to restructure, in terms of both the foregone profits and the needed subsidies. The right hand side is the benefit to the politician of high labour spending. When the cost exceeds the benefit, the politician cannot convince the manager not to restructure. To understand why privatisation works in this model, we can compare (12) to (3) and (6).

The difference between (12) and (3) is the presence of the term αk in (12): the cost of getting the firm not to restructure is higher for the politician after privatisation. Privatisation works because, to convince the manager who has control rights to have high labour costs, the politician must compensate him (and shareholders) for foregone profits, which are proportional to the privatised cash flow stake α. In contrast, when the politician controls the firm, he does not need to pay for the profits foregone by the private investors. The politician pays for the profits foregone by the private shareholders with subsidies, and the cost to him of a dollar of subsidies is k. The term αk thus measures the cost to the politician of convincing the manager with control rights not to restructure.

The difference between (12) and (6) is that (12) has αk where (6) has α. When the manager bribes the politician to allow low labour spending, his foregone profits from high labour spending are also fully internalised, except now the cost of a dollar of foregone profits is exactly a dollar. With privatisation rather than bribes, the cost of a dollar of foregone profits is k rather than a dollar, so privatisation is not quite as effective as corruption [(12) is harder to satisfy than (6)]. However, corruption and privatisation work in similar ways: they get the politician to internalise the cost of profits foregone by the manager and outside shareholders. Since corruption has its own problems, privatisation may be the best available way to stimulate restructuring.

When does (12) hold and (3) fail? First, even for a fixed α and $k = m$, the left hand side of (12) is higher than that of (3) because, once control rights are turned over from the politician to the manager, the politician has to compensate the manager for the foregone profits if he wants high employment. By making the politician internalise the cost of the inefficiency borne by the manager and shareholders, this transfer of control encourages restructuring.

Second, when $k > m$, the left hand side of (12) rises with α, and hence higher private ownership is conducive to restructuring. As cash flow ownership is transferred from the Treasury to the manager (and outside shareholders), the politician must pay for excess labour spending not in terms of relatively cheap to him profits foregone by the Treasury, but in terms of relatively expensive to him subsidies. As a result, as more cash flows are privatised, condition (12) is more likely to become satisfied even when (3) fails. When subsidies are costlier to the politician than foregone profits, privatisation of cash flows and not just the transfer of control rights raises the overall cost to the politician of preventing restructuring. In this case, which we regard as the most plausible, a high α is essential for the restructuring to take place.

A high k is naturally interpreted as a tough monetary policy stance. Because a tough monetary stance makes subsidies costly to the politician, it facilitates restructuring. Indeed, condition (12) shows that there is an interaction between k and α: the harder is the monetary policy stance, the lower is the management ownership necessary to bring about restructuring. This result may describe the restructuring in Poland of public but managerially controlled firms during the regime of a restrictive monetary policy, which occurred even before privatisation (see Pinto *et al.* 1993). At the same time, when monetary policy is extremely loose, as it was in Russian in 1993, even high management ownership does not induce managers to give up huge government subsidies and restructure. Indeed, if k is low, no α might be high enough to satisfy (12). More generally, both a high k, meaning a restrictive monetary policy, and a high α might be needed to assure restructuring. We have made this argument informally in our earlier paper on the Russian privatisation (Boycko *et al.* 1993).

We began this paper by asking: how does privatisation work? In this section, we proposed a channel through which privatisation widens the separation between the manager and the politician, and in this way stimulates restructuring. By transferring control from politicians to the managers, privatisation makes politicians accountable for the profits used on excess labour spending, since they need to subsidise the firm to convince managers to incur this spending. By transferring cash flow rights from the Treasury to the managers (and outside shareholders), privatisation forces politicians to pay for these foregone profits not through the relatively cheap mechanism of failing to remit profits to the Treasury, but through a more expensive mechanism of extracting subsidies from the Treasury. Privatisation thus works because, first, it makes politicians pay for the private share of profits, and, second, it raises the cost of such payments.

III. DESIRABLE OWNERSHIP STRUCTURES

In the previous sections, we examined two types of control over firms: that by politicians and that by managers. Managers were not distinguished from outside shareholders. The reality is more complicated. In many countries, enterprise employees get significant control rights even before privatisation. In addition, managers do not always have the same preferences as outside shareholders. In thinking about desirable control structures, we can rank potential shareholders in terms of their concerns for labour spending versus profits. Thus employees are even more concerned about labour spending relative to foregone profits than the politicians. After all, the politicians' interest in labour spending is derived from pressure from the unions and the (potentially) unemployed. Managers in reality are in between politicians and outside shareholders, since managers have some concern for empire building/employment whereas outsiders have none.

The fundamental implication of our analysis is that the closer are shareholders' tastes to those of the politicians, the less likely restructuring is to occur. When these shareholders get control rights, it is relatively cheaper for politicians to convince them not to restructure through the use of subsidies.

This simple logic has several implications. First, it suggests that worker control is bad for restructuring. Workers are unlikely to want layoffs necessary for restructuring to begin with, especially if they can get subsidies. Formally, if we replace the manager's objective function (2) by one that puts some weight on labour spending, it is easy to check that restructuring is less likely. This result confirms well established scepticism about worker control (as opposed to control-free cash flow ownership common in the United States and other countries – see Hansmann (1990)). It is also consistent with scepticism about significant worker ownership in privatisation (Lipton and Sachs, 1990; Boycko *et al.* 1993).

Second, very similar logic suggests that, from the point of view of restructuring, control by large outside investors, who are unlikely to care about employment, is superior to control by managers, who care about it more. The reason, as before, is that large investors are harder to convince through subsidies not to restructure since their tastes are farther away from those of the politicians. In addition, large outside investors, unlike managers, need not be cash constrained, and hence could afford a larger ownership stake α, which also makes effective subsidisation harder. This result suggests that the presence of large outside investors is conducive to efficiency (see Shleifer and Vishny, 1986). It accords well with recommendations for core investors for East European privatisation programmes (see Frydman and Rapaczynski, 1991; Lipton and Sachs, 1990, and Phelps *et al.* 1993), which also happens to be a common practice in other countries, such as Mexico and France.

The result on desirability of large shareholders should be interpreted carefully. The reason that outside shareholders promote restructuring is their interest in profits. If large shareholders are politicised, in the sense that they are pressured or bribed to bring their objectives in line with those of the politicians, they can become detrimental to restructuring. In Russia, for example, politicians want to create industrial holding companies that become core investors in privatised firms. This strategy is designed to increase political influence on firms, not to reduce it. Indeed, throughout the world, government holding companies come to represent the tastes of the politicians, and as a result, slow down rather than encourage restructuring.

A more subtle example of the same potential danger would be privatisation in Poland, in which several government-sponsored mutual funds are to become controlling shareholders of privatising companies through a free allocation of shares to these funds, which in turn are to be owned by Polish citizens. This programme is intended to be a quick way to bring core investors to privatised firms, provided that those investors maximise profits. If, in contrast, the government-regulated mutual funds come to represent the preferences of politicians, they might work to prevent restructuring rather than facilitate it. To be effective, large blockholders must be private parties whose objective is to maximise profits.

IV. CONCLUSION

This paper started with an empirically plausible assumption that the inefficiency of state firms results from their pursuing well specified objectives of politicians, such as excess labour spending. We have presented a model in which privatisation effectively drives a wedge between politicians and managers, i.e., depoliticises firms and leads to their restructuring, even when politicians can use subsidies to convince privatised firms not to restructure, In this model, privatisation and an effective stabilisation policy can work together to make restructuring more likely, by making it too costly for politicians to subsidise firms.

At a more general level, this paper tried to show that the critical agency problem that explains the inefficiency of public firms is the agency problem with politicians rather than that with managers. We believe that managerial discretion problems are usually minor relative to political discretion problems. Privatisation works because it controls political discretion.

Russian Privatisation Centre

Harvard University

University of Chicago

References

Boycko, Maxim, Shleifer, Andrei and Vishny, Robert W. (1993). 'Privatizing Russia.' *Brookings Papers on Economic Activity*, no. 2, pp. 139–92.

Coase, Ronald H. (1960). 'The problem of social cost.' *Journal of Law and Economics*, vol. 3, pp. 1–44.

Dewatripont, Mathias and Maskin, Eric S. (1990). 'Credit and efficiency in centralized and decentralized economies.' Harvard University (mimeo).

Donahue, John D. (1989). *The Privatization Process*. New York: Basic Books.

Frydman, Roman and Rapaczynski, Andrzej (1991). 'Markets and institutions in large-scale privatization.' In *Reforming Central and Eastern European Economies* (ed. V. Corbo, F. Coricelli and J. Bossak). Washington, D.C.: The World Bank.

Grossman, Sanford J. and Hart, Oliver D. (1986). 'The costs and benefits of ownership: a theory of vertical and lateral integration.' *Journal of Political Economy*, vol. 94, pp. 691–719.

Hansmann, Henry (1990). 'When does workers' ownership work? ESOPs, law firms, codetermination and economic democracy.' *Yale Law Journal*, vol. 99, pp. 1749–816.

Kikeri, Sunita, Nellis, John and Shirley, Mary (1992). *Privatization: The Lessons of Experience*. Washington, DC: The World Bank.

Kornai, Janos (1979). 'Resource *vs.* demand-constrained systems.' *Econometrica*, vol. 47, pp. 801–19.

Leff, Nathaniel (1964). 'Economic development through bureaucratic corruption.' *American Behavioral Scientist*, vol. 8, pp. 8–14.

Li, Daokui (1992). 'Public ownership as the cause of a soft budget constraint.' Harvard (mimeo).

Lipton, David and Sachs, Jeffrey D. (1990). 'Privatization in Eastern Europe: the case of Poland.' *Brookings Papers on Economic Activity*, pp. 293–341.

Lopez de Silanes, Florencio (1994). 'Determinants of privatization prices.' Harvard (mimeo).

Megginson, William L, Nash, Robert C. and van Randenborgh, Mathias (1994). 'The financial and operating performance of newly privatized firms.' *Journal of Finance*, vol. 49, pp. 403–52.

Mueller, Dennis C. (1989). *Public Choice*. Cambridge: Cambridge University Press.

Phelps, Edmund S., Frydman, Roman, Rapaczynski, Andrzej and Shleifer, Andrei (1993). 'Needed mechanisms for corporate governance and finance in Eastern Europe.' *Economics of Transition*, vol. 1 (2).

Pinto, Brian, Belka, M. and Krajewski, S. (1993). 'Transforming state enterprises in Poland: evidence on adjustment by manufacturing firms.' *Brookings Papers on Economic Activity*, pp. 213–70.

Rose-Ackerman, Susan (1978). *Corruption: A Study of Political Economy*. New York: Academic Press.

Schmidt, Klaus (1990). 'The costs and benefits of privatization (mimeo), MIT.

Shapiro, Carl and Willig, Robert D. (1990). 'Economic rationales for the scope of privatization.' In *The Political Economy of Public Sector Reform and Privatization* (ed. E. N. Suleiman and J. Waterbury). London: Westview Press, pp. 55–87.

Shleifer, Andrei (1994). 'Establishing property rights.' *Proceedings of the World Bank Annual Conference on Development Economics*, pp. 93–117.

Shleifer, Andrei and Vishny, Robert W. (1986). 'Large shareholders and corporate control.' *Journal of Political Economy*, vol. 94, pp. 461–88.

Shleifer, Andrei and Vishny, Robert W. (1993). 'Corruption.' *Quarterly Journal of Economics*, vol. 108, pp. 599–618.

Shleifer, Andrei and Vishny, Robert W. (1994). 'Politicians and firms.' *Quarterly Journal of Economics*, vol. 109, pp. 995–1025.

Tirole, Jean (1991). 'Privatization in Eastern Europe: incentives and the economics of transition.' *NBER Macroeconomics Annual*, vol. 5, pp. 221–67.

Vining, Aiden and Boardman, Anthony (1992). 'Ownership *vs.* competition: efficiency in public enterprise.' *Public Choice*, vol. 73, pp. 205–39.

[18]

PRIVATISATION

The conceptual framework

INTRODUCTION

In the last decade many countries have introduced privatisation programmes. In 1995 the value of state sell-offs is reported to have reached a record figure of US$73bn with at least forty-five countries in the process of privatising some industries (*Economist*, 13 January 1996, p. 5). This figure may exaggerate the degree of true privatisation since some governments choose to describe the sale to the private sector of only a small part of the total shareholding as a privatisation. Nevertheless, there can be no doubting the profound effect of world-wide privatisation on industrial organisation both in the developed and the developing world.

Table 1.1 UK privatisation proceeds

Year	*£mn at 1994–5 prices*
1979–80	0.4
1980–1	0.2
1981–2	0.5
1982–3	0.5
1983–4	1.1
1984–5	2.0
1985–6	2.7
1986–7	4.5
1987–8	5.1
1988–9	7.1
1989–90	4.2
1990–1	5.3
1991–2	7.9
1992–3	8.2
1993–4	5.4
1994–5	6.4
1995–6	2.4
1996–7	4.0e
1997–8	2.5e
1998–9	1.5e

Source: H.M. Treasury, 1995.
Note: e = estimates.

THE IMPACT OF PRIVATISATION

This book is concerned with privatisation in the UK where, since 1979, over £60bn of UK business assets have been transferred from the state sector to the private sector. At first the annual value of sales was low but, as reflected in the figures in Table 1.1, since the mid-1980s sales have regularly exceeded £5bn per annum, reaching a figure of over £8bn in 1992–3. Table 1.2 provides a summary listing of the main industrial privatisations since 1979 in the UK. Whole industries, such as water, electricity and gas supply, have been affected, along with large sections of the transport, aerospace and telecommunications industries. Because of the size and scope of the privatisation programme, the UK is an obvious candidate for studying the economic effects of this policy. Also, sufficient time has now passed since the early privatisations to begin to assess their longer-term economic impact.

Table 1.2 Major privatisations in the UK

Organisation	*Year of first share sale*	*Industry*
British Petroleum	1979	Oil
National Enterprise Board Investments	1980	Various
British Aerospace	1981	Aerospace
Cable & Wireless	1981	Telecoms
Amersham International	1982	Scientific goods
National Freight Corporation	1982	Road transport
Britoil	1982	Oil
British Rail Hotels	1983	Hotels
Associated British Ports	1983	Ports
British Leyland (Rover)	1984	Car producer
British Telecom (BT)	1984	Telecoms
Enterprise Oil	1984	Oil
Sealink	1984	Sea transport
British Shipbuilders & Naval Dockyards	1985	Ship building
National Bus Company	1986	Transport
British Gas	1986	Gas
Rolls-Royce	1987	Aero-engines
British Airports Authority	1987	Airports
British Airways	1987	Airlines
Royal Ordnance Factories	1987	Armaments
British Steel	1988	Steel
Water	1989	Water
Electricity distribution	1990	Electricity
Electricity generation	1991	Electricity
Trust Ports	1992	Ports
Coal industry	1995	Coal
Railways	1995–7	Railways
Nuclear energy	1996	Electricity

In the UK, as in many other countries, the political pressure for privatisation came from a combination of disillusionment with the results of state ownership and from a belief that private ownership would bring substantial economic benefits. State-owned industries were viewed as highly inefficient, slow at developing and introducing new technologies, subject to over-frequent and damaging political intervention and dominated by powerful trade unions (Veljanovski, 1987). Privatisation seemed to offer a means of ridding the state of the financial burden of loss-making activities, while at the same time spreading share ownership and curtailing union power (Arbomeit, 1986). Moreover, privatisation sales offered a tempting source of state funding at a time when economic policy was geared to reducing the public sector borrowing requirement (PSBR).

From the beginning, government ministers have stuck tenaciously to the argument that the privatisation programme has been an outstanding success story, especially in terms of increasing efficiency. For example, John Moore, the Financial Secretary to the Treasury in charge of the privatisation programme in the mid-1980s, stated in a speech in November 1983 that:

> The privatisation programme is coherent, and well thought out. It holds substantial advantages for the management of the industries, their employees, the consumer and the taxpayer. And it also, of course, brings benefits to the PSBR and furthers our objectives of reducing the size of the public sector. But these important by-products are secondary to the main theme. Our main objective is to promote competition and improve efficiency.
>
> (Moore, 1983)

In a later statement he returned to the subject now certain that the source of performance gains lay in the nature of state ownership:

> To begin with, the priorities of elected politicians are different from and often in conflict with the priorities of effective business managers. Yet, in state-owned industries politicians are in charge, which means that whenever politicians cannot resist getting involved in what should be management decisions, political priorities take precedence over commercial ones. Politicians may overrule commercial judgements in order to build a new factory in an area where voters need jobs or they may refuse to close an uneconomical plant. They can become involved in policies affecting the hiring and the size of the workforce.
>
> (Moore, 1992, p. 117)

Inefficiency is, allegedly, the inevitable result. Similarly, Tim Eggar, Minister for Industry and Energy, felt able to summarise recently the certain and enormous economic benefits that had resulted from the government's privatisation programme as 'price reductions; the shake up of old management practices leading to large efficiency improvements and dramatically falling costs; and . . . improvements in standards of service' (Eggar, 1995, p. 7).

THE IMPACT OF PRIVATISATION

A more critical commentary, however, would note that the programme has been dogged from the outset by some incoherence. In particular, the government had a number of objectives for privatisation that are potentially contradictory. For example, the promotion of quick and successful asset sales sits uneasily alongside a desire to promote competition in industries previously supplied by state monopolies and to raise funds to reduce the PSBR. Monopolies with their more or less guaranteed profits fetch a higher price in the stock market than an identical firm facing intense competition in the product market. In addition, the promotion of small shareholdings, by favouring the small investor during flotation sales, may be inconsistent with the imposition of an effective capital market constraint on managerial behaviour. The government has based its case for privatisation largely on the benefits that it produces in terms of competition in the product market and the pressure private investors place on management to manage efficiently. However, a number of state-owned companies were already operating in competitive markets and others retained their monopoly at privatisation. Moreover, large share-holders are arguably more likely than small investors to manage their share portfolios actively to maximise income and capital gains; a point we return to later.

This book is concerned with the primary rationale for privatisation both in the UK and elsewhere and as evidenced in the above statements by government ministers, John Moore and Tim Eggar, that is to say, the impact of privatisation on efficiency. The remainder of this chapter is concerned with developing a conceptual framework for the analysis of privatisation and efficiency, in which some of the above contradictions will feature. The concern is with why ownership may matter from an economic point of view. Chapter 2 provides a brief history of each of the eleven organisations that are the subject of this study. In chapter 3 the principles and method of performance assessment are discussed, including the meaning of 'efficiency'. Chapter 4 is concerned with a review of earlier studies of public versus private efficiency and the effects of privatisation.[1] Chapters 5–8 provide a detailed investigation of pre- and post-privatisation performance for a selected group of eleven enterprises privatised in the UK in the 1980s. Performance is assessed using a variety of performance measures: labour and total factor productivity, value-added, the rate of profit, and an efficiency frontier method. Data are also provided on the distribution of business income, wage relativities and employment pre- and post-privatisation. Chapter 9 looks at how privatisation has affected the internal organisation of the firms in this study. Chapter 10 provides conclusions and draws lessons for industrial policy in the UK and overseas, especially for other countries pursuing privatisation policies. The chapter also attempts to answer the central question: has privatisation been successful in improving efficiency?

PRIVATISATION: THE CONCEPTUAL FRAMEWORK

PROPERTY RIGHTS, PUBLIC CHOICE AND INCOMPLETE CONTRACTS: AN AGENT–PRINCIPAL FRAMEWORK

In the privatisation literature state enterprises are said to be inefficient because:

a. state-owned industries suffer from excessive political intervention;
b. management in state industries have vague, fluctuating and often conflicting objectives. Political time frames are often incompatible with the longer time cycles that successful investment needs;
c. politicians and civil servants fail to monitor managerial behaviour as effectively as the private capital market and, amongst other things, this leads to over-investment (Rees, 1989; Pryke, 1981) and the trading of more output for lower profits (Pint, 1991);
d. trade unions in the public sector are able to succeed in obtaining above market wages, employment levels and conditions of work at the expense of consumers (so-called rent-seeking behaviour) (Windle, 1991);
e. bankruptcy is not a credible threat when there are seemingly unlimited taxpayers' funds to call upon;
f. managerial salaries in the public sector are politically determined and rarely compare well with the pay of equivalent jobs in the private sector. Consequently, the quality of management suffers;
g. there is a lack of performance related rewards in the public sector;
h. public sector firms are insufficiently consumer orientated when operating in monopoly markets; and
i. state ownership confuses the regulation of the activities of industry with the role of ownership so that state regulation is less effective.

Clearly, there are some difficulties with these arguments. For example, the suggestion that some labour groups (workers) receive an above market wage while others (managers) earn a below market rate seems slightly contradictory. Or if paying a below market rate to one group reduces their quality, then paying an above market rate to another group would presumably lead this part of the workforce to be of a better than average quality. Nevertheless, research suggests that the record of state ownership in the UK accords with a number of these weaknesses, including politically motivated pricing, distorted investment programmes and uneasy industrial relations (NEDO, 1976; and see chapter 4). In their influential study of privatisation Vickers and Yarrow conclude that:

> The history of the nationalized industries has shown that . . . a system of control that relies heavily upon agents' internalization of the public interest objectives is unlikely to produce good performance. In the event . . . the results of the policy failure have included widespread goal displacement, lack of clarity in corporate objectives, overlapping

> responsibilities and excessive ministerial intervention in operational decisions. These in turn have had detrimental effects on the pricing, investment and internal efficiency performance of the nationalized industries.
>
> (Vickers and Yarrow, 1988, p. 151)

Given these perceived failures of state ownership, Rees (1989, p. 108) predicts that privatisation will lead to 'higher prices, lower outputs, higher labour productivity, lower employment, and lower wage rates, since these are the consequences in the model of tightening the profit constraint'. Other results of privatisation are said to be: more commercial management; greater consumer focus and more imaginative marketing; improved capital usage; less damaging state interference; and more effective regulation of industries in the public interest (Veljanovski, 1987).

A useful starting point for the economic analysis of privatisation is agent–principal theory. Agency situations arise when one party (principals, such as shareholders) delegate to another party (agents, such as managers) decisions over the use of their property or property rights (Jensen and Meckling, 1976; Arrow, 1985; Fama and Jensen, 1983). This arrangement may be economically efficient from a specialisation or comparative advantage perspective, but agency relationships raise the prospect of divergent goals. The agenda of the agents may well not be the same as those of the principals, especially since agents can be expected to be self-interested. In particular, principals are at risk of slacking and other dysfunctional behaviour by agents that reduces the underlying value of the property rights.

This can be illustrated as follows: in both the public and private sectors managerial utility can be expressed as a function of profit (Π) and quantities of inputs. Hence $U = U(,I)$ where $U(.)$ takes the usual shape and is a twice continuously differentiable concave function and I is a vector of inputs. The manager's utility will be related to profit if he or she owns shares, benefits from profit-related pay, gains prestige from high profit or where higher profit improves job security. Inputs enter the utility function because the manager's income may rise when there are more employees and a larger capacity to manage or extra employees may mean more free time. Profit is the product of costs deducted from revenue. The cost efficiency of the firm will be weaker the smaller the relationship between the manager's utility and profit, and the stronger the relationship between the manager's utility and the volume of discretionary inputs. Assuming that managers in the public and private sectors pursue either profits or output (or some combination of the two) expressed as Φ, and both require management effort, the management objective is to maximise $\Phi - (\lambda - 1)E$ where E is managerial effort and $\lambda > 1$ reflects the disutility of such effort.

The aim of principals wishing maximum profits must therefore be both to maximise E and to ensure that management effort is directed at maximising profit and not at maximising output and employing discretionary inputs. In practice, the agent knows the amount of useful effort he or she puts into the management of the business. The principal, however, knows the outcome but cannot monitor effort directly. Assuming that costs depend upon (a) environmental random variables that represent factors impacting on the performance of the firm that are outside the agent's control, such as the business cycle, M_i, and (b) the agent's effort at controlling and reducing production costs, E, then total costs, C_i, take the form $C_i = f(M_i, [\lambda - 1]E)$.

The principal monitors C_i but in a world of imperfect information cannot be certain whether an inflated C_i is the result of changes in M_i or E. To ensure that E is maximised the principals must write and enforce a contract with the agent to maximise effort. Given that E is known to the agent but not the principals, an incentive system must be designed to maximise E irrespective of the M_i states so that agent maximisation of effort becomes the dominant strategy. The differences between public and private ownership, therefore, can be reduced to the efficacy of the incentive mechanism.

This discussion suggests that if privatisation is to lead to more managerial effort leading to efficiency gains in the organisation, it must involve improved policing of agent behaviour or more constraints on managerial discretion. In other words, a change in ownership involves a new agent–principal relationship with new forms of information and incentive regimes in a world of incomplete contracts.

Ownership and competition

When a state-owned monopoly is privatised, the government might also introduce competition into the product market (that is, remove the company's monopoly). Economists have a predilection for competition. The first fundamental theorem in welfare economics states that, under certain conditions, a competitive equilibrium in a market economy is Pareto efficient since when this exists no one can be made better off through a resource reallocation without making someone else worse off. The second fundamental theorem broadly states that most such Pareto-efficient outcomes can be achieved in a perfectly competitive economy, provided redistribution is dealt with first.

> As with all theorems, certain assumptions have to be made if the theory is to hold. In particular, the first theorem assumes the absence of externalities in consumption or production, and the technical conditions required for the second are relatively onerous. But broadly speaking the two theorems together amount to saying that competition produces efficiency and, if the outcome is inequitable, this can be dealt with as a separate issue.
>
> (Waterson, 1995, p. 132)

THE IMPACT OF PRIVATISATION

Empirical study of the effect of competition on productivity in manufacturing has borne out that it affects both the level and growth rate positively (Nickell, 1993). Competition sharpens the incentives for management to manage the firm's assets efficiently. Also, where there is competition, the firm's profits reflect and identify differences in managerial ability creating a link between the product and capital markets. At the same time, however, privatisation may have no effect on competition. Monopolies might be sold-off with their monopoly powers wholly or largely intact while many state-owned firms have traditionally operated in competitive markets. Thus conceptually, the impact of ownership and competition (in the product market) are quite distinct, and while the positive effect of competition on performance is a relatively uncontroversial one in economic theory, the impact of ownership *per se* is much less well determined. In this book, the primary focus is on the impact of ownership (although where competitive conditions change this is noted since the results may be influenced by the change in the product market).

If competition in the product market does not alter when privatisation occurs then the source of any performance improvement will lie in a change in the capital market, that is to say directly in the change of ownership. Privatisation subjects enterprises to the discipline of the competitive capital market, which many believe imposes a more effective constraint on managerial discretionary behaviour than political control (Crain and Zardkoohi, 1980; Pera, 1989, p. 181). The result, it is claimed, is higher efficiency even under similar product market conditions.

The argument is that in the private sector owners can trade their shares in the capital market and this constrains managerial behaviour. If management lose the confidence of their shareholders the share price falls, which may trigger a hostile takeover bid (Alchian, 1965; Jensen and Meckling, 1976; Fama, 1980). Alternatively, management may be deposed by large shareholders when performance disappoints at company annual general meetings (AGMs) or on other occasions (Aoki, 1983; Leech, 1987). In contrast, in the public sector there are no shares to trade and managerial appointments depend upon government decisions which may not be heavily weighted by economic results (Zeckhauser and Horn, 1989, p. 35).

The possible impact of both the product and capital markets on performance can be discussed with the aid of Figure 1.1. Position A represents a monopoly supplier in the public sector. With no or very limited product market competition and taxpayer funding, incentives for management to achieve high efficiency in their firms are poor. Hence the expectation is that efficiency will be low. By contrast, position D represents a competitive firm raising funding from the private capital market. Here the expectation is that there are high incentives for management to operate their firms efficiently. Both the product market (competition) and the capital market (tradeable

	Monopoly	Competition
Public ownership	A	B
Private ownership	C	D

Figure 1.1 Alternative ownership and competitive regimes

shares) constraints apply. B and C are in effect intermediate positions, they represent mid-way states in which either the product market or capital market constraints on behaviour are limited. The expectation would be that the performance of firms in positions B and C will be higher than firms in position A but not as high as those in position D. The expectation would be that maximum efficiency gains will arise when privatisation is combined with the introduction of competition in the product market; that is, where there is a move from point A to D. Smaller gains might be anticipated when the movement is from position A to C (privatising a monopolist) or from B to D (privatising a firm in a competitive market). Gains would also be anticipated when exposing a state-owned monopoly to competition (moving from A to B) or when exposing a privately owned monopoly to competition (moving from C to D).

Differences in behaviour under state and private ownership may be compounded by differences in objectives. In the private sector although profit may not always be pursued rigorously and consistently there is, nevertheless, a clear bottom line. If losses continue to be made ultimately the firm will fail. In the state sector, however, objectives are often vague and tend to change according to the political climate, leading to uncertainty about long-term strategy within the industries. Public enterprises pursue multiple and often blurred or ill-articulated objectives which may help to mask inefficiency. Privatisation should change and clarify the objectives of the enterprise as well as affecting managers' incentives to achieve these goals (Bös, 1991). At its most simple, profit maximisation will replace wider and less well articulated goals to do with welfare maximisation. But it is important to note that whether this actually translates into higher efficiency and how the efficiency gains are distributed in terms of profits and prices is complex. For example, De Fraja (1993) argues that because consumer surplus enters into the government's social welfare function, but not the shareholders' profit function, the government has more to gain from a given improvement in the firm's efficiency. Higher efficiency leading to lower prices benefits the consumer but not shareholders. If managers' utility enters the social welfare function then the government will pay the managers more, inducing a higher effort level. 'The results contained in the present paper considerably strengthen the hand of those favouring public ownership by showing that the latter is not only not necessarily less productively efficient, but in some circumstances more productively efficient...' (De Fraja, 1993, p. 24).

This result emphasises the dangers of drawing a set of conclusions about relative performance in the state and private sectors. Taking into account objectives, which can be expected to be different in the public and private sectors, complicates the analysis of performance and this is pursued in chapter 3. At the same time, De Fraja's analysis is only one possible outcome and differs from that of the public choice and property rights literatures detailed below. It also seems to conflict with the arguments of some economists, such as Bös and Peters (1989), who show that under certain conditions the monitoring of employees can be more effectively undertaken in private sector firms.

Property rights

Especially important in shaping attitudes towards public and private ownership have been the public choice and property rights literatures in economics. Although they developed separately, and have two distinct analytical traditions, they produce highly complementary conclusions. Lindblom defines property rights as follows:

> Property is a set of rights to control assets: to refuse use of them to others, to hold them intact, or to use them up. Property rights are consequently grants of authority made to persons and organizations, both public and private and acknowledged by other persons and organizations.
>
> (Lindblom, 1977, p. 26)

A standard property rights approach to public and private ownership acknowledges that there are agency problems in all forms of ownership, but that because ownership is transferable through a competitive capital market in the private sector, a better use of resources results. Monitoring by residual claimants is more efficient than monitoring through the political process. The literature lays heavy emphasis upon the attenuation of property rights where public ownership exists and, in turn, explores the consequences of attenuated property rights for efficiency.

Drawing upon seminal work by Coase (1937), the firm is perceived to be a 'nexus of contracts' between management, labour, suppliers, shareholders and other stakeholders (Jensen and Meckling, 1976; Fama, 1980; Aoki, 1983; Hart and Holmstrom, 1987; Aoki *et al.*, 1990). The boundary of the firm is determined by the relative costs of transacting for inputs in the market as against employment within the firm given: (a) information asymmetries between contractors; (b) an inability to write complete contracts covering all contingencies; and (c) the costs of monitoring contract compliance (Marschak and Radner, 1972; Arrow, 1974, 1987; Williamson, 1975; Holmstrom and Tirole, 1989). In certain circumstances it will be more cost efficient in terms of transaction costs to employ inputs directly, in other cases it will be more efficient to contract in the market. In terms of the privatisation debate, this analysis draws attention to the important role of contracting for inputs and of monitoring their performance within firms. If employment within firms is to be more efficient than contracting in the market then the inputs must be efficiently managed. Equally, the success of one firm compared to another derives from more efficient contracting leading to higher performance.

Alchian and Demsetz (1972) have argued that the firm is a team of factor suppliers with contracts established and monitored by management. It is the role of management to ensure that there is no free-riding or slacking in the team, but, since there are costs in terms of time and effort in devising an optimal monitoring-reward system, to perform this task well management need an incentive (also see Jensen and Meckling, 1976). In the property rights literature the incentive is profit (usually referred to in the property rights literature as 'the residual'). This leads to the expectation that private sector organisations in which rights to profits are clearly defined will perform better than those in the public sector where rights, it is claimed, are diffused and uncertain (Alchian, 1965, 1977; Furubotn and Pejovich, 1972 and 1974; De Alessi, 1980; McCormick and Meiners, 1988). Consequently, the monitoring of management by owners is likely to be much more effective in the private sector. In sum, the property rights literature is concerned with the *incentives* to monitor agent behaviour effectively under public and private ownership.

Public choice, incomplete contracts and agency relationships

In contrast, public choice theory is concerned more directly with actual *behaviour* in the public sector. At the core of this literature is the argument that politicians and state bureaucrats pursue their own utility rather than the public interest (Downs, 1967; Niskanen, 1971, 1987; Tullock, 1965; Buchanan, 1972, 1978; Blankart, 1983; Mitchell, 1988; Mueller, 1989; Aranson, 1990). Policies are arranged to maximise votes, thereby securing the careers of the politicians, and departmental budgets are expanded so that bureaucrats benefit from better jobs and higher salaries (Migue and Belanger, 1974; Orzechowski, 1977). It is also claimed that public monitoring of spending is inhibited in the state sector because bureaucrats will have more information than taxpayers about the consequences of budgetary changes (Olson, 1965; Kristensen, 1980; Breton and Wintrobe, 1982). Civil servants gather information and can lobby for their budgets as a matter of course in their jobs. By contrast, it will usually be quite rational behaviour for any individual member of the public not to seek out the information needed to monitor state spending adequately. For any individual, the costs of information gathering and lobbying (the political transaction costs) are likely to far exceed the benefits that would accrue directly from success in changing policy. This may not be true, however, for interest groups, such as trade unions representing employees in the public sector or major suppliers. In consequence, the public sector is fertile ground for rent-seeking activity. In particular, the argument suggests that trade unions will inflate wage demands and staffing levels and contractors will gather high profits (Tullock, 1976; Bhagwati, 1982). The expectation in the property rights literature is that this will be especially true in countries where state industries raise little or no capital on the open market (as, for example, in the UK) and hence are not open to the sanction of the private capital market.

Together the property rights and public choice literatures suggest that state-owned and privately-owned firms will differ in behaviour and hence performance because of differences in: (a) management's objective function; and (b) constraints. In effect, the fundamental differences between state and private enterprise reduce to a matter of incentives in the face of incomplete information leading to differences in behaviour (Hart and Holmstrom, 1987; Holmstrom and Tirole, 1989; Shapiro and Willig, 1990, p. 55). Hence, incompleteness of contract becomes the starting point for the theory of ownership. If contracts were complete ownership would not matter since managerial discretionary behaviour would be avoided through the contract (Grossman and Hart, 1986; Hart, 1993, pp. 140–1). It is the inability of principals to write complete contracts for their agents covering all possible contingencies and to perfectly monitor and enforce such contracts that leads to scope for managerial discretionary behaviour or agency problems (Hart, 1995).

Two types of information problem may exist where there are incomplete contracts: *adverse selection* (as a result of hidden information) and *moral hazard* (hidden action) (Jensen and Meckling, 1976; Arrow, 1985; Laffont, 1989). In both the public and private sectors there are agent–principal relationships which are characterised by asymmetric information leading potentially to adverse selection and moral hazard (Ross, 1973; Mitnick, 1980; Jackson, 1985; Rees, 1985; Bös and Peters, 1991). This necessitates the creation of efficiency incentive systems. In the economics literature, the solution to an agent–principal problem involves the development of an

Private ownership	Public ownership
Shareholders	Public
↓	↓
Agent:	Tiers of agents:
Directors	Elected representatives (MPs)
	↓
	Government ministers and 'sponsoring' departments (for example, Department of Industry for British Coal)
	↓
	Boards of 'quangos' and nationalised industries

Figure 1.2 Flows of information between principals and agents in the public and private sectors

effective incentive package that binds the agents to follow the objectives of the principals.

In the private sector an important agency relationship exists between shareholders (principals) and directors (agents). At its simplest, the shareholders own the enterprise and appoint directors to manage it on their behalf. The implications of this relationship for efficiency in the private sector are explored below. In the public sector, by contrast, the agent–principal relationship is more complex because the ultimate owners of state assets, the principals, are the public. Between the public and the managers of the assets (the boards of state industries) exist layers of agencies (Aharoni, 1982). The greater complexity of the agency relationship is illustrated in Figure 1.2.

The existence of layers of agents seems to provide more scope for 'noise' to distort the information flow between principals and resource managers (Smith, 1990, p. 55). Hence privatisation can be viewed as changing the nature of the agent–principal relationship to reduce this noise and therefore facilitate the introduction of more effective incentive systems that bind agents to the principals' goals (Rees, 1985). The failure of the ballot box, especially in the face of rent seeking groups, to control agents in the public sector is well documented (see, for example, Crew and Rowley, 1988; Mitchell, 1988; Carroll, 1990). Arrow's impossibility theorem (1963) states that it is not possible for multiple principals to generate social choices that are consistent with transitivity, Pareto efficiency and independence of irrelevant alternatives in the absence of a dictator. Though the probabilistic voting literature can demonstrate that under certain circumstances political competition for votes may lead to socially efficient outcomes (Wintrobe, 1987; Mueller, 1989, p. 214; Peltzman, 1990, 1992), the more general view is that in practice the ballot box is much less reliable than market signals (Borcherding, 1977). In terms of Hirschman's (1970) terminology, 'voice' through the political process is a more inferior indicator of public demands than 'exit' (sale of shares) in the competitive capital market.

According to public choice theory, the result of the agent–principal relationship in the public sector is an over-expansion of state budgets leading to waste or inefficiency. Various models have been put forward leading broadly to this conclusion. For instance, Navajas (1984) assumes that state enterprises can be modelled according to a minister wishing to maximise the difference between the sum of total consumer surpluses plus profit, and managerial income. This occurs in an environment where there is asymmetric information and incompatible preferences. Rees (1984) uses a model that assumes managers want to maximise output, and hence income and utility, and workers want to maximise real wages and employment. More generally, models have been developed based on managerial utility maximisation (for a review see Lawson, 1994) but with different variables entering into the utility function.

In the words of a leading proponent of public choice theory, William A. Niskanen, government officials (bureaucrats) pursue their own utility which is held to be a function of 'salary, perquisites of the office, public regulation, power, patronage, output of the bureau, ease of making changes, and ease in managing the bureau' (Niskanen, 1971, p. 38). All but the last two relate to the size of the bureau and, therefore, the expectation is that public outputs will be over-supplied. Niskanen (1973, p. 33) concludes that the output of a monopoly government bureau will be twice as large as provision in competitive private markets (though for critical reviews of this conclusion see Jackson, 1982, pp. 131–5; Cullis and Jones, 1987, ch.6; and Dunleavy, 1991, pp. 156–62). Others have suggested that too low a rate of discount will be used when appraising investments and there will be excessive employment of labour (see, for example, Buchanan and Tullock, 1962; Buchanan, 1968, 1986; Tullock, 1976; Breton, 1974; Orzechowski, 1977; Breton and Wintrobe, 1975). Tullock (1979, p. 34) argues that as a result, and as a rough rule of thumb, public sector outputs will be twice as costly as they would be if privately supplied.

Whatever the precise outcome in terms of over-production and other inefficiencies, there can be no doubting the powerful effect of the property rights and public choice theories on the academic literature on privatisation since the 1970s. Together they have provided a formidable *a priori* argument in favour of reducing state budgets and, wherever possible, transferring state activities to the private sector.

CRITICISMS OF THE PROPERTY RIGHTS/PUBLIC CHOICE APPROACH

This literature, however, is not free from weakness. Drawing a sharp distinction between the public and private sectors may be misleading. Arguably ownership is best viewed as a continuum of organisational types. In the UK, these range from the archetypal government bureaucracy (for example, the Foreign Office) through various types of agencies (such as trading funds, 'next steps' agencies and public corporations), through to private sectors firms heavily dependent on government contracts (for example, construction and defence businesses), limited liability companies, and lastly the archetypal entrepreneurial small business (such as the corner grocery store) (Dahl and Lindblom, 1953; Rainey, Backoff and Levine, 1976; Bozeman, 1987; Dunsire *et al.*, 1988; Perry and Rainey, 1988; Rainey, 1991). At the same time *all* firms, whatever their legal ownership, are subject to *some* degree of state influence, namely through regulations, taxes and the impact of macroeconomic management on demand, prices and interest rates.

An emphasis upon ownership as a continuum always involving some state intervention suggests that it might be too simplistic to presume some readily identifiable public versus private split in organisational design and orientation. Public sector and private sector firms may have similarities that define their behaviour and performance more clearly than the presumed differences. Interestingly, two of the privatised firms whose performance is studied in detail in this book, Rolls-Royce and British Aerospace, have remained highly dependent upon state contracts, while a number of other firms have remained state regulated, as detailed later.

Two further criticisms can be made of the approach to ownership differences in the property rights and public choice literatures: first the attitude to motivation in the public sector; and second the supposed working of the capital market in the private sector.

At the heart of the public choice model is the neoclassical rational actor or maximising individual. Agents are considered to behave rationally in a self-regarding way and through the pursuit of self-interest they optimise their preferences in a consistent fashion. This is held to be as true of politicians and employees in the state sector as it is elsewhere in the economy. The resulting perspective on motivation in the public sector contrasts markedly with the Weberian notion of disinterested officials pursuing the public interest which underpinned public ownership in the UK in the 1940s.[2] The chief architect of post-war nationalisation, the Labour minister Herbert Morrison, applied the phrase 'high custodians of the public interest' to the new boards of state industries.

Motivation

From its inherent assumptions about individual motivation based on rational self-seeking behaviour, public choice theory leads to the conclusion that state employees pursue their own interests even when they clearly conflict with the public interest. This may be a correct view of the public sector, but on the other hand it may seriously misrepresent how employees in the public sector actually behave. Certainly, the organisational behaviour literature for a long time has argued that the motivational needs of individuals in organisations are more complex than as represented by neoclassical utility-maximising man (Maslow, 1964; Herzberg, 1966). Maslow argued that individuals have a hierarchy of needs, which range from physiological needs at the lowest level (such as food and warmth), through safety needs, love needs, esteem needs, to self-actualisation at the highest level. Neoclassical economics tends to emphasise low level needs, whereas the concept of 'high custodians' is more commensurate with esteem and self-actualisation needs important to high income groups.

Since the management of public enterprises are often recruited from the private sector and have reputations to defend, and senior civil servants and politicians frequently come from higher social backgrounds, from a Maslow perspective we might expect attitudes and behaviour to be similar and concerned with a 'job well done'. Self-interest becomes inter-related with a wider group interest. From doing the job well peer group recognition results (Posner, 1984). In which case, utility maximisation will not necessarily lead to starkly different performance outcomes in the public and private sectors as implied in the public choice literature (for such a discussion of the role of group interest and public choice theory, see Lewin, 1991 and Udehn, 1996). The inclusion of esteem, pride or group respect in people's utility functions is compatible with Gary Becker's more inclusive notion of utility maximisation (Becker, 1976). Furthermore, Fama notes how the labour market for management may capitalise performance in managerial remuneration producing a direct incentive for managers to satisfy owners independent of the precise form of the ownership (Fama, 1980; also Frech, 1980). In its simplest terms, effective management has its own rewards in terms of salary and promotion prospects.

The work on bureaucracy by Downs (1957, 1967), which spawned a good deal of the later public choice literature, recognised that employees in the public sector could have broader motives than purely egotistical ones (such as loyalty to the bureau or nation, pride in the proficient performance of work, and even serving the public interest). Downs work also stands out because he recognised the importance of intra- and inter-bureau relationships. Much of the public choice literature takes a homogeneous view of the public sector. All state bureaucrats are assumed to act identically or, at least, differences in behaviour between officials is considered to be relatively unimportant. This simplification may result in a distorted view of the performance of bureaux and state industries, especially if contrasted with an idealised, entrepreneurial private sector. Downs (1967) reminds us that bureaucracy exists in the private sector too.

In any event the notion that public sector managers may wish to expand their bureaux, for example by using low discount rates when appraising investments, is not the same thing as saying they will be able to do so. Although there may be no private capital market, government employees face extensive political monitoring of their behaviour and performance, including media scrutiny and official audits and enquiries. Certainly the notion that politicians and public servants do pursue the public interest, at least some of the time, should not be entirely discounted (Fiorina and Noll, 1978). This may help to explain why budget maximising models of behaviour have been strikingly unconfirmed by empirical evidence. As Mueller concludes in his review of the public choice literature: 'systematic support for the bureaucracy–size relationship is sparse and contradictory' (Mueller, 1989, p. 339; for a similar view, see Green and Shapiro, 1994). Hood *et al.* (1984), after studying the manner in which the UK civil service reacted to changes in public spending budgets between the early 1970s and the early 1980s, concluded that: 'the link between budgetary increases and bureaucratic utility is neither clearly demonstrable nor universally applicable' (p. 163). There seemed to be no clear relationship between an increment in budget and an increase in bureaucratic benefits represented by changes in total staff and top staff within departments. Dunsire *et al.* (1989) also noted that in times of retrenchment there was no evidence that top civil servants unduly protected their own grades, as might be expected if the utility maximising model is a sufficient predictor of behaviour. Moreover, overall they found no evidence that the salaries of top civil servants had grown faster than the pay of junior staffs or pay in comparable private sector work. A study of changes in public spending in the USA came to a similar conclusion (Peters, 1989).

The fact that the biggest increases in public spending in the UK since the 1960s have occurred in the area of transfer expenditures and outside central government, notably in the NHS and local authorities, also fits uneasily into a public choice framework. If civil servants pursued their own utility and this was linked to the size of the budget, the expectation would be that Whitehall would have protected central government spending and concentrated cuts elsewhere. Moreover, it is difficult to explain the apparent lack of strong opposition within government to privatisation including contracting out, though Dunleavy (1986, 1991) explains this in terms of 'bureau reshaping', which is most costly for the lower grades. Similarly, if state ownership is more compatible with the pursuit of managerial utility than private ownership, the expectation would be that the management of state industries would have opposed privatisation. In fact, the opposite has been true. The top management of state industries have embraced privatisation enthusiastically as an opportunity to shake free from political control.

The private capital market

The second criticism of the public choice and property rights literatures is concerned with the operation of the private capital market. While the disincentive effects of the attenuation of property rights in the public sector are emphasised, a more sanguine attitude is adopted about arrangements in the private sector. In the sole proprietor business there is a clear and direct incentive to be efficient, for slacking and other such behaviour will affect the pecuniary income of the entrepreneur directly. In small partnerships and private companies there may be a slightly less direct but nevertheless still a significant relationship between an individual owner's efforts and his or her income (Farrell and Scotchmer, 1988). However, sole proprietor businesses, partnerships and small companies are not the obvious alternatives to state ownership. Public enterprises are usually replaced by public joint-stock companies (the main exceptions in the UK have been the management buy-outs during the sale of the National Freight Consortium and the break-up of the state-run bus industry).

Mitchell (1983, p. 89) reminds us that, in relation to state spending, 'nobody spends somebody else's money as carefully as he spends his own', but presumably this maxim also applies to the private sector. In public joint stock companies ownership and control are divorced, producing the agent–principal relationship introduced earlier. Capital is raised from the investing public in the shape of equity and the financial institutions in terms of equity and loans, while the control or management of assets is in the hands of professional managers (directors, mainly executive directors). The latter act as agents for the shareholders' interests. The utility of shareholders is advanced by maximising profits (or more precisely the net present value of the firm's current and future profits) as this increases dividends and promotes growth in share values.

Managerial activities which are not intended to increase the utility of the owners of resources are possible because of information asymmetries and incomplete contracts between the directors of boards and their shareholders. Shareholders lack the information to know whether profits are being maximised, and contracts which heavily constrained managerial discretionary behaviour would restrict the ability of management to react to unforeseeable contingencies on behalf of shareholders.

There is a respected literature in economics, dating especially from Berle and Means (1932), which highlights the existence of managerial discretionary behaviour in the private sector when ownership and control are divorced (Baumol, 1959; Marris, 1964; Williamson, 1964; Jensen and Meckling, 1976; Zahra and Pearce, 1989). A more traditional approach in economics has private sector managers maximising profits and retaining or distributing those earnings in the interests of shareholders. By contrast, managerial theories of the firm stress the importance of the separation of ownership and control in modern corporations, leading to discretionary (non-profit) behaviour by managers in the private sector. Interestingly, statements made about management motivation in large private corporations in this literature appear almost identical to those made by Niskanen *et al.* regarding the behaviour of state bureaucrats.

The public choice and property rights literatures concentrate upon the lack of incentive for management in the public sector to minimise inefficiency because public sector management have no rights to profit. But in the public joint stock company, while shareholders will be interested in high profit, directors may be more interested in their own utility. This may be better advanced by director perks, high salaries and bonuses or an 'easy life' rather than by generating more profit. Even though directors may hold shares in the company, and stock options and profit related bonuses schemes have proliferated in recent years, it is still the case that management are largely rewarded by salary. Figures from the British Institute of Management a few years ago, for instance, revealed that the percentage of managers owning shares in their companies was still only around 36 per cent (Mansfield and Poole, 1991). Also, unlike civil servants whose pay and conditions tend to conform to nationally agreed levels, private sector management appear to have considerably more discretion to raise their own pecuniary and non-pecuniary incomes.

In the public choice and property rights literatures the divorce of ownership and control is recognised. But the literature suggests that the capital market restricts managerial discretionary behaviour in the private sector better than political control in the public sector (Fama and Jensen, 1983; Jensen, 1983; Millward and Parker, 1983, pp. 215–17). Firstly, there is a bankruptcy constraint in the private sector. Private sector companies can go bankrupt, while loss making state industries are usually supported from taxpayers' funds.[3] In the UK, the coal and rail industries in particular have a long history of public subsidy and periodic capital write-offs.

Secondly, in the private sector shareholders can attend Annual General Meetings and call directors to account (there are no public AGMs for state enterprises) and more importantly shares can be traded. Most of the relevant literature emphasises selling shares when performance disappoints; a minority of economists have also emphasised the possibility that larger shareholders might depose management (Aoki, 1983; Leech, 1987). Shares will be sold in companies which produce disappointing profits leading to a fall in the share price and this, in turn, increases the likelihood of takeover by new management (this reasoning is similar to that in Marris's (1964) model of the firm, in which managerial utility is a function of the growth rate of the firm, which is limited by the negative effect on the share price of investing for growth). It is the ability to transfer property rights and the associated threat of takeover in the private sector which are emphasised in the property rights literature as the mechanism by which managerial behaviour is constrained in the public joint stock company (Manne, 1965; Alchian, 1965; and, for more recent arguments along the same lines, see Madden, 1981; Coffee, 1986). By contrast, no such tradeable property rights tend to exist for public sector organisations except in 'mixed' public and private enterprises (Boardman and Vining, 1989). The inability to trade property rights in state industries also means that specialisation in ownership cannot occur. It is held that this further reduces effective monitoring of the management in state industries (De Alessi, 1980, pp. 27–8). In the private sector, individuals and perhaps more importantly the institutional investors can specialise and build up information on industries, leading to more effective monitoring of management.

In practice, however, though the private capital market is efficient, in the sense that prices appear to adjust to firm-specific information (Fama, 1991), there is considerable uncertainty as to whether it does distribute funds to areas of highest return to act as an effective constraint on managerial behaviour. A large number of studies of the market for corporate control now exist and suggest that it works imperfectly.

The capital market can act as a fully effective constraint on managerial discretionary behaviour only if there are insignificant information imperfections and transactions costs. In practice, although specialist intermediaries assist, shareholders usually will not have sufficient information about company performance to ensure perfect monitoring of management, except perhaps in small companies where the directors are the shareholders or are connected through family relationships. Under company law audited accounts and periodic reports have to be presented to shareholders, but statements can be disguised and important information omitted (Hindley, 1970; Salamon and Smith, 1979). The ability of shareholders to influence management has also been questioned even when they are adequately informed (Holmstrom and Tirole, 1989, p. 88). Inertia along with the transaction costs of trading shares, may mean that funds are not moved even when a higher return could be earned elsewhere. This will apply particularly to small shareholders, where the transaction costs of share dealing are likely to offset gains and where individual shareholders may free ride in the hope that others sell. By retaining their shares, they would hope to benefit subsequently from any improved performance (Grossman and Hart, 1980).

Firms with highly diffused shareholdings do not necessarily perform worse than those with highly concentrated shareholdings (Demsetz and Lehn, 1985), but nevertheless recent studies have argued that corporate control is likely to be more effective where there are large blocks of shares (Shleifer and Vishny, 1986; Caves, 1990; Leech and Leahy, 1991; Boycko *et al.*, 1996). In this literature, however, there is particular disagreement regarding the effect of large *managerial* shareholdings. On the one hand, managers personally benefit from higher profits which should encourage efficiency. On the other hand, their large shareholdings may mean protection from hostile takeover bids (Demsetz, 1983; Fama and Jensen, 1983). Empirical studies of the relationship between firm performance and the percentage of stock held by directors continue to produce mixed results (relevant studies up until the early 1980s are reviewed in Millward and Parker, 1983, p. 216; for more recent studies see Demsetz and Lehn, 1985; Lloyd *et al.*, 1986; Kesner, 1987; Kim *et al.*, 1988; Schellenger *et al.*, 1989; Oswald and Jahera, 1991). Empirical evidence suggests that managerial emoluments may be more closely correlated with firm size than with profitability (Scherer, 1980, pp. 29–41).

Where ownership is concentrated, the benefits to the individual from monitoring management behaviour and trading in shares are more likely to exceed the transaction costs of share trading, whereas where ownership is widely dispersed there may be no individual or group with the incentive or voting power to exercise control and ensure profit maximisation. In this sense it has been suggested that a single owner as in the public sector might improve agent monitoring (Estrin and Perotin, 1991, p. 67; Sappington and Stiglitz, 1987), though allowance needs to be made for the possibility that public officials pursue their own private agendas (Shapiro and Willig, 1990, p. 75). It has been suggested that privatised industries need dominant experienced shareholders 'to compensate for the weaknesses of managers never before exposed to best business practice' (McDonald, 1993, p. 49).

This conclusion, however, has unfavourable implications for the UK privatisation programme where there has been an emphasis upon encouraging small shareholdings. In so far as this impairs the capital market's monitoring of managerial discretionary behaviour, there is a potential conflict with the goal of the privatisation programme, raising efficiency. Also, recent research at the theoretical level has demonstrated that where a privatised firm does not operate in a perfectly competitive market, to enable the state to exert pressure on management to prevent monopoly pricing, it may be welfare optimal for the state not to sell all of its shares in the public firm (Bös, 1988). In the UK, however, privatisation has been associated with total disposals and the creation of an alternative regulatory structure (this issue is taken up below). The main exception has been where privatisation has occurred and the government has retained a golden share (Graham and Prosser, 1988). Currently eighteen privatised firms in the UK have golden shares. It is difficult, however, to reconcile the importance of the takeover threat to raising efficiency in privatised firms with the existence of such shares for they create uncertainty as to whether a takeover would be permitted, thus reducing the likelihood of a bid. Also, the golden share usually rules out a foreign takeover. The removal of the golden share which led to Ford's takeover of Jaguar in 1989 may be seen as a belated recognition of the contradiction in government thinking about the desirability of takeovers. The takeover threat also loses credibility when the government lays down the level of maximum individual shareholdings allowed in the company's articles of association, as in the cases of Rolls-Royce, BT and British Airways. For example, in the case of British Airways at privatisation no one person was allowed to hold more than 15 per cent of the issued shares and non-UK nationals were limited to a total holding of 25 per cent.

There also appears to be a contradiction between the high expectations of property rights theorists in the ability of the capital market to constrain managerial behaviour and the results of research into the effects of takeovers. Some studies suggest that the takeover threat produces short-termism, which penalises investment in, for example, training and research and development, leading to a long-term decline in competitiveness (Aoki, 1984; Dertouzos *et al.*, 1989, p. 144; Shleifer and Summers, 1991; Williamson, 1991; but, for an opposing view, see Ball, 1991). Compared with their UK counterparts, German and French managers have far more security from hostile takeovers because of the structure of shareholdings, the concentration of voting rights and the terms of management contracts (Berglof, 1990; Franks and Mayer, 1990). At the same time both the German and French economies have outperformed the UK economy since 1945, implying that the link between an active market in takeovers and economic efficiency is ambiguous.

Other studies have cast doubt on whether it is necessarily firms with flagging profits that attract the hostile takeover bid (Singh, 1971, 1975; Jenkinson and Mayer, 1994). Moreover, in recent years management have learnt to protect themselves from the personal costs of a bid through methods which either make successful takeovers more difficult or provide generous compensation for loss of office, such as 'poison pills', 'golden parachutes' and the like (Jacobs, 1991). Also, studies by Singh (1975), Meeks (1977) and Ravenscraft and Scherer (1987) have found that many acquisitions and mergers do not necessarily produce the expected profits. Indeed, around 50 per cent of acquisitions and mergers are said to fail, in the sense of not achieving the expected performance gains. This has led to suggestion that takeovers are a product of management empire building rather than a means of ensuring that management pursues shareholder welfare. Acquisitions increase the size of the firm and therefore the management's span of control. They can also improve management job security because making the firm bigger can reduce exposure both to particular market segments and the likelihood of a hostile takeover bid (Mueller, 1980; Roll, 1986; Hughes and Singh, 1987; Jarrel *et al.*, 1988; Caves, 1989; Hughes, 1989; Morck *et al.*, 1990). The finding that average returns to bidding shareholders from making acquisitions are at best only slightly positive (Jensen and Ruback, 1983; Franks and Harris, 1989) and in some studies significantly negative (Firth, 1979 and 1980; Bradley *et al.*, 1988) conforms to the idea that takeovers are motivated by the pursuit of managerial rather than shareholder utility.

Lawriwsky (1984, p. 217) at the end of a detailed study of the relationship between private sector industries and the capital market concluded that the degree of control over management varies and is far from predictable and that a mixture of 'internal organisation and external constraints are important determinants of company performance'. He also found that the relationship between the external capital market constraint and conduct and performance varied according to a number of factors, including organisational form, control type and size. In the private sector large size was 'associated with freedom from stock market restraints – and this is what distinguishes large firms from small and medium-sized firms'. Studies by Kuehn (1975) and Singh (1975) suggest that as the ratio of the stock market value of the company to its book value (known as the valuation ratio) falls, the probability of takeover increases. This suggests some capital market constraint on managerial behaviour. But the larger the firm the smaller the threat seems to be and in any case the constraint does not work perfectly. This may suggest that large firms foster managerial discretionary behaviour irrespective of the type of ownership. This is an important conclusion in the light of the fact that a number of the privatised industries (such as BT and British Gas) are giants in the stock market.

The evidence suggests, therefore, that a capital market discipline exists but may operate far from perfectly. The takeover threat *may* encourage managers to minimise costs or achieve static efficiency gains but an undesirable consequence may be lower long-term investment or dynamic efficiency. The distinction between static and dynamic efficiency is explored at more length in chapter 3. As Jenkinson and Mayer comment:

> managers who constantly live under the threat of removal may discount the long-term future performance of the company at a higher rate than a manager with a more secure tenure. Why initiate long-term projects whose fruits may be enjoyed by others?
>
> (Jenkinson and Mayer, 1994, p. 52)

To make matters worse, long-term investment may reduce short-run profits provoking a hostile stock market response.

The above discussion should not be interpreted, however, as a complete dismissal of the capital market as a useful constraint on corporate behaviour. The threat of takeover *is* a constraint which clearly does not exist in the public sector. Also, large private sector firms can and occasionally do go bankrupt. Neither are the public choice and property rights theorists necessarily wrong about relative behaviour in the public and private sectors. Nevertheless, quite clearly privatisation involves a move from one intricate agent–principal relationship to another and the outcome is not entirely clear (Bös, 1991; Bös and Peters, 1991; Bös, 1993). The motivation of public sector employees may be more complex than portrayed in the public choice literature, especially in its more populist forms. Moreover, it is important not to fall into the trap of comparing a flawed state enterprise with an idealised image of the operation of firms in the private capital market. Gibbard and Varian (1978, p. 665) warn against the use of caricature models in economics which exaggerate or distort reality. Arguably, in recent years the public choice and property rights theories have taken on a semblance of caricatures to support the wholesale transfer of industries from the public to the private sectors.

In reality the effects of ownership on managerial behaviour and hence on organisational performance are likely to be complex (Gravelle, 1984; Rees, 1984; Bös and Peters, 1989; De Fraja, 1993). In so far as a convincing case for privatisation cannot be made by deduction alone, it is necessary to resort to empirical study of public versus private efficiency. This book is concerned primarily with such empirical study.

PRIVATISATION AND REGULATION

Often following privatisation the state retains an interest in the operations of an enterprise, once again reflecting the importance of seeing ownership as a continuum rather than as discrete public versus private sectors. This is particularly the case with firms that operate in industries with natural monopoly characteristics, that is to say, industries where cost conditions are such that it would be inefficient to have more than one or a very small number of suppliers; but it also applies to certain strategic industries, notably those in the defence sector. Natural monopolies tend to be found where the production technology requires a high (often durable and largely irreversible) fixed cost and a much smaller variable cost so that one firm can produce the industry's output more cheaply than a number of smaller firms. The distribution networks in the electricity, gas, telecommunications and water industries are examples of natural monopolies. Where the production technology precludes competition in the product market, the monopolist must be prevented from abusing its dominant position when it is transferred to the private sector. Consequently, a regulatory system is usually introduced and, in the UK, regulation has taken the form of legislation that lays down certain operational requirements. Typically, this includes: an operating licence for the company, which sets out its public service obligations in detail;

a pricing formula to determine maximum prices (and therefore indirectly maximum profits); and a regulatory office headed by a director general. The regulatory office polices the licence, regulates market entry and negotiates and monitors the pricing formula and service standards.

In the UK prices are mainly regulated under a RPI–X structure, in which prices are allowed to rise by the rate of inflation (as measured by the RPI) less an efficiency factor 'X'. The efficiency factor is set for each industry periodically (typically every five years) to reflect the scope for cost savings in the industry. For example, if the X factor was set at 3 per cent then overall prices in the industry would be permitted to rise by the RPI–3 per cent each year until the next price review.

The RPI–X price-cap system of regulation begins with negotiation over the appropriate level at which X should be set. At privatisation X has tended to be set at a relatively low level to ensure the success of the flotation and because government and the regulator have typically underestimated the scope for cost savings. But in subsequent price reviews the efficiency factor has been raised to much more demanding levels. Table 1.3 summarises the evolution of price regulation for British Gas, British Telecom and British Airports Authority – the three regulated enterprises included in the eleven organisations which are the main focus of the studies in this book. In all cases the price cap has become more demanding. Similar price regulation exists for the electricity, water and railway industries in the UK but is not discussed here as these industries are not included in our later studies.

Industries came into state ownership for a variety of political, social and economic reasons, but one reason, interestingly, was the failure of state regulation of privately-owned utilities such as gas and water (Millward and Singleton, 1995). A main difference between public and private ownership can be attributed to the transaction costs faced by government when attempting to intervene in production activities. The expectation might be that such intervention would be generally less costly under public ownership because the enterprises are directly owned by the state. Managerial behaviour in state firms would be directly monitored and controlled reducing the scope for managerial discretion. If this is the case then the expected result would be a fall in managerial effort after privatisation with continued regulation and a decline in operating efficiency.

Certainly privatisation involves a change in information, incentives and controls over enterprises, as discussed earlier, and it may reduce the amount of intimate information about an enterprise available to the government or regulator (Sappington and Stiglitz, 1987; Shapiro and Willig, 1990). At the same time, the disadvantages of state ownership have been rehearsed and relate to the *incentives* for principals to monitor their agents effectively. In general terms, state ownership will be a superior form of regulation when the monitoring-control costs are lower under state ownership and these cost

THE IMPACT OF PRIVATISATION

Table 1.3 The evolution of price regulation: BT, British Gas and BAA

Organisation	*Main features of the price regulation*	*Comment*
British Telecom (BT)	1984–9 RPI−3% 1989–91 RPI−4.5% 1991–3 RPI−6.25% 1993–7 RPI−7.5% Rentals for lines and connections limited to RPI+2%. Median user bill and leased lines have a cap of RPI−0%.	Applies to inland calls, line rentals, leased lines and international calls (since 1991). Apparatus supply, mobile services and value-added networks are unregulated.
British Gas	1987–92 RPI−2% 1992–4 RPI−5% 1994–7 RPI−4% Standing charge to rise by no more than the RPI.	Excludes gas input costs, which can be passed on to the consumer less a 1% efficiency factor (since 1992).Price regulation applies to small (<25,000 therm) users. Supply to large users is unregulated and competitive. Full competition in all markets to be permitted after 1998.
British Airports Authority (BAA)	1987–92 RPI−1% 1992–4 RPI−8% 1994–5 RPI−4% 1995–7 RPI−1%	Applies to landing charges, passenger fees and aircraft parking charges at Gatwick, Heathrow and Stansted. All other services (for example, parking fees and retail services) are unregulated but profits made on these are taken into account under the price cap.

Notes: 1 The RPI−X price cap is an index applied either to a weighted basket of services provided by the company or to the company's average revenue. The basis of the price index is: BT – weighted quantities in previous year; British Gas – average revenue per therm; BAA – average revenue per passenger.

2 The above table is intended as a general guide only. The pricing rules are complex and subject to variation.

savings are not offset by any reduced operating efficiency in the state sector resulting from inferior agent-monitoring incentives. Another way of stating this is to say that the superiority of each form of ownership and regulation depends upon the *net* advantages from state intervention in managerial decision making. For example, we might expect there to be large net advantages from political control of an activity like defence.

In privatised but regulated industries, the regulator needs to take a view on the development of a number of key variables, notably operating expenditure, capital expenditure, asset valuation and the cost of capital, over the regulatory period to establish both fair prices to the consumer and fair profits for shareholders. At the same time, it will be in the interests of the management of the regulated firm to try to exaggerate all of these costs and values in an attempt to secure a slacker pricing regime in the form of a lower X factor. The role of the regulator is to collect and pass judgement on the information supplied by the regulated enterprise to ensure that cost reductions are pursued vigorously and that profits are not so low that necessary investment levels are damaged. If the regulator had perfect information then this regulatory activity would simply be a matter of routine. In practice, however, the regulator will have imperfect information, for example, on cost-reducing activities and the effect of exogenous factors (such as the business cycle) on performance (Sappington and Stiglitz, 1987).

Regulatory failure might occur under both state ownership with direct control and private ownership with regulatory structures like those created in the UK. But there is a substantial literature in economics which focuses on state regulation of private-sector firms and the nature of the potential resulting inefficiencies, which it is important to review, albeit briefly (for more details see, for example, Bailey, 1973; Laffont and Tirole, 1990, 1993; Foster, 1992; Armstrong *et al.*, 1994). Whereas state ownership has been associated with excessively labour-intensive production because of limits on external capital raising (Rees, 1984), both theoretical and empirical research suggest that private sector state-regulated firms spend revenues which cannot be turned into profits because of profit ceilings. While this could lead to managerial slack in the form of excessive management salaries and perks, other possible outcomes include either over-staffing or over-capitalisation of the business depending upon the precise circumstances. Over-capitalisation has been especially singled out as a problem of profit regulation (Averch and Johnson, 1962; Sappington and Stiglitz, 1987; Pint, 1991). Profit regulation can take the form of a ceiling on the permitted rate of return or cost of service regulation, where the regulator sanctions a profit mark-up on an agreed cost of providing the service, as in most US utilities. Either way, when the profit is controlled, directly or indirectly, there are disincentives for management to reduce costs. Instead management is likely to dissipate potential excess profits (for example, through higher management salaries and better perks) and exaggerate the true cost of service. Moreover, by expanding its asset base (the rate base) the company can increase its total profits without exceeding the rate of return ceiling.

The RPI−X pricing formula was established in the UK with a view to avoiding the efficiency disincentives associated with rate of return or cost of service regulation in the economics literature (Littlechild, 1983). Pure rate of return regulation is essentially a 'cost-plus' method of regulation with disincentives to cut costs. RPI−X regulation in its pure form would create incentives to reduce costs since any cost savings achieved above and beyond the X level will raise profits to shareholders. The X factor is set following negotiations over the capacity of the firm to reduce its real operating costs as a result of new technology, economies of scale and reductions in slacking. If management succeed in cutting costs by more than X then shareholders benefit through higher profits. This means, however, that over time the prices will deviate more and more from the costs of supply leading to allocative inefficiency (for an explanation of allocative efficiency see chapter 3). The purpose of the periodic price reviews is therefore to bring prices back closer to costs of supply. At the same time, the price reviews must not be too frequent otherwise shareholders could achieve little in the way of profit gains thus diminishing efficiency incentives. If the X factor was immediately adjusted when costs were reduced by a larger amount then effectively the price cap would become a rate of return or cost of service regulation and the incentive to reduce costs by more than X would be removed.

The incentive to seek out cost reductions depends, therefore, upon the length of time between the price reviews. The shorter the period, the smaller the incentive. Moreover, in so far as a forthcoming price review leads management to search for ways of dissipating excess profits so that the next price cap is less hostile, efficiency will suffer. Equally, those regulated privatised firms which face potential competition (including British Gas and BT) may aim to restrict profit growth with a view to deflecting the regulator's interest from encouraging new competition; while low profits signal to potential new entrants to the industry that there is apparently little scope for profit making in the industry. Turning to wages and employment, if efficiency incentives are dulled by regulation then we would expect there to be less managerial interest in reducing over-staffing and in removing labour rents in regulated firms. Similarly, there may be less incentive to reorganise the business, out-source and negotiate tougher contracts with suppliers.

In the UK the RPI$-$X regulatory control for pricing was designed so as not to reduce efficiency incentives, but in practice the X factor seems increasingly to be set with a view to achieving an agreed satisfactory profit level between the enterprise and the regulator. In so far as this is the case, UK price regulation moves closer to being a *de facto* profit regulation. Also, the constant threat that the regulator may choose to intervene and change the price cap even within the agreed review periods (as has occurred, most recently, in the UK electricity industry) increases the risk that high profits will not be permitted even when earned through efficiency gains (gains in efficiency above and beyond the X factor). The effects of such a breach of trust in the regulatory system are reduced incentives for management to cut costs and a rise in the cost of capital to the industry, as potential investors are driven away by the uncertainty, especially where the investment would be sunk (Helm and Thompson, 1991, p. 238). Michael Reidy, Executive

Director Corporate Affairs of PowerGen, one of the regulated power generating companies in the UK, has commented: 'From a regulatee's perspective, this uncertainty is significant. We have to commit resources to trying to guess what is around the next corner' (Reidy, 1995, p. 124).

The regulator needs to know the marginal costs (cost function) and demand function of the regulated enterprise to set prices optimally. He or she may look at best practice costs from other utilities in the UK (when they exist) or from elsewhere in the world, but such 'yardstick competition' has its problems in terms of obtaining relevant comparisons (Shleifer, 1985). Also, the regulator becomes responsible for managing the level of competition in the industry. The regulators have favoured more competition but have been aware of the need to make market entry attractive to newcomers, especially in the face of the dominant, privatised incumbent. By managing the competition the regulator has attempted to ensure a profit environment conducive to new entrants while still protecting the consumer. This is an uneasy balance. It has, in particular, necessitated the regulator setting interconnection or access charges so that new entrants can use the incumbent's monopoly system or network without discrimination. Too high an access charge would deter competition, while too low a charge would lead to an excessive expansion of the industry resulting in under-utilisation of capacity. The regulator has also had to be vigilant to prevent the incumbent operator cross-subsidising those parts of its business subject to competition from charges in those parts still retaining a high degree of monopoly. If such cross-subsidisation occurred then it would be difficult for competition to develop.

Regulation in the UK has, therefore, been associated with an unexpected gradual increase in regulatory involvement. For example, at BT this has included deciding restrictions on services that could be offered, technologies that could be used, market entry by new competitors, requirements on internal accounting systems and approval of budgets in BT's apparatus supply business. In other words, this is 'a degree of direct management intervention almost unprecedented even in BT's public sector days' (Souter, 1995, p. 109).

Given the potential inefficiencies associated with state regulation of private sector firms the expectation would be, everything else being equal, that regulated privatised firms will have performed less well since privatisation than their counterparts operating in more competitive environments. Certainly earlier empirical studies on the effect of ownership on managerial behaviour and performance, reviewed in chapter 4, have suggested that, especially where the private sector operator remains state regulated, production efficiency may be no higher than in the state sector. Vickers and Yarrow (1988, p. 3) conclude that 'it can be argued that the degree of product market competition and the effectiveness of regulatory policy typically have rather larger effects on performance than ownership *per se*'.

CONCLUSION

After reviewing various possible ways of regulating public sector firms, Gravelle concludes that none of the methods ensures efficiency, but he warns us that to draw from this the conclusion that the answer is to substitute private ownership is

> to commit the 'grass is greener' fallacy: if one of the alternative systems of property rights (public firms) produces inefficient results then the other system (private ownership) must be adopted. This is to ignore the theoretical and empirical evidence which indicates that privately owned firms must also be allocatively and X-inefficient.
>
> (Gravelle, 1982, p. 102)

In this chapter certain concepts and theories relating to incentives and behaviour in the public and private sectors have been presented. Agent–principal theory, public choice theory and the study of property rights can be invoked to mount a case against state ownership. At the same time such theories are not conclusive as they rely on a particular view of human motivation and the assumption that the private capital market acts as an efficient disciplinarian. Empirical support for public choice concepts is especially thin and more generally the notion that privatisation will improve economic performance remains an empirical question. Also, the possible impact of continued state regulation of privatised enterprises needs to be considered as regulation can introduce its own set of efficiency disincentives.

The following chapter provides some background information on the eleven UK privatised organisations whose performance is the main focus of this book.

NOTES

1 Throughout this book the word public, as in public ownership and public enterprises, is used interchangeably with the term state, for example state ownership and state enterprises. A public enterprise should not be confused with a public joint stock company in the UK which is a private sector company with publicly traded shares.
2 Weberian after Max Weber the German sociologist who studied the operation of ideal bureaucracies (Weber, 1912).
3 Although, of course, occasionally bankrupt private sector companies are also rescued by public funds.

References

Aharoni, Y. (1982) 'State-Owned Enterprise: an Agent without a Principal', in L.P. Jones (ed.) *Public Enterprise in Less-Developed Countries*, Cambridge: Cambridge University Press.

Alchian, A.A. (1965) 'Some Economics of Property Rights', *Il Politico* 30: 816–829.

Alchian, A.A. (1977) *Economic Forces at Work*, Indianapolis: Liberty Press.

Alchian, A.A. and Demsetz, H. (1972) 'Production, Information Costs and Economic Organization', *American Economic Review* 62: 777–795.

Aoki, M. (1983) 'Managerialism Revisited in the Light of Bargaining-Game Theory', *International Journal of Industrial Organisation* 1: 1–21.

Aoki, M. (1984) *The Cooperative Game Theory of the Firm*, Oxford: Oxford University Press.

Aoki, M., Gustafsson, B. and Williamson, O.E. (eds) (1990) *The Firm as a Nexus of Treaties*, London: Sage.

Aranson, P.H. (1990) 'Theories of Economic Regulation: from Clarity to Confusion', *Journal of Law and Politics* 6: 247–287.

Arbomeit, H. (1986) 'Privatisation in Great Britain', *Annals of Public and Cooperative Economy* 57: 153–179.

Armstrong, M., Cowan, S. and Vickers, J. (1994) *Regulatory Reform: Economic Analysis and British Experience*, Cambridge, Mass.: MIT Press.

Arrow, K.J. (1963) *Social Choice and Individual Values*, New Haven, Conn.: Yale University Press.

Arrow, K.J. (1974) *The Limits of Organization*, New York: Norton.

Arrow, K.J. (1985) 'The Economics of Agency', in J.W. Pratt and R.J. Zeckhauser (eds) *Principals and Agents: the Structure of Business*, Boston, Mass.: Harvard University Press.

Arrow, K. (1987) 'Reflections on the Essays', in G. Feiwel (ed.) *Arrow and the Foundations of the Theory of Economic Policy*, New York: NYU Press.

Averch, H. and Johnson, L.L. (1962) 'Behavior of the Firm under Regulatory Constraint', *American Economic Review* 52: 1052–1069.

Bailey, E.E. (1973) *Economic Theory of Regulatory Constraint*, Lexington, DC: Heath.

Ball, J. Sir (1991) 'Short Termism – Myth or Reality?', *National Westminster Bank Quarterly Review*, August, 20–30.

Baumol, W.J. (1959) *Business Behaviour, Value and Growth*, London: Macmillan.

Becker, G.S. (1976) *The Economic Approach to Human Behaviour*, Chicago: University of Chicago Press.

Berglof, E. (1990) 'Capital Structure as a Mechanism of Control: a Comparison of Financial Systems', in M. Aoki, B. Gustafsson and O.E. Williamson (eds) *The Firm as a Nexus of Treaties*, London: Sage.

Berle, A.A. and Means, G.C. (1932) *The Modern Corporation and Private Property*, New York: Macmillan.

Bhagwati, J. (1982) 'Directly Unproductive Profit-Seeking Activities', *Journal of Political Economy* 90: 1069–1087.

Blankart, C.B. (1983) 'The Contribution of Public Choice to Public Utility Economics: a Survey', in J. Finsinger (ed.) *Public Sector Economics*, London: Macmillan.

Boardman, A.E. and Vining, A.R. (1989) 'Ownership and Performance in Competitive Environments: a Comparison of the Performance of Private, Mixed and State-Owned Enterprises', *Journal of Law and Economics* 32: 1–33.

Borcherding, T. (1977) 'The Sources of Growth in Public Expenditures', in T. Borcherding (ed.) *Budgets and Bureaucrats: the Sources of Government Growth*, Durham, NC.: Duke University Press.

Bös, D. (1988) 'Privatization, Internal Control, and Internal Regulation', *Journal of Public Economics* 36: 231–258.

Bös, D. (1991) *Privatization: a Theoretical Treatment*, Oxford: Clarendon Press.

Bös, D. (1993) 'Privatization in Europe: A Comparison of Approaches', *Oxford Review of Economic Policy* 9 (1): 95–111.

Bös, D. and Peters, W. (1989) 'A Principal–Agent Approach on Manager Effort and Control in Privatized and Public Firms', University of Bonn, Discussion Paper A-252.

Bös, D. and Peters, W. (1991) 'Privatization of Public Enterprises: a Principal–Agent Approach. Comparing Efficiency in Private and Public Sectors', *Austrian Economic Papers* 18 (1): 5–16.

Boycko, M., Shleifer, A. and Vishny, R.W. (1996) 'A Theory of Privatization', *Economic Journal* 106: 309–319.

Bozeman, B. (1987) *All Organizations are Public: Bridging Public and Private Organizational Theories*, San Francisco, Cal.: Josey-Bass.

Bradley, M., Desai, A. and Kim, E.H. (1988) 'Synergistic Gains from Corporate Acquisitions and their Division Between the Stockholders of Target and Acquiring Firms', *Journal of Financial Economics* 21: 3–40.

Breton, A. (1974) *The Economic Theory of Representative Government*, London: Macmillan.

Breton, A. and Wintrobe, R. (1975) 'The Equilibrium Size of a Budget–Maximizing Bureau: A Note on Niskanen's Theory of Bureaucracy', *Journal of Political Economy* 83: 195–207.

Breton, A. and Wintrobe, R. (1982) *The Logic of Bureaucratic Control: an Economic Analysis of Competition, Exchange and Efficiency in Private and Public Organizations*, Cambridge: Cambridge University Press.

Buchanan, J.M. (1968) *The Demand and Supply of Public Goods*, Chicago: Rand McNally.

Buchanan, J.M. (1972) *Theory of Public Choice*, Michigan: University of Michigan Press.

Buchanan, J.M. (1978) in *The Economics of Politics*, IEA Readings 18, London: Institute of Economic Affairs.

Buchanan, J.M. and Tullock, G. (1962) *The Calculus of Consent: Logical Foundations of Constitutional Democracy*, Ann Arbor: University of Michigan Press.

Buchanan, J.M. (1986) *Liberty, Market and State: Political Economy in the 1980s*, Brighton: Wheatsheaf.

Carroll, K.A. (1990) 'Bureau Competition and Inefficiency: a Re-evaluation of Theory and Evidence', *Journal of Economic Behaviour and Oraganization* 13: 21–40.

Caves, R.E. (1989) 'Mergers, Takeovers and Economic Efficiencies: Foresight vs. Hindsight', *International Journal of Industrial Organization* 7 (1): 151–174.

Caves, R.E. (1990) 'Lessons from Privatization in Britain: State Enterprise Behaviour, Public Choice and Corporate Governance', *Journal of Economic Behaviour and Organization* 13 (2): 145–169.

Coase, R.H. (1937) 'The Nature of the Firm', *Economica* 4: 386–405.

Coffee, J. Jr. (1986) 'Shareholders versus Managers: the Strain in the Corporate Web', *Michigan Law Review* 85: 1–109.

Crain, M. and Zardkoohi, A. (1980) 'X-inefficiency and Nonpecuniary Rewards in a Rent-Seeking Society: a Neglected Issue in the Property Rights Theory of the Firm', *American Economic Review* 70 (4): 784–792.

Crew, M.A. and Rowley, C.K. (1988) 'Toward a Public Choice Theory of Monopoly Regulation', *Public Choice* 57: 49–67.

Cullis, J.G. and Jones, P.R. (1987) *Microeconomics and the Public Economy: a Defence of Leviathan*, Oxford: Basil Blackwell.

Dahl, R.A. and Lindbolm, C.E. (1953) *Politics, Economics, and Welfare*, New York: Harper & Row.

De Alessi, L. (1980) 'The Economics of Property Rights: a Review of the Evidence', *Research in Law and Economics* 2: 1–47.

De Fraja, G. (1993) 'Productive Efficiency in Public and Private Firms', *Journal of Public Economics* 50: 15–30.

Demsetz, H. (1983) 'The Structure of Ownership and the Theory of the Firm', *Journal of Law and Economics* 26: 375–390.

Demsetz, H. and Lehn, K. (1985) 'The Structure of Corporate Ownership: Causes and Consequences', *Journal of Political Economy* 93: 1155–1177.

Dertouzos, M.L., Lester, R.K. and Solow, R.M. (the MIT Commission on Industrial Productivity) (1989) *Made in America: Regaining the Productive Edge*, Cambridge, Mass.: MIT Press.

Downs, A. (1957) *An Economic Theory of Democracy*, New York: Harper & Row.

Downs, A. (1967) *Inside Bureaucracy*, Boston, Mass.: Little Brown.

Dunleavy, P. (1986) 'Explaining the Privatization Boom: Public Choice versus Radical Approaches', *Public Administration* 64 (2): 13–34.

Dunleavy, P. (1991) *Democracy, Bureaucracy and Public Choice: Economic Explanations in Political Science*, London: Harvester Wheatsheaf.

Dunsire, A., Hartley, K., Parker, D. and Dimitriou, B. (1988) 'Organisational Status and Performance: a Conceptual Framework for Testing Public Choice Theories', *Public Administration* 66: 363–388.

Dunsire, A., Hood, C. and Huby, M. (1989) *Cutback Management in Public Bureaucracies: Popular Theories and Observed Outcomes in Whitehall*, Cambridge: Cambridge University Press.

Eggar, T. (1995) 'The Regulation of the Former Nationalised Utilities: a Government View', in D. Helm (ed.) *British Utility Regulation: Principles, Experience and Reform*, Oxford: Oxera Press.

Estrin, S. and Perotin, V. (1991) 'Does Ownership Always Matter?', *International Journal of Industrial Organization* 9: 55–72.

Fama, E.F. (1980) 'Agency Problems and the Theory of the Firm', *Journal of Political Economy* 88: 288–307.

Fama, E.F. (1991) 'Efficient Capital Markets II', *Journal of Finance* 46 (5): 1575–1617.

Fama, E.F. and Jensen, M.C. (1983) 'Separation of Ownership and Control', *Journal of Law and Economics* 26: 301–325.

Farrell, J. and Scotchmer, S. (1988) 'Partnerships', *Quarterly Journal of Economics* 103: 279–298.

Fiorina, M.P. and Noll, R.G. (1978) 'Voters, Bureaucrats and Legislators: a Rational Choice Perspective on the Growth of Bureaucracy', *Journal of Public Economics* 9: 239–254.

Firth, M. (1979) 'The Profitability of Takeovers and Mergers', *Economic Journal* 89: 316–328.

Firth, M. (1980) 'Takeovers, Shareholder Returns and the Theory of the Firm', *Quarterly Journal of Economics* 94: 110–120.

Foster, C.D. (1992) *Privatisation, Public Ownership and the Regulation of Natural Monopoly*, Oxford: Blackwell.

Franks, J.R. and Harris, R.S. (1989) 'Shareholder Wealth Effects of Corporate Takeovers: the UK Experience 1955–1985', *Journal of Financial Economics* 23: 255–249.

Franks, J.R. and Mayer, C. (1990) 'Capital Markets and Corporate Control: a Study of France, Germany and the UK', *Economic Policy* 10: 189–231.

Frech III, H.E. (1980) 'Property Rights, the Theory of the Firm and Competitive Markets for Top Decision-Makers', *Research in Law and Economics* 2: 49–63.

Furubotn, E.G. and Pejovich, S. (1972) 'Property Rights and Economic Theory: a Survey of the Recent Literature', *Journal of Economic Literature* 10: 1137–1162.

Furubotn, E.G. and Pejovich, S. (1974) *The Economics of Property Rights*, Cambridge, Mass.: Ballinger.

Gibbard, A. and Varian, H. (1978) 'Economic Models', *Journal of Philosophy* 75: 665–667.

Graham, C. and Prosser, T. (1988) 'Golden Shares: Industrial Policy by Stealth', *Public Law*: 413–431.

Gravelle, H.S. (1984) 'Bargaining and Efficiency in Public and Private Sector Firms', in M. Marchand, P. Pestieau and H. Tulkens (eds) *The Performance of Public Enterprises*,

Amsterdam: North-Holland.
Gravelle, H.S. (1982) 'Incentives, Efficiency and Control in Public Firms', *Journal of Economics*, supplement 2: 79–104.
Green, D.P. and Shapiro, I. (1994) *Pathologies of Rational Choice Theory: a Critique of Applications in Political Science*, Yale: Yale University Press.
Grossman, S. and Hart, O. (1980) 'Takeover Bids, the Free-Rider Problem and the Theory of the Corporation', *Bell Journal of Economics* 11: 42–64.
Grossman, S. and Hart, O. (1986) 'The Costs and Benefits of Ownership: a Theory of Vertical and Lateral Integration', *Journal of Political Economy* 94: 691–719.
Hart, O.D. (1993) 'Incomplete Contracts and the Theory of the Firm', in O.E. Williamson and S.G. Winter (eds) *The Nature of the Firm: Origins, Evolution and Development*, Oxford: Oxford University Press.
Hart, O.D. (1995) *Firms, Contracts and Financial Structure*, Oxford: Oxford University Press.
Hart, O.D. and Holmstrom, B. (1987) 'The Theory of Contracts', in T.F. Bewley (ed.) *Advances in Economic Theory*, Cambridge: Cambridge University Press.
Helm, D. and Thompson, D. (1991) 'Privatised Transport Infrastructure and Incentives to Invest', *Journal of Transport Economics and Policy* 25: 231–246.
Herzberg, F. (1966) *Work and the Nature of Man*, New York: World Publishing.
Hindley, B. (1970) 'Separation of Ownership and Control in the Modern Corporation', *Journal of Law and Economics* 13: 185–222.
Hirschman, A.O. (1970) *Exit, Voice and Loyalty: Responses to Decline in Firms, Organizations and States*, Cambridge, Mass.: Harvard University Press.
Holmstrom, B. and Tirole, J. (1989) 'The Theory of the Firm', in R. Schmalensee and R. Willig (eds) *Handbook of Industrial Organization*, Amsterdam: North-Holland.
Hood, C., Huby, M. and Dunsire, A. (1984) 'Bureaucrats and Budgeting Benefits: How Do British Central Departments Measure Up?', *Journal of Public Policy* 4 (3): 163–179.
Hughes, A. (1989) 'The Impact of Merger: a Survey of Empirical Evidence for the UK', in J. Fairburn and J.A. Kay (eds) *Mergers and Merger Policy*, Oxford: Oxford University Press.
Hughes, A. and Singh, A. (1987) 'Takeover and the Stock Market', *Contributions to Political Economy* 6: 73–85.
Jackson, P.M. (1982) *The Political Economy of Bureaucracy*, Oxford: Philip Allan.
Jackson, P.M. (1985) 'Economy, Democracy and Bureaucracy', in R.C.O. Matthews (ed.) *Economy and Democracy*, London: Macmillan.
Jacobs, M.T. (1991) *Short-term America: the Causes and Cures of our Business Myopia*, Harvard, Mass.: Harvard Business School.
Jarrel, G., Brickley, J. and Netter, J. (1988) 'The Market for Corporate Control: the Empirical Evidence since 1980', *Journal of Economic Perspectives* 2: 49–68.
Jenkinson, T. and Mayer, C. (1994) *Hostile Takeovers: Defence, Attack and Corporate Governance*, London: McGraw-Hill.
Jensen, M.C. (ed.) (1983) 'Symposium on the Market for Corporate Control', *Journal of Financial Economics* 11.
Jensen, M.C. and Meckling, W.H. (1976) 'Theory of the Firm: Managerial Behaviour, Agency Costs and Ownership Structure', *Journal of Financial Economics* 3 (4): 305–60.
Jensen, M.C. and Ruback, R. (1983) 'The Market for Corporate Control: the Scientific Evidence', *Journal of Financial Economics* 11: 5–50.
Kesner, I.F. (1987) 'Directors Stock Ownership and Organizational Performance: an Investigation of Fortune 500 Companies', *Journal of Management* 13 (3): 499–507.
Kim, W.S., Lee, L.W. and Francis, J.C. (1988) 'Investment Performance of Common Stocks in Relation to Inside Ownership', *Financial Review* 23 (1): 53–64.
Kristensen, O.P. (1980) 'The Logic of Political-bureaucratic Decision Making as a Cause of Government Growth', *European Journal of Political Research* 8: 249-264.
Kuehn, D. (1975) *Takeovers and the Theory of the Firm*, London: Macmillan.

Laffont, J.J. (1989) *The Economics of Uncertainty and Information*, Cambridge, Mass.: MIT Press.

Laffont, J.J. and Tirole, J. (1990) *Privatization and Incentives*, Cambridge, Mass.: MIT Press.

Laffont, J.J. and Tirole, J. (1993) *A Theory of Incentives in Procurement and Regulation*, Cambridge, Mass.: MIT Press.

Lawriwsky, M.L. (1984) *Corporate Structure and Performance*, London: Croom Helm.

Lawson, C. (1994) 'The Theory of State-owned Enterprises in Market Economies', *Journal of Economic Surveys* 8 (3): 283–309.

Leech, D. (1987) 'Ownership Concentration and the Theory of the Firm: a Simple Game Theoretic Approach', *Journal of Industrial Economics* 35 (3): 225–240.

Leech, D. and Leahy, J. (1991) 'Ownership Structure, Control Type Classifications and the Performance of Large Companies', *Economic Journal* 101: 1418–1437.

Lewin, L. (1991) *Self-Interest and Public Interest in Western Politics*, Oxford: Oxford University Press.

Lindblom, C.E. (1977) *Politics and Markets: The World's Political-Economic Systems*, New York: Basic Books.

Littlechild, S.C. (1983) *Regulation of British Telecommunications' Profitability*, London: HMSO.

Lloyd, W.P., Jahera, J.S. and Goldstein, S.J. (1986) 'The Relationship between Returns, Ownership Structure and Market Value', *Journal of Financial Research* 9 (2): 171–177.

Madden, G.P. (1981) 'Potential Corporate Takeovers and Market Efficiency: a Note', *Journal of Finance* 36: 1191–1198.

Manne, H.G, (1965) 'Mergers and the Market for Corporate Control', *Journal of Political Economy* 73: 110–120.

Mansfield, R. and Poole, M. (1991) 'Advancing the Horizons: the Central Role of the Manager', paper presented to the British Academy of Management Conference, University of Bath.

Marris, R. (1964) *The Economic Theory of 'Managerial' Capitalism*, New York: Free Press.

Marschak, J. and Radner, R. (1972) *Economic Theory of Teams*, New Haven: Yale University Press.

Maslow, A.H. (1964) *Motivation and Personality*, New York: Harper & Row.

McCormick, R.E. and Meiners, R.E. (1988) 'University Governance: a Property Rights Perspective', *Journal of Law and Economics* 31: 423–442.

McDonald, K.R. (1993) 'Why Privatization is Not Enough', *Harvard Business Review*, May–June: 49–59.

Meeks, G. (1977) *Disappointing Marriage: a Study of the Gains from Mergers*, Occasional Paper 51, Cambridge: Cambridge University Press.

Migue, J.L. and Belanger, C. (1974) 'Towards a General Theory of Managerial Discretion', *Public Choice* 17: 27–43.

Millward, R. and Parker, D. (1983) 'Public and Private Enterprise: Comparative Behaviour and Relative Efficiency', in R. Millward, D. Parker, L. Rosenthal, M.T. Sumner and N. Topham (eds) *Public Sector Economics*, London: Longman.

Millward, R. and Singleton, J. (1995) *The Political Economy of Nationalisation in Britain 1920–1950*, Cambridge: Cambridge University Press.

Mitchell, W.C. (1983) 'Fiscal Behaviour of the Modern Fiscal State: Public Choice Perspectives and Contributions', in L. Wade (ed.) *Political Economy: Recent Reviews*, Boston, Mass.: Kluwer-Nijhoff.

Mitchell, W.C. (1988) *Government As It Is*, Hobart Paper 109, London: Institute of Economic Affairs.

Mitnick, B. (1980) *The Political Economy of Regulation*, New York: Columbia University Press.

Moore, J. (1983) *Why Privatise?*, Press Release, London: HM Treasury.

Moore, J. (1992) 'British Privatization: Taking Capitalism to the People', *Harvard Business Review*, January–February: 115–24.

Morck, R., Shleifer, A. and Vishny, R.W. (1990) 'Do Managerial Objectives Drive Bad Acquisitions?', *Journal of Finance* 45 (1): 31–48.

Mueller, D.C. (1980) *The Determinants and Effects of Mergers: an International Comparative Study*, Cambridge, Mass.: Oclgeschlager Gunn & Hain.

Mueller, D.C. (ed.) (1989) *Public Choice II*, Cambridge: Cambridge University Press.

National Economic Development Office (NEDO) (1976) *A Study of UK Nationalised Industries: their Role in the Economy and Control in the Future*, London: HMSO.

Navajas, F.H. (1984) *Managerial Incentives and Control in Public Enterprises*, unpublished D.Phil thesis, University of Oxford.

Nickell, J. (1993) 'Competition and Corporate Performance', Applied Economics Discussion Paper Series 155, Institute of Economics and Statistics, University of Oxford.

Niskanen, W.A. Jr. (1971) *Bureaucracy and Representative Government*, Chicago: Aldine.

Niskanen, W.A. Jr. (1973) *Bureaucracy, Servant or Master?* London: Institute of Economic Affairs.

Niskanen, W.A. Jr. (1987) 'Bureaucracy', in C.K. Rowley (ed.) *Democracy and Public Choice*, Oxford: Basil Blackwell.

Olson, M. (1965) *The Logic of Collective Action*, Cambridge, Mass.: Harvard University Press.

Orzechowski, W. (1977) 'Economic Models of Bureaucracy: Survey, Extensions and Evidence', in T. Borcherding (ed.) *Budgets and Bureaucrats: the Sources of Government Growth*, Durham, NC.: Duke University Press.

Oswald, S.L. and Jahera, J.S. Jr. (1991) 'The Influence of Ownership on Performance: an Empirical Study', *Strategic Management Journal* 12: 321–326.

Peltzman, S. (1990) 'How Efficient is the Voting Market', *Journal of Law and Economics* 33: 27–63.

Peltzman, S. (1992) 'Voters as Fiscal Conservatives', *Quarterly Journal of Economics* 57 (2): 327–361.

Pera, A. (1989) 'Deregulation and Privatization in an Economy-Wide Context', OECD *Economic Studies* 22 (Spring): 159–204.

Perry, J.L. and Rainey, H.G. (1988) 'The Public–Private Distinction in Organization Theory: a Critique and Research Agenda', *Academy of Management Review* 3 (2): 182–201.

Peters, B.G. (1989) *Comparing Public Bureaucracies: Problems of Theories and Methods*, Tuscaloosa, Ala.: University of Alabama Press.

Pint, E. (1991) 'Nationalization vs. Regulation of Monopolies: the Effects of Ownership on Efficiency', *Journal of Public Economics* 44: 131–164.

Posner, M. (1984) 'Privatisation: the Frontier between Public and Private', *Policy Studies* 5 (1): 22–32.

Pryke, R. (1981) *The Nationalised Industries: Policies and Performance since 1968*, Oxford: Martin Robertson.

Rainey, H.G. *Understanding and Managing Public Organizations*, San Francisco, CA.: Jossey-Bass.

Rainey, H.G., Backoff, R.W. and Levine, C.L. (1976) 'Comparing Public and Private Organizations', *Public Administration Review* 36: 233-246.

Ravenscraft, D. and Scherer, F. (1987) *Mergers, Sell-Offs and Economic Efficiency*, Washington, DC.: The Brookings Institution.

Rees, R. (1984) 'A Positive Theory of Public Enterprises', in M. Marchand, P. Pestieau and H. Tulkens (eds) *The Performance of Public Enterprises: Concepts and Measurement*, Amsterdam: New Holland.

Rees, R. (1985) 'The Theory of Principal and Agent: Parts 1 and 2', *Bulletin of Economic Research* 37 (1): 46–69 and 37 (2): 70–90.

Rees, R. (1989) 'Modelling Public Enterprise Performance' in D. Helm, J. Kay and D. Thompson (eds) *The Market for Energy*, Oxford: Oxford University Press.
Reidy, M. (1995) 'Privatisation, Regulation and the Electricity Market', in D. Helm (ed.) *British Utility Regulation: Principles, Experience and Reform*, Oxford: Oxera Press.
Roll, R. (1986) 'The Hubris Hypothesis of Corporate Takeovers', *Journal of Business* 59: 197–216.
Ross, S.A. (1973) 'The Economic Theory of Agency: the Principal's Problem', *American Economic Review* 62: 134–139.
Salamon, G.L. and Smith, E.D. (1979) 'Corporate Control and Management Misrepresentation of Firm Performance', *Bell Journal of Economics* 10 (1): 319–328.
Sappington, D. and Stiglitz, J.E. (1987) 'Information and Regulation', in E.E. Bailey (ed.) *Public Regulation: New Perspectives on Institutions and Policies*, Cambridge, Mass.: MIT Press.
Schellenger, M.H., Wood, D.D. and Tashakori, A. (1989) 'Board of Directors Composition, Shareholder Wealth and Dividend Policy', *Journal of Management* 15 (3): 457–467.
Scherer, F.M. (1980) *Industrial Market Structure and Economic Performance*, second edition, Chicago: Rand McNally.
Shapiro, C. and Willig, R.D. (1990) 'Economic Rationales for the Scope of Privatization', in E.N. Suleiman and J. Waterbury (eds) *The Political Economy of Public Sector Reform and Privatization*, Boulder: Westview Press.
Shleifer, A. (1985) 'A Theory of Yardstick Competition', *Rand Journal of Economics* 16: 319–27.
Shleifer, A. and Summers, L. (1991) 'Breach of Trust in Hostile Takeovers', in A. Auerbach (ed.) *Corporate Takeovers: Causes and Consequences*, Chicago: Chicago University Press.
Shleifer, A. and Vishny, R.W. (1986) 'Large Shareholders and Corporate Control', *Journal of Political Economy* 94: 461–488.
Singh, A. (1971) *Takeovers, their Relevance to the Stock Market and the Theory of the Firm*, Cambridge: Cambridge University Press.
Singh, A. (1975) 'Takeovers, Economic Natural Selection and the Theory of the Firm: Evidence from the Post-war UK Experience', *Economic Journal* 85: 497–515.
Smith, P. (1990) 'The Use of Performance Indicators in the Public Sector', *Journal of the Royal Statistical Society* Series A 153 (1): 53–72.
Souter, D. (1995) 'A Stakeholder Approach to Regulation' in D. Helm (ed.) *British Utility Regulation: Principles, Experience and Reform*, Oxford: Oxera Press.
Tullock, G. (1965) *The Politics of Bureaucracy*, Washington, DC.: Public Affairs Press.
Tullock, G. (1976) *The Vote Motive*, London: Institute of Economic Affairs.
Tullock, G. (1979) 'Bureaucracy and the Growth of Government', in *The Taming of Government*, London: Institute of Economic Affairs.
Udehn, L. (1996) *The Limits of Public Choice: a Sociological Critique of the Economic Theory of Politics*, London: Routledge.
Veljanovski, C. (1987) *Selling the State*, London: Weidenfeld & Nicolson.
Vickers, J. and Yarrow, G. (1988) *Privatization: An Economic Analysis*, Cambridge, Mass.: MIT Press.
Waterson, M. (1995) 'Developing Utility Regulation in the UK', in D. Helm (ed.) *British Utility Regulation: Principles, Experience and Reform*, Oxford: Oxera Press.
Weber, M. (1912: 1964) *The Theory of Social and Economic Organization* (translated by A.M. Henderson and T. Parsons), New York: Free Press.
Williamson, O.E. (1964) *The Economics of Discretionary Behaviour: Managerial Objectives in a Theory of the Firm*, Englewood Cliffs, NJ.: Prentice Hall.
Williamson, O.E. (1975) *Markets and Hierarchies: Analysis and Antitrust Implications: a Study in the Economics of Internal Organisation*, London: Free Press.
Williamson, O.E. (1991) 'The Firm as a Nexus of Treaties: an Introduction', in M. Aoki, M.B.

Gustafsson and O.E. Williamson (eds) *The Firm as a Nexus of Treaties*, London: Sage.

Windle, R.J. (1991) 'The World's Airlines: a Cost and Productivity Comparison', *Journal of Transport Economics and Policy* 25: 31–49.

Wintrobe, R. (1987) 'The Market for Corporate Control and the Market for Political Control', *Journal of Law, Economics and Organization* 3: 435–448.

Zahra, S.A. and Pearce, J.A. II (1989) 'Boards of Directors and Corporate Financial Performance: a Review and Integrative Model', *Journal of Management* 15 (2): 291–334.

Zeckhauser, R.J. and Horn, M. (1989) 'The Control and Performance of State-owned Enterprises', in P.W. MacAvoy, W.T. Stanbury, G. Yarrow and R.J. Zeckhauser (eds) *Privatization and State-owned Enterprises: Lessons from the United States, Great Britain and Canada*, Boston, Kluwer.

Pergamon

World Development Vol. 27, No. 1, pp. 157–168, 1999

Printed in Great Britain
0305-750X/98/$ — see front matter

PII: S0305-750X(98)00118-1

A Theory of Privatization, or Why Bureaucrats are Still in Business

GEORGE YARROW
Hertford College, Oxford University, Oxford, UK

Summary. — Privatization is a dynamic phenomenon, and changes in ownership arrangements require explanations based upon changes in background variables. Without movements in these variables bureaucrats are likely to stay in business, even if reform would increase efficiency. It is argued that changes in one such variable, the cost of government finance, have played a particularly significant role in triggering privatizations and related reforms. The increasing cost of government finance, resulting from higher levels of general public expenditure and taxation, also explains the policy sequence, observed in many countries, in which comprehensive ownership reform is preceded by a period of increased financial stringency for state-owned enterprises (SOEs). © 1998 Elsevier Science Ltd. All rights resrved.

1. INTRODUCTION

The worldwide spread of privatization policies during the 1980s and 1990s has been a remarkable phenomenon, which has first halted and later reversed an apparently inexorable upward trend in the state sector's share of global output. Accompanying the policy switch there has also ben a rapid growth in the analysis of privatization, with particular emphasis placed upon work concerned with the evaluation of the many, detailed policy options that occur within any broad program of ownership reform. That is, a large part of the analytic work has been driven by normative agendas and has been aimed at improving the formulation and implementation of privatization programs.

Rather less common have been studies attempting to explain the emergence and development of privatization policies, and, in particular, to explain why at a particular time in history so many disparate economies, possess ed of different institutional structures and at different stages of economic development, have pursued similar policy strategies. Moreover, the positive theories of privatization that have emerged have not been fully satisfactory in providing an account of the phenomenon. This weakness is in turn related to the absence in economic theory of any generally accepted, positive theory of state-owned enterprises (SOEs), such as might bear comparison with, say, textbook models of privately owned, profit-maximising enterprises.

The theoretical position here may account for some of the puzzlement that can be detected throughout *Bureaucrats in Business* (*BIB*, 1995). On the one hand, the authors clearly believe that divestiture and other related reforms can substantially improve economic performance, a position that is now well supported by extensive evidence on the effects of such policies throughout the world. On the other hand, it is clear that quite a number of countries have not followed the path of reform with any great enthusiasm and that, as *BIB* points out, SOEs today account for nearly as large a share of developing countries' economies as they did almost two decades ago. The obvious question, on which much of *BIB* is focused, is *why*?[1]

In this paper, I seek to explore aspects of the apparent tension between the potential efficiency benefits of SOE reform and the relatively leisurely pace at which change has occurred in many parts of the world. Section 2 is focused on the expected effects of ownership reform on incentives and market performance. Here there is a well-established and now extensive literature (see Yarrow and Jasinski, 1996), and I will do nothing more than summarize some central themes and emphasize one or two key points. In particular, I will stress the crucial importance of product market competition and of accompanying regulatory reform (including the option of simple deregulation) in determining the impact of privatization or of SOE reforms on incentives and market performance. Policies that do not involve significant changes in regulation and/or competitive conditions are unlikely to have much of an impact on economic efficiency, as demonstrated, for example, by the limited contribution made by performance contracts to SOE performance (see *BIB*).

The later sections of the paper concentrate on the question of what triggers major SOE reforms. A number of immediate points can be made in relation to this question. First, the global interest in privatization and associated reforms indicates that some general, common influences have been at work. Second, since privatization and regulatory reform represent changes in public policy, we should look for explanatory factors that have also changed over the relevant period. For example, explaining privatization on the basis that private ownership is inherently more efficient than public ownership is unsatisfactory in that it does not, in itself, offer any account of why governments worldwide first built up and later reduced their SOE sectors.

I will argue that the most common trigger for privatization and SOE reform is fiscal pressure. Demands for increased public expenditure across a wide variety of activities (i.e. not just in the SOE sector) and across a wide range of countries have tended to raise the opportunity costs of public finance; and the results of an increasing cost of finance include tightened SOE budgets, curtailed investment programs, and divestiture of SOEs. On the other hand, since the political benefits derived from the operation of SOEs—which include distributional effects—may vary considerably, the pace of change in any particular country will also be influenced by a variety of local political factors.

2. INCENTIVES AND EFFICIENCY

Two of the most important lessons that come out of the economic analysis of privatization are that:

(a) the incentives facing the managers of an enterprise are jointly determined by a whole range of factors emanating from the various market and policy environments in which the relevant firm operates, including product markets (e.g., the intensity of competition, the power of buyers), capital markets (e.g., corporate governance, takeover and bankruptcy threats, financial structure of the firm), managerial labour markets (e.g., the value of reputation, the transferability of human capital) and the regulatory system (e.g., whether or not the firm is regulated, the specific regulations in force);

(b) the policy environments in which firms operate are themselves functions of the incentive structures faced by policy makers, which in turn depend upon a range of political and institutional factors at work in what might, metaphorically, be called "the market for regulation".[2] These factors include interest group pressures, transparency and scrutiny of decisions, the influence of public opinion, the degree of regulatory discretion, bureaucratic goals, the balance of political forces, and the extent of judicial oversight of regulation.

As a first approximation, privatization can be viewed as one means of reducing the impact of political factors on economic incentives, behaviour and performance (Vickers and Yarrow, 1991). More specifically, divestiture reduces political influence and increases the influence of capital market factors, although the precise impact of ownership transfer in any particular case will depend upon the specific characteristics of the relevant market for regulation and of the relevant capital market.

(a) *The significance of regulatory reform*

The rationale for seeking to reduce political influence on economic decision making is, most usually, to improve incentives for economic efficiency at the level of the enterprise. Underlying the case for privatization is the view that there is "government failure", in the sense that public policy is likely to operate in ways that, for one reason or another, impede the efficient functioning of markets. Or, putting matters another way, the market for regulation is itself highly imperfect and can be expected to produce inefficient levels and mixes of state intervention.

In a number of cases of privatization this relatively simple view of the policy process is all that is required. For example, where an SOE operating in a competitive market is transferred to the private sector and all direct links between the firm and the state are severed, the monitoring activities of politicians and bureaucrats will indeed be replaced by those of capital market participants. In many other cases, however, relatively high levels of state intervention may persist beyond privatization, for example in the form of specific regulations that apply to the enterprise itself and/or to the market(s) in which it is involved. Such persistence of intervention may occur in response to perceived market failures and/or (and more likely in practice) to politically unwelcome redistributive effects that might result from deregulation.

Where regulation continues after privatization, there is obviously a lesser degree of de-coupling of enterprise (managerial) incentives from factors at work in the market for regulation. In particular, enterprise incentives, conduct and performance will tend to continue to be sensitive to political and bureaucratic agendas. It is also worth noting here that, since privatization policies are simply particular types of government activity, they are themselves vulnerable to inefficiencies arising from political and bureaucratic influences. For example, divestiture may be accomplished in ways that provide for ongoing protection of favoured political constituencies, even where this involves some sacrifice in overall economic performance. Ultimately, therefore, there may be cases where privatization is only effective if accompanied by relatively radical political and constitutional reforms (which, according to the metaphor, will have the effect of changing the structure of the supply side of the market for regulation).

If, then, we are interested in the question of why bureaucrats are still in business on a large scale, or in the question of how privatization policies can be made more effective, it is to analysis of the relevant markets for regulation that we should turn. Before doing so, however, there is one slight detour that is worth taking first. It concerns the relationships between enterprise incentives, ownership and product market competition.

(b) *The significance of product market competition*

Consider SOE incentive structures where the relevant firm (1) is a monopoly and (2) operates in a reasonably competitive market. In case 1, the firm will survive and operate (at a slightly greater or lesser scale) whether it is efficient or not, whereas in case 2 inefficiency is liable to be punished by loss of market share. Arguably, in the monopoly case, public officials could compensate for the lack of direct incentives on enterprise management by means of an incentive contract that gears managerial rewards to efficiency performance. Officials will, however, tend to have relatively little information upon which to base their monitoring activities: in effect, the product market monopoly is associated with an information monopoly. For example, how will bureaucrats know what level of unit cost reduction might be realistic or what new services might be introduced that would better meet consumer preferences?

Much of the economic analysis of regulated monopoly, whether publicly or privately owned, has focused on the asymmetry of information between firms and regulators. For example, the managers of the firm might be assumed to know the level of unit cost that is attainable or the level of effort that is applied to reducing cost, while the regulator is assumed not to have this information. The regulatory task is then to design an optimal incentive structure that causes the regulated firm's managers to reveal information or to choose the effort level that contributes maximally to public policy objectives.

Useful though such principal-agent models of regulation have been, they tend to be limited by (i) the fact that they abstract from the problem of the incentives faced by regulators and (ii) their highly restrictive assumptions about information conditions. While information asymmetries clearly exist and are important factors in the analysis of regulation, what is arguably much more problematic about regulated monopoly is the absence of dynamic incentives to discover, utilize and reveal new information (i.e. things that, at the outset, are known neither to the regulator nor to the firm). Thus, in practice, one of the most important empirical findings that has been made over recent years in respect of the performance of regulated utilities is that the introduction of competitive pressures into previously monopolized areas has led to cost reductions substantially greater than those initially thought feasible by any of the major interested parties. Or, to take another example, firms newly exposed to competition have been provided with incentives to discover their own cost structures for the first time: a regulated monopoly may have no significant incentive to calculate its marginal costs in an accurate way, but such information clearly becomes much more valuable to managers in a competitive environment. Again, therefore, the problem is not so much that the firm knows its marginal costs and the regulator does not, but rather that neither party knows those costs and there is a lack of incentives to discover them (for example, bureaucrats may either have no incentives to determine marginal costs or they may lack the information required to set effective incentive structures).

The information sets of bureaucrats can be expected to be larger in the competitive case (case 2) since performance benchmarks will be available from the market. In principle, therefore, the improved incentives made feasible by increased information—perhaps embodied in a performance or management contract—should reinforce the direct incentives of market competition in promoting efficiency. On the other side of the coin, the direct incentives provided by competition complicate the task of writing an optimal contract. Given that final incentives are jointly determined, the specification of the performance contract needs to take account of the interactions between its provisions and those competitive pressures in the market that directly influence commercial behavior. This is a complex task which leaves considerable scope for error, or, perhaps more importantly, for the exercise of bureaucratic discretion. The beneficial incentive and information effects of competition can, therefore, be partly undermined if the complexities of determining efficient contracts lead to greater intrusion of bureaucratic agendas into the policy process.

Nevertheless, competitive markets will tend to have decisive performance advantages over monopolistic markets, even when some of the competing firms are SOEs. Consider, for example, the incentives generated by the two market structures for the discovery and introduction of product changes that increase consumer satisfaction. In a competitive market innovation is stimulated both by a carrot and by a stick. The carrot is the increased cash flows (from higher prices or higher volumes or both) that the enterprise will enjoy if it is an innovator; the stick is the reduced cash flows (from lower prices or lower volumes) that the enterprise will suffer if it is a laggard.[3] In contrast, price controls may prevent a monopoly from enjoying financial benefits from product improvements. More important, a monopolist, whether regulated or unregulated, will not face damaging financial consequences if it fails to innovate in a timely fashion, since no other firm will steal its market as a result.

This last point is what lies behind Adam Smith's view that:

> Monopoly, besides, is a great enemy to good management, which can never be universally established but in consequence of that free and universal competition which forces every body to have recourse to it for the sake of self-defence.

It should, however, be noted that the target of Smith's attack here is persistent or "perpetual" monopoly (i.e. monopoly that cannot readily be challenged), rather than temporary monopoly. Later in the *Wealth of Nations* (1976) he goes on to argue that:

> By a perpetual monopoly, all the other subjects of the state are taxed very absurdly in two different ways; first, by the high price of goods, which, in the case of a free trade, they could buy much cheaper; and, secondly, by their total exclusion from a branch of business, which it might be both convenient and profitable for many of them to carry on. It is for the most worthless of all purposes too that they are taxed in this manner. It is merely to enable the company to support the negligence, profusion, and malversion of their own servants, whose disorderly conduct seldom allows the dividend of the company to exceed the ordinary rate of profit in trades which are altogether free, and very frequently makes it fall even a good deal short of that rate.

Since, in practice, most persistent monopolies exist by virtue of state interventions which give enterprises special privileges, de-monopolization can be expected to be a powerful force making for improved efficiency incentives. Indeed, it is precisely because it tends to have such a major effect on market conduct and performance that de-monopolization is frequently resisted strongly by those groups liable to be adversely affected by it. Thus, whereas much of the economic analysis of privatization has tended to stress the possibility of market failure/efficiency as a rationale for continuing state intervention, the reality is that the persistence of intervention is, in most cases, much more likely to be associated with demands from well-placed interest groups for protection against the effects of market forces.

3. STATE OWNERSHIP AS REGULATION

To account for obstacles to privatization it is first necessary to have a view about the objectives of the relevant decision makers and of the perceived contribution of SOEs to those objectives. As noted in Section 1, one factor in the relative paucity of general, positive theorizing on privatization is the absence of any general, positive theory of state ownership. The theoretical literature on public enterprise is dominated by normative issues such as the optimal pricing and investment policies for state-owned firms. In addition, although there exists a considerable body of empirical material on the conduct and performance of SOEs, generally accepted models have been difficult to come by in this area.

Even in mature, industrialized economies, SOEs have tended to be quite diverse. They have operated in a range of market environments, have sometimes had markedly different histories, and have been justified in many different ways. This in turn indicates that state ownership can be a very flexible policy instrument, or, putting it more accurately, that state ownership is a means of increasing the flexibility of policy by increasing the range of immediately available policy instruments. For, under state ownership, all the decision variables of the firm (prices, investment, employment, location, and so on) potentially become instruments of public policy.

Nevertheless, despite the diversity of circumstances in which it is found, there are very definite patterns in the incidence of state ownership. While acknowledging that SOEs can have a very wide variety of purposes, a major task of analysis is to attempt to explain the main features of those patterns. For example, it must be explained why, in developed market economies, the bulk of the economic activity accounted for by SOEs has been in the communications, energy, water and transport sectors.

Characteristics that these sectors have in common include economies of scale and of density, which in the absence ofstate intervention might be expected to lead to high levels of concentration and to a tendency for physically similar goods and services to be sold at (sometimes vastly) different prices to customers located in different areas. (Compare, for example, the costs of delivering electricity to an isolated village with the costs of delivery to a large town which has power stations nearby.) In response to regulatory demands from affected groups, the tendency of state intervention has been to suppress these price differences to a greater or lesser degree by creating monopoly rents which are then used to subsidize supplies to the high-cost customers. That is, governments have sought to redistribute economic resources among different consumer groups, here defined chiefly by location.

It is not the case, of course, that state ownership is the only means by which cross-subsidization can be achieved. Regulated private monopoly or explicit subsidies financed from general taxation are obvious alternatives. The point is simply that, given the goal of cross-subsidization, these alternatives may have disadvantage is that make public ownership appear more attractive. For example, explicit subsidy might make the costs of regulation more transparent and hence reduce its political payoffs—for example, by increasing the opposition from those who lose out—while regulated private ownership might be less effective in achieving secondary political goals such as protecting employment in the industry or using the enterprise to cross-subsidize upstream and/or downstream industries.

As a second example of the use of public ownership to meet regulatory objectives, consider the case of the "rescue" of a failing firm, motivated by a political desire to protect the interest groups that would be adversely affected by bankruptcy and liquidation. State ownership has the potential advantage that financial assistance can be targeted precisely on the firm in trouble—compare this with the costs of the alternative optionof subsidizing all firms in the industry—but the matching disadvantage is that the unequal treatment of similar firms in the industry will create negative political feedback from rival interests who are adversely affected by the targeted subsidies. This latter factor (i.e. discriminatory treatment) therefore increases the political costs of state ownership of only part of a competitive industry, but it is a factor that does not operate when the whole of the domestic industry is in public ownership.

4. PRIVATIZATION AS REGULATORY REFORM

Privatization can take many forms, but here the focus will be on divestiture of SOEs. Divestiture unaccompanied by the introduction of any new regulations concerning the commercial operation of the enterprise concerned is perhaps the simplest form of privatization. In such a case privatization implies that the state has relinquished control (or potential control) of variables such as prices, investment and employment levels, and ownership transfer is therefore unambiguously associated with deregulation. The extent of deregulation will, however, depend upon exactly how the enterprise had been governed within the public sector. Where the SOE had been used actively to promote policy goals such cross-subsidization—so that its behavior was somewhat different from the behavior of an unregulated privately owned firm—the deregulation will be substantive. In contrast, in cases where the SOE had already been required to operate at arm's length from government and to meet rigorous financial constraints, the extent of deregulation associated with the act of divestiture might be highly limited. In the latter case, the more substantive deregulation may well have occurred earlier, for example when the enterprise was first required to behave commercially.

As noted above, however, it is not inevitable that ownership transfer leads to deregulation. Particularly in utility industries, privatization is frequently accompanied by the establishment of new regulatory regimes, and in such cases detailed analysis may be required to determine the extent to which the stance of regulatory policy has really shifted. For example, where public monopoly is replaced by private monopoly the change in ownership could represent no more than a relatively minor adjustment in policy. On the other hand, privatization may be part of a wider shift in regulatory policy that leads to much more fundamental behavioral changes in the market, as when divestiture is accompanied by measures to promote competition (such as the elimination of statutory entry barriers) and by (usually implicit) abandonment of cross-subsidization objectives. It is, therefore, the overall shape of the package of regulatory reforms that is likely to be of most economic significance, not privatization per se. The divestiture of an SOE may represent anything from a minor adjustment of regulatory policy to a major regulatory reform depending upon the measures that accompany it.

5. WHY PRIVATIZE?

A common account of the emergence of privatization policies is based on the proposition that state ownership is simply a less efficient way of organizing production than private ownership. When this is coupled with a public interest theory of policy,[4] the implications are fairly direct: privatization is desirable in terms of economic efficiency and occurs for precisely this reason.

Although it is not difficult to find examples of manifest inefficiency within the public sector, it is nevertheless easy to see why this "explanation" of privatization is less than compelling. If it is true (a) that publicly owned enterprises are less efficient than similar privately owned firms and (b) that policy makers seek to promote economic efficiency, there remains the puzzling question of why the various activities to be privatized were taken into the public sector in the first place.

One possible response to the puzzle is the argument that state-ownership was a "mistake", attributable to the influence of socialist thinking in earlier parts of the century. On reflection, however, theories predicated on the basis of systematic and worldwide "mistakes" stretching over several decades lack a certain credibility. Among other things, they fail to acknowledge the significance of case studies of nationalization which reveal many examples where the extension of the public sector was a pragmatic response to problems being encountered by key interest groups in the economy.

The underlying difficulty with analyses of privatization that are based only upon propositions about the relative efficiencies of public and private production is that they tend to be fundamentally static in character. The initial creation of state-owned enterprises and their subsequent privatizations represent changes in policy, and it is therefore natural to seek explanations for them in terms of changes in economic conditions. Thus, if the aim is to explain privatization in terms of the differential efficiency of the private and public sectors, the analysis must rest upon a hypothesis of increasing relative efficiency of private enterprise. This complicates matters of course, since, even if public ownership were demonstrably less efficient than private ownership, it is not at all obvious why its relative performance should deteriorate over time.

Similar objections can be made to some of the other theories of privatization that have been put forward over recent years. In an early example of the genre, Sappington and Stiglitz (1987) develop a model in which the main difference between public and private ownership lies in the transactions costs faced by the government when attempting to intervene in production activities. There is then a tradeoff between the advantages of greater ease of intervention (public ownership) andof greater credibility of promises not to intervene (private ownership).

Shapiro and Willig (1990) explore models in which privatization not only reduces the information available to regulators but also has the effect of reducing the effort levels of the managers of the enterprise concerned (the enterprise continues to be subject to regulation). On the other hand, they argue that public ownership has the disadvantage that, as a result of the superior information that it makes available, it provides politicians and bureaucrats with more opportunities to pursue their own agendas/goals, to the potential detriment of economic efficiency. In consequence, there is a tradeoff between the conflicting incentive effects.

These and other principal-agent models tend to be limited by the very strong assumptions that they tend to make about information conditions. For example, to anyone familiar with the operation of government bureaucracies the assumption that public ownership gives politicians full information about the production possibilities of the firm is heroic in the extreme. Indeed, it is far from obvious that the information available to regulators is reduced by privatization. While privatization may reduce a government's rights in respect of the acquisition of information from the firm, any such loss is balanced by the fact that privatization provides incentives for competing operators in the capital market (brokers, fund managers, individual investors) to seek out and analyze information that could affect share prices.

The main point to be made here, however, is that the various principal-agent models are static in nature, and that at best they can only be regarded as preludes to dynamic theories capable of explaining the changes in policy that go under the name of privatization. Moreover, the variables upon which the principal-agent models place emphasis are not ones that are likely to provide convincing bases for the development of more dynamic analyses. For example, it is difficult to see why there might have been a worldwide shift in the ease of obtaining information from either publicly or privately owned firms, or in the ability of politicians and bureaucrats to insert their own agendas into enterprise decision making. Indeed, in general, it would seem more realistic to view factors such as information conditions and political discretion as idiosyncratic or context specific, in the sense that they tend to be dependent upon the particular institutional, political and cultural circumstances pertaining in different countries and different economic sectors.

6. THE OVERALL SIZE OF THE STATE SECTOR

A more promising starting point from which to embark upon an analysis of privatization is to consider the overall portfolio of activities for which the state is responsible in a given economy. For, in general, privatization is nothing more than the transfer to the private sector of some part of this wide portfolio of activities and, even in those cases where privatization programs have been the most radical, the state has continued to play a major role in economic activity.

One, albeit imperfect, measure of the size of the overall government portfolio is the level of public expenditure,[5] which showed a strong tendency to rise relative to GDP or GNP throughout most of the world over the first three-quarters of the 20th century. To give just one example, in Britain government expenditure as a percentage of GNP was around 8% in 1890, 12% in 1910, 29% in 1932 and 38% in 1961. The ratio peaked in the mid-1970s, when public expenditure reached over 49% of GDP. Since then it has fallen back somewhat, albeit with notable cyclical fluctuations.

For present purposes it is not necessary to go into great detail about the factors giving rise to upward pressures on public expenditure programs: it is sufficient to note that public expenditure has tended to rise strongly relative to national income throughout much of the 20th century. The significance of this trend is that governments have been compelled to increase the tax burden in order to finance the higher expenditures and that the economic costs of raising additional finance have therefore tended to increase over time.

The problem is that much of the output of the state sector is either not priced (as when education or health services are supplied free of charge) or is priced in ways that do not reflect the relevant costs of supply (as when electric power is provided to rural communities at subsidized prices). Indeed, if activities were priced on a commercial basis, in many cases the rationale for state provision would disappear. In practice, then, the state relies heavily upon tax revenues to finance its activities, and taxes are levied on individuals at rates that do not vary with the state benefits received by the individuals concerned.

Given this lack of correspondence between benefits received from state activities and the incidence of taxation required to finance those activities, taxation gives rise to distortions in economic incentives. There will be a tendency for economic agents to substitute into those goods and services that are not taxed (or are subsidized) by the state and out of those goods and services that are taxed. Further, the magnitude of the substitution (or change in behavior) will tend to be greater the greater the level of activity of the state, for the greater the level of activity of the state the higher will tend to be the relevant taxes and subsidies.

Letting the "deadweight" or efficiency loss caused by taxation be E, the total cost of government intervention can be written as $T + E$, where T is the level of tax revenue. The first component (T) represents income transferred from consumers and producers to the government and the second component (E) represents the real resource loss to the economy as a whole that is incurred as a result of effecting the transfer of funds.

Assuming that all the tax revenue is used to provide government supplied goods/services and transfer payments, including the administrative services required to collect the tax revenues, total government expenditure G will be equal to the tax yield T. In these circumstances the relationship between the level of government expenditure and its "costs" can be explored by examining how the quantity $T + E$ varies with T. Thus, for example, the marginal "cost" of government expenditure is $(\Delta T + \Delta E)/\Delta T = 1 + \Delta E/\Delta T$. The second term in this expre ssion, $\Delta E/\Delta T$, is the marginal resource cost of government finance, which will be represented by λ.

It can be assumed that, in general, the marginal costs imposed by government expenditure are an increasing function of the level of government expenditure relative to national income. On the other side of the coin, government expenditure can be assumed to generate economic benefits in the form of advantages to those individuals and groups using state-provided services and receiving transfer payments. While the total of such benefits will rise with the level of government expenditure, marginal benefits might be expected to fall with the size of the budget since higher benefit activities will tend to be given priority when resources are restricted.

Similar points also apply to the relationship between expenditure and political/regulatory benefits, which are the benefits that will be relevant to decision makers. Total political payoffs can be assumed to be an increasing function of government expenditure, while marginal payoffs will be a decreasing function of expenditure. The equilibrium level of government expenditure will then be determined by the condition that marginal political/regulatory benefits are equal to marginal costs.

Within this framework, increases in government expenditure relative to GDP can be explained either by growth of demand for government expenditures or by a reduction in the marginal costs of government finance. While the latter of these possibilities may have been a significant factor in many countries—particularly where marketization has shifted an economic activity toward forms that are more readily taxable—it appears clear that demand growth has generally been the faster of the two, and that is it has therefore tended to have the effect of raising the marginal resource cost of government finance. It can be hypothesized that it is this increasing cost of raising government finance and the related increase in the supply price of government expenditure that has the driving factor behind privatization programs in non-communist economies, as will now be explained.

7. PRIVATIZATION AND THE PORTFOLIO OF STATE OUTPUTS

Total government expenditure is accounted for by a large variety of different activities, each of which can be viewed as an individual output of the state sector. In addition to the problem of determining the overall size of the state sector, therefore, there are important issues to be settled concerning the precise portfolio of outputs that the state will supply. For example, to what extent should the public sector be a provider of health care, or of higher education, or of transportation systems? Thus, movements in the overall expenditure total do not necessarily imply equiproportionate movements in its various components, nor does a static level of expenditure imply an absence of shifts in the mix of different activities undertaken by the state.

If the focus is switched to aparticular activity of the state sector, we can let q represent the level of the activity (i.e. q is some measure of the level of output) and g represent the size of the budget implicitly allocated to that activity. It can reasonably be assumed that, other things equal, higher outputs require higher budgets. Over time, both the output and the budget allocation can be expected to shift as circumstances change. A particular activity may be expanded or contracted and, within this framework, complete privatization can be said to occur when the level of the relevant activity falls to zero. That is, the state no longer engages in the particular activity.

To formalize this line of reasoning a little, let $B(q)$ be the benefits derived from an activity level q before deduction of the cost. For example, if the activity were the construction of a road, $B(q)$ would be a measure of the present value of the benefits accruing to road users less the damages inflicted via effects such as environmental degradation, noise, and so on. Benefits and damages would, in this calculation, be weighted to reflect the distributional preferences of the relevant decision maker.

For simplicity it will be assumed that, when $q > 0$, there is a linear relationship between the budget and the output level: $g = \alpha + \beta q$ where α and β are positive constants. It will also be assumed that $g = 0$ when $q = 0$, implying that α is an avoidable cost. For example, in the case of an SOE the fixed cost element can be interpreted as the value of the assets of the firm. More precisely, α can be interpreted as the opportunity cost of retaining assets in the public sector rather than selling them on the capital market.

Given these assumptions, the net benefits from the state activity can be written as:

$$NB(q) = B(q) - (1+\lambda)[\alpha + \beta q], \tag{1}$$

where λ is the marginal resource cost of a unit of government revenue, which is determined, among other things, by the general level of taxation/expenditure (G) relative to GDP (Y). That is, $\lambda = \lambda(G/Y)$).

For small adjustments in a particular government activity, λ can be taken as parametric. Large changes in expenditure will, however, significantly affect the value of λ, and this should properly be taken into account in policy evaluations. For example, a large-scale cut-back in government spending on a major activity would, by reducing the value of λ throughout the state sector, produce higher net benefits from other government activities, as well as from the activity in question. The magnitude of this increase in net benefits will be equal to the product of total government expenditure and the fall in the cost of finance.

The equilibrium level of the state activity will be determined by two conditions. First, there is the local condition that marginal benefit be equal to marginal cost, $B'(q) = (1+\lambda)\beta$. Second, there is the condition that any local maximum (say q^*) defined by the marginal benefit equals marginal cost condition should also be a global maximum. In particular, net benefit at q^* needs to be non-negative, otherwise the equilibrium policy is for the state not to engage in the activity in question. This latter condition can be written as

$$B(q^*) - (1+\lambda)\beta q^* \geqslant (1+\lambda)\alpha, \tag{2}$$

which, in the privatization context, can be interpreted as saying that the benefits associated with the SOE, net of the costs of current financial transfers, should be at least equal to the value of the revenue yield from privatization.

Now consider the position in respect of a state activity for which benefits and costs are static in real terms (so that $B(q)$, α and β are constant over time). If the marginal resource cost of government revenue, λ, is increasing over time, the net benefit derived from the activity will fall over time. Assuming that condition (2) initially continues to hold, the equilibrium level of the activity will initially fall. During this stage of the process the budget allocated to the activity is squeezed. In the case of SOEs there may be a reduction in the amount of finance made available for new investment or, more generally, the enterprise's budget constraint may be hardened. Past some critical value of λ, say λ^c, however, condition (2) ceases to hold and there is a discontinuous jump in the level of state provision to zero, representing the shift to privatization of the activity. Thus, over time, the typical sequence is tighter budgets followed by privatization.

While it is changes in the cost of government finance that, in this analysis, trigger the regime shift, it can be noted that other factors play a role in influencing the timing of the reform. For example, β can be interpreted as a measure of the efficiency of the SOE: the higher the value of β the less efficient is the enterprise. As can be seen from (2), the critical value of λ is a decreasing function of β. Hence, other things being equal, privatization will tend to occur earlier the less efficient is the SOE. Similarly, the value of the political benefits deriving from state ownership will affect the timing of reform, and this value can be expected to vary widely across countries and industries according to the specifics of each particular set of circumstances.

The analysis indicates that privatization should be a normal part of the management of the public sector. Over time, as preferences, institutions, political influence and technologies shift, it is natural for the portfolio of state activities to adjust. For example, the high income elasticity of demand for some of the goods that are supplied or subsidized by the state, such as education and health care, will tend to drive up the demand for government expenditures. As demands for these activities increase, however, others (for which income elasticities of demand are lower) will tend to be "crowded out" as the cost of government revenues rises.

Other things being equal, then, we might expect to see the adoption of privatization policies occurring first where the marginal resource cost of government revenue, λ, is high and rising. The variable λ may not itself be directly observable, but the hypothesis can be tested by reference to proxy variables likely to be correlated with the resource cost of government revenue. For example, it was argued above that λ can be expected to be an increasing function of the overall rate of taxation, in which case privatization will be linked to high and rising rates of taxation. More generally, privatization will tend to be triggered by fiscal crises.

In respect of the types of activities likely to be privatized, the obvious candidates are those outputs of the state whose benefits rise less slowly than national income and which are not subject to counteracting reductions in costs. The SOE sector of the economy tends to fulfill these conditions: for example, public ownership to subsidize the development a particular sector of the economy, create a national telephone network, create a national electricity system, and so on, may become less and less of a priority as the desired developments proceed.

Similarly, consider the use of SOEs to cross-subsidize the supply of a commodity to one section of the population, for example, subsidization of telephone services in rural areas by higher prices in urban areas. In this case, the implicit tax (on urban consumers) is non-transparent and does not figure directly in fiscal calculations, but the underlying analysis is similar. That is, the implicit tax combines with explicit taxation to magnify resource allocation distortions, and the efficiency cost of the cross-subsidization will tend to increase over time. In contrast, there is no obvious reason to expect that the income-elasticity of demand for redistribution of resources will be particularly high.

Finally, it can be noted that the analysis also suggests that shorter-term fluctuations in the level of overall economic activity and in the state of public sector finances can have important implications for the timing of privatizations. Cyclical movements in the economy will generally be associated with movements in government expenditures and taxes relative to GDP. In a recession there will tend to be a relative increase in demand for financial resources to support those adversely affected by changed economic conditions (e.g., the unemployed) and, given the short-run inflexibility of government expenditure programs, compensating reductions in other areas may be difficult to achieve. The expenditure to GDP ratio therefore tends to rise. It is, however, unlikely that the tax revenue to GDP ratio will, in the absence of an increase in tax rates, increase in a similar fashion. Indeed, where, as is often the case, marginal tax rates (with respect to economic activity) are greater than average rates, the tax yield will tend to fall relative to GDP in recessions.

The net result of recessionary tendencies in an economy can, therefore, be expected to be an increase in fiscal pressures on the government, implying that, other things being equal, privatization is more likely to be triggered by recessionary conditions than by boom conditions (alternatively, recession will tend to accelerate divestiture programs).

8. CONCLUSIONS

The brief analysis developed above is rather different from the theories of privatization based on principal-agent analysis which have been popular in theoretical economics. It does, however, appear to be much closer to the empirical realities. For example, agency theory might be used to support the argument that private enterprise is inherently more efficient than public enterprise, either in nearly all circumstances or at least in situations not involving natural monopoly. Acceptance of such a proposition, however, is not very helpful as a theory of privatization. It can offer no explanation of how enterprises got to be in the public sector in the first place, or, given that they did, why privatization occurred when it did and not earlier or later.

In contrast, the approach developed above locates a theory of privatization within a more general theory of state behavior. Moreover, while a large number of factors can influence the preferred policy outputs of the state at any one particular time, the increasing cost of government finance appears to be a factor that is of particular empirical significance in explaining the emergence of privatization programs.

More specifically, a rising cost of goverment finance induced by increased demand for state expenditure (for example, due to demands for governm ent services that have high income elasticities of demand) will put longer-term pressures on government outputs whose perceived benefits are rising less fast. These latter type of outputs are arguably characteristic of the SOE sector of very many economies in the late 20th century.

The alternative approach does not imply, of course, that efficiency differences between public and private enterprises are not an important influence on policy decisions. Other things being equal, if public sector options are less efficient than private sector alternatives, state ownership will appear that much less attractive and divestiture will be triggered at a lower value of the cost of government finance. The reason why relative efficiency is not stressed in the current analysis is simply that it is a factor that is likely to be relatively stable over time.

Finally, the specific political benefits associated with SOEs will vary from case to case, so that, while the general trend toward privatization is clear, the timing of individual divestitures will be heavily affected by local circumstances. Given the variations that occur in such circumstances, it is not to be expected that all bureaucrats will leave business at a broadly similar time.

NOTES

1. *Bureaucrats in Business* is also concerned with the question of how reform can be speeded up, an issue that I will not address in the this paper.

2. According to this metaphor, state interventions of various types (e.g., the promulgation of a new regulation, the granting of a subsidy) are outputs supplied by some arm of the state (e.g., legislature, ministry, regulatory agency) in response to explicit or implicit demands from one or more sections of the population (e.g., producers, labour unions, consumers, taxpayers).

3. The valuation placed upon the changes in cash flows by enterprise managers, and hence the strength of the dynamic incentives, will depend upon a range of factors, including ownership. For example, a relatively soft budget constraint will reduce the severity of the stick in the SOE case, and it might also have the indirect effect of reducing the value of the carrot to a competing, privately owned firm (since the latter may be able to gain less volume from the protected SOE).

4. Public interest theories abstract from agency problems in the political system and assume that policy makers maximize social welfare, most commonly defined in terms of economic efficiency.

5. This measure fails to take proper account of the significance of state "outputs" that take the form of rules and regulations. It is, for example, easy to imagine an economy in which the level of public expenditure is small in relation to GDP but in which the state meddles in all sorts of minor details of private activities.

REFERENCES

Bureaucrats in Business: The Economics and Politics of Government Ownership, World Bank Policy Research Report (New York: Oxford Univ. Press, 1995).

Sappington, D. E. M. and J. E. Stiglitz. 'Privatization, information and incentives,' *Journal of Policy Analysis and Management* (1987).

Shapiro, C. and R. D. Willig. "Economic rationales for the scope of privatization," in E. N. Suleimann, and J. Waterbury (Eds.), *The Political Economy of Public Sector Reform and Privatization* (Oxford: Westview Press, 1990).

Smith, A. *An Inquiry into the Nature and Causes of the Wealth of Nations*, edited by R. H. Campbell, and A. S. Skinner (Oxford: Clarendon Press, 1976).

Vickers, J. and G. Yarrow. 'Perspectives on privatization,' *Journal of Economic Perspectives* (1991).

Yarrow, G. and P. Jasinski (Eds.), *Privatization: Critical Perspectives on the World Economy* (London: Routledge, 1996).

Part III
Regulation Theory and Policy

[20]

Information and Regulation

David E. M. Sappington and Joseph E. Stiglitz

Governments are involved in a large number of regulatory activities, from regulating utilities, to regulating financial institutions, to regulating automobile safety and setting emission standards. Regulations are but one means that the government has of attempting to elicit certain desired outcomes. To some extent, regulations represent a half-way house between methods that involve more direct controls (nationalization of an industry) and those that involve the use of more indirect control mechanisms (taxes and subsidies). The theme of this chapter is that central to an understanding of both the choice among these methods of control—and, when regulation is opted for, the design of the regulatory scheme—is an understanding of the problems posed by imperfect and costly information.

The discussion proceeds as follows. The first section contains an overview of the basic issues associated with government control. The analysis is broken down as follows. First, the reasons for government control are outlined. The essence of the information problems under consideration here is then described, and it is noted that the particular control problems on which we and the literature focus are properly viewed within the context of a broader range of control problems. The different control structures under taxation, regulation, and public enterprise are illustrated. The reasons that the structure and hierarchy of control are not inconsequential are then outlined. The role that franchise bidding can play in the regulatory arena is considered. We next examine the apparent duality between problems of optimal taxation, regulation, and monopoly pricing—a duality that if not properly treated, can given misleading results. The regulatory problem of rent extraction from an established firm is then outlined and thereby serves as an introduction to the second section of the chapter.

The second section focuses on regulation as a method of control. It begins with a formal statement of the regulator's problem of rent extraction. It identifies the problems caused for the regulator by imperfect information and reviews proposed methods for dealing with these problems. In particular, regulatory schemes that involve auditing, comparisons across firms, and comparisons over time are considered. An attempt is also made to relate the "new" models of regulation under imperfect information to the "classic" models of regulation (e.g., the analysis in Averch and Johnson 1982).

A caveat is in order before proceeding. We attempt to provide an evenhanded overview of the literature on the design of regulatory policy in the presence of limited information. But it is likely that we fail to cite some important references and manage to cite papers with which we are most familiar (e.g., our own) too often. We apologize in advance for any shortcomings on these two accounts. We also note at the outset two complementary surveys that are recommended. The one most closely related to ours is by Caillaud et. al. (1985). The other is an overview of the contracting literature by Hart and Holmstrom (1985).

Reasons for Government Control

As noted at the outset, government control is observed in at least three distinct forms: indirect control, regulation, and nationalization. Government action in one of these forms generally arises from a belief that markets do not always work well. One of the central results of modern economics is the fundamental theorem of welfare economics. The theorem establishes conditions under which competitive market allocations are Pareto efficient and under which Pareto-efficient allocations can be sustained by competitive markets. When these conditions fail to hold, markets will not, in general, be efficient. Thus, in principle, there is scope for government intervention.

Much of regulation is aimed at three broad classes of market failure:

1. *Imperfect competition.* Under a variety of circumstances the market will not be competitive. (What is required for economic efficiency is more than just rivalry; what is required is that firms be price takers, which they may not be, even when there are many firms in a market.) This is particularly relevant where there are large nonconvexities, giving rise to natural monopolies. This provides the motivation for government intervention in utilities.[1]

2. *Imperfect information.* The fundamental theorem of welfare economics assumes that there is perfect information. Recently Greenwald and Stiglitz (1986) have shown that when there is imperfect information, there is almost always scope for government intervention (even if the government is restricted to imposing commodity taxes and subsidies) which is Pareto improving. Imperfect information provides the basis of two broad sets of government regulatory activities: First, in insurance markets the likelihood

of the event occurring that is insured against is increased by the provision of insurance; to offset this, the insurer attempts to *regulate* the actions of the insured. Since the government, either implicitly or explicitly, is involved in a large number of insurance activities, it attempts to impose regulations that reduce the incidence of events that are insured against.[2] Second, consumer protection and worker protection legislation is largely based on the presumption that individuals cannot look after themselves as well as the government, largely because they are imperfectly informed and it is costly for them to gather information:

3. *Externalities*. Whenever there are externalities, competitive market solutions will be inefficient. Government regulations aimed at controlling pollution, for example, are directed at alleviating the problems posed by these externalities.

Critics of government activities suggest that even when the simple competitive model does not yield efficient outcomes, a broader interpretation of the competitive process will. For instance, in the case of externalities, there are incentives for individuals to get together to eliminate such inefficient outcomes. This assertion is loosely referred to as the Coase theorem. It ignores of course all the standard public good/free rider problems. Moreover it ignores the transactions costs involved in these private deliberations: the government can be thought of as the mechanism that has, indeed, been set up to deal with these externalities. Finally, in small group situations it ignores the bargaining problems and the inefficiencies that arise in bargaining under imperfect information.[3]

With perfect information the three approaches of regulation, nationalization, and control via tax/subsidy schemes are equivalent.[4] To see this, assume the government wishes to effect a particular outcome. It can either *induce* the private firms to do what the government would like them to do through taxes and subsidies, or it can, via the regulatory mechanism, *order* the firms to do what it wishes them to do. Alternatively, the government can carry out the task itself (with nationalization). Indeed, in some sense, regulation can be viewed simply as the imposition of a nonlinear tax/subsidy schedule, with large penalties being imposed for noncompliance with the orders of the regulator (sufficiently large that the regulated is always induced to voluntarily comply with the wishes of the regulator).[5] With perfect information none of the controversies about the efficiency of government control or its form would arise.

With imperfect information regulation, nationalization, and tax/subsidy schemes are not equivalent; and the form of regulation becomes of importance. Research to date has not delineated clearly the distinctions among these alternative control mechanisms. Our objective is to identify some of the salient differences. To see what is at issue, we focus our attention on the regulation of utilities, but it should be apparent how the analysis can be adapted to other regulatory contexts.

The information theoretic approach to these issues begins by attempting to delineate who knows what when, and who has the right to take what actions under various circumstances. The natural assumption is that those involved in production (i.e., in running the utility) have more information concerning (1) the technology of production (both current technology and the possibilities for technological improvements), (2) the demand structure for the commodity, and/or (3) relevant factor costs than do outside parties.[6] Others (the government, the regulator) may come to know about some of these variables, but only with a lag, and indeed, in a rapidly changing environment, the information that they acquire may be of only limited relevance to the current situation. It is this limited information that poses the central problem for the government. The government can only order the firm to do something that is feasible, but it may not know what is feasible. And even if it were to know what is feasible, what it would wish the firm to do depends on factor costs, technology, and consumer preferences, about which it may be less informed than the firm—for example, if the costs of reducing pollution are enormous, the government might not wish the firm to reduce its pollutant levels by very much; if the costs are insignificant, it may wish a large reduction. But if the government must rely on the firm to tell it what the costs are, what is the government to do? It cannot, in general, rely on the firm to tell it the truth—for instance, what manager of the firm would truthfully tell the government his reservation wage, or the opportunity cost of his time? Much of the detailed modeling we describe in the second section of this chapter is aimed at devising methods by which the firm is induced to reveal this information truthfully (although at a cost, often in the form of "distorted" behavior).

The information problems with which we are concerned arise because of the impact that they have on the government's attempt to control the firm and to "extract" rents from it. We now turn to consider directly the problem of control.

The Hierarchy of Control

The simplest model of control involves two parties: the party that establishes the controls (the principal) and the party that operates under these controls (the agent). The simplest model of regulation, for example, considers the interaction between one regulator and a single firm. In fact, this is the type of model that has been afforded the vast majority of attention in the literature, as the review in the second section makes clear. In reality, however, the control problem is far more complicated.

Take, for instance, the case of regulation. And for simplicity, suppose that there is only a single firm in the economy and that this firm produces the sole commodity that is consumed by society. Thus with only a single market we need not be concerned with distinctions between partial and general equilibrium analyses. Even in this simple setting there are a host of control problems that are intricately intertwined.

In the traditional nineteenth-century model of such a firm, there was no division between ownership and management: the owner-manager took whatever actions were required to maximize his (expected) utility, and since little attention was paid to any disutility of effort, it was usually presumed that he simply maximized his (expected) profits or the (market) value of the firm.

It is now recognized that this provides an inadequate description of most modern corporations where ownership is widely held. The earlier naive models simply substituted the "board of directors" for the "owner" and ignored any problems the owner (or board of directors) faced in controlling the management. But the members of the board of directors (other than those who are part of management itself) usually have very limited information, both concerning what the management is doing, and what the firm's full opportunity set is—that is, they have limited information concerning technology, markets, and factor prices. These information limitations provide management with considerable discretion.[7]

But even this view, which emphasizes the distinction between owner-managed and nonowner-managed firms, does not provide a good description of corporations in which shares are widely held. For it is not apparent that shareholders can effectively exercise even the limited control associated with ownership. As has been repeatedly emphasized, good management is a public good: all shareholders benefit from having the firm run in a better way. There is, however, a cost to learning whether the current management is performing its job well (and of course to attempting to replace inadequate management). There is thus an incentive for each small shareholder to attempt to free ride on the management efforts of others.[8]

But shareholders are not the only ones affected by the actions of the firm. Debtors, though they do not share in large gains, will be adversely affected by large losses. The institutional structure by which one bank acts as the lead bank reduces the "free rider" problem, which in any case is much less than that for shareholders, since individual banks are likely to have large positions with particular firms. The threat of banks to cut off credit, and the explicitly specified rights of banks to intervene in the firm under stipulated conditions, enable the banks to exercise some indirect control over management. This suggests that the appropriate way to view a firm is as an agent for multiple principles.[9] And as is by now well known, the equilibrium to multiple-principal agent problems is not Pareto efficient (see Braverman and Stiglitz 1982, Bernheim and Whinston 1984, Arnott and Stiglitz 1985). This basic depiction of the simplest control structure within a firm is illustrated in figure 1.1.

Figure 1.1 also illustrates an additional problem of control within the regulated setting. When regulation is introduced, there is another "principal" who can exercise some control over the firm's activities. However, the effectiveness of the regulator's control is reduced by her limited information. For example, the regulated utility can claim that at current rates of return, capacity expansion is unprofitable; it can attempt to create a "crisis." The regulator may find it difficult to ascertain whether the crisis is real.

There is another important aspect of the control structure in a regulated setting. Generally, the regulator is either elected or appointed by an elected official. To ensure that the regulator is acting according to the interests of her constituency, she may be subject to a variety of controls. Thus, in practice, the regulator is most often both a principal (to the firm) and an agent (of her constituency, or the "government"). Note too that the judiciary often serves as an independent check on the activities of both the regulator and the firm.

Figure 1.2 illustrates the basic hierarchy of control under nationalization. It is still important for managers within the public enterprise to create incentive systems for their subordinates. Furthermore the judiciary will still exercise control over the activities of the enterprise. The distinctive element of nationalization is that the board of directors, rather than being elected by shareholders, is appointed by the government. Initially, this fact was interpreted to mean that no separate regulatory authority was needed, since it was generally assumed either that the firm acts according to the government's wishes or that effective control can be exercised via the board of directors.

More recently, discussions have correctly emphasized the similarity between nationalized and nonnationalized (including regulated) industries: the actions of the firm are still controlled by managers, who have

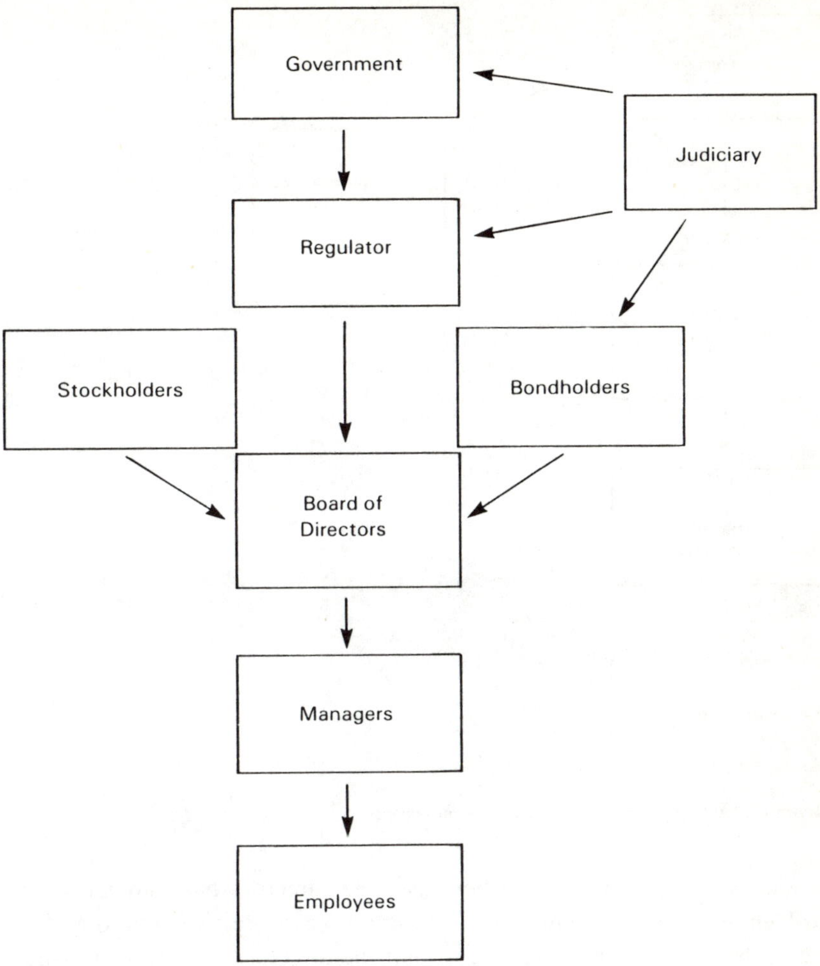

Figure 1.1 Control structure in a regulated setting

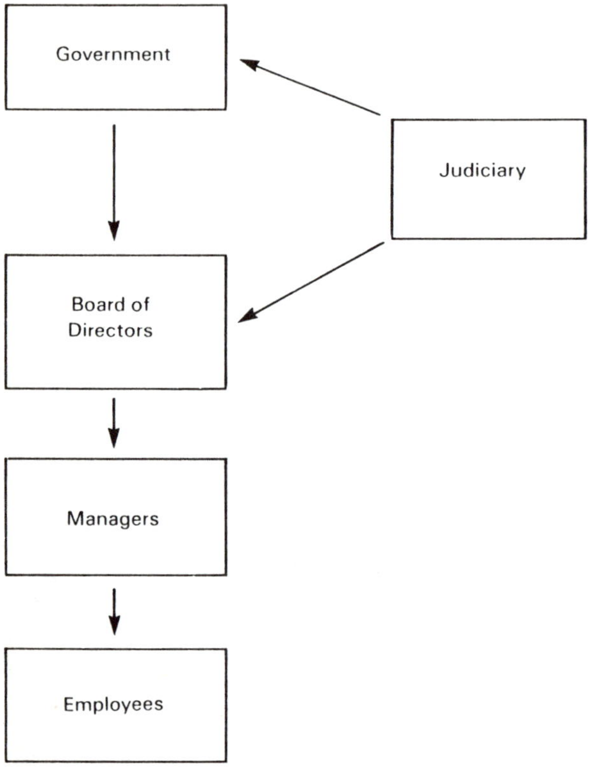

Figure 1.2 Control structure under nationalization

considerable discretion. In either case, the directors have an incentive problem in inducing the managers to undertake the desired actions and to reveal their private information, so that the directors can ascertain what actions should be undertaken.

But this is not the only problem. Often, the directors of an enterprise come to identify with the problems of the firm. Thus they see themselves as representing the interests of the firm—its workers and other members of the nationalized industry—within the government (e.g., in seeking greater government subsidies). Thus, in at least one country which has nationalized many industries, the focus of current concern is on the "socialization" of nationalized industries, trying to alter the behavior of the firm to pursue national objectives rather than private objectives.

Moreover the possibility of large government subsidies replaces the indirect control exercised by banks (and credit markets in general) by the indirect control exercised by political institutions. The differences in incentives (to management, or to the board of directors) should be apparent.[10]

Why Is Control Important?

We have proceeded in our discussion emphasizing the differences in the structure of control associated with different institutional structure.[11] At first glance it is not obvious why differences in firm behavior must necessarily be associated with differences in institutional structure. For instance, vertical integration need not have any effect on the behavior of either the upstream or downstream firm, if all contingencies are contracted for. That is, just as we argued for the equivalence between regulation and indirect control in the presence of perfection information, there is a similar equivalence, even in the presence of at least certain kinds of information imperfections, between a vertically integrated and a nonvertically integrated industry. So long as the set of observables remains unchanged, the same set of contracts for each of the actors can be designed. And with the same set of contracts, behavior of each of the actors will presumably be the same.

But contracts are never complete. Thus the debt contract allows the creditor to intervene in specified ways in specified circumstances, but it does not specify precisely what he will do—that is, what kinds of direct or indirect control mechanisms he will employ. (The reason that contracts are not fully specified should by now be obvious. For a detailed discussion, see Williamson 1975.) Because contracts are not complete, different institutional structures differ according to which party has "residual control," namely who can take what actions when unspecified contingencies arise and who has the right to intervene in the activities of others and under what circumstances. And because of incomplete contracting, it may not be possible for a principal who has the right to intervene to commit himself in advance not to intervene.

There remains, however, the question of why control is important. In the traditional competitive (Arrow-Debreu) model, control is not important; the manager of the firm simply maximizes the firm's market value. Any other manager would do precisely the same thing that the firm's current manager does. Indeed, the manager's beliefs about the likelihood of any given state of nature have no impact on the firm's actions.

In the Arrow-Debreu economy there is unanimity among all shareholders concerning what actions the firm should take. However, when there is not a complete set of Arrow-Debreu securities, there may be disagreements, both about whether the firm should maximize its stock market value, and what will be the consequences (e.g., for future market value) of any particular course of action.[12] Though these disagreements are of some theoretical interest, the disagreements between the interests of the debtors and creditors are undoubtedly of greater significance. In particular, the firm's shareholders are concerned only with those returns in the states of nature in which the firm does not go bankrupt, the firm's debtors only with the likelihood of bankruptcy, and the returns in the bankrupt states (which affect what can be recovered). There is a real conflict of interest, and as the probability of bankruptcy looms large, this conflict of interest becomes of sufficient importance that the debtors can no longer trust the manager: they wish to intervene, and the debt contract gives them the right to do so.

It is important to realize that in nationalized enterprises, the government stands in the position as a creditor, either losing the returns on its investment or being "forced" to extend further funds to the enterprise. (The issues are more complicated in regulated enterprises, where shareholders may not be allowed to retain profits from "good" decisions and where ratepayers may be "forced" to pay for "bad" decisions.)

But the government's involvement in these decisions is broader. We argued earlier that it is only under the highly idealized conditions of the Arrow-Debreu model that there would be complete congruence between the objectives of the firm and Pareto efficiency. Thus, in principle, the government might wish to intervene to alleviate some important observed inefficiency in the firm's behavior (e.g., the firm fails to take into account the cost to the government, in unemployment insurance, of closing a plant). In practice, the government seems equally likely to intervene for distributional reasons (e.g., to ensure that some remote areas obtain services at subsidized rates). In some cases the two are hard to distinguish (largely because of the informational concerns that are the central concern of this chapter). Is the government's attempt to reduce the prices paid by a certain class of consumers an attempt to restrict the exercise of monopoly power, or is it an attempt to subsidize that class of consumers?

Auctions as a Means of Control

It is precisely because of the difficulty of separating out these distributional questions from more narrowly defined efficiency issues that some economists have argued for a more limited role of government: the gains from efficiency enhancing interventions may be more than offset by the losses from efficiency decreasing interventions.

Let us assume, for the moment, that the government is simply concerned with efficiency issues; problems of distribution, it is frequently argued, are the proper province of taxation. Let us also assume that the government and potential producers share the same perfect information about consumers' preferences. For simplicity, also consider the case where the regulator's objective is to maximize some well-defined measure of consumers' welfare, such as consumers' surplus. Thus we are abstracting from any problems associated with controlling the regulator. (We will similarly abstract from the control problems within the firm.) Finally, suppose that there are a number of firms who have or can acquire technological information but that this information is unavailable to the regulator.

Auctions have been proposed as a means to render inconsequential the regulator's limited knowledge in this setting. Loeb and Magat (1979), for example, suggested that the regulator might grant a monopoly franchise and subsidize the monopolist for his output according to the magnitude of consumers' surplus generated. The subsidy ensures marginal cost pricing and least cost production. And, with sufficiently competitive bidding, the government can appropriate all monopoly rents. In as much, the regulator effects the outcome that she would have if she had perfect knowledge of the most efficient technology.

Of course for this scheme to perform as well as this analysis suggests, a number of conditions must be satisfied. In particular, there are a number of important institutional assumptions implicit in the theory. For example, unlimited subsidies are presumed feasible (and costless). If subsidies are not feasible (for political or other reasons), so that the firm's only income must be derived from its sales revenue, efficient pricing will not result unless the producing firm is able to price discriminate perfectly. Furthermore, when firms differ in their abilities to price discriminate, a firm may be willing to bid more for the franchise, not because it is a more efficient producer but because it has developed better methods of discrimination.

It is also important for this proposed auction scheme that the bidding be sufficiently competitive to eliminate all monopoly rents. In practice, it is costly for firms to prepare a bid (which entails determining the expected present discounted value of the profits associated with the monopoly franchise). And since these costs are generally sunk costs, only a small number of firms may bid for the monopoly rights.[13]

Thus, though it is true that the presence of technological information dispersed among many firms can help alleviate control problems that arise when the regulator's information is limited, auctions are not necessarily a panacea.

There are some circumstances under which, even in the absence of the ability to discriminate perfectly, an auction will yield efficient outcomes. Assume all individuals are identical and that only linear prices (i.e., a constant price per unit consumed) are feasible. Then an auction in which the government imposes a lower bound on the utility level of the consumers will yield Pareto-efficient outcomes, provided the utility level is set appropriately. The markups of price over marginal cost will not be uniform. Rather, they will correspond to Ramsey prices, after Frank Ramsey (1927).[14] In the simple case of independent demand curves, goods with inelastic demand will have proportionately higher markups.

This result follows from the duality between the optimal pricing problem of a monopolist and the problem of optimal taxation: the latter maximizes utility subject to a profit constraint, whereas the former maximizes profit subject to a utility constraint. The Lagrangian functions associated with these two problems have the same form, and for appropriately chosen values of the constraints yield identical solutions. But this result requires some critical assumptions, which we will return to shortly.

The Locus of Control

To this point, the analysis has largely been concerned with a partial equilibrium analysis. General equilibrium considerations also warrant attention, for they further complicate problems of control. To illustrate this point, consider a setting related to the setting of the preceding section. In particular, suppose there are a number of regulated markets in the economy, with one good produced in each market. Suppose also that the regulator in each market knows how consumer demand varies with the product's price in that market but lacks global demand information. The regulator is again presumed to have as her goal the maximization of consumers' surplus. Similarly, suppose that there are a large number of potential producers of each product who are perfectly informed about the costs of producing that one product but none of whom has global technological information. For simplicity, also assume that the firms in each sector are identical in their ability to price discriminate.

It is immediate from the preceding discussion that if the regulator in each sector is permitted to subsidize the producer under her jurisdiction—and if none of the other sources of market failure noted earlier arise—she can effect her most desired outcome within that sector through an auction. And even without subsidies, the most preferred price vector can be ensured if potential producers can sign binding contracts with consumers. This is accomplished by awarding the franchise to the firm that, with its signed contracts, generates the highest amount of consumer's surplus. Competition will eliminate any rents to the monopolist and will ensure that the least cost producer in each sector wins the franchise.[15]

If subsidies are not allowed, price will not equal marginal cost in each sector. It is apparent that this solution is not as desirable as the solution when subsidies are feasible. But given the restriction, the outcome is the same one that would arise under a system of direct control and full knowledge of technological possibilities.

More subtle questions arise if there are multiple products in each sector, but subsidies across sectors are still not allowed. Will the pattern of prices required to break even be Pareto efficient? This question seems similar to that posed earlier, where we argued that the duality between the optimal tax problem and the monopoly pricing problem ensured the efficiency of the pricing structure. But there we ignored the interactions between the regulated sector and the rest of the economy, interactions that would be taken into account with direct government control. We will show that there is less to this duality result than meets the eye in a general equilibrium analysis. The global optimum to the government's problem will take into account the impact of each firm's pricing decisions on (1) the tax revenues (and profits) generated elsewhere in the economy and (2) the prices of other commodities. The decentralized, partial equilibrium approach outlined earlier will not do so.

Thus, if coal is used as an input into electricity, a railroad monopoly would ignore the effect of its pricing structure on the price the utility has to charge to break even. Since price in that sector exceeds marginal cost, there are real welfare effects from this apparent pecuniary externality (see Ebrill and Slutsky 1985; McFarland 1985). Similarly, a change in the price of electricity may affect the demand for oil, and hence the revenues the government receives from the windfall profits tax.

There is an additional problem with this decentralized approach to regulation. The least cost producer of a single product is not necessarily the least cost producer of two or more products. Thus, when franchises are awarded on the basis of performance within a particular market, the producer that is globally most efficient may be overlooked, particularly if the franchises are not all awarded simultaneously.

It is also the case that in practice, the monopolist is usually granted a limited monopoly. Thus, being concerned with the entry of competitors (producing "related" products), the monopolist will choose prices with entry deterrence in mind. To illustrate, suppose that there is some "inefficient" technology for producing some commodity. The associated production cost puts a constraint on what the monopolist can charge for its output. If the demand for the product is very inelastic, the monopolist will have to charge less than the unconstrained Ramsey price. If the stand-alone technology has diminishing returns, the monopolist will consider only his residual demand curve (taking into account the amount supplied by others) in calculating the "Ramsey" prices. In as much, these prices may differ markedly from those the government would charge.

Of course all of these problems could be avoided if the monopoly franchise were defined "appropriately." In particular, if the entire economy were defined as the franchise, the distinction between the partial and general equilibrium approaches would disappear. But, for the proposed bidding schemes to operate well in this setting, there would have to be a number of firms with detailed *global* technological information. Clearly this is an unlikely possibility. For effective operation of the scheme, the government would also need to know global demand functions. Such knowledge is also unlikely. Indeed, one apparent reason for delegating authority to individual regulators within individual markets is to have them develop expertise and make informed judgments using that expertise. With limited abilities to acquire and process information, regulators cannot be expected to develop anything close to global expertise.

Thus some degree of decentralization is inevitable. But we have shown that even with complete information about local demand and cost structures, regulators will generally be unable to effect the outcome that is globally optimal.

Our analysis has suggested that defining the franchise appropriately is of critical importance. Even limiting ourselves to the static entry deterrence and residual demand problems, this is not an easy matter.[16] In a dynamic setting, awarding a broad franchise may result in "correct" prices today. But broad franchises imply that some new, more efficient technologies that develop may not be employed.

The duality between the standard optimal tax problem and the standard monopoly pricing problem will fail to hold for another reason when consumers differ and their characteristics are not completely known to the government or monopoly firm. Under such circumstances the government may employ nonlinear price schedules to allocate the burden of the fixed costs of the utility in an equitable manner. In setting its price structure, the government may know that some individuals are better able to pay than others but can only distinguish among them on the basis of, say, the quantity of electricity consumed. Formally, the set of Pareto-efficient discriminating pricing structures are those that maximize one group's utility subject to other groups attaining particular levels of utility, while ensuring that no group consumes the (price-quantity) "bundle" designed for a different group. These latter constraints are referred to as the self-selection constraints.[17]

The optimal pricing problem of the monopolist is not fully dual to the problem of Pareto-efficient taxation in this setting, for the monopolist is concerned only with maximizing revenue subject to the self-selection constraints. In particular, for indivduals who are inframarginal (i.e., who derive strictly positive consumer surplus from consuming the product), the monopolist is only concerned with how a change in pricing policy affects his demand and revenues, and not how it affects their utility.[18] Moreover, there are important situations where the government prefers a pooling outcome (where individuals' characteristics cannot be discerned from their consumption patterns), though a monopolist would always discriminate.[19]

It is thus apparent that the formal similarity between the government's pricing problem and that of the monopolist is just that: a formal similarity. The government would not in general simply wish to delegate the problem of pricing to a monopolist, even if it could capture the rents through an auction. Our analysis has shown that a monopolist would not behave as would the government if the government had access to the monopolist's information about technology and demand.

In practice, the problem faced by the government is that it neither knows the technology nor the demand structure. Thus it finds it difficult to ascertain what the marginal costs are, and hence what the implicit tax is on any particular service. The government also has difficulty determining the deadweight losses associated with any particular discriminatory pricing scheme. It knows that the monopolist need not be acting in the public interest, but it may now know how to take appropriate corrective action.

Rent Extraction from Established Firms

These important informational problems, as large as they may loom in political debates, have not played quite so central a role in recent literature on the regulatory problem. This literature has been more concerned with the problem of extracting rents from a utility in a partial equilibrium setting where there is an established firm, so that a "fair" auction of the franchise is not feasible. If the government attempts to extract too much rent from the firm, the firm may terminate operations. The government must make an inference concerning the technology but must extract the information through the standard method of framing the choices of the firm in such a way as to induce it to reveal its true characteristics, so the firm's behavior is distorted. The second section describes more formally how this is done, and identifies some important situations where the associated distortions are limited in magnitude.

Before presenting these results, several general observations are in order. First, this literature focuses on the rent-extraction problem, not the incentive problem of providing the manager with the appropriate impetus to work hard.[20] It focuses on imperfections of information relating to technology, rather than to factor prices. In fact, these informational problems are related: the regulator finds it difficult to know whether some factor (e.g., "management") is being paid more than its opportunity cost. Thus, observed inefficiencies may arise from an incompetent (but overpaid) management working as hard as they can, rather than a competent management sloughing off on the job. (Indeed, it is possible that it is often no more difficult to make good managerial decisions than to make bad managerial decisions. Since much of the effort involved in making better managerial decisions entail costs not borne by the manager himself (e.g., he hires a contractor to do some research), the importance of effort disutility is hard to ascertain).

Second, it will become apparent that the structure of the regulator's policy is highly dependent on what she knows, what she can monitor, and how quickly she can learn. We suspect that in the static environments underlying most of the models to be presented, the government would eventually learn most of the relevant aspects of technology, and thus the informational asymmetry would disappear. But in the real world, technologies (as well as demands and factor prices) are constantly changing. Thus the magnitude of the informational problem is related to how fast the environment changes and how fast the regulator learns.

Third, we turn to "revelation problems," where the regulated firm is induced to reveal his information by the choices he makes. The regulator also learns a considerable amount from auditing, namely from directly monitoring the actions or performance of the regulated. The design of optimal monitoring behavior would be the subject of a separate review.[21]

Some Simple Models of Regulator-Firm Interaction

In this section we focus on the implications of the recent literature on the economics of information for the direct interaction between a regulator and regulated firm(s). We attempt to describe a general framework within which existing work can be analyzed. We discuss the essential similarities and differences among the various models in the literature and also some important regulatory models not normally associated with that literature (e.g., the Averch-Johnson 1962 model). We close with a brief discussion of important issues that have been afforded relatively little attention in the literature. Though our formal review of the literature is slanted toward models that concern the regulation of public utilities, the basic insights of the literature apply more generally. Note also that the focus of the entire analysis here is on a small part of the entire hierarchy of control. This concerns the direct interaction between the regulator and the firm (figure 1.1). Furthermore the "firm" is treated as a "black box," and the assorted control problems within the firm are not addressed.

The central features of the models that we will discuss here are the following. First, the nature of the information asymmetry between regulator and firm is crucial. As noted earlier, what is known to each party at various points in time largely determines the properties of the optimal regulatory policy. Second, the policy tools available to the regulator and the costs of using them are of paramount importance. Bounds on penalties that the firm can be forced to bear and large (perhaps infinite) costs of auditing the firm's activities will severely limit the regulator's ability to influence the firm's decisions. Third, whether or not interaction between the regulator and firm is repeated will be shown to play a major role in shaping optimal regulatory policy. Fourth, the manner in which the regulator's strategy varies with the number of firms under her control will be considered.

A General Model

We begin with a description of a simple but fairly general model that allows us to consider in some detail the first two of these four features—the nature of the information asymmetry and the set of policy tools available to the regulator. The model thus presumes nonrepeated interaction between a regulator and single firm. We return later to discuss repeated play and multiple firms.

A common element of most principal-agent analyses is that the principal (here, the regulator) is the Stackleberg leader in the "game" played with the agent (here, the regulated firm). That is, the regulator specifies the terms of an incentive scheme before any other actions take place. Following the announcement of how the firm's compensation and the regulator's actions will depend on observable variables, the firm and then the regulator may alternate actions that influence the ultimate outcome of the regulatory process. Some models have each party undertake only one action. In other models it is important that the parties alternate actions, with both the regulator and firm undertaking at least two distinct moves. Both possibilities are incorporated in the general model we construct here.

Often the firm's initial action ($\mathbf{a}_1^F$) is simply some communication about its information ($\mathbf{I}^F$) to the regulator. Based on this communication and her own information ($\mathbf{I}^R$), the regulator undertakes an action ($\mathbf{a}_1^R$) according to the terms of the announced regulatory policy.[22] This action might include an audit of the firm's communication or a decision as to whether to allow the firm to continue operations. There is assumed to be an outcome ($\mathbf{Z}_1$) that is observed by both the regulator and firm following their initial actions. This outcome could include the firm's message to the regulator and/or the result of the regulator's audit of this report.

Next the firm undertakes a second action ($\mathbf{a}_2^F$). This action might be a production or pricing decision, for example. Then the regulator undertakes a second action ($\mathbf{a}_2^R$), which might represent an observation of industry performance, an audit of the firm's activities, and/or a payment to the firm. Following these actions, a second outcome ($\mathbf{Z}_2$) is commonly observed. This outcome might include realized prices and outputs, and/or the result of an audit of the firm's activities (e.g., realized costs). Note that all actions, outcomes, information sets, and so forth, may well be vectors.

The regulatory policy ($\mathbf{R}$) consists of the regulator's actions and the payment schedule, $\tilde{P}(\cdot)$. This schedule specifies payments to the firm as a function of observable variables $\mathbf{Z}_1$, $\mathbf{Z}_2$, $\mathbf{a}_1^F$, and $\mathbf{a}_2^R$. Thus the firm's compensation can depend on its communications with the regulator, its performance, and the regulator's actions, for example. The regulatory policy is presumed chosen to maximize the regulator's expected utility given her initial information $\hat{E}\{U^R(\cdot)|\mathbf{I}^R\}$. Here and throughout the ensuing analysis, E represents expectations over unknown variables. $U^R(\cdot)$ is the regulator's utility function. This function may have as arguments payments (P) to the firm, the regulator's actions ($\mathbf{a}_1^R$, $\mathbf{a}_2^R$), the firm's utility level (U^F), and the (vector of) outcome(s) of the regulatory process ($\mathbf{X}$). Typically the regulator is regarded as acting to maximize the expected level of consumers' surplus or a weighted average of producers' and consumers' surplus.[23] The firm is generally thought to maximize its own expected profits.

Thus a fairly general representation of the regulator's problem (RP) is the following:

$$\underset{\mathbf{R}}{\text{Maximize}} \quad E\{U^R(\mathbf{X}, P, \mathbf{a}_1^R, \mathbf{a}_2^R, U^F)|\mathbf{I}^R\}, \qquad (RP)$$

subject to

$$\mathbf{a}_1^{\mathrm{F}} \in \underset{\mathbf{a}}{\operatorname{argmax}}\, E\{U^{\mathrm{F}}(P, \mathbf{a}, \mathbf{a}_2^{\mathrm{F}})|\mathbf{H}_1^{\mathrm{F}}\}, \qquad (AS_1)$$

$$\mathbf{a}_2^{\mathrm{F}} \in \underset{\mathbf{a}}{\operatorname{argmax}}\, E\{U^{\mathrm{F}}(P, \mathbf{a}_1^{\mathrm{F}}, \mathbf{a})|\mathbf{H}_2^{\mathrm{F}}\}, \qquad (AS_2)$$

$$\mathrm{E}\{U^{\mathrm{F}}(P, \mathbf{a}_1^{\mathrm{F}}, \mathbf{a}_2^{\mathrm{F}})|H_i^{\mathrm{F}}\} \geq \bar{U}^{\mathrm{F}}, \quad i = 1, 2, \qquad (\mathbb{R})$$

$$\tilde{P} \in \hat{\mathbf{P}}, \qquad (FP)$$

$$\mathbf{a}_i^s \in A_i^s, \quad i = 1, 2, \quad s = R, F, \qquad (FA_1^s)$$

where

$$P = \tilde{P}(\mathbf{Z}_1, \mathbf{Z}_2),$$

$$\mathbf{Z}_1 = \tilde{\mathbf{Z}}_1(\mathbf{a}_1^{\mathrm{F}}, \mathbf{a}_1^{\mathrm{R}}, \mathbf{I}^{\mathrm{F}}, \mathbf{I}^{\mathrm{R}}),$$

$$\mathbf{Z}_2 = \tilde{\mathbf{Z}}_2(\mathbf{a}^{\mathrm{F}}, \mathbf{a}^{\mathrm{R}}, \mathbf{I}^{\mathrm{F}}, \mathbf{I}^{\mathrm{R}}),$$

$$\mathbf{X} = \tilde{\mathbf{X}}(\mathbf{a}^{\mathrm{F}}, \mathbf{a}^{\mathrm{R}}, \mathbf{I}^{\mathrm{F}}, \mathbf{I}^{\mathrm{R}}).$$

In the statement of (RP), $\mathbf{H}_i^{\mathrm{F}}$, $i = 1, 2$, denotes the history of outcomes that are known to the firm at the time it undertakes action $\mathbf{a}_i^{\mathrm{F}}$. Thus, for example, $\mathbf{H}_2^{\mathrm{F}} = \{\mathbf{I}^{\mathrm{F}}, \mathbf{R}, \mathbf{a}_1^{\mathrm{F}}, \mathbf{Z}_1\}$. Also $\bar{U}^{\mathrm{F}}$ is the reservation expected utility level of the firm.

The act-selection (AS) constraints in (RP) capture the fact that the firm chooses its actions to maximize its expected utility, given all available information. The individual rationality ($\mathbb{R}$) constraint guarantees that **R** promises the firm at least its reservation level of expected utility, so that the firm will not choose to employ its resources elsewhere.

The fourth constraint in (RP) defines feasible payment (FP) schedules. For example, upper bounds on rewards and lower bounds on penalties (e.g., bankruptcy limitations) may be imposed by appropriate specification of $\hat{\mathbf{P}}$, the set of feasible payment schedules. The (FA_i^s) constraints simply define the set of feasible actions ($\mathbf{a}_i^s$) for both the regulator ($s = R$) and the firm ($s = F$). These constraints might, for example, structure communication between the firm and the regulator, and/or dictate that the regulator cannot expropriate the firm's assets.

Special Cases: Adverse Selection and Moral Hazard

Many models of regulation in the literature are special cases of (RP). These models differ only in the interpretation of actions, in the restrictions placed on payment schedules, and in the nature and timing of the information that becomes known to the regulator and firm. Before describing a few of these models, let us reiterate that problems of control only arise for the regulator if the firm's private information is better than her own and/or if she cannot costlessly observe the firm's actions. Absent these difficulties, the regulator can effect $\mathbf{a}_1^F$ and $\mathbf{a}_2^F$ to maximize her own expected utility (subject only to individual rationality concerns for the firm). This outcome is known as the first-best outcome. It is achieved in the presence of perfect information with a "forcing" contract. The regulator specifies the actions that she wants carried out and ensures the firm its reservation utility level if and only if these actions are carried out. Otherwise, the firm is penalized and is thereby "forced" to effect the desired behavior.

The dual concerns of private information and unobservable actions reflect two classes of problems. When the actions of the firm are unobservable and when the actions enter the firm's utility function in a nontrivial manner, a moral hazard problem is said to exist. For example, in Laffont and Tirole's (1986) model of public enterprise, personally costly effort supplied by the manager to reduce costs cannot be observed by the government. Here, a moral hazard problem exists because it is costly for the government to induce the manager to supply an "appropriate" level of effort.

A problem of adverse selection is said to exist when the firm has nontrivial information about its capabilities (e.g., its technology) that is not shared by the regulator. For example, in Baron and Myerson's (1982) model, the regulated firm knows its cost structure perfectly while the regulator does not.

When Is the First-Best Outcome Feasible?

It is important to note that the regulator may be able to achieve the first-best outcome even though problems of moral hazard and adverse selection are potentially present. This ideal outcome will be feasible if (1) the firm is risk-neutral toward monetary payoffs, (2) the regulator and firm share the same information initially (i.e., $\mathbf{I}^R = \mathbf{I}^F$ at the time when $\mathbf{R}$ is announced), (3) $\hat{\mathbf{P}}$ is unrestricted, and (4) the outcome ($\mathbf{X}$) of the regulatory process is observable. The first-best is effected in this scenario by equating the firm's compensation schedule with the regulator's utility function (i.e., $P = U^R(\cdot)$). Thus the expected payment to the firm is the expected level of the regulator's utility. In addition, to effect the desired distribution of rents, the firm is required to make a lump sum payment to the regulator prior to beginning production equal to the difference between its expected payoff under this scheme and its reservation utility level. Due to symmetric beliefs the regulator and firm will concur on the appropriate magnitude of this lump sum payment (k). And because the firm is risk-neutral, it need be awarded no risk premium for undertaking this venture.

When the firm's objective function is made to coincide with the regulator's, it is apparent that the firm will act as the regulator would require it to if she shared the firm's private information. Thus any problems of moral hazard and/or adverse selection are avoided.[24] It is this intuition that underlines the subsidy scheme proposed by Loeb and Magat (1979). They note that if the firm is subsidized with the level of consumers' surplus it generates, the firm will effect marginal cost prices and engage in the socially optimal level of cost-reducing activities.

Aside from the important general equilibrium effects discussed in the first section, there are a number of other reasons why, in practice, it may not be possible to effect the first-best outcome. For one, the firm (or its investors) may have some aversion to risk. Second, the firm's information about its environment may be better than the regulator's information from the start of the regulatory regime. Third, the firm may not have the resources to make the requisite payment before demand and cost functions become known, and legal limitations on the firm's liability may allow the firm in some adverse circumstances to renege on the promised lump sum payment (k). In the presence of binding bankruptcy constraints of this sort, (i.e., when the definition of $\hat{\mathbf{P}}$ in (RP) places binding restrictions on the compensation schedule), it will no longer be optimal for the regulator to reward the firm according to the social objective (i.e., set $P = U^{R}(\cdot)$) and accept a payment less than k when the firm's profits are too low. Such a policy provides inappropriate incentives to the firm. Since it cannot be forced to bear the full "downside" risk from its activities, for example, the firm may well undertake actions that are too risky from the perspective of the regulator. (A more detailed discussion of this point is provided by Stiglitz and Weiss 1981.)[25] Furthermore the firm may be tempted to declare bankruptcy under circumstances where the net social surplus from continued production is positive. To counteract these tendencies, the regulator will effect a policy that induces an outcome different from the first-best outcome. The nature and intent of the distortions are analogous to those that will be introduced when the firm's information is initially better than the regulator's.[26] These distortions are described next.

When the firm's information about its environment is strictly better than the regulator's from the onset of the regulatory regime, the regulator's problem becomes more difficult. It is on this problem that much of the recent literature has focused. In this case the regulator must make the terms of the regulatory contract sufficiently attractive to the firm whatever its private information might be. (Technically, the individual rationality (IR) constraint in (*RP*) must be satisfied for all values of $\mathbf{I}^F$.) This will generally entail some rents for the firm under favorable circumstances (e.g., low costs or high productivity).

Auditing

Obviously the rents of the firm can generally be reduced if the regulator is able to verify directly the firm's private information through some costly investigation (e.g., an audit of the firm's costs). It is well known, for example, that if an unbounded penalty can be imposed on the firm when it is found to have falsely reported ($\mathbf{a}_1^F$) its private information, then a perfect audit of the firm's report ($\mathbf{a}_1^R$) need only be carried out with arbitrarily low probability to ensure the firm will always truthfully reveal its private knowledge.[27] Thus aside from the cost of obtaining this direct observation of the firm's private knowledge, the regulator can effect the first-best outcome.

Of course this conclusion may be sensitive to the quality of the audit. If the firm's compensation is based on the realization of an imperfect monitor of its private information, some risk is necessarily imposed on the firm. Thus the first-best outcome cannot be attained if the firm is averse to risk. If the firm is risk-neutral, though, an imperfect signal may allow the regulator to effect the first-best outcome. Necessary and sufficient conditions for this to be the case are recorded in Riordan and Sappington (1985b).[28] A sufficient (though not a necessary) condition is that the dimension of the signal space be at least as great as the dimension of the space of the firm's private information.

Bounds on penalties that the firm can be forced to bear following an unfavorable audit (like bankruptcy constraints) will also inhibit the regulator's ability to achieve the first-best outcome. Baron and Besanko (1984b) examine the regulator's optimal strategy when an imperfect monitor of the firm's costs is available to the regulator and when payments to the firm are bounded from below. Intuitively, to maximize expected surplus net of auditing costs the regulator will optimally investigate any report of costs above a critical level and impose the maximum feasible penalty on the firm if the audit and original report are sufficiently inconsistent.

When moral hazard complicates the incentive problem, the optimal use of imperfect cost information is a bit different. Laffont and Tirole (1986) examine a setting in which the firm's manager can reduce operating costs through the expenditure of effort. The disutility associated with such effort is common knowledge, though the level of effort expended is unobservable.

The manager also has private information about the marginal cost of production that would prevail in the absence of any cost-reducing effort. Thus the model incorporates both adverse selection and moral hazard problems. After production occurs, the regulator observes an informative signal about realized production costs.

To induce the manager to exert effort to reduce costs, the regulator must promise the manager a reward if realized costs are small relative to predicted costs. On the other hand, the manager must be rewarded for predicting that costs will be low; otherwise, incentives will exist to exaggerate cost projections. Laffont and Tirole demonstrate that the optimal incentive scheme is linear in the difference between predicted and realized costs. Payments increase more rapidly with this difference the smaller are predicted costs, providing the requisite incentive both to reveal truthfully cost estimates and to put forth the effort required to reduce costs.

Self-Selection

Absent access to an auditing technology, the regulator will generally have to rely on other policy instruments. Many studies have focused on the optimal use of prices, subsidies, and taxes to deal with the adverse selection problem. A large number of these studies have adopted the assumption that there is a single technological parameter (e.g., marginal cost of production) that is known to the firm, whereas the regulator only knows the statistical distribution of this parameter (e.g., see Baron and Myerson 1982).[29] Communication about this parameter between the regulator and firm is presumed costless. In terms of (*RP*) these models have $\mathbf{a}_1^F$ as a report by the firm to the regulator concerning its technological parameter, and $\mathbf{a}_1^R$ may be a decision by the regulator as to whether the firm's operations should be terminated. If the firm produces, $\mathbf{a}_2^F$ includes production by the firm at the regulated price, and $\mathbf{a}_2^R$ includes a verification of the firm's output and the payment of compensation to the firm. Thus the firm's compensation can depend on both its initial report to the regulator and other observable variables (e.g., its production level).[30] Most models of this type (with the aforementioned exceptions) presume the firm's costs cannot be observed by the regulator at any cost.

The solutions to models of this type have a number of common and central features. First, the firm is generally able to command rents from its superior information. Second, distortions in production decisions are generally effected. Third, firms with different information (e.g., costs) will generally be induced to behave differently (e.g., produce different levels of output). These features arise from a few fundamental considerations. For simplicity, these considerations are illustrated here, assuming that the sole information asymmetry concerns which of two possible values ($c_1 < c_2$) characterize the firm's two (constant) average production costs. Also the regulator's presumed objective is to maximize the expected level of consumers' surplus.

Ideally the regulator would have the firm with costs c_i produce output $Q(c_i)$ at price $p_i = c_i$, $i = 1, 2$, where $Q(\cdot)$ is the demand curve. Given a choice among these two prices, however, the firm with low costs will select p_2 and thereby earn rents. To induce the low-cost firm to choose the lower price, an additional payment of at least the magnitude of these rents must be promised the firm. Faced with this trade-off, it will be optimal for the regulator to reduce the rents that must be afforded the low-cost firm by raising p_2 above c_2, and thereby reducing the number of units of output on which the firm can exercise its cost advantage.[31] In extreme cases the optimal level of p_2 may be so high that the firm with high costs will not produce at all. But the more certain is the regulator that the firm's costs are c_2, and the smaller is the cost advantage of the lower cost firm (i.e., the smaller is $[c_2 - c_1]$), the closer to marginal cost c_2 will be the optimal price level p_2.[32]

Thus the optimal regulatory policy will induce the firm to set a lower price the lower are its costs so that ex post, the firm's true costs can generally be inferred from the price it has set. However, this "self-selection" only results because the regulator has made a binding commitment not to use against the firm the cost information that she will ultimately infer. We will return at the close of this section to consider how the optimal regulatory policy changes in the absence of such ability to precommit.

Distortions other than prices in excess of marginal cost will generally arise when the regulator's set of policy tools is more extensive. For example, if variable production costs are affected by observable fixed costs differentially according to the firm's technological parameter, the regulator will generally instruct the firm to operate with other than the cost-minimizing level of fixed costs (see Sappington 1983b).[33] And more generally, the regulator is likely to base the firm's final compensation on observable inputs and/or outputs that interact in a nontrivial manner with the source of the firm's private information. Doing so will generally distort the use and/or production of these inputs and/or outputs from efficient levels. And even if these variables of indirect interest can only be observed with some error and at some cost, the regulator is likely to incur the requisite costs provided the signal is sufficiently informative about the variable in question.[34]

Averch-Johnson

One form of input distortion that has received widespread attention in the regulatory literature is the overcapitalization bias considered by Averch and Johnson (A-J) (1962). The question of interest here is how their analysis is related to the general model described in (*RP*). There appear to be two crucial sources of information asymmetry in the A-J model. First, input prices (i.e., the cost of capital, r) are known to the firm but not the regulator. Second, the firm has superior information about the functional form of its technology. One might interpret the regulator's beliefs about r as having positive density on some interval $(r, \bar{r})$. The fact that the regulator always sets the allowed rate of return, s, in excess of the true cost of capital suggests that the regulator sets $s = \bar{r}$. Such a policy might be optimal if there are infinite costs associated with forcing the firm into bankruptcy. Baron and Taggart (1980) have also shown that the A-J regulatory policy can only be optimal if the regulator has no knowledge of the firm's cost structure. Otherwise, the optimal regulatory policy would employ the firm's choice of capital stock as an informative signal about its technology.[35]

A critical assumption in the A-J model is that r is exogenous. In fact the firm's cost of capital is likely to be sensitive to regulatory policy. One possibility is that if s is set below the current cost of capital, the firm's scale will be reduced (due to the difficulty in raising new capital), thereby reducing the firm's operating risk which in turn reduces the firm's cost of capital. A second possibility is that improved performance by the firm (e.g., reducing organizational "slack") will reduce its cost of capital. Thus the implicit assumption that the firm will go bankrupt if s is set below r may be an extreme one.

In practice, the regulator will also couple rate-of-return regulation with direct controls on the firm's choice of capital. Holmström's (1984) analysis suggests that these controls will be less stringent the less disparate are the objectives of the regulator and the firm and the more severe is the information asymmetry between the two parties.[36] When the firm's information is much better than the regulator's it is much better able to determine the socially optimal level of investment. Thus, provided its interest does not diverge too drastically from the social interests, the firm will be afforded greater freedom in selecting investments.

Repeated Interactions

To this point we have focused on models in which the interaction between the regulator and the firm is not repeated. In practice, regulation is most often an ongoing affair. Thus we turn to the question of how repeated interaction alters the conclusions derived from static models. Of central concern is how the firm will alter current behavior in order to influence future regulations when these regulations are based on current performance. Thus the main issue here is analogous to that faced in planning and labor settings. In the Soviet incentive problem (e.g., see Holmstrom 1982a; Loeb and Magat 1978; Weitzman 1976), when future production targets increase with current output, firms may intentionally operate below their capabilities. Similarly, if future piece rates are revised downward as output is produced more rapidly, workers will reduce current effort levels (see Stiglitz 1975).

To begin, note that there are conditions under which the conclusions of static models carry over exactly to their dynamic counterparts. For example, consider the adverse selection problem in which the regulator can costlessly commit herself to execute faithfully the terms of any regulatory policy announced at the outset of the regulatory regime. Furthermore suppose, for example, that the firm's cost structure (which it knows perfectly) is the same in every period, as is the regulator's imperfect information about these costs. Thus the regulator can never observe the firm's historic costs. Under these circumstances the optimal dynamic regulatory policy will be to institute the optimal single period policy in every period of the regulatory regime.[37] When the firm's costs are not perfectly correlated over time, the optimal dynamic regulatory policy will differ from its static counterpart, though the nature of the output distortions is the same in both.[38]

The severity of the information asymmetry about costs between regulator and firm may be of no consequence in repeated adverse selection problems if the regulator can observe the past performance of the firm. Sappington and Sibley (1985) propose a regulatory mechanism that gurantees that total surplus is maximized and that the firm is held to its reservation profit level in every period. The regulator is required only to know the firm's demand curve and discount rate and to be able to observe with a lag of one period (e.g., a year) the firm's historic expenditures (which the firm may manipulate strategically to exceed minimum possible production costs). She need have no knowledge of the firm's technology. The scheme awards the firm in each period the increment in consumers' surplus that its activities generate and imposes a tax equal to the difference between revenues and expenditures in the preceding period. The scheme is effective because it makes the objectives of the regulator and firm essentially coincidental.[39]

The ability to observe historic expenditures can ultimately render inconsequential even more severe forms of information asymmetry between regulator and firm. Vogelsang and Finsinger (1979) explore the case in which the regulator has virtually no information about the technology or demand structure of a multiproduct monopoly firm.[40] They propose an elegantly simple scheme that induces the firm to set prices that converge to their Ramsey levels. The scheme constrains a Laspeyre's index of the firm's prices in each period not to exceed the realized expenditures of the preceding period. The weights in the index are the quantities produced by the firm in the preceding period. Thus the larger are the realized profits of the firm in any period, the more severely will the subsequent price index be constrained. Eventually, profits are eliminated, and total surplus is maximized.[41]

It is also the case that repeated interaction with observable past performance can resolve problems of moral hazard. Radner (1984) and Linhart, Radner and Sinden (1983) show that provided the discount rate of the manager is sufficiently low and his personal costs from being dismissed are sufficiently great, he can be induced to act nearly in the regulator's interests without the imposition of undue risk.[42] The intuition commonly ascribed for their result is that with repeated play, the law of large numbers permits the regulator to distinguish more accurately between lack of diligence or effort by the firm and "bad luck" (that will be statistically offset by "good luck" over time). Consequently she is better able to motivate the desired behavior on the part of the firm. She may do so, for example, by threatening to terminate the management of the firm if performance over time is deemed sufficiently poor.

Comparisons among Agents

Repeated interaction is one source of multiple observations that allow the regulator to control better the actions of the firm. Another such source is the comparison of the performances of two or more agents. The use of comparative performance can be a powerful tool for the regulator. The work of Demski and Sappington (1984), for example, indicates that the first-best outcome can be ensured when the regulator is dealing with two risk-neutral firms whose costs are correlated (however slightly), even if the firms initially have perfect knowledge of their costs that is not shared by the regulator. In a related model, Nalebuff and Stiglitz (1983a) demonstrate how the first-best outcome can be achieved as a Nash equilibrium among privately informed regulated firms, even if they are risk-averse.

A regulatory scheme that rewards each firm according to its relative performance can mitigate the incentives that firms might otherwise have to perform poorly (e.g., exaggerate costs or shirk on effort). Essentially, the performance of one firm serves as a natural monitor of the behavior of another. Of course the value of the monitor will often depend on how similar are the characteristics (e.g., technologies and demand functions) of the firms. The greater the similarity, the more about unobservable firm behavior that can be inferred from relative performance. Because comparative performance can help alleviate the problems caused by information asymmetries, a regulator may even find it advantageous to permit entry into an industry that is known to be a natural monopoly. This possibility, which is suggested in Nalebuff and Stiglitz (1983a), is analyzed in Demski et. al. (1985). They show that the optimal regulatory policy may even entail replacing the incumbent firm with a higher-cost entrant at times in order to mitigate the incumbent's incentives to exaggerate costs.

Note too that with multiple potential producers, ex ante competition for the right to serve as a regulated monopolist can limit the ex post rents of the monopoly firm (see Demsetz 1968; McAfee and McMillan 1984).[43] Loeb and Magat (1979), for example, argue that bidding for this right can replicate the first-best outcome if the monopoly firm is subsidized according to the consumer's surplus that it generates and if there is sufficient competition for the right to operate the franchise. Riordan and Sappington (1985a) demonstrate that when potential producers receive independent estimates of the expected value of the franchise, "sufficient competition" entails an infinite number of bidders. With fewer potential producers some rents will accrue to the winning bidder. Furthermore, to limit these rents, it will generally be optimal for the regulator to induce the producer to set the price for its output strictly in excess of marginal production costs. The distortions at the production stage foster more competitive bidding and thereby limit the rents of the monopolist. (For related observations, see Laffont and Tirole 1985 and McAfee and McMillan 1986.) The magnitude of the distortions will generally be greater if the smaller is the highest private assessment of the value of the franchise (i.e., the smaller is the "winning bid").

A brief explanation of these conclusions is the following. The distortions at the production stage limit the rents that accrue to the producer when realized production costs are small. The more pronounced the distortions, the greater the rent reduction. Thus, by promising to effect more severe distortions the smaller the winning bid, potential producers are dissuaded from understating their true valuations of the franchise. Not only does a firm run a greater risk of losing the franchise to a competitor by understanding its true valuations, but, conditional on winning the franchise, it also secures a less profitable operation the smaller its bid.

Note that competitive bidding for a monopoly franchise allows the regulator to deal with two difficult problems. Bidding can both limit the rents of the eventual monopolist and help to identify the firm that is best suited for the productive task. Intuitively the firm with the lowest costs can afford to bid the most for the franchise.[44] Of course more congruent costs will promote more aggressive bidding. Again, then, greater similarity among participants will generally allow the regulator to approximate the first-best outcome more closely.

In general, specification of the optimal regulatory policy in the presence of multiple firms is a difficult and subtle exercise. Simple tournaments, for example, where a prize is awarded for the best performance, work less effectively as idiosyncratic differences among firms (e.g., abilities) become large relative to common environmental shocks (e.g., changes in key factor prices).[45] Nalebuff and Stiglitz (1983b) have shown that imposing a penalty on the "loser" can provide better incentives than rewarding the "winner." The authors also demonstrate that in more sophisticated incentive schemes, multiple equilibria can result or no equilibrium may exist at all. A key concern is to avoid excessive imitation by firms. If they are penalized too heavily for failures while being rewarded only meagerly for superior performance, incentives for efficient risk taking may be dulled, and technological progress thereby hindered. This and other related issues warrant substantially more attention.[46]

Limited Commitment

Before concluding, we briefly consider an important issue that has been avoided to this point. The issue concerns changes in regulatory policy that become necessary when the regulator cannot precommit herself for an indefinite period to carry out the terms of the announced policy. Recall that a credible commitment never to employ against the firm in the future information that can be inferred from its current performance generally allows the regulator to motivate better current performance. For example, with commitment, the firm can be induced to produce more output in every period the lower are its costs, thereby increasing consumers' surplus. However, without significant compensation for doing so, the firm will not allow itself to be identified as a low-cost producer if the regulator will subsequently eliminate all its future rents (as she will do absent a binding commitment not to). Thus the costs of tailoring the firm's performance to its capabilities (i.e., achieving "separation") increase when the regulator's ability to precommit is abrogated.

In the extreme case, where the length of the regulatory regime is infinite and the firm's discount rate is zero (as in Roberts 1984), no separation will be, or indeed can be, effected. Separation could only be achieved under these circumstances by offering the firm what amounts to an infinite bribe. With a finite planning horizon and/or positive discount rate (as in Britto et al. 1985; Baron and Besanko 1985), the payment required to induce separation will not be infinite. Therefore the optimal regulatory policy will generally entail a initial period of time in which no separation occurs, followed by a period in which separation is effected.[47] Thus with costless commitment it will generally be optimal to induce separation with continuing distortions (e.g., prices in excess of marginal cost). Absent the ability to commit, the optimal regulatory policy will generally induce more severe distortions for some period of time before all distortions are eliminated.[48]

Suggestions for Future Research

To this point, our concern has been with reviewing the insights the literature has to offer regarding the design of regulatory policy in the presence of important information asymmetries. Before concluding, we turn our attention to issues and questions in the field that warrant additional investigation.

First, note that our analysis (like the bulk of the literature) has focused on one particular principal-agent relationship. There are other such relationships of interest that characterize the regulatory environment, however. For example, owners of regulated firms must structure incentives for their managers to act on the behalf of owners. Similarly the managers must motivate employees to behave appropriately. Furthermore it may be necessary for the Congress to provide adequate incentives for the regulator to perform her job diligently. Significant research remains to be done before we can understand the delicate interplay among these many principal-agent problems.[49]

A related line of research concerns the optimal control of a regulated firm that is under the jurisdiction of more than one regulator. When the interests of these regulators are not entirely congruent, problems of conflicting regulatory mandates arise. The rationale for overlapping regulatory jurisdictions warrants additional consideration, as does the optimal structuring of incentives for the firm given such overlap.[50] Political considerations are one reason for the separation of regulatory powers. Another may be that the information required to design appropriate regulatory policy optimally resides with different regulatory bodies.[51]

It is also the case that while the literature we have reviewed contains observations regarding the general nature of efficient regulatory mechanisms, specific policy recommendations are generally absent. For instance, though we know that managers of electric utility firms should generally be forced to bear some of the social burden derived from incorrect decisions regarding nuclear power plants, the optimal extent of the burden is certainly not apparent. The optimal distribution of risk among ratepayers, shareholders, regulators, and managers of public utilities deserves much closer scrutiny. As noted earlier the issue is complicated because of a multitude of information asymmetries and interrelated principal-agent problems.

One additional information asymmetry also limits policy prescriptions on crucial regulatory matters. Because most economists lack crucial institutional knowledge of the particular industries in which policy issues arise, they are unable (or, at least, would be unwise) to offer precise policy recommendations. What seems important, then, is a sharing of private information concerning theoretical insights and institutional detail.

Notes

This chapter was written in part while J. E. Stiglitz was a visiting scholar at the Hoover Institution. Financial support from the Hoover Institution and the National Science Foundation is gratefully acknowledged. The views expressed in this chapter are not necessarily those of Bellcore. We are grateful to Elizabeth Bailey, David Besanko, Steven Salop, Jean Tirole, and an anonymous referee for helpful comments.

1. Recent literature (e.g., Baumol, Panzar and Willig 1982) has focused on the importance not only of nonconvexities but also of sunk costs. In the absence of sunk costs, efficient outcomes may be sustained, even with natural monopolies. On the other hand, even with very small sunk costs (which are pervasive in the economy), it may not be possible to sustain competitive and efficient outcomes even in the presence of small nonconvexities. See Dasgupta and Stiglitz (1985).

2. Notice, however, that private insurance firms would similarly attempt to "regulate" the behavior of the insured if they had the same powers to do so.

3. That is, when the two sides to the bargain have imperfect information concerning each other, a costly self-section process operates to enable them to differentiate themselves. For a more extended discussion of this, see Farrell (1985).

4. There are some problems that arise in the presence of nonconvexities; some allocations may not be able to be supported by linear tax-subsidy schemes. In general, however, they can be supported by nonlinear tax/subsidy schemes (see also note 5.)

5. Nonlinear tax/subsidy schemes are schemes where the payments to or from the firm are not simply proportional to the relevant variable. Thus a linear price system for pollutants would entail the polluter being charged an amount which is proportional to the amount of pollution. Simple nonlinear schedules include the pollutant being charged a fixed amount per unit of

pollution in excess of some threshold amount, or being charged a fixed amount per unit of pollution up to some threshold amount and a larger, fixed amount per unit of pollution beyond that level. Regulations often are written as if they impose a zero charge up to the threshold level and an infinite fine beyond that level. Of course the penalties imposed are seldom infinite; the polluter has the option not only to ignore the regulator but also any ensuing court order. Usually, however, the penalties for doing so are likely to be sufficiently great that compliance is achieved.

6. This ignores of course the fact that information within the utility is not shared equally by everyone. There are important control problems within the organization, as well as between the organization and the government. Our focus is on the latter class of problems, though we briefly discuss the former.

7. Thus the information literature (including the principal agent literature (Ross 1983; Stiglitz 1974) has provided a rigorous justification for the "managerial" theories of the firm, discussed earlier by Berle and Means (1932) and March and Simon (1958), among others.

8. Thus all the major alleged mechanisms for shareholder control have only limited effectiveness. While the ineffectiveness of shareholder meetings has long been recognized, the problems associated with the takeover mechanism have only recently attracted attention. See, for instance, Grossman and Hart (1980, 1981), and Stiglitz (1972, 1982, 1985).

9. There are other affected parties as well: when there are positive mobility costs (including specific human capital), workers are affected by the well-being of the firm.

10. Some discussions have emphasized the differences between "soft" budget constraints of government enterprises and their "hard" counterparts in private enterprises. There is much to the distinction, but it should not be overdrawn, particularly in the regulatory context. The firm can "persuade" the regulator to increase prices, in much the same way it attempts to persuade the government to increase subsidies. In addition, private firms often try to convince governments to provide them with subsidies when the threat of bankruptcy is imminent.

11. In traditional economic theory, all individuals are assumed never to make mistakes; any seemingly deviant behavior can be accounted for simply by inappropriate incentives. By contrast, recent work has focused on the consequences of errors (which are viewed to be inevitable) for organizational design. See, for instance, Sah and Stiglitz (1985).

12. These issues were discussed in Stiglitz (1970), parts of which were subsequently published in Stiglitz (1972). There, he noted in the context of a simple mean-variance model that shareholders would not wish the firm to maximize the market value unless they planned to sell all of their shares and that there would not be unanimity if shareholders' plans for selling shares differed. He also showed that there would be unanimity in favor of the Pareto-efficient allocation if shareholders neither planned to buy nor sell shares. A large subsequent literature (e.g., see Ekern-Wilson 1974) extended the latter result to a larger class of "spanning" conditions and showed that unanimity on the value maximizing condition could obtain under slightly weaker conditions than those associated with having a complete set of Arrow-Debreu securities. But as Grossman and Stiglitz (1980) and Radner (1974) point out, if among the actions of the firm is the choice of a debt-equity ratio, then essentially a full set of Arrow-Debreu securities is required. Moreover, as Stiglitz originally pointed out, and as Grossman and Stiglitz emphasize, in any economy with trading (either because of life cycle considerations or because different individuals obtain different information), the assumption that all individuals are planning neither to sell nor to buy securities seems inapplicable.

The importance of differences in beliefs for the behavior of the firm, in the absence of a complete set of Arrow-Debreu securities, is discussed in Stiglitz (1972).

13. In the second section we discuss how the government can enhance effective competition in the auction. That discussion also abstracts from a number of institutional drawbacks to auctions that are analyzed by Williamson (1976).

14. Boiteaux (1956) was the first to study the problem in the context of utility pricing. In the past decade an enormous literature on these issues has developed. For a survey in the context of the taxation problem, see Atkinson and Stiglitz (1980); in the context of optimal pricing, see Baumol and Bradford (1970).

15. And if one had complete confidence in the competence of the monopolist, one would trust that he would take advantage of any efficient innovation within the broadly defined confines of the franchise. But, given the informational problems within the firm that were previously discussed, we are concerned with issues of organizational slack, so we do not have complete confidence that all efficient innovations are adopted.

16. Note that we have ignored the fact that, in practice, Ramsey pricing is often misapplied, focusing on the conclusion that commodities with inelastic demands should be taxed more heavily. This ignores (1) the potentially important cross elasticity effects and (2) the important distributional concerns that often require that commodities with elastic demands be taxed more heavily (Atkinson-Stiglitz 1972, 1980).

17. Of course the government might not discriminate. Indeed, if there is an optimally chosen income tax designed to redistribute income optimally, then under certain separability conditions, if the consumers' surplus associated with consuming the output is high enough, a fixed-fee access charge along with a marginal cost price is optimal. Whatever redistribution is to be done is best done through the tax system.

18. Formally the outcome may still be within the set of Pareto-efficient outcomes, where zero weight is placed on the utility of all individuals. But this does not correspond to any "reasonable" social welfare function.

19. This is seen most clearly in the context of insurance. There, if individuals have the same risks, but differ in their risk aversion, a monopolist would price discriminate, but an egalitarian government would provide complete insurance to everyone at the actuarially fair odds.

20. Some exceptions are noted later.

21. Thus the regulator might base his review process (e.g., to ascertain, whether bad outcomes are the result of lack of effort or bad luck) on the level of certain observed outcomes such as output. Thus it might make the probability of a review an increasing function of the time since last review and a decreasing function of the integrated output since the last review. (It should be obvious that if the firm knew for certain that a review was to arrive at a certain date, its behavior at the time of review would be altered; hence, to be effective, reviews must be stochastic.)

In a complete analysis of review behavior, one must also discuss the incentives of the reviewers. Thus, if at time t a bank audit turns up a loan that should have been declared in default at the time of the previous audit, the incentives for revealing that may be different if the current auditor is different from the previous auditor than when they are the same person. On the other hand, the cost of the audit may be greatly increased by having different auditors.

22. Here we presume the regulator will choose her actions (which are assumed to be observable to all parties) and compensate the firm as she initially promised to do when she announced the regulatory policy. Before closing, we will briefly consider the possibility that the regulator cannot make such binding commitments.

23. In practice, regulators might well act to maximize their own expected benefits (e.g., income, tenure, and fame) subject to some restrictions imposed by their legal mandate. This possibility has been noted, for example, by Stigler (1971).

24. This insight is offered by Stiglitz (1974) in his analysis of the sharecropping problem. It is also recorded in a general theoretical setting by Harris and Raviv (1979), Holmstrom (1979), and Shavell (1979). Riordan's (1984) interesting solution to the peak-load pricing problem

with demand uncertainty also relies on the risk-neutrality of the firm and the symmetry of initial beliefs about the regulatory environment.

25. Stiglitz and Weiss (1981) demonstrate that in the presence of bankruptcy constraints, the optimal policy for a lender may be to deny credit to a potential borrower rather than to simply increase the charge for borrowing (i.e., raise the interest rate). Their basic insight is that an increase in the interest rate (which is paid only in the absence of bankruptcy) entails a greater effective increase in the expected cost of borrowing to those whose projects are more likely to succeed than those who are likely to declare bankruptcy. Thus an increase in the interest rate may serve only to attract less desirable borrowers. Moreover a higher interest rate may induce borrowers to undertake projects that are more risky.

26. These distortions are described in some detail in Sappington (1983a) and characterized in general by Kahn and Scheinkman (1985).

27. This observation has been made in a variety of settings other than the regulatory arena, Becker (1968), for example, notes that sufficiently large penalties need be imposed only rarely to deter criminal activity. Stiglitz (1975) shows that moral hazard problems can be costlessly resolved when the agent's action can be inferred perfectly from his performance with positive (though arbitrarily small) probability. The general observation is also recorded in Townsend (1979). Riordan and Sappington (1985b) demonstrate that the basic conclusion is true even if the result of the regulator's audit is not publicly observed, so that the firm's payment can only depend on the regulator's claim about the audit's finding and not directly on the finding itself.

28. Their analysis considers both the case in which the signal is publicly observed and that in which only the principal (regulator) can observe the signal. The first-best outcome is less likely to be feasible in the latter case, as any (regulatory) contract that employs the signal must be constrained to eliminate any incentives for the regulator to misrepresent her private observation of the signal.

29. This same assumption characterizes a host of models in related literatures. See, for example, the treatment of the insurance market in Rothschild and Stiglitz (1976) and Stiglitz (1977), the sharecropping problem in Stiglitz (1974), the optimal tax problem in Mirrless (1975), and the general treatment of signaling and screening models in Stiglitz and Weiss (1985). Self-selection problems with two or more parameters are mathematically far more difficult.

30. Some studies in the literature do not formally model the initial communication between the firm and the regulator. Thus, for example, payment to the firm is based only on the final outcome of the regulatory process. There is no loss of generality here if there is only a single firm with information that is initially perfect and if the regulator never takes an action before the firm makes its production decision. Absent these conditions, however, the presence of an initial costless communication phase may increase the regulator's expected payoff. This is true, for example, in the models of Nalebuff and Stiglitz (1983a), Weitzman (1976), Holmstrom (1982a), and Demski et al. (1985) which are described in greater detail later.

31. Technically, since the regulator's objective function is maximized at the first-best outcome, a small deviation from first-best prices (or levels of output) will have no effect on the regulator's utility level (by the envelope theorem). Thus some increase above first-best (marginal cost) prices will be optimal to limit the rents of the firm should it have lower costs for all realizations of costs except the very lowest (here c_1).

32. This basic intuition is explained in greater detail and generality in the regulatory setting in, for example, Baron and Myerson (1982) and Sappington (1982, 1983a, b). It also underlies corresponding conclusions in the optimal tax literature (e.g., Mirless 1971; Atkinson and Stiglitz 1976), the insurance literature (e.g., Rothschild and Stiglitz 1976; Stiglitz 1977), and in studies on nonlinear pricing (e.g., Goldman, Leland, and Sibley 1984; Maskin and Riley

1984). A general characterization of the solution to adverse selection problems of this nature is described in Cooper (1984).

33. Besanko (1984) also reports the gains from technological distortions.

Note that these distortions generally persist whether or not the firm's private information is initially perfect. Induced distortions in observable decision variables generally remain optimal whenever the firm's information is initially better than the regulator's. For details, see Sappington (1982, 1984).

Note also that production technologies may be intentionally distorted for a different reason. In the case of pollution control, for example, the regulator may mandate the installation of a particular technology (e.g., scrubbers) rather than impose a tax on pollutants. Though the direct control is inefficient in the sense that it does not induce firms to use their superior technological information to effect the optimal level of pollution abatement, indirect control will not be feasible when it is prohibitively costly to monitor pollution emissions.

34. It seems likely that a nonconcavity in the value of this information will exist (see Radner and Stiglitz 1984; Singh 1985). Thus signals that are only slightly correlated with the variable in question will not be "purchased" by the regulator.

35. Besanko (1984) shows that if the critical technological asymmetry in the A-J model can be reduced to a single parameter (e.g., as in the analysis of Baron and Myerson 1982), then the optimal regulatory policy will have the allowed rate of return vary inversely with the firm's level of invested capital, thereby moderating the firm's tendency toward overcapitalization.

36. Holmstrom's (1984) analysis of the delegation problem (with a single agent) can be regarded as a special case of (*RP*). Specifying a range within which the agent's observable actions (e.g., his capital choice) can fall amounts to a presumption that infinite penalties will be imposed if an action outside of this range is observed.

37. This observation is recorded in Rothschild and Stiglitz (1976) and analyzed in detail by Baron and Besanko (1984a).

38. Baron and Besanko (1984a), for example, examine the multiperiod extension of Baron and Myerson's (1982) model when future costs are positively but imperfectly correlated with current costs. They find distortions (prices in excess of marginal costs) that are designed to limit the firm's rents continue to characterize the optimal regulatory policy, but the magnitude of these distortions is generally diminished in periods after the first.

39. Thus the logic that underlies the scheme is similar to the basic insight of Loeb and Magat (1979). The ability of the regulator to observe historic expenditures, though, resolves the question of the distribution of rents between consumers and the firm. It should be noted, however, that the resolution may not be complete under the scheme proposed by Sappington and Sibley (1985) if there is no separation of ownership and management in the firm, and if expenditures in excess of minimal production costs provide direct utility to the owner-manager.

40. Technically, it need only be known that the firm's cost structure is characterized by decreasing ray average cost (see Panzar and Willig 1977). (This assumption assures that the firm's profits are always nonnegative under the proposed regulatory scheme.) In particular, note that (as in the models of Loeb and Magat 1979 and Sappington and Sibley 1985) the critical information asymmetry cannot be reduced to a single technological parameter whose realization is known to the firm and whose distribution is known to the regulator. It is in this sense that the information asymmetry is more severe in these models.

41. As Sappington (1980) has shown, the scheme is not immune to strategic behavior by the firm (e.g., intentional cost inflation). However, it can be shown that the authors' basic conclusions continue to hold in the presence of such behavior. In particular, prices still converge to Ramsey levels, though the speed of convergence may be slow. Finsinger and Vogelsang (1981, 1985) have also proposed attractive mechanisms for inducing managers of

public enterprises to use their superior cost and demand information to effect optimal pricing decisions. Their schemes, which require no cost or demand information to implement, effectively reward the managers in each period an amount that approximates the increment in total measured surplus that their activities generate. An interesting overview of schemes of this type is contained in Tam (1985).

42. See the analysis of Radner (1981) for a precise statement of the result, along with additional intuition.

43. Williamson (1975) cites a variety of reasons why successful franchise bidding operations may be difficult to implement.

44. Optimal franchise auctions do not necessarily guarantee that the firm with the lowest production costs will be awarded the franchise. If firms adopt mixed bidding strategies, for example, the winning bid may be submitted by other than the least-cost firm. Furthermore, as Jean Tirole has pointed out to us, when the optimal incentive scheme involves "pooling" or "bunching," the franchise may be awarded with positive probability to other than the least cost producer (see also Myerson 1981).

45. This and related results are found in Lazear and Rosen (1981) and Green and Stokey (1983).

46. The analysis of Holmstrom (1982b) and Mookherjee (1984) provide promising insights concerning the design of incentive mechanisms for multiple agents.

47. The model of Baron and Besanko (1985) is such that absent the imposition of ex post individual rationality constraints, the duration of either the initial phase or the subsequent separation phase shrinks to zero.

Freixas et al. (1985) also examine an interesting two-period model in which the regulator lacks commitment ability. The authors' analysis makes evident the losses that arise when the regulator cannot precommit to future incentive schemes. An important related multiperiod model is that of Lewis (1986).

48. A related concern in the regulatory setting is whether some forms of commitment are more readily achieved than others. For example, Sappington (1986) suggests that when commitment to a monitoring technology (i.e., the expense of observing the firm's realized costs) is more readily achieved than commitment to the frequency of use of any existing technology, there may be gains to committing to an inefficient technology. This is one of many instances where inefficiencies at one stage of the regulatory hierarchy can help compensate for the absence of commitment abilities at another stage.

49. For some thoughts on this matter, see Demski and Sappington (1986).

50. The research of Baron (1985) represents an important contribution along these lines. He examines the optimal design of regulatory policy given conflicting objectives of a public utility commission and the Environmental Protection Agency.

51. Our review has been limited to models in which the firm has better information than the regulator. It is also possible of course that the regulator's knowledge of certain aspects of the regulatory environment is better than the firm's. Interesting theoretical work on the optimal design of incentive schemes by an "informed" principal is provided by Myerson (1983). Insights concerning the optimal design of incentive structures for a single agent by many principals are recorded in Braverman and Stiglitz (1982) and Bernheim and Whinston (1984).

References

Arnott, R., and Stiglitz, J. 1985. "The Welfare Economics of Moral Hazard." Princeton University mimeo. March.

Atkinson, A., and Stiglitz, J. 1980. *Lectures in Public Economics*. New York: McGraw-Hill.

Atkinson, A., and Stiglitz, J. 1976. "The Design of Tax Structures: Direct vs. Indirect Taxation." *Journal of Public Economics 6*: 55–75.

Atkinson, A., and Stiglitz, J. 1972. "The Structure of Indirect Taxation and Economic Efficiency." *Journal of Public Economics 1*: 97–119.

Averch, H., and Johnson, L. 1962. "Behavior of the Firm under Regulatory Constraint." *American Economic Review 52*: 1052–1069.

Baron, D. 1985. "Noncooperative Regulation of a Nonlocalized Externality." Stanford University Discussion Paper. February.

Baron, D. 1984. "Regulatory Strategies under Asymmetric Information." In M. Boyer and R. Kihlstrom, eds., *Bayesian Models in Economic Theory*. Amsterdam: North Holland, pp. 155–180.

Baron, D., and Besanko, D. 1985. "Commitment in Multiperiod Information Models." Working Paper at Stanford University. May.

Baron, D., and Besanko, D. 1984a. "Regulation and Information in a Continuing Relationship." *Information, Economics and Policy 1*: 267–302.

Baron, D., and Besanko, D. 1984b. "Regulation, Asymmetric Information and Auditing." *Rand Journal of Economics 14*: 447–470.

Baron, D., and Myerson, R. 1982. "Regulating a Monopolist with Unknown Costs." *Econometrica 50*: 911–930.

Baron, D., and Taggart, R. 1980. "Regulatory Pricing Procedures and Economic Incentives." In M. Crew, ed., *Issues in Public Utility Economics and Regulation*. Lexington, Mass.: Lexington Books.

Baumol, W., and Bradford, D. 1970. "Optimal Departures from Marginal Cost Pricing." *American Economic Review 60*: 265–283.

Baumol, W., and Klevorick, A. 1970. "Input Choices and Rate-of-Return Regulation: An Overview of the Discussion." *Bell Journal of Economics 1*: 162–190.

Baumol, W., Panzar, J., and Willig, R. 1982. *Contestable Markets and the Theory of Industry Structure*. New York: Harcourt, Brace, Jovanovich.

Becker, G. 1968. "Crime and Punishment: An Economic Approach." *Journal of Political Economy 76*: 169–217.

Berle, A. and Means, G. 1932. *The Modern Corporation and Private Property*. New York: Macmillan.

Bernheim, D., and Whinston, M. 1984. "Common Agency." Harvard Institute of Economic Research Paper No. 1074.

Besanko, D. 1984. "On the Use of Revenue Requirements Regulation under Imperfect Information." in M. Crew, ed., *Analyzing the Impact of Regulatory Change*. Lexington, Mass.: Lexington Books, pp. 39–58.

Boiteaux, M. 1956. "Sur la Question des Monopoles Publics Astreints a l'Equilibre Budgetaire" *Econometrica 24*: 22–40.

Braverman, A., and Stiglitz, J. 1982. "Sharecropping and the Interlinking of Agrarian Markets." *American Economic Review 72*: 695–715.

Britto, R., Hamilton, J., Slutsky, S., and Stiglitz, J. 1985. "Taxation and commitment." Mimeo. June.

Cooper, R. 1984. "On Allocative Distortions in Problems of Self-Selection." *Rand Journal of Economics 15*: 568–577.

Dasgupta, P., and Stiglitz, J. 1985. "Sunk Costs, Competition and Welfare." Princeton University Working Paper. July.

Demsetz, H. 1968. "Why Regulate Utilities?" *Journal of Law and Economics 7*: 55–65.

Demski, J., and Sappington, D. 1986. "Hierarchical Regulatory Control." Bell Communications Research mimeo. July.

Demski, J., and Sappington, D. 1984. "Optimal Incentive Schemes with Multiple Agents." *Journal of Economic Theory 33*: 152–171.

Demski, J., Sappington, D., and Spiller, P. 1985. "The Disciplinary Role of Switching Suppliers: A Regulatory Interpretation." Working Paper at Bell Communications Research. June.

Ebrill, L., and Slutsky, S. 1985. "Pricing Rules for Intermediate and Final Good Regulated Industries." University of Florida Working Paper. March.

Ekern, S., and Wilson, R. 1974. "On the Theory of the Firm in an Economy with Incomplete Markets." *Bell Journal of Economics and Management Science 5*: 1971–180.

Farrell, J. 1985. "Allocating and Abrogating Rights: How Should Conflicts be Resolved under Incomplete Information." GTE Laboratories mimeo.

Finsinger, J., and Vogelsang, I. 1981. "Alternative Institutional Frameworks for Price Incentive Mechanisms." *Kyklos 34*: 388–404.

Finsinger, J., and Vogelsang, I. 1985. "Strategic Management Behavior under Reward Structures in a Planned Economy." *Quarterly Journal of Economics 100*: 263–270.

Friexas, X., Guesnerie, R., and Tirole, J. 1985. "Planning under Incomplete Information and the Ratchet Effect." *Review of Economic Studies 52*: 173–191.

Goldman, M., Leland, H., and Sibley, D. 1984. "Optimal Nonuniform Prices." *Review of Economic Studies 51*: 305–319.

Greenwald, B., and Stiglitz, J. 1986. "Externalities in Economies with Imperfect Information and Incomplete Markets." Princeton University Working Paper. January.

Green, J., and Stokey, N. 1983. "A Comparison of Tournaments and Contracts." *Journal of Political Economy 91*: 349–364.

Grossman, S., and Hart, O. 1980. "Takeover Bids, the Free Rider Problem, and the Theory of the Corporation." *Bell Journal of Economics 11*: 42–65.

Grossman, S., and Hart, O. 1981. "The Allocational Role of Takeover Bids in Situations of Asymmetric Information." *Journal of Finance 36*: 253–270.

Grossman, S., and Stiglitz, J. 1980. "Stockholder Unanimity in Making Production and Financial Decisions." *Quarterly Journal of Economics 94*: 543–566.

Harris, M., and Raviv, A. 1979. "Optimal Incentive Contracts with Imperfect Information." *Journal of Economic Theory 20*: 231–259.

Holmstrom, B. 1982a. "The Design of Incentive Schemes and the New Soviet Incentive Model." *European Economic Review 17*: 127–148.

Holmstrom, B. 1979. "Moral Hazard and Observability." *Bell Journal of Economics 10*: 74–91.

Holmstrom, B. 1982b. "Moral Hazard in Teams", *Bell Journal of Economics 13*: 324–340.

Holmstrom, B. 1984. "On the Theory of Delegation." In M. Boyer and R. Kihlstrom, eds., *Bayesian Models in Economic Theory*. Amsterdam: North Holland, pp. 115–142.

Kahn, C., and Scheinkman, J. 1985. "Optimal Employment Contracts with Bankruptcy Constraints." *Journal of Economic Theory 35*: 343–365.

Laffont, J., and Tirole J. 1985. "Auctioning Incentive Contracts." MIT Working Paper. October.

Laffont, J., and Tirole, J. 1986. "Using Cost Observation to Regulate Firms." *Journal of Political Economy*, forthcoming.

Lazear, E., and Rosen, S. 1981. "Rank-Order Tournaments as Optimum Labor Contracts." *Journal of Political Economy 89*: 841–864.

Lewis, T. 1985. "Reputation and Contractual Performance in Long Term Projects." Working Paper at the University of British Columbia. June.

Linhart, P., Radner, R., and Sinden, F. 1983. "A Sequential Principal-Agent Approach to Regulation." Bell Laboratories Discussion Paper.

Loeb, M., and Magat, W. 1979. "A Decentralized Method for Utility Regulation." *Journal of Law and Economics 22*: 399–404.

Loeb, M., and Magat, W. 1978. "Success Indicators in the Soviet Union: The Problem of Incentives and Efficient Allocations." *American Economic Review 68*: 173–181.

March, J., and Simon, H. 1958. *Organizations*. New York: Wiley.

Maskin, E., and Riley, J. 1984. "Monopoly with Incomplete Information." *Rand Journal of Economics 15*: 171–196.

McAfee, R., and McMillan, J. 1986. "Competition for Agency Contracts." Working Paper at University of Western Ontario. January.

McAfee, R., and McMillan, J. 1984. "Incentive Contracts and Selection of Agent by Principal." Working Paper at University of Western Ontario. May.

McFarland, H. 1985. "Ramsey Pricing of Inputs with Downstream Monopoly Power and Regulation." EPO Discussion Paper 85-2. U.S. Department of Justice.

Mirrlees, J. 1971. "An Exploration in the Theory of Optimum Income Taxation." *Review of Economic Studies 38*: 175–208.

Mookherjee, D. 1984. "Optimal Incentive Schemes with Many Agents." *Review of Economic Studies 51*: 433–446.

Myerson, R. 1983. "Mechanism Design by an Informed Principal." *Econometrica, 51*: 1767–1798.

Nalebuff, B., and Stiglitz, J. 1983a. "Information, Competition and Markets." *American Economic Review 73*: 278–283.

Nalebuff, B., and Stiglitz, J. 1983b. "Prices and Incentives: Towards a General Theory of Compensation and Competition." *Bell Journal of Economics 14*: 21–43.

Panzar, J., and Willig, R. 1977. "Free Entry and the Sustainability of Natural Monopoly." *Bell Journal of Economics 8*: 1–22.

Radner, R. 1981. "Monitoring Cooperative Agreements in a Repeated Principal-Agent Relationship." *Econometrica 49*: 1127–1148.

Radner, R. 1974. "A Note on Unanimity of Stockholders' Preferences among Alternative Production Plans." *Bell Journal of Economics 5*: 181–186.

Radner, R. 1984. "Repeated Moral Hazard with Low Discount Rates." Bell Laboratories Discussion Paper.

Radner, R., and Stiglitz, J. 1984. "A Nonconcavity in the Value of Information." In M. Boyer and R. Kihlstrom, eds., *Bayesian Models in Economic Theory*. Amsterdam: North Holland, pp. 33–52.

Ramsey, F. 1927. "A Contribution to the Theory of Taxation." *Economic Journal 37*: 47–61.

Riordan, M. 1984. "On Delegating Price Authority to a Regulated Firm." *Rand Journal of Economics 15*: 108 115.

Riordan, M., and Sappington, D. 1985a. "Awarding Monopoly Franchises." Working Paper at Stanford University and Bell Communications Research. Revised December.

Riordan, M., and Sappington, D. 1985b. "Optimal Incentive Contracts with Public and Private Ex Post Information." Working Paper at Stanford University and Bell Communications Research. June.

Roberts, K. 1984. "The Theoretical Limits to Redistribution." *Review of Economic Studies 51*: 177–196.

Ross, S. 1973. "The Economic Theory of Agency: The Principal's Problem." *American Economic Review 63*: 134–139.

Rothschild, M., and Stiglitz, J. 1976. "Equilibrium in Competitive Insurance Markets: An Essay on the Economics of Information." *Quarterly Journal of Economics 90*: 225–243.

Sah, R., and Stiglitz, J. 1985. "Human Fallibility and Economic Organization." *American Economic Review 76*: 292–297.

Sappington, D. 1986. "Commitment to Regulatory Bureaucracy." Bell Communications Research Working Paper. January.

Sappington, D. 1984. "Incentive Contracting with Asymmetric and Imperfect Precontractual Knowledge." *Journal of Economic Theory 34*: 52–70.

Sappington, D. 1983a. "Limited Liability Contracts between Principal and Agent." *Journal of Economic Theory 29*: 1–21.

Sappington, D. 1983b. "Optimal Regulation of a Multiproduct Monopoly with Unknown Technological Capabilities." *Bell Journal of Economics 14*: 453–463.

Sappington, D. 1982. "Optimal Regulation of Research and Development under Imperfect Information." *Bell Journal of Economics 13*: 354–368.

Sappington, D. 1980. "Strategic Firm Behavior under a Dynamic Regulatory Adjustment Process." *Bell Journal of Economics 11*: 360–372.

Sappington, D., and Sibley, D. 1985. "Regulatory Incentive Schemes Using Historic Cost Data." Working Paper at Bell Communications Research. Revised August.

Shapiro, C., and Stiglitz, J. 1984. "Equilibrium Unemployment as a Worker Discipline Device." *American Economic Review 74*: 433–444.

Shavell, S. 1979. "Risk Sharing and Incentives in the Principal and Agent Relationship." *Bell Journal of Economics 10*: 55–73.

Singh, N. 1985. "Monitoring and Hierarchies: The Marginal Value of Information in a Principal-Agent Model." *Journal of Political Economy 93*: 599–609.

Stigler, G. 1972. "The Theory of Economic Regulation." *Bell Journal of Economics 2*: 3–21.

Stiglitz, J. 1985. "Credit Markets and the Control of Capital." *Journal of Money, Credit, and Banking 17*: 133–152.

Stiglitz, J. 1975. "Incentives, Risk and Information: Notes Towards a Theory of Hierarchy." *Bell Journal of Economics 6*: 552–579.

Stiglitz, J. 1977. "Monopoly, Non-Linear Princing and Imperfect Information: The Insurance Market." *Review of Economic Studies 44*: 407–430.

Stiglitz, J. 1970. "On the Optimality of the Stock Market Allocation of Investment." Paper presented at the Far Eastern Meetings of the Econometric Society, Tokyo, Japan, June 27–29.

Stiglitz, J. 1972. "Some Aspects of the Pure theory of Corporate Finance: Bankruptcies and Takeovers." *Bell Journal of Economics and Management Science 3*:458–482.

Stiglitz, J. 1974. "Risk Sharing and Incentives in Sharecropping." *Review of Economic Studies 41*:219–256.

Stiglitz, J. 1982. "Self-Selection and Pareto Efficient Taxation." *Journal of Public Economics 17*:213–240.

Stiglitz, J., and Weiss, A. 1983. "Alternative Approaches to Analyzing Markets with Asymmetric Information." *American Economic Review 73*:246–249.

Stiglitz, J., and Weiss, A. 1981. "Credit Rationing in Markets with Asymmetric Information." *American Economic Review 71*:393–410.

Stiglitz, J., and Weiss, A. 1983. "Incentive Effects of Terminations: Applications to the Credit and Labor Markets." *American Economic Review 73*:912–927.

Stiglitz, J., and Weiss, A. 1985. "Sorting Out the Differences between Screening and Signaling Models." Bell Communications Research Discussion Paper.

Tam, M. 1985. "Reward Structures in a Planned Economy: Some Further Thoughts." *Quarterly Journal of Economics 50*:279–290.

Townsend, R. 1979. "Optimal Contracts and Competitive Markets with Costly State Verification." *Journal of Economic Theory 21*:265–293.

Vogelsang, I., and Finsinger, J. 1979. "A Regulatory Adjustment Process for Optimal Pricing by Multiproduct Monopoly Firms." *Bell Journal of Economics 10*:157–171.

Weitzman, M. 1976. "The New Soviet Incentive Model." *Bell Journal of Economics 7*:251–257.

Williamson, O. 1976. "Franchise Bidding for Natural Monopolies—In General and with Respect to CATV." *Bell Journal of Economics 7*:73–104.

Williamson, O. 1975. *Markets and Hierarchies: Analysis and Antitrust Implications*. New York: The Free Press.

[21]

Public versus Regulated Private Enterprise

Robert D. Willig

A comparison of public enterprise with regulated private enterprise shows that the efficiencies of privatization stem from the insulation it brings from arbitrary political and self-serving influences. The critical insulation springs from the costliness of interventions when there is a regulatory compact in place that protects private property from expropriation while it also corrects for market failures. That same insulation means that public enterprise is a better form of organization for activities that call for a response to public interest exigencies which cannot be specified in advance or reliably adjudicated after the fact. The analysis emphasizes that an appropriate regulatory compact requires institutional support. International organizations that seek to implement privatization should consider promoting credible regulatory commitment by requiring countries to execute explicit regulatory compacts and by bringing to bear the weight of their continuing relationship as a means of motivating the countries to conform to such strictures.

Since the early 1980s there has been a dramatic spread of appreciation of the social benefits of private enterprise. National leaders have been outspoken on the need to foster private initiative in the interests of productivity and growth and have been taking substantive steps to move economic activities to the private sector. More than eighty countries have launched privatization initiatives, and 6,800 state-owned enterprises have been privatized since 1980 (Kikeri, Nellis, and Shirley 1992). Hoped-for events on the horizon in Central and Eastern Europe, the former U.S.S.R., and China may render the progress to

Robert D. Willig is professor of economics and public affairs at Princeton University. He would like to thank Carl Shapiro for his partnership in developing many of the ideas expressed in this paper, which builds on and draws on their joint work, Shapiro and Willig (1990).

Proceedings of the World Bank Annual Conference on Development Economics 1993

date toward private enterprise largely a prelude and harbinger of massive movements to come.

The World Bank has been a leading force in this movement. In the past decade 182 Bank operations have supported privatization in 67 countries (Kikeri, Nellis, and Shirley 1992). The widely articulated rationales for the movement toward privatization have generally focused on perceptions of waste, lethargy, inefficiency, and poor quality of output in the operations of state-run enterprises, as contrasted with expectations of dynamism, cost-effectiveness, high quality, and creative productivity in the operations of private enterprises. At the same time there appears to be a countervailing reluctance to spin activities out of direct public control, a reluctance linked both to the protection of status quo benefits and to concern over the ability of private enterprise to respond to and serve the public interest.

Experience and analysis have taught key lessons about the relationship between the structure of an economy and the ability of privatization to satisfy its goals and expectations. (For an excellent exposition of this topic, see Guislain 1992.) The first lesson is that in order to be effective, the divestiture of state-owned enterprises requires a suitable set of institutions, a suitable legal system, and a strategy that is tailored to the country's circumstances. The second is that achieving desirable performance requires a market-friendly institutional framework. The third lesson is the importance of a microeconomic structure that is open to competition. And the fourth is that in cases where the privatized enterprise provides infrastructure services that are natural monopolies there must be an effective system of regulation to curb the potential abuse of monopoly power. (See Ordover and Pittman 1992 for a powerful articulation of the view that in emerging market economies privatization of infrastructure supply is desirable even if regulation is ineffective.)

In addition to the four institutional categories just described, there is another that is essential to the success of privatization and that drives the difference between public and regulated private enterprises—the government's ability to confine its influence over the privatized firm. That is, the government must commit itself to laissez-faire or to a limited and predefined regulatory mechanism. Even where the other four categories of institutional prerequisites are in place, if the government does not have the capacity to tie its own hands and insulate the firm from arbitrary intervention, the expected benefits of privatization are unlikely to be realized.

This commitment to maintain an anonymous and arm's-length relationship is a critical component of a market-friendly economic environment. Efficient systems of taxation and financial disclosure, environmental and consumer protection, enforcement of contracts and protection of intellectual property, and labor and antitrust regulations will apply to all firms in relatively similar ways. To be sure, if the government fails to commit itself to an anonymous and circumscribed system of taxation and, for example, arbitrarily confiscates business proceeds, private enterprise cannot function effectively. When viewed against the backdrop of generally applicable and uniform codes that describe government-business relationships, however, such arbitrary behavior will be relatively visible and distinguishable from the ordinary course of affairs. In contrast, where there is an ongoing system of regulation that is applied to a particular firm because, for instance, it is a monopoly supplier of infrastructure services, it will be much more difficult to distinguish arbitrary interventions from the ordinary workings of the announced idiosyncratic regulatory relationship.

It may be the case that the government cannot commit itself to a confined regulatory mechanism. If institutions cannot be found to solve this commitment problem, the country may not be able to improve on the inadequate performance of public enterprises in critical infrastructure sectors.[1] As a consequence, the performance of the regulated private enterprise may be worse than that of the public enterprise from the perspective of the public interest. The next section argues that many of the disparate rationales for privatization reduce to one: that the privatized enterprise, albeit regulated, is more insulated than the counterpart public enterprise from arbitrary government intervention. Subsequent sections offer a theoretical analysis of the relative efficiency of public and regulated private enterprises, under two assumptions: first, that the government can commit itself to an optimal regulatory mechanism, and second, that the government is unable to make such a commitment. In the latter case, the paper suggests a possible role for international organizations in providing the necessary commitment to a regulatory regime.

Privatization as Insulation

If an archetypical economist were asked why, in one word, society would benefit from the privatization of state-owned enterprises, the answer would probably be "efficiency." It is widely accepted that government enterprises are managed to achieve a variety of objectives that relate to the complexities of politics, while private enterprises are largely managed to earn profits, and cost efficiency and market responsiveness are important to that pursuit. The more competitive the markets in which the private enterprise operates, the more it is compelled by its objectives of profits and survival to operate efficiently.

But this response does not answer two fundamental questions. First, why do the authorities not make public enterprises equally efficient by offering managers the same financial incentives as their private sector counterparts? Second, since all private enterprises are subject to a variety of regulations, how is it that the authorities are able to devise efficient regulations for the private sector while those that apply to public enterprises are so poorly constructed? To quote Bos (1993): "A priori, it is not clear why the state, failing to run the firms well as owner, should now suddenly have become an efficient regulator."

The empirical answer to the first question seems to be that such public sector reform just doesn't work. Robinson (1992) uses the example of electricity supply in Great Britain to make this point.

> Despite good intentions . . . it proved impossible to have "arm's-length" relationships between the nationalized corporations and government. Instead, governments of both major parties found irresistible the temptation to interfere with the decisions of state-owned industries so that, in practice, the corporations had little control over pricing and investment decisions.

In another instance (according to a 1989 World Bank report) Brazil, in the interest of eliminating operational inefficiency, adopted a system whereby state-owned enterprises had to compete with private corporations under the same conditions. The government, however, proved incapable of abiding by its own rules and instead provided the enterprises with financial support. A similar point is made by Hemming and Mansoor (1988), who are skeptical that government can be persuaded to interfere less than in the past.

The answer to the second question is that political reality is inevitably injected into regulation, to some extent, when the magnitude of the effect and the route that it takes are dependent on the details of the regulatory structure and process. Most directly, regulators are often political actors themselves or serve at the pleasure of those in political office. At the opposite extreme are regulators who are appointed for long and secure terms and who are not subject to active oversight from political bodies. Robinson (1992) stated that "an independent regulatory body is capable of providing the industry with a much clearer set of ground rules, which avoids much of the confusion between commercial and political objectives associated with nationalization." However, Noll, in his 1989 survey *The Politics of Regulation,* concludes that "the absence of direct political oversight—with public hearings, explicit directions through legislation or executive order, and occasionally punishment of agency miscreants—does not imply a lack of political control and an opportunity for runaway bureaucracy."

From these perspectives, the answers of the archetypical economist are not incorrect, just a bit superficial. The efficiency gains from privatization stem from the fact that state-owned enterprises are subject to politicized directives while private enterprises enjoy a degree of insulation. Stated this way, it is clear that the efficiency comparison turns, first, on the presumed inefficiency of the politicized directives and, second, on whether regulation indeed offers the presumed greater insulation.

Public Enterprise versus Private Enterprise with Committed Regulation

The performance of public and regulated private enterprises is analyzed here by comparing models of these two different forms of organization in a common setting, focusing on differences in information and incentives.

In a public enterprise, the tasks of responding to the profitability or cost conditions facing the organization and determining the effect of the organization's activities on the public are the responsibility of an appointed official. The enterprise's sphere of activity is directed toward maximizing that official's objective function. In contrast, the private enterprise is controlled by a private manager whose objective is maximization of profit. The organization's profit levels and consequent choices of activity levels are affected by a mechanism established by the regulator, who has access to the information concerning the public impact of the enterprise's activities but has no direct knowledge of profitability or cost conditions. The regulator of the private enterprise has the same objective function as that of the official who heads the public enterprise.

To establish a normative framework, we postulate the presence of a framer, a public-spirited agent who must choose whether the economic activity is to be public or private and who sets up the governance structure for the chosen form. The framer has an objective function that tends to be different than that of the public manager or the regulator, and the framer has no direct access to the private information concerning their common objective function, demand and cost conditions, and the public impact of the enterprise's activities. The analysis is thus cast in the following terms: what is the optimal form of ownership and control, and how does this choice depend on various features of the economic environment? The framer recognizes that political forces will influence subsequent public sector and regulatory decisions, but his or her power is confined to setting up the organizational structure that will best serve the public interest.

The Model of Public Enterprise

The official in charge of the public enterprise receives private noncontractible information, θ, regarding the technology of production. A distinction need not be drawn between marketed and nonmarketed outputs of production: both are encompassed in the reduced-form profit function $\pi(x, \theta)$, where x denotes the enterprise's action or activity level. The π function incorporates the cost of the investments needed for the enterprise to operate. The impact on the governmental treasury of the enterprise's choice of action is simply π. The random variable θ is defined so that profits are increasing in its level. While θ is initially unknown at the time when the framer must choose between public and private enterprise, the framer has a prior density of $f(\theta)$ on the interval between θ_0 and θ_1.

The notion of "action," symbolized by x, is very general, encompassing such examples as output, quality, location, and employment. However, for analytic tractability, x is taken to be one-dimensional. An important assumption is that the marginal return to increasing the activity level is higher when the profitability parameter θ is higher; that is, $\pi_{x\theta} > 0$, where subscripts denote partial derivatives. Thus, other things being equal, efficiency requires higher levels of activity when costs are lower.

By virtue of his or her position in the public sector, the government official also observes information, ϕ, that bears on the external social benefits generated by the enterprise's operations. The external social benefits (or costs, if negative) associated with action x are given by $S(x, \phi)$. There are numerous examples of such benefits or costs: consumer surplus of those utilizing the enterprise's output; worker surplus generated by employment in the enterprise; environmental damages caused by a manufacturing facility; spillover effects of a major factory on related industries or on overall regional development; national security benefits associated with the operation of a defense facility; or the effect of the telephone system on national cohesion. The expression $S(x, \phi)$ represents anything that affects the public interest without also appearing in the enterprise's profits.

The first decision is whether to make the investment required to operate the enterprise. If the investment is made, the next step is to decide what level of x to direct the enterprise to implement. For simplicity, we model the investment decision as a discrete yes or no choice, and we further assume that the investment is always warranted under the objectives of the framer and the government official. The overall social welfare function that the framer seeks to maximize is given by $W = S(x, \phi) + k\pi(x, \theta)$, the external benefits from the enterprise's activities plus the enterprise's profits, with a magnification factor applied to the net contribution made by the enterprise to the public treasury. This magnification factor, $k \geq 1$, equals the marginal social cost of raising public funds, including any distortions caused by the taxes required to finance public sector operations.

The government official also has a similar, but possibly different, objective function given by $V^M = W + \alpha J(x, \epsilon)$. The expression $J(x, \epsilon)$ represents the official's private agenda, or whatever divergences arise between the objectives of a public official who is subject to political pressure and the genuine long-run public interest. The variable α parameterizes the extent of the divergence between the official's objectives and those of the framer—either the saliency of the private agenda or the power of political forces that impel divergence of decisions from the long-run public interest. The variable ϵ, which is observable only by the official, captures the idiosyncratic nature of the hidden private or political agenda that cannot be foreseen by the framer or observed by others. (Formally, the expected value of J_x with respect to the prior on ϵ is assumed to be 0.) The key point is that because the framer cannot know who will be appointed or what his or her private aims will be, it is impossible systematically to counteract a private agenda. Given that the government official's private goals are not publicly observable, the framer cannot charge a third party, such as the court, with the responsibility of penalizing the official for pursuing his or her private agenda.

The Model of Regulated Private Enterprise

The model of regulated private enterprise captures the same underlying economic and informational environment as that just described, while incorporating a fully articulated treatment of the relationship between the enterprise and its regulator. The public official, now playing the role of a regulator, observes the public interest impact variable, ϕ, and the private agenda variable, ϵ. As before, the party who will be operating the enterprise, in this case the private manager, observes the private information about profitability, θ.

The private investment decision is necessarily more complex than the public investment decision described above. It is still a simple yes or no decision, and it is assumed that the outcome of the decision is commonly observable. The added complexity arises because in order to attract private investment, the regulator must commit to a regulatory mechanism that offers the expectation of at least a competitive rate of return on the private firm's sunk capital, whether physical investment or the purchase of assets previously owned by the public sector. So, in the case of private enterprise, a regulatory contract must be specified prior to the investment decision.

We model regulatory schemes as follows, on the assumption that the actions of the regulated firm are commonly observable. (For a discussion of the generality of such schemes, see Caillaud, Guesnerie, and Tirole 1988; Baron 1989; Laffont 1992.) The regulator commits to provide the schedule $T(x)$, specifying that if the firm chooses action x, it will receive the money transfer $T(x)$ from the treasury. If T is positive for the applicable value of x, it will constitute a payment to the firm; if negative, it can be interpreted as a tax, a penalty, or a franchise fee.

In response to the announced regulatory incentive scheme, $T(x)$, the private firm first chooses whether to commit its funds to the requisite investment. It is modeled to do so if and only if the investment brings the firm nonnegative expected profits, where the expectation is based on the $T(x)$ schedule, the firm's information or priors on the profitability variable θ, and the firm's anticipations of its corresponding choices of activity level, x. Second, after it has made its investment, and possibly after more private information about θ has been revealed to the firm's private manager, the private manager chooses what level of x to implement. This choice is made to maximize the total profit of the firm, inclusive of the regulatory transfer.

With anticipation of the schedule's impact on the investment and activity decisions of the private enterprise, the regulator chooses to commit to the schedule $T(x) = T(x; \phi, \epsilon)$ when the regulator knows the public interest variable ϕ and the private agenda variable ϵ. This choice maximizes the expected value of the regulator's objective function V^M, where the expectation is taken over the prior distribution on the enterprise's profitability variable, θ. The maximization presumes that the firm will select the level of x that maximizes its total profit, in light of the firm's knowledge of θ and of the entire T schedule. The maximization is constrained by the need to provide the enterprise with nonnegative expected total profits in order to induce the needed investment by the enterprise.[2]

If the regulator will not learn about the public interest and private agenda variables until after the time that the investment commitment must be made by the private enterprise, a more complex (and more realistic) process must be followed. Here the regulator commits, before the time of the private investment decision, to the menu of schedules $T(x; \phi, \epsilon)$, for each relevant (ϕ, ϵ), promising to choose one from the menu at the later date when the values of ϕ and ϵ will become known to the regulator. This commitment is sufficient to induce the private investment, since each schedule on the menu provides nonnegative expected profits for the private enterprise. Once (ϕ, ϵ) is learned by the regulator, the corresponding $T(x; \phi, \epsilon)$ will be selected from the menu, since it is the best schedule on the menu for the regulator under those conditions.[3]

The framer's evaluation of these scenarios is given by

$$W = S(x, \phi) + \pi(x, \theta) - (k - 1)T(x; \phi, \epsilon)$$

since $\pi(x,\theta) + T(x; \phi, \epsilon)$ is the enterprise's total profit and the drain on the treasury is $T(x; \phi, \epsilon)$.[4]

Circumstances with Equivalence

Several circumstances can be identified in which the performances of public and regulated private enterprise are equivalent. Here the regulator exerts sufficient indirect control over the private enterprise to achieve the same results as would the official with direct control of a public enterprise. Under these circumstances the framer is indifferent between public and private enterprise. Identifying such circumstances in the abstract is important for recognizing the key characteristics that make the organizational forms perform differently in reality.[5]

In one such instance, there is no private information about the profitability variable, θ, before the private investment decision must be made; perhaps this information is revealed only through the physical process of investment or once the private owners have taken possession of the newly privatized public assets. In contrast, private information concerning public impacts, ϕ, and the private agenda, ϵ, is known to the regulator when commitment must be made to the regulatory mechanism, before the time of the investment decision. Then it is optimal for the regulator to pay the firm according to the schedule

$$T^*(x; \phi, \epsilon) = (1/k)[S(x, \phi) + \alpha J(x, \epsilon)] + G(\phi, \epsilon)$$

where $G(\phi, \epsilon)$ is independent of the activity level x and is set as small as possible consistent with inducing the firm to make the required investment.[6]

The mechanism operates by causing the firm to internalize the objectives of the regulator, inasmuch as the firm's total profit of $\pi + T$ takes on a positive linear relationship to the regulator's objective function. As a result, when the firm does learn its private information, it is motivated to make the same choice of activity level that the informed official would direct the public enterprise to choose. Because the firm knows no more than the regulator about θ before the investment is made, the firm can be induced to invest while being held to zero expected profit. Hence, with this mechanism, the regulator induces the same actions and achieves the same expected payoff as does the official under public enterprise.

Another set of circumstances in which equivalence holds is characterized by private information concerning θ, ϵ, and ϕ that is revealed only after the investment commitment must be made. Here the regulator commits to the menu of payment schedules given by $T^*(x; \phi, \epsilon)$, as defined above, with the understanding that the regulator will choose a particular schedule from this menu after the investment decision is made and the private information is revealed to its recipients, but still before the activity level must be chosen by the firm. The firm is motivated to invest, and the regulator is motivated to choose the T^* from the menu that corresponds to the revealed values of ϕ and ϵ.[7] The outcome is again internalization of the regulator's objectives by the firm, and the same choices of activity levels and the same expected drain on the treasury that would be the result of public enterprise.[8]

The third case of equivalence is characterized by $k = 1$, so that transfers from the treasury are not a matter of concern to the framer, the regulator, or the government official. Here, before the investment decision, the firm knows its value of θ and the regulator is aware of that fact but does not know the pertinent value of θ. Hence, to ensure that the investment will be made, the regulator must commit to a payment schedule or to a menu of schedules that provides nonnegative profit for all levels of $\theta \geq \theta_0$. Since $k = 1$, the regulator is not adverse to adding enough funds to any payment schedule to ensure its profitability. Consequently, it is optimal for the objectives of the regulator to offer the firm the above internalization schedules T^*, but with a different portion G that is here sufficiently large to guarantee the firm nonnegative profit even if its profitability level θ is as small as θ_0. The outcome is that the regulated private firm chooses the same activity levels that the public enterprise would choose but that the drain on the treasury caused by regulation is greater than that caused by public enterprise. However, since in this case the drain is not a matter of concern, the framer would find no difference between the performance of public and private forms of organization.

In light of these sets of abstract circumstances in which equivalence holds, to understand the differences between public and regulated private enterprises it is necessary to consider an environment in which there is noncontractible private information about profitability prior to the investment decision and in which there is concern about the drain on the treasury ($k > 1$).[9]

Comparative Performance

Information rents, which are a necessary feature of an optimal regulatory mechanism when the firm has superior information about its profitability before the time of the investment decision, drive the differences between public and regulated private enterprise.[10] Since the firm must be paid enough to cover its costs when the firm knows that its profitability is minimal, the payments will necessarily yield the firm more than it needs to cover its costs when profitability is higher.

The more costly (or the larger) the activity level sought by the regulator, the greater will be the concomitant level of information rent paid to the firm. To see this intuitively, let $x(0)$, $x(1)$, and $x(2)$ be the respective activity levels sought by the regulator for the circumstances that the profitability variable has its lowest level $\theta(0)$, a higher level of $\theta(1)$, and a still higher level of $\theta(2)$. To induce investment where $\theta(0)$ prevails, $T[x(0)]$ must be big enough to make $T + \pi$ nonnegative in this circumstance. Where, instead, $\theta(1)$ prevails, the firm can earn a positive profit of $\pi[x(0), \theta(1)] - \pi[x(0), \theta(0)]$ by choosing the activity level that the regulator intended for $\theta(0)$. Thus, to induce the firm to choose $x(1)$ here, the regulator must make $T[x(1)]$ big enough to offer a greater rent. Further, where $\theta(2)$ prevails, the firm can earn still more profit by choosing $x(1)$. To induce the firm to select $x(2)$ instead, $T[x(2)]$ must offer yet more rent to the firm.

This intuitive argument indicates why the increments in the optimal $T(x)$ schedule cover the incremental costs to the firm of the higher activity levels, plus increments to the information rents earned by the firm. As a consequence, the information rents not only decrease the regulator's payoff, since $k>1$, but they also present the regulator with higher marginal costs to his objective function of obtaining various levels of activity. These marginal costs include a component of incremental information rents that are absent from the considerations of the official who chooses the activity levels of the public enterprise directly.

Three critical comparisons emerge. First, the government official achieves a greater value of their common objective function than does the regulator. Although the full comparison is more complex, the payout of information rents alone suffices to explain this comparison. Second, the regulator chooses to induce less costly (here, lower) levels of activity for the regulated private enterprise than those chosen directly by the official for the public enterprise. This follows as a result of the higher marginal costs perceived by the regulator. And third, the activity levels that result from regulation are less responsive to changes in the objective function of the regulator and official than the activity levels chosen for the public enterprise. That is, when the marginal value of their activity levels is altered by changes in the public interest (ϕ) or private agenda (ϵ) variables, the equilibrium levels of x change less under regulation than they do under direct public control.[11]

The foundations are finally in place for analyzing the differences between public and regulated private enterprise from the normative perspective of the framer. As a starting point, if the objectives of the regulator and the official coincided perfectly with those of the framer, so that $\alpha = 0$, the framer would prefer the public enterprise for two reasons. First, it avoids the drain on the treasury associated with the information rents that arise under regulation. Second, outcomes respond to realizations of the public interest random variable with full efficiency.

As the saliency (α) of the private agendas of the official and the regulator grows, the evaluation by the framer of both forms of organization falls, since outcomes will be chosen that deviate from those that would be optimal for the framer's public interest objective function. The framer's evaluation of the outcomes of public enterprise falls faster with respect to α than does the framer's evaluation of the outcomes of regulated private enterprise. The reason is that the equilibrium activity levels under the latter form of organization show less response to the increasingly salient private agenda of the regulator and the official. At some level of α, the framer prefers the regulated private form of organization over the public enterprise. This critical level is smaller, the smaller is the variance in ϕ, and the larger is the variance in ϵ.

The Insulation Question Revisited

It has emerged from the analysis that privatization insulates an enterprise from political influences that lead to inefficiency. As compared with public enterprise, the regulated private enterprise is relatively unresponsive to the noncontractible influences of its regulator, and when these influences largely spring from a politicized or self-serving private agenda, this unresponsiveness works for the public interest.

The insulation arises from the fact that in order to attract the requisite sunk investment by private capital, privatization intrinsically requires an institutional framework that works to protect private property—that commits the process of regulation or governmental intervention to a mechanism which promises non-negative expected financial returns. Privatization also intrinsically creates a separation between governmental regulators and the productive enterprise, making it likely, if not inevitable, that the enterprise possesses private information about its costs and potential profitability, both before and after irreversible investment decisions must be made.

The combination of respect for private property and separation of private information implies, as a matter of economic logic, that it is relatively expensive for the government, or its appointed regulators, to alter the activities of the enterprise in reaction to noncontractible influences. Such alterations can be bought, but at a distinctly higher price than incremental cost, which would be the applicable price for a directly controlled public enterprise. It is the higher price of influence that underlies the insulation resulting from privatization.

While insulation from inefficient political and self-serving influences may be the prime fundamental benefit of privatization, the corresponding unresponsiveness to nonmarket public interest exigencies may render regulated private enterprise the wrong organizational form for some activities. For example, the desirable maintenance of order in a prison is rife with unpredictable and non-contractible exigencies that strongly influence the external benefits and costs of the various custodial and enforcement activities. As such, the analysis suggests that public enterprise would be the superior form of organization for this job. In contrast, although the operation of hotels may have an external public interest impact that arises from regional development strategies, to the extent that the impact is predictable or is based on contractible information, it does not provide a valid rationale for the public enterprise form of organization.

Public and Regulated Private Enterprises under Nondiscretionary Governance

In the models of public and regulated private enterprise analyzed above, the government official is accorded complete discretion by the framer to direct the activities of the public enterprise, and the regulator is accorded complete discretion by the framer to establish the regulatory mechanism. In view of the presumption that the objectives of both officials may deviate from the objectives of the framer, it is worthwhile considering forms of nondiscretionary governance that limit the officials to implementing the directions of the framer (perhaps as detailed in enabling legislation).

Nondiscretionary regulation of a private enterprise requires that the framer mandate specific regulatory mechanisms that are contingent on only contractible information. Thus the applicable mechanism cannot be influenced by either private information about the public interest, ϕ, or private information about the regulator's private agenda, ϵ. The comparison for the framer between discretionary and nondiscretionary regulation entails a tradeoff between the distortions induced by the regulator's private agenda and the ability of regulation to respond to noncontractible information on variations in the public interest benefits from the enterprise's activities.

Nondiscretionary control of a public enterprise requires that the framer mandate specific actions for the enterprise that are contingent on only contractible information. The applicable choices cannot be influenced by private information on costs or profitability, θ, in addition to the independence of the choices from ϕ and ϵ, because the private nature of all these categories of information makes it infeasible to accord the government official discretion to react to θ without also according discretion to react to ϕ and ϵ as well. The outside observer cannot discern the difference.

Hence a significant advantage of nondiscretionary regulation of private enterprise over nondiscretionary management of public enterprise is the ability of the former to yield outcomes that are responsive to private information about costs and profitability. This advantage is linked to the fact that a regulator of private enterprise can be more effectively monitored—and thus more effectively constrained—by the framer because the regulator does not have access to the private information on costs and profitability that is possessed by the government official. With less private information, the regulator is less able to disguise his or her pursuit of a private agenda.

This general effect favoring privatization arises from its intrinsic separation of information on cost and profitability from the power to influence activities for the sake of noncontractible public effects and private agendas. As a result of this separation, the framer can better restrain the influence of the private agenda on the interventions of the regulator of the private enterprise.

In the most dramatic form of this effect, optimal nondiscretionary regulation is no regulation at all.[12] Here, private enterprise with a commitment of laissez-faire from the framer yields optimal results from the framer's perspective. In contrast, in this case discretionary regulation or public management would yield lower net social benefits as a result of the influence of the private agenda on the activities of the enterprise, and nondiscretionary public management would yield lower net social benefits as a result of the unresponsiveness of the enterprise's activities to cost and profitability conditions.

Government Commitment to Privatization

Government commitment plays several explicit and implicit roles in the scenario involving regulated private enterprise. First, and most directly, the regulator made a commitment, before the firm committed capital, to use a particular regulatory mechanism (or to select later from an announced menu of mechanisms). These mechanisms all promised nonnegative expected returns.

Of course, the regulator could achieve a higher level of his or her objective function by reneging on the announcement after the private investment is sunk and utilizing a mechanism that promises nonnegative returns on only the unsunk portions of the enterprise's costs. If the private firm had anticipated that the regulator would renege, it would not have been willing to sink any costs, and privatization would not occur. (On this point, see Vickers and Yarrow 1988.) In this sense, privatization requires institutional protection against blatant expropriation or reneging on a regulatory commitment.

Second, it was presumed that the regulator would select or implement the mechanisms faithful to any contingencies on contractible information that were stipulated by the framer (that is, mandated by enabling legislation). Here the regulator would prefer to use a mechanism that reflected his or her own objectives. Such an adjustment might be difficult and costly to stop where the legislated contingencies were imperfectly clear.

The anticipation of such difficulties would not deter the firm from investing so long as the adjusted mechanism provided nonnegative expected private returns. But the inability of institutions to hold the regulator to the mandated mechanism would vitiate the desirable properties of nondiscretionary regulation. With foreknowledge, the framer would be unlikely to alter the decision to privatize because nondiscretionary public management would likely be infeasible as well and because the framer would likely prefer discretionary regulation to discretionary public management for the same reasons that drove the preference for nondiscretionary regulation (that is, the desire to insulate the enterprise from the official's private agenda).

Third, and most subtly, commitment is important in extending the analysis beyond its unrealistic static confines. In particular, the private enterprise faces many periods during which it must choose activity levels and is affected by regulatory mechanisms. The extension of the one-period analysis to this domain is considerably more complex and depends sensitively on the intertemporal correlations of the informational random variables. (See Baron 1989 and Laffont 1992 for overviews of the known results.) For the case in which each period's cost variable for the enterprise has the same realization, the standard result (attributed to Baron and Besanko 1984b) is that the dynamic optimum requires commitment to repetition of the optimal one-period mechanism.

A regulator who cannot commit for more than one period at a time will be impelled to use the information about the firm's costs that was gleaned in prior periods to improve his or her outcome in the period to come. Aware of the workings of this ratchet effect that compresses information rents over time, the firm requires correspondingly greater rents in the early periods and reveals more private information over time. Although the firm never fully reveals its private information if it is drawn from a continuum, the information may be revealed if it is drawn from a discrete set of possibilities (see Laffont and Tirole 1988). Here, as the extent of the asymmetric information and the corresponding flow of information rents diminish over time, the outcomes move closer to those that the regulator would choose in the absence of information and control barriers. However, the parties involved in the regulatory relationship have incentives to create the ability to commit to mechanisms over time, and if so, the optimum is stationary repetition of the static optimal mechanism.

In summary, the capacity for dynamic commitment to a regulatory mechanism is a necessary prerequisite for effective privatization. Without commitment, alteration in the regulatory regime can have the same effect as outright expropriation of sunk investment, and the aware private sector will not support privatization. Moreover, it would appear that without commitment to the dynamic regulatory regime, the insulation that regulation provides from arbitrary politicized or self-serving directives may weaken over time. With dynamic commitment, private property and private information are simultaneously protected, making effective privatization both feasible and desirable.

Perhaps international organizations that advise and finance privatization programs can take on the complementary role of promoting credible regulatory commitment. The organization might require the adoption of an explicit regulatory compact and assume the role of cosigner to the agreement. Where the legal system of the country does not have the capacity to adjudicate disputes over the compact, the organization might provide that service.

The organization's power to enforce conformance to its findings would arise from its continuing financial relationship with the country. In the same way that such a continuing relationship impels borrowers to eschew deliberate and opportunistic default, the relationships might create the incentives for adherence to explicit regulatory compacts and to the overriding principle of protection of privatized property.

Notes

1. In the United States the federal court system serves as a guarantor of limits on regulatory discretion over private enterprises. Frequent litigation is brought in this venue by parties affected by regulation who

claim that an independent regulatory agency has exercised its power "unreasonably" or has engaged in "arbitrary and capricious actions." The U.S. Supreme Court has interpreted the constitution (most notably in Federal Power Commission et al. v. Hope Natural Gas Co., 1944) as protecting from regulation the right of regulated utilities to earn a "fair rate of return" on "used and useful" assets employed in regulated activities. The resulting litigation is protracted, complex, and expensive. In part, the disputes are difficult to resolve because the legislation that provides independent regulatory agencies with their powers is deliberately vague. More specific regulatory compacts would likely be more readily adjudicated.

2. In general, the regulator has an endogenous decision concerning whether to induce investment in the various states of nature. However, for simplicity, it is assumed here that the regulator will find it preferable to induce investment in all relevant states of nature.

3. The analysis would be far more complex here if the desirability of the investment to the regulator depended on the revealed values of ϕ and ϵ or if the firm had more options than just whether or not to invest a set amount.

4. To see that this specification of social welfare is consistent with the one used under public enterprise, suppose that the regulator could perfectly capture the firm's profits for each realization of θ with a franchise fee equal to its profits, making $T = -\pi$. Substituting this value of T into W in the equation returns the framer's objective function under public enterprise, namely $S + k\pi$.

5. Sappington and Stiglitz (1987) use the same approach in an analytic setting without private information about public impacts and without a private agenda for the public official.

6. This internalization procedure was inspired by Loeb and Magat (1979), who were the first to show that a firm with private information about costs could be motivated with a schedule of transfer payments to produce optimally for social welfare, and by Sappington and Stiglitz (1987), who argued that other features of the environment must underlie choices between private and public enterprise, since the Loeb-Magat mechanism could make the two equivalent where it is applicable.

7. Here we need to assume that θ is stochastically independent of ϕ and ϵ, and we are relying on the assumption that the regulator and the firm share common priors on the random variables.

8. This proposition is an adaptation of the results derived in a somewhat different context by d'Aspremont and Gerard-Varet (1979) and explicated and applied by Pratt and Zeckhauser (1987).

9. Even under these conditions, equivalence still emerges in two additional environments. First, if the regulator can partially observe the firm's private information (that is, can observe a variable that is correlated with the firm's information), if there is no limit to the penalties that the regulator can impose on the firm, and if the firm is risk neutral, then, as Baron and Besanko (1984a) show, the information problem between the regulator and the firm is not essential (see Riordan and Sappington 1988). Second, if two identical firms with knowledge of θ compete to win the franchise of becoming the regulated enterprise, then, as Sappington and Stiglitz (1987) point out, the regulator need surrender no rents, and equivalence again holds. In proceeding, we assume that ex post auditing and penalties alone are insufficient to impel truthful revelation of private information and that competition for the franchise is imperfect.

10. The seminal development of models of regulation with information rents is due to Baron and Myerson (1982). For comprehensive discussions, see Caillaud, Guesnerie, and Tirole (1988); Baron (1989); and Laffont (1992).

11. This comparison requires the additional structure on the model that is termed the "normal case" by Shapiro and Willig (1990): (a) $\pi_{xx\theta} \geq 0$, and (b) the nonnegativity of the third partial derivative with respect to x of $S + \alpha J + k\pi$. Stipulation (a) follows, for example, if θ is a cost parameter and $C(x, \theta) = c + m(\theta)n(x)$, where $m' < 0$ and $n'' \geq 0$. Stipulation (b) holds in a conventional quadratic model, or, if x were output, with convex inverse demand, convex marginal revenue, and concave marginal cost functions.

12. Analytically, this case arises when $k = 1$, or when θ is revealed after the investment decision, and when the revenues provided by the market to the firm equal the gross social benefits of the firm's activities—for example, if x represents the firm's output sold in a perfectly competitive market. Then the optimal T schedule represents a lump-sum transfer (of possibly $0). Furthermore, the framer would impose optimal Pigouvian taxes to correct any externalities the marginal impacts of which were assessed from contractible information.

References

Baron, David P. 1989. "Design of Regulatory Mechanisms and Institutions." In Richard Schmalensee and Robert Willig, eds., *Handbook of Industrial Organization*, vol. 2. Amsterdam: North-Holland.

Baron, David P., and David Besanko. 1984a. "Regulation, Asymmetric Information and Auditing." *Rand Journal of Economics* 15(4): 447–70.

———. 1984b. "Regulation and Information in a Continuing Relationship." *Information Economics and Policy* 1(3): 267–302.

Baron, David P., and Roger B. Myerson. 1982. "Regulating a Monopolist with Unknown Costs." *Econometrica* 50 (July): 911–30.

Bos, Dieter. 1993. "Privatization in Europe: A Comparison of Approaches." *Oxford Review of Economic Policy* 9 (Spring): 95–111.

Caillaud, Bernard, Roger Guesnerie, and Jean Tirole. 1988. "Government Intervention in Production and Incentives Theory: A Review of Recent Contributions." *Rand Journal of Economics* 19(1): 1–26.

d'Aspremont, Claude, and Louis-André Gerard-Varet. 1979. "Incentives and Incomplete Information." *Journal of Public Economics* 11: 25–45.

Guislain, Pierre. 1992. *Divestiture of State Enterprises: An Overview of the Legal Framework*. World Bank Technical Paper 186. Washington, D.C.

Hemming, Richard, and Ali Mansoor. 1988. *Privatization and Public Enterprises*. IMF Occasional Paper 56. Washington, D.C.: International Monetary Fund.

Kikeri, Sunita, John Nellis, and Mary Shirley. 1992. *Privatization: The Lessons of Experience*. Washington, D.C.: World Bank.

Laffont, J. J. 1992. "The New Economics of Regulation Ten Years After." Institut d'Economie Industrielle Document de Travail 22. Toulouse, France.

Laffont, J. J., and Jean Tirole. 1988. "The Dynamics of Incentive Contracts." *Econometrica* 56 (September): 1153–75.

Loeb, M., and W. Magat. 1979. "A Decentralized Method for Utility Regulation." *Journal of Law and Economics* 22: 399–404.

Noll, Roger. 1989. "The Politics of Regulation." In Richard Schmalensee and Robert Willig, eds., *Handbook of Industrial Organization*, vol. 2. Amsterdam: North-Holland.

Ordover, Janusz, and Russell Pittman. 1992. "Competition Policies for Natural Monopolies in a Developing Market Economy." Economic Analysis Group Discussion Paper 92-9. U.S. Department of Justice, Washington, D.C.

Pratt, John W., and Richard Zeckhauser. 1987. "Incentive-Based Decentralization: Expected Externality Payments Induce Efficient Behavior in Groups." In George R. Feiwel, *Arrow and the Ascent of Modern Economic Theory*. Basingstoke, U.K.: Macmillan.

Riordan, Michael H., and David E. M. Sappington. 1988. "Optimal Contracts with Public Ex Post Information." *Journal of Economic Theory* 45.

Robinson, Colin. 1992. "The Results of UK Electricity Privatisation." Working Paper, University of Surrey, Guildford, U.K.

Sappington, David E. M., and Joseph E. Stiglitz. 1987. "Privatization, Information and Incentives." *Journal of Policy Analysis and Management* 6(4): 567–82.

Shapiro, Carl, and Robert Willig. 1990. "Economic Rationales for the Scope of Privatization." In Ezra N. Suleiman and John Waterbury, eds., *The Political Economy of Public Sector Reform and Privatization*. Boulder, Colo.: Westview Press.

Vickers, John, and George Yarrow. 1988. *Privatization: An Economic Analysis*. Cambridge, Mass.: Massachusetts Institute of Technology Press.

Yarrow, George. 1986. "Privatization in Theory and Practice." *Economic Policy* 1 (April): 323–77.

[22]

Appropriate Regulatory Technology
The Interplay of Economic and Institutional Conditions

Leroy P. Jones

Appropriate regulation means maximizing the benefits from removing market failures in relation to the costs of government intervention. Monopoly markets fail because of both allocative and cost inefficiencies. The former are measured by Harberger's little *triangles and the latter by* big *rectangles. Regulation that mitigates allocative inefficiency while exacerbating cost inefficiency is inappropriate because the costs of intervention outweigh the benefits. In developing and formerly socialist countries the potential benefits from intervention are larger because the realm of market failure is greater, but the costs of intervention are also larger because government failures are more likely. The marginal benefits of regulation decline linearly as intervention increases, while costs rise exponentially. Therefore intervention should only attempt to control egregious allocative inefficiencies through low-cost mechanisms. The Chilean and New Zealand methods represent quite different ways of doing this and thus provide appropriate models for developing and formerly socialist countries.*

In 1991 Mongolia adopted the American Telephone and Telegraph (AT&T) model for dealing with its telephone monopoly, breaking it up into twenty-three separate companies. The question is whether this transfer of regulatory technology was appropriate for a country with only 2 million people, very low telephone penetration, and only a handful of economists, accountants, lawyers, and managers trained to work in market economies, and without specific regulatory bodies or even the institutional framework for enforcing legal obligations.

Leroy P. Jones is professor of economics at Boston University. He would like to thank Mukesh Chawla for effective research assistance and Guy Beatson, Henry Ergas, Jean-Jacques Laffont, David Sappington, and Ingo Vogelsang for helpful comments.

Proceedings of the World Bank Annual Conference on Development Economics 1993

The example of Mongolia, albeit extreme, illustrates the general issue addressed in this paper: how to regulate market power in developing and formerly socialist countries. On the one hand, these countries have smaller economies, which exacerbates the problems of market power. On the other hand, they have weak institutions and smaller endowments of appropriate human capital, which makes dealing with these problems more difficult. The interplay of these economic and institutional conditions is the focus of this paper. The goal is to help identify regulatory institutions that are appropriate to these conditions. Or, by analogy with the effort to identify technology appropriate to the factor endowment of developing countries, the search is for regulatory technology appropriate to the factor and institutional endowments of developing countries and formerly socialist economies.

Benefits and Costs of Regulation

The benefits of regulation can be thought of as the welfare gains from correction of *market failure* to achieve a Pareto-efficient outcome. The costs of regulation are those that follow from *government's failure* to rectify matters without introducing additional distortions. Both benefits and costs need to be defined broadly. The costs include the opportunity cost of the public and private resources devoted to the regulatory process, as well as the possibility that imperfect institutions operating with imperfect information may create new perversions in the attempt to eliminate old ones. Similarly, market failures include not only the problems created by market power but also those associated with imperfections variously labeled as transaction, agency, contracting, or information costs.

Failures in Regulating Monopoly Pricing

To make these ideas more concrete, consider the market failures that occur in the production and management practices of a natural monopolist who is producing a nontradable good (table 1).

Although these lists are by no means comprehensive, they indicate the classes of costs and benefits associated with regulation. They also suggest that there is considerable variation in the magnitude and signs of the costs in various institutional environments. The point is simply that appropriate regulatory policy is designed to maximize the net benefits for a particular industry, country, and time. Although the list is intentionally even-handed in balancing the arguments of the left and the right, in particular cases the costs and benefits will be anything but balanced. How large might the various costs and benefits be?

Magnitudes of Net Benefits

Arguments for no regulation. The set of regulatory options notably includes no regulation at all. The case can be and has been made that the costs of

Table 1. *Market Failure versus Government Failure*

Market failure	*Government failure*
1. A profit-seeking monopolist will reduce the quantity offered and thus increase the price at which it sells. The resulting allocative inefficiency is the first evil of monopoly and is reflected in Harberger's little triangles (figure 1), as described in any introductory economics text.	1. Government efforts to regulate monopoly reduce welfare by the opportunity costs of the resources devoted thereto. This includes not only the costs of the regulatory body but also the costs of the regulated firm and of the consultants hired by both sides.
2. If ownership is divorced from control[a] and agency problems prevent the owner from fully imposing his objectives on the manager, the manager will use his discretion in ways that divert some of the monopoly rents to serve his own objectives (Williamson 1975). This may take the form of overspending on perquisites (activities such as entertainment and fancy means of transport that serve corporate goals but also contribute to the manager's utility). It may take the form of increased managerial leisure, which results in less supervision of subordinates and higher costs. It may take the form of reduced bargaining with suppliers and labor. All these increase the measured costs of the firm (the big rectangle in figure 1). The magnitudes can be substantial. One study of U.S. corporations finds that up to two-thirds of monopoly rents are diverted to employees alone (Karier 1985). I will refer to this interchangeably as the second evil of monopoly, the corporate governance problem, the X-efficiency problem, or the rectangle problem.	2. Regulators are not perfect. One consequence is that they are not fully able to accomplish the goals of regulation. Much more dangerously, imperfect regulation may introduce new distortions. One heavily studied manifestation of this phenomenon is the Averich, Johnson, Wellisz (AJW) effect, whereby excessively generous estimates of a "fair" rate of return lead to excess investment (Kahn 1992). Under different institutional arrangements, the opposite effect can occur, with underinvestment following from enterprise fears that government will use price regulation to expropriate future earnings (Levy and Spiller, in this volume). Reversing our field once again, there is a considerable body of literature which argues that, far from exploiting the regulated, the regulators go to bed with them. This regulatory capture provides a fig-leaf of consumer-protection respectability but actually leads to high prices in the short run and protection from competitive entry in the long run. Many other examples are possible.[b]
3. While some of the behavior described above will increase both the firm's and society's costs (perks and sloth), others will appear as mere transfers from the owner to stakeholders in the firm (Krueger 1974). A higher wage for workers is the most obvious example. However, the literature on rent-seeking reminds us that where there are rents to be had, people will expend real resources in their pursuit. One need not accept the extreme version (that the resources expended will *fully* absorb the rents) to recognize that much, if not all, of the rectangle represents real welfare losses.	3. Government regulators have the power to grant or deny rents to firms. In some institutional settings it would be viewed as ungracious, if not positively immoral, for those favored by regulation not to share some of the rents with those who granted them. This can be viewed merely as one of the sources of regulatory capture. However, civil servants are not unaware that some government jobs are "wet" (with high potential for receiving such gifts), while others are "dry." They will naturally spend resources to gain access to a "wet" position, and—as in the first column—real social costs are incurred.

a. A similar story can be told for an owner-operator. As he becomes rich on monopoly profits, he will be wise to take some of the increased income in increased leisure and perquisites, with effects similar to those described in the text. Given the monomania of many big entrepreneurs, this may often be of minimal import for the first generation of tycoons but will take on increasing importance for their heirs.

b. Regulating a multiproduct firm (such as telecommunications) by imposing a single average price allows the firm to cross-subsidize, charging high prices in noncompetitive markets (such as home service) and precluding entry via lower prices in more competitive markets.

Figure 1. *The Algebra of Little Triangles and Big Rectangles: Welfare Loss from the Presence of Market Power*

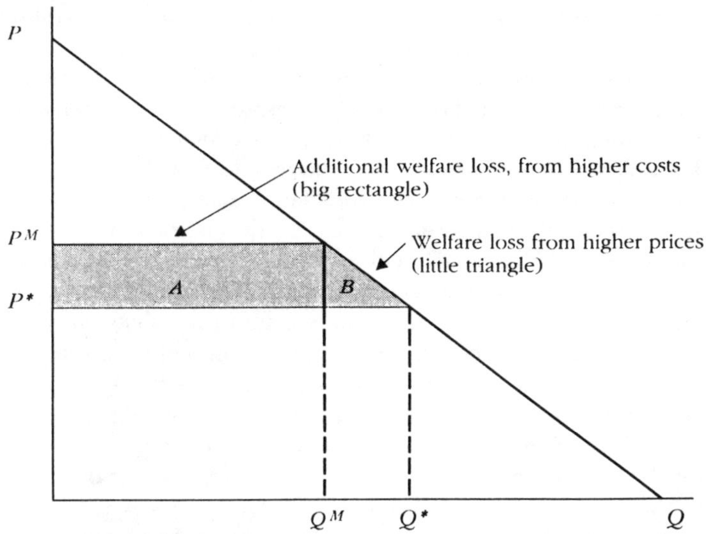

regulation exceed the benefits. Consider only the first evil of monopoly. Figure 1 gives the standard derivation of the size of the Harbergerian triangle for the simplest case: a single product, linear demand, and constant costs. The welfare loss from monopoly pricing is indicated by shaded area *B*. The welfare loss from higher costs is indicated by shaded area *A* + *B*. The price elasticity of demand is defined as $\epsilon = (\Delta Q/Q)/(\Delta P/P)$. The price distortion factor is defined as $d = \Delta P/P$. Then $\Delta Q = \epsilon\, dQ = Q^* - Q^M$, $\Delta P = dP$, and $Q^M = Q^* - \epsilon\, dQ$. The respective areas become:

(1)
$$B = \tfrac{1}{2}\Delta P\,\Delta Q$$
$$B \approx \tfrac{1}{2}(dP^*)(\epsilon\, dQ^*)$$
$$B \approx \tfrac{1}{2}\epsilon\, d^2 P^* Q^*$$

(2)
$$A + B = \Delta P Q^M + \tfrac{1}{2}\Delta P\,\Delta Q$$
$$A + B \approx (dP^*)(Q^* - \epsilon\, dQ^*) + \tfrac{1}{2}\epsilon\, d^2 P^* Q^*$$
$$A + B \approx dP^* Q^* - \tfrac{1}{2}\epsilon\, d^2 P^* Q^*$$

(The triangle algebra is from Harberger; the rectangle algebra is added.) For example, let elasticity equal 1 and distortion equal 10 percent. Then $B = 0.5$ percent of revenues and $A + B = 9.5$ percent of revenues.

Equation 1 shows that the welfare loss is proportional to the total revenues of the enterprise, where the factor of proportionality is one-half the product of the price elasticity of demand and the square of the price-distortion factor (that is, the ratio of the price increase to the base price). Thus if elasticity is in the vicinity of 1, the welfare cost of a monopolist's raising prices by 10 percent is in the vicinity of half of 1 percent of revenues ($0.5 \cdot 1 \cdot 0.1 \cdot 0.1$). This vicinity is clearly a low-rent district and remains so even if the estimate is off considerably. One might therefore wonder why anyone would undertake empirical work on the subject; it is not surprising to find that the original Harberger estimate of the cost of monopoly in the United States was 0.1 percent of gross national product (GNP) and that subsequent refinements have boosted that figure to only a few percent. (For a survey of the literature, see Scherer and Ross 1990.)

A gain of 1 percent of revenues may be small in relative terms, but it could nonetheless be large in absolute terms for, say, a large electric utility. How might the costs compare? That depends on the institutional mechanism chosen, but consider the classic U.S. model in which "cost plus fair rate of return" is determined in an advocacy setting. The first cost is that of the public utility commission; the second is the cost to the enterprise of preparing petitions, responses, and cases; and the third is that of the economists and lawyers hired as consultants. Although an institution that generates demand for economists cannot be all bad, two things seem clear: the opportunity costs are substantial, and they will be substantially higher in developing countries and formerly socialist countries, where the requisite talent is in short supply. Confining ourselves to the United States, I am not aware of any study that actually quantifies these costs, but would anyone be surprised if they were of the order of magnitude of 1 percent of revenues, or even higher? Costs might thus exceed benefits on this ground alone.

Matters look even bleaker if we take into account the second evil of regulation. This can take many forms, but consider only the classic American variant. If I reimburse you for costs, you have no reason to minimize any costs and every reason to maximize capital costs, since the absolute value of the "plus" will then rise (assuming that the "plus" rate of return is above the opportunity cost of investment and there is unexploited market power; Kahn 1992). Such cost- or X-inefficiencies give rise to big rectangles of welfare loss. A look at figure 1 or at Leibenstein's (1976) *Beyond Economic Man* might convince one that the triangles are considerably smaller than the rectangles. Once again, a little algebra makes this clear. Equation 2 shows that the welfare loss from cost efficiency is, as a first approximation, proportional to revenues where the factor of proportionality is simply the cost-distortion factor (exactly analogous to the price-distortion factor above).[1] The result is slightly more accurate if we subtract the second term in the equation, which is simply the little triangle. Accordingly, if costs rise by 10 percent, the welfare loss is 9.5 percent of revenues (0.10 minus the corresponding triangle). If, therefore, a costless regulatory body succeeded in reducing the exercise of market power by 10 percent but at the same time precipitated a rise in costs of 10 percent, the net welfare loss from regulation would be about 9 percent of total sales.[2] There is, of course, no reason why the price and cost distortion factors should be of equal magnitude, but the point is that the cost distortion is far more important, and even a little cost inefficiency will wipe out the gains from a sharp price cut.

If these back-of-the envelope calculations are even roughly correct, it is easy to see how the costs of regulation could exceed the benefits. In fact, it is difficult to see how they could not exceed the benefits. Accordingly, it is not mere indifference that leads some policymakers to argue against regulation in the developing countries and the formerly socialist countries. We are most unlikely to make things better in any event, the reasoning goes, so why not simply relax and enjoy it—let the robber-barons make their piles now and generate the savings needed for growth? The markets will eventually catch up to them, and later generations will dissipate their wealth. The reader may correctly infer that I reject that conclusion. Nonetheless, these are some important lessons here, which I recapitulate below.

THE CASE OF LARGE DISTORTIONS. The first weakness in the no-regulation argument is that it is predicated on relatively modest price distortions. In a Harberger-type study of an entire industrial economy, this is reasonable, since many sectors have no distortions and problems in the potentially most distorted sectors have already been ameliorated by regulation. If, however, we want to know what the potential gains are in moving from zero to perfect regulation in a particular sector, the magnitude of the distortion may be considerably larger. This is obvious from figure 1: as the distorted price line (P^M) rises, the triangle becomes larger and the rectangle smaller, so that at the extreme of zero production the rectangle disappears and the losses from allocative problems and X-inefficiency (corporate governance) problems become equal. No one would go to this extreme, and a natural limit is found at the distortion effected by a pure profit-maximizer. A model by Galal and others (forthcoming) reveals that the profit-maximizing price distortion is (d/c^*), where ϵ is evaluated at Q^*.

$$d^* = \frac{1}{2\epsilon}. \tag{3}$$

That is, for an elasticity of 1 (at the welfare maximum where price equals marginal cost), the profit maximizer would raise prices 50 percent, yielding (from equation 1) a welfare loss of 12.5 percent.

At this level of welfare loss, the elasticity component of the proportionality factor becomes important. There is an inverse relationship between the elasticity and the optimal price distortion: the more inelastic the demand (the smaller the elasticity), the more the profit maximizer will raise prices. Lower elasticity thus goes with higher distortions. The former reduces the welfare effect, but the latter increases it, and since the latter is squared, it dominates. Lower elasticities generate greater maximum potential allocative losses from monopoly (approaching 100 percent for elasticities in the teens), while higher elasticities generate lower losses (approaching 1 percent for high-single-digit elasticities). Accordingly, society has little to fear from monopolists facing elastic demand and much to fear from those facing inelastic demand.

How large might the relevant elasticities be? There is obviously considerable variance over sectors, countries, and estimation methods, but it is clear that in some critical industries they can be quite small. In sectors such as electric power, short-term demand is highly inelastic; values in the vicinity of 0.20 are not uncommon. In such a sector the optimal distortion is given by equation 3 to be 2.5, and the corresponding welfare loss (from equation 1) is 62.5 percent of revenues. This is certainly large.

Long-term elasticities, however, are always higher because people have time to adjust. A short-term elasticity of 0.2 might, for example, correspond to a long-term elasticity of 2.0, and the latter yields a welfare loss of only 6 percent. In such an industry, which measure of welfare loss is correct, 60 percent or 6 percent? The answer is a weighted average, where the weights are a function of the discount rate of the monopolist. The monopolist will maximize the net present value of a stream of profits, taking into account the fact that higher prices now yield lower demand later. Given the very high discount rate for entrepreneurial capital in developing countries (say, 30 percent), the first few years loom large in this decision, and the average can be closer to 60 than to 6 percent. In sum, little triangles are not always so little, and the scope for allocative gains from regulation is thus sometimes substantial.

In such sectors it is obviously quite possible to have substantial net gains from regulation so long as one avoids mechanisms that motivate cost inefficiencies or other distortions. In well-developed market economies such sectors will be largely confined to regulated public utilities, explaining low additional potential gains in Harbergerian-type studies. How will matters differ in developing countries and formerly socialist countries?

INDUSTRIAL CONCENTRATION IN DEVELOPING COUNTRIES. Is the problem of market power more or less serious in developing countries than in industrial countries? To my knowledge, the empirical work does not allow a definitive answer to this question, but enough information is available to permit informed conjecture. Begin by decomposing the question into two parts. First, for a given industry operating in both developing and industrial countries, how does concentration vary? Second, what is the share of highly concentrated sectors in relation to the entire economy?

The first question can be further decomposed, since within an industry concentration depends tautologically on the relationship between plant size and market size. With other factors held constant, developing countries have smaller markets. If technology were standardized, all countries would have the same minimum efficient scale of plant, but larger and richer countries would have more plants and thus less concentration. Technology, however, does adjust, but not fully. The elasticity of plant size to market size has been shown across a wide range of studies to be approximately 0.5 (Caves 1989). Since plant size thus declines less rapidly than market size, empirical studies show rising concentration as we move to smaller economies (Scherer and Ross 1990, pp. 82–89).

But matters are more complicated than this. For example, the foregoing conclusion would predict less concentration in the largest developing countries than in the smallest industrial countries,[3] but this need not be so because other things are not necessarily held constant. Sutton (1992) shows that although the inverse relationship between market size and concentration holds for industries with low expenditure on advertising, research and development, and other endogenous sunk costs, it does not hold where such costs are high. The same literature emphasizes that market structure also varies with the degree of price competition. Exogenous price competition (independent of market structure) depends on the ability of a small number of producers to collude. This in turn depends on the government's capacity to prevent such collusion and the ability of the press to publicize it. In many developing countries government policies (such as licensing requirements) have worked to increase, rather than to reduce, industrial concentration. That is, rather than prohibiting a firm from erecting barriers to entry, they erect them for it through licensing. Furthermore, enforcement mechanisms and other countervailing institutions are weak.

Other factors that affect concentration include openness to trade and the quality of the transport system. For any particular country a host of such factors enter in, but for present purposes it is only necessary to establish that most developing countries have small economies and that concentration will thus be larger for a given sector. Available empirical data are thin, but they support this view (Lee 1984).

The other half of the question may be answered more quickly. In developing countries agriculture accounts for a much larger share of gross domestic product (GDP) and manufacturing for a smaller share. Therefore the share of concentrated sectors will be smaller because of systemic differences in industrial structure.

In sum, the scope for welfare improvement will be larger because the modern sector is more concentrated, but that sector will generate a smaller fraction of GDP. How do these two offsetting tendencies net out? For the sake of argument, assume that the share of concentrated sectors is 10 percent of GDP. This is the order of magnitude of public enterprise sectors in developing countries, and these sectors overlap substantially with concentrated sectors (Jones and Mason 1982). Assume further that half of this is in utilities with short-term elasticities of 0.2 and long-term elasticities of 2.0, yielding welfare gains in the vicinity of 30 percent. Assume that the other half of the concentrated sector is in oligopolistic industries that imperfectly exploit their market power but have similar elasticities. The welfare gain could be something like 10 percent in the oligopolistic subsector, and the average for the sector would be 20 percent of total sales. Since concentrated sectors tend to be intermediate-intensive, 10 percent of value added would translate into sales of about 25 percent of GDP. The potential welfare gain would be 20 percent of that, or 5 percent of GDP. This is on the order of double what improved Harbergerian analysis yields for the United States and appears plausible (although I suspect it errs on the low side). Pending research, let us take it as a working stylized fact.

The next question is whether 5 percent of GDP is enough to worry about. Five percent of GDP is, after all, of the same order of magnitude as total corporate and personal income tax collections in the average developing country;[4] it amounts to 28 percent of total taxes and thus—allowing for borrowing and deficit finance—to perhaps a fifth of total government expenditure. Big is in the eye of the beholder, but I see this as big.

INDUSTRIAL CONCENTRATION IN FORMERLY SOCIALIST COUNTRIES. Data on industrial concentration in the formerly socialist countries have not been analyzed as thoroughly as for industrial countries, but available data from Russia permit the following preliminary generalizations.

- Enterprises are typically bigger than in the West, but markets are smaller, and individual *enterprises* are therefore more likely to dominate particular industries (IMF and others 1991, pp. 16–17, 36–40).
- Even worse, enterprises are widely incorporated into *groups* (for example, cement, fertilizer, or heavy equipment) so that at this level concentration frequently approaches 100 percent.
- Because transport networks are less developed, regional monopolies are common.
- Even where there are many producers, there is often only one middleman because the wholesale and retail trade sectors are monopolized.
- Competition from foreign trade is often minimal,
- Countervailing forces are weak or absent; consumer advocacy groups are nascent, antimonopoly and regulatory bodies are in their infancy, and the legal system is underdeveloped.

If we start with the fact that enterprise monopolies account for 30 to 40 percent of mining and manufacturing output, a crude adjustment for group monopoly as well as oligopoly suggests that highly concentrated industries must account for at least half, and probably two-thirds, of total output. Like the developing countries, formerly socialist countries have much more concentrated markets than is common in industrial countries. However, the share of modern sectors in GDP is much closer to that in industrial countries. Accordingly, it seems safe to conclude that imperfectly competitive markets are a considerably larger problem in formerly socialist countries than in developing countries and that the potential welfare gains discussed in the preceding section should be increased substantially in formerly socialist countries.

THE SECOND EVIL OF MONOPOLY. This far I have argued that little triangles might sometimes be large enough to worry about in both developing and formerly socialist countries. Now let us consider the rectangles. The second problem with the no-regulation argument is that it ignores the market failures of monopoly-induced sloth and rent-seeking. The resulting cost inefficiencies are measured in terms of big rectangles, so the cost of even modest distortions can be substantial.

How big might these rectangles be? Under the same conditions that yielded a 5 percent triangle in developing countries, and on the basis of equation 2, the rectangle would be about 15 percent of GDP. This calculation assumes that rents would be fully converted into costs, but 5 to 10 percent strikes me as a plausible estimate of the gains from eliminating market power in developing countries. In formerly socialist countries these gains would be considerably larger.

Once again, there are potential gains from well-designed regulatory mechanisms. As I discuss below, the ability of price regulation to deal with this problem is probably quite limited, but cost inefficiencies do provide an argument for some of the structural remedies in oligopolistic markets.

THE POLITICS OF REGULATION. A final, and rather different, problem with the no-regulation argument is that it ignores the political reality of popular pressures to regulate, usually associated with calls for distributional equity. Such appeals are easily overstated in the context of developing countries. For example, the truly poor do not have access to electricity at all, or they have a single bare bulb dangling from the ceiling. The comparatively well-off have refrigerators and air conditioners and consume other energy-intensive products. Thus raising utility prices in such countries harms mostly the top third of the income distribution. If those increases are captured by the government (through taxes or public enterprise profits) and are used to help the poor, income distribution will *improve*. If, however, profits accrue to rich private owners, the transfer is still from middle-class consumers.

Helping the middle class is, of course, an important political goal; they are the ones who vote and who riot in the streets. Because the room for Pareto-efficient reallocations (which make someone better off without making someone else worse off) to this class is small, politicians naturally turn to what I (in Jones 1985) call *politically* efficient reallocations, which make someone better off without making anyone else *aware* that they are worse off. In this latter sense, Pareto-inefficient price regulation is politically efficient because the beneficiaries of lower prices are aware of it but the losers are not. Most governments are therefore likely to regulate, for better or worse.[5]

SUMMARY. The no-regulation argument is something of a rhetorical straw man, set up to make the following points:

- The benefits of regulation are easily overstated because little triangles are often just that—little.
- The costs of regulation are often unrecognized and include both significant resource costs and potentially much larger regulation-induced distortions.
- The net benefits of regulation can easily be negative. The doctor's creed, "first of all, do no harm," should be adopted by regulators.
- There is, nonetheless, considerable scope for welfare-enhancing regulation, but the targets must be carefully selected, and mechanisms must be designed to minimize the costs in relation to the benefits.

- Particular attention should be paid to the big rectangles associated with cost-inefficiencies, where most of the really big numbers lie. This applies to both targeting the benefits from removing market failures and avoiding the costs associated with government failures.

Price Regulation

Regulatory technology is characterized by diminishing marginal benefits and increasing marginal costs. The benefits from removing allocative inefficiencies (although not X-inefficiencies) diminish because of the squared distortion term. Eliminating the first 1 percent of a 20 percent allocative distortion is approximately forty times as beneficial as removing the last 1 percent (assuming unit elasticity). Costs rise because of information problems. It is not difficult to determine whether a company's prices are above the efficient level: international comparators convey a great deal of information. Figuring out, however, that a firm is a few percent above the efficient level is probably impossible. The trite but true lesson is to keep it simple: try to control the more egregious problems and leave the smaller issues aside. How do various regulatory mechanisms measure up under this criterion? I start with price regulation.

The Effect of Cost-Plus Pricing on Incentives

It should be apparent that U.S.-style cost-plus regulation does not fare very well. For one thing, it is conducted in an advocacy setting and incurs high costs to obtain the last few percentage points of accuracy. Even if this is cost-effective in the United States, it is highly unlikely to be of use in countries in which professional skills are scarce.

Leaving this problem aside, the fundamental flaw is that cost-plus pricing encourages cost inefficiency. Many incentive mechanisms have been proposed to deal with this problem by leaving some fraction of cost savings to the enterprise. (In this context, "incentive" refers to the problem of motivating the firm to act like a true profit maximizer in minimizing costs.) Laffont and Tirole (1993) point out that such schemes can be arrayed on a scale from zero to one according to the percentage of cost savings that accrue to the enterprise. At one extreme (see figure 2) are ex-post cost-plus contracts that give the firm no incentive to economize. At the other extreme, under a fixed price cap, the firm has full incentive to economize. Incentive schemes are anything in between. Those on the cost-plus end of the spectrum are termed low powered in their ability to induce efficiency, while those at the price-cap end are termed high powered. Note that the spectrum reflects a classic efficiency-equity tradeoff because all the benefits have to be given to the enterprise in order to maximize the quantum of benefits to be distributed.

In practice, the U.S. version of cost-plus pricing does not fall at the zero end of the spectrum. It is not ex post in the sense that the firm simply sends in bills and

Figure 2. *Incentive Power of Pricing Schemes*

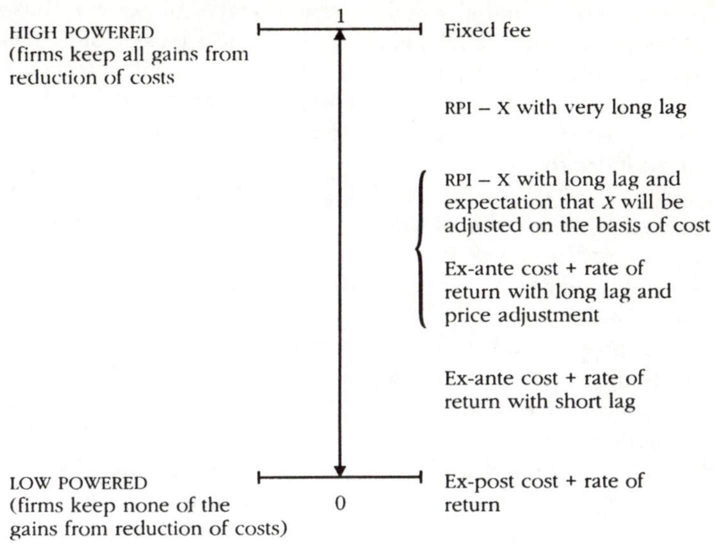

is reimbursed for its costs (including the opportunity cost of capital). Rather, it is ex ante; the last period's costs serve as the basis for the current period's prices. This method generates some surplus, which in turn is used as the basis for determining the next period's prices, and so forth. The resulting regulatory lag adds power to the scheme. If prices are fixed for a period of years, any cost savings in the interim accrue to the firm. If prices were fixed forever, it would be equivalent to a price cap and fully high powered. However, with a finite regulatory lag, the enterprise knows that when the next price is set, lower costs this period will be taken into account in setting a lower price next period. Some cost reductions will be appropriated by the government for consumers (or for itself in higher taxes), and the incentive effect is thus less than complete. Nonetheless, the longer the lag, the higher the power of the system.

Are Price Caps a Better Formula?

It is easy to see why the incentive power of regulation might be raised by switching to a price-cap formula such as the United Kingdom's "rate of price inflation minus *X*" (RPI – X). If an enterprise is told that for the next, say, three years it can raise prices at no more than, say, RPI – 2, will it not have every incentive to lower costs? Costs, after all, are not even mentioned. The answer is that this will be fully high powered only if that rate is reasonably expected to last forever. If not, then we must ask how *X* will be determined for the next period. The manager might think that if profits were 30 percent, *X* would rise significantly, as opposed to what it would be if profits were 10 percent. Accordingly, there is the same danger of a ratchet effect as with cost-plus pricing: the fact that profits may be expropriated in the future reduces the incentive to cut costs now. That costs are not explicit in the formula does not mean that they are not implicit in the *X*. If *X* is not determined as a function of revealed profits and costs, how is it determined?

One advantage of RPI − X is that it is typically associated with a relatively long lag. However, this dimension of choice can easily be added to cost-plus schemes. The proper comparison is between two managers in the same environment; one can raise prices 2 percent a year under cost-plus and the other can raise prices the same amount under RPI − X. I have yet to see a convincing argument as to why the two managers would behave any differently, given a common set of regulators and a common expectation of what figures regulators will examine.

A related advantage of RPI − X is that it allows a longer lag because it explicitly adjusts for one of the major exogenous environmental variables (Vogelsang 1989). Allowing the price to vary with the rate of inflation thus promotes a longer lag before prices have to be adjusted. Given higher rates of inflation in developing and formerly socialist countries, this is no small advantage. Much the same thing, however, can be accomplished with a crude tool (such as the fuel-adjustment clause in U.S. regulations, which calls for a surcharge on electricity bills if the prices of energy inputs rise more than a specified amount). The adjustment can also be accomplished in a far more sophisticated way. In Chile the telephone company adjusts charges every two months on the basis of a Divisia index of the prices of inputs into each service (Galal 1992).

In sum, the incentive power of a price regulation system does not depend fundamentally on whether it is couched in cost-plus or RPI − X terms. Rather, it depends on the length of the regulatory lag and the expectations of how prices will be adjusted at the end of that lag.

Price Adjustment Techniques: New Zealand versus Chile

One major advantage of RPI − X is that in practice—although by no means necessarily—it has been associated with relatively simple implementation mechanisms. Perhaps the ultimate in simplicity is found in New Zealand, whose system has been described as "regulation without regulators."[6] That is, there are no industry-specific regulatory bodies, and restraints are embodied in regulations.[7] This authority seems to be used with considerable restraint. For example, in the case of telecommunications, the regulations provide that "the standard residential rental for a phone line will not rise faster than movements in the Consumer Price Index unless the profits of Telecom's regional operating companies are unreasonably impaired" (New Zealand, Ministry of Commerce,

1992). It also stipulates that rural rates will not be higher than residential rates and includes a service requirement. Prices of other services are regulated only by competition or the threat thereof. The latter provision is particularly important and will be elaborated on in the next section.

The RPI − 0 pricing mechanism has some clear advantages. First, it is extremely economical in terms of the cost of regulation. It is not quite costless because there is a communications division within the Ministry of Commerce. However, this division is small, and the bulk of its time is spent on entry issues rather than pricing. Second, its cost-incentive power is quite high because of the indefinitely long regulatory lag with a fixed price in relation to inflation. Furthermore, the regulation gives the firm an escape clause that allows prices to rise faster if profits are "unreasonably impaired." Given the recent rapid rate of technological progress in the telecommunications industry and the scope for internal efficiencies in the recently privatized enterprise, this provision is unlikely to be needed for some time, but it presumably is a comfort to the firm to have it there just in case.

The scheme nonetheless falls short of being completely high powered. There is always the danger that some future government will impose price controls. A judicious manager will take this into account and will keep profits from rising to unreasonable levels. Ideally, of course, he would do this by lowering prices. Alternatively, he might not work quite so hard to exploit cost-cutting opportunities. Given the latter possibility, the scheme is something less than fully high powered. Furthermore, it does not attack the second evil of monopoly, instead leaving that corporate governance problem to the private sector.

Still, the New Zealand compromise has much to recommend it. The primary emphasis is on cost-efficiency incentives, with considerably weaker controls on the allocative inefficiencies of monopoly pricing. Given the relative sizes of rectangles and triangles and the importance of correcting the worst of the triangle abuses, the direction of the bias in the compromise cannot be questioned, although one might quibble about the magnitude.

Chile employs a rather different model (Galal 1992, pp. 11–13). The system can be described as cost-plus-fair-return because firms are allowed a rate of return equal to the risk-free rate plus a premium based on the systematic risk of the industry and the difference between the risk-free rate and the return on a diversified investment portfolio. (It could as well be described as RPI − X because the price cap is adjusted every two months to reflect inflation.) Which phrase is chosen is immaterial because the real distinction lies elsewhere.

The first critical feature is specificity. If New Zealand is near the zero end of the vagueness-specificity continuum, Chile is at the opposite end. For one thing, the adjustment period is explicit and reflects a long lag of five years. Moreover, a range of regulatory technology is spelled out in law. In addition to the sophisticated fair-rate-of-return and inflation-adjustment mechanisms already described, long-run marginal costs are calculated in the context of a five-year investment plan (designed to minimize the system costs of meeting projected demand), markups from marginal to average costs are apportioned via Ramsey pricing, and so on. There is more, but the general point of sophisticated specificity is clear. Note that this mechanism reduces the firm's uncertainty and focuses any debate on technological parameters. This approach is similar to that of the U.S. model, which allows for only "reasonable" costs. The difference lies in the ex-ante specificity about how the parameters are to be determined. In the United States it is in an advocacy proceeding guided by general principles, but in Chile the principles are detailed in advance.

The second critical point is that the model relies on data not simply from the firms themselves but from similar firms in other countries. In principle, such benchmark or yardstick pricing is unassailable. Given a sufficiently large set of sufficiently similar firms, one could readily use econometric techniques to establish a best-practice technological frontier. Add data on local prices and the cost of capital and it would be possible to generate the right price for the company. The problem, of course, is that there is a shortage of sufficiently similar firms, and adjustment must be made for local conditions—that is, using data from the regulated firms themselves. In the case of electricity distribution in Chile, this problem is minimized because there is a number of similar distribution networks. Data are gathered from the set as a whole, and a local best-practice benchmark is established (Galal and others forthcoming). Forced to meet prices generated by this frontier, a given firm has no incentive to shirk so long as its own costs are a small fraction of the total.

An appealing property of this approach is that, unlike any of the other schemes discussed, it solves the corporate governance problem so long as at least one firm in the sample has solved it. For Chile Telecom this condition does not hold because the comparators are imperfect (foreign) and are drawn from a set of regulated private firms or public enterprises, where cost minimization is not likely. Nonetheless, the technological benchmark model is clearly a major step in the right direction.

A third feature of the system is that if the regulator and the firm disagree, they can appeal to a technical arbitration board. Finally, the system is reasonably economical as to the cost of regulation; the bulk of the work consists of a study that is produced every five years.

The New Zealand and Chilean systems are quite different, but they define the boundaries of what might be practical. The system used in New Zealand is extremely simple. It minimizes the costs of both of the major regulatory failures, at the expense of the two major market failures. Chile's system makes considerable progress on the two market failures as well, but at the expense of some complexity and information requirements. Many intermediate solutions are possible. For example, New Zealand's system could be designed so that X is estimated on the basis of exogenous data on the rate of productivity change in the industry and adjusted for changes in relative price trends. I would suggest that the feasible choice for regulatory design lies on the continuum between the two countries. The precise point on that continuum would be a function of specific country and industry conditions.

Underinvestment: Expropriation versus Exploitation

Thus far I have focused on the way in which regulatory expectations can lead firms to raise costs. However, they can also induce underinvestment if it is feared that regulators will expropriate future earnings. In a monopoly environment, underinvestment is a serious economic problem. A World Bank study (Galal and others forthcoming) of divestiture in Chile, Malaysia, Mexico, and the United Kingdom found that much of the welfare gain came from an expansion of investment and that most of the benefits accrued to consumers. Levy and Spiller (forthcoming) study regulation in five countries, with a primary focus on observed underinvestment.

There are, of course, other explanations for underinvestment than the fear that regulators will expropriate future earnings. First, the company may have underestimated demand. Second, public enterprises underinvest when they are bound by public borrowing constraints rather than by the economic merits of their particular projects. Finally, underinvestment is exactly what a profit-maximizing monopolist would do to reduce quantity, create excess demand, and increase prices under a friendly regulatory regime. In this guise, underinvestment is simply one manifestation of the first evil of monopoly.

Whatever the source, the associated welfare loss is measured by the relevant little triangle. The operations of France Telecom in the 1960s provide a nice example of this phenomenon (Anastasopolus 1973, p. 164). Despite offering abysmal service, the company was consistently highly profitable. The actual rents, which were high, were absorbed by higher costs, thus illustrating the second evil of monopoly.

In other countries the same phenomenon also illustrates the third (rent-seeking) evil of monopoly. Excess demand plus price regulation means that some people are willing to pay a considerable amount for a phone line. In some instances a legal market is created to reallocate old lines and auction off new lines. In others the problem is resolved by queuing and by bringing pressure. In many developing countries, however, it is necessary to pay several hundred or several thousand dollars to someone with the right connections. These rents may go to employees or to political appointees, but they do not go to finance the expansion of telephone service. In such a setting an expansion of service would damage prominent decisionmakers and—even if they are not strictly profit-maximizers—this likelihood may explain why the shortage exists and persists. Whatever the reason, underinvestment is expensive. What can be done about it?

Mechanisms to Create Positive Regulatory Expectations

In cases where underinvestment reflects a fear of expropriation, Levy and Spiller (in this volume) emphasize the importance of institutional factors:

> For a regulatory system to encourage private investment, three complementary mechanisms must be available to restrain arbitrary adminis-

> trative action: substantive restraints on the discretion of the regulator, embedded in the design of the regulatory system; formal or informal procedural constraints on changing the regulatory system; and institutions that enforce these substantive and procedural constraints.

These conditions are profoundly important but are covered in other papers in this volume.

Another mechanism is reputational. It has been suggested that the threat of expropriation can be mitigated by covenants—or conditions—in lending agreements with international financial institutions. Those who doubt the potential efficacy of this mechanism must explain why else the countries involved in the Latin American debt crisis did not default on their loans. The answer presumably has to do with reputation, which is a precious international commodity. Still, one might wonder at what point international agencies would go to the mat to enforce a pricing contract. Even if this prevented a wholesale expropriation, at what margin would the deterrent operate? Given the inevitable accounting and legal questions, would it be possible to deter, say 25 percent exploitation?

The strength of reputational deterrents will vary with whose property is being expropriated. By granting part or all of the license to foreigners or selling shares to dispersed private domestic shareholders, the probability of expropriation is reduced. Both mechanisms were used in the U.K. divestiture.

If one were not sure which problem would crop up, or simply wanted a little insurance, a more complete contract should be considered. This statement rests on the principle that achieving two goals requires two instruments. A contract will be required that explicitly incorporates pricing and investment rules and that makes expansion an explicit condition of the license. In the United States a utility is typically expected to provide service to anyone willing to pay. This is obviously not feasible in developing countries, but Mexico applies the same principle by requiring that the number of lines in service must expand by 12 percent a year, that all towns with more than 500 people must have service by a fixed date, that the number of public telephones must increase at a specified rate, and that the maximum waiting time for a phone must be reduced to six months by 1995 and to one month by 2000 (Tandon forthcoming).

This seems a sensible solution. It is particularly appealing because once the investment is in place, the potential for enhancing profits by cutting quantity is substantially reduced. One drawback is that the firm would require a higher expected return in this case, and if credibility were an issue, that return might be very high indeed.

Laffont and Tirole (1993, pp. 100–03) suggest four other mechanisms, three of which are straightforward: reimburse a high fraction of the investment costs; rely on repetitive regulatory interaction to develop credibility over time; and, where possible, allow the firm to use its capital to produce nonregulated commodities. A fourth—somewhat facetious–suggestion would entail installing a captured regulator. The same thing can be accomplished by granting the license to a relative or compatriot of the president. The problem may then be overinvestment (if AJW conditions obtain).

Although this course is not to be recommended, it does serve to remind us that capture will be the likely outcome in many countries. In fact, I would hazard a guess that the phenomenon of capture and resulting exploitation will be the problem in considerably more countries than will be the danger of expropriation. This may simply be the result of bias in the sample of countries I know well. However, there is some logic in the inherent imbalance in power relationships between regulator and regulated. Large public utilities (and other firms with sufficient market power to worry about) are going to be owned or run—or both—by rich, powerful individuals. Regulatory commissions are going to be run by technocrats or midlevel politicians. An amusing illustration occurred in Chile under Allende, when the two phone companies were run by generals and the regulatory agency by a colonel.

Although no wholly satisfactory solution to underinvestment is available, some combination of the foregoing ideas may substantially ameliorate the problem in particular contexts.

Other Regulatory Issues

In part because of space limitations and in part because they are obvious, regulatory issues other than natural monopolies will be dealt with more perfunctorily. They are included only to provide a balanced perspective. Others, especially problems of antitrust and aggregate concentration regulations, however, are quite complex and are decidedly underresearched in the context of developing and formerly socialist countries. They are included to suggest further areas of research.

Structural Remedies

Structural remedies alter market structures in ways that promote or simulate competition. They are by definition institutionally appropriate, since they primarily require one-time policy actions rather than ongoing monitoring.

Optimal regulatory policy. This is one area that needs no research; the simplest and most effective regulatory mechanism is competition.

Tariff policy. A considerable share of the concentrated industries in developing and formerly socialist countries produces tradables. In this case the simplest solution is to reduce tariff protection. I do not suggest ignoring the importance of infant industry regulation. As we know from the experiences of the Republic of Korea and Japan, such protection can be quite effective if it is done right. Doing it right means not extending the protection to teenage—let alone geriatric—industries. Provide a firm schedule of tariff reductions tailored to the conditions of individual industries, and tell the babies they have a fixed number of years to grow up.

Reducing government barriers to entry. Domestic competition can also be enhanced in ways that are not only administratively economical but actually save resources. Most developing and formerly socialist governments discourage rather than promote competition by imposing such entry barriers as general licensing requirements and cumbersome import procedures. They also prevent competitors from impinging on the territory of natural monopolies, which have all too often been de facto unnatural monopolies (such as provision of telephone equipment or cellular services). Such barriers should be eliminated, not on a fixed schedule, but immediately. The problem is not complex in economic terms, but it does face considerable political barriers.

Breaking up large units in the formerly socialist countries. Competition can also be fostered without new entrepreneurship by breaking up large existing enterprises. The potential here is particularly large in the formerly socialist countries, where, as noted earlier, economic ideology promoted huge units. This step will require careful attention to economies of scale and scope. The danger is apparent from the example of Mongolia cited earlier. Given the country's human resource endowment, the fact that competition will not be materially affected, and the very limited scale of telephone penetration in the country, it is highly likely that welfare will be reduced rather than enhanced by this policy. Substituting blind capitalist ideology for blind socialist ideology is not necessarily an improvement. The intermediate step of breaking the company into semiautonomous profit centers could both improve current corporate governance and help prepare for eventual dismantling without sacrificing economies of scale and scope.

Mongolia, however, is almost certainly the exception rather than the rule. The formerly socialist countries are littered with conglomerate behemoths that cover huge areas and produce everything from soup to nuts. In such cases a few fences and a little legal work could yield clear efficiency gains, unless economies of scope are considerably larger in the formerly socialist countries than in the United States.

Much more important than breaking up companies is the need to break up groups of companies. In Russia today a critical battle is being fought to prevent the reconstitution of the old branch ministries as holding companies that control shares in subordinate enterprises. If this battle is lost, the privatization process in the short run will have changed nothing internal to the public enterprise sector: the same old people will be making the same old decisions in the same old way. To be sure, they will eventually have to respond to market forces, but that could take a long time.

Breaking up large units in developing countries. The scope for breakup in developing countries is less, but it is by no means absent. Egypt's large public enterprise sector has historically been organized into vertically oriented groups. For example, all fertilizer companies were in one holding company and all cement companies in another. The government has decided to commercialize most of these enterprises as a first step toward privatization. However, giving the firms a profit orientation while grouping them together under one controlling body has obvious dangers for consumers and less obvious dangers of perpetuating old management with old people under a new name. As a partial solution, the government is committed to reducing the number of holding companies substantially and reassigning portfolios so that, for example, cement and fertilizer firms are spread across holding companies.

In addition, the so-called natural monopolies appear less natural with the progress of technology. In the case of electricity the core grid is necessarily a monopoly, but the separate generating plants are not. For example, in Chile, which followed this model, the generating units were free to compete in selling power to the grid. The separate distribution units, although noncompetitive, at least gave regulators a comparative basis for regulating prices and costs.

Threat of Entry

The literature on contestable markets has taught us to look not only at actual but also at potential market structure. Market power may not be fully exploited if there is fear that high prices and high profits will attract entry. In the regulatory context, this line of reasoning is extended to include the threat of regulation. Thus it is argued that New Zealand's otherwise rather toothless price regulation scheme nonetheless has a significant constraining effect on the exercise of market power. According to an official of the Electricity Corporation:

> Unless we can be confident that what we are doing will stand up to robust scrutiny and price on that basis, then what we are doing is just extracting monopoly rents. We'd be proving everyone right who says we are just a dirty monopoly and we'll end up price regulated. That is the last thing we want. (quoted in Spicer and others 1992, p. 145)

Similar claims have been made to explain the pricing of local telecommunications services. Determining how much of this is self-serving rhetoric and how much a reflection of actual pricing policies is a subject for analysis. Pending that, only note that threat of entry or more rigorous regulation can have an attenuating effect on otherwise unregulated pricing behavior.

Aggregate Concentration

This paper has emphasized concentration in particular markets. However, there is another important form of concentration: the share of business groups in the total economy. Well-known examples include Japan's prewar *zaibatsu* and postwar *keiretsu,* Korea's *jaebul,* India's industrial houses, and Pakistan's twenty-three families. Such aggregate concentration has been of concern in the United States at least since the time of Thomas Jefferson. Berle and Means (1932) calculated that the 100 largest nonfinancial corporations held 49 percent of nonfinancial corporate assets and that if their relative growth rate continued, they would hold 100 percent by 1972. As with most such Malthusian arguments, this one failed to materialize (Scherer and Ross 1990). It has proved exceedingly difficult to identify any deleterious conduct resulting from this particular structure. That is, if aggregate concentration cannot be found to result in the exercise of market power, why worry about it? This is why one observer has termed aggregate concentration "a phenomenon in search of significance" (Brozen 1982).

In developing and formerly socialist countries, however, matters may be considerably different. If a particular family or business group is large in relation to the entire economy, it can use its power to gain privileged access to scarce resources. Such resources include underpriced credit, import licenses, tariff protection, and a host of favors granted by the government and the private sector in disequilibrium markets (Leff 1978, p. 666). As Leff notes, "The group pattern of industrial organization is readily understood as a microeconomic response to well-known conditions of market failure in the less developed countries. . . . The group can be conceptualized as an organizational structure for appropriating quasi-rents which accrue from access to scarce and imperfectly marketed inputs."

Aggregate concentration may not be a problem in industrial countries in which markets are closer to equilibrium, but it can be serious in countries in which markets are distorted. The locus of the problem is factor markets, where nonprice rationing of credit and other government-controlled inputs conveys unfair advantage across many product markets, even where those product markets themselves are uncontrolled. This issue deserves considerably more attention than it has received thus far.

Conclusions

An examination of the issues involved in adapting regulatory technology to developing and formerly socialist countries allows us to draw the following conclusions.

- Markets are more distorted in developing countries and formerly socialist countries because they are generally smaller in relation to minimum efficient plant size; because they have made less progress in developing institutions to deal with market power; because the room for rent-seeking behavior is greater; and because information is less widely available. If a Harbergerian framework yields estimates of the allocative inefficiency losses attributable to market power of a few percent in the United States, it might amount to 5 percent in developing countries and considerably more in formerly socialist countries.

- The losses attributable to X-inefficiencies or corporate governance failures are considerably larger, perhaps on the order of 10 percent of GDP in developing countries and, again, considerably higher in formerly socialist countries.

These estimates, based on simple linear models and highly generalized stylized facts, are imperfect. Nonetheless, they suggest that without much more work, one cannot simply dismiss out of hand the need for regulation in these countries on the basis of the finding that the gains from further improvements are small in the United States.

Turning to the cost side,

- The costs of intervention are also higher in developing and formerly socialist countries. The opportunity cost of scarce human capital devoted to regulation is higher, and the potential for adding new distortions is greater. Regulatory design should therefore focus on minimizing these costs. In particular, since allocative costs are an exponential function of the magnitude of the price distortion, the marginal benefits of regulation decline with more regulation, and the costs rise because of increasing information requirements. It is therefore vital to keep regulatory mechanisms simple and to focus on controlling the most serious abuses.

The implications of this philosophy suggest that:

- The U.S. version of cost-plus regulation is not recommended because the direct costs of regulation are high in an advocacy setting (the first government failure) and because cost incentives are low powered (the second government failure).
- The New Zealand RPI − 0 system neatly solves both of the government failure problems but may have only marginal impact on the allocative and corporate governance forms of market failure.
- Chile has resolved both market failure problems and the second government failure problem, but at increased cost (the first government failure).
- New Zealand's effort represents the minimum that should be done; Chile's, the maximum that should be attempted. Most countries will fall somewhere in between, with a relatively long regulatory lag and *X* set using as much exogenous data as possible.

Other regulatory problems, including competition and aggregate concentration, are dealt with more briefly.

- Competition is the most effective way to regulate market power. Structural means of ensuring a competitive marketplace include tariff policy, entry policy, and the breakup of large units.

- Given the institutional endowment of developing and formerly socialist countries, antitrust legislation is likely to be extremely costly in terms of market failure. The income elasticity of demand for such legislation is accordingly very high, and it can be argued that there should be little effective demand below, say, $2,000 per capita.
- Aggregate concentration conveys market power across product markets through privileged access to scarce credit and government licenses. This problem deserves considerably more attention.

In sum, institutional and factor endowments in developing and formerly socialist countries differ from those in industrial countries. This means that the nature of the problem changes. For example, both aggregate and market concentration are more serious problems in developing countries and formerly socialist countries. It also means that the tools available for solving the problems are scarce and must be used sparingly.

Notes

1. The distortion factor is *not* squared, which explains why triangles are small and rectangles are large in the case of small distortions. For large distortions, see equation 3 and the accompanying explanation.

2. In figure 1, add another horizontal line 10 percent above P^M and let that be the unregulated price; let *PM* be the price and cost achieved by regulation, and let P^* be the competitive price and cost. The loss would be exactly 9 percent.

3. India's GNP is about ten times that of Israel, and recent work suggests that China may have the world's third largest economy.

4. A sample of eighty-two developing countries shows that total tax collections average 18.1 percent of GDP, with about a third each from income, foreign trade, and other domestic taxes (Burgess and Stern 1992, pp. 14–17).

5. Bradburd (1992) provides schedules of the losses associated with different assumptions and offers significant refinements. Bradburd's bottom line is somewhat closer to the pure no-regulation view. This is attributable in part to a difference in subjective judgment as to just what constitutes "big" in a policy context, in part to my placing somewhat more emphasis on short-term elasticities, and in part to my giving more weight to the second evil of monopoly.

6. The term was used by Guy Beatson in a speech at the World Bank in December 1992.

7. The 1986 Commerce Act "makes provision for the imposition of price control generally, or on particular firms, or even specific products and services, in circumstances where the Minister of Commerce is satisfied that conditions of effective competition do not exist and control is necessary; to protect users or consumers or, as the case may be, suppliers" (McCabe forthcoming).

References

Anastasopolus, J. P. 1973. "The Strategic Anatomy of Government-Controlled Enterprise." Ph.D. dissertation. Columbia University, New York.

Berle, Adolf, and Gardiner Means. 1932. *The Modern Corporation and Private Property*. New York: Macmillan.

Bradburd, Ralph. 1992. "Privatization of Natural Monopoly Private Enterprises: The Regulation Issue." World Bank Country Economics Department Working Paper. Washington, D.C.

Brozen, Yale. 1982. *Concentration, Mergers, and Public Policy*. New York: Macmillan.

Burgess, Robert, and Nicholas Stern. 1992. "Taxation and Development." Development Economics Research Program Paper 42: 14–17. London School of Economics.

Caves, Richard E. 1989. "International Differences in Industrial Organization." In Richard Schmalensee and Robert Willig, eds., *Handbook of Industrial Organization*. New York: North-Holland.

Galal, Ahmed. 1992. "Regulation, Commitment and Development of Telecommunications in Chile." World Bank, Policy Research Department, Washington, D.C.

———. Forthcoming. "Chilgener." In Ahmed Galal, Leroy Jones, Pankaj Tandon and Ingo Vogelsang. *Welfare Consequences of Selling Public Enterprises: Case Studies from Chile, Malaysia, Mexico, and the United Kingdom*. New York: Oxford University Press.

Galal, Ahmed, Leroy Jones, Pankaj Tandon, and Ingo Vogelsang. Forthcoming. *Welfare Consequences of Selling Public Enterprises: Case Studies from Chile, Malaysia, Mexico, and the United Kingdom*. New York: Oxford University Press.

IMF (International Monetary Fund), World Bank, Organization for Economic Cooperation and Development, and European Bank for Reconstruction and Development. 1991. *A Study of the Soviet Economy*. Washington, D.C.

Jones, Leroy P. 1985. "Public Enterprise for Whom? Perverse Distributional Consequences of Public Operational Decisions." *Economic Development and Cultural Change* (January): 333–34.

Jones, Leroy, and Edward Mason. 1982. "Economic Determinants of the Size and Structure of the Public Enterprise Sector in Mixed Economy LDCs." In L. P. Jones, ed., *Public Enterprise in Less Developed Countries*. New York: Cambridge University Press.

Kahn, Alfred. 1992. *The Economics of Regulation*. Vol. 2. New York: Wiley.

Karier, Thomas. 1985. "Unions and Monopoly Profits." *Review of Economics and Statistics* 67 (February): 34–42.

Krueger, Anne. 1974. "The Political Economy of the Rent Seeking Society." *American Economic Review* 64: 291–303.

Laffont, Jean-Jacques, and Jean Tirole. 1993. *A Theory of Incentives in Procurement and Regulation*. Cambridge, Mass.: Massachusetts Institute of Technology Press.

Lee, N. 1984. "Business Concentration in Developing Countries." In Charles Kirkpatrick, N. Lee and F. I. Nixson, eds., *Industrial Structure and Policy in Less Developed Countries*. London: George Allen and Unwin.

Leff, Nathaniel. 1978. "Industrial Organization and Entrepreneurship in the Developing Countries." *Economic Development and Cultural Change* 32 (July): 661–75.

Leibenstein, Harvey. 1976. *Beyond Economic Man*. Cambridge, Mass.: Harvard University Press.

Levy, Brian, and Pablo Spiller. Forthcoming. "Regulatory Institutions and the Performance of Private Telecommunications: A Comparative Analysis of Five Country Studies." World Bank, Policy Research Department, Washington D.C.

McCabe, Patrick G. Forthcoming. "New Zealand: The Unique Experiment in Deregulation."

New Zealand, Ministry of Commerce. 1992. "Telecommunications Information Leaflet No. 1." April 21. Wellington.

Scherer, F. M., and David Ross. 1990. *Industrial Market Structure and Economic Performance*. 3d ed. Boston, Mass.: Houghton Mifflin.

Spicer, Barry, Robert Bowman, David Emanuel, and Alister Hunt. 1992. *The Power to Manage*. Auckland, New Zealand: Oxford University Press.

Sutton, John. 1992. *Sunk Costs and Market Structure*. Cambridge, Mass.: Massachusetts Institute of Technology Press.

Tandon, Pankaj. Forthcoming. "Telefonos de Mexico." In Ahmed Galal, Leroy Jones, Pankaj Tandon and Ingo Vogelsang. *Welfare Consequences of Selling Public Enterprises: Case Studies from Chile, Malaysia, Mexico, and the United Kingdom*. New York: Oxford University Press.

Vogelsang, Ingo. 1989. "Price Cap Regulation of Telecommunication Services." In Michael Crew, ed., *Deregulation and Divestiture of Utilities*. Boston, Mass.: Kluwer.

Williamson, Oliver. 1975. *Markets and Hierarchies*. New York: Free Press.

Part IV
Comparative Performance between Public and Private Enterprises

[23]

Public and private enterprise: comparative behaviour and relative efficiency

Robert Millward and David M. Parker*

1. Introduction

In recent years there appears to have been some shift in the literature on the economics of public enterprises from prescriptive welfare economics to an examination of the actual behaviour and performance of publicly owned firms. Notably there has been growing interest in the relative behaviour and efficiency of public and private enterprises to see whether there is any difference and to identify the cause of observed differences.

The economics literature in the 1960s contained numerous studies which prescribed for public enterprises the adoption of 'optimal' pricing and investment policies to achieve economic efficiency.[1] The literature emphasised the case for prices to be set according to marginal economic costs, the need for social cost-benefit studies where 'spillover' effects existed and investment to be determined by discounted cash flow techniques using an optimal rate of discount. Both prices and investment were to be determined so as not to distort the allocation of resources between the public sector and private sectors of the economy. This prescriptive welfare literature, stressing allocative efficiency, arguably reached a high point of respectability in the UK with the publication of the Government's 1967 White Paper on the Nationalised Industries which endorsed marginal cost pricing and introduced a Test Rate of Discount for public enterprise investments, supposedly equivalent to the opportunity cost rate in the private sector.

It would be wrong to say that interest in allocative efficiency declined in the public enterprise literature in the 1970s, but it was qualified and complemented by a growing interest in the behaviour and performance of public ownership. In the UK one cause of this was the apparent failure to implement the 1967 guidelines. There was some indifference to the guidelines within the industries and in addition government intervention in pricing and investment policy in the 1970s as part of anti-inflation policy became the dominant characteristic of government dealings with the industries.[2] Largely independent of these issues however there has been a growing neo-institutionalist literature, especially in the USA, concerning the economic theory of organisational forms

*Thanks are due to the editors and other participants in this volume for comments and suggestions.

which, as a by-product, has considered whether differences in the performance of public and private enterprises can be traced to differences in forms of ownership. To a degree the theoretical literature has links with studies in the field of business economics which consider the goals of firms where ownership and control are divorced.[3] Also, by considering motivation and incentives, the literature strongly complements earlier work on the internal efficiency of organisations.

As in many areas of applied economics there is a chasm between analytical work and empirical tests. The problem is compounded here because for some types of comparison like the relative costs of producing certain outputs, it is important that public and private firms are assessed on a like-with-like basis. In particular it is usually an advantage for the two types of firm to be producing the same type of good or service. This is rarely found in the UK where public firms often have national monopolies. Hence much of the empirical work under review relates to North America where public and private firms coexist in electricity, water supply, transport, refuse collection, though studies for industries in Australia, Indonesia and Switzerland have also been published.

An interest in the relative behaviour of public and private enterprise need not imply any judgements about what is good or bad and part of this survey is concerned with such 'positive' theories of public firms. Since in addition judgements *are* made, usually in the context of 'efficiency' we need to understand measures of efficiency. One type is 'economic efficiency' which is treated extensively in many books on microeconomics and public finance. Our interest in this concept stems partly from its use as a normative criterion of performance and, since policy guidelines for public enterprises have been derived from considerations of economic efficiency, partly from its possible implications for the behaviour of public firms relative to private. In the next section we therefore provide a brief introduction to this topic. The main sections of the survey are therefore:

- Economic efficiency
- Economic organisation, contractual forms and ownership
- The behaviour of the public firm
- The measurement of efficiency
  (this section may be omitted by readers acquainted with problems involved in the estimation of cost functions and with the recent literature on measures of productivity).
- Empirical comparisons of public and private firms
  (productivity in transport – the cost of electric power in USA – cost studies in water supply, refuse collection, and others – market structure and ownership – pricing, politics and profitability).

2. Economic efficiency

The classic concern of public finance has been with methods of raising taxation which do least harm to the allocation of resources. Little attention initially was devoted to the analysis of the public services for which finance was being raised – law and order and defence being seen not only as inescapable commitments of governments but also as delimiting the scope of public services. During this century both the range of public services and the economic analysis of them have expanded considerably. Little of this work was however initially directed to analysing *the behaviour of public enterprises* for two reasons. Firstly, the major objective – which is also characteristic of the study of taxation – has been that of devising optimal solutions, that is, as we shall show shortly, of developing *prescriptions for policy*; if industries are publicly owned, what should be their pricing and investment policy?

Secondly, though the *theory of public goods* can be viewed in part as an explanation of why some goods are financed through government, its relevance for public enterprise is limited. The focus of this theory is on goods which are necessarily supplied simultaneously to large groups of consumers. The technology of schemes for flood protection, noise abatement, clean air, pest control, national defence, etc. are such that if one person in a defined group is supplied so also necessarily are other members of the group. An individual in such a population will not fully reveal his preferences for these goods; the provision of the service will not be contingent on the amount he is willing to pay and if the service is supplied he cannot be excluded from enjoying the benefits. Hence the amounts which consumers are prepared to pay for such schemes cannot be revealed through market prices and the revenue would have instead to come from central or local taxation – even though the actual construction or running of such schemes could, so far as the analysis above is concerned, be undertaken by private firms, on contract from government agencies. Thus at the heart of the theory of public goods is the systematic underrevelation of preferences by users. That part of this survey which is concerned with public production is however devoted to goods and services where full preference revelation is assumed – coal, railways, electricity and gas supply, airlines, water supply being typical examples of areas inhabited by public enterprise.

The rest of this section therefore briefly[4] considers the policy prescriptions for the operation of public enterprises or the control of private enterprise which emanate from the precepts of economic efficiency. Tangential to this we also consider whether these theoretical issues have any implications for the relative behaviour of public and private enterprises; that is, if public enterprises did follow the policy prescribed would that imply a different behaviour from private enterprises? Models of economic efficiency usually consider an economy with a number of different 'firms'. The latter are often defined by the location and/or technology of production rather than by their organisational features. Production efficiency is deemed to exist when (a) it is not possible by shifting inputs or outputs from one firm to another, to raise the quantity of any product without lowering the quantity of another product, (b) it is not possible to lower the use of any one input, given a certain pattern of outputs, without increasing the use of other inputs. Clearly this would require that the marginal product of any input should be the same in each firm producing the same kind of good. This would further imply that the ratio of the marginal products of two inputs should be the same in firms producing the same goods. The ratio of the marginal products of two inputs is often referred to as the marginal rate of technical substitution and this has to be the same in all firms even when they produce different products, for otherwise a reallocation of inputs could raise the output of one firm without decreasing that of another. Clearly one way of attaining production efficiency would be to try and ensure that each firm is faced with a common set of prices for inputs. In such circumstances standard microeconomic analysis implies that each firm will choose its input combination so that the marginal technical rate of substitution is equal to the (common) relative prices of the inputs.

A second major issue of economic efficiency and one which has tended to dominate the policy prescriptions for public enterprises relates to the scale and patterns of outputs. To analyse this it is useful to work with a hypothetical example. Consider a product, say coal, which can be produced under conditions of constant returns to scale – doubling all constant quality units of management, labour, capital equipment and coal deposits is assumed to double coal output. Whether or not wage-rates, the price of equipment and the availability of good managers changes with the volume of production is not of central significance for the moment and hence, for simplicity we assume they do not vary. The geological conditions of mines vary considerably so that it is usually not possible to continue to open new mines with the same technical working conditions. Thus although constant returns to scale prevail, average production costs (including a 'normal' return to capital) in the 'marginal' mine, as shown by LL′ in Fig. 5.1, would rise as the industry expanded and so coal is produced at rising long-run marginal costs (LL′). In the short run, variations in production can take place only by changes in the intensity of use of a given stock of equipment and mines. The associated changes in the amount of the variable factor, say labour, could

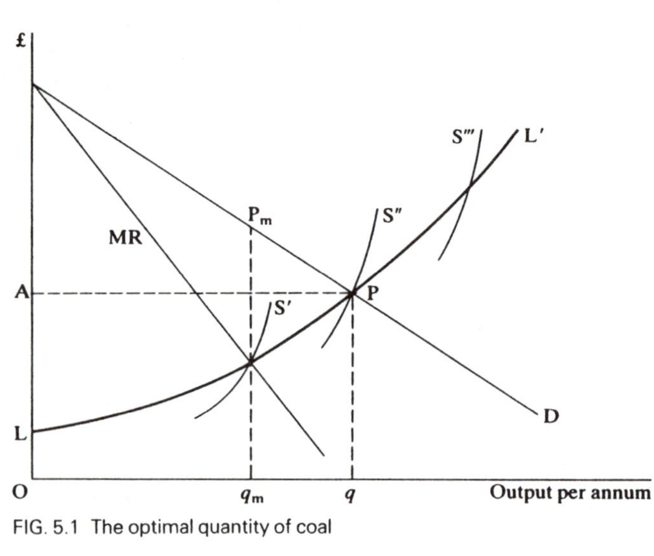

FIG. 5.1 The optimal quantity of coal

therefore be expected to be subject to diminishing returns. Thus with given stocks of equipment and mines short-run marginal costs associated with such capacity levels would be indicated by lines like S′, S″ and S‴ in the diagram. The standard precepts of economic efficiency suggest that output should be expanded to the point where marginal cost equals the valuation of extra output by consumers. The latter is indicated by the ordinates of the curve D in Fig. 5.1, so that the optimal amount in this case is where price equals marginal cost.

If this rule is followed in every sector of the economy then the associated allocation of resources is optimal in the following sense. Increases in output beyond *q* would involve the use of resources whose valuation to consumers is less than their marginal costs, that is, less then their value in other parts of the economy. A contraction of output below *q* would involve releasing resources whose value to consumers in other parts of the economy is less than their value in coal mining. The precise positions of the demand curves for each commodity will reflect the pattern of relative valuation of different goods and services. This pattern will be determined – and space precludes a rigorous demonstration of this – by the distribution of income in the economy which itself will reflect, amongst other things, the initial ownership of resources. There is no unique economically efficient allocation of resources but rather a limited range of allocations, all efficient but varying with the distribution of income.

One implication is that if governments have views about the desirability of a certain distribution of income this should be attained by lump-sum redistributions of income, that is by taxes and transfers unrelated to the volume or value of production, input supplies and sales. They should not, that is, break the link between marginal costs and the marginal valuations of output. Indeed since government production in other areas like education and defence are financed by taxation then such taxes would, ideally, also have to be lump-sum. However, transfers of income unrelated to occupation, sales, etc. are virtually impossible to devise; in practice therefore some taxes will be related to the rewards of inputs and the prices of outputs. Moreover the rule of pricing at marginal cost only works if it is applied in each and every sector. If there are 'uncontrolled' sectors where price is not equal to marginal costs – such as private sector monopolies – the 'first best' marginal cost rule may no longer be appropriate for the 'controlled' public sector. For both these reasons a literature[5] has developed on 'second-best rules' which are designed to promote efficiency in resource usage subject to such constraints. Essentially this involves analysing what the appropriate relationship between price and marginal cost should be in the 'controlled' public sector given that there are distortions in other parts of the economy. This is a complex literature which at present provides no simple policy guidelines. It is not explored further, the not unreasonable justification for this omission being that where considerations of economic efficiency have entered the public/private debate at the empirical level, it is the 'first-best rules' which have dominated so far.

Returning then to our main theme, if the production of coal in the above diagram is under public ownership, we may think of the public enterprise as controlling production in all the mines and facing a demand curve D. The long-run marginal cost to the enterprise of expanding production by opening up new mines is to be taken as LL′. Associated with various volumes of capacity are short-run marginal cost functions such as those shown by the S lines. In essence then the efficiency rule would require the public firm to expand the usage of any *given* capacity to the point where price equals short-run marginal cost and to expand capacity as long as long-run marginal cost is less than price. If the public enterprise did behave in this way then its optimal output is at q where price, P, is equal to both short- and long-run marginal cost. In the case of private ownership, *if* the industry is competitive then the same result would emerge. Consider a situation where each of the myriad of mines is worked by separate companies who pay royalties to the owners of land for permission to exploit the coal deposits. Each of the mining companies is unable to influence the price of coal and therefore produces where price equals the *firm's* short-run marginal production costs. The latter are not shown in Fig. 5.1 but the horizontal sum of the short-run marginal production cost curves of each of a given number of firms would constitute the industry's short-run supply function such as S′ in Fig. 5.1. Long-run expansion involves the entry of new mining companies working more and more geologically difficult deposits. Thus the *industry* marginal cost is approximately equal to the average production cost of the marginal mining company. The marginal company will just earn normal profits, so that it will operate where its own average production costs are at a minimum – and therefore equal to its marginal costs and the market price. Thus the long-run supply curve of the industry is LL′. In long-run equilibrium, the perfectly competitive industry produces at q where price is equal to the average production costs of the marginal mining company. Any differences between production costs in the marginal company and production costs in other companies will be competed away in the form of royalties from the mining companies to accrue as differential rent to the owners of the inelastic factor of production, coal deposits.[6] Hence each mining company's average costs (covering both production and royalties) all equal qP. Moreover, since landlords reap where they do not sow, the taxation of the royalty rents by the state would not affect the quantity of such natural resources available to the country.

Of course, if for some reason private ownership involves monopoly, then the demand curve facing the one mining company would be D in the diagram and the marginal revenue of the firm is no longer equal to price, but to the MR line. The private monopolist[7] produces at q_m. Put otherwise, if a public and a private firm faced the same cost and demand conditions, prices in the public firm will be less than in the private firm and the difference will be greater the smaller is the elasticity of demand over the relevant range (cf. Funkhouser and MacAvoy 1979, who compare public and private enterprise prices largely on this basis). However, this is not a strong theoretical reason for expecting differences in the behaviour of public and private enterprise unless the propensity of private ownership to lead to monopoly is stipulated. In particular the constant returns to scale technology is quite consistent with expansion occurring through a growth in the number of firms in a highly competitive setting. Moreover, even if private ownership did lead to monopoly, public provision is not the only alternative for attaining efficient output levels. Fixing of the price at P and monitoring of rates of return by a regulatory body could force the private firm to sell quantity *q* in the diagram. To say the least, this is not an easy exercise and the question of price regulation is considered later in the survey in the context of the empirical studies.

At this point it is useful to mention one other argument which, as we shall see later, is sometimes used for public ownership – even though it is not directly connected with questions of economic efficiency as conventionally defined. This is the problem of *declining industries.* Consider for example the impact of a substantial fall in the demand for coal on the employment of labour in the competitive coal industry. Previously we assumed mining labour was available at a fixed wage independent of the scale of mining output; of more interest is the case where mining labour is not in perfectly elastic supply to the mining industry; thus the industry marginal cost line LL′ can now be interpreted to slope upwards for a further reason – expansion of the industry raises wage rates for each mining company. Thus, starting from the equilibrium position at P, a large leftwards shift in the demand function would initially involve a decline in employment and wage rates as the industry moves down its short-run supply curve S″. The long-run adjustment would involve bankruptcies of mining companies, closure of mines and further declines in prices, employment and wages as the industry moves down the long-run supply curve LL′.

Now governments of the twentieth century have not been able to ignore such developments, especially where large and rapid employment changes are involved and the effects are concentrated in specific regions – compare the coal, railway and steel industries in Britain. If a government objective is to slow down the rate of contraction and spread the adjustments over a longer period, it might do this by taking the industry into public ownership and ignore considerations of economic efficiency. Initially, for example the level of output and employment might be maintained despite the decline in price, with the government accepting the financial implications and also accepting that large amounts of resources are not being released to other parts of the economy where, in the long run, their value to consumers exceeds their value in coal mining.

On the face of it then, publicly owned declining industries would have lower prices, more capacity, larger outputs and more employment than in comparable privately owned declining industries. However, public ownership is not the only policy instrument available. If the industry remained in private ownership, its rate of contraction could be reduced by government subsidies to the mining companies per unit of coal sales. This would shift the supply curves to the right with the same potential impact on output and employment. The subsidies would be financed by tax payers, including, of course, any tax receipts from owners of coal deposits. Hence the underlying hypothesis about the differential behaviour of public and private enterprise is analytically weak (cf. Pashigian 1976) unless it can be argued, on other grounds, that the propensity to subsidise is likely to be bigger when industries are publicly owned than when they are privately owned.

Finally we consider the strongest case where considerations of economic efficiency suggest different behaviour between public and private enterprise, i.e. *economies of scale and natural monopoly.* When increasing returns to scale operate for a product, a given percentage increase in constant quality units of equipment, labour, management, etc. leads to a more than proportionate increase in output. Thus even when the prices of inputs do not vary with the scale of operations – as we shall assume for simplicity – the long-run average costs of the product decline as output expands (in contrast to the previous case of constant returns to scale where with given input prices long-run average cost would be constant). An expansion of the size of generating plants, transmission lines and distribution networks in electricity for example, can lead to more than proportionate increases in output per unit of time simply because of the engineering characteristics of such assets. Thus the industry long-run marginal cost (MC) lies below average cost (AC) in Fig. 5.2 and the economically efficient scale of operations is at q (or zero output, a vital qualification which we will consider later).

Following the marginal cost rule, a public enterprise setting a uniform price per unit of output of P would have sales receipts less than its total costs. Hence resort would have to be made to levying on consumers an additional charge unrelated to the size of purchases (such as an annual rental charge for connection to the electricity system) or to carrying a deficit financed ultimately from taxation. In the case of private ownership the first firm into the field is likely to be able to undercut potential competitors since its costs (in real terms) would fall as it expanded sales. No such possibility arises with constant returns to scale. The present case is therefore often termed a natural monopoly. The private profit maximising monopolist with marginal revenue, MR, will sell q_m at

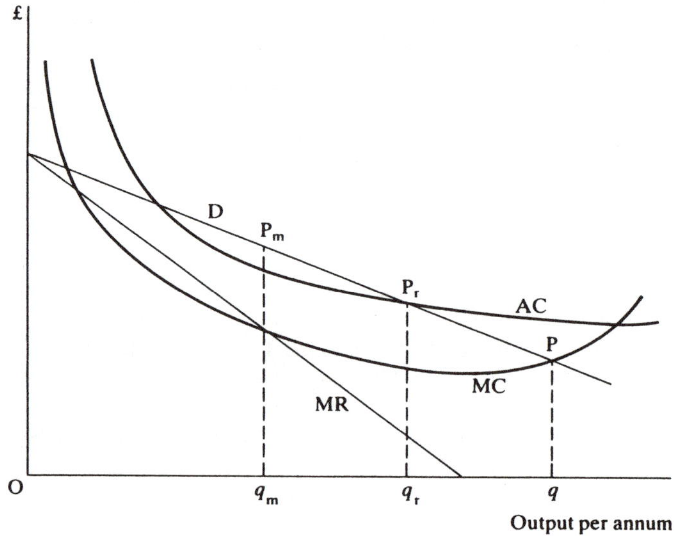

FIG. 5.2 The decreasing cost industry

a price P_m – and this is true whether or not connection charges are levied since such lump-sum charges affect only whether a customer is connected, not how much he buys.

On the face of it then private ownership involves a problem which is solved by public ownership which is predicted to involve a larger output and lower price. However we must, as before, ask whether the solution to the problem intrinsically requires public ownership and in this case there are two rather different issues involved. Whilst economies of scale with private ownership might involve monopoly *in* the field it is quite consistent with competition for the field (Demsetz 1968). In particular, government could invite bids for the contractual right to supply, exclusively, electricity to some defined area over some defined period (as local governments sometimes do for contracts for refuse collection). Provided there is active competition in the bidding process, the entry or franchise fee would be bid up to the level of monopoly profits; the successful bidder would finish up with average costs, including the franchise fee, equal to P_m in the diagram, or even higher if lump-sum connection charges are possible. At the time the contract is due for renewal, potential entrants would again bid, with of course the first entrant's assets open for sale if necessary.

Now there are lots of problems with contracting – the size of transactions costs, the information advantages of the first entrant (cf. Williamson 1971) – but even if there were not it is clear from the diagram that competition for monopoly of the field will only, at best, eliminate monopoly profits; it will not yield the efficient scale of operations, q. As an alternative to contract bidding, consider the case where the government allows a private monopolist to emerge but regulates its prices. (We shall postpone to a later section of this survey the possibility that price regulation, in so far as it affects the rate of return on capital and hence the degree of capital intensity, affects costs.) By specifying that prices have to be lowered when monitored rates of return are seen to be above normal, the regulator would drive down prices and profit rates from the unconstrained monopoly position and therefore induce an expansion of output beyond q_m. The limit of this, however, is q_r in Fig. 5.2, since any further reductions of the exogeneously given uniform price below P_r would lower the monopolist's rate of return below what could be earned elsewhere in the economy. An important qualification is necessary if lump-sum consumer charges are possible and here we find ourselves finally in a situation exactly analogous to the public enterprise. If such charges were sufficient to allow a public enterprise to break even, i.e., earn a normal rate of return, with a per unit price of P then so also would they allow the private monopolist, faced with a regulated price of P, to earn a normal rate of return. If the lump-sum charges are insufficient then the public enterprise would have to carry a deficit if it sold q at price P and the deficit would be financed from taxation. Exactly the same result would emerge however by government capital subsidies to a private monopolist facing a regulated price of P. Products which it is difficult for consumers to resell, like electricity, are of course ripe for discriminating charges both as between different units of output (like the two-part tariff we have been suggesting) and across consumers. However, the major problem, at least analytically, is that if such limited[8] discriminatory charges are inadequate for normal rates of return, there is no obvious way of knowing whether the subsidies are warranted – that is, whether *any* production at all is warranted. The basic problem of increasing returns to scale is that one is faced with an indivisibility (the extreme example being an uncongested bridge with zero running costs) and the *marginal* cost rule is really inappropriate for an *indivisible* change. Imagine the case, for example, where the demand curve is everywhere to the left of the AC curve. There is no price which yields enough revenue to cover total costs and yet production might still be warranted to the extent that consumers' total valuation, as indicated by the area under the demand curve, exceeds total costs at some output levels. To ascertain empirically the area under the demand curve is however a formidable exercise when discriminatory charges are not possible. The only consolation in the present context is that the same issue arises whether the industry is in private or public ownership.

In summary, economic efficiency considerations predict that public enterprise will build more capacity, employ more labour and sell more output at lower prices than private enterprises if, and only if, two conditions are met:

(a) public enterprise operations are based solely on considerations of economic efficiency;
(b) either
 (i) any tendency for private ownership to lead to monopoly is unconstrained by price regulation
 or
 (ii) subsidies to public enterprise are more likely than subsidies to private enterprise even when both face the same economic problems.

These hypotheses about the *actual* behaviour of public enterprise will, at a later point in the survey, be compared with other hypotheses.

3. Economic organisation, contractual forms and ownership

The traditional analysis of economic efficiency was primarily concerned with the broad objectives of firms in the area of pricing, input choice and scale of operations. It paid little attention to factors internal to the firm affecting the success with which given objectives were achieved. The very terms 'public' and 'private' relate however to different organisational forms. An important question therefore is whether the two organisational types involve any systematic differences in the success with which objectives are achieved, irrespective of what are the objectives. Hypotheses on this issue have emerged as a by-product of a growing literature on the theory of economic organisation. The focus here will be on three issues: (a) the factors theoretically affecting the success of *management* in achieving the owners' objectives, i.e. factors affecting what is sometimes called 'organisational slack' (Williamson 1963a) or 'X inefficiency' (Leibenstein 1966); (b) the minimisation of the costs of a given output, a common corporate objective which will be used here for illustration – the whole issue of efficiency of different kinds is considered in section 5; (c) the degree to which the ownership features of public and private firms imply different performances from management.

FIRMS VERSUS MARKETS

Recent developments in the theory of economic organisation suggest that the 'firm' can be thought of as a nexus of contracts between varying parties, notably labour, management, financiers, raw material suppliers. Since all exchanges of resources involve contracts, formal or informal, then each organisational form and each transaction in the economy will be characterised by particular types of contractual arrangements. It is often helpful to focus on broad groupings of contract types. In so far as we are interested in public and private *firms*, then it would seem useful first of all to draw a distinction between the direction of resources within firms as opposed to their direction across markets.

A producer can make a market contract with resource owners for goods and factor services. Alternatively, he can 'employ' such resource owners, i.e. enter into a contract which essentially gives the producer more flexible control over the resource owners. A car producer could buy pressed body parts from other producers; accounts work could be undertaken by an independent accountancy firm for a fee; office and factory cleaning could be 'contracted out'; haulage work could be undertaken by an independent haulier. A classic explanation of such 'vertical disintegration' would be the economies of scale that accrue from specialisation at each stage of production (Stigler 1951). The alternative is to manufacture own body parts, employ own accountancy staff, cleaners and hauliers. The broad distinguishing feature of this alternative is the greater flexibility given to the producer in his direction of the resource owners. For example, accountancy staff may always be on hand and maintain confidentiality; own haulage capacity will always be available for a firm's use at short notice. Other contractual forms are possible beside the simple ones of employment or market contracting with autonomous suppliers – for example franchising agreements, between say producers and retailers or the establishment of subsidiary companies to specialise in certain work or services. Whilst space precludes further exploration of these other forms, they do carry the implication that the economic boundaries of the 'firm' are blurred (Rubin 1978). The important point in the present context is that differing contractual forms will have differing benefits and costs and one might expect that the chosen form is that which yields the largest net benefits. Difficulties in contracting in markets with autonomous suppliers is now understood to be an important reason for the existence and expansion of firms. Market contracting costs seem to result from information problems. Coase (1937) identified a number of costs of transacting in markets which essentially arise from information imperfections, notably the difficulties market contracting faces where uncertainty about future events exists, where long-term decisions regarding resource use are involved, or where difficulties exist in discovering mutually beneficial prices.

This 'transaction costs' approach to explaining the existence of resource allocation within firms rather than in markets has been developed and refined in recent years and a considerable literature now exists (Stigler 1961, Demsetz 1969, Alchian 1969, Alchian and Demsetz 1972, Hirshleifer 1973, Arrow 1975, Spence 1975).[9] Outstanding in this literature, however, is the contribution of Oliver Williamson (1973, 1975, 1976a, 1976b, 1979), who has identified a number of possible costs of market transacting to explain why resources are sometimes organised in 'firms', or what he prefers to refer to as 'hierarchies'. In particular:

(a) costs resulting from what he calls 'bounded rationality'. He argues that individuals have a limited ability to absorb and process the complex issues necessary to reach a position of completely objective and rational behaviour. Therefore, people are sometimes unable to identify easily, and hence cheaply, future contingencies and write these, and adaptations thereto, into market contracts. Successive short-term contracts may overcome this but at the price of larger transactions costs.
(b) costs resulting from 'opportunism', i.e. where one or other of the parties to a contract withholds information pertinent to a mutually beneficial contract, or has special skills, information or position which allow that party to bid up the recontracting price, thereby imposing costs on the other party. Such 'opportunist' behaviour will be especially prevalent where the number of potential bidders for a contract is smaller, i.e. where competition for a contract is limited, giving market power to one of the parties to the contract.
(c) costs results from 'information impactedness', i.e. a producer may have varying information about potential contractors, some of whom, though genuine, are unable to convince the producer that they have the ability, as well as the will, to fulfil a contract. This problem is exacerbated by 'opportunism' in market contracts and suggests that where there are asymmetries in the levels of information available to the parties to a contract, the party with the least information may suffer costs, and contracts unfavourable to that party may be negotiated.

In other words, Williamson is essentially saying that contracting parties in markets sometimes require considerable information about current and future circumstances, which may be unavailable. Firms or hierarchies, however, may have more sophisticated information bases. To illustrate, Williamson, along with Wachter and Harris (1975), has suggested that the recruitment of labour within firms may have advantages over market contracting with autonomous suppliers of labour in markets, where: (a) complex contingent claims contracts would be required in a market contract to offset a lack of information about future conditions; (b) there are information asymmetries favouring workers, which would reduce the benefits of purchasing labour in markets; (c) firms need to create an environment in which labour will have incentives to train other labour in skills important to the long-term success of the firm. Hence we would expect employment contracts to be preferred in circumstances where labour has to be moved between tasks or geographically to meet changing requirements which are difficult to predict accurately; where workers once trained would be able to exert considerable pressure upon management to obtain exceedingly favourable contracts unconstrained by potential suppliers of alternative labour services in the labour market; and where workers would be unwilling to train if they saw them as potential competitors in future recontracting.

Williamson also rejects the idea of a frictionless capital market in which shareholders have perfect knowledge. Instead he argues that shareholders suffer from bounded rationality and the capital market in general suffers from information impactedness. Therefore he suggested that capital markets involve significant transaction costs and conglomerate firms acting as mini, internalised, capital markets may avoid such costs and be superior allocators of capital, since they can benefit from superior information relating to the allocation of capital. Thus in the case of two important inputs, labour and capital, there may be circumstances in which employing resources is more efficient than contracting for resources with autonomous suppliers in markets.[10]

INCENTIVES WITHIN FIRMS

Organising resources within firms also involves costs which parallel the 'transaction costs' found in markets. By considering the costs in hierarchies we gain a further understanding of why different organisational forms are adopted for allocating resources and, importantly, we can identify the role of management within firms. This leads to a consideration of the way incentives to management may differ in public and private firms.

The basic unit of analysis in an organisation is taken to be the individual, whether a member of the labour force or management, for it is the individual who owns, supplies or hires factor services. It is assumed individuals have utility functions which include both pecuniary and non-pecuniary variables and which they attempt to maximise or at least pursue.[11] Pecuniary items are financial receipts, notably wages, bonuses and salaries and non-pecuniary items are other 'rewards' such as a pleasant working environment, a pretty secretary, a quiet life ('low stress') and ability to avoid work or effort ('shirking'). Given that there are these two broad forms of income we may conjecture that where individuals are unable to alter their pecuniary income directly, by say working harder, they will attempt to raise their income and hence utility by raising non-pecuniary income. In particular, individuals will raise their non-pecuniary income by pursuing an 'easier life' at work as long as this has no effect on their pecuniary income. Since 'shirking' and related activity raises a firm's costs of production in the form of reduced labour productivity or directly increasing other costs, a major function of management is checking the pursuit of non-pecuniary income by the labour force. The same point, and we return to this later, applies to management. Managers will also pursue non-pecuniary variables, unless they are prevented from doing so by, say, external factors, such as pressure from shareholders, or by the existence of pecuniary incentives such as profit sharing agreements or plain entitlement to profits. In contrast, where resources are allocated in markets competition and exchange in the market place, at least where competition does exist, will produce rewards to factors of production which reflect their productivity, producing incentives to be efficient. In such circumstance an increase in 'shirking' would reduce an individual's productivity, leading to a fall in the supply of services and hence a decline in his pecuniary income. In firms the marginal products of individual workers have to be directly identified by management and at the same time the productivity of management also needs to be metered, if pecuniary payments are to be related to their productivity.

Incentives for labour inputs to perform efficiently and contribute to the success of the firm are determined by management and can take two broad forms: (a) incentives can be related to 'prices'; for example, payments to factors can be related to output through the adoption of piecework modes of payment, productivity bonuses, profit sharing schemes and at least for some grades of the labour force the 'carrot' of promotion with associated higher earnings is an apparent spur to greater effort; (b) directives and control procedures can be implemented; these procedures include the introduction of set working hours and meal breaks, job specifications, direct supervision of work, standards relating to the quantity and quality of work, managerial directives, disciplining procedures, and the use of work study and similar techniques.

The form and success of such 'incentives' is not the subject of this review, *per se*;[12] we are more concerned with the motivation of management, in the private and public sectors of the economy, to identify and introduce the optimal 'incentives' structure in their firms to ensure minimum production costs at any given output level. Firms are in a sense hierarchies in which incentives to be efficient are necessary at *all* levels. The costs of introducing, operating and enforcing incentives related to 'prices' or of making directives and control procedures, will rise where internal signals or information flows between different levels of the firm hierarchy become blurred or incomplete. Therefore an important function of management in firms is to develop efficient information flows, which will involve introducing organisational forms and employment contracts which economise on the costs of monitoring.

In addition, the terms of the employment contract between labour and management may economise on monitoring costs by creating incentives to limit 'shirking'. However complex, detailed contracts are costly to write and enforce; therefore actual employment contracts usually contain relatively few provisions, each of which serve several purposes. The reasons for this relate to the market 'transaction cost' arguments and particularly the problems of writing long-term detailed contracts emphasised above.[13] More specifically, writing detailed employment contracts is difficult where the future use of inputs cannot be fully foreseen or specified easily, where future work requirements are unclear, or where the nature of the work concerned is non-routine. In such cases, to allow flexible use of labour, employment contracts tend to outline only general duties or areas of responsibility. A contract for piecework introduces direct incentives to be efficient but can only be adopted where the work is routine, easy to detail and agree at the time of employment and where the quantity and quality of the product can be cheaply identified and monitored.

In other cases, management has to monitor labour inputs and outputs directly (McNeil 1974, Goldberg 1974a, Leibenstein 1979). Furthermore, even where inputs and/or outputs can be more clearly detailed in the employment contract, monitoring activity is not redundant. Inputs and/or outputs will need to be monitored if the employment contract is to be enforced; that is there will be 'enforcement costs' (McManus 1976). Where the details of a job can be clearly specified and agreed at the time of employment the *quality* of performance will still need to be monitored.

There are likely to be particular difficulties in establishing detailed employment contracts with inputs and in monitoring inputs and outputs, including enforcing contracts where there are problems in identifying the productivity of individuals within a firm and hence in relating pecuniary rewards to productivity. In particular, in such cases the self-policing 'price' incentives referred to above cannot be relied upon to stimulate effort. Identifying each individual's productivity becomes especially difficult where 'team production' occurs, that is where each input contributes simultaneously to a given task. For example, where four men are jointly involved in lifting items on to lorries the contribution or effort of each individual cannot be easily identified. Each individual has no separable output; only the team has an output and the assessment of each person's contribution involves monitoring costs.[14]

Where such joint production occurs the opportunity for individuals to increase their non-pecuniary income by 'shirking' increases. Some or all individuals in a 'team' could gain extra pecuniary income if 'shirking' was curbed, as rewards available to the team would rise as output rose, but there is no automatic incentive for any particular individual to reduce his 'shirking' unless he can be certain that other individuals in the 'team' will do likewise. In other words, 'non-shirking' in a 'team' is a public good in the sense that the benefits of 'non-shirking' will be shared out indiscriminately amongst all the 'team'. Individuals in a team who do not 'shirk' will share the benefits of 'non-shirking' with those who do. In such circumstances which are characteristic of many production activities, we can expect that close monitoring of factor inputs and/or outputs will be needed and this will require, especially when large numbers are involved, management time, effort and resources.

AGENTS, PRINCIPALS AND INCENTIVES FOR MANAGEMENT

Since management monitoring of factor inputs requires time and effort, management itself needs incentives. In the small firm, where the owner of the firm is the manager, incentives exist for the owner-manager to minimise 'shirking' and other activities which raise costs of production. Any such inefficiencies will reduce the residual income left to the entrepreneur after payments to contracted factor inputs, thereby reducing his pecuniary income. Hence his freedom to take 'income' in non-pecuniary forms, e.g. an afternoon on the golfcourse, involves a direct cost in terms of a lower pecuniary income.

Turning to large firms in the private sector, which are often the nearest equivalents to publicly owned enterprises, control of the firm's resources lies with a management whose pecuniary income takes the form largely of salaries – though links with profits are not uncommon. Ownership rights in such firms are held by shareholders (stockholders), including small shareholders taking no direct active part in management policy and large institutional investors, such as banks, insurance companies and pension funds, which also, at least in the UK, refrain from interference, at least openly, in the management of the firms in which they invest. In some cases shares may be held by directors of the firm or other senior management, although in the UK the shareholdings of directors are a very small percentage of total shareholdings.

A number of studies relating to managerial and behavioural theories of the firm suggest that there is a significant divorce of ownership and control in the private sector and that this may lead to an alteration in the objectives of firms away from the pursuit of profit to some other goal, such as sales, growth or utility maximisation or 'expense preference', where profit is a constraint rather than a goal.[15] By implication there will be differences across firms in the degree of success in achieving the owners' objectives – there will, that is, be variations in 'organisational slack' and 'X inefficiency'.

Such behaviour will presumably only be possible where a firm's 'owners' are unable or unwilling to invest time, effort and resources to limit managerial behaviour to the pursuit of high efficiency and profits. Hence, the pressure placed by 'owners' on management to monitor factor inputs or outputs efficiently becomes an important determinant of efficiency differences between firms. A useful way of analysing this, and one which is particularly helpful in the context of comparison of public and private firms, is from the perspective of 'agency relationships' and property rights.

In agency relationships 'principals' appoint 'agents' to undertake stipulated duties. If both principals and agents are maximisers of their respective utilities then there is no good reason for assuming that agents will act in the best interests of principals, unless some limit to the discretionary behaviour of agents is introduced. Such a limit will normally be imposed and hence generate monitoring costs for the principals.[16] In firms where ownership and control are divorced, the owners of the firm are the principals who appoint directors ('agents') to manage the firm on their behalf. This agency relationship involves an attenuation (restriction) of the property rights of owners over their firms' assets.[17] Such property rights consist of the right to receive the reward from the employment of resources, the right to direct the use of resources and the right to transfer these ownership entitlements to others, which may be summarised as the rights to benefit from, control and dispose of resources.

In a business with the traditional single 'entrepreneur', the owner's property rights are unattenuated, except in so far as they may be constrained by general legislation relating say to the environment, employment or taxation. The entrepreneur can direct the use of resources, sell his property rights and, importantly, fully benefit from the use of his property through having complete entitlement to any residual income remaining in the firm after payments to all contracted inputs. It is this entitlement to the residual income which leads to the presumption that there are incentives to minimise production costs in owner-controlled firms (cf. Cho 1977). Where ownership and control are divorced the property right to control resources is transferred to management, while the right to benefit from ownership (to benefit from the residual income) remains with the 'owners' of the firm. Management are given powers to hire, fire and organise inputs; the ultimate right to dispose of the ownership rights in the firm remains with the 'owners'.

In such cases, we might infer that where principals are unable to limit managerial freedom significantly and where management pursue their own rather than owners' utility, incentives to minimise costs are lower than where ownership and control are not divorced. To limit managerial behaviour which diminishes owners' utility, 'owners' will need to monitor management activities. Such monitoring activity will be costly in time, effort and resources and hence there are 'agency costs' where ownership and control are divorced. Contracts between shareholders and directors and other similar agreements may limit these costs as would the linking of management salaries to profits. So will company law, which defends shareholders against managerial fraud and lays down minimum information requirements relating to companies' affairs. However, the costs will not disappear and, in particular, detailed contracts will again be difficult to write, monitor and enforce.

THE OWNERSHIP FUNCTION IN LARGE PRIVATE SECTOR COMPANIES

The argument that privately owned joint stock companies are likely to be more efficient than public enterprises, frequently derives from study of the different attributes of ownership in publicly and privately owned companies, that is the differing property rights or, alternatively, agency relationship involved (Alchian 1965, Alchian and Demsetz 1972, Demsetz 1964, 1966, 1967, de Alessi 1969, 1974a, 1974b, 1975, 1977, Furubotn and Pejovich 1972, 1974). We have noted that management requires incentives to monitor inputs efficiently and that if management has no direct interest in the residual income of the firm then these incentives could be imposed by pressures from 'principals'. In the case of private sector companies a great deal depends upon the ability of shareholders to limit managerial behaviour to the pursuit of maximum efficiency and profits. It has been suggested that shareholders are able to do this at firms' annual general meetings when they can elect and fire directors, act in consort with other shareholders to establish block votes to impose policy changes and generally badger management. On the other hand, it appears that AGMs are rarely occasions where shareholders and management clash.

Three other factors are perhaps of more significance. Firstly there is the market for shares enabling shareholders to signal their confidence in management policy through day-to-day buying and selling of shares. This involves some expense and effort but will usually be less costly than organising direct action at AGMs. By selling, shareholders can signal disapproval of management policy, which may in itself change management attitudes as share prices fall, and in the extreme could encourage 'take-over' of the firm, possibly by more effective management. In addition, the ability to buy and sell shares in companies permits specialisation in shareholding. Thus individuals with a special interest or expertise in shipbuilding will be able to specialise in owning shares in shipbuilding concerns. Poor managerial decisions are more likely to be spotted by owners who specialise. Secondly, it has been suggested that competition in the market for top management, from lower levels of management within the firm or from potential management outside, may be a further constraint on managerial behaviour in the private sector. Furthermore, 'principals' will be able to reflect their confidence in the quality of the management they are hiring, in the salaries they pay their managers, and so transfer the costs of any *anticipated* higher production costs (Alchian 1977a, Alchian and Demsetz 1972, Furubotn and Pejovich 1972, Fama 1980). Thirdly, company law in so far as it requires regular independent audits and financial statements, would appear to be a further restriction upon managerial freedom of action.

In other words, in private companies where ownership and control are divorced, the existence of markets for ownership rights and management, along with legislation regulating the publication of information relating to the company, limit the costs to owners of monitoring management behaviour. Of course, the extent to which these constraints actually do limit managerial behaviour is an empirical matter and unfortunately studies to date provide no firm conclusions. Some undertaken in the UK and USA suggest that in manager controlled firms a lower profit is earned than in firms where a clear divorce between ownership and control does not exist (see for example, Monsen, Chiu and Cooley 1968, Radice 1971, Palmer 1973, Round 1976, McEachern 1978).[18] Some research into the relationship between the pay and tenure of top management and the goals of large firms has suggested that profit maximisation is not so important as growth and sales maximisation, a result which is consistent with the proposition that management can adopt discretionary behaviour to increase their own rather than owners' utility.[19] Not all empirical studies, however, support such a view and there is a similar lack of consensus about the actual operation of capital markets in modern industrial economies. On the one hand, there are those who endorse an 'efficient markets hypothesis' and who support the view that owners do limit the behaviour of management by buying and selling shares. On the other hand, a number of studies have pointed to inefficiencies in capital markets. In particular, some studies have stressed that the costs of buying and selling shares or uncertainty about the current and future performance of firms, or shareholder inertia in the face of costs of obtaining information about firms and shares, permit management to deviate from policies which maximise shareholders' utility.[20]

Therefore, although shareholders in the private sector do appear to have powers to limit managerial behaviour, there is some suggestion that the agency relationships, which exist where ownership and control are divorced, are important and permit at least some degree of discretionary behaviour by management which reduces owners' utility. On the other hand, it seems reasonable to presume that there will be a minimum level which a firm's profits cannot fall without provoking a response from shareholders at an AGM or in the stock market.

THE OWNERSHIP FEATURES OF PUBLIC ENTERPRISE

Agency relationships also exist for public enterprise. For example, in the UK the public in effect delegate powers to ministers and government departments, who themselves delegate powers to the boards of the public corporations. Hence the boards act as agents of government and more indirectly the public. Where such agency relationships exist property rights and in particular rights to the residual income of enterprises are affected. The boards, their chairmen and other senior management in public enterprises will normally have no direct interest in the residual since they do not benefit directly from a high residual, although status, career prospects and survival in office could be linked to the performance of their enterprise.

In addition, government departments and ministers are usually prevented from directly benefitting from the residual. In the UK it would be judged improper for civil servants or politicians to receive financial benefits from public enterprises. Therefore, while civil servants may have an incentive to promote the size and scope of public ownership, as this may mean more and better paid civil service posts, and politicians may promote low prices and high employment in public industries to win votes, there may be no direct incentive for government to pressure public boards (or similar agencies) to minimise production costs and maximise the residual.

The public, of course, have a direct interest in the performance of public enterprises, as they consume the products or services supplied by these enterprises and act as ultimate financiers of the industries losses through the tax system. Just as shareholders in joint stock companies need to monitor management in these companies, so the public need to monitor the activities of the public enterprise. In both instances a divorce of ownership and control occurs. However, there is a difference between joint stock companies and public enterprises from an agency and property rights perspective. Whereas in joint stock companies the residual may act as a direct incentive for shareholders to monitor management and in the extreme shareholders may terminate their property rights by selling shares, in the case of public ownership, the public, the 'principals', find the monitoring of their 'agents' more costly. Each owner, that is each member of the public, will normally find that the cost of influencing the policy of the enterprise or government policy will considerably outweigh any benefits that he or she will gain from a change in policy. Unlike shareholders in joint stock companies who can sell their shares, their property rights, the cost of terminating ownership rights in public industries is much greater since these ownership rights are compulsory by virtue of residence. Migration from one jurisdiction to another will terminate these rights and would be a costly action if undertaken just for that reason. Alternatively, the public may actively support political changes which will terminate public ownership, for instance by supporting a political party which will 'denationalise'. This also is a high cost strategy, involving time, effort and perhaps money, and which may have uncertain results. In both cases, whether moving residence or political action, the cost to an individual is likely to be far greater than any resultant benefit the individual might receive. We may therefore conclude that, on a priori grounds at least, the lack of a capital market where ownership rights can be exchanged makes the cost of monitoring agents by principals far greater in the case of public ownership than in the case of private ownership where capital markets exist (Alchian 1965b). Similarly, whereas in the case of private ownership specialisation in ownership reduces monitoring costs by permitting ownership by those who have special knowledge of an industry's affairs, in the case of public ownership specialisation is impossible. All members of the public hold an equal and very small share in the ownership of the enterprise and are unable to sell or trade this ownership.

We may conclude from this fundamental difference between private and public ownership that, since that cost of terminating property rights in publicly owned industries is high in relation to resultant benefits, the public may be expected to acquiesce in their continued ownership of the respective industries and to playing a very passive role as 'owners', conceding all control over the industries to government and management. Supportive of this view is the oft-cited lack of interest or even outright opposition to public industries discovered in public opinion polls.

Finally, it should be re-emphasised that problems of agency relationships can, on a priori grounds, be expected to exist in the private sector. Whilst the analytical literature points to these problems being greater in the public sector, in the end the question is an empirical matter. The empirical studies considered in the last section of the survey are therefore of prime importance.

4. The behaviour of the public firm

The previous section has two broad implications for the analysis of public firms. Firstly it focuses attention on economic organisation, i.e. on the contractual arrangements distinctive to 'public' ownership and in particular the form of constraints on the behaviour of individuals working in public enterprise. Secondly in portraying the citizen of a political jurisdiction as the ultimate owner of the enterprise and in contrasting his powers as owner with those of the shareholder of the private firm, it makes explicit the potential importance of civil servants and politicians in any explanation of the behaviour of public firms, even though these issues cannot be handled solely within the framework of the property rights theory of the firm.

The latter set of issues thrusts us into a very wide-ranging and complex areas. For example, to understand the behaviour of a public enterprise, it is not irrelevant to ask why it was bought into public ownership. One approach might be to analyse which particular income groups or occupational categories benefit from specific acts of nationalisation. One could then contrast the behaviour of the enterprise with that which would have occurred under private ownership. Useful though this approach may be, it has to be recognised that if the coal mines and railways had not been nationalised in for example the UK in the 1945–50 period, the whole political climate could well have been different (if not explosive) and hence 'what otherwise would have occurred' with private ownership requires treatment of a barely discernible scenario. Secondly, in so far as the motivation of politicians is relevant to the behaviour of public firms, an analysis of vote-getting and related electoral issues is necessary. This is an area where economists have started to make a contribution – under the heading of public choice theory (see Mueller 1976). Nevertheless, the area is in an embryonic state, much is still highly theoretical and studies of public enterprise behaviour which draw explicitly on public choice theory are few in number.

The empirical work on public firms has not therefore been able to draw on a well articulated set of theoretical concepts. There are several broad approaches which individually or in combination have provided a starting point for empirical work. One approach has already been mentioned in section 2, i.e. the comparison of public and private under the rather restrictive assumption that public enterprise operations are based on the precepts of economic efficiency. We now consider three further approaches.

THE ORIGINS AND STATED ECONOMIC OBJECTIVES OF PUBLIC OWNERSHIP

Economists, by nature, are prone to attach little weight to the public statements of political leaders usually because the statements on economic matters are vague by the standards of logic required in economic theory or a vested interest is suspected to lie in the background. No doubt these strictures are in part applicable to what we know of the stated reasons for public ownership and the stated objectives of public enterprises. Nevertheless, economists have not yet tested models to explain acts of nationalisation and it would therefore be foolish to ignore the extensive public debate on these subjects. Some of the electoral aspects of public ownership are considered later in this survey. Students should also read some of the economic history of nationalisation movements (see Eldon Barry (1965), Chester HMSO 1975, Trebing (1976)). Here we propose to illustrate some of the issues by several features of note in the origins and stated economic objectives of public ownership in Britain.

Firstly the public ownership of key industries in Britain in the 1945–50 period can be viewed in part as an expression of a political philosophy with a long history which would embrace Spencean socialists, Chartism, Marxism, 'gas and water' socialism, Syndicalism and Guild socialism – though the role of this philosophy in explaining public ownership has perhaps been overstated. A major theme was the redistribution of economic power and hence the political power that goes with it. Whilst this cannot easily be translatable into conventional economic terminology, it did above all imply a downgrading of the role of profit and the use of public industries to promote the general economic welfare of the poor. Private profit was to be 'confiscated' and used to improve the welfare of the workers in the industry and the public at large. The Nationalisation Acts did not include profit as an objective. The industries were required to break even and any profits earned were to remain in the industries to improve services and working conditions. To many in the labour movement profits came from the surplus value created by the workforce and therefore belonged to the workers. The introduction of public ownership was intended to change the pattern of production and income distribution and for the Labour Party public ownership had its roots in Clause IV of the Party's constitution which aimed to secure for workers 'the full fruits of their industry and the most equitable distribution thereof'. Moreover, Herbert Morrison, who inspired the establishment of an early public corporation to run London Transport and who was perhaps the key architect of the public corporation in Britain, expected (1933) that one benefit of nationalisation would be the provision of 'socially necessary' services and all the Nationalisation Acts contained a 'public purpose' clause requiring that the new enterprises provide cheap and abundant coal and gas, electricity supply to rural areas, an 'adequate' railway system, etc.

Secondly, the nationalised industries were also to be a tool in national economic planning. Here the background of the inter-war period is vital. To many in the labour movement private ownership had failed the nation and permitted mass unemployment and social deprivations. Economic planning would overcome this and amongst other things this required public ownership of the commanding heights of the economy. In fact up to the mid 1970s unemployment was not a major problem in the British economy though the investment programmes of the nationalised industries have been adjusted on occasions, as with other items of public expenditure, to meet the requirements of macroeconomic management. Perhaps the best illustration of the general phenomenon is the way in which the industries' prices were controlled in the 1970s as an arm of counter-inflation policy, the choice of this instrument being motivated in part by the belief that this would especially benefit people with low incomes (cf. Millward 1976).

Thirdly, it can be argued that the promotion of economic efficiency and of management efficiency *did* play a very important part in arguments for public ownership. How this was to be reconciled with the first two points was never and has never subsequently been satisfactorily resolved. Notwithstanding what we have argued in the previous section on economic efficiency, it was felt that economies of large-scale production could lead to monopoly abuse if the industries were left in private ownership. After the slump of the 1920s and 1930s the labour movement felt there was a need to reorganise and rationalise a number of key industries and pressure groups allied to the labour movement, such as the Railway Nationalisation Society, declared the need for efficient management of publicly owned industries, (Eldon Barry 1965: 237). Herbert Morrison (1933) expected that one benefit of public ownership would be that the industries would be efficiently and economically conducted. This was a view which had found some sympathy in the case of electricity supply in the unlikely quarter of the employers' pressure group the Federation of British Industries (now the Confederation of British Industries) in the mid-1920s. Though some Conservative back-benchers opposed the establishment of a publicly owned Central Electricity Board to rationalise and develop the nation's electricity supplies, the FBI supported the move on the grounds that it would mean cheaper electricity. Thus the argument that public ownership was necessary for the exploitation of economies of scale and rationalisation seems to have found some favour even outside the labour movement.

Moreover the view that management efficiency was important for the proponents of nationalisation can be defended in the structure and form which public ownership eventually was to take. The acceptance by 1945 of *public corporations* as the vehicle for public ownership resulted from a belief that such corporations would be the best method to ensure efficient operation of publicly owned industries. Direct government control through government departments was rejected on the grounds that government ministers did not stay long enough in one department to gain expertise in an industry's affairs and the civil service had no experience and received no training in the running of industries. It was hoped that the boards of public corporations could play a role somewhat like the boards of joint stock companies, an argument put forward by the Liberal Party in its 'Yellow Book' in 1928 and which Morrison acknowledged as a source of his faith in public ownership through public corporations, cf. HMSO Chester 1975:385–6. Since joint-stock companies separated ownership and control in industry, why should public corporations which did the same be any less efficient? Thus the final legislation was designed with the intention that the Corporations would be independent of government in a significant way, thereby promoting initiative, enterprise and a basically commercial ambience. The assets were vested in new bodies which were given a corporate status free from Treasury supervision of personnel and from day to day supervision by the Minister or Parliament. The fixed terms of the Board's members were seen to provide some immunity from the changes in the political party in office. These features were buttressed by the clauses which required the industries to break even and which have been described (HMSO Chester 1975:1046) as the sheet anchor of the thinking of the Ministers who introduced the nationalisation legislation. It was hoped, that is – and how subsequent experience has proved this a vain hope! – that any threats of wage claims leading to deficits would be converted to a trade-off between wages and prices. Moreover the break-even clause was intended to reinforce independence from government by divorcing the accounts from the national budget – though not entirely since for some corporations specific privision was made for deficit grants and capital finance was also linked to the Treasury.

BUREAUCRACY

A further feature of public firms stems from the analysis in section 3 of the survey. This is the line of argument which links the property rights analysis of the public firm to the behaviour of *management* without necessarily giving an explicit role for politicians and civil servants. Managers of public firms are seen, in this approach, to have more scope than in private firms for promoting their own welfare at the expense of the owners' welfare. The specific manifestations of this will depend on the specific control framework in each firm but some general points can be made. In the simplest type of production theory the employment of a factor of production is extended until its pecuniary income is equal to its marginal value product and the marginal physical product of a factor is larger, the bigger is the volume of co-operating factors of production. Where a factor has several uses, its time will be allocated among activities such that each activity yields the same marginal value product. Where the factor is management, it has to be recognised that such an allocation of time will rarely coincide with the management's preferred allocation of time. For owners supervising management, there are costs (in terms of time and effort) in devising the monitoring reward systems such that the total input of management and its allocation of time between activities corresponds more closely to profit-maximising patterns. As a result of the ownership characteristics of public firms, the incentive to devise and monitor such reward systems is less.

The first implication of this is that since the physical productivity of management is always difficult to discern and the span of control is often used as a rough proxy, then management will itself attempt to raise the volume of co-operating resources beyond profit-maximising levels in order that management's own pecuniary income is raised. Capital equipment is an obvious example and the predication is (de Alessi 1969, 1974b) that public enterprises will use lower interest rates than private firms in evaluating the time-stream of revenue and costs of an investment project. Consider two projects which yield the same stream of revenue net of operating costs but where A involves a capital outlay now whereas B involves capital expenditures spread out through time. *Ceteris paribus*, the lower is the interest rate used for discounting the larger will be the present value of B's future capital expenditures and the more favourable becomes A, that is, the more favourable becomes the project which activates large volumes of co-operating resources *now*.

The second implication is that management will have more scope for promoting its non-pecuniary income – of attaining an allocation of its time nearer to its preferred allocation and of obtaining types and volumes of co-operating resources which more fully promote management welfare rather than that of the owners. Moreover and paradoxically, public enterprises, and especially those closely integrated with government, sometimes lay down strict operating guidelines for pecuniary income when the productivity of management is less easy to judge in terms of profitability. If pecuniary income is so constrained and yet detailed monitoring of management is limited, the 'cost' to management of extending non-pecuniary income is reduced. Job perks of comfortable surroundings are commonly quoted but some authors have extended this to more strategic aspects of the firm's behaviour. Since the design of complicated price structures to reflect complex cost characteristics, hard bargaining with buyers and sellers, customer complaints about the product and industrial relations problems all make life difficult to management, then for example de Alessi (Fall 1974) predicts that, as compared to private firms there will in public firms *ceteris paribus*, be less product differentiation, higher prices paid for inputs and lower prices received for outputs, higher quality products (to minimise customer complaints) and better conditions for a larger work force.

BALLOT BOX MODELS

The main prediction of the bureaucracy approach is that public enterprises will expand their output and capital equipment beyond profit-maximising levels. By its focus on the attenuated rights of citizen-owners its theoretical force depends on a muted role for government. Explicit models of the effect of government on public enterprises are small in number though growing. Their main focus has been politicians motivated by the desire for re-election[21] and their ability to influence the operations of public enterprises to enhance voter support. This is seen to take the form of directly conferring economic benefits on voters or in some cases to use public enterprise operations to raise the volume of campaign resources in cash or in kind.

Considering first the direct appeal to voters, attention has concentrated on two key blocs of votes, consumers and owners, and a contrast drawn with the behaviour of a firm maximising profits. Two simple ideas are involved. The significance of an individual consumer to a profit maximising firm is as a source of profit whilst to the public firm it arises from the possibility of his having one vote; similarly the significance of an owner arises from his having one vote whereas for the profit maximising firm it arises from the size of the owner's entitlement to profit. Secondly any departure from the profit-maximising price structure involves a net gain to an individual if the rise in his tax bill as citizen owner is less than the saving he makes as a consumer (ignoring the consumer surplus elements of any increase in consumption). The aggregate of all such net gains over all individuals cannot be positive but this still leaves the possibility that some change in the price structure may involve a larger *number* of gainers than losers (cf. Peltzman 1971).

If we assume that taxes are related to income, then there will be no possibility of raising votes if each individual has the same preference for goods and services and the same income level and each qualifies for one vote. Consider however the case where preferences are different, implying that the demand for the product of the enterprise varies across individuals. A price reduction will yield greater benefits to those with heavy demands for the product whilst enterprise losses associated with this will be spread evenly over the taxpaying population. If the heavy demanders of the product are numerous their net economic gains will mean larger gains in votes than are lost from the minority group paying the uniform tax but consuming only small amounts of the product. A good illustration of this possibility is the case of urban bus transit systems in the USA. The smaller is the proportion of car-owning non-users of buses in the voting population of any metropolitan area the bigger, *ceteris paribus*, would we expect to be the financial losses on publicly owned transit systems; evidence collected by Pashigian (1976) for 40 transit systems in the years 1960 and 1970 is consistent with this hypothesis. When tax liabilities differ, more complex possibilities are involved.

This approach has several implications. Firstly, we would expect a downward price bias since prices *above* the profit-maximising level injure both consumers and taxpayers. Secondly, non-voting users – such as those users located outside the jurisdiction of citizens who own the enterprise – can be expected to pay higher prices than owners. (On this whole general area see the N. Topham survey in this volume.) Thirdly, Peltzman (1971) has argued that in public firms differences in the costs of supplying different customer groups are not likely to be reflected in the price structure as closely in public firms as in private firms. Thus two customers with similar demand functions for the product but who occasion, perhaps because of location, different costs to the enterprise will not face the same set of prices if they are supplied by a profit-maximising firm but, *ceteris paribus*, might be treated equally by the public firm since each consumer has at most only one vote. Finally in this context we may note the case were the size of the subsidy to the enterprise is fixed and the key decision involves the rate of price subsidy across the customer population. Sometimes it may be possible to focus on one dimension of the good or service being supplied – for example whether the subsidy to travellers on a commuter rail service (cf. Cooter and Topakian 1980) should vary with trip length or be generalised across all users. A hypothesis consistent with this general approach would be that the fare would be set to maximise the subsidy to that group of voters whose trip length was the median of all voters. The median trip length is such that 50 per cent of voters have smaller trip lengths than the median and the remaining 50 per cent of voters have trip lengths greater than the median. Hence with fares set to maximise the subsidy to the group of voters whose trip length is the median, the number of voters desirous of a bigger subsidy per mile and a smaller lump-sum generalised element would be less than 50 per cent and hence 'outvoted'. Similarly those wanting a bigger lump-sum element and a smaller subsidy per mile would be 'outvoted'.

Finally we may note that, on the face of it, an important class of voters would be the employees of the public enterprise. In fact little systematic work has been performed on this area. In the British context the problem of being unable to compare public and private firms in the same industry undermines what otherwise would have been a good data base, namely the coincidence in some cases of parliamentary constituency boundaries with groups of employees working in divisions or plants of nationalised industries. In the American context it is the municipal firm which dominates numerically in many of the empirical studies, such that the proportion of the voting population who are consumers of the municipal utility is likely greatly to exceed the proportion who are workers in the firm. Crain and Zardkoohi (1978), however, have argued that public firms will extend employment beyond profit-maximising levels with the aim, in the USA context, of increasing the army of campaign workers. The further implication that the labour-capital ratio[22] is higher in public firms than private is of some interest since in contrast the bureaucracy approach puts much stress on the advantages to management of size, and specially, large volumes of capital equipment, i.e. is pointing to higher capital-labour ratios in public firms.

5. The measurement of efficiency in firms

(This section may be omitted by readers acquainted with problems involved in the estimation of cost functions and with the recent literature on ideal measures of productivity.)

In the previous section various hypotheses about the *behaviour* of public firms have been explored. In some cases these have carried direct implications about pricing, output levels, capacity size and employment in public firms relative to private firms. An expectation that, for example, prices in public firms will be less than in private firms faced with the same cost and demand conditions can be deduced from several of the approaches discussed. The empirical studies considered later in this survey will be examined in part in relation to these hypotheses about behaviour. In this section we introduce a further general consideration, namely that of efficiency. Whether or not a lower price level is a good or a bad thing involves a *normative judgement*. One needs a standard by which things are to be classified as good and bad. When the term 'efficient' is used in relation to pricing levels or output or resource usage, the writer is characterising behaviour according to some such standard even though this is sometimes not stated explicitly. We suggest that 'the efficiency of an enterprise' is a phrase which has a normative significance only in relation to the objectives of the enterprise. If the objective is to raise the real income level of the poor, then an efficiency measure would have to reflect that – the size of costs per unit of output or the level of the achieved rate of profit on capital may be completely inappropriate.

The efficiency measures that have been used by economists are much less sophisticated in scope. Even so the problems of measurement and interpretation remain complex. Three commonly found measures are: (a) productivity, (b) costs, (c) profits. In this section we consider precise formulations of these measures for firms and assess the extent to which they successfully measure the achievement of the following objectives:

(i) maximising the income of owners,
(ii) economic efficiency in the allocation of resources in the economy as a whole.

Clearly enterprises which are ruled by other objectives will, rightly or wrongly, often be seen to be inefficient by such measures. At the least, however, a clear understanding of the measures will indicate what has not been measured.

PRODUCTIVITY

The fundamental idea behind productivity comparisons of firms is to measure the *volume* of resources used to produce a *given* pattern of outputs. For firms producing several products and/or using several inputs, the aim of obtaining a volume measure is complicated, as we shall see, by the necessity of aggregating outputs and inputs with weighting systems which usually involve the use of prices. Consider therefore to start with enterprises which are known to produce only one product with one input. Firms A and B in the next diagram are observed to produce the same output but B uses larger amounts of labour. Provided that all labour working in the firms involves a cost to the enterprise, the difference in the volume of labour employed is a measure of the relative efficiency with which the enterprise owners' income is being enhanced. Similarly, provided that all labour employed involves a cost to the economy, the differing amounts of employment are a measure of the relative economic inefficiency of firm B. The qualification is important since in an economy with large-scale unemployment the alternative use value of the 'surplus' labour may be insignificant.

With this as background we now consider some of the general problems of measuring productivity. Firm C in Fig. 5.3 is producing a different output level to Firm A and in such circumstances it is tempting to compare the two firms by examining output per unit of input, Y/X. The fact that the firms are producing different output levels may be due to several factors including the different ownership characteristics of A and C. If at the same time technology is such that different output levels involve different output/input ratios then a simple comparison of Y/X would be confusing the two issues. Suppose however that it is known with certainty that the production technology involves constant returns to scale. Within each firm a given percentage increase in labour yields on equal percentage increase in output – though the labour/output ratio differs across firms. We would then be sure that measured differences in Y/X between

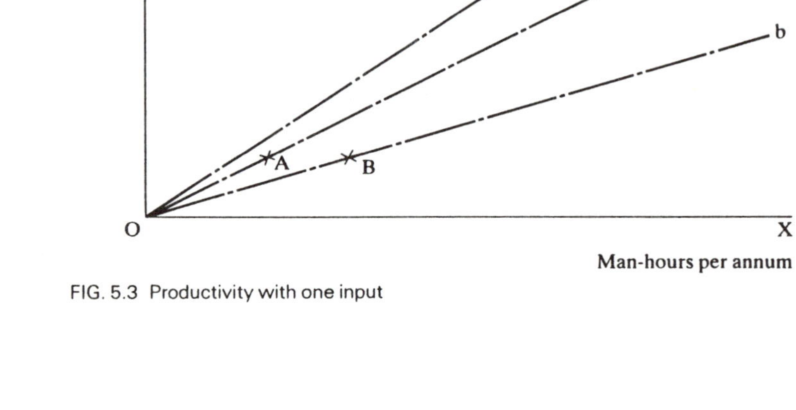

FIG. 5.3 Productivity with one input

A and C would be mirrored in different volumes of X were each firm to produce the same output level.

One obvious point may also be noted at this stage. Measures of value of output per man and costs per unit of output are not substitutes for the Y/X measure since they may be picking up factors other than productivity. If P is the price of the product then PY/X may be measuring, in part, differences in prices between firms. Such price differences may be due to factors unconnected with ownership (such as the particular markets served) and in some cases they may be due to ownership characteristics (such as government imposed price constraints on public firms). Similarly the price of labour, W, might be higher in public firms because management are under less financial pressure to bargain with unions or the difference may be due to differing work locations; a measure of unit costs, WX/Y, would pick up these factors. The productivity measure Y/X is, in other words, designed to be independent of these problems and figures of value of output per man or costs per man are not necessarily reflecting differences in productivity.

Productivity comparisons are usually *presented* in the form of growth rates or indexes. The assumption of constant returns to scale would imply that the production function for firm A takes the form shown by the broken line 'a' in Fig. 5.3, whilst for B it is line 'b' and for firm C it is 'c'. Each enterprise exhibits varying skills in the deployment of labour in production. We could in fact think of there being a general production technology for this product involving certain returns to scale between Y and X but with a shift factor, T, representing different institutional arrangements. Thus

$$Y = \mathrm{f}(X, T) \qquad [1]$$

A common presentation of the productivity differences would then be the *growth rate of productivity as T changes*, that is as we move from one ownership structure to the next. To prepare the way for the more complex cases of several inputs we may note that for infinitely small changes the growth rate of output associated with a change in T is

$$\frac{\mathrm{d}\log Y}{\mathrm{d}T} = \frac{\mathrm{d}\log \mathrm{f}(X, T)}{\mathrm{d}T} = \frac{\partial \log \mathrm{f}}{\partial T} + \frac{\partial \log \mathrm{f}}{\partial \log X}\frac{\partial \log X}{\partial T} \qquad [2]$$

The growth of output thus arises in part from a growth in input associated with the change ($\partial \log X/\partial T$) multiplied by the elasticity of output with respect to input ($\partial \log \mathrm{f}/\partial \log X$). The remaining element in the growth rate of output is that due purely to the institutional change ($\partial \log \mathrm{f}/\partial T$); this is therefore the growth rate of productivity which we see from rearranging [2] is

$$\frac{\partial \log \mathrm{f}}{\partial T} = \frac{\mathrm{d}\log Y}{\mathrm{d}T} - a\frac{\partial \log X}{\partial T} \qquad [3]$$

The elasticity of output, denoted by a in the above, will be equal to 1 if there are constant returns to scale so that the productivity measure for an infinitesimally small change would be the growth rate of output minus the growth rate of input.

For a discrete change from ownership structure t to ownership structure t' the productivity measure[23] emerges simply as

$$r_y - r_x \qquad [4]$$

where $r_{y'}$ the growth rate of output, would be measured as the log of $Y_{t'}/Y_t$ and r_x, the growth rate of input, measured as the log of $X_{t'}/X_t$. We cannot always assume constant returns to scale especially for products like electricity and transport. In fact empirical studies often have to start with no prior information. Production functions like [1] would then have to be estimated and if they cannot be estimated because of insufficient data the use of simple productivity measures would be misleading indicators of productivity unless there are compelling reasons to assume constant returns to scale.

Turning to the situation where firms use several inputs, the same basic issues apply. Instead of [1] we have

$$Y = \mathrm{f}\,(X_1, X_2, \ldots, X_i, \ldots, X_n; T) \qquad [5]$$

which again is deemed to depict a general production technology for the product but now with n inputs. Instead of [3] we therefore have

$$\frac{\partial \log \mathrm{f}}{\partial T} = \frac{\mathrm{d} \log Y}{\mathrm{d}T} - \sum_i a_i \frac{\partial \log X_i}{\partial T} \qquad [6]$$

where $a_i = \partial \log \mathrm{f} / \partial \log X_i$.

This 'total factor' growth rate of productivity comprises the growth rate of output minus the sum of the growth rates of inputs each weighted by the elasticity of output with respect to changes in that input. For a discrete change from t to t' we have, instead of [4]

$$r_y - \sum_i a_i r_i \qquad [7]$$

where r_i is the growth rate of input X_i and where a_i would have to be treated as an elasticity averaged over the old and new output levels. In fact, unless there have been prior studies, the estimation of the elasticities would be close to estimating the whole production function. A short cut is available involving the use of factor shares of total cost as weights, instead of the elasticities. As we shall show shortly, apart from bringing in new efficiency considerations, the short cut requires an assumption of constant returns to scale for which no compelling *a priori* reason may exist.

There is a related reason for not presuming too much about the production function. So far we have assumed the firms produce just one product. In practice railways, for example, produce freight-ton miles as well as passenger-miles. Moreover the *dimensions* of output can be complex. Electricity can be supplied at different voltages and in geographical areas with varying terrain for laying power lines. Refuse collection can be once weekly, twice weekly, collected from flat or house or only at the curbside. If these factors are not made explicit in the output measure, then the comparison would be reflecting issues other than productivity. Whilst electricity supply by a public firm to a remote part of mid Wales may be unprofitable or indeed inefficient in the economy's use of resources, this does not necessarily imply that the firm has a low productivity or cost effectiveness. What we wish to show in the present context is whether *given the same job*, public firms are less cost effective than private firms. Whether or not the range of outputs is efficient is an important, though separate issue.

In these circumstances with different products or output dimensions denoted by Y_1, Y_2, etc. the production function in [5] has to be replaced by

$$g(Y_1, Y_2, \ldots, Y_i, \ldots, Y_m) = f(X_1, X_2, \ldots, X_n; T) \qquad [8]$$

In the productivity measure [6], the symbol Y essentially has to be replaced by $g(Y_i, \ldots Y_m)$. Now

$$\frac{\mathrm{d}\log g}{\mathrm{d}T} = \sum_j \frac{\partial \log g}{\partial \log Y_j} \frac{\partial \log Y_j}{\partial T}$$

where $\partial \log g / \partial \log Y_j$ is the elasticity of inputs with respect to a change in Y_j in the initial situation. For the discrete change, the productivity measure in [7] becomes

$$\sum_j v_j r_j - \sum_i a_i r_i \qquad [9]$$

where r_j is the growth rate of output Y_j and where v_j is the elasticity of input with respect to output Y_j averaged over the old and new output levels. The growth rate of productivity now consists of the sum of the growth rates of the various outputs minus the sum of the growth rates of inputs weighted by their respective input and output elasticities. Thus now we require further information about the production function. A short cut is again available by using revenue shares instead of v_j but, as we shall see later, apart from bringing in new efficiency considerations, this also requires an assumption of constant returns to scale. There is now even less basis for assuming this on *a priori* grounds since it requires that a given percentage increase in all inputs increases the volume of each product by the same percentage.

COSTS

The productivity measures discussed so far are essentially measuring the degree to which different firms would use different volumes of resources if they produced the same set of outputs. From the point of view of economic efficiency or the income of owners, they can be interpreted as reflecting the varying facility with which the enterprises combine and use inputs to produce outputs. To illustrate (cf. Farrell 1957, Rowley 1977), Fig. 5.4 shows the input combinations of six firms all assumed to be producing the *same* output. Firm E uses less inputs than firm E′, firm F uses less than F′ and firm G uses less than G′. Provided the technology is sufficiently adaptable to allow small changes in the factor combination then firms exemplified by E, F and G could be shown as being on one production line K whilst the other group are on another line, K′, which, be it

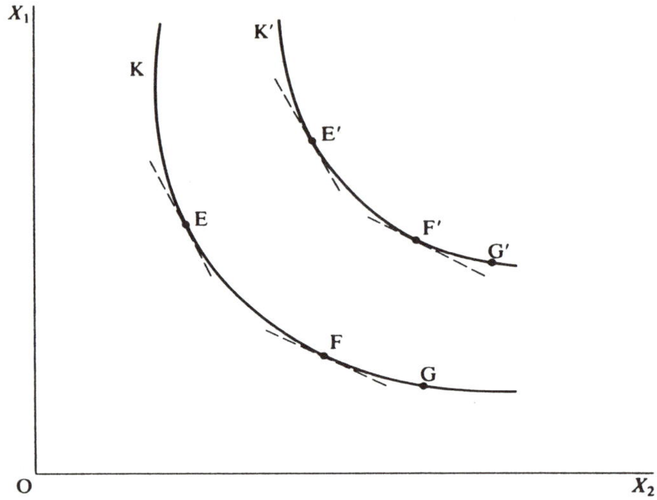

FIG. 5.4 Productivity and input price inefficiencies

noted involves the *same* level of output. On the previous measures then, a positive growth of productivity would be recorded in moving from E′ to E or from G′ to E but none in the move from G to E, which is what is required.

In particular the productivity measures are independent of factor prices. Suppose now that firms E and E′ faced an exogenously given factor price ratio equal to the slopes of the (parallel) dotted tangents at E and E′. Both firms would have chosen the least cost factor combination to produce the given level of output, notwithstanding that the institutional structure of E′ involves a lower productivity level. The input price ratio is equal to the slope of the production lines which reflects the relative marginal products of the two inputs in the respective firms. Firm G is assumed to face the same price ratio so its chosen input combination is not the least cost combination open to it. It is less 'price efficient' than E in its choice of inputs even though, in terms of productivity, there is no difference between the two. This is then a source of inefficiency with respect to the objective of maximising owners' income additional to that involved in the productivity measure [7]. The same point applies for economic efficiency provided factor prices are reflecting economic costs. Now the essential difference between firm E and firm G (and between E′ and G′) lies in the extent to which the relative marginal products of the two inputs correspond to the input price ratio. It can be shown[24] that this difference is, with constant returns to scale, precisely equal to the difference between the output elasticities of inputs and their respective share of total costs. If then constant returns to scale prevail, we can replace a_i, in the productivity measures of equations [6], [7] and [9] by the share of outlays on input X_i in total cost and this will have achieved three things. Firstly it means that the estimation of output elasticities in the production function is circumvented; all we need is data on expenditure on inputs. Secondly it means that the measure will not only reflect the productivity differences such as those between E and E′ but it will also pick up the price inefficiencies of G relative to E. Thirdly it will pick up the two sources of difference between E and G′, assuming both face the same input prices; that is, the G′ firm has a lower productivity and is less price efficient than firm E. Although the two effects cannot be unscrambled, the simplicity of the factor share weighted productivity measure explains its pervasive use.

However, the assumption of constant returns to scale is crucial. We have already given reasons why we cannot *a priori* be sure of this property and why therefore several writers adopt the approach of estimating the whole production function. In practice it is usually the *cost function* which is estimated. In part this is because data on the volume of input supplies is not always readily available; in other cases data on input prices are limited so that all one has are figures of costs in different firms, some indications of output dimensions and little information on differences in input prices between firms.

Thus for the simple one product/one input case instead of estimating [1], total costs are estimated as

$$C = f(Y, P_x, T) \qquad [10]$$

where P_x is the price of X, which we are assuming for the time being is the same in all firms. Two of the approaches used for estimation are as follows. Firstly one collects data from each of the population of firms for the years in question on total costs, output and input prices and then examines how in general costs vary with output and prices and whether, with the latter two held constant, costs are sensitive to the institutional structure, that is whether they are higher in public firms than private. Whichever way the cost-function is initially specified,[25] it would obviously be desirable to allow that the results could yield various possible scale economies. A typical form of the function would be, with total costs expressed in log form and now allowing several inputs and outputs,

$$\log C = A + a_1 \log Y_1 + a_2 \log Y_2 + a_3 \log P_l + a_4 \log P_k + a_5 D \qquad [11]$$

where P_l is the wage rate, P_k the price of capital and where A, a_1, a_2 etc. are assumed constant and their values derived from the estimation. Here the cost function has been constrained to have constant elasticities with respect to output ($a_1 = \partial \log C/\partial \log Y_1$ etc.), their size reflecting the types of return to scale. The major point about [11] however is that the institutional structure is included in the form of a dummy variable D which takes a value of 1 under one ownership structure (say public) and 0 under private. Hence the coefficient $a_5 = \partial \log C/\partial D$ shows the percentage change in costs when one shifts from the set of private firms to the set of public firms, holding outputs and input prices constant. An alternative method of presentation might be to estimate two cost functions, one public and one for private and then examine whether the coefficients are significantly different.

If firms face different input prices it is important to examine the reasons for the difference. There is some evidence for example that wages and salaries in the public sector grew faster than in private sector in the UK in the late 1960s and the early 1970s (Dean 1975, 1977, Hawkesworth 1976). However, a public firm's wage bill may differ from that of a private firm simply because, though wage rates of given skill grades are the same, a different mix of skilled and unskilled workers is employed. In principle this means that different categories of labour input should be reflected in the production function and a range of associated wage rates in cost functions like [11]. The question then reverts again to whether the public firm has chosen a less cost-effective factor combination than the private firm and this will be picked up in the productivity measures and in the a_5 coefficient. Similarly if wage rates of a given grade of labour tend to be higher in the public firm because of the work location this again, in principle, will be picked up in these measures.

It may be the case however that public firms, *ceteris paribus* do pay higher wages or face lower interest charges than private firms. It is a frequent supposition (cf. Pryke 1971, Wallace and Junk 1970, Neuberg 1977) that public firms get their capital cheaper, i.e. at lower interest rates, than do private firms, notwithstanding that governments sometime require public firms to use a discount rate (cf. in the UK, the Test Discount Rate) in evaluating investment projects, different from the rate of interest actually charged. Such differences would not show up in the productivity or cost function measures for these treat input prices as exogenous to the firm. Although public firms, in the above circumstances, would have relatively more expensive labour and less expensive capital than the majority of private firms, it could still be the case that the factor combination chosen is just as cost effective as the combination that private firms would choose *when faced with the same input prices* – and indeed there could be some private firms in the sample in precisely such circumstances. To illustrate, firm F in the previous diagram has no different productivity than firm E and if F faces an input price ratio indicated by the dotted tangent at F then it is also price efficient. In productivity measures like [7], the two firms would be revealed to have the same efficiency. If, in the absence of data on production elasticities, input shares are used as weights, the measure would record no change as long as there are constant returns to scale and as long as each firm chooses that input combination which minimises costs for the given input prices.[24] Similarly in the estimated cost function [11] and assuming good data on input prices are available, the dummy coefficient would only pick up an ownership effect if the public firm's input choice differed from what private firms would choose at such input prices.

If then the difference in prices is intrinsic to the ownership characteristics *other measures are necessary*. When it is felt, on grounds of economic efficiency in resource allocation, that the cost to the nation of capital supplied to public firms is larger than the nominal cost, then the total costs of the public firms in the sample are sometimes revalued at a higher shadow cost. Thus in calculating total factor productivity in British public enterprise, Pryke (1971) revalues the weight attached to capital by using the rate of return then earnable in private manufacturing industry. In Neuberg's electricity cost functions (1977) the total costs of public firms are revalued upward to account for a higher shadow cost of capital. Such revised productivity measures or the a_5 coefficient in a revised cost function would then pick up the fact that at the same standardised interest rate, public firms will use relatively more capital and hence, to this extent, would be recorded as economically less efficient than private firms. These then would be measures geared to economic efficiency. They are not geared necessarily to the objective of maximising the income of owners, since for the owners the true cost of a factor may be its nominal price. On the other hand, when the input price differences are attributable to management – for example when a weak management bargains ineffectively with trade unions – one needs a measure which includes the input price differences. Thus, for cost functions, the input prices would have to be excluded as independant variables. When constant returns to scale prevail the simplest replacement for the factor-share weighted productivity measure would be costs per unit of output. In summary the way in which input prices are treated significantly affects the conclusions that can be made from the efficiency measures.

PROFITS

Variations in profitability across firms are commonly used by the media and laymen as indicators of efficiency. Figure 5.5 on p.234 shows that the profitability of publicly-owned industry in the UK has, in the post-war period, been consistently less than in private industry. There are three elements which contribute to the variability of profits across firms. Firstly there is the productivity of each firm as defined earlier. Secondly there is the degree to which firms are 'input price efficient' – i.e. choose input combinations which minimise costs. Thirdly, there is the volume and range of products chosen and the level of prices set for each product. It is clearly possible then for a public firm to have a lower rate of profit than a private firm even though its productivity performance is superior. It is also possible for a public firm to be more cost efficient than a private firm and yet still have a lower rate of profit because of factors connected with the volume and range of its products and the structure and level of its product prices. Some of these issues will be discussed in the next section of the survey. Here we conclude the basic theme of this section by examining firstly how the productivity measure can be estimated when there are several products and secondly the extent to which the choice of products and product prices is itself a question of efficiency.

When firms have the same productivity performance and are equally efficient with respect to exogenously given input prices, any differences in their promotion of owners' income essentially lies in the range of outputs produced, their quality dimensions, the rate of production and the level of prices. When public and private firms face the same set of exogenously given product prices then the more 'price-efficient' firm from the point of view of the owners is that where rates of production or range of outputs more nearly corresponds to the point where marginal costs equal price since this is the profit-maximising position. This would also be an economically efficient outcome if marginal costs reflected the economic costs to the country.

Putting matters this way allows us to return again to the productivity measure which, as we saw, becomes difficult to estimate if there are many

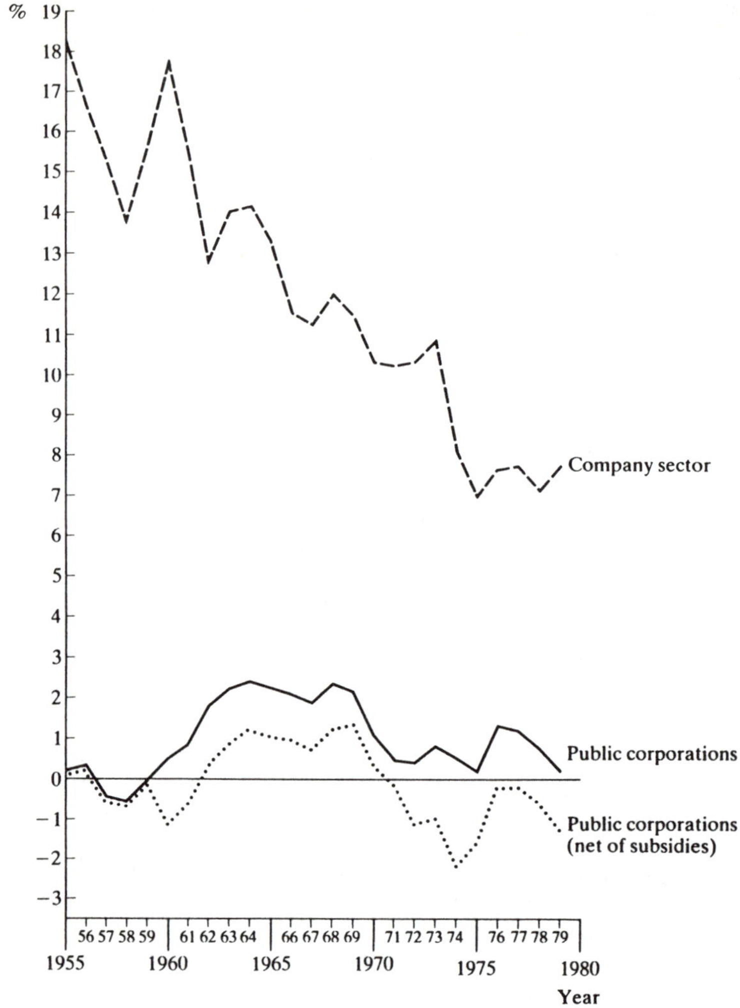

FIG. 5.5 Rate of profit in public and private industry in the UK 1955–79 (Gross trading profits including stock appreciation but net of capital consumption as a percentage of net capital stock)
Source: *National Income and Expenditure Blue Books*, Central Statistical Office, HMSO.

products since knowledge of the input elasticity of each product is required. Now with constant returns to scale it can be shown[24] that the difference between relative product prices and relative marginal costs is precisely reflected in the difference between the elasticities of products and their respective shares of revenues. Hence we can circumvent the estimation of elasticity by replacing v_j in equation [9] by product Y_j's share of total revenue and any difference in 'price efficiency' will be picked up by a productivity measure where inputs are weighted by factor shares and products by revenue shares. Of course again the constant returns to scale assumption is crucial. If this cannot reasonably be assumed and if it is desired to include a price efficiency effect one could estimate a profit function taking output, unit costs and product prices as independent variables and include an institutional dummy as in the cost function discussed before.

When, of course, the firms are not price takers it is not in the owners' interest for prices to be equal to marginal costs. If the objective is profit then the measure should be profit even though that measure will be reflecting pure productivity considerations, input price efficiency and differences in product prices intrinsic to ownership. The last mentioned will reflect monopolistic elements in earned profits in the same way that any monopsonistic elements in factor prices would be reflected in a measure of costs per unit of output.

In conclusion let us summarise how owners' income and economic efficiency are reflected in each of the measures we have considered:

(a) The proportionate difference in costs between public and private firms, as revealed by cost functions which treat output and input prices as independent variables, reflect 'pure' productivity differences plus differences in input price efficiency, provided such prices are truly exogenous to the enterprise.
(b) With the same proviso but also a further one of constant returns to scale, factor-share weighted productivity measures will reflect the same thing.
(c) If input prices are in part endogenous, reflecting the bargaining context and market structure, the level of unit costs would be a better indication of efficiency with respect to a profit objective but for economic efficiency such a measure would reflect both monopsonistic power and the performance of management.
(d) If input prices facing the firms are not, on economic efficiency grounds, deemed to reflect economic costs, shadow prices could be used but the measure would also be reflecting input price efficiency.
(e) Difference in profits, usually measured as a rate of profit on capital, will reflect all the forces mentioned already plus 'product price efficiency' and any monopolistic market power.

6. Empirical comparisons of public and private firms

If the sole focus of interest in the performance of enterprises was the income accruing to owners, there would be considerably more public/private studies than exist at present. The relevant indicator would be profitability, usually expressed as the rate of profit on capital advanced by owners. Since the owners' interest so measured does not vary with the location or type of products or inputs, cross industry and cross country comparisons could be made, with allowances perhaps for the way in which the cycles of booms and depressions have affected the observations. There are basically three reasons why economists have not been satisfied with studies which restrict themselves to profit measures. Firstly there has been an interest in the behaviour of public and private enterprises independently of any question of efficiency. Secondly where efficiency considerations have been introduced these have often embraced the objective of economic efficiency rather than simply the objective of enhancing owners' income. Thirdly the previous section has shown that little can be deduced about the *sources* of inefficiency from summary measures like profitability; a firm might be minimising the costs of its chosen output levels even though the volume of production in different areas is not adjusted to the point where relative prices equal relative marginal costs; the latter may be due to price restraints imposed by government or it may indeed reflect poor management decisions.

As a result empirical comparisons of public/private have been restricted to areas where the two types of institutions have been doing a broadly similar job – especially producing a similar type of output but more generally where differences and the types of differences can be isolated and attributed to ownership rather than other factors. This has meant a rather patchy collection of studies, scattered across different countries and even then involving results subject to varying interpretations. Since the coverage of particular product areas like transport or water supply have not been systematic nor has that of particular countries (with the USA perhaps an important exception) we propose to discuss the studies in terms of the themes of (a) productivity, (b) costs, (c) market structure versus ownership, (d) pricing, politics and profitability.

PRODUCTIVITY IN TRANSPORT

Few public/private comparisons have been able to approach the essence of the 'ideal' productivity measure discussed earlier in this survey, i.e. to measure the degree to which different volumes of resources are used to produce a given pattern of outputs. Two recent studies of Canadian railways and Australian airlines have however got closer than any others. Moreover they were both designed as attempts to test the proposition that the structure of property rights is such that pressure on management from owners is less in public firms than private firms and that this will manifest itself in lower productivity and/or higher unit costs. Discussion of these studies reveals problems which, we shall show, are at the heart of attempts to compare the public and private sectors of industry in the UK.

Railways throughout the world have in this century had radically to reduce their capacity in the face of competition from new long-distance modes of transport. The Canadian railways were no exception but by the mid-1950s the system had settled down to two main companies – the publicly owned Canadian National and the private Canadian Pacific, in competition with each other over many routes and subject less and less to rate regulations. For each of the years from 1956 to 1975, Caves and Christensen (1980) calculated the growth rate in productivity in moving from one rail company to the other using a presentation with some similarities to equation [9] which we reproduce here

$$\sum_j v_j r_j - \sum_i a_i r_i \qquad [9]$$

where r_j is the growth rate of output j in moving from one institutional structure to another and measured as the log of $Y_{jt'}$ output in institutional structure t' minus the log of $Y_{jt'}$ output in the other institutional structure. The growth rate, r_i, of input i is measured in an analogous way. The input elasticity of product j is denoted by v_j and the output elasticity of input i by a_i. Such elasticities are averaged over the old and new output levels and essentially act as weights for aggregating the growth rates. The authors identified four grades of labour input which, together with fuel, equipment, materials and structures formed the main input categories. Data on passenger miles and freight-ton miles were available as two indicators of output. The growth rate in productivity in any year as one shifts from CP to CN, is measured as the sum of the growth rates of the two outputs (aggregated by weights to be discussed shortly) minus the (weighted) sum of the growth rates of inputs. Taking 1967 as an example, the growth rate of productivity so calculated was 0.041 which implied that productivity in the public firm was some 4.1 per cent higher than in the private firm (see Table 5.1). Analogous figures for the other years are reproduced in Table 5.1 from which Caves and Christensen concluded there was little difference in productivity and hence no support for the proposition that the property rights structure of public firms leads to lower 'production efficiency' than in private firms.

TABLE 5.1 Productivity in Canadian railways (Percentage growth rate in productivity in moving from CP to CN)

1956	1957	1958	1959	1960	1961	1962
(−)5.5	(−)8.1	(−)7.6	(−)7.1	(−)8.1	(−)8.6	(−)7.6
1963	1964	1965	1966	1967	1968	1969
(−)4.1	(−)5.1	(−)3.2	2.5	4.1	6.4	4.9
1970	1971	1972	1973	1974	1975	—
4.5	2.5	2.9	2.1	0.8	2.9	—

Source: Calculated as the logarithms of the entries in the last column of Table 2, Caves and Christensen 1980, showing CN total factor productivity relative to CP.

This is, of course, only one aspect of economic efficiency. Canadian railways have for a long time been subject to control with respect to the hauling of grain and flour and the transport of such crops for export has been subject to rate regulation. In addition the abandonment of track in the prairies, where regulation has held grain rates below variable costs, has also been controlled by government. Railways rates then do not reflect marginal costs in some areas and Caves and Christensen suggest this phenomenon affects Canadian National more than the privately owned Canadian Pacific. Indeed, in order to exclude this factor, Caves and Christensen did not weight outputs by revenue shares since, as was argued earlier, this would have picked up such 'inefficiencies' in product pricing. Instead data on the cost elasticity of each product were obtained from some separate work on US railroads and used as product weights. As note 24 demonstrates, such weights will be reflecting any differences in input price efficiencies as well as the underlying input elasticities of each product.

A similar point applies to the way inputs were each weighted not by their output elasticities, a_i, but by their shares of total cost. If there are differences in the facility with which each firm adjusts its input combination to the input prices it faces, these will be reflected in the measure which, given the aim of reflecting productivity and/or unit costs, is no bad thing as long as input prices are truly exogenous to the enterprise. It could be however that any differences in input prices such as cost of capital are intrinsic to the ownership differences. Caves and Christensen do not discuss this, apparently relying on the observation that railroads purchase inputs in unregulated factor markets. Finally their measure could be a distortion of productivity differences if constant returns to scale do not apply since the use of cost shares as a proxy for the theoretically ideal weights of the output elasticity of each input would then obscure the differences in productivity due simply to scale of operation. Fortunately Caves and Christensen were able to claim that the information on returns to scale from US studies was such that the hypothesis of constant returns to scale could not be rejected for the broad range of output over which the Canadian railways were operating.

The case of Australian airlines has some similarities to the above in being another instance where a public firm (Trans Australian Airlines) coexists with a private firm (Ansett Transport Industries) in the same product area in the same country. Indeed the very possibility of this comparison stems from a peculiar institutional structure. Where the two airlines operate on inter-state routes, government policy has been to equalise practically every aspect of their operations, that is, routes, ports of call, frequency of stops, aircraft capacity and types, import licences for aircraft, take-off times, engineering and airport facilities, seating arrangements, fares, freight rates. Since available aircraft are the same in each airline as, apparently, are the prices of all inputs, then productivity measures can focus on output per man provided the use of materials and fuel is not too dissimilar.

In Davies' oft-quoted studies (1971, 1977, 1980) for the period 1958–74, the most striking statistics are those which indicate freight tonnage per employee vastly higher in the private firm. The first column of Table 5.2 shows figures for three years which are representative of the results for the whole period. Two immediate questions are whether freight tonnage is the only dimension to output and whether constant returns to scale operate. Forsyth and Hocking (1980) point out that the private airline operates on local short routes as well as the inter-state routes and hence ton kilometres is a better measure of output. The second column of Table 2 shows, for the same three years, their adjusted figures which also exclude operations in Papua New Guinea where, it is claimed the airlines operate in very different circumstances. The differences in labour productivity so calculated are now less marked. Moreover the private airline carries a much larger volume of freight than the public firm so there is a danger of attributing productivity differences arising from scale of operation to ownership factors unless constant returns to scale prevail.

In any case freight is not the only output – it accounts for less than 20 per cent of each airline's revenue and the employment figures relate to all

TABLE 5.2 Labour productivity in Australian airlines

	Freight tonnage per employee (Davies)	Freight-ton km per 1000 employees (Forsyth-Hocking)	Passengers per employee (Davies)	Passenger-km in 1000s per employee (Forsyth-Hocking)	Revenue in $1000 per employee (Davies)
1964/5	5.0 (12.1)	29 (32)	287 (352)	245 (251)	8.5 (9.7)
1969/70	5.8 (9.3)	40 (42)	390 (414)	341 (336)	13.1 (14.1)
1973/4	6.0 (10.0)	48 (50)	496 (532)	433 (431)	19.1 (21.4)

Sources: Davies 1980, Table 1; Forsyth and Hocking 1980, Table 1
Note: Figures shown are for the public airline, TAA, with figures for the private airline, ATI, in brackets

activities. From Davies' point of view this difficulty disappears with the fact that output per man in the other product category, passengers, is also, he argues, higher in the private firm, as the third column of Table 5.2 shows. When the Forsyth-Hocking adjustments are made to the passenger figures, however, we see from the fourth column of Table 5.2 that the public firm is, if anything, showing a better performance, again subject to the returns to scale qualification. It is therefore necessary to use some form of weighting system to aggregate outputs in the manner of the productivity measure of expression [9]. All that is available is the data shown in the last column of Table 5.2. In the words of Forsyth and Hocking 'the significance of revenue per man is obscure' as a productivity measure. The observed proportionate differences between the two firms (of the order of 5 per cent) are at best a very crude approximation to a measure of the sum of the rates of growth (in moving from TAA to ATI) of freight ton kilometres and passenger kilometres (disaggregated by routes and each weighted by revenue shares) minus the growth rate of labour. Such a measure would be consistent with expression [9] if constant returns to scale prevail. It would in any case be picking up efficiency factors additional to productivity – namely the degree to which passenger and freight volumes on both the inter-state and local routes were expanded to the point where marginal costs equal the price per kilometre. Having said all this, the major conclusion that can be drawn from the case of Australian airlines is similar to that for Canadian railways – there is no significant evidence that productivity is lower in public firms than private firms. It may be noted here that in both countries the public firm does not have a monopoly of its service and we return in a later section of this survey to explore the relationship between market structure and ownership.

PRODUCTIVITY IN PUBLIC AND PRIVATE INDUSTRY IN THE UK

The reservations about figures of revenue per man apply with equal force to the sort of comparisons that have sometimes been made between the private manufacturing sector and the public enterprise sector in the UK. In fact the figures of the value of net output per man for one particular year, 1971, shown in the first row of Table 5.3 are of even less significance than the Australian figures since there is no basis for presuming that non-labour inputs are the same in each sector. G. and P. Polanyi (1972, 1974) felt in particular that the nationalised industries had excessive capital and thus expressed net output as a ratio of expenditure on labour and capital, and obtained the figures shown in the second row of Table 5.3 which they called 'productivity indicators'. Such ratios are meaningless as productivity measures for two reasons. Firstly the use of a value measure of output would not be unreasonable if prices are equal to marginal costs in each sector and for each product within each sector and if constant returns to scale prevailed since in such circumstances revenue shares are an exact proxy for each product's cost elasticity as required in expression [9]. It is well known however that UK governments have in some periods held prices down in the public sector in the interests of counter-inflation policy and generally intervened in the relationship between prices and costs of different products (Millward 1976). Whilst the Polanyis' measure could reasonably be interpreted as in part reflecting one aspect of economic inefficiency it is not a measure of productivity. Indeed the figures in row B are primarily reflecting differences in the profitability of the two sectors. The Polanyis view the annual costs of capital as consisting of two components; one part is the return that could have been earned by the use of capital elsewhere in the economy (estimated at 10 per cent); the other part is the depreciation in the capital stock. Since 10 per cent was the sort of return being earned in the private sector it is not surprising that their 'productivity' indicator for manufacturing comes out near to 1.0. As Fig. 5.5 on p.234 shows, the rate of return on capital in the nationalised industries has been consistently lower than the private sector so that the results shown in row B of Table 5.3 are not at all surprising.

The second major problem is that the two sectors are producing completely different products. This means that, in the present state of the art, it is impossible to use the kind of productivity model discussed in the previous section and in particular to use expression [9]. Moreover the concept of returns to scale embracing the two sectors is now meaningless, as also would be comparisons of costs per unit of output. Of course one could calculate productivity changes over time in each sector. This is precisely what Pryke (1971) has done in his extensive work on UK public enterprise. Roughly speaking[26] Pryke calculated for the manufacturing sector a growth rate of productivity with some similarities to expression [9], treating labour and capital as the main inputs and with the change in question being that from one year to another (rather than from one ownership form to another). His results showed productivity, so conceived, growing at an average of 2 per cent per annum in manufacturing in the period 1948–68, as can be seen in section C of Table 5.3. Similar calculations were performed for various nationalised industries and Pryke felt able to conclude that the performance of the nationalised industries was probably slightly better than private manufacturing. However, since Pryke's method implicitly involved the use of revenue shares as weights for products and

TABLE 5.3 Some 'productivity' measures for public and private industry in the UK

	Nationalised industries	Manufacturing
A. Value of net output (£) (1971) ÷ number of employees	2529	2040
B. Value of net output (1971) ÷ (wages bill + capital consumption + 10% capital stock)	0.67	0.99
C. Annual average % growth rates of output per unit of composite input		

	Nationalised industries					
	Electricity	Coal	Railways	Gas	Airways	Manufacturing
1948–58	3.6	0.4	0	0.7	7.8	1.5
1958–68	3.1	3.0	2.4	3.7	9.1	2.4
1948–68	3.4	1.7	1.1	2.2	8.4	2.0

Sources: Section A and B from G. and P. Polanyi 1974, Table 6; Section C from Pryke 1971, Table 9

cost shares as weights for inputs, his measures are picking up 'price inefficiencies' as well as pure productivity factors. More significantly, Pryke's approach at most allows one to compare the two sectors in terms of their *respective* growth rates of productivity *over time*. It is not possible to compare productivity *levels* in the two sectors nor therefore to calculate, for any year, the change in productivity in moving from the private sector to the public sector.

THE COST OF ELECTRIC POWER IN THE USA

The American electricity supply industry has probably been studied, with respect to public/private comparisons, more intensively than any other industry in the world. Essentially this is due to the very large number of both private and public firms. The objectives of the studies of costs have not always been made explicit though they can be viewed as being relevant to the hypothesis tested for the transport productivity studies – that the ownership structure of public firms implies less pressure on management to raise productivity and lower unit costs.

Now whilst the aim has usually been to measure the degree to which different volumes of resources are used in producing and distributing given patterns of electricity supply, data limitations forced the studies to be directed to differences in *costs* between firms, allowing for any differences in output levels and in input prices. That is, one attempts to estimate whether costs would be different in public and private electricity firms if they faced the same input prices and produced the same output levels, as we have illustrated in the context of equation [11] in an earlier part of the survey. One implication of this is that usually returns to scale are estimated rather than presumed. In addition the studies, for the large part, treat input prices as exogeneous to the firms. Most importantly of all however at this point is to note that by treating costs as the main indicator of efficiency, one is including a measure of the 'input price inefficiencies' of different firms as well as their production inefficiencies.

Whilst the US electric utility industry is possibly '... as close to perfection in public/private comparability as any other imaginable real world case' (Yunker 1975:66) it does contain problems arising from the size distribution of firms. Most of the research studies of the industry discussed in this survey were completed during the last five years and refer to cross sections of data drawn from within the period 1964–72 and sampled from a basic population which included all but the smallest firms. Many of the latter, in the case of municipally owned firms, as Wallace and Junk (1970) have noted, continue to generate their own power thriving on a subsidised cost of capital. In this period there were 67 Federal projects, involving largely hydroelectricity, producing 12 per cent of the nation's power, wholesaling about half of this to other utilities. Of the 536 municipal firms in the basic population many were small and the 210 private firms in the basic population produced 77 per cent of the nation's power.

Yunker's study (1975) was explicitly motivated by a desire to test the property-rights proposition that the ownership structure put less pressure on management in public firms which are thereby 'economically inefficient', the best indication of which he felt was a measure of unit costs. He estimated costs as a function of output and the number of customers for 1969. Concerned at the different size distribution in the public and private industries, he restricted attention to private and municipal firms producing 0.5 to 4 million megawatt hours per annum and further restricted to firms with at least 1,000 customers since some firms sell to only a very small number of business or government users. Looking at the remaining 24 public and 49 private firms his equation suggested costs were lower in public firms but the results were not statistically significant. He concluded therefore that there was no evidence that private firm costs were lower than public firm costs. Yunker had however no data on input prices and therefore any production inefficiencies in public firms might be obscured if public firms had lower input prices. Put otherwise, he had not estimated what costs would be in the two sets of firms if both had faced the same input prices. Moreover the firms, in a sense, differed in their output composition in that some were just distributing whilst others were generating, transmitting and distributing.

Meyer (1975) felt that cost studies could reveal the degree to which new technologies or organisational methods were being adopted. He also lacked data on input prices which he felt might vary regionally and therefore attempted a partial offset by grouping the basic population geographically, excluded firms which were not engaged in all three functions and then drew a quota sample, 30 public and 30 private; a review of size of firms by volume of generation indicated that the composition of the public and private samples was quite similar. He found that from observations for each of the three years 1967, 1968, 1969 the cost structures of the two types of firm were significantly different in all the different functions. Generating costs per megawatt hour declined with the number of megawatt hours and were generally lower for public firms. Total transmission costs were primarily determined by the number of customers, with the results pointing to lower costs for public firms. The percentage of sales to resale customers was not found to affect either transmission or distribution costs. Neither were distribution costs per megawatt hour affected by the split of sales between residential and non-residential consumers but they were affected in a complex way by both output and the number of customers, but Meyer did not identify the pattern of the differences between public and private. In each of the above estimates he excluded maintenance costs which were found, separately, to be primarily determined by plant size, and maintenance costs per megawatt of capacity were significantly lower in public firms. Similar separate estimates of (a) sales and account expenses and (b) general and administration expenses, again pointed to lower costs in public firms.

The work of Yunker and Meyer was important in being the first attempts to allow systematically for output levels in assessing relative cost efficiency in electricity but the estimates related simply to *operating costs* embracing, therefore, only labour, fuel and raw materials. Data deficiencies were the main problem but it does mean that, in addition to the problem of input prices, the results have significance only if the similar size composition of firms in the two samples control precisely for differences in capacity and technology, that is for capital costs and Meyer's public sample included the Federal projects which involve much larger production units than in many other firms. Neuberg (1977) overcame some of these problems in his detailed study of distribution where he also argued that some of the complex features of customer characteristics and location could be picked up by allowing for miles of overhead distribution line (S_2) and the square mileage of the territory (S_3). From the basic population of firms he excluded the Federal projects and some 25 private firms not involved in distribution. Then a questionnaire survey was made of the remaining private firms and a sample of the municipal firms, finishing up with data from 90 private firms and 75 municipal firms for the year 1972. Costs embraced distribution proper, sales, customer accounts and a proportion of general and administrative expenses. Neuberg was concerned to allow for the suggestion that public firms had a lower cost of capital than private firms. He therefore credited all firms with the same cost of capital using a 10 per cent interest rate and adjusted each firm's costs accordingly. Neuberg's main results are illustrated in the following cost function. It expresses costs per final customer as a function of output, wages rates and ownership. In log form we have

$$\log C_n = 6.1 - 0.40 \log Y + 0.01 \log Y^2 + 0.25 \log (S_1/Y) - 0.92 \log (S_2/Y) + 0.97 \log (S_3/Y) + 0.30 P_L - 0.09 D \qquad [12]$$

where Y is the number of ultimate customers, S_1 is megawatt hours of electricity, P_L is the wage rate and D takes a value of 1 for public and 0 for private firms.[27] Thus in moving from the set of private firms to the set of public firms, holding output and wage-rates constant, costs fall by about 10 per cent.

If the incentive to minimise costs is weak in publicly owned electric distributing firms, this might manifest itself in the prices paid for bought-in power, clearly here a major input. De Alessi (1975) indeed argued that municipal buyers have less incentive to bargain and more incentive to conclude convenient agreements. There was however no evidence in support of this proposition in the prices paid by public and private firms to his sample of firms for the year 1969. There were 209 firms in the sample and all were generating electricity and then transmitting it (as wholesale sellers) to the public and private retail distributors. Allowing for the size of the wholesaling firm, input prices, the number of customers, the degree to which customers had multiple sources, regional effects, de Alessi found that electric power sold to municipally owned retail distributors did not involve any higher prices than that sold to private retail distributors.

Neuberg did not of course cover the actual production of electricity. We therefore finally consider the study by Pescatrice and Trapani (1980) who considered generation data for the years 1965 and 1970. They were able to estimate a cost of capital for each firm and in addition explored differences in generating technology. They argued that capacity could be similar in age and in the general method of production but differ in technology and this would be reflected in unit costs. From the basic population they therefore excluded firms for which adequate data were not available and which were not generating by a common production method, that is by coal, gas or oil. For each of the remaining 33 private firms and 23 municipal firms, they calculated a weighted average age of equipment. An equation was then estimated for costs per megawatt hour as a function of output (the number of megawatt hours generated), the prices of labour, capital and fuel, the age of equipment and finally the ownership form. The results indicated that a shift from private firms to public firms lowered average costs by the order of 25 per cent, a significant contribution to which was the considerably higher level of technology embodied in the plant of public firms.[28]

Thus none of the cost studies support the proposition that public electricity firms have a lower productivity or higher unit costs than private firms, allowing for differences in output and in factor prices though one qualification may be mentioned at this point. The possibility that public firms have a lower cost of capital is dealt with explicitly in Neuberg's work. In Pescatrice and Trapani's study, figures on cost of capital for each firm were available and whilst their cost function would not pick up any 'economic inefficiencies' arising from an unduly low cost of capital, at least, by treating the cost of capital as an explicit variable, public firms are not credited with lower costs simply because their cost of capital is less. Such data, however, all related to one year; if *in the past* cost of capital in public firms, *relative* to that in private firms, was lower than at present then the new technology which that might have induced will in part be reflected in current operating cost data and any relative cost superiority attributed to the ownership factor would be overstated. Such problems can be overcome only by a vastly superior data base than exists at present.

STUDIES OF UNIT COSTS IN WATER SUPPLY, REFUSE COLLECTION AND OTHER AREAS

Estimating cost *functions* has the decided advantage of offering possibilities for separating ownership issues from effects due to scale of operation and quality dimensions of output. The remaining cost studies that we now consider do have one common feature, also found in electricity but not so markedly, namely problems arising from public firms producing at a different scale or different dimensions of output to private firms.

Funkhouser and MacAvoy (1979) have examined the large number of private and public firms coexisting in many industries in Java, Sumatra and Bali. The nationalisation of Dutch companies in Indonesia in the 1950s and 1960s was such that during the 1960s and 1970s public and private firms coexisted in shipping, rubber, palm oil, cement, fertilisers, trading, banking, insurance and construction (embracing contractors, engineers and architects). Data was collected for one year, 1971, from balance sheets, banks and tax records supplemented in the case of public firms by reports to the Ministry of Finance and, in the case of private firms for which data was generally inaccessible, by extensive interviews. Whilst Funkhouser and MacAvoy felt able to claim that, for each firm in the same industry, production conditions, demand conditions and public policies on import licenses and local taxes were roughly the same, no data was available on input prices nor on capital employed and the two types of firm did not always sell the same product or market in the same area. The basic cost information then was production costs (excluding interest and depreciation – cf. Yunker and Meyer for electricity) plus a single dimension measure of output yielding figures of direct costs per ton in cement, fertilisers and shipping and per kilogram in rubber and palm oil; in finance and construction the output measures were in value terms. Such data were available from 54 public and 40 private firms and the authors suggested that unit variable costs were significantly higher in public firms. Whilst higher costs (and lower profit margins) were most noticeable in finance and construction, averaging over all industries unit costs in private firms were some 12 per cent lower than the industry averages. A restricted sample was constructed by pairing public and private firms in the same industry on the basis of comparable level of sales. For the resulting 31 paired observations, the cost difference disappears, both types of firms showing unit costs some 11 per cent below the full industry average. The significant public firms excluded from these samples are large public companies in fertilisers and cement and some very small companies in rubber and trading. As Funkhouser and MacAvoy comment, '. . . the public companies "out of scale" with respect to their industries appear to have had higher costs as well as lower profit margins' (1979: 365). Thus there is no evidence that public firms are less cost efficient than private firms of the same size. However, the problem is complicated by another of their findings, namely that unit production costs did not, generally, tend to vary with scale. Since the majority of firms at the top end of the scale spectrum are public, the basic sample of private firms is not sufficiently spread to allow one convincingly to conclude that their costs would have been lower than public firms if they had operated at such output levels.[29]

Scale effects are also important in the work by Crain and Zardkoohi (1978, 1980) on *water supply* in USA, which they found was an industry subject to increasing returns to scale. They examined data from the American Water Works Association on 1970 cost figures embracing operation, maintenance, administration and depreciation. Utilities with inadequate data were excluded and in addition any public firm larger than the biggest private firm was excluded. This left 24 private and 88 public. Pooling all firms they estimated unit costs (C = costs per million gallons of water) as a function of the wage rate (P_L), the price of capital (P_k), output (Y = million gallons of water supplied) and with a dummy variable for ownership effects. The approach was therefore similar to that exhibited in equation [12] above for Neuberg's study of electricity. The results suggested that shifting from private to public raised unit costs by an order of 25 per cent. Of particular interest are the cost functions for the separate samples.[30] Thus in log form for the public firms we have

$$\log C_n = 0.93 - 0.24 \log Y + 0.67 \log P_L + 0.33 P_k \qquad [13]$$

and for the private firms

$$\log C_p = 1.97 - 0.14 \log Y + 0.84 \log P_L + 0.16 \log P_k \qquad [14]$$

The coefficient on the output variable shows the elasticity of average cost with respect to output. Thus for the sample of private firms we see that the fall in average costs for a 100 per cent rise in output is 14 per cent ($= \partial \log C_p / \partial \log Y$). Such economies of scale are even larger for public firms where the elasticity is (−) 0.24. Large public firms who would presumably benefit most from such economies are however excluded from the sample. On the other hand, there are no comparably large private firms and where firms of the same size are taken the private firms show lower unit costs for any given set of input prices. Both this case and the Indonesian case shows the danger of sampling from a basic population where public and private do not coexist over the whole spectrum of scales of operation. Nevertheless for American water utilities the evidence is consistent with the proposition that public firms have higher costs than private firms.

There have, finally, been studies of unit costs in areas which are often not embraced in the public 'enterprise' sector in so far as that term is commonly used to encompass public agencies levying prices, i.e. direct user charges. Thus both public and private provision of refuse collection services, health and fire services can be found though only refuse collection has been studied in any depth in terms of cost efficiency. Since taxation rather than user charges is the more common source of finance, they are rather different animals to electricity, railways, etc. The broad results of the studies are that public provision involves higher unit costs than private provision. A fruitful line of inquiry for future research may well be that of examining the extent to which the source of finance and associated budgeting procedures affects cost efficiency. In this survey however we merely provide a brief outline of the findings.

Apart from the fact that an impressive volume of work has now been done on *refuse collection*, one source of interest is the complex characteristics of output reinforcing the general problem in cost studies of ensuring that the public and private firms are compared under similar circumstances. Since public and private refuse collectors rarely work the same geographic area then costs should ideally be expressed as a function of the various dimensions of output, viz.

frequency of service, customer density, location of pick-up points, weight and type of garbage, climatic factors, topographic variations, distance from disposal site. Unless such variations are covered, cost measures would be picking up efficiency considerations related to the choice of the quality and quantity of output.

A second source of interest lies in the fact that, whilst in the UK refuse is generally collected by departments of local authorities, in several other countries a variety of patterns is found. A Columbia University survey of 1975 (see Savas, Policy Analysis 1977) involved data on mixed residential waste collection in 2052 cities embracing one third of the US population. In nearly 20 per cent of cities citizens self-hauled their garbage to disposal sites. In 40 per cent of the cities self-hauling was allowed to coexist with arrangements where householders could alternatively pay user charges (in some cities regulated) to private firms. In some cities private firms had to have hauling licences and in some cities area franchise agreements had been reached with municipal authorities. After allowing for other variables which might affect costs, such as location and frequency of service, Edwards and Stevens (1978) found that in 77 cities sampled the price charged per household showed no significant variations as between these various arrangements.

This study and one by Bennett and Johnson (1979), who considered residential refuse collection in Fairfax, Virginia, contrast with several studies which have found private firm/household arrangements to be more expensive than municipal provision (Hirsch 1965, Pier, Vernon and Wicks 1974, Savas, Policy Analysis 1977, Pommerehne and Frey 1977). It is not surprising to find municipal provision cheaper than private firm/household agreements since municipal provision invariably involves an area monopoly for a specific type of garbage, which means that it can reap economies from the contiguity of customers quite apart from any economies of scale which may be open to both types of firm. A more valid comparison would therefore be between municipal firms and those private firms operating in cities where self-hauling is prohibited and where the firms have area franchises or exclusive contracts under which the householder has no choice of service level, does not pay user charges and where the municipal authority pays the private contractor. The Edwards and Steven study found prices (as contract fees or user charges on households) in such cases to be lower than where 'free market' private firm/household agreements existed. The difference was attributed to economics of contiguity and scale.

Most studies have found that franchise and contract arrangements also involve lower costs than municipal provision, though it has not always been possible to control properly for differences in input prices. Sampling from the Columbian University survey B. J. Stevens (reported in Savas, Policy Analysis 1977) found municipal provision involved significantly higher costs after standardising for the total volume and weight of refuse, household density, wage rates, temperature, frequency and location of service.[31] Savas (Policy Analysis 1977) considered the case of Minneapolis, where in 1971 a new system of residential waste collection was introduced, with one area served by the local

Sanitation Division and another by a consortium of private firms. It emerged that the cost per ton for the Sanitation Division, excluding overheads, was some 10 per cent higher in 1971 than the consortium's contract income per ton and costs expressed per household were 15 per cent higher (Savas, Policy Analysis 1977). However, this cost difference disappeared by 1975!

General evidence pointing to lower costs for private franchise and contract arrangments has been found in countries other than the USA. Kitchen's cost data (1976) for 48 Canadian municipal areas for 1971 suggested that the costs of public provision were higher than private sector provision after standardising for wage rates and many of the dimensions of output. Pommerehne and Frey from a sample of 103 Swiss cities in 1970, embracing half the Swiss population, confirmed that user charge arrangements are more costly than other forms of provision and that private contract provision is some 20 per cent cheaper than public residential refuse collection.

Turning to *hospital* services we are dependent upon one major study by Clarkson (1972) who compared proprietary (for profit) with non-proprietary short-term stay general hospitals with a 50 to 99 bed capacity. Non-proprietary included government owned hospitals as well as non-profit making charitable institutions. Clarkson argued that differences in performance between non-proprietary and proprietary hospitals would exist partly because certain rights or claims to benefits in non-proprietary organisations are not for sale as they are in proprietary organisations; in addition managers or workers in non-profit organisations do not have exclusive claims on the residual income remaining after costs have been met. From his sample of hospitals in California, Clarkson felt able to make two broad conclusions. Firstly, there is evidence that non-proprietary hospitals have different and more explicit rules than proprietary hospitals, including a greater tendency to have formal budgets approved by a governing board, written staff regulations and standing committees of the staff. Clarkson suggested that non-proprietary hospitals were less likely to use price and wage information provided by markets and were more likely to use other sources of information such as opinion polls; this latter conclusion may be questioned, since the majority of non-proprietary as well as proprietary hospitals in the sample did not use opinion polls. Secondly, from payroll data covering 26 separate worker classifications for short-term general hospitals in Los Angeles and San Francisco, supported by other *ad hoc* indicators of inputs, Clarkson concluded that variability in the choice of factor input combinations was higher in non-proprietary than proprietary hospitals, a result which is attributed to the lower concern with market prices. However, sample sizes are not made explicit and the input variability observed may result from factor price differences and technology. Wage rates differ across hospitals, as Clarkson acknowledges, so that efficient input usage would require differing factor combinations. Moreover, technology in this industry may allow a fair amount of factor substitutability and various input combinations may be therefore equally efficient. Finally, the problem of output dimensions is side-stepped. In the field of health care output and, therefore, input requirements will vary not only according to quantity but also quality.

In the case of *fire services* Ahlbrandt (1973) calculated costs of public provision from data collected relating to cities and fire districts in the Seattle-King County area and from some additional cities within the state of Washington. The estimated costs were contrasted with the actual cost for a competitive firm supplying Scottsdale, Arizona, as well as other communities in that state. The private firm's rate of profit was regulated and Ahlbrandt considered that costs would be held in check by potential competition from alternative municipal provision or other producers. His results showed costs to be significantly lower for the private firms. However, Ahlbrandt conceded that much of the cost difference arose from differences in the employment of fire fighters and equipment, resulting in differences in the quality and quantity of services supplied, notwithstanding that this may be reflecting superior knowledge of demand characteristics under private contracting.

MARKET STRUCTURE VERSUS OWNERSHIP

A characteristic of the cost studies discussed so far is the attempt to isolate those features of the behaviour and efficiency of public and private firms which are not intrinsic to ownership differences. One further feature is however rather difficult to unscramble from the institutional setting. In Western mixed economies the coexistence of public and private firms is often found where large economies of scale and contiguity are believed to exist. Geographic areas then often finish up with one firm, either a regulated private utility or a public enterprise. There are important exceptions. Of the studies already cited, Indonesian public firms and the Canadian National railway faced competition. In US electricity many private utilities are unregulated. When we observe the relative behaviour and efficiency of public and private firms, it is clearly important to distinguish the effects of the presence of competition and regulation from the role of the ownership factor. To date only a small number of studies have considered this problem.

Meyer (1975), it may be recalled, had found electricity operating costs to be significantly lower in public firms than private. Each of the firms in the sample was presumed to have a monopoly of its area of supply and in order to examine whether the cost differences were reflected in prices he calculated for one year, 1969, the average revenue per kilowatt hour for various customer groups. For the groups 'residential', 'small commercial' and 'other' he found that the public firms' prices were lower than for private firms and suggested that the margin was consistent with the cost differences, given that purchased kilowatt hours per customer were found to be similar in both types of firm. For the 'resale' group, consumption per customer was much bigger in public firms and, given block tariffs, he felt this accounted for the considerably lower price charged by public firms. Whilst consumption per 'large commercial' user was sufficiently lower in the sample of public firms, to expect higher prices in public firms than private firms, Meyer found that the two sets of prices were very similar and indeed average revenue was noticeably lower than in any other customer group (except resale). 'Large commercial accounts . . . ' suggests Meyer (p.398) '. . . have a competitive threat open to them, which is not available to other customers, since they may be large enough to make setting up generating capacity for themselves an economically and financially feasible alternative.'

Indirect though this example may be, one can search in vain for clear examples where competition affects the relative prices of public and private firms. Other evidence on the effects of competition relates, perhaps surprisingly, to cost efficiency. Caves and Christensen (1980) had found no significant difference in productivity between the two Canadian railroads and concluded that the performance of the publicly owned Canadian National showed '. . . the impact of competition in offsetting the negative aspects of public ownership. Our results indicate that the impact of competition can be substantial' (p.974). In presuming that publicly owned firms are cost inefficient the authors (cf. also Spann 1977) do not appear to have been aware of the recent evidence on costs in electricity but have rather relied on Davies' work on airlines (see pp.238–9 for a criticism of this), studies of the inefficiencies of *price* structures in US electricity and on studies of fire services (Ahlbrandt 1973) and hospital services (Clarkson 1972, Lindsay 1976) which are rather different animals to public corporations. There is at present, no general support for the proposition that public enterprises are less cost efficient than private firms. The Canadian railroads experience confirms that – it cannot, *per se*, be adduced in support of a role for competition. Of rather more direct relevance is the exploitation by Primeaux (1977, 1978) of the fact that there are some American cities – a total of 49 in 1966 if those with populations less than 25,000 are excluded – where public electricity firms faced competition from other firms, mainly private. Consumers can in some of the cities switch from one firm to another whenever they want; in other cities, new customers have a choice of supply but thereafter they are committed to that firm. Primeaux compared the costs of these municipal firms with other municipals of the same size and with the same power source but which had a monopoly of their area. Allowing for differences in levels of sales, capacity, fuel costs, the cost of purchased power, the rate of consumption per consumer, and geographical area he found that costs were significantly lower in the municipals facing competition. He concluded therefore that the effects of competition in making firms more cost conscious offset any excess capacity effects that would be associated with the duplication of facilities. As a footnote to this we may note that for refuse collection in Minneapolis Savas suggested that the mere coexistence of the two types of firms in the city (doing the same job but in different areas) seemed to reduced cost differences. In summary there is some evidence pointing to competition improving the cost efficiency of public firms but the relative magnitude of this effect on public and private firms has not yet been explored.

Given their access to government subsidies, it is not clear even on theoretical grounds why competition should affect public firms though it may be that the performance of managers in different firms is more readily comparable. Turning now to the effects of *regulation*, the theoretical issues have received much more attention but little agreement between writers, (cf. Stigler 1971, de Alessi, Fall 1974). Space precludes any extended discussion of the regulation literature. On the one hand regulated firms are well placed to collude and have an incentive to influence regulators who in any case have little vested economic interest of their own in acquiring the full information needed for effect. Thus in the Australian airline case discussed earlier, Forsyth and Hocking argue that while '. . . it might appear that the industry is regulated by the Department of Transport, in fact it is to a large degree self-regulating. The airlines agree issues between themselves and submit their proposals to the Department of Transport. The Department has imperfect information about the operations of the airlines and this gives some freedom of operation' (1980: 182–3). On the other hand, regulators might well be under pressure from vested interests – consumers, potential contractors – a force making for active regulation.

Precise evidence on the effects of regulation *vis-à-vis* the effects of ownership is inconclusive as yet. Regulation usually involves control of tariffs or fares and the prescription of a maximum average rate of return on capital. Suppose that the latter is less than what an unconstrained firm would earn. Theory suggests (Averch and Johnson 1962, Baumol and Klevorick 1970) that the imposition of such a required rate of return would reduce actual profits but that some of these profits can be restored if the firm raises its output and capital/labour ratio, ensuring all the time that the *average* rate of return is not exceeded. Thus the regulatory constrained profit maximising position involves 'over-capitalisation'. Of particular relevance to the public/private issue is a finding of Crain and Zardkoohi (1980) that changes in the capital/labour ratio in private water utilities were not responsive to changes in the relative prices of capital and labour – which one would expect for an unconstrained private firm. Since the public water firms in the sample were found to have higher costs than the private utilities, the authors concluded that the overcapitalisation effects of regulation of the private firms were offset by ownership factors. Davies (1971, 1977, 1980) comes to similar conclusions about Australian airlines but there is some doubt attached to his claim that the public airline is less cost efficient. Evidence of regulation effects on private electricity utilities in the USA have been found (Courville 1974, Spann 1974) but in the one study to date which examined such effects in conjunction with ownership factors, the costs of public electric firms were significantly lower than the private utilities. Pescatrice and Trapani (1980) found very little evidence of the standard 'static' overcapitalisation effects of regulation. Since however they attributed the cost superiority of public firms to more technically advanced production methods, they speculated that the input distortion arising from regulation was manifesting itself in the excessive acquisition by private utilities of equipment with old fashioned technology.[32]

In summary, whilst the results are rather mixed, there is some evidence that competition does reduce the costs of public firms and regulation raises the costs of private firms. Neither finding is inconsistent with the findings about the effects of 'ownership' on costs – namely that, balancing the results of electricity and railroads against water, airlines and refuse collection, there is no general indication that private firms are more cost efficient than public firms.

PRICING, POLITICS AND PROFITABILITY

The unprofitability of the UK nationalised industries has been a favourite debating theme for some time. Figure 5.5 shows rates of profit in the UK public and private enterprise sectors. Whether or not allowance is made for subsidies and for the pervasive problems of measuring profits and capital, the rate of return has been consistently and considerably lower in the public sector. For reasons already discussed it is not possible, at a sectoral level, to compare the productivity or even cost efficiency of these two institutional types in the UK. Some of the cyclical movements in the prices and profitability of the public sector, relative to the private sector, can sometimes be traced to the machinations of macroeconomic policy (Millward 1976). For deeper insight in this context we turn to the USA where the coexistence of public and private in the same product areas is more common.

Very broadly the main findings have been that, standardising for other factors, (a) prices are lower and output higher in public firms than in private firms, (b) for different types of product and consumers, relative prices are not as closely geared to relative marginal costs in public firms as they are in private firms, (c) one or both of the above two factors have contributed to the lower profit rates sometimes found in public firms.

These findings emerged from the earliest comparisons of public and private firms and led some to the conclusion that public enterprises were generally inefficient (Peltzman 1971, de Alessi, Fall 1974). Subsequent work on productivity and costs in electricity and transport in the USA suggests that such a conclusion cannot be drawn. In any case, one of the major problems in assessing the findings on 'price inefficiencies' and output levels is to what extent they can be uniquely attributed to a particular hypothesis about the behaviour of public firms relative to private. In what follows we shall try to link these results to three different explanations, discussed earlier in this survey: (a) public firms as a vehicle for harnessing the political support of voters, (b) the straight property rights prediction that public firms are more bureaucratic than private firms, (c) public firms as an instrument of government economic and social policy especially in the area of income redistribution and macroeconomic policy.

Considering first the average level of prices, in US electricity some of the earliest interpretations have to be revised in the light of the subsequent work on costs. Peltzman (1971) assumed that managers of public firms were interested in the continued existence of the enterprise and their jobs, the vehicle for which was political support. In particular he expected that prices would tend to lie below the profit maximising level and examined the 1966 electricity bills, in various customer classes, of a sample of firms each serving at least 10,000 customers and embracing both municipal firms and private firms, the latter tending to operate in cities with larger populations. A straight comparison of the bills revealed the customers of public firms had consistently lower bills and Peltzman attributed this to the preferential tax treatment of public firms. He had not however properly standardised for production costs[33] and, as we have already seen, Meyer's detailed study of electricity operating costs had concluded that, in conjunction with block tariffs, they were consistent with the differences in prices between public and private firms. An indirect implication of all this is that electricity profit rates in the public sector will not be too far out of line with profits in the private sector. In Table 5.4 we reproduce some data from Mann (1970) which broadly bears this out. The rate of return on capital varies much more across the sample of public firms than it does for private but the average return is quite similar. Many US electricity firms have a monopoly of their geographic areas and hence different prices reflecting different costs is plausible. In contrast many Indonesian public firms face some sort of competition in which case, with broadly similar prices, differences in costs could well be reflected in differences in profit margins. Funkhouser and MacAvoy's study of Indonesian firms (1979) had started with a working hypothesis that public firms were a vehicle of government economic and social policy with the specific objective of so setting prices as to maximise consumer benefits subject to profits not falling below prescribed levels. As already hinted, whilst profit margins were found to be generally lower in public firms than in competing private firms, especially in finance and construction and in large firms, the authors attributed this to differences in costs or to public firms being 'out of scale'.

In the monopoly context it would be surprising not to find some association between prices and costs. Different tests from the above are needed to see if there is anything over and above cost differences which is influencing the general level of prices. Pashigian (1976) found differences in prices and profits between public and private firms remained, after allowing for costs, in his study of urban bus transit systems, each of which had semi-monopolistic positions in their respective cities and were generally subject to fare regulations. Of the systems in the 117 largest US cities several were excluded because of data limitations, leaving Pashigian with a sample of 58 transit systems with 1970 data of which 40 had adequate data for a 1960–70 comparison. Pashigian estimated an equation for prices (revenue per vehicle) as a function of operating costs and of regulatory and ownership factors. Since costs had been allowed for and did prove to be an important factor, then the remaining differences in prices

TABLE 5.4 Rates of profit in public and private electric utilities in USA, 1966 (percentages)

Rate of return	Proportion of public firms	Proportion of private firms
Less than 5	18	5
5–7	23	25
7–8	6	36
8–10	12	30
More than 10	41	4
Average rate of return	7.1	6.7

Note: Rate of return equals electric utility operating income as a percentage of net electric fixed assets. There were 494 (non-Federal) public firms in the sample and 185 private firms (but the average figure for the latter of 6.7 is based on 213 observations).
Source: Mann (1970)

between transit systems which were not attributable to costs but rather to regulatory and ownership factors were mirrored in differences in gross profit margins (revenue net of operating costs, expressed as a proportion of revenue).

Now Pashigian did find evidence that publicly owned transit systems had lower prices, after allowing for costs, and therefore lower profit margins, than private firms.[34] He observed however that this could be consistent with several explanations. Thus in so far as these systems represent declining industries or are subject to economies of scale both with respect to the transporter's costs and the users' waiting time they are, so one argument goes, either naturally unprofitable or become unprofitable from heavy regulation of fares; particularly unprofitable systems are therefore abandoned by private utilities and operated by publicly owned systems. To add substance to these arguments one would have to add the presumption that governments are more willing to subsidise publicly owned firms than private ones. On this basis the occurrence of government ownership would be greater in those cities where, allowing for the growth of population, car ownership had grown most and thereby undermined the profitability of bus transit systems. In fact, Pashigian finds precisely the opposite to be the case; urban bus transit systems have tended to become publicly owned in cities where the level of car ownership is low. Now the lower for any city is the level of car ownership the larger tends to be the proportion of low income families and the larger is the proportion of the city population travelling to work by transit. Thus it could be that urban authorities are consciously holding down fares and taking firms into public ownership as part of more general policies to redistribute income to the poor. An alternative explanation, for which Pashigian finds supportive evidence, rests on electoral issues. Transit systems, whether publicly or privately owned, are sometimes regulated by a district based metropolitan authority, sometimes by a city council, sometimes by a state commission. As one rises from district to city to state the more non-bus users there are in the voting population to which the regulatory body is answerable and the larger therefore is the number of non-users who would have to finance subsidies. Thus Pashigian finds that private utilities have lower prices, allowing for cost differences and therefore lower profit margins, when they are regulated by city or district bodies than by state agencies,[35] a phenomenon he attributes to voter opposition to subsidies from rural and semi-rural areas. Similarly the proportion of firms which are publicly owned is bigger the lower is the level of the regulatory body. Thus the earlier observation that a shift to government ownership has occurred less where car ownership has grown more, is consistent also with an electoral hypothesis that car-owning non-users constitute a voting opposition to strong regulation and heavy subsidies.

One final question in the context of the general level of prices is that, if political factors are present, under what circumstances are they stronger than others? Pashigian's findings suggest that private firms are not immune from political factors, a tendency which was revealed in Mann's study (1974) of electricity where he did standardise for cost differences between firms. For 196 publicly owned electric firms, he calculated whether monthly residential bills during 1967, allowing for size of plant and various cost categories, were a function of the apparent degree of political activism in the firm's county (measured by the proportion of the county population who cast votes in the last Presidential election) and/or of the strength of the majority party. He found no role for political activism but prices did tend to be significantly less the larger was the percentage vote difference between the majority and minority parties. A similar exercise for 46 private utilities found however the same variable to be important so that publicly owned firms were not as distinctive as first thought.

Turning now to the structure of prices of different products and different consuming groups Peltzman did in this case find some evidence consistent with his stress on political factors. He argued that though the cost of supplying Group A might be greater than the cost of supplying Group B, price differences would not completely reflect this since a lower price for Group B might gain less votes than were being lost from Group A. The prediction is therefore that the tariff structure of public electricity firms is less differentiated with respect to customer groups and less reflective of differences in costs as between groups. The only cost data which Peltzman had related to the whole system of each firm. He argued however that the cost per kilowatt hour for a firm supplying a group of consumers with particular cost characteristics would be equal to the system-wide unit costs less amounts that get bigger the larger is the ratio of that group to the total customer population. Prices were then regressed on system-wide unit operating and capital costs and variables to reflect the varying proportions of residential/non-residential customers and, within each, high and low consumption. For private firms he found that the prices of high consumption residential customers were significantly related to these variables whereas the public firm prices were not; a similar result emerged for non-residential customers. In confirmation of this de Alessi found that the 1966 selling prices of municipal wholesaling firms were less significantly related to regional variables than were the prices of private firms. Indeed by putting the price of one group as an independent variable in the price equation for the other group, Peltzman found that his residential and non-residential prices were highly and significantly intercorrelated for public firms but not for private firms. Thus costs of particular groups are reflecting themselves in public firms in the overall tariff structure rather than the prices of particular groups. Suggestive evidence on the same lines can be found in Peltzman's other work[36] on liquor prices in state-owned and private stores.

Independently of cost differences, one might expect that, since electricity is non-storeable and consumers can change monopoly area suppliers only inconveniently by shifting residence, firms will operate price discrimination. On the grounds that private firms are more geared to maximising their owners' wealth and less geared to the ballot box than public firms, more price discrimination might be expected in private firms. Peltzman hypothesised that, given the same average price, standardising for differences in the number of customers, their income levels and any regional effects, a more enthusiastic execution of price discrimination would raise the volume of kW sales per customer. The results indicated significantly higher volumes for private firms. He also found that private utilities tended to have a larger number of rate schedules but this result was not standardised for other variables. De Alessi's careful examination (1977) of rate schedules in 1970 involved allowing for regional differences in income and state regulation, differences in city sizes, the residential/non-residential mix and sources of power, by the selection of matching pairs of municipal and private firms. He finished up with 20 pairs and found that public firms had significantly lower numbers of peak schedules and of total schedules.

Private utility electricity tariff structures seem therefore to be more profit orientated than those of public firms. A key problem again however is whether this is consistent with more than one explanation. In some countries, railroad rates have been equal across customer groups, independently of any cost differences, partly as a heritage from the days of the rail monopoly of long distance transport and associated rate regulation. In the UK the Nationalisation Acts often required the provision of gas, electricity, railway services throughout the country, which was meaningless if for example the prices levied in remote areas were to reflect costs. Such uniformity in rates, fares and tariffs is therefore consistent with the use of industries to further wider goals of economic and social policy (Millward 1978). As a further alternative to the electoral explanation, it may be noted that the drawing up and monitoring of price schedules related to complex cost structures would be economically attractive for a management with a strong economic incentive to raise profits; de Alessi (Fall 1974, 1977) contrasts therefore with Peltzman in attributing the 'price inefficiencies' of public firms to the reduced pressure on management arising from the attentuated property rights of the owner of public firms. To distinguish between bureaucratic and electoral hypotheses requires more stringent tests.

One attempt to date, though not conclusive, warrants mention. Rail transport for travellers in the San Francisco Bay area is managed by the Bay Area Rapid Transit District (BART) a publicly owned body managed by a board of directors directly elected by voters in the counties and cities it serves. Cooter and Topakian (1980) attempted to explain the fares charged in one year (1975/6) to passengers commuting from 33 stations grouped on four arms radiating from the central business district. Their focus was on short-run allocation decisions (since capital investment in an expansion of BART was not likely) and on the structure of fare subsidies rather than the total subsidy from the Metropolitan Transport Commission which was treated as given. At any one station the subsidy conferred on the average passenger, i.e. with average trip length for passengers embarking from that station, would be the cost to BART of that journey less the relevant fare. Rail costs in the short-run would be restricted to fuel, engine wear and tear, track maintenance. How these should be allocated across different segments of track is itself a complicated exercise. The dotted line in Fig. 5.6 shows Cooter and Topakian's estimate of the various possible subsidy structures open to BART given the total subsidy available, the cost assumptions and other assumptions relating to demand elasticities.[37] The mileage of the passenger estimated to receive the largest daily subsidy was estimated as 13.5 miles and was equivalent to a per mile subsidy of 19 cents plus an amount unrelated to mileage and working out at (−) 127 cents. This may be

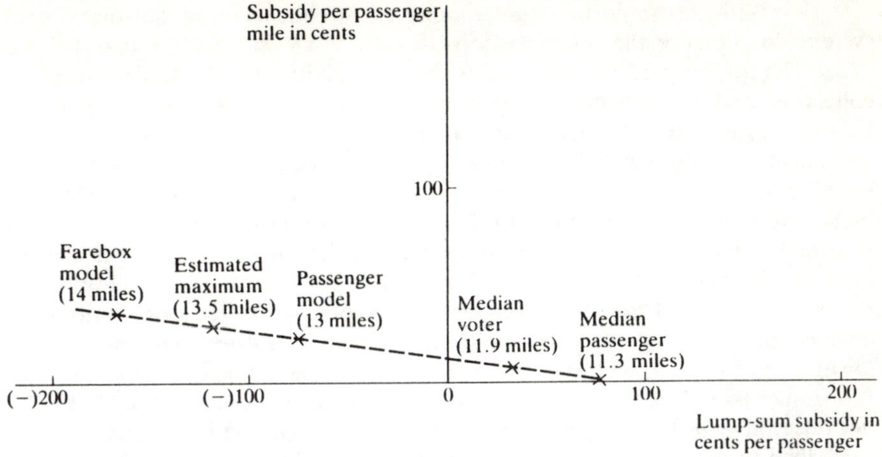

FIG. 5.6 Subsidy structures on the San Francisco Bay Area Rapid Transit District Railway 1975/6
Source: Adapted from Fig. 1 of Cooter and Topakian 1980

compared with the predictions from models of BART's behaviour. Thus Cooter and Topakian calculated the subsidy structure that would emerge from a bureaucracy model; two variants were covered, one where BART is deemed to maximise total revenue (the farebox model) and another where passenger mileage is maximised. Finally, by examining the distribution of the voting population, they considered an electoral hypothesis by estimating what subsidy structure would maximise the subsidy accruing to the passenger whose trip length was median and what subsidy structure would maximise the subsidy accruing to the voter (whether or not he used the railway) whose distance from the central business district was median. In the latter case it was presumed the voting non-user would have a preference similar to his rail travelling neighbour on the grounds that road congestion costs would vary symmetrically with the subsidy structure. As can be seen from Fig. 5.6 the bureaucratic models predicted best, yielding a subsidy structure favouring journeys between 13–14 miles. Unfortunately these results were extremely sensitive to the cost and demand assumptions – so much so that Cooter and Topakian had to allow that no hypothesis could be rejected under a reasonable range of assumptions.

7. Conclusions

It seems likely that in the future the data basis for comparing public and private firms will improve. At present observations are often available only for selected years with long time series conspicuous by their absence. This is not a problem unique to this area of applied economics but the requirement of comparing the two institutional forms on a similar product basis certainly makes life more difficult.

With this important reservation, a first conclusion is that there is no systematic evidence that public enterprises are less cost effective than private firms. The poorer performance, in this respect, exhibited in the studies of refuse collection and water supply (and possibly the Indonesian case) has to be balanced against the absence of any significant difference in Canadian railways and Australian airlines and the superior performance in US electric power. The separate components of cost effectiveness have not been easily identifiable. A 'pure' productivity comparison, to date, has been reported only for Canadian Railroads. Any differences in what we have called 'input price inefficiencies' have usually been mixed up with other factors. Yet a further possibility is that the two types of firms face different input prices for reasons intrinsic to ownership. There does seem reason to think that public firms sometimes have a lower cost of capital, with due reservations about the difficulty of that concept; few studies have made explicit allowance for this; Neuberg (1977) tried but it did not offset his conclusion that US municipal electric firms had lower distribution costs than private firms; for the very small municipal firms it may be important (see Wallace and Junk 1970). The possibility that wages are higher in public firms has not been widely explored though Hamermesh (1975) did not find that unionised US bus drivers and construction workers received higher compensation in government than in private industry.

Some proponents of the property rights theory of the firm have certainly predicted that unit costs would be higher in public firms, after allowing for any differences in input prices and scale of operation.[38] This line of analysis is particularly attractive in its attempt to understand organisational forms by looking at the contractual underpinnings and to base the analysis firmly on individuals within the organisation. In contrast to the property rights approach to individuals in firms, the role of management labour markets remains relatively unexplored. Is it possible, for instance, that competition amongst managers helps to equalise performance levels in the public and private sectors? Do managers' salaries reflect their likely contribution to raising profits (cf. Fama 1980)? In other words, does the management labour market operate so as to transfer the costs of any management inefficiency from shareholders to managers' own salaries, thereby creating incentives for management to pursue efficiency? In a perfect labour market, with perfect information, we would predict this outcome; in practice, information is imperfect and the extent to which managerial salaries do reflect managerial efficiency is a grey area. A further problem is that public and private firms often coexist where markets are in any case regulated. Perhaps both public enterprises and regulated private firms attract a similar kind of management in that dealings with para-statal bodies are part of the job. It is likely also that further studies will give a better picture of the respective roles of ownership, competition and regulation.

Clear differences between public and private firms do appear when we turn to pricing and profitability. In particular the broad picture emerging from North American electricity supply and transport is that where firms have monopoly coverage of a geographic area, the prices of private firms are more closely geared to the marginal costs of different products and services and, *ceteris paribus*, public firms have lower prices and bigger output levels. This is consistent with what can be gleaned in the UK by looking at the nationalised industries on their own. Since British economists have for long been preaching that prices should be related to marginal costs, they are well aware that practice differs. Whether however the behaviour of public firms here is attributable to political influence or to the empire building of bureaucratic management and civil servants or to explicit execution of social objectives with respect to the poorer regions and groups is still largely an open matter. That voting pressure plays at least some part in the USA is convincingly suggested by Pashigian's work (1976) on urban bus transit systems. One other potential influence merits final mention. 'Labour' was instrumental in furthering public ownership, yet paradoxically they finished up in Britain with no explicit representation on the boards of the nationalised industries and no preferential rights apart from due recognition of centralised bargaining; moreover with the exception of Hamermesh's US study the role of trade unions has been largely unexplored.

Notes

1. See for instance R. Turvey (1968) and J. R. Nelson (1964).
2. 'The criteria for control of nationalised industries, which have been established by government in the past, have not only been invalidated by subsequent government price restraint policies but have in any case taken insufficient account of the circumstances of individual nationalised industries. As a result it is doubtful whether they have made a material contribution to improving the allocation and effective use of resources.' (HMSO 1976).
3. Baumol (1958, 1959), Marris (1963, 1964), Williamson (1963, 1964, 1970).
4. For an extensive discussion see Rees (1976).
5. See Baumol and Bradford (1970), Rees (1976) and more generally Atkinson and Stiglitz (1980).
6. Equal to the area APL on Fig. 5.1. Very similar issues are involved if mine managers are not equally efficient; a rental return accrues to the more efficient mining companies since management is not in perfectly elastic supply to the industry.
7. We ignore the complication that the one company would be a monopsonistic leaser of coal deposits.
8. If perfect price discrimination is possible, then the demand curve also indicates marginal revenue. Total revenue would then equal the area under the demand curve, i.e. the total valuation by consumers. If in such circumstances the enterprise cannot break even, no production is warranted on grounds of economic efficiency.
9. For a review of the argument that the firm is an economy in miniature and that information problems are central to the literature on the internal organisation of resources see Spence (1975). For a further view on issues raised in this section see Marris and Mueller (1980).
10. For a review of some other reasons for the growth of firms and especially the role of monopoly policy see Kessler and Stern (1959) especially pp.1–20.
11. Whether maximisation of a generalised utility function is a meaningful or useful approach is a debate which we will not enter into here; for a sceptical view see Leibenstein (1979) especially p.495. Pursuit rather than maximisation of utility

would presumably satisfy Leibenstein and does not appear to alter the essential argument.

12. On the problems of control and information in organisations and hence the need for enforcement and operating rules for members of organisations, see for example, Alchian and Kessel (1962) and Arrow (1964). On the design of incentives within firms see for example, Hurwicz (1973), Mirrlees (1976), Harris and Raviv (1978), Kleindorfer and Sertel (1979), and references therein and Cohen (1980).
13. If employment contracts completely specified all duties, leaving no room for discretionary behaviour without recontracting or writing contingent claims contracts, then allocating resources within firms would presumably suffer from the same information and contracting costs as allocating in markets.
14. On the general background to the concept of 'teams' see Marschak and Radner (1972) and Radner (1972); on the problems of 'shirking' in teams, Alchian and Demsetz (1972), and Furubotn and Pejovich (1972). For a complementary approach see Radner and Rothschild (1975). In Alchian and Demsetz's approach factor complementarity is the root cause of 'team production'. McGuire in his study of 'clubs' (1972) has argued: 'Increasing applications of one factor, in combination with others enhance the marginal products of the other factors (and *vice versa*). This reciprocal conferral of marginal benefits leads to multifactor operation; economies are internalised in production clubs called "firms".' McManus (1976), especially pp.348–9 argues, however, that the problem in identifying marginal products lies in the technical characteristics of the inputs and outputs rather than 'team production' as such. Auster (1978) emphasises the importance of simultaneity in time of factor contribution in making the identification of marginal products difficult.
15. Baumol (1962), Marris (1964), Rees (1974). The argument that, where ownership and control are divorced, management may pursue goals other than maximum profit, has been explored in some detail since the late 1950s, but does predate this period. For instance, in 1935 Sir John Hicks discussed management pursuit of 'the quiet life', in 1947 Rothschild emphasised 'long-run survival' as a goal of management, and in 1952 Papandreou anticipated the later work of Simons, Cyert and March and suggested that the goals of firms arose out of interactions within firms. For a review of theories relating to the goals of firms see, for instance, Cyert and Cedrick (1972). On utility maximisation see Williamson (1963, 1964, 1970) and Alchian, November (1965).
16. In some circumstances agents may incur costs to guarantee behaviour conducive to the interests of principals, referred to as 'bonding costs'. The difference between the value of a firm without 'monitoring' and 'bonding' costs and with these costs defines the 'total gross agency costs', that is the costs of the agency relationship. See Jensen and Meckling (1976) and more generally on the theory of agency Ross (1973) and Mitnick (1975).
17. The agency and property rights literature have in the main developed independently, even though the issues they deal with are clearly complementary. For an early study which does discuss the two approaches together see Alchian (1965b). For a general study of the concept of property rights see Becker (1977).
18. For a recent review of these and other studies, see the various contributions to *Managerial Finance* 4, 1978.
19. McGuire, Chiu and Elbing (1962), Marris (1964), Meeks and Whittington (1975), McEachern (1978), Boyes and Schlagenhauf (1979). Some studies of pricing policy have also suggested that management may not pursue profit maximisation policies (e.g. Lanzillotti 1958). Other studies, however, question the view that the divorce of

ownership and control is as widespread as some suggest or that it is especially important in determining firms' objectives (for example, Kania and McKean (1976), Cooper (1977) and Nyman and Silberston (1978)). Differences in the results of empirical studies may arise from differing definitions of owner and management control and from differences in the samples of firms studied. For recent support for this view see Glassman and Rhoades (1980).

20. Kaysen (1965), Grabowski and Mueller (1975), Kuehn (1975), Singh (1975), McEachern (1976), Smiley (1976) and Owen (1979), Brown (1978) suggest stock market prices do adjust to information but not instantaneously. Some other studies also support, sometimes with some reservations, an 'efficient markets' approach and hence the view that shareholders do react in the stock market to managerial policy; for example, see Sullivan (1977) and Koutsoyiannis (1978). The power of shareholders and the efficiency of the capital market is clearly still something of a grey area.
21. In the USA there is often a close link between management and politicians, especially at the municipal level.
22. Crain and Zardkoohi invoke a further argument for expecting a less capital-intensive technique. The owner of a private investment can pass on his accumulated wealth to heirs but for a public investment the expected benefits after death cannot, suggest Crain and Zardkoohi, be capitalised and bequeathed to heirs. Hence citizens would want managers of public firms to use techniques of production with short gestation periods; a similar argument is seen to apply for citizens who may be switching their jurisdiction. This argument however loses some weight to the extent that heirs reside in the same constituency and thereby reap some of the benefits of the public investment and to the extent that other jurisdictions are making similar public investments.
23. An *index* measure of productivity change would be the growth rate of output divided by the growth rate of input which for a discrete change would be measured as r_y/r_x. For the many input/many product case discussed later the index measure is

$$\sum_j v_j r_j \Big/ \sum_i a_i r_i$$

where a_i is the elasticity of output with respect to input x_i and v_j is the elasticity of input with respect to output Y_j, both elasticities being averaged over the old and new output levels. For further discussion of these 'Divisia' measures of growth see Crew, Kleindorfer and Sudit (1979) and Caves and Christensen (1980).
24. Consider for simplicity the case of two inputs (X_1, X_2) yielding one output, Y. The output elasticity of X_1 is

$$a_1 = \frac{\partial Y}{\partial X_1}\frac{X_1}{Y} = \frac{X_1}{Y/\partial Y/\partial X_1}$$

Now the crucial property of constant returns to scale is that the sum of the output elasticities is equal to 1. Intuitively the explanation is that, since the output elasticity of an input is the proportionate response of output to an increase in the input then when all inputs are increased, the proportionate responses of output must add up to unity if constant returns to scale prevail. This property is usually written in the following form:

$$Y = X_1\frac{\partial Y}{\partial X_1} + X_2\frac{\partial Y}{\partial X_2}$$

Substituting in the expression for a_1 and denoting input prices by P_{x1} and P_{x2} yields

$$a_1 = \frac{X_1}{X_1 + X_2\left(\dfrac{\partial Y/\partial X_2}{\partial Y/\partial X_1}\right)} = \frac{X_1 P_{x1}}{X_1 P_{x1} + X_2 P_{x2}\left(\dfrac{\partial Y/\partial X_2}{\partial Y/\partial X_2}\dfrac{P_{x1}}{P_{x2}}\right)}$$

Clearly then the output elasticity a_1 is equal to the share of expenditure on X_1 in total costs if the expression in the last brackets is equal to 1, that is if

$$\frac{\partial Y/\partial X_2}{\partial Y/\partial X_1} = \frac{P_{x2}}{P_{x1}}$$

which is the standard requirement for the least cost input combination, namely that relative input prices equal relative marginal products. Moreover for a firm which is technologically efficient and operating under constant returns to scale, the degree to which it is 'price efficient' with respect to its input choices, is reflected in the degree to which the input's share of total costs corresponds to the output elasticity of that input.

When a firm produces several products (say Y_1 and Y_2), the relevant weight for each product in the productivity growth measures is that product's input elasticity, that is the proportionate increase in the bundle of inputs divided by the proportionate increase in the volume of that product. Under certain circumstances a proxy to that elasticity is the cost elasticity of the product. To show this, it should be recognised that we now have a production function of the following form

$$Y(Y_1, Y_2) = X(X_1, X_2)$$

The input elasticity of product Y_1 is

$$V_1 = \frac{\partial X}{\partial Y_1}\frac{Y_1}{X} = \frac{\partial Y}{\partial Y_1}\frac{Y_1}{Y}$$

If the production function is linearly homogeneous of degree D then

$$Y = \left(X_1\frac{\partial Y}{\partial X_1} + X_2\frac{\partial Y}{\partial X_2}\right)\frac{1}{D}$$

where D is a constant and would be equal to unity for constant returns to scale. Hence

$$Y = \left(X_1 + X_2\frac{\partial Y/\partial X_2}{\partial Y/\partial X_1}\right)\frac{\partial Y/\partial X_1}{D}$$

If the firm is price efficient in its choice of inputs then

$$Y = (X_1 P_{x1} + X_2 P_{x2})\frac{\partial Y/\partial X_1}{D P_{x1}}$$

For small changes in the usage of inputs $\partial Y/X_1$, D and P_{x1} will not change. Hence

$$\frac{\partial Y}{\partial Y_1} = \frac{\partial Y/\partial X_1}{D P_{x1}}\frac{\partial(X_1 P_{x1} + X_2 P_{x2})}{\partial Y_1}$$

Substituting back into the expression for V_1 yields

$$V_1 = \frac{\partial(X_1 P_{x1} + X_2 P_{x2})}{\partial Y_1}\frac{Y_1}{X_1 P_{x1} + X_2 P_{x2}}$$

which is the cost elasticity of product Y_1, that is the proportionate change in total costs divided by the proportionate change in Y_1. When not even cost elasticity data is available the revenue shares of each product can be used as proxies for input elasticities under certain circumstances. The expression for the input elasticity of product Y_1 can be presented as

$$V_1 = \frac{Y_1}{X/\partial X/\partial Y_1}$$

If constant returns to scale prevail, the input elasticities of all the products add up to unity, that is

$$X = Y_1 \frac{\partial X}{\partial Y_1} + Y_2 \frac{\partial X}{\partial Y_2}$$

Substituting into the previous equation yields

$$V_1 = \frac{Y_1}{Y_1 + Y_2\left(\frac{\partial X/\partial Y_2}{\partial X/\partial Y_1}\right)}$$

Denoting the product prices by P_{y1} and P_{y2}, we have

$$V_1 = \frac{Y_1 P_{y1}}{Y_1 P_{y1} + Y_2 P_{y2}\left(\frac{\partial X/\partial Y_2}{\partial X/\partial Y_1}\frac{P_{y1}}{P_{y2}}\right)}$$

Thus the input elasticity of product Y_1 is equal to that product's share of total revenue if relative product prices equal relative marginal product costs, i.e.

$$\frac{\partial X/\partial Y_2}{\partial X/\partial Y_1} = \frac{P_{y2}}{P_{y1}}$$

25. This survey does not presume any prior knowledge of econometric methods. For a good discussion of dummy variables see Stewart (1976) ch. 3–10.
26. The precise calculation that Pryke makes is not entirely clear from chapters 2 and 6 of his book (1971) but a statistical appendix has been available from D Pryke at Liverpool University. It appears that for each sector, such as manufacturing, an *index* of productivity for year t' with year t as base is calculated by

$$\sum_j R_j Y_{jt'} \Big/ Y_{jt} \div \sum S_i X_{it'} \Big/ X_{it}$$

where R_j is the share of value added in manufacturing taken by product j and S_i is the share of total costs taken by input i. These weights appear to be averages from two years, 1954 and 1958 and applied irrespective of the values for t' and t. Apart from that, the index is similar to the ideal index given in footnote 23 with the difference that $r_j = \log(Y_{jt'}/Y_{jt})$ and $r_i = \log(X_{it'}/X_{it})$. The costs of one of the inputs, capital, was estimated by Pryke in a manner analogous to that used by the Polanyis and described in the text of this survey; 10 per cent was the assumed rate of return. The average annual rate of growth of productivity between year t and t' is then calculated as the log of the above index, divided by the number of years between t' and t.
27. For those interested in significance tests, the F and t tests were significant at the 0.01 level for all coefficients except S_3 and D; the latter was significant at the 0.09 level.

Both Neuberg and Meyer estimated, in addition, separate cost equations for public and private and found they were significantly different, using Chow tests.

28. For further discussion of the Pescatrice and Trapani study see Millward (1981).
29. Bearing this in mind, as well as the absence of data on input prices and capital employed, one feels Funkhouser and MacAvoy may have overstated the case in the following observations: 'For the public enterprises in question, higher costs ... cannot be traced either to their operating with different factor input ratios or their desire to provide more output. Indeed it seems that all cost elements in the public firms are higher and it is this phenomenon which requires explanation' (p.366).
30. In the pooled sample all coefficients were significant with t and F tests at the 0.05 level. The cost structures of the two separate samples were found to be significantly different. For further discussion of the Crain and Zardkoohi results see Millward (1981).
31. The cost of contract collection was not significantly different from municipal provision in cities with populations less than 50,000 (quoted in Savas, Policy Analysis 1977). The Pier, Vernon and Wicks study (1974) found public provision to be cheaper but the only variable in their cost function was number of pick-ups.
32. Recall however our earlier observations about changes over time in the relative cost of capital. For further discussion of regulation in the public/private context see Millward (1981).
33. Similarly in his 1975 study, de Alessi had hypothesised that management in public firms would not bargain hard in obtaining selling prices. His results suggested that such public firm prices were some 30 per cent lower than in private firms but he had no explicit cost variable in the equation for selling prices.
34. For the group of public and private firms regulated by state bodies. Where regulation was by city or district there was no significant difference.
35. Whether private utilities were regulated by city rather than district had no significant effect on the profit margin. At the same time, the profit margin of public firms tends to be bigger the lower is the level of the regulatory body, a phenomenon which Pashigian does not discuss and which does need reconciling with the experience of private firms.
36. See the last part of his 1971 article.
37. In what follows their 'best' cost assumption and constant demand elasticities are taken for illustration.
38. See in particular the expectation that management will be inferior in public firms in Alchian (1965:827), Rowley (1977:13), Davies (1971:150), Crain and Zardkoohi (1978:398), Pommerehne and Frey (1977:223), Peltzman (1971:111), de Alessi (May 1974:646, Fall 1974:7, 1977:9).

References and further reading

Ahlbrandt, R. (1973) Efficiency in the provision of fire services, *Public Choice*, **16**, 1–15.

Alchian, A. A. (1959) Private property and the relative cost of tenure, in Bradley, P. D. (ed.), *The Public State in Union Power*, University of Virginia Press: Charlottesville.

Alchian, A. A. and Kessel, R. A. (1962) Competition Monopoly and the Pursuit of Pecuniary Gain, in *Aspects of Labour Economics*, Bureau of Economic Research, Princeton.

Alchian, A. A. (1965a) The basis of some recent advances in the theory of management of the firm, *Journal of Industrial Economics*, **November**, 30–41.

Alchian, A. A. (1965b) Some economics of property rights, *Il Politico*, **30**, 816–29, reprinted in Alchian, A. A., *Economic Forces at Work.*

Alchian, A. A. (1969) Information cost, pricing and resource unemployment, *Western Economic Journal*, **7**, 109–28, reprinted in Alchian, A. A., *Economic Forces at Work.*

Alchian, A. A. (1977a) Corporate management and property rights, in Mann, H. (ed.), *Economic Policy and the Regulation of Corporate Securities*, 227–57, American Enterprise Institute: Washington, reprinted in Alchian, A. A., *Economic Forces at Work.*

Alchian, A. A. (1977b) *Economic Forces at Work*, introduction by Coase, R. H., Liberty Press: Indianapolis.

Alchian, A. A. and Demsetz, H. (1972) Production, information costs and economic organisation, *American Economic Review*, **62**, reproduced in Furubotn, E. G. and Pejovich, S. (1974) and Alchian, A. A., *Economic Forces at Work.*

Alchian, A. A., Klein, B. and Crawford, R. G. (1978) Vertical integration, appropriable rents and the competitive contracting process, *Journal of Law and Economics.*

Amacher, R. C. and Tollison, R. D. (1976) Property rights within government and devices to increase government efficiency, *Public Finance Quarterly*, **4**, 151–8.

Arrow, K. J. (1975) Vertical integration and communication, *Bell Journal of Economics*, **6**, 173–83.

Arrow, K. J. (1964) Control in large organisations, *Management Science*, **10**, 397–408.

Atkinson, A. B. and Stiglitz, J. E. (1980) *Lectures on Public Economics*, McGraw Hill: New York.

Auster, R. (1975) Some economic determinants of the characteristics of public workers, in Leiter, R. D. and Sirkin, G. (eds), *Economics of Public Choice*, **2**, 185–98.

Auster, R. (1978) Shirking in the theory of the firm, *Southern Economic Journal*, **45**, 867–73.

Auster, R. and Morris Silver (1976) Comparative statics of the utility maximising firm, *Southern Economic Journal*, **42**, 626–32.

Averch, H. and Johnson, L. L. (1962) Behaviour of the firm under regulatory constraint, *American Economic Review*, **52**, 1052–69.

Barry, E. E. (1965) *Nationalisation in British Politics: The Historical Background*, Cape.

Baumol, W. J. (1958) On the theory of Oligopoly, *Economica*, **25**, 187–98.

Baumol, W. J. (1959) *Business Behaviour Value and Growth*, Macmillan: London.

Baumol, W. J. (1962) The theory of the expansion of the firm, *American Economic Review*, **52**, 1078–87.

Baumol, W. J. and Bradford, D. (1970) Optimal departures from marginal cost pricing, *American Economic Review*, **60**, 265–83.

Baumol, W. J. and Klevorick, A. K. (1970) Input choices and rate of return regulation: an overview of the discussion, *Bell Journal of Economics*, **1**, 162–90.

Becker, L. C. (1977) *Property Rights: Philosophic Foundations*, Routledge and Kegan: London.

Beesley, M. and Evans, T. (1978) *Corporate Social Responsibility: A Reassessment*, Croom Helm: London.

Bennett, J. T. and Johnson, M. H. (1979) Public versus private provision of collective goods and services: garbage collection revisited, *Public Choice*, **34**, 55–63.

Berle, A. and Means, G. (1933) *The Modern Corporation and Private Property*, Macmillan: London.

Blair, R. D. and Kaserman, D. L. (1980) Vertical control with variable proportions: ownership integration and contractual equivalents, *Southern Economic Journal*, **46**, 1118–28.

Boyes, W. J. and Schlagenhauf (1979) Managerial incentives and the specification of functional forms, *Southern Economic Journal*, **45**, 1225–32.

Brown, S. L. (1978) Earnings, changes, stock prices and market efficiency, *Journal of Finance*, **33**, 17–28.

Buchanan, J. M. et al. (1978) The economics of politics, in *Institute of Economic Affairs Readings*, **18**: London.

Carrol, T. M., Ciscil, D. H. and Chisholm, R. K. (1979) The market as a commons: an unconventional view of property rights, *Journal of Economic Issues*, **13**, 605–27.

Caves, D. W. and Christensen, L. R. (1980) The relative efficiency of public and private firms in a competitive environment: the case of Canadian railroads, *Journal of Political Economy*, **88**, 958–76.

Chester, D. N. (1952) Management and accountability in the nationalised industries, *Public Administration*, **Spring**, 27–47.

Chester, T. E. (1976) The public sector – its dimensions and dynamics, *National Westminster Bank Quarterly Review*, **February**, 31–44.

Cho, J. H. (1977) Moral implications of acquisitive instinct under the separation of ownership and control, *Review of Social Economy*, **35**, 143–8.

Clarkson, K. W. (1972) Some implications of property rights in hospital management, *Journal of Law and Economics*, **15**, 363–84.

Coase, R. H. (1937) The nature of the firm, *Economica*, **November**, 386–405, reproduced in Boulding and Stigler (eds) (1953) *Readings in Price Theory*, and Neel, R. E. (ed.) (1973) *Readings in Price Theory*.

Coelho, P. R. P. (1976) Rules, authorities and the design of not-for-profit firms, *Journal of Economic Issues*, **10**, 416–28.

Cohen, S. I. (1980) Incentives, iterative communications and organisational control, *Journal of Economic Theory*, **22**, 37–55.

Comanor, W. S. and Leibenstein, H. (1969) Allocative efficiency, x-efficiency and the measurement of welfare losses, *Economica*, **36**, 304–9.

Coombes, D. (1971) *State Enterprise: Business or Politics*, Allen and Unwin: London.

Cooper, D. (1977) Some limitations of tests of the effect of control on firm performance, *Revista Internazionale di Scienze Economiche e Commerciali*, **24**, 167–74.

Cooter, R. and Topakian, G. (1980) Political economy of a public corporation: pricing objectives of BART, *Journal of Public Economics*, **13**, 299–318.

Copeland, T. E. and Smith, K. V. (1978) An overview of non-profit organisations, *Journal of Economics and Business*, **30**, 147–54.

Courville, L. (1974) Regulation and efficiency in the electric utility industry, *Bell Journal of Economics*, **5**, 53–74.

Crain, W. M. and Zardkoohi, A. (1978) A test of the property rights theory of the firm: water utilities in the United States, *Journal of Law and Economics*, **40**, 395–408.

Crain, W. M. and Zardkoohi, A. (1980) Public sector expansion: stagnant technology or property rights, *Southern Economic Journal*, **46**, 1069–82.

Crew, M. A. and Kleindorfer, P. R. and Sudit, E. F. (1979) Managerial discretion and public utility regulation, *Southern Economic Journal*, **45**, 696–709.

Crew, M. A. and Sudit, E. F. (1979) Incentives for efficiency in the nationalised industries: beyond the 1978 White Paper, *Journal of Industrial Affairs*, **7**, 11–15.

Crew, M. A. and Rowley, C. K. (1970) Anti-trust policy: economics versus management science, *Moorgate and Wall St. Review*, 19–34.

Cyert, R. M. and Cedrick, C. L. (1972) Theory of the firm, past, present and future: an interpretation, *Journal of Economic Literature*, **10**, 398–412.

Davies, D. G. (1971) The efficiency of public versus private firms: the case of Australia's two airlines, *Journal of Law and Economics*, **14**, 149–65.

Davies, D. G. (1977) Property rights and economic efficiency – the Australian airlines revisited, *Journal of Law and Economics*, **20**, 223–6.

Davies, D. G. (1980) Property rights in a regulated environment: a reply, *Economic Record*, **June**, 186–9.

de Alessi, L. (1969) Implications of property rights for government investment choices, *American Economic Review*, **59**, 13–24.

de Alessi, L. (1974a) Managerial tenure under private and government ownership in the electric power industry, *Journal of Political Economy*, **82**, 645–53.

de Alessi, L. (1974b) An economic analysis of government ownership and regulation: theory and the evidence from the electric power industry, *Public Choice*, **Fall**, 1–42.

de Alessi, L. (1975) Some effects of ownership on the wholesale prices of electric power, *Economic Inquiry*, **13**, 526–38.

de Alessi, L. (1977) Ownership and peak-load pricing in the electric power industry, *The Quarterly Review of Economics and Business*, **17**, 7–26.

Dean, A. J. H. (1975) Earnings in the public and private sectors, *National Institute Economic Review*, **74**, 60–70.

Dean, A. J. H. (1977) Public and private sector manual workers pay 1970–77, *National Institute Economic Review*, **82**, 62–66.

Demsetz, H. (1964) The exchange and enforcement of property rights, *Journal of Law and Economics*, **7**, 11–26.

Demsetz, H. (1966) Some aspects of property rights, *Journal of Law and Economics*, **9**, 61–70.

Demsetz, H. (1967) Toward a theory of property rights, *American Economic Review,* **57**, 347 59.

Demsetz, H. (1968) Why regulate utilities?, *Journal of Law and Economics*, **11**, 55–65, in Rowley, C. K. (ed.) (1972), *Readings in Industrial Economics*, **2**, 173–86.

Demsetz, H. (1969) Information and efficiency: another viewpoint, *Journal of Law and Economics*, **12**, 1–22.

Downs, A. (1967) *Inside Bureaucracy*, Little Brown: Boston.

Edwards, F. R. and Stevens, B. J. (1978) The provision of municipal sanitation services by private firms: an empirical analysis of the efficiency of alternative market structures and regulatory arrangements, *The Journal of Industrial Economics*, **27**, 133–47.

Elliott, R. F. (1977) Public sector wage movements, *Scottish Journal of Political Economy,* **24**, 133–51.

Fama, E. F. (1980) Agency problems and the theory of the firm, *Journal of Political Economy*, **88**, 288–307.

Farrell, M. J. (1957) The measurement of production efficiency, *Journal of the Royal Statistical Society*, series A, **120**, 253–81.

Florestano, P. S. and Gordon, S. B. (1980) Public versus private: small government contracting with the private sector, *Public Administration Review*, **Jan/Feb.**, 29–34.

Forsyth, P. J. and Hocking, R. D. (1980) Property rights and efficiency in a regulated environment: the case of Australian airlines, *Economic Record*, **June**, 182–5.

Fosler, R. S. (1978) State and local government productivity and the private sector, *Public Administration Review*, **38**, 22–27.

Foster, C. D. (1971) *Politics, Finance and the Role of Economics*, Allen and Unwin: London.

Funkhouser, R. and MacAvoy, P. W. (1979) A sample of observations on comparative prices in public and private enterprise, *Journal of Public Economics*, **11**, 353–68.

Furniss, N. (1978) Property rights and democratic socialism, *Political Studies*, **26**, 450–61.

Furubotn, E. G. and Pejovich, S. (1972) Property rights and economic theory: a survey of recent literature, *Journal of Economic Literature*, **December**, 1137–62 and in Fels, R. and Siegfried, J. S. (eds), *Recent Advances in Economics: A Book of Readings*, Irwin: London.

Furubotn, E. G. and Pejovich, S. (1974) *Economics of Property Rights*, Ballinger Pub. Company: Cambridge, Mass.

Gay, D. E. R. (1978) Property rights and the theory of the firm under Hungary's new economic mechanism, 1968–73, *Rivista Internazionale de Scienze Economiche e Commerciali*, **25**, 1021–8.

Glassman, C. A. and Rhoades, S. A. (1980) Owners versus manager control effects on bank performance, *Review of Economics and Statistics*, **62**, 263–70.

Goldberg, V. P. (1974a) Public choice – property rights, *Journal of Economic Issues*, **8**, 555–79.

Goldberg, V. P. (1974b) Protecting the right to be served by public utilities, *Research in Law and Economics*, **1**.

Gordon, R. A. (1961) *Business Leadership in the Large Corporation*, CUP: London.

Grabowski, H. G. and Mueller, D. C. (1975) Life-cycle effects of corporate returns on retention. *Review of Economics and Statistics*, **57**, 400–9.

Gravelle, H. S. (1976) Public enterprises under rate of return financial targets, *The Manchester School of Economic and Social Studies*, **44**, 1–16.

Gravelle, H. S. E. and Katz, E. (1976) Financial targets and x-efficiency in public enterprise, *Public Finance*, **31**, 218–34.

Gunderson, M. (1979) Earnings differentials between public and private sectors, *Canadian Journal of Economics*, **12**, 228–42.

Hamermesh, D. S. (1975) The effect of government ownership on union wages, in Hamermesh, D. S. (ed). *Labour in the Public and Non-Public Sectors*, Princeton University Press: Princeton.

Harris, M. and Raviv, A. (1978) Some results on incentive contracts with application to education, employment, health, insurance and law enforcement, *American Economic Review*, **68**, 20–30.

Hawkesworth. R. I. (1976) Public and private sector pay, *British Journal of Industrial Relations*, **14**, 206–13.

HMSO (1961) *The Financial and Economic Obligations of the Nationalised Industries*, Cmnd. **1337**.

HMSO (1968) *Ministerial Control of the Nationalised Industries*, HC **371**.

HMSO (1967) *Nationalised Industries: A Review of Economic and Financial Objectives*, Cmnd. **3437**.

HMSO (1975) *The Nationalisation of British Industry 1945–1951*, Sir Norman Chester.

HMSO (1976) *A Study of UK Nationalised Industries: A Report to the Government by the National Economic Development Office*.

HMSO (1978) *The Nationalised Industries*, Cmnd. **7131**.

Hirsch, W. Z. (1965) Cost functions of the urban government service: refuse collection, *Review of Economics and Statistics*, **47**, 87–92.

Hirshleifer, J. (1973) Where are we in the theory of information?, *American Economic Review*, **63**, 31–9.

Hirshleifer, J. and Milliman, J. W. (1967) Urban water supply: a second look, *American Economic Review*, **58**, 169–78.

Hurwicz, L. (1973) The design of mechanisms for resource allocation, *American Economic Review*, **63**, 1–30.

Jacob, N. L. and Page, A. N. (1980) Production, information costs and economic organisation, *American Economic Review*, **70**, 476–78.

Jensen, M. C. and Meckling, W. H. (1976) Theory of the firm: managerial behaviour, agency costs and ownership structure, *Journal of Financial Economics*, **3**, 305–57.

Kania, J. J. and McKean, R. N. (1976) Ownership, control and the contemporary corporation: a general behaviour analysis, *Kyklos*, **29**, 272–91.

Kaysen, C. (1965) Another view of corporate capitalism, *Quarterly Journal of Economics*, **79**, 51–51.

Keating, B. (1979) Prescriptions for efficiency in non-profit firms, *Applied Economics*, **2**, 321–32.

Keating, B. and Keating M. A. (1975) A non-profit firm model, *Atlantic Economic Journal*, **3**, 36.

Kessler, F. and Stern, R. N. (1959) Competition contract and vertical integration, *Yale Law Journal*, **69**, 1–129.

Kitchen, H. M. (1976) A statistical estimation of an operating cost function for municipal refuse collection, *Public Finance Quarterly*, **4**, 56–76.

Klein, B., Crawford, R. G. and Alchian, A. A. (1978) Vertical integration, appropriable rents and the competitive contracting process, *Journal of Law and Economics*, **21**, 297–326.

Kleindorfer, P. R. and Sertel, M. R. (1979) Profit maximising design of enterprises through incentives, *Journal of Economic Theory*, **21**, 318–39.

Koutsoyiannis, A. (1978) Managerial job security and the capital structure of the firm, *Manchester School*, **46**, 51–75.

Kuehn, D. (1975) *Takeovers and the Theory of the Firm: An Empirical Analysis for the United Kingdom 1957–1969*, Macmillan: London.

Lanzillotti, R. F. (1958) Pricing objectives in large companies, *American Economic Review*, **48**, 921–40.

Leavitt, H. J. (1978) *Managerial Psychology: An Introduction to Individuals, Pairs and Groups*, 4th edn, University of Chicago Press.

Lecraw, D. S. (1977) Empirical tests for x-efficiency: a note, *Kyklos*, **30**, 116–20.

Leibenstein, H. (1975) Aspects of the x-efficiency theory of the firm, *Bell Journal of Economics and Management Science*, **6**, 580–606.

Leibenstein, H. (1966) Allocative efficiency versus x-efficiency, *American Economic Review*, **June**, 392–415.

Leibenstein, H. (1972) Comment on the nature of x-efficiency, *Quarterly Journal of Economics*, **86**, 327–31.

Leibenstein, H. (1976) *Beyond Economic Man: A New Foundation for Microeconomics*, Harvard University Press: Cambridge, Massachusetts and London.

Leibenstein, H. (1978) X-inefficiency xists – a reply to an xorcist, *American Economic Review*, **68**, 203–11.

Leibenstein, H. (1978) On the basic proposition of x-efficiency theory, *American Economic Review, Papers and Proceedings*, **68**, 238–32.

Leibenstein, H. (1979) A branch of economics is mission: micro-macro theory, *Journal of Economic Literature*, **17**, 477–502.

Lindsay, C. M. (1976) A theory of government enterprise, *Journal of Political Economy*, **84**, 1061–77.

McCain, R. A. (1975) Competition, information, redundancy: x-efficiency and the cybernetics of the firm, *Kyklos*, **28**, 286–308.

McEachern, W. A. (1976) The managerial revolution and corporate performance, *Challenge*, **19**, 36–40.

McEachern, W. A. (1978) Ownership, control and the contemporary corporation: a comment, *Kyklos*, **31**, 491–6.

McGuire, M. (1972) Private good clubs and public good clubs: economic models of group formation, *Swedish Journal of Economics*, 85–9.

McGuire, M., Chiu, J. S. Y. and Elbing, A. O. (1962) Executive income, sales and profits, *American Economic Review*, **52**, 753–61.

McKean, R. N. (1965) The unseen hand in government, *American Economic Review*, **55**, 496–505.

McKean, R. N. (1972) Property rights within government and devices to increase government efficiency, *Southern Economic Journal*, **39**, 177–86.

McManus, J. C. (1976) The costs of alternative organisations, *Canadian Journal of Economics*, **9**, 334–50.

McNeil, I. R. (1974) The many futures of contracts, *Southern California Law Review*, **47**, 691–816.

Mann, P. C. (1970) Publicly owned electric utility profits and resource allocation, *Land Economics*, **46**, 478–83.

Mann, P. C. (1974) User power and electricity rates, *Journal of Law and Economics*, **17**, 433–43.

Mann, P. C. and Seifried, E. J. (1972) Pricing in the case of publicly owned electric utilities, *Quarterly Review of Economics and Business*, **12**, 77–89.

Marks, M. (1980) State and private enterprise, *The Business Economist*, **11**, 3–16.

Marris, R. (1963) A model of the 'managerial' enterprise, *Quarterly Journal of Economics*, **77**, 185–209.

Marris, R. (1964) *The Economic Theory of Managerial Capitalism*, Macmillan: London.

Marris, R. and Mueller, D. C. (1980) The corporation, competition and the invisible hand, *Journal of Economic Literature*, **18**, 32–63.

Marschak, J. and Radner, R. (1972) *The Economic Theory of Teams*, Yale.

Martin, J. E. (1976) Applications of a model from the private sector to federal sector labour relations, *Quarterly Review of Economics and Business*, **16**, 69–78.

Meeks, G. and Whittington, G. (1975) Directors pay, growth and profitability, *Journal of Industrial Economics*, **24**, 1–14.

Meyer, R. A. (1975) Publicly owned versus privately owned utilities: a policy choice, *Review of Economics and Statistics*, **57**, 391–99.

Millward, R. (1976) Prices and incomes policy and the UK nationalised industries, in Laidler, D. E. W. (ed.), *Study on the Possible Part Played by Certain Primary Non-Employment Incomes in the Inflationary Process in the UK*, Commission of the European Communities, Medium Term Economic Policy Series, **6**, 124–81.

Millward, R. (1976) Price restraint, anti-inflation policy and public and private industry in the UK, *Economic Journal*, **86**, 226–42.

Millward, R. (1978) Public ownership, the theory property rights and the public corporation in the UK, *Salford Papers in Economics 78–1*.

Millward, R. (1982) The comparative performance of public and private ownership, in Lord Eric Roll (ed.), *The Mixed Economy*, Macmillan: London.

Mirrlees, J. (1976) The optimal structure of incentives and authority within an organisation, *Bell Journal of Economics*, **7**, 105–31.

Mitnick, B. M. (1975) The theory of agency: the policing paradox and regulatory behaviour, *Public Choice*, **24**, 27–42.

Monsen, R. J. Jr. and Downs, A. (1965) A theory of large managerial firms, *Journal of Political Economy*, **73**, 221–36.

Monsen, R. J. Jr., Chiu, J. A. and Cooley, D. E. (1968) The effect of separation of ownership and control on the performance of the large firm, *Quarterly Journal of Economics*, **82**, 435–51.

Moore, T. G. (1970) The effectiveness of regulation of electric utility prices, *Southern Economic Journal*, **36**, 365–75.

Morrison, H. (1933) *Socialisation and Transport*, Constable & Co.: London.

Mueller, D. C. (1976) Public choice: a survey, *Journal of Economic Literature*, **14**, 395–433.

Munkirs, J. R., Ayers, M. and Grandys, A. (1976) Rape of the ratepayer: monopoly overcharges in the 'regulated' electric utility industry, *Anti-trust Law and Economics Review*, 57–68.

Nelson, J. R. (ed.) (1964) *Marginal Cost Pricing in Practise*, Prentice-Hall: London.

Neuberg, L. G. (1977) Two issues in the municipal ownership of electric power distribution systems, *Bell Journal of Economics*, **8**, 303–23.

Niskanen, W. A. (1971) *Bureaucracy and Representative Government*, Aldine–Atherton: New York.

Nyman, S. and Silberston, A. (1978) The ownership and control of industry, *Oxford Economic Papers*, **30**, 74–101.

Ostergaard, G. N. (1954) Labour and the development of the public corporation, *The Manchester School*, **22**, 192–226.

Owen, G. (1979) Stopping the rot in companies, *Financial Times*, **27 Sept.**, 22.

Palmer, J. (1973) The profit performance effects of the separation of ownership from control in large US industrial corporations, *Bell Journal of Economics*, **4**, 293–303.

Park, Y. J. (1979) On x-efficiency and output differences, *Rivista Internazionale di Scienze Economiche e Commerciali*, **26**, 73–83.

Pashigian, B. P. (1976) Consequences and causes of public ownership of urban transit, *Journal of Political Economy*, **84**, 1239–59.

Peel, D. A. (1973) Some implications of utility maximising firms: a note, *Bulletin of Economic Research*, **25**, 148–51.

Peltzman, S. (1971) Pricing in public and private enterprises and electric utilities in the United States, *Journal of Law and Economics*, **14**, 109–47.

Pescatrice, D. R. and Trapani, J. M. III (1980) The performance and objectives of public and private utilities operating in the US, *Journal of Public Economics*, **13**, 259–75.

Pier, W. J., Vernon, R. B. and Wicks, J. H. (1974) An empirical comparison of government and private production efficiency, *National Tax Journal*, **27**, 653–6.

Polanyi, G. and Polanyi, P. (1972) The efficiency of nationalised industries, *Moorgate and Wall Street Review*, **Spring**, 27–49.

Polanyi, G. and Polanyi, P. (1974) *Failing the Nation: The Record of the Nationalised Industries*, Fraser Ansbacher Limited: London.

Pommerehne, W. M. and Frey, B. S. (1977) Public versus private production efficiency in Switzerland: a theoretical and empirical comparison, *Urban Affairs Annual Review*, **12**, 221–41.

Prescott, E. C. and Visscher, M. (1980) Organisation capital, *Journal of Political Economy*, **88**, 446–61.

Primeaux, W. J. (1977) An assessment of x-efficiency gained through competition, *Review of Economics and Statistics*, **59**, 105–8.

Primeaux, W. J. (1978) The effect of competition on capacity utilisation in the electric utility industry, *Economic Inquiry*, **April**.

Pryke, R. (1971) *Public Enterprise in Practice*, MacGibbon and Kee: London.

Pryke, R. (1981) *The Nationalised Industries: Policies and Performance since 1968*, Martin Robertson.

Radice, H. K. (1971) Control type, profitability and growth in large firms: an empirical study, *Economic Journal*, **81**, 547–62.

Radner, R. (1972) Teams, in McGuire, C. B. and Radner, R. (eds), *Decision and Organisation: A Volume in Honour of Jacob Marschak*, ch.10, North-Holland: Amsterdam.

Radner, R. and Rothschild, M. (1975) on the allocation of effect, *Journal of Economic Theory*, **10**, 358–76.

Rees, R. (1974) A reconsideration of the expense preference theory of the firm, *Economica*, **41**, 295–307.

Rees, R. (1976) *Public Enterprise Economics*, Weidenfeld and Nicholson, London.

Richardson, H. (1973) On public ownership, *New Society*, **28 June**, 748–9.

Robson, W. A. (1962) *Nationalised Industry and Public Ownership*, 2nd Edition, Allen and Unwin: London.

Ross, S. A. (1973) The economic theory of agency: the principal's problem, *American Economic Review*, **62**, 134–9.

Round, D. K. (1976) The effect of the separation of ownership and control on large firm profit rates in Australia: an exploratory investigation, *Revista Internazionale di Scienze Economiche e Commerciali*, **23**, 426–35.

Rowley, C. K. (1980) Industrial policy in the mixed economy, British Association for the Advancement of Science, Salford, in Lord Eric Roll, (ed.), *The Mixed Economy*, Macmillan: London.

Rowley, C. K. (1971) *Steel and Public Policy*, McGraw-Hill, London.

Rowley, C. K. (1976) The x-efficiency factor, *New Society*, **15 January**, 97–8.

Rowley, C. K. (1977) Efficiency in the public sector, paper 2 in Bowe, C. (ed.), *Industrial Efficiency and the Role of Government*, Department of Industry, HMSO: London.

Rubin, P. H. (1973) The expansion of firms, *Journal of Political Economy*, **81**, 936–49.

Rubin, P. H. (1978) The theory of the firm and the structure of the franchise contract, *Journal of Law and Economics*, **21**, 223–33.

Samuels, W. J. (ed.) (1976) *The Chicago School of Political Economy*, Michigan State University: Michigan.

Samuels, W. J. and Mercuro, N. (1976) Property rights, equity and public utility pricing, in Trebing, H. M. (ed.), *New Dimensions in Public Utility Pricing*, MUS Public Utility Studies, Michigan State University: Michigan.

Sandler, T. (1975) The challenge of property rights, the human prospect discussion, *Futures*, **7**, 523–25.

Sandler, T. and Cawley, T. (1980) A hierarchical theory of the firm, *Scottish Journal of Political Economy*, **27**, 17–29.

Savas, E. S. (1974) Municipal monopolies versus competition in delivery of urban services, in Hawley, W. D. and Rogers, D. (eds), *Improving the Quality of Urban Management*, Saga Publications: Beverly Hills, California, 473–500.

Savas, E. S. (1977) An empirical study of competition in municipal service delivery, *Public Administration Review*, **Nov/Dec**, 717–24.

Savas, E. S. (1977) Policy analysis for local government: public versus private refuse collection, *Policy Analysis*, **3**, 49–74.

Schmid, A. A. (1976) The economics of property rights: a review article, *Journal of Economic Issues*, **10**, 159–68.

Shapiro, D. L. (1973) Can public investment have a positive rate of return?, *Journal of Political Economy*, **81**, 401–13.

Silver, M. and Auster, R. (1969) Entrepreneurship, profit and limits on firm size, *Journal of Business*, **42**.

Simon, J. L. (1968) State Liquor Monopolies, in Turvey, R. (ed.), *Public Enterprise: Selected Readings*, Penguin: Harmondsworth, 365–77.

Singh, A. (1975) Take-overs, national selection and the theory of the firm: evidence from the post-war UK experience, *Economic Journal*, **85**, 497–515.

Smiley, R. (1976) Tender offers, transactions costs and the theory of the firm, *Review of Economics and Statistics*, **58**, 22–32.

Smith, S. (1975/6) Pay differentials between federal government and private sector workers, *Industrial and Labour Relations Review*, **29**, 179–97.

Spann, R. M. (1974) Rate of return regulation and efficiency in production: an empirical test of the Averch-Johnson thesis, *Bell Journal of Economics*, **5**, 38–52.

Spann, R. M. (1977) Public versus private provision of government services, in Borcherding, T. (ed.), *Budgets and Bureaucrats: The Sources of Government Growth*, Duke University Press: Durham NC.

Spence, A. M. (1975) The economics of internal organisation, *Bell Journal of Economics*, **6**, 163–72.

Stein, B. A. (1976) Collective ownership, property rights, and control of the corporation, *Journal of Economic Issues*, **10**, 298–313.

Stewart, J. (1976) *Understanding Econometrics*, Hutchinson: London.

Stigler, G. J. (1951) The division of labour is limited by the extent of the market, *Journal of Political Economy*, **59**, 185–93.

Stigler, G. J. (1961) The economics of information, *Journal of Political Economy*, **69**, 213–25.

Stigler, G. J. (1971) The theory of economic regulation, *Bell Journal of Economics*, **2**, 3–21.

Stigler, G. J. (1976) The xistence of x-efficiency, *American Economic Review*, **66**, 213–6.

Stigler, G. J. and Friedland, C. (1962) What can regulators regulate? The case of electricity, *Journal of Law and Economics*, **5**, 1–16.

Stiglitz, J. E. (1975) Incentives risk and information: notes towards a theory of hierarchy, *Bell Journal of Economics*, **6**, 552–79.

Sullivan, T. G. (1977) A note on market power and returns to stockholders, *Review of Economics and Statistics*, **59**, 108–13.

Tawney, R. H. (1921) *The Acquisitive Society*, G. Bell & Sons: London.

Tivey, L. (1978) *The Politics of the Firm*, Martin Robertson: London.

Trebing, H. M. (1976) The Chicago school versus public utility regulation, *Journal of Economic Issues*, **10**, 97–126.

Tulkens, H. (1976) The Publicness of public enterprise, in Shepherd, W. G. (ed.), *Public Enterprise: Economic Analysis of Theory and Practice*, Lexington Books: Lexington.

Tullock, G. (1965) *The Politics of Bureaucracy*, Public Affairs Press: Washington DC.

Tullock, G. (1971) Public decisions on public goods, *Journal of Political Economy*, **79**, 913–28.

Turvey, R. (ed.) (1968) *Public Enterprise Economics*, Penguin: Harmondsworth.

Turvey, R. (1968) *Optimal Pricing and Investment in Electricity Supply*, Allen and Unwin: London.

Wallace, R. L. and Junk, P. E. (1970) Economic inefficiency of small municipal electricity generating systems, *Land Economics*, **46**, 98–104.

Weisbrod, B. A. (1978) The forgotten economic sector: private but non-profit, *Challenge*, **21**, 32–6.

Williamson, O. E. (1963a) Managerial discretion and business behaviour, *American Economic Review*, **53**, 1032–57, reprinted in Furubotn and Pejovich (1974).

Williamson, O. E. (1963b) A model of rational managerial behaviour, in Cyert, R. M. and March, J. G. (eds), *A Behavioural Theory of the Firm*, Prentice-Hall: Englewood Cliffs, NJ.

Williamson, O. E. (1964) *The Economics of Discretionary Behaviour, Managerial Objectives in a Theory of the Firm*, Prentice-Hall: Englewood Cliffs, NJ.

Williamson, O. E. (1970) *Corporate Control and Business Behaviour*, Prentice-Hall: Englewood Cliffs, NJ.

Williamson, O. E. (1971) The vertical integration of production: market failure considerations, *American Economic Review Papers and Proceedings*, **61**, 112–23.

Williamson, O. E. (1973) Organisational forms and internal efficiency. Markets and hierarchies: some elementary considerations, *American Economic Review, Papers and Proceedings*, **May**, 316–25.

Williamson, O. E. (1975) *Markets and Hierarchies: Analysis and Antitrust Implications: A Study in the Economics of Internal Organisation*, Free Press: London.

Williamson, O. E. (1976a) The modern corporation as an efficiency instrument, in Pejovich, S. (ed.), *Government Controls and the Free Market: The US Economy in the 1970s*, Texas Press, 163–94.

Williamson, O. E. (1976b) The economics of internal organisation: exit and voice in relation to markets and hierarchies, *American Economic Review*, **66**, 369–77.

Williamson, O. E. (1977) Firms and markets, in Weintraub, S. (ed.), *Modern Economic Thought*, University of Pennsylvania Press, Blackwell, ch.10, 185–202.

Williamson, O. E. (1979) Transaction cost economics: the governance of contractual relations, *Journal of Law and Economics*, **22**, 233–61.

Williamson, O. E., Wachter, M. L. and Harris, J. E. (1975) Understanding the employment relation: the analysis of idiosyncratic exchange, *Bell Journal of Economics*, **6**, 250–78.

Young, D. R. (1974) The economic organisation of refuse collection, *Public Finance Quarterly*, **2**, 43–72.

Yunker, J. A. (1975) Economic performance of public and private enterprise: the case of US electric utilities, *Journal of Economics and Business*, **28**, 60–67.

[24]

Measuring the Performance of State-Owned Enterprises

INTRODUCTION

Are SOEs more or less efficient than private enterprises? If SOEs are less efficient, what are the systematic determinants of this difference? The efficiency of SOEs is an important issue since greater efficiency of the SOEs is a pure gain to the economy rather than a transfer. The larger the share of SOEs in the economy, the more salient is the gain from increased efficiency. Jones (1981c), assuming that there is room for at least 5 percent overall improvement in efficiency, has calculated the resulting efficiency bonus. For example, a 5 percent increase in SOE sector efficiency was about 1 percent of GDP in 1980/81 in Pakistan. If these additional funds were transferred to the government, it would provide revenue equal to 53 percent of direct taxes, or 82 percent of all foreign grant assistance. Stated differently, this efficiency bonus would be enough to finance a 46 percent increase in total government expenditures on education.

Using the same calculations, in Egypt, e.g., such an increase in SOE efficiency is equal to an increase of about 5 percent of GDP, and if these additional funds were transferred to the government, they would provide revenue equal to 75 percent of all direct taxes, or enough to triple governmental expenditure on education. A 5 percent increase in SOE efficiency amounts to 1.7 percent of GDP in South Korea (Jones, 1981c); almost 2 percent of GDP in Turkey, or 10 percent of tax revenue; 1.5 percent of GDP in Tanzania, enough to finance all its spending on health; 1.4 percent of GDP in Bolivia, 14 percent of its tax revenue, and 2.2 percent of GDP in Mali, twice the expenditure on health (World Bank, 1983, p. 75). A 5 percent increase in turnover of Zambia's manufacturing holding company would free resources equal to almost 90 percent of the country's expenditures on education (Shirley, 1983, p. 17).

The assumption of a 5 percent increase in overall efficiency implies improved capital utilization as well as more efficient use of intermediate inputs and labor. Jones (1981c) argues that this gain in efficiency may be attained by installing an appropriate signaling system that will guide managers to act in the interest of society as a whole. Such a system, according to Jones, is composed of two major components. The first is a *performance evaluation* system in which national goals are translated into explicit enterprise objectives and quantified in a performance criterion. The second is an *incentive system* in which managerial welfare is linked to national welfare by a pecuniary or non-pecuniary bonus system based on achievement of particular target values of the criterion variables.

In reality, signaling systems of SOEs are usually woefully inappropriate and inadequate, creating negative and unintentional results. Problems in the signaling system stem from several inherent characteristics of SOEs, discussed in Chapter 4. These enterprises are hybrids, expected to achieve multiple economic, social and political goals without any clear and agreed on trade-offs among them. SOEs have plural principals, or different control organs, with different perceptions of what the priorities in achieving different goals should be. The ambiguity caused by the plethora of goals and the plural principals allows both controllers and managers to pursue objectives they see as important and makes an objective performance evaluation extremely difficult, if not impossible. If goals cannot be specified, there is no way to judge performance.

The problem is compounded by the fact that an SOE can be evaluated by numerous possible criteria of success. The success of the firm can be rated by measuring its internal efficiency. Alternatively, the SOE may be judged by its contribution to goals such as social welfare, economic growth, employment creation, social equity or workers' satisfaction. Differences of opinion about goals to be pursued may lead to different evaluation of SOEs' performance.

The efficiency of private firms and SOEs may be compared on several levels. First, efficiency of socialist countries and capitalist countries may be compared. If socialist countries have established a more efficient mode of production, this will affect the macro results for the economy as a whole. Second, efficiency of the SOE sector in a mixed economy may be measured. Third, and more relevant to this book, the efficiency of SOEs and privately owned firms in a similar setting within a mixed economy may be compared. Finally, it is necessary to establish the reasons for whatever systematic differences in efficiency are found. Before attending to these tasks, however, it is necessary to define terms such as *efficiency* or *performance* in order to have agreed-upon criteria for performance measurement.

THE ECONOMIST'S CRITERIA FOR PERFORMANCE

Economists focus mainly on efficiency as a criterion for performance. There are basically three types of efficiency. Internal efficiency is defined as the ratio of outputs (the products) to the inputs (resources used in production). If the firm can create more outputs with the same inputs or the same outputs with less inputs, it increases efficiency. In neoclassical economic theory, the concern is with allocative efficiency, and the firm is expected to be always efficient in the sense defined here—namely, to be on the production frontier. Under certain assumptions about the technology of production and the preferences of individuals, the market price mechanism works in achieving the efficiency conditions in which marginal cost is equal to price and Pareto optimum is achieved. Allocative efficiency requires, of course, that the social costs of producing a given level of output desired by consumers be at a minimum. The second type of efficiency is *dynamic efficiency:* measuring the rate of change of output per unit of input. Thus, an economy is *production-efficient* if the supply of any good or service cannot be increased without reducing the supply of some other good, including all possibilities of foreign trade. Allocative efficiency requires also that it is impossible to make anyone better off without making someone worse off; in addition to production efficiency, all final consumers must have exhausted all possibilities of mutually beneficial exchange.

Leibenstein (1966) pointed out, quite correctly, that firms do not always operate under these conditions. As a result of motivational factors within the firm, motivational factors from external sources and nonmarket input efficiency, firms may be what he termed *x-inefficient*.

The degree of x-inefficiency may be defined as the difference between maximum and actual effectiveness in the utilization of inputs. The theory of x-efficiency is more akin to managerial theories because it assumes that effort of individuals is a discretionary variable, that no identity of interests exists between the firm and individuals, that rationality is selective and that individual motivation is a significant variable.

Most observers believe that x-inefficiency is more prevalent in SOEs; that is, they are less efficient than they could have been if all possible variations of individual and collective motivational structures had been exhausted. In Pakistan, the Chamber of Commerce and Industry claimed, "Briefly, the taken over industries are caught in the whirlwind of spiraling costs and expenses, pinpointing the gross negligence in controlling and checking them" (1979, p. 27, quoted in Jones, 1981c, p. II-5).

One way for SOEs to be efficient is to guide them along the commercial principles discussed in Chapter 4. If SOEs operate in perfectly competitive markets, the ubiquitous competitive process will lead each SOE to an efficient use of resources. In fact, under perfect competition conditions, with many buyers and sellers and perfect and costless information, managers do not have any discretion. In real life, managers do have discretion, markets are less than perfect and uncertainty is ubiquitous. Still, many economists would argue that the bulk of the services to society of non-monopolist SOEs comes through their commercial activities. Therefore, their performance must be evaluated like private enterprises, and their managers should be compensated according to their success in achieving the measures agreed on. It is also argued that a lack of commercial discipline is dangerous. As one student of SOEs put it: "If the public comes to regard the railways or any other nationalized industry as a special service which can and should be subsidized year after year from the taxpayers' money, then there will not be the slightest prospect of achieving financial solvency. . . . a concerted attempt to scotch this pernicious idea should be made" (Robson, 1962, p. 288).

A more realistic situation for many SOEs is that of *monopoly*. In this case, a profit-maximizing firm knows that the more it sells, the more it drives the price down. It will prefer to restrict output to the point where its marginal revenue equals marginal costs. At that point, prices are higher than marginal cost. This means inefficient use of resources and reducing consumers' welfare.

Economists expect SOEs to maximize social welfare, not profits. It follows that one must have a definition of welfare from which the behavior of the enterprise must be determined and its performance assessed. This behavior is operationally defined by economists in terms of the prices to be charged by the enterprise and guidelines for investment decisions. As Bös (1981) argues, "pricing of publicly supplied goods is the primary vehicle for embedding public enterprises adequately into a market economy" (p. 1). Welfare is defined, in terms of the theory of benefit–cost analysis, as the difference between social benefits and social costs. Social benefits are equal to the benefit to the SOE, measured by its revenues plus the consumer surplus.* Consumer surplus is measured in the benefit–cost analysis by the consumers' willingness to pay. Empirically, it is not very easy to calculate willingness to pay—and therefore consumers' surplus—and the analysis is fraught with many difficult theoretical questions such as the empirical estimates of external effects, intangibles, the choice of optional rate of time preference or rate of opportunity costs. Therefore, before continuing, it is important to estimate the size of the welfare losses. Technically, the question is that of the quantitative importance of allocative efficiency measured by the difference between marginal cost pricing and that of profit maximization.

*There is a debate among economists about whether one should use the Marshallian consumer surplus or the Hicksian consumer surplus. In the first, individual income is held constant. In the second, individual utilities are held constant. Since individual utilities cannot be measured empirically, applied economists tend to use Marshallian concepts, in an attempt to measure the area under the market demand curve.

Economists have attempted to measure the welfare losses resulting from resource misallocation because of monopolistic structure and conduct. Harberger (1954), by making a number of simplifying assumptions, estimated these losses in the U.S. manufacturing sector to be less than 0.1 percent of GNP. Several other empirical studies confirmed these results (Schwartzman, 1960; Worcester, 1973). At least two others, however (Kamerschen, 1966; Cowling and Mueller, 1978), estimated that the welfare losses were in the range of 4 to 7 percent, and Harberger's results were criticized on various grounds (Bergson, 1973; Cowling and Mueller, 1978). Most writers on this subject assess welfare losses from monopoly by summing a series of partial equilibrium estimates. Kay (1983), using a general equilibrium framework, found that the size of welfare loss depends on the weight given consumption because the consumer buys the consumption goods but sells labor. More fundamentally, he found the bounds within which welfare losses to lie to be very wide. He concluded that "there is sufficient rationale for anti-trust policies. The test of the utility of the fire brigade is not whether fire losses are large but whether they would be large if fire proceeded unchecked" (Kay, 1983, p. 331).

Whether or not welfare loss is significant, one would certainly like to avoid it in the case of SOEs. The loss of the efficient allocation merits cannot be rectified by imposing financial targets or profit-limit rules. These rules are not necessary or sufficient to guide allocation toward efficient patterns. In this case, economists developed the so-called marginal cost pricing rule: efficient allocation requires that the monopolist public utility should price its output at marginal costs. Any deviations of price from marginal cost must entail some welfare loss. Unfortunately, marginal costs are extremely hard to define and measure because there are differences between short-run and long-run marginal costs, marginal costs are different for each gradation of time horizon and it is extremely difficult to allocate joint costs (e.g., among bus lines) or to compare marginal costs of different technologies (coal and oil in electricity generation) (see Nelson, 1964; Shanks, 1963, pp. 56–71). Thus, given present knowledge, a good portion of the theoretical solution is not amenable to practical application (see, e.g., Nove, 1973, Turvey, 1971).

Even if marginal costs can be calculated—e.g., for the peakload in electricity—the marginal cost pricing rule means that the SOE will lose; since costs are declining, marginal costs are less than average cost. These losses may be covered by cross subsidization among different units or by subsidies from the treasury. Even if we neglect the practical problems involved, direct subsidies have to be paid ultimately through taxes, and taxation may have its own distortion effects on efficiency. A host of alternative pricing rules, including two-part and multipart tariffs, has been developed in response to the recognition that adherence to marginal cost pricing sometimes yields operating deficits (Turvey, 1971; Reed, 1973).

Further, marginal cost pricing may not lead to allocation efficiency. Remember that the rationale for this method was that other sectors of the economy are perfectly competitive and charge marginal costs. However, if prices exceed marginal costs in other parts of the economy, using marginal cost pricing for the monopoly may not be justified. This situation leads to the theory of second best (Lipsey and Lancaster, 1956/1957), since elimination of distortions in one market might not advance welfare if distortions existed elsewhere in the system. Any deviation of an SOE's prices from marginal cost can be interpreted as an implicit subsidy or tax. Therefore, SOEs' pricing rules are a special case of the design of a set of optimal taxes on all sectors (Atkinson and Stiglitz, 1980; Diamond and Mirrless, 1971).

Finally, prices and costs may misrepresent true social costs and benefits since they do not take into account externalities. If cost is reduced by discharging pollution into rivers or corrosive wastes into the air, then marginal cost pricing is socially undesirable. Therefore, many would advocate adjusting all costs and prices to take account of external effects and then using marginal cost pricing. In many cases, other public policies that absorb or offset the repercussions directly are preferable. For example, a bus line may help the aged. One possibility is to maintain the line with cross subsidies. Another is to aid the aged directly. Once we get into this area, we have to find an effective allocation of all governmental programs to decide on proper measures for SOE behavior and the means of assessing their performance since SOEs are not necessarily the only, or the best, alternative for achieving national goals. In most countries, SOEs are exposed to all sorts of political pressures, bureaucracies are not able to calculate all possible effects of policies and the ready access to subsidies may erode managerial incentives to achieve efficiency. Therefore, it is often argued, it is more practical to achieve social ends through other policies and to judge SOEs by their ability to generate surplus.

Financial statements must be corrected to reflect differences between private and public relevant profits. To arrive at social profits, a series of adjustments has to be made. Thus, if wages are valued above their marginal product in an alternative employment, the opportunity cost of labor is used. If unskilled labor has been hired from the pool of unemployed, this opportunity cost is zero. Another adjustment is made for the costs of borrowed funds. SOEs may have received these funds at subsidized rates, not at the market rate. Adjustments are made also for imports and exports, if the exchange rate is overvalued. Other types of adjustment are for government-set prices, taxes paid to government, subsidies received, for the effect of underpriced SOEs produced goods for reason of redistribution of income and for the effect of regional imbalances. More generally, a public manager is expected to look for the interests of all citizens of the country. The manager, therefore, has to be judged by public profits, or social benefits less social costs.

Economists have developed an impressive analytical artillery to calculate the public profits. Their solution rests on the foundation of a set of preferences provided by government. These preferences set out the goals of society and the rate at which one goal is appropriately traded off against another. The preference set can be used to generate socially optimal shadow prices that embody the social opportunity cost of society's resources. Using the social rate of discount, the relative social profitability of alternative operations can be calculated. Activities that are unprofitable when measured in private (market) prices may prove appropriate when evaluated on the basis of social (shadow) prices. Indeed, Handoussa (1980) showed for Egypt that social profits were positive and higher than accounting profits. Of course, not the government directly but the manager (the agent of the state) is charged with the realization of social welfare through the SOE, and as the theory of agency cost highlights, the private interests of the enterprise manager need not be served best by operating the SOE according to the criteria prescribed by the state. Here, too, economic theory offers an analytical answer. With knowledge of both private preferences of the manager and the preferences of society, government can tailor managerial incentives. With appropriate incentives the objectives of the manager can be made identical to those of society.

Unfortunately, in the real world the shadow price prescriptions of economists founder on the rock of uncertainty. Setting accurate shadow prices requires complete information of the social opportunity cost of resource utilization, and such information is unavailable. Moreover, firms do not operate in a neoclassical world; rather, they have a certain size and are therefore managed hierarchically. Much of the available information on costs to the enterprise is collected at the firm's level, and such information is not always presented to the government decision-makers. Decision-makers are not characterized by omniscience; rather, the typical government executive—in the LDCs in particular—is overburdened with too many responsibilities and does not have the time to learn even available information or reflect on its significance. Further, social planning includes decisions that will affect future generations, and trade-offs between the present and the future have to be embodied in the social discount rate. The future, however, is unknown. Projects such as building a nuclear generator or exploring for oil are fraught with uncertainty and extremely hard to quantify, and, as Wells (1973) pointed out, engineers have a different notion of efficiency.

The difficulties in implementing the economist's solutions to performance evaluation do not end with problems of uncertainty, high costs of information or its unavailability at any price and the difficulties in allocating precious time of overburdened government officials. In oligopolistic markets, private firms are likely to adjust their behavior in response to any initiatives by SOEs (Jones and Vogelsang, 1982). In some cases, governments might use the threat of entry into hitherto privately controlled oligopolistic sectors of industry to improve market performance. In addition to these well-known problems, as already shown, making coherent social choices is extraordinarily difficult, not only because the environment is suffused with ambiguity but also, mainly, because of power struggles. In responding to political demands,

SOE managers may choose their high-priority clientèle, excuse the lack of compliance with political demands by citing technical requirements or simply refuse to conform.

Economists have also developed techniques of project appraisal to help SOEs determine the social efficiency of their investment plans and to enable governments to evaluate the social efficiency of establishing new SOEs and the performance of existing ones (Little and Mirrlees, 1974). However, in practice it is extremely difficult to make operational the socially optimal behavior criteria. As Scherer (1980) notes, in particular when SOEs operate in sectors:

> [R]*ichly interconnected with other sectors . . . the general solutions* [*of second best analysis*] *are so complex that it may be impossible to deduce unambiguously even the direction in which particular controlled prices should be adjusted in order to improve resource allocations. . . . no central authority could conceivably obtain the masses of information on demand elasticities, cross elasticities, cost functions and prices needed to devise fully articulated, second-best pricing policies for even a single major industry.* [*Pp.* 27–28]

In summary, economists devoted most of their attention in analyzing SOEs to the derivation of optimal and efficient pricing and investment rules. Much less economic analysis is available on how costs could be minimized. Most economic analysis of pricing and investment implicitly assumes that monitoring costs are zero. In fact, those with the greatest knowledge of the ways by which costs can be reduced are on the employees and managers of the SOEs. The gains of efficiency, however, accrue to all taxpayers and consumers, and employees may even lose by greater efficiency. Given the asymmetry of goals and of information, the problem of achieving cost minimizing is insoluble.

If managers are offered incentives, they can meet targets and get incentives based on profits simply by raising prices. Rees (1968) has suggested linking managerial rewards to the SOEs' profit, but also to improve pricing rules to prevent managers from abusing their monopoly power. However, to calculate prices "on the basis of expected marginal costs" (Rees, 1968, p. 272), again requires that the monitors will have information on the firm's cost structure. Bös (1978) suggested a system of minimization of Laspeyres price index, subject to profit constraint. An even more basic limitation of economists' solutions is that they are based on certain assumptions about the definition of social costs and social benefits that are not necessarily agreed to by all. Most important, governments' decisions with regard to SOEs, as shown in previous chapters, are not necessarily motivated by the goal of maximizing social welfare. For example, the distribution of power among different actors may be more important. Normative guidelines do not give us an idea as to what might be the actual behavior of governments and of SOEs. Moreover, a survey of the economic literature on SOEs would give the impression that we live in a certain world with perhaps some uncertainty as a special case. Some new theoretical developments introduced uncertainty, but assume that individual consumers are risk-neutral—an unpalatable assumption if uncertainty is recognized. Further, most analyses assume that welfare distribution is acceptable or has been optimized. All these difficulties led Nove (1973) to conclude that "commercial operation of nationalized industries raises a host of problems which are now, as a rule, swept under the carpet or ignored" (p. 132).

ORGANIZATIONAL EFFECTIVENESS AND VITALITY

Efficiency must be defined in terms of achievement of goals. Without clear cut and measurable goals it is impossible to measure performance. If goals are stated in static terms, their achievement allows repetition, learning and specialization and creates greater efficiency in production but may also hinder innovations and adaptation to changing market needs. Even operational efficiency may be difficult to achieve. Managers can be held responsible for the performance of their subordinates (and, thus, the enterprise) only if they have the power to hire/fire and reward/penalize them. In SOEs, appointments and the size of employment are often controlled by ministerial selection boards, and managers are neither allowed to appoint all subordinates nor always allowed to decide on the size of the labor force.

Performance evaluation thus involves a dilemma. The more operating routines are retained and repeated, the easier is the performance evaluation. However, very little innovation will occur, and very little novel activity will be available from which to select adaptive response when environmental circumstances change. The very attributes that make actions efficient limit the visibility of alternatives and prevent the intrusion of new ideas or different perspectives, even when changes are required by changing environments. In an SOE, managers are often penalized more for one failure than they are rewarded for several successes.

One way to achieve organizational effectiveness is to guarantee that all the actors in the organization devote all their energies to performance and employ their knowledge creatively toward achieving the goals of the organization. Such an organization, according to Miller (1977), possesses "organizational vitality." Organizational vitality refers to the capability for future achievement in contrast to effectiveness, which measures past success. It may also be said that vitality ensures future effectiveness.

Organizational vitality depends on the existence of implemental capability, which is the totality of competence and skills required to accomplish an objective and motivation, that causes the individual to deal with the objective and carry it out with purposeful effort. In referring to the motivation of all those participating in the organization, we may speak of a suitable organizational climate.

One way to achieve a suitable organizational climate for ensuring the achievement of goals is the selection of managers according to their identification with the goals of one sector or another. All other things being equal, it is reasonable to assume that a manager who identifies with the sector's goals will achieve them far better than a manager who does not believe in them. As one example, Pierre Dreyfus, CEO of Renault, recites in his memoirs how Renault, at a time of a run on the French franc, at its own initiative, supported the currency by accelerating the conversion to francs of receipts in foreign currency (Dreyfus, 1977, p. 35). Unfortunately, those who believe in the right ideology are not necessarily the best and most effective managers. As one example, rapid Africanization meant that SOEs were managed by weak and inexperienced leaders. The political claims in this case had costs in terms of efficiency.

The greater the identification of managers and workers with their organization's goals and a consensus among all stakeholders on these goals, the less important it becomes that these goals be defined and quantifiable by outsiders: the unanimous agreement should lead to concerted efforts to achieve the goals, even if they are not sharply defined. Of course, the achievement of goals does not depend solely on ideological views, and all other things are not necessarily equal. No less important for the achievement of goals is the manager's implemental capability, competence in utilizing and employing optimally the resources at the organization's disposal and competence in getting a maximum of further resources required for the achievement of tasks.

The dominant characteristic of firms whose goals are conflicting and ambiguous is the tension created by the various actors' attempts to place emphasis on different goals. All those dealing with issues concerning the SOE agree that the central problem in monitoring such a firm stems from the inability to weigh various goals and frequently from the manager's perception that the goals of the political controllers are illegitimate, at least in terms of how the manager perceives the goals of the organization. Such a conflict returns us full circle to the question: How and by whom are the goals actually pursued by the organization formulated, and how can stakeholders' satisfaction with the organization's performance be ensured?

MEASURING EFFECTIVENESS

Efficiency measures gauge whether things are done right and effectiveness is purported to measure whether the right things are done. Thus, effectiveness has as much to do with missions and goals as with unit costs, productivity and resource conservation. It is, therefore, an elusive concept, not easily quantifiable. The criteria for evaluation may be subjective, based on value judgments and personal preferences. Further, organizational effectiveness encompasses a large number of criteria.

There are at least three ways to define organizational effectiveness (Cameron, 1980). The first is the inputs or resources method. According to Yuchtman and Seashore (1967), an organization is more effective insofar as it can obtain resources from the environment. To the extent that these resources exist, there is a clear connection between the inputs the organization receives and its products. Yuchtman and Seashore (1967) propose ten indexes for measuring organizational effectiveness according to the resources approach. Steers (1975, p. 549) listed fifteen criteria used by researchers in evaluating organizational effectiveness. Campbell (1976, pp. 36–38) listed thirty.

The second approach focuses on the organization's stakeholders or beneficiaries—individuals or groups whose participation is essential to the proper functioning of the organization—including workers, suppliers, customers and users. According to this point of view, organizational effectiveness is measured by the degree of satisfaction of different stakeholders. The effectiveness of the organization "derives from the management of demands, particularly the demands of interest groups upon which the organization depends for resources and support" (Pfeffer and Salancik, 1978, p. 2). One way to measure effectiveness, according to this point of view, is by the absence of criticism "for it means that no one views the operation of a particular program or organization as inimical to his own interests or goals and that some may even perceive it as beneficial" (Sapolsky, 1972, p. 232). According to this standard, Sapolsky suggests that the Polaris program was successful. This success "was not assured at its establishment" (p. 243).

> *[It] depended upon the ability of its proponents to promote the Polaris. Competitors had to be eliminated; reviewing agencies had to be outmaneuvered; congressmen, admirals, newspapermen, and academicians had to be coopted. Politics is a system requirement. What distinguishes programs in government is not that some play politics and others do not, but rather, that some are better at it than others. [Sapolsky, 1972, p. 244]*

A third approach views the organization as being effective if it functions without internal tensions. This approach focuses on the processes within the organization and examination of the meshing, coordination and cooperation among the organization's units and groupings, as well as the degree of communication among its various parts. This approach is akin to the human relations school of thought.

The differences between these approaches are quite substantial. An organization may be effective according to one approach and ineffective according to another. Some of the approaches also focus on one specific aspect of the organization's extremely complex structure. Thus, harmony within the organization does not necessarily guarantee achievement of goals and may even lead to decay. Technological innovation, e.g., often entails changes, tensions and conflicts.

SOCIALIST VERSUS CAPITALIST COUNTRIES: A COMPARISON OF THEIR EFFICIENCY

One way to understand the problems involved in measuring performance of SOEs is to ask the question, are socialist countries more or less efficient than capitalist ones? The discussion is intended only as an illustration of the difficulties in assessing relative efficiency in agreed terms and not as a comparison of different economic systems. Bergson (1968) one of the major researchers of this question, claims that there is no evidence to support the Marxist view that socialism is more efficient than capitalism. In fact, "Socialism, exemplified by the USSR, is markedly less efficient than capitalism, as exemplified by the U.S.A., though perhaps about as efficient as capitalism as exemplified by Italy" (Eckstein, 1971, p. 239). This conclusion was reached by comparing the static efficiency (output per unit of inputs at a given time) and concluding that it is worse for the USSR than for the United States, France and Germany and on par with Italy.

Bergson (1968) also compared what he termed the *dynamic efficiency*, or the rate of change of output per unit of inputs, and found that it is better in the USSR than in the United States and the United Kingdom but worse than that in Germany, France and Italy. These conclusions are based on calculations for the economy as a whole and assume that the only difference between the economies is the system. It is further assumed that each country faces constant or decreasing returns to scale, identical technology and homogeneous labor and capital. Of course, if in reality there is, e.g., a technology gap between the United States and the USSR, and the former is in fact using more advanced technology, it is possible that the USSR is more efficient but that this efficiency is more than offset by the technology gap. Further, the two countries differ in their historical and cultural heritage, not only in the system.

Theoretically, these problems can be solved by comparing the efficiency of the German Democratic Republic and the Federal Republic of Germany. These two countries may be said to be identical in most of the aforementioned respects, differing only in their economic systems. Several researchers have compared the performance of the two Germanies (Schnitzer, 1972; Gregory and Leptin, 1977). These studies show that the static efficiency of the Federal Republic of Germany has been higher throughout the postwar period. Comparison of the dynamic efficiency is more problematic, since it is sensitive to the year for which the comparison was made, and the data used is based on different national accounting systems. While the rate of growth of aggregate labor productivity for the period 1950 to 1958 was a third greater in the Democratic Republic than in the Federal Republic of Germany (Gregory and Leptin, 1977, p. 529), it was about equal for the period 1960 to 1973. It may well be that these differences are the result of differential wartime destruction in the two Germanies. More important for our discussion, these studies are based on a comparison, rooted in the tradition of neoclassical economics, between utilized inputs and the available level of outputs as measured in the national accounts. Marxism's major attack on capitalism, however, was not cast in these terms. The efficiency discussed in Marxist theory is the relationship between available inputs and the social utility of outputs. Capitalism, socialists would argue, is inefficient because it fails to utilize the available resources, allowing idle capacity as well as unemployment.

Further, socialists refer to the social utility of outputs. According to them, much of the capitalist outputs consist of social ills like hard drugs or waste like that caused by the frequent change of car models or by advertising. Baran and Sweezy, two Marxist economists, calculated that car model changes in the late 1950s were costing the United States 2.5 percent of its GNP every year (1968, p. 141). When they combined all they perceived as "surplus" or social wastes—military expenditures, real estate services, advertising, legal services, waste in distribution—they concluded that total surplus as a percentage of GNP in the United States was 56.1 percent in 1963 (p. 374).

The picture is further complicated by the fact that "efficiency depends predominantly on the stage of development, and so in reality is little affected by the social system" (Eckstein, 1971, p. 238). At the same time, Marxist economists would argue that the stage of development is not independent of the social system. Of course, the USSR also devotes some of its resources to the production of goods defined by Baran and Sweezy as not socially desirable, from military expenditures to vodka. In short, what is socially desirable is a value-laden question (e.g., is censorship a waste?) Ellman concludes:

> *Neither the neoclassical hypothesis nor the Marxist hypothesis are [sic] corroborated by the evidence. Whether or not both, either, or neither, are considered to be definitely refuted depends on how precisely the hypotheses are formulated (e.g., do the hypotheses refer to some measure of central tendency or can they be refuted by a single observation?), which theory of economic growth one utilizes, which time period one considers, what proportion of the output of each system one judges to be waste, and on what the level of waste of resources outside and inside production is judged to be. . . . The two systems are equally good at producing tendentious arguments.* [1979, *p.* 257]

When a term like *performance* is used, factors other than economic efficiency should be taken into account because one system may have more or less skewed income distribution than another (for the evidence on this point, see Bergson, 1984), the distribution of power may be different (state ownership may reduce the power of the private business firms) or workers may be happier in one system than they are in another. It is therefore extremely important to be crystal clear on how performance is measured. The major problem in measuring the performance of SOEs is similar to that analyzed previously: different persons would like the SOEs to achieve different goals. Therefore, they measure their performances differently.

THE FINANCIAL PERFORMANCE OF SOEs: PROFITS

Most studies of SOEs' performance measure the results of the operations of these firms by calculating accounting profits. Thus, a study of sixty-four SOEs in twenty-six countries in the 1960s measured flow of funds, investment ratios, surplus after investments and transfers (excluding loans from the government budget) as a percentage of current activity. The researchers found that when a normal depreciation (estimated by the authors to be 24 percent of activity as a whole) was included and subsidies excluded, these enterprises showed a loss equal to 16 percent of total activity (defined as operating revenues less operating expenses) (Gantt and Dutto, 1968). (By using this base, the authors avoided the problem of calculating current value of assets, an almost insurmountable difficulty in countries with high rates of inflation.) Some results of this study are reproduced in Table 5.1. All ratios are percentage of activity as defined here.

Despite low cash flows and operating deficits, SOEs' investments were high, amounting on the average to 74.3 percent of current activities of which two-thirds were the net investment and one-third was the renewal of assets. According to the capital/output ratios calculated by the writers, the SOEs they studied as a group increased their output by 5 percent a year, the fastest growth being in electricity (28.4 percent) and the smallest in railroads (0.1 percent).

Table 5–1 shows also the financial position of the firms after taking investment needs into account. On the average, for each monetary unit of current activity, the corporations needed an additional two-thirds of the unit to cover investment requirements. The largest needs are in electricity enterprises because of high growth. The railroads had low investment requirements but large operating deficits. About half of the external finances needed were provided by government transfers. Although differences were found among regions and industries, flow of funds as a percentage of activity was low, in particular in Latin American railways. The authors conclude that "government-owned enterprises, rather than serving as a focal point for collecting financial resources for their own investment or for other purposes, have generally placed a financial burden on parent governments" (Gantt and Dutton, 1968, p. 128).

Table 5.1 Indicators of performance of SOEs in LDCs by area and industry

	Industry						
Area and Indicators	Railways	Other Transport	Petroleum	Electricity	Communications	Other Industries	Overall Mean
Europe							
Flow of funds as percentage of activity	−20	−0.5	10.1	27.4	24.8	−12.4	0.7
Gross investment ratios as percentage of activity	17.7	14.8	24.1	49.3	20.3	162	80.7
Surplus after investment as percentage of activity	−37.7	−15.3	−14	−21.9	4.5	−174.4	−80
Transfer excluding loans from government budget	29.2	3.3	1.3	1	−8.1	74.6	33.2
Latin America							
Flow of funds as percentage of activity	−57.1	−3.8	43.3	21	26.7	−6.6	2.1
Gross investment ratios as percentage of activity	32.3	46.3	70	114.2	51.5	48.5	58.4
Surplus after investment as percentage of activity	−89.4	−50.2	−26.7	−93.2	−24.9	−55.1	56.3
Transfer excluding loans from government budget	90.6	44.5	−1.6	59.6	14.5	45.7	42.3

(cont.)

Area and Indicators	Industry						
	Railways	Other Transport	Petroleum	Electricity	Communications	Other Industries	Overall Mean
(cont.)							
Africa							
Flow of funds as percentage of activity	18.2	30.2	—	21.4	−27.3	31.7	19.5
Gross investment ratios as percentage of activity	26.8	24.7	—	100.9	13.8	449	80.6
Surplus after investment as percentage of activity	−8.6	5.5	—	−79.5	−41.1	−417.4	−61.1
Transfer excluding loans from government budget	0.6	−1.5	—	8.4	42.1	100.6	13.4
Asia							
Flow of funds as percentage of activity	16.6	14.5	—	37.7	−10.2	—	16.4
Gross investment ratios as percentage of activity	29.1	19.1	—	208.7	47.9	—	91.2
Surplus after investment as percentage of activity	−12.5	−4.5	—	−171.1	−58.1	—	−74.8
Transfer excluding loans from government budget	−0.1	6.4	—	56.1	58	—	34.8

Asia *(cont.)*							
Overall Mean							
Flow of funds as percentage of activity	−13.5	10.9	33.8	27.2	5.7	−6.3	8
Gross investment ratios as percentage of activity	27.5	30.1	56.9	129.2	37.7	131.7	74.3
Surplus after investment as percentage of activity	−41	−19.3	−23.1	−102	−32	−138.1	−66.3
Transfer excluding loans from government budget	35.3	17.8	−0.7	33.7	28.6	63.3	32.9

SOURCE: Gantt, Andrew H., and Guiseppe Dutto, 1968, "Financial Performances of Government-Owned Corporations in Less-Developed Countries," *IMF Staff Papers* 15:108, 111, 113, 115.

In a more recent International Monetary Fund (IMF) study, Short (1984) found that nonfinancial SOEs in twenty-four developing countries earned an average operating surplus before depreciation of about 1.3 percent of the GDP in 1977. The net budgetary burden (defined as government subsidies, transfers and net lending to SOEs, less dividends and interest payments to government) averaged more than 3 percent of GDP, of which current subsidies and transfers were 1.4 percent of GDP. In developed countries, for the same year, the budgetary burden of SOEs for seven countries averaged 2 percent of GDP (Short, 1984). The budgetary burden is partially the result of government policy but partially a result of losses and the inability of SOEs to generate funds for investment. The losses ultimately have to be paid by the taxpayers. Individual country studies also show a dismal picture of losses and self-financing close to nil. Shirley (1983, p. 12) shows that gross profits as a percentage of sales for Turkey's manufacturing SOEs was 1 percent in 1973, −4.7 percent in 1974, −10.3 percent in 1975, −23.2 percent in 1976, −20.3 percent in 1977, −16.6 percent in 1978 and −2 percent in 1979. In 1976, SOEs in Turkey required 1 percent more labor and 43.6 percent more capital per unit of output than private enterprises. In comparing these figures, readers should bear in mind that the average SOE in Turkey is about 50 percent more capital-intensive than a private enterprise. From 1965 to 1975 average labor productivity in Turkey rose by 9 percent per annum in the private sector and 7 percent in the SOEs. In 1979, average labor productivity was 30 percent higher in the private than in the state-owned manufacturing sectors (Shirley, 1983, p. 16). These poor results may have been caused by bureaucratic interference and the imposition of price ceilings on the output of SOEs that reduced their growth potential.

Frank found the performance of five African economies—Kenya, Tanzania, Nigeria, Ghana and Uganda—"hardly short of disasterous." He attributes this abysmal performance to bad management and to the fact that investment has been made "with political patronage in mind and to the benefit primarily of powerful political figures" (in Ranis, 1971, p. 97). Killick (in UNIDO, 1983), in a later survey of manufacturing firms in four African countries, found that they contributed little to economic growth, that they were a drain on public finance and that they discouraged the growth of private industry. The World Bank survey of sub-Saharan Africa reports, "Public enterprises have thus far caused serious fiscal burdens" (1981, p. 38). Gillis (1980, p. 267) observed that SOE savings in Korea, Uruguay, Pakistan and Indonesia represented 10 to 15 percent of gross investments. However, in each of the first three countries the SOEs were unable to generate enough funds to finance their investments. Diaz found that subsidies in Argentina, through the cheap operation of railroads and other SOEs, reached 3 percent of the GNP (in Ranis, 1971, pp. 218–219).

The profit record of most SOEs in other LDCs shows a similar dismal picture of many ill-conceived investments and huge capital needs. A report of an international workshop on financial profitability and losses of SOEs, held in Yugoslavia in June 1981, (Ahmed, 1982) shows that in many individual SOEs the financial losses are heavy:

Bangladesh: "The overall financial picture of the public enterprises . . . shows substantial negative returns." [p. 23]
Somalia: "The production enterprises run at a heavy loss." [p. 24]
Tanzania: "The majority of the public enterprises are being run at heavy losses." [p. 24]
Algeria: "The general picture of the financial situation of the Algerian public enterprises was one of losses." [p. 24]
Sri Lanka: "A majority of public enterprises were making heavy financial losses." [p. 25]
Thailand: "Though 'on an aggregate basis' public enterprises make profits, the size of the profit has been decreasing for the last few years." [p. 25]
Tunisia: "In certain sectors such as mining, textiles and transportation, the enterprises are suffering financial losses." [p. 26]
Jamaica: "By and large the public enterprises are being run at substantial losses." [p. 26]

For the aggregate of SOEs reported on in the conference, 70 percent operated at financial losses. In Nigeria, the average annual losses as a percent of sales of 44 SOEs studied for the period 1975-1979 was 55.1 percent. Only the SOEs in the service and in the finance and investment sectors were profitable, while agrobusiness SOEs lost on the average 70.9 percent of their sales revenue. Manufacturing firms lost on the average 4.2 percent of sales (Fubara, 1984, p. 10).

According to the World Bank, SOEs in Mexico, excluding state petroleum company, showed a net loss of 1.2 percent of GDP in 1980, and Senegal's SOEs recorded a deficit in 1977/1978 and again in 1979/1980 (1983, p. 74).

Ramandaham (1984b, p. 136) cites more examples:

Zambia: "Parastatal performance was negative in terms of net profit in mining, tourism, agriculture and miscellaneous industry, and also, on the whole, in 1978." (*Third National Development Plan*, Lusaka), p. 416.
Sudan: "The financial performance of the public sector enterprises registered deterioration" (over 1970/75). "The past record of financial performance of public enterprises clearly indicates that their net contribution to domestic capital formation has been minimal." [*The Six Year Plan of Economic and Social Development* 1977/78–1982/83, Vol. 1 (Khartoum, 1977) pp. 13 and 68.]

Table 5.2 shows profits and subsidies of SOEs in selected developing countries as a percentage of GDP at market prices. In all of them the return on investment is low and sometimes negative, and self-financing of investment is close to nil.

In some cases, the situation may be worse than Table 5–2 reveals. Thus Trebat (1983, p. 177) reports that Chile's SOE losses as percentage of net worth in 1978 were 3.12 percent and Mexico's SOEs' net losses as percentage of 1972-74 were 3.8 percent. On the other hand, in Brazil, the ratio of net profits to net worth was 11.4 percent in 1974 and 7.9 percent in 1978.

In Thailand, total deficits of SOEs are expected to double in the two years to end in September 1986 and to be equal to 3.5 percent of GNP (*The Economist*, December 21, 1985, p. 75).

In many cases, the losses wiped out the total equity several times. "The oldest and largest of Uganda's public enterprises, the Uganda Development Corporation, had an accumulated deficit of 128 million Uganda shillings, as compared with its total share capital of 159 million shillings, by the end of 1977. (It was 90 percent of the value of its fixed assets.) (Ramandaham, 1984b, p. 126). Table 5.3 indicates how high the accumulated deficits have been as a percentage of paid-up capital in certain Indian and Pakistani SOEs.

In Liberia, SOEs are experiencing acute cash flow problems and large operating losses. They have financed their losses largely through arrears in payment to the government and to other SOEs and increasing debts to sup-

Table 5.2 Profits and subsidies of SOEs in selected countries as a percentage of GDP at market prices

Country	After Tax Profit/Loss (−) Before Depreciation	After Tax Profit/Loss (−) After Depreciation[a]	Current Subsidies	Gross Margin (Surplus/Deficit before Subsidies, Interest and Depreciation)
Industrialized Countries				
Australia (1974–1977)	1	—	n.a.	2.2
Canada (1978–1980)	1.1	0.4	n.a.	n.a.
France (1978–1981)[b]	1.2	n.a.	0.7	1.1
Italy (1978–1980)	−0.3	−2	n.a.	n.a.
Japan (1978–1980)	1	−0.1	n.a.	n.a.
Netherlands (1978)	2.3	0.6	n.a.	n.a.
Norway (1977–1980)	0.8	n.a.	n.a.	n.a.
Developing Countries				
Africa				
Botswana (1978–1979)	1.7	0.9	n.a.	4.9
Ivory Coast (1978–1979)	2.8	n.a.	n.a.	n.a.

(cont.)

Country	After Tax Profit/Loss (−) Before Depreciation	After Depreciation[a]	Current Subsidies	Gross Margin (Surplus/Deficit before Subsidies, Interest and Depreciation)
Developing Countries *(cont.)*				
Malawi (1978)	2.9	1.5	0	n.a.
Mali (1978)[c]	−2	−3	n.a.	−0.9
Senegal (1974)[d]	4.9 (0.0)	3.2 (−1.4)	n.a.	n.a.
Tunisia (1978–1980)	3.4	0.6	n.a.	n.a.
Asia				
Burma (1978–1980)	1.7	n.a.	n.a.	n.a.
India (1978)	1.7	0.4	0.6	3.6
Korea (1978–1980)	2.1	n.a.	n.a.	n.a.
Thailand (1978–1980)	1.2	n.a.	0.1	n.a.
Europe, Middle East				
Portugal (1978–1980)	n.a.	n.a.	4.5	n.a.
Turkey (1978–1980)	0.8	−0.1	2.7	−1.4
Western Hemisphere				
Argentina (1976–1977)	2.1	n.a.	1	n.a.
Barbados (1978–1980)	0.3	n.a.	1.3	n.a.
Bolivia (1974–1977)	2.4	n.a.	0.1	8
Chile (1978–1980)[b]	1.5	n.a.	0.3	8.2
Columbia (1978–1980)	1	n.a.	0.3	1.5
Dominican Republic (1978–1979)[b]	0.3	n.a.	0.7	n.a.
Guatemala (1978–1980)	0.3	n.a.	0	0.5
Guyana (1978 1980)	6.5	n.a.	1.1	13.5
Jamaica (1978–1980)[b]	1.3	n.a.	1.2	n.a.
Mexico (1978)[b]	1.5	n.a.	0.9	4.9
Panama (1978–1979)	0.6	−1.8	0.4	n.a.
Paraguay (1978–1980)	1.4	n.a.	0.1	2.2
Peru (1978–1979)	0.6	n.a.	0.1	n.a.
Uruguay (1978–1980)	2.3	n.a.	0.3	3.8

NOTE: Gross margin is sales revenue less operating expenditures excluding depreciation and interest. Profits equal gross margin plus current transfers and subsidies less interest, dividends, and taxes. These data are not fully comparable because of differences in the treatment of SOE taxes, subsidies and finance charges.

[a]At replacement cost for most countries. The basis of measurement for several African countries is unknown.

[b]Major enterprises only.

[c]Eight large enterprises only.

[d]Figures in parentheses exclude the phosphate company.

SOURCE: P. Short, 1984.

Table 5.3 Accumulated deficits of selected SOEs in India (1981–1982) and Pakistan (1980–1981)

Enterprise	Deficit as percentage of equity
India	
Indian Firebricks & Insulation Co. Ltd.	279
Bharat Coking Coal	191
Heavy Engineering Corporation Ltd.	170
Jessop Co. Ltd.	211
Mining & Allied Machinery Corp. Ltd.	240
Triveni Structurals Ltd.	156
Biecco Lawrie Ltd.	627
National Instruments Ltd.	667
Central Inland Water Transport Corp. Ltd.	353
Garden Reach Shipbuilders & Engineers Ltd.	123
Scooters Ltd.	604
Bharat Ophthalmic Glass Ltd.	259
Rehabilitation Industries Corp. Ltd.	627
Tannery & Footwear Corp. of India Ltd.	222
Banana & Fruit Development Corp. Ltd.	269
National Textile Corp. (Delhi, etc.) Ltd.	173
NTC (Maharashtra North) Ltd.	116
NTC (Maharashtra South) Ltd.	120
NTC (UP) Ltd.	228
NTC (W. Bengal, etc.) Ltd.	242
Elgin Mills Ltd.	317
Cotton Corp. of India Ltd.	269
Jute Corp. of India Ltd.	1,297
Hindustan Prefab Ltd.	129
Hindustan Steel Works Construction Ltd.	251
Engineering Projects (I) Ltd.	719
Pakistan	
Antibiotics Pr. Ltd.	363
Kurram Chemical Co. Ltd.	196
Pakdyes & Chemical Co. Ltd.	134
Pakistan PVC Ltd.	360
Ravi Rayon Ltd.	100
Ravi Engineering	495
Nätional Fertilizer Marketing Ltd.	472
Bannu Sugar Mills	1,067
Utility Stores Corp.	167
Printing Corp. of Pakistan	264

SOURCE: V. V. Ramandadham (1984) *The Nature of Public Enterprise* (New York: St. Martin's Press) pp. 127–128.

pliers and local banks. In many LDCs, because of similar circumstances, the SOEs are vulnerable to court action by creditors. This situation often forces the government to inject more cash into the SOEs. The poor aggregate financial performance of the SOEs is damaging to the economy as a whole and is a growing burden to the treasury.

In Mexico, the only SOE to earn a substantial profit in the first 9 months of 1984 was PEMEX, the oil SOE (earning $2.38 billion). The rest lost $789 million between them, of which the federal electricity commission lost $550 million. In Argentina, the accumulated losses of the SOE sector in 1983 were estimated at $1.7 billion, or about 2 percent of GDP. Even the Argentinian oil company, YPF, managed to be probably the only loss-ridden oil company in the world (*The Economist*, February 16, 1985, p. 67). Capital-intensive mammoth projects in the SOE sector led to its growing indebtedness and reliance on governmental transfers. In Argentina, the total indebtedness of the SOE sector was $14.2 billion, or 23 percent of the GDP (*The Economist*, February 11, 1985, p. 67).

The financial performance of the SOEs in the developed countries may be seen from Table 5.4, showing net income (or loss) of the largest Western European SOEs for the selected years in the decade 1969–1984. Several interesting observations can be made. First, most oil companies are very profitable. Second, the largest losers are the declining industries (coal, steel). Third, British Aerospace, after privatization, is much more profitable than when it was an SOE, and than other SOEs in other industries.

Accounting profits are not a good measure of efficiency of SOEs since accounting conventions define "profits" in different and still acceptable ways. Many SOEs use historical cost accounting, and this gives unfair advantage to older firms with historically low depreciation charges. In fields such as energy, water or transportation, SOEs are natural monopolies that have declining average cost curves, profits being determined by government decisions, so that accounting profits may be the result of taking advantage of the monopoly power despite inefficient use of resources.

Other SOEs are not business enterprises and were not established for profit purposes. Others are established by the government to develop new technologies. Evaluating their activities by the criterion of profitability is most misleading. Frequently, private-sector firms were nationalized to prevent their going bankrupt. Serious rehabilitation efforts are required to make such companies profitable again. Here, too, profitability is not the only criterion. In other cases, SOEs serve as a tax instrument, and their high profits derive from the monopoly granted them, not from the efficiency with which they are managed. High profits may also result from inadequate maintenance. Then again, higher profits may simply reflect market imperfections, not efficiency.

Profitability is certainly not the sole index of managerial efficiency in an SOE. Profitability and cost minimization can be used as a criterion only if they are the avowed objectives of the enterprise. SOEs are also seen as instru-

Table 5.4 Net income (or loss) of the largest western European state-owned firms (in thousands of dollars)

Industry	Fortune 500 Rank 1984	1969	1974	1979	1983	1984
Metals and Heavy Engineering						
British Steel (UK)	88	(54,766)	170,455	(600,796)	(1,452,230)	(381,804)
Cockerill (Bel)	173	22,127	18,139	(122,423)	(658,907)	73,107
Halsider (It)	*	—	50,413	(309,730)	—	—
Salzgitter (Ger)	146	9,875	20,503	(1,997)	272,863	(153,279)
Svenska Varv (Swed)	*	—	—	98,724	61,961	—
Svenskt Stae (Swed)	343	—	—	(6,882)	3,962	24,164
VIAG (Ger)	239	—	23,684	25,325	31,684	37,993
VOEST-Alpine (Aust)	130	1,981	9,901	(29,124)	(2,062)	27,117
Sacilor (Fr)	110	—	24,385	(358,452)	(710,785)	(920,006)
Usinor (Fr)	105	16,176	29,041	—	(713,874)	(845,921)
British Shipbuilders (UK)	368	—	—	(124,573)	(213,718)	(346,053)
Valmet (Finland)	452	—	—	5,509	6,984	15,185
Preussag (Ger)	94	—	24,289	23,739	41,860	47,575
Motor Vehicles						
Alfa Romeo (It)	*	—	(89,432)	(109,920)	—	—
BL (UK)	100	46,769	(56,318)	(306,632)	(229,656)	107,516
Renault (Fr)	30	29,191	7,261	241,520	(206,769)	(1,435,861)
Volkswagenwerk (Ger)	16	126,904	(312,585)	371,534	(51,083)	85,916
SEAT (Sp)	427	—	6,463	(224,855)	(249,251)	(224,905)

Electric and Electronics						
CGE (Fr)	46	18,784	25,654	—	52,611	67,533
Thomson (Fr)	61	19,279	34,339	64,457	(140,776)	(2,402)
Norsk Hydro (Nor)	109	—	—	28,985	66,839	130,399
Bull (Fr)	321	—	—	—	(82,023)	55,921
ICL (UK)	*	—	—	71,284	59,772	—
Petroleum						
Britoil (UK)	242	—	—	28,859	217,226	226,245
BP (UK)	2	232,320	1,140,117	3,439,582	1,562,873	1,474,466
CFP-Total (Fr)	11	—	292,457	1,137,282	101,548	149,476
Elf-Aquitaine (Fr)	7	62,741	238,229	1,310,132	488,451	742,576
ENI (It)	3	16,800	(91,256)	89,040	(928,925)	(50,119)
OMV (Aust)	181	—	13,153	19,616	133	12,002
Saarbergwerke (Ger)	206	—	(10,157)	—	(81,067)	(28,777)
VEBA (Ger)	55	—	12,118	50,367	5,208	(21,011)
ENPETROL (Sp)	111	—	—	25,226	2,775	19,526
Statoil (Nor)	106	—	—	—	187,369	143,745
Neste (Fin)	80	—	3,056	30,560	11,121	11,763
PETROGAL (Port)	233	—	—	26,414	1,786	3,612
Hispanoil (Sp)	454	—	—	—	11,117	36,909
Butano (Sp)	*	—	—	(23,836)	(5,502)	—
Petroliber (Sp)	*	—	—	—	4,500	—

(cont.)

Industry	Fortune 500 Rank 1984	1969	1974	1979	1983	1984
(cont.)						
Mining and Chemicals						
National Coal Board (UK)	59	(21,314)	(315,777)	(37,671)	(185,498)	0
Charbonage de France (Fr)	295	(10,865)	(2,573)	18,249	(29,215)	(24,326)
DSM (Neth)	57	30,650	192,995	44,446	57,328	144,289
Enterprise Miniere et Chimique (Fr)	317	—	42,770	22,988	(16,829)	6,689
Montedison (It)	56	66,198	173,602	22,193	(211,882)	(47,218)
Saint-Gobain (Fr)	58	28,960	146,386	154,350	53,135	58,761
Ruhrkohle (Ger)	49	—	—	3,249	15,293	41,042
Rhone-Poulenc (Fr)	74	92,612	179,556	186,019	12,857	227,473
Pechiney (Fr)	120	60,367	154,589	233,124	(60,771)	62,398
Holding Companies						
IRI (It)	5	—	—	—	—	—
Statsfortag Group (Swed)	348	—	16,869	45,000	35,060	7,008
EFIM (It)	198	—	—	—	(509,307)	(323,694)

Aerospace						
Aerospatiale (Fr)	180	8,876	(76,569)	1,956	(46,903)	37,969
British Aerospace (UK)	156	6,703	40,421	86,844	124,757	144,235
Messerschmidt-Bolkau-Blohm (Ger)	247	—	—	24,024	35,896	34,408
Rolls-Royce (UK)	265	10,140	—	(133,475)	(292,565)	26,711
SNECMA (Fr)	305	—	—	15,527	(7,077)	6,707
Avions Marcel Dassault-Breguet (Fr)	277	—	—	64,020	51,661	49,377
Matra (Fr)	316	—	—	47,108	4,463	7,838
Tobacco						
SEITA (Fr)	*	—	—	(55,532)	(14,396)	—
Tabacalera (Sp)	299	—	9,086	10,985	9,551	7,344

*not in Fortune 500 of 1984

—data not available

SOURCE: Fortune Directory of the 500 Largest Industrial Corporations Outside the U.S.—August 1970, pp. 143–150, August 1975, pp. 156–167, August 11, 1980, pp. 190–205, August 20, 1984, pp. 200–219, August 19, 1985, pp. 168–187.

ments for the execution of social and economic policies of the government, as tools for winning the next election, or as a means for distributing political patronage. They are also expected to be sensitive to the needs of people (Otter, 1984).

Since economies are riddled with market imperfections and distortions, financial profitability is not necessarily consistent with positive social surplus. Firms in oligopolistic industries control prices, they are sometimes protected by high tariff barriers and market prices for imports do not reflect their opportunity costs.

Lower profits or loss may point to indirect subsidy or to low controlled prices for an SOE's profits. At the same time, the government also determines many of the company's costs. The government may set wage ceilings, fix raw material costs, subsidize interest rates or give SOEs their investment funds at preferential rates. The company's profits are the outcome of policies regulating input and output prices, which the company does not set. In these cases the degree of profitability of such a firm cannot be used to indicate the level of efficiency with which it exploits its inputs. Thus, if a subsidy given to farmers is granted directly, an SOE making fertilizers may be profitable; if the same subsidy is given as a reduced price of fertilizers, the firm would show losses that are not necessarily a reflection of its efficiency. In Indonesia weaving SOEs were profitable because state ownership guaranteed a supply of raw materials, obtaining a quota of yarn (that was in short supply) and "virtually ensured the profitability of the recipient" (Hill, 1982, p. 1019). With the abolition of yarn quotas in 1966, the financial position of these SOEs gradually deteriorated.

Finally, SOE managers may hide profits or at least attempt to smooth them. As Grayson (1981) notes in the case of national oil companies (NOCs),

> *If returns are too high, owner governments assume (1) that the NOC charges outrageous prices, (2) that it pays inadequate wages, (3) that it ignores some or most of its nonfinancial objectives, or (4) that it commits all three sins simultaneously. In fact, a national oil company's public position resembles that of the multinationals. The moment that ROI seems more than 'reasonable', governments and the news media begin to talk about 'excess' or 'windfall' profits. A very profitable NOC would lose some of its managerial independence—the government might ask it to undertake a new nonfinancial project, for instance. On the other hand, running the NOC at a loss would also erode managerial authority (Grayson, 1981, p. 254).*

The burden of the social welfare programs is often used as an excuse for inefficiency. In fact, the major reason most economists insist on the separation of the economic and social tasks of these enterprises is to allow a better assessment of their performance. Today, unfortunately, it is impossible to relate SOEs' profitability or rate of self-financing to the ownership factor or to bad management. Losses could have been a result of resource diversion for various means; remember that in Mexico, most losses come from electricity, used to subsidize the private sector. These uses, in turn, created a budgetary burden but may also have reduced incentives for cost controls, resulting in greater losses and higher indebtedness. Some developing countries also face acute shortages of trained managers, engineers and foreign exchange.

The major reason for losses, however, is the political milieu in which SOEs operate. According to Ghai, SOEs in Africa are frequently used as a means of patronage and a source of wealth and power for political and administrative leaders.

> *The role of the State has therefore been to enable groups which have acquired control over the State apparatus to establish an economic basis for themselves . . . The distinction between the government and the enterprises tends to become blurred and the government has often a vested interest in hiding the inefficiency of enterprises (in Reddy, 1983, p. 182).*

On the other hand, in countries in which SOEs operate under control structures with less governmental interference, the financial results were much better (UNIDO, 1983), as Brazil, Chile, Peru, Thailand and Uruguay, more SOEs showed positive accounting profits than losses. The German or Austrian SOEs fared as well as private enterprises.

The financial results of SOEs are important insofar as they have an impact on the resource utilization of the country. However, these results are not necessarily an indicator of efficiency or performance. A comparative study of the relative performance of public and private manufacturing enterprises in India (Dholakia, 1978) found that although SOEs were not very profitable, they have shown much larger increases in total factor productivity. Over the 15-year period 1960–1975, the total factor productivity has increased by 89 percent in the SOEs and by only 3 percent in the private sector (p. M-8). "The severe criticism of the management of public enterprises solely on the ground of low profitabilty, may often turn out to be misleading inasmuch as it represents a partial view of the overall performance" (p. M-9). SOEs have been absorbing an increasing amount of scarce national resources and used these resources with "most rapidly increasing efficiency" (p. M-4). At the same time, Ramamurti (1985b, p.10) found that senior bureaucrats and selected journalists used as external evaluators of Indian SOEs "espouse one set of standards for judging performance but use a different set of standards (in which profitability plays a very important role) for *actually* judging performance (p. 18). His study shows that profits are a more important criterion for performance evaluation of SOEs in practice than they should be according to official policy or economic theory. Perhaps because SOEs are judged in practice by their accounting profitability, public perception is that SOEs are less efficient than private enterprises. Is that perception true? Can one discern systematic differences in behavior or results between private and state-owned firms? If such differences exist, what are the reasons?

COMPARING PRIVATE FIRMS AND SOEs

Theoretical Arguments

According to the proponents of the property rights school of thought, individuals respond to incentives, and the pattern of incentives at any time is influenced by the property rights structure. Individual managers are assumed to maximize their utility subject to the limits established by the existing organizational structure. They respond to incentives, and different property assignments have different effects on the penalty/reward system. Individual businesspersons in private enterprise are profit maximizers, who are attempting to achieve efficiency. When owners are not the managers, they incur costs in contracting, policing, negotiating and enforcing their property rights. Private property rights are exclusive and voluntarily transferable. In some cases, the government limits the individual owner's rights to change the form, place, substance or use of an asset. Thus, zoning laws put restrictions on the free use of land. Attenuation causes the market value of the assets to decrease.

In an SOE it is virtually impossible to transfer the ownership rights belonging to the state from one individual or group to another. Taxpayers who wish to change their portfolio of assets cannot sell their shares in an SOE. In theory, at least, they can change citizenship and move to another country in which the portfolio of assets held by the state is more to their liking. These taxpayers may, of course, cast their votes in the elections, attempting to change the preferences of the state and its policies. However, they do not have any easy or direct way to transfer their share of the property rights in any one of the SOEs. The inability to transfer ownership rights is said to mean that state ownership is inherently less efficient than private property.

First, it is argued that owners of a private firm have an incentive to monitor management behavior to ensure efficiency in the production of goods and services. In contrast, a taxpayer-owner of an SOE, being one of many diffused owners, does not have a similar incentive to scrutinize management. The greater the personal financial investment, the greater the interest in the operations of the firm. Owner-managers have the highest stake and, therefore, care more. If ownership is diffused and separate from management, the additional monitoring costs may make the firm less efficient. However, the owner can still motivate managers by linking their pecuniary compensation with the profits of the firm, allowing the managers to capture part of any monetary gains, e.g., through stock options. In an SOE the manager (and the government's bureaucrat) has no wealth invested in the firm and no rights to profit sharing. Lack of a link between the firm's economic performance and the manager's personal pecuniary gains, it is claimed, will have detrimental effects on efficiency.

Second, transferability of shares encourages specialization of ownership. According to Armen Alchian (1965, 1977), since owners of shares in a private firm can sell these shares in the capital market, shareowners will be those who find their highest valued use as an input. Others will simply exercise their exit right and sell the shares. Ownership, Peltzmann (1971) argued, can be viewed as a productive input that organizes managerial inputs and fulfills the functions of risk bearing. If a market for these rights is not available, as is the case in an SOE, the distribution of taxpayer-owners or even that of the government bureaucrats, acting as their agents, will not reflect their highest valued use as an input, at least not as frequently as in an investor-owned private enterprise.

This line of thinking is based on the axiomatic assumption that individuals operate to maximize their utility. In some of the theoretical presentations, this assumption is said to imply that utility includes both pecuniary and non-pecuniary gains (e.g., Furubotn and Pejovich, 1972, 1974). Under this configuration, one may hypothesize that SOE managers will be individuals who possess different utilities, valuing, e.g., prestige or power more than the additions to their wealth. In most studies, however, utility is equated with pecuniary gains. It is hypothesized that the more wealth the manager owns in a firm, and the more the manager's income is a function of this wealth by the linking of personal net monetary gains to the operational results of the firm, the higher the manager's incentives to invest more time, energy and efforts in ensuring organizational efficiency.

Berle and Means (1932) detected a growing tendency for the separation of ownership and control, at least in the United States. The separation of ownership and control means that diffused owners cannot really control management and that many large private firms are run by a self-perpetuating group of managers. As Dahrendorf correctly noted, a class theory based on the relationships between the owners of means of production and the workers "loses its analytical value as soon as legal ownership and factual control are separated" (1959, p. 136). Separation of ownership and control may reduce efficiency, and the manager may not single-mindedly pursue profits. Adam Smith certainly thought so: "The directors of such companies, however [are] the managers rather of other people's money than their own. Negligence and profusion, therefore, must always prevail, more or less, in the management of the affairs of such a company" (1937, p. 700).

One should, therefore, expect to find that the more dispersed the ownership, the lower the level of profits and efficiency. Pondy (1969) found that as ownership was separated from management, the ratio of administrative to operating personnel in forty-five manufacturing firms increased. His explanation for this finding is the "stronger preference for hierarchical expansion *per se*" of the professional manager (p. 57).

The vast literature on the separation of ownership from control has not reached any clear conclusions. There is considerable debate on the proportion of shares needed for effective control by the owners, as well as to whether shares held by one family or a pension fund should be counted as one. Certainly, concentrated ownership is not synonymous with the degree of involvement of the owners in the affairs of the corporation, and a pension fund, e.g., may not exercise its ownership rights in the same way as a private owner. Different researchers have used different approaches to these questions and have come out with different results. Berle and Means (1932) used 20 percent ownership as defining effective control, while Larner (1970), Palmer (1972) and Sheehan (1967) used 10 percent. Villajero (1962) used 5 percent and McEachern (1975) used 4 percent as sufficient control. Gordon (1945) added the shares held by what he termed "a small compact group of individuals," and Villajero (1962) included the holdings of investment companies and insurance firms in his measures of control. In view of these differences in definitions, Larner (1970) maintained that separation of ownership and control is growing, and Zeitlin (1974), using the same data, argued that there was no discernible trend.

Further, in most studies of the effects of ownership, the differences were not statistically significant. In some, the statistical techniques were defective, partly due to failure to control for government regulation. At any rate, the results did not resolve the questions. Some of these empirical studies support the hypothesis that individuals work more productively if they can appropriate the managerial gains of their work. Others do not. (For a summary see Nyman and Silberston, 1977. See also De Alessi, 1973; Gordon, 1945; Larner, 1966; McEachern, 1975, 1976; Jensen and Meckling, 1976, p. 305; Leibenstein, 1976, p. 44.) It stands to reason that additional factors, like the structure of the markets in which the enterprise operates, influence the profit rate. (See Demsetz, 1983.) In any event, it is clear that when a company is not run by its owner, there are likely to be agency costs.

Franchise agreements are a profitable device for reducing monitoring costs. Shelton (1967) compared two sets of franchises, one set operated by owner-managers and another by experienced managers employed by the parent company, motivated by bonuses that could be as high as a third of their salaries. His results show clearly that higher net returns are associated with owner-management. For example, the net revenue/sales ratio averaged 1.8 percent for franchise employees and 9.5 percent for owner-managers.

Even though it is difficult to monitor managerial behavior in a diffused ownership firm, it may be argued that managers in private firms receive bonuses and stock options that may be an incentive for seeking efficiency. The shareholders (as well as the capital market) may discipline the managers to behave in a profit-maximizing and efficient way (Stano, 1975). Thus, one major difference between private firms and SOEs is claimed to be in the incentive structures. Private enterprises "operate for profit and public ones must at least avoid losses" (Davies, 1981). A manager in an SOE does not increase his or her present monetary gain because of benefits that will accrue to the organization. Government controllers have even less personal monetary gain from increased efficiency of SOEs. Since shares are not transferable, private individuals are said to have no incentive to devote their time and energy to detect inefficient management in SOEs. They cannot use their resources to acquire the firm, apply their skills to reorganize it and, thus, appropriate gains to themselves. Even if an individual would be willing to reorganize such a firm, bearing all costs of implementing corrective actions, his or her personal gains in terms of lower taxes will be miniscule or even zero. In a private firm, even when ownership is diffused, managers always face the possibility that certain individuals, constantly searching for monetary gains, will take over a laggard firm. The very existence of those alert entrepreneurs puts pressures on managers to perform efficiently (Manne, 1965, p. 110). State ownership does not have a similar ingenious institutional device. Moreover, the government bureaucracy does not bear personal costs if firms are inefficient. They may also be constrained by a host of bureaucratic rules and regulations.

As a result of these factors, SOE managers are said to have no incentive to run efficient operations, and the monitoring system of their operations suffers from the same weakness. In fact, it may be argued that managers of SOEs have more opportunities to further their interests at the expense of the owners-taxpayers. They can insure themselves by employing larger staffs and more capital aids to assist them in decision making (De Alessi, 1974a). They can increase the size of the organization simply because larger size means higher salaries, more perquisites and higher budgets. To achieve high growth, they can use lower discount rates in evaluating investment opportunities, thus implementing larger projects, using more capital (De Alessi, 1969, 1974a, 1974b). They can monitor work less effectively (Davies, 1981) or simply opt for an easier life. In short, they will manage the firms less efficiently and take fewer risks than their private sector counterparts. Therefore, SOEs will use more labor and capital for a given output and will have lower profits, and their managers will enjoy more leisure than managers in privately owned firms similarly situated.

This explanation does not seem to be very convincing. Large business enterprises are very complex, and the decisions made by their managers involve a trade-off between short- and long-term considerations. In fact, many claim, the need to show quarterly results means that large private enterprises, at least in the United States, tend to develop myopic behavior, ignoring the long-term needs of the firm. Managers seeking to maximize their gains in an uncertain environment may decide to cut R&D costs or to minimize maintenance costs. Moreover, several studies point out that managers of private business enterprises attempt not to achieve efficiency but to maximize the growth of the firm (Baumol, 1959) or that they prefer to spend more on staff and perquisites (Williamson, 1964). Further, managers are not necessarily motivated by pecuniary incentives. They have been portrayed by Maccoby (1976) as gamesmen, playing the games of power and of prestige and attempting to win games, not because of their stock options but because of the rules of the game. No empirical evidence supports, however, the hypothesis that firms that have higher incentives are better and more efficiently managed. Further, in a democracy, the electorate can voice their concern about higher prices, putting pressure on Parliament to demand efficiency from SOEs.

The earlier quote from Davies (1981) suggests a totally different explanation—i.e., a difference in management's perception of the objectives to be pursued by the enterprise. Private-sector managers know they are expected to be efficient and to make profits. SOE managers perceive their role differently: they have to avoid losses, but they may see their major role as managing the environment rather than managing the business in an efficient way. Since SOEs have many stakeholders, all of whom have to be satisfied, the managers spend more of their time in public relations activities, in making explanations or in negotiations with external authorities. The more of the manager's extremely scarce time that is devoted to the management of the environment, the less time is left for the efficient management of the enterprise.

We have considered differences in behavior caused by behavior of managers and their controllers that is based on their different self-interest. Lindsay (1976, p. 1062) suggests another reason that leads him to believe that SOEs are inherently less efficient than private enterprises: customers of SOEs affect supply behavior, not only by their decisions in the market but also through political channels. This demand-based political influence is strongest when the enterprise supplies services that economists classify as public goods; i.e., those goods in which the consumption by one individual does not reduce the amount available to others. In these cases, one encounters problems like the familiar free rider problem observed by Olson (1965). When the SOE produces outputs of private goods to be sold in the market, no free riders exist. Still, taxpayers can and do pressure government to force SOEs to supply them goods at below market value because of an alleged or real social value of the output. For example, the government may instruct a railroad to maintain unprofitable services, not because of its market value but because it wants to help the elderly or simply because the constituents of the political representative of a certain town put pressure to maintain the service at prices that do not cover the cost. The market value of the consumption without any governmental intervention is simply the amount individuals are willing to pay for the services. If this value is below cost, the service will not be offered. When the service is supplied by government directly or by an SOE, political pressures may force its continuation at a loss. The loss, of course, is covered either by direct subsidy, by cross subsidization or by continuous losses of the SOE that are covered by governmental capital appropriation.

The same phenomenon is true also in the case of a private enterprise. In many market-oriented economies, government restrictions on economic activity are a pervasive fact of life. These restrictions give rise to rents in a variety of forms, and people often compete for the rents. This competition is for directly unproductive profit-seeking activities, e.g., through lobbying. As long as the cost of lobbying is lower than the expected benefits, rational profit maximizers will lobby in an attempt to get government subsidies or other forms of largesse. It is important to remember that the alternative to state ownership in many cases is regulation rather than a totally free market. In the case of water supplies, for example, there is a need to maintain a significant excess capacity for fire protection. Whether the additional cost of this protection is absorbed into the rates or paid by the property owners is a question decided by the regulators, not by the firm supplying the water—be it public or private.

Property rights theorists correctly point out that the very existence of private transferable property rights allows the flourishing of new entrepreneurs, eagerly looking for new opportunities. They also remind us that the threat of takeover bids may act as a constraint on managers. Still, in a mixed economy, a significant percentage of economic power is concentrated in the hands of the managers of a few hundred large firms. Many of them—in both private firms and SOEs—are motivated by considerations of power and achievement, not by personal pecuniary gains (see Chapter 8).

In many cases, the preservation of a nonprofitable service may generate a variety of external benefits, not captured by the accounting conventions. A government wishing to internalize these benefits may use public ownership or other means. Thus, "[t]he preservation of rail service avoids negative social and environmental impacts, such as air and noise pollution, increased traffic congestion and accidents, or increased risk from shipment of hazardous materials" (Fisher, 1982, p. 267). If business firms move away because of an abandonment of rail services, this factor may also increase the net fiscal burden on the state. Infant industry agreements, job preservations, or strategic considerations may lead a government to impose tariff restrictions. Potential entry of new companies may be deterred by minimum wage laws, health and safety regulations or environmental restrictions. In most of these cases, allocative efficiency is not the politician's ideal, and prospects of rents are created for both private firms and SOEs.

Another theoretical approach predicts SOEs to be less efficient than private enterprise for reasons of a different sort. The "public choice" school of thought is directed by the so-called theory of bureaucracy (Niskanen, 1971). Niskanen (1971) proposed that bureaucrats attempt to achieve more pay, power and prestige. Since in public bureaucracy there is no "bottom line," these "three p's" can be maximized by budget maximization. The coalition of bureaucrats and special interests pushes the budget to a higher level. According to this line of thinking, SOE managers attempt to maximize growth. De Alessi (1969) found some evidence that public managers use larger staff. They also use higher capital–labor ratios: the excess capital make productivity look higher to their monitors. This theory was tested mainly on public bureaucracies (for a summary, see Borcherding et al., 1982, pp. 136-145). However, it may be applied to SOEs, too.

EMPIRICAL EVIDENCE

Much of the debate on comparative efficiency of privately owned firms and SOEs is waged primarily on ideological grounds, generating much heat but very little light.

It is extremely difficult to compare efficiency in private enterprises and SOEs because it is not very easy to find two firms operating in the same country that are exactly comparable. Electric utilities in the United States are one exception described "as close to perfection in public–private comparability as any other imaginable real-world case" (Yunker, 1975, p. 66). California private electric utilities, however, have conceded that their costs are higher than state-owned electric firms but argued that their territories are more difficult to serve (Neuberg, 1977, p. 310, footnote). Different electric firms also have different input costs because one uses hydroelectric power and another coal or fuel or because the cost of capital to the SOE is lower: municipal firms in the U.S. can tap funds by issuing tax-exempt bonds. At the same time, it may be argued that differences in input costs are a result of absence of pressure on management to bargain.

Despite these difficulties, there is a growing number of studies comparing private enterprises and SOEs comparatively situated, i.e., cases in which both operate in the same country and the same environment. These studies were carried out mainly in the United States on electric power and refuse collection. There have been also a few studies in other countries.

Electricity and Telephone

Yunker (1975) estimated costs as a function of output and number of customers for 1969 on private and municipally owned firms producing 0.5 to 4 million megawatt hours per annum. He found that the costs of the public firms were lower but the results were not statistically significant. Further, Yunker did not control for input prices and for the different mixes of generation, transmission and distribution.

Meyer (1975) attempted to offset the problem of input prices by grouping the population geographically, assuming input prices vary regionally. He then chose a random sample of thirty firms in each ownership category. Real estate taxes, income taxes and interest costs were included in the general and administrative cost components but were excluded from the operating costs. He found for the years 1967, 1968, and 1969 that generating costs per megawatt hour declined with the size of the output and were lower for the SOEs. Transmission costs were also lower for SOEs and varied with the number of customers.

His study, however, was criticized on several methodological grounds, including the fact that he failed to exclude the cheaper federal hydroelectric plant (Meyer, 1975). Of course, if private plants burn fuel and a public firm uses hydropower, the cost difference is not necessarily a result of ownership. Meyer did, however, show that the cost coefficients are lower for SOEs. Wallace and Junk (1970) compared large private utilities with small municipalities. They found, not surprisingly, the former to be more efficient but mainly because of the economies of scale. When size and use of hydroelectric power was controlled for, municipal firms were found to be more efficient (Hellman, 1972; Yunker, 1975). Peltzmann (1971), however, attributed the difference to the tax-exempt status enjoyed by the municipalities. Spann (1977) concluded, on the basis of a different sample, that private firms adjusted for scale were no less efficient than municipal ones, and probably more so with respect to operating costs and investment per kwh.

Neuberg (1977) compared costs of distribution systems of 90 private and 75 municipal firms for 1972. He found the operating costs of public firms were 23 percent cheaper than private firms. This figure falls to 15 percent when capital costs are included.

Pescatrice and Trepani (1980) estimated simultaneously the cost and input demand functions and explored differences in generating technology, using generation data for the years 1965 and 1970 for 33 private firms and 23 municipal firms. They found SOEs minimize cost and have 24 (in 1965) to 33 (in 1970) percent lower per unit cost than their privately owned counterparts. Moreover, the rate of technical progress in SOEs was found to be considerably higher than in private firms.

Vaughn and Rives (1982) hypothesized that

> *Ownership form can affect the firm's taste for price discrimination rather than its level of sales and output. At the same time, rate of return regulation (ROR) can affect the private firm's output decisions while not changing its taste for price discrimination. Finally the public firm's decisions may be affected if the firm cross-subsidies* [*sic*]. [*p.* 385]

Therefore, the rate of return of SOEs may be lower, even though they are equally efficient.

The property rights theory would also predict that SOEs would charge lower prices that favor large users with much political power. Moore (1970) estimated profit-maximizing prices for sixty-two privately owned and twenty-seven municipally owned U.S. electric utilities. The prices charged by the latter were 10 to 22 percent below the profit-maximizing level, while those of private firms were between 0 and 5 percent below this level (see also Peltzman, 1971, Baldwin, 1975).

Mann and Seifried (1972) report for 128 U.S. municipally owned electric utilities that the rates are more cost related for domestic users than for commercial and industrial users and that industrial users reap most of the benefits. Jackson (1969) and Mann and Mikesell (1971) report that the price behavior of privately owned U.S. electric utilities is similarly cost related across different user categories. This evidence corroborates much anecdotal evidence from other countries that SOE electric firms are used to benefit large industrial users. It does not show, however, that these firms are more or less efficient. Gordon (1981) compared five state-owned and three investor-owned electricity firms in Canada. There were no fundamental differences among these firms. For example, all operated both in high-cost, remote areas and in lower-cost, heavily urbanized areas. They used different combinations of power sources and had different load factors. State-owned Hydro Quebec had the lowest cost (11.6 mills/kwh) and investor-owned Newfoundland Light and Power, the highest (393 mills/kwh). Hydro Quebec, however, had a high load factor and a high concentration of hydroelectric power, while Newfoundland Light and Power sells to a low-load residential service. A trend within utilities over the 1967 to 1976 period showed that all except one had a decreasing cost performance and that the SOEs had a better cost structure (Gordon, 1981, pp. 253–260).

Like the electric utilities, telephone companies operate in monopolistic environments, and the terms and conditions for these services are subject to the approval of a regulatory commission. A comparison of seven investor-owned and three state-owned telephone companies did not demonstrate major performance differences (Gordon, 1981, pp. 263–269): "When operating costs are totaled . . . investor-owned and government-owned telephone companies displayed very comparable performance" (p. 267). Bell-Canada has fewer employees per 1,000 telephones, apparently because of economies of scale.

It is also argued that price discrimination is a means for wealth maximization. SOE managers are reported to adopt fewer rate schedules than private managers. Peltzman (1971) hypothesized that the primary objective of SOE managers in public utilities is to maintain both their managerial tenure and political support for the firm; that is, managers would use the price mechanism to redistribute wealth within their political constituency, conferring benefits on voter-consumers, trading profits for political support. Therefore, there will be a tendency to average costs uniformly across classes; they will forego opportunities for price discrimination in the rate structure; prices will rise less frequently, and prices for nonvoters (consumers who are not residents of the community) will be higher than for resident-voters. The rate structure of those consumer groups that are more politically active or have lower costs of organizing will be lower regardless of the group's size or relative usage. Peltzman indeed found that the tariff structures of municipal electric utilities reflected less closely the costs of serving specific customer groups. He also found that privately owned firms engaged in greater price discrimination within customer groups and sell more output. De Alessi (1977) corroborated this hypothesis. He concluded that SOEs use less peak load pricing and that their rate structure is less complex than that of private firms. These results were corroborated by an international study of telephone rate structure. Littlechild (1983b) found that privately owned telephone systems are significantly more likely to use three or more time-of-day pricing periods for toll calls than SOEs. He also concluded that "separating a traditional PTT into its component postal and telephone business is unlikely to have much effect on telephone tariff policy unless the telephone business is also transferred to private ownership" (Littlechild, 1983b, p. 375).

Moore (1970) found evidence suggesting that municipal firms have greater capacity and built more plants at higher costs than private firms. He also reported that although fuel costs per kilowatt hour were not different for various ownership groups, operating costs per kilowatt hour were higher for municipally owned firms. De Alessi, in a summary of many studies, concluded that SOEs in electric power relative to privately owned firms charge lower prices, use less price discrimination, have more favoritism toward business relative to residential users and show less frequent rate changes, longer managerial tenure and less speed in adopting cost-reducing innovations (De Alessi, 1947a).

Blair (1976) also argues that rate structure in an SOE is particularly vulnerable to political influences. Prices will be based on subjective criteria such as "fair and equitable" and "less discriminatory."

In contrast, it should be noted that EDF in France has been a pioneer in the introduction of peak load pricing. The reason for the differences may be related more to the U.S. SOEs. Further, in many countries governments required uniform rates across customer groups and geographical areas for macroeconomic and social reasons. Whether the reasons for the rate structure are management inefficiency, electoral considerations or social welfare ideology cannot be deduced from these studies.

Foreman–Peck and Waterson (1985) focused on electricity generation in the United Kingdom, using data for 1937, when electricity in Britain was still generated by competing firms, selling their outputs to the national grid operated by the Central Electricity Board (CEB). At that time, CEB selected certain firms to supply it with electricity. They concluded that "the best municipal undertakings are on a par in static efficiency terms with the best companies and that they do not appear to show any biases towards the employment of particular factors of production" (p. 93). They also conclude "that in the absence of CEB regulation, the local authority sector would have been less efficient on average than the private sector" (p. 93).

Refuse Collection

In contrast to electricity, there are very small economies of scale in refuse (solid waste) collection. In the United States, refuse collection is sometimes performed by a municipal sanitation department, sometimes by private firms enjoying franchises to certain areas, or by competing firms. Most comparative studies in this area focus on the user charges levied, not on cost. Thus, Bennett and Johnson (1979) report on their home county of Fairfax, Virginia, that householders must contract with one of 29 competing firms or with the municipal solid waste division. The cost for municipal collection was $126.80 for one weekly collection, while the mean charges for private collectors was $85.76 with estimated standard deviation of $18.20 (p. 59). The authors do not explain the wide dispersion of prices charged by private collectors. They propose that these differentials are a result of the "transient nature of the population" (p. 61). The difference in user charges between private firms and the municipality is largely mitigated by the fact that municipal charges are deductible from both federal and state taxes.

Spann (1977), reviewing various activities including electric utilities and garbage collection concluded that, for the majority of the activities "private producers can provide the same services at the same or lower costs than can public producers" (p. 88).

The many studies of refuse collection often fail to take into account factors such as the volume and type of garbage, distance from disposal site and split between residential and commercial sites. Savas (1982) summarizes his and other studies, estimating municipal collection to be on the average 29 to 37 percent more costly than contract or franchise collection (pp. 93–94). This finding is attributed to the use of more persons to do the job, higher rates of absenteeism and the use of less productive vehicles (Spann, 1977, p. 82; Savas, 1979). Savas (1977a) also found that conventional municipal budgets understate the cost of the service by an average of 23 percent. Since the full costs are not revealed, municipalities tend to prefer their own refuse collection.

Hirsch (1965), however, found more significant differences between public and private cost of residential refuse collection in his study of 24 cities and municipalities in St. Louis and Missouri. Kemper and Quigley (1976) report, from an analysis of 101 Connecticut jurisdictions, that private collection appears to be 30 percent more expensive than municipal collection, which in turn appears to be about 25 percent more expensive than contract collection.

Kitchen (1976) studied 48 Canadian municipalities for 1979, each with a population in excess of 10,000. He found municipal collection is more costly than private collection.

Since most studies are based on user costs, differences in trucks used and other factors may influence the result. Still, most of the studies do point out that private refuse collection is cheaper.

Water

Other researchers in the United States compared the supply of water by municipal utilities and privately owned firms. Crain and Zardkoohi (1978) argued that a municipally owned water firm would tend to have more employees. They explained the propensity for increased employment as stemming from the desire to elevate the proportion of the population that supports the enterprise. They also report that the marginal product of labor was higher and the marginal product of capital lower for privately owned compared to municipally owned firms. In one case, a private firm became public and experienced a decline in output per employee of 40 percent. In another, a public firm became private and output per employee increased by 25 percent.

Mann (1979) compared 315 public and 56 private water utilities in the United States. The mean daily production of the publicly owned utilities was much larger than privately owned utilities, they experienced much greater maximum daily demand and per capita use, served more population that is less dense and rely more heavily on surface water sources as opposed to groundwater sources used by private firms. The publicly owned firms had much more debt costs and paid much less in taxes. They employed more employees per 10,000 population served but fewer per 1,000 customers served; this difference is apparently explained by the lower density. Both their monthly charges and their weighted annual labor cost per employee were lower, and they served fewer customers relative to the size of the population. Their operating cost per million gallons supplied was $198.50 compared to a mean of $203.09 for the private firms. Their total costs were higher because of the much higher debt charges (mean $64.10 compared to $36.46 for the private firms). In his regressions, Mann combined operating costs and debt charges, thus reaching the conclusion that total unit costs decrease, among other things, with private ownership (Mann, 1979, p. 22). He also claims that "one cannot assert unambiguously the sources of the [unit operating costs] differences. Regulatory environment may have a greater effect than ownership *per se*" (p. 25). Mann and Mikesell (1976) and Morgan (1977) showed that U.S. state/municipal suppliers of water are costlier by 15–20 percent than private suppliers.

Other Services

Scottsdale, Arizona, receives its fire protection under contract from a private company. A comparison of this city to three other Phoenix-area cities of comparable size, age and demographies demonstrated that Scottsdale ranked number one in speed of responses to alarms, and its average per capita cost for fire protection was $6.48 compared to $11.58 average in the three other cities (Poole, 1983, p. 109). Ahlbrandt (1973) compared Scottsdale to the Seattle area, showing Seattle municipal fire departments had 39 to 88 percent higher cost per capita.

Pashigian (1976) examined 58 U.S. bus transit systems, all of which had monopolies in their particular areas. He reports that private bus companies were more successful than municipally-owned companies in reducing the diversion of passengers from local transport to private autos. He also found that the convergence of urban transit systems from private to public ownership occurs earlier in cities where users have more voting strength. Blankart (1979) reports from Germany that municipal bus transport costs were higher per kilometer than the contract price paid to private bus operators for comparable services.

Borcherdring *et al.*, (1982) summarized findings from more than fifty studies and in most of them SOEs had higher unit cost structures. The empirical evaluation of the reasons for the differences is fraught with many difficulties. No two firms are perfectly comparable, and even a single firm is not comparable over time. The size may be different and the distribution of clients and their density may not be identical.

Many studies rely on cost estimates for only one year, and have to make many assumptions. Certainly, the subject of comparing SOEs to private firms is in the embryonic stage.

Unfortunately, there are very few other studies comparing SOEs and private firms. Nunnenkamp (1981) compared the efficiency of SOEs and private firms in Taiwan. His analysis compares performance at the level of aggregate industries such as food, textile or basic metals—and therefore heterogeneous products and different types of these firms in the two sectors. Nunnenkamp found that in half the industries SOEs were less efficient. In general, he found "a lower technical efficiency in the public sector (although the differences between the various industries are considerable)" (p. 107). He also found SOEs had advantages in terms of economies of scale, but noted that "it is to be expected that SOEs' advantages will diminish with an increasing engagement of private enterprises in industries characterized by far reaching economies of scale" (p. 107). This study compares all manufacturing at the aggregate. It is thus highly influenced by factors such as type of product or firm's size.

The studies of electrical utilities in the United States do not provide support to the superiority of private ownership, although many researchers clearly have an ideological bias, attempting to substantiate such superiority (see De Alessi, 1980; Borcherding et al., 1982).

At least one study of short-line railroads in the U.S. (John Due, summarized in Fisher, 1982, p. 240) also shows that city-owned railroads had comparable cost of ton/miles of freight. Goodermote and Mancke (1983) report that the fears that the British National Oil Company (BNOC) will be inefficient "appear to be unfounded. As BNOC gained experience and territory it also earned grudging respect from the oil industry" (p. 70). In many cases, government policies dictate higher costs, e.g., when the SOE is required to use high-cost inputs (as in the case of coal sold to electricity producers in the United Kingdom or when more manpower is used for social reasons.) Whether or not such a policy is misguided is an important question, but it is not easy to isolate managerial efficiency in such cases.

Pryke (1971), one of the ardent believers in public ownership, studied the performance of the state-owned sector in the United Kingdom. In his first study (1971), he found the state-owned sector to perform better than the private sector and reported on very favorable productivity of the U.K. nationalized industries. In a follow-up study for the period since 1968, Pryke reversed his earlier conclusions, taking a much less favorable view of the subject. He believes his "views have changed because the facts have altered and because [he] know[s] more about the subject" (Pryke, 1981, p. vii). He found that the real return for the private industrial and commercial sector had fallen to 3 and 4 percent and that the average return of SOEs in the 1970s plummeted to about zero. Detailed comparisons of the state-owned British Airways and the private British Caledonian, state-owned cross-channel ferries and hovercraft services and the sale of gas and electric appliances by the state-owned firms indicated that state-owned firms performed less well than private enterprises. He sees the reasons for inefficiency as stemming mainly from the size of the SOEs and their monopoly power:

> *The fact that the nationalised undertakings are so large and are in public ownership converts what would otherwise be a collection of local difficulties and decisions into a national problem about which pressure groups and trade unions become concerned and politicians adopt policies. Corner shops have been quietly closing for years, but if retailing had been nationalised there would have been a great outcry some years ago when it became known that the Shops Board had a ten-year plan to close many of its uneconomic local outlets, and the process would probably have been slowed down. If the Coal Board did not exist and the railways had not been nationalized the problems of closing down loss-making pits and withdrawing unprofitable rail services would be less formidable. Moreover, if the electricity industry has been less centralized, different utilities would have chosen different types of reactors and some of them at least would have made the right choice. The great advantage of decentralized decision-making is that bets are hedged, change is gradual and issues are not politicised.* [*Pryke, 1981, p. 265*]

While I fully agree that many of the reasons given by Pryke for the politicization of the SOEs are because they are too centralized and mainly too subject to governmental political interference, I would question the effect of their size. Had the United Kingdom nationalized only one grocery shop, its board would have faced the same almost insurmountable problems in attempting to close it. The member of Parliament for the area would surely have demanded explanations in Parliament, and the government might have decided that the closure was not worth the political uproar. Had there been a coalition government in the United Kingdom, and the minster for that shop felt that he would lose power by the closure, the same thing would have happened. The problem, again, is not size but the institutional structure and processes.

Pryke's (1981) second point is well taken: had there been more than one electricity firm, they might have experimented with different reactors. However, if all these electricity firms had been state owned and tightly controlled by one minister of energy, the minister (or his or her staff) would have felt such experiments to be a waste of money. A committee of experts would have been nominated inside the ministry to repeat the staff work already done at the level of the different corporations. It is highly probable that such a committee would have found one reactor to be better than the others and forced all the enterprises to purchase it. If these enterprises were told in the past to freeze their prices as a part of the national government's anti-inflation measures, they would all be starved for cash and would have to crawl to the Treasury to ask for funds. The Treasury would then nominate another committee of experts and would recheck all the figures and work done at the enterprise level and at the ministry of energy level. Their decision would be the one the enterprises would have to adopt to obtain the necessary funds.

Gordon (1981) in Canada compared airlines, in addition to electricity and telephone utilities. Air Canada was relatively less efficient in using people and capital than were the privately owned U.S. carriers and Canadian Pacific Air. However, such a comparison "cannot be definitive because of the differences among airlines in routes flown" (p. 281). In steel, the state-owned Sidbec had a sales turnover broadly similar to the industry's but a low return, caused by its flat rolling mills operations running at low volumes (p. 287).

These studies compare firms that are heavily regulated. They thus combine a mixture of the effects of property rights with those of limited competition and regulation. In addition, except for the studies of Blankart and Pryke, they were all carried out in the United States or Canada.

IMPACT OF COMPETITION

Both socialist and capitalist economists accept that competing firms are more efficient than monopolies and that industrial structure has very important ramifications for efficiency. They also agree that "The differences between government monopolies and government firms with private competitors might be greater than the differences between government firms and private firms in competition with one another" (Peltzmann, 1971, p. 146). Still, it is possible that "the managers of political firms . . . are less constrained by market considerations . . . and find it easier to obtain subsidy and to mask bad management under the guise of fulfilling other 'social' costs. Government firms . . . can survive for long periods . . . [with] grossly inefficient management" (De Alessi, 1974a, p. 7). Therefore, even under competition, an SOE would be less efficient than a private firm. Conversely, "One would expect competition to exert some market pressure on government enterprises to hold down costs . . . and to eliminate some of the opportunities for directing behavior on the part of bureaucracies" (Spann, 1977, p. 75).

There are, however, very few cases in which the effects of property rights can be isolated from those of noncompetitive markets and regulation. One of the few cases studied is that of the Canadian railroad industry. In Canada, two large railroads of roughly equal size are in operation. One is the privately owned Canadian Pacific, which has spanned the North American continent since 1885. The other is the state-owned ("Crown corporation," as such firms are called in Canada) Canadian National. This firm has been a nationwide competitor of Canadian Pacific since 1923, when the government decided to take over and consolidate several failing railroads. The two railroads account for 90 percent of Canadian railway gross revenues. Since World War II, restrictions on their ability to compete for traffic have been removed.

Caves and Christensen (1980) measured the production efficiency of the two railroads using total factor productivity (TFP), or real output per unit of real resources expended, as a measure. They reported the following:

> *Contrary to what is predicted in the property rights literature, we find no evidence of inferior efficiency performance by the government-owned railroad. In fact, our evidence indicates that the CN [Canadian National] has achieved larger gains in productivity than the CP [Canadian Pacific] since 1956. In the late 1950s and early 1960s the CN had a level of productivity approximately 90 percent as high as the CP, but this gap has been closed. We conclude that in the case of Canadian railroads the beneficial effects of competition have been sufficient to overcome any tendency toward inefficiency resulting from public ownership.* [*Caves and Christensen, 1980, pp. 960–961*]

R.A. Daly and Co. Ltd., studied the same railroads for the period 1971 to 1976. Their analysis suggests that Canadian Pacific's railway operations were more efficient, but Canadian National has been closing the gap. Daly concluded, "By most measures utilized, CP appears to be the most efficient transporter, but its lower exposure to rail lines which must be operated in the public interest must be considered. Measures of labor efficiency indicate that [CN has tightened] its managerial control in recent years" (in Gordon, 1981, p. 278). Caves and Christensen concluded:

> [T]*hat public ownership is not inherently less efficient than private ownership—that the oft-noted inefficiency of government enterprises stems from their isolation from effective competition rather than their public ownership* per se. *Of course, our findings do not provide any evidence in favor of public ownership over private ownership. There*

> *may be criteria other than productive efficiency which provide the basis for preferring either public or private ownership, but that is another question.* [*1980, p. 974*]

In a later publication, Caves and Christensen were joined with two other authors and continued their investigation, this time comparing the economic performance of U.S. with Canadian railroads. They concluded that the degree of economic regulation had a strong influence on the economic performance of the North American railroads. "When one controls for the influence of regulation, there is little indication that ownership form influences performance" (in Stanbury and Thompson, 1982, pp. 146–147). They observed no substantial differences in productivity growth rates between Canadian National and Canadian Pacific. The substantially less-regulated Canadian railroads had a distinctly better performance than the more regulated U.S. railroads in terms of productivity growth rates. The productivity levels of the two Canadian railroads and their growth rates exceeded that of all U.S. railroads except three small ones. They concluded that the

> [*S*]*pecific explanation for the superior economic performance of the two Canadian railroads must ultimately lie in the area of organizational design and control. . . . For example . . . as the Canadian railroads were deregulated the marketing organizations of those companies were radically altered . . . Canadian railroads have much more elaborate "costing" systems than those of their U.S. counterparts . . . perhaps the greatest costs associated with transportation regulation are not those associated simply with misallocation of traffic between modes . . . or expenses incurred in maintaining services that would not be provided in a competitive setting, but those associated with a lack of innovation.* [*In Stanbury and Thompson, 1982, pp. 147–148*]

One of the most quoted papers on comparisons of state-owned and private firms is that of Davies (1971). He compared the performance of the two domestic Australian air carriers. The two were in the same country and the same line of business and were operating in the same lines. Both were regulated. Davies studied their performance for the 16-year period from 1958/1959 to 1973/1974. He concluded, "The evidence indicates that the private firm [Ansett Airlines], operating under the rules and customs associated with exchangeable private property rights, is more productive than the public enterprise ['Trans-Australia Airlines] (1977, p. 226). William A. Jordan, however (in Stanbury and Thompson, 1982, pp. 161–199), claims that Davies used consolidated figures for Ansett and its four subsidiaries but that only one of these subsidiaries was similar to the state-owned Trans-Australia Airlines in providing interstate trunk operations. Based on a more detailed breakdown of the figures, Jordan claims:

> *[O]wnership is not a relevant factor in airline performance where regulatory monopolies exist. . . . the evidence regarding ownership does not necessarily apply to performance in a deregulated environment. Indeed, it could well be that the performance similarities among federally regulated airlines, regardless of ownership, are a common response to a dominant environment produced by a regulatory monopoly, and that performance differences due to ownership would develop with the removal of such regulation. For example, in the absence of regulation, would a government-owned airline respond in the same ways as a privately owned airline if it faced bankruptcy because of the competition of rival carriers? Might not the government-owned airline (supported by its employees and suppliers) turn to the government for subsidies (such as direct payments and low-interest loans) or for the allocation of an increased share of government traffic, rather than make the painful adjustments that a small, privately owned airline would tend to make in similar circumstances? If so, the performance of the government-owned airline would diverge from that of the privately owned airline.* [*p.* 194]

Certain cases exist, to respond to the implicit question posed by Jordan, in which a state-owned airline had to take the same painful adjustment that a privately owned small airline does. El Al Airlines was literally allowed by the government to file for bankruptcy. Since December 1982, it has been operated and directed by a court-appointed receiver. Its new fleet of airplanes was acquired by the government and leased to it for operations. The firm made many painful changes in employment and work rules and installed many more cost-saving measures. The Sri Lanka airline was also allowed to be closed, and a new firm was immediately created to take some of its employees. To be sure, managers, employees and other interest groups did fight to receive subsidies. However, when they understood they would not receive these subsidies, they took draconic measures to become more competitive. The point is that managers of SOEs may be hypothesized to learn with time how to negotiate with their environment—in particular, the part in it that gives them the authority and the legitimacy. In fact, private firms also approached their respective governments demanding subsidies and aid. The U.S. steel firms have been doing that, and others attempted but were less successful.

Again, the emphasis is on the importance of the common response to a dominant environment produced by a regulatory monopoly. There, no differences have been found, either in the famous Australian case or in North America, that can be explained by ownership differences. The question, therefore, remains, are any differences caused by ownership in a nonregulatory environment?

Davies (1981) compared Australian private and state-owned banks. Seven large banks, each with an extensive network of branches, control 92 percent of assets and deposits of the Australian trading banks. Six are privately owned and one, the Commonwealth Trading Bank, is owned by the government. This bank and the Bank of New South Wales are the largest and are similar in size and other important characteristics. The banking legislation passed in the years 1956 to 1959 attempted to put state-owned and private commercial banks on equal footing so that the banks in both sectors operate under virtually identical legal constraints. Prior to 1955, private commercial banks were not allowed to own savings banks. Since then, each one of the major commercial banks has a saving bank subsidiary.

Davies (1981) hypothesized that a private bank will hold a higher proportion of its assets in loans while state-owned banks will hold a higher proportion of government securities, reflecting their risk aversion. Indeed, the private banks held a larger share of total investments in higher yielding but riskier nongovernment securities than the state-owned banks, and in every year except one, the ratio of loans to assets was higher for the private compared to the state-owned banks. In 10 of 11 years, the state-owned bank had a higher ratio of Australian public securities to total assets. No test of significance for the difference is provided.

A comparison of the state-owned Commonwealth with privately owned savings banks shows that the proportion of assets held in relatively riskless, low-yielding Australian public securities by the state-owned bank is larger than that of the private enterprise for all years except 1970 and 1971, when the ratios were identical for the two institutions. This is the only substantial piece of evidence that runs counter to the risk hypothesis (Davies, 1981, p. 127).

Davies (1981) further hypothesized that managers of state-owned banks will arrange their bank affairs so they can enjoy a less arduous life. Another hypothesis was that SOE managers would attempt to increase the size of the organization, "which in turn leads to correspondingly higher salary, as well as more power and prestige" (p. 129). Davies concluded that the state-owned bank had a higher ratio of expenses to net earnings and lower ratio of profits to assets, to expenses, to employees, to deposits and to capital.

In France, the three largest banks were nationalized immediately after World War II and most of the other financial institutions, in 1982. Following nationalization, chairmen of all banks were replaced by political appointees, loyal to the government line. Still, it is believed that nationalization was a complete waste of taxpayers' money. The newly appointed managers, according to *Institutional Investor,* "have been quick to identify with their new fiefdoms and, more surprisingly, have become quite vocal in defending their turf" (February 1983, p. 112). To be sure, the French government requires banks to maintain credits to sick companies at artificially low interest rates for a long time. However, *Euromoney* (July 1983, p. 66) quotes one bank manager in France: "Nationalization responded to certain political and economic objectives of the parties that took over power in France. . . . There was no economic reason to do it . . . and many Western governments, either with conservative or social democratic systems, are able to manage their economic goals through a private or semi-private banking system."

Finsinger (1983a) studied the performance of insurance markets in the Federal Republic of Germany and concluded that SOEs and mutual companies outperformed privately owned joint stock companies. Competition seems to be important in keeping SOEs efficient.

In some other cases, for historical or other reasons, SOEs were allowed to compete in the market. British Petroleum is one such example, and it does not seem that the firm is less efficient or gives its managers an easier life or better working conditions than the private oil multinationals. Monsen and Walters (1983) showed that SOEs are less profitable than private enterprises in Europe in areas like automobile production, but then in 1983, Peugeot's losses were greater than those of Renault's.

Primeaux (1975, 1977) reported that there are 49 cities with a population exceeding 25,000 in the United States where consumers can choose between more than one electric company. These cases are categorized as competitive. In a cross-sector regression equation designed to explain intercity variation, the competitive variable is used as a dummy variable and explains the cases of cities with relatively low rates. The duopolistic rivalry, according to Primeaux, causes efficiency that is greater than the loss of economies of scale.

Private competitive firms avoid any costs that would reduce their ability to compete. SOEs are often forced to carry additional costs because they are state owned. SOEs may be forced to operate on a scale that is prefixed by the size of the political unit, not by efficiency considerations (Spann, 1977). SOEs may be forced to deliver their services also to remote, sparsely populated areas.

Funkhauser and MacAvoy (1979) compared private firms and SOEs in Indonesia. In observing industries with both public and private firms, average profit margins for SOEs were 0.22 and for private firms −0.36. In fact, in all four samples used by the authors, SOEs had lower profit margins than private companies (p. 363). These results may be explained as stemming from the economist's prescription of optimal departures from marginal cost pricing (Baumol and Bradford, 1970). Baumol and Bradford, however, assume that SOEs add to consumer benefits by having lower profit margins, but the cost of production is assumed to be the same as in private firms. Funkhauser and Mac Avoy found that the reason was higher costs than the private firms. This higher cost was explained by them as "a 'tax' on operation to meet the requirements of local political organizations" (p. 367). SOEs' "goals are met by payments to factors [of production]—resulting in higher operating costs rather than by increased dividend payments" (p. 367).

Hill (1982), too, compared privately owned firms and SOEs in Indonesia. His sample included firms operating in a competitive environment: the weaving industry. According to him, government's goal in entering this industry was to reduce the dominance of Chinese entrepreneurs. His study shows that in 1976 there were 14 Indonesian weaving SOEs, operating 4,448 looms—or 318 looms on the average—as opposed to 75 looms in the average private firm. To get comparable data he chose only those firms operating fully automatic mechanized looms (M3) or semi-automatic looms (M2). His sample included 10 firms using technique M2—and in each category there were two SOEs. He then calculated the ratio of SOEs to private firms by technique.

For the fully automatic firms, the SOEs required 1.59 times the capital for a given value-added measured at market price (capital was measured as the replacement cost of all fixed assets). To find out how efficiently equipment is being used, the ratio of machinery output was calculated. This time SOEs reached 1.02 times capital compared to the private firms. The difference between these two measures show that SOEs had more capital invested in buildings and inventories.

By subtracting the labor costs from the value-added denominator, Hill (1982) obtained the capital/surplus ratio. Here, the ratio SOEs/private was 3.44. In other words, labor costs were much higher in the SOEs. Indeed, labor costs as a percent of total costs were 2.56 times higher in SOEs than in private firms, although wages were similar. Thus, SOEs employed many more workers. Finally labor hours per M^2 of cloth was 1.26 times higher in SOEs.

When semi-automatic equipment was used, all ratios were much higher per unit of value added; SOEs required 5.38 times capital, 1.66 times machinery. Capital surplus ratio was 18.01, labor hours per 1000 M^2 was 1.88, and labor cost as a percentage of total costs was 2.58. All in all, SOEs were found to require both more capital and more labor per unit of production. Still, all four SOEs covered their current expenditures from current revenues and one was "almost able to cover its full cost of production" (p. 1018).

Hill did not say how the four SOEs were chosen from the 14 operating in Indonesia. One of these SOEs, he reported had "aging machinery" (p. 1019). It had a sole agent who charged for the raw materials more than material prices and more than the selling price that he himself determined (p. 1019). Management was replaced and losses went down for three months from Rp 150 million to Rp 1.6 million.

Hill draws two implications from the above. First, "State enterprises are vulnerable for personal gains . . . [and] abuse. Secondly, the internal environment of government weaving mills may not be the major determinant of their performance. The quality of mill management is obviously very important" (p. 1019). One of the firms "had almost 12 month's stock of production on hand" (p. 1022) at a peak period of demand for cloth where three months is considered the upper limit in this industry. It is difficult to say how representative these SOEs were. Hill (1982) does mention two state-owned mills with significantly different results.

In another study of LDC, Victor Levy (1982) compared the allocational and technical efficiency of private and public firms in the chemical, mineral and food-processing industries in Iraq for 1962–1968 (1963–1968 for chemicals). In all three industries, SOEs were not using labor at its optimum amount: the value of marginal product of labor is above the wage rates. Instead, they were found to be overcapitalized. As to efficiency, SOEs were found on the whole to be "more efficient than private firms in the food and mineral industries" (p. 247) and no differences of efficiency were found in chemicals.

One advantage of competition from the professional manager's point of view is that the government and perhaps other stakeholders tend to reduce demands for achieving other social and political objectives when the firm faces direct competition in its spheres of activities. Governments tend to use SOEs to achieve these external objectives when the additional costs can be hidden from the public. One dubious advantage of subsidies to industrial users through the price mechanism of SOEs is that the subsidy is hidden—thus, it does not cause a public outcry. In fact, one way to interpret the property rights theory in terms of political economic argument is that government favors certain strong interest groups and uses SOEs to grant them more subsidies and more largesse. In Sri Lanka, e.g., the minister of industry called the managers of a U.S. MNE subsidiary, demanding that they curtail their output because their SOE competitor was inefficient and could not compete with them (*Financial Times*, October 10, 1984, Sri Lanka *Supplement*, p. 4).

Thus, an alternative explanation may be that government bureaucracies may allow more latitude and more discretion to managers of SOEs in a competitive environment; that is, when competition exists, one would expect government to allow the firm to pursue pure efficiency goals and demand from the managers less in terms of social goals. If this hypothesis is true, the problem with an SOE is not necessarily the nontransferability of shares but the institutional process of control. In fact, we know that the performance of the SOE sector in France, the United Kingdom or Italy has been deteriorating when measured in pure economic criteria of return on investment, profits or returns on assets in the 1960s and 1970s when government required these firms to freeze prices, bail out ailing firms, and in the case of Italy, direct increasing investments to the Mezzogiorno.

IRI, during the 1950s, enjoyed considerable autonomy, and all accounts analyzing its history seem to agree that in that period it was innovative, well managed and efficient. With time, however, it was required to direct its funds to the Mezzogiorno and to become the major rescuer of failing private firms (which preferred to be nationalized rather than to make the painful adjustment assumed as coming so naturally to a privately owned firm). As a result, it became inefficient, debt-ridden and a tremendous burden on the government budget. IRI's management tried to resist governmental pressures, and GEPI was created because IRI did not want to acquire more ailing firms. The U.K. nationalized industries suffered heavy losses because the government did not allow them to raise prices as an integral part of its attempt to combat inflation (NEDO, 1976; Daniels, 1977). In fact, it is extremely difficult for managers to maintain morale and lead the firm on the efficiency route when they are expected also to carry out and advocate to middle management other projects that are less acceptable to them. Managers also learn very fast how to lean on government once such behavior is legitimized.

However, since the French government reversed its earlier policies in 1983/1984 and insisted that its SOEs must be profitable or their managers would be sacked, the financial performance of these SOEs has dramatically changed. Péchiney, for example, posted a consolidated net for 1985 of FFr 750 million and FFr 550 for 1984, contrasted to a loss of FFr 4.46 billion in 1982 and 480 million in 1983. The turnaround has been attributed largely to the recovery plan instituted by George Besse, the group's chairman (*Financial Times*, February 19, 1986). Mr. Besse was named to head Régie Nationale des Usines Renault, replacing a chairman who had planned to shed jobs gently.

It seems, therefore, that efficiency differentials are the result of market structure and institutional controls as much as ownership type. SOEs operating in a competitive environment may be as efficient as privately owned firms. Competitive market pressures may be sufficient to yield productive efficiency even when shares are nontransferable.

Competition can be stimulated by institutional means, too. Tendler (1968) shows that, in the case of Brazil, competition for funds among different state-owned electricity generating firms "demonstrated a novel way of spurring performance in state enterprises" (p. 152). She notes:

> *A traditional argument against state production is that such ventures are not exposed to the rigors of market competition. In the Brazilian electric power sector, the government went into a naturally monopolistic industry, but left alone the branch of the industry (distribution) that required supply by only one company. By taking on generation only, state power production could contain many companies. In lieu of competition in the product market, competition for financing could stimulate state enterprise to behave like competitive private enterprise. Although the performance of the Brazilian state power companies in many cases, and at many points, fell below the standards of efficiency suggested here, there is no doubt that the successful cases can be explained in part by the competitive atmosphere in which they had to exist. (p. 52).*

In some cases, private enterprise seems to be more efficient (and certainly more profitable) because its operations are concentrated in the profitable parts of the business. In many cases, the SOE has to supply a certain service to all customers for the same price regardless of the costs. Public utilities often cross subsidize one part of their operations from the profits in other parts of the system. Parts could be either geographical, as when the rail service to a certain small community is cross subsidized by the profits from other lines, or based on time, such as when the bus or subway services in the peak rush hour are profitable and they subsidize the losing operations during other times of the day. In the telephone industry, long-distance phone call rates were fixed in a way that cross subsidized the local calls. Whether or not it is economically justifiable to use a cross-subsidization system is a point often discussed in the economic literature. It is argued by many that a system of differentiated prices that will take into account the real costs of operations district by district or hour by hour will be less costly to operate, more efficient, more equitable and fairer.

The argument for or against this type of differential pricing is not the subject of this book. The point, however, is that when such a system is not in operation, there is a strong incentive for a new entrant to the business to operate only part of the system at a lower cost, charging lower prices. Indeed, one argument for state ownership is that private operators will cream off the profitable work. In fact, the entry of private entrepreneurs in such cases may be beneficial: if cross subsidization is unavailable, consumers will have to pay the real cost of the service. To be sure, the criterion of willingness to pay assumes certain values; the elderly who need mobility to do their shopping or visit their children may not be able to pay. If government wants to subsidize certain services, however, it can do so openly through its budgets. The wider latitude to hide costs is not a good enough theoretical reason for using SOEs. In some countries, this wider latitude may even increase the opportunity for corruption (Levy, 1982).

POLITICS AND EFFICIENCY

Organizations are often seen as instruments for accomplishing complex tasks efficiently, with explicit, defined, and measurable goals. They are structured to achieve these goals and accomplish tasks effectively and efficiently. As shown in Chapter 4, SOEs have a multitude of goals and are required by different parts of government to stress different objectives. Government is not a single controller, speaking with one voice; it is a plethora of ministries, bureaus, agencies and departments pursuing a variety of conflicting goals. Managers are not innocent bystanders in this game. They, too, attempt to exert influence on their environment (Aharoni, 1982) and to coopt their controllers (Selznick, 1949). Corporations are essentially political constructs, and the manager's behavior may be governed by political more than by economic considerations.

Large corporations are managed not only by the top management but also by what Mintzberg (1983) called "the internal coalition"—that is, the full-time career managers of the firm. Chandler took the position that "career managers preferred policies that favored the long-term stability and growth of their enterprise to those that maximized current profits" (1977, p. 10). According to Baumol (1959), Roberts (1959) and Marris (1964), this preference is largely because of the association between size and managerial compensation and other perquisites. Professional managers tend to avoid controversy, criticism and risk. They are also, according to Monsen:

> [P]*robably more responsive to pressures from the various constituent groups of the firm such as workers, consumers, suppliers, or stockholders, and the government. The professional manager is apt to respond to conflicting demands from these groups by balancing one off against the other or by utilizing compromise as an issue settling device. The owner-manager, who views each dollar given to workers, suppliers, consumers or the government as coming from his own pocket, is less likely to compromise.* [1969, *p.* 48]

Since governmental impact on the economy has increased, the professional managers would be inclined to "shift their battleground from the firm level to the political level. Control of the government may then become the means for establishing 'control' of the firm" (Papandreou, 1952, p. 203). While state ownership may lead to politicization and inefficiency, there is much more to performance, innovation and efficient management than just ownership.

The first best requirement for efficiency is competition. However, many SOEs are monopolies. Privately owned monopolies have no reason to be more efficient than state-owned ones. They may capture the bodies that are supposed to regulate them. To the extent that pecuniary incentives and self-interest operate, they may merely mean that monopoly power will be exploited more fiercely. A privately owned monopoly may escape both political and market discipline. In other cases, SOEs are said to be less efficient because their management know losses are borne by the state. This fact, even if true, is not necessarily a function of ownership but that of certain institutional design. Governments are not required legally or otherwise to cover losses of SOEs instead of allowing them to go bankrupt!

To a large extent, efficiency depends on the design of the system, which as discussed in chapter 4, is composed of the rules of interactions of both the internal and external parts of the organization. Within the organization, resource-allocation decisions are influenced by the structure of tasks and authority, by the reward and punishment structure and by the values and beliefs of its internal coalition. Most decisions in the organization tend to reflect its past history and accumulated experience. Organizations, however, are also dependent on their environment and must ensure fit with the external environment to survive. Thus, competition can also be among different SOEs for funds from the government. Further, public policy and public outputs have many, very subtle dimensions. Internalization of externalities, well accepted by economists since Coase's (1937) seminal work, is true in SOEs, and even more so. Measuring efficiency is important, but the process of interaction of goals and means is even more important. Some of the higher costs of SOEs may be least-cost means to achieve certain social, political and redistributive goals. Some of the measured inefficiencies are in fact transfers to certain interest groups. Transfers through SOEs are politically preferable because they are invisible. Unfortunately, no test has yet been devised to measure the effectiveness of this method of transfer, and to separate these transfers and managerial effectiveness. It is almost impossible to separate what economists may see as waste from the political transfers in the form of higher wages or payments to other interest groups. It is also impossible to assess the extent to which government direct budget expenditures would have been increased if SOEs would not have been used to achieve these transfers with far less discrimination. Much more understanding of the process through which public production and provision is determined is needed (Aharoni, 1981b).

CONCLUSION

It is widely believed that SOEs are inherently less efficient than a private firm: first, the management of SOEs is not expected to achieve profits, and profit orientation is impaired by controlled prices, by political intervention in the SOE's strategy, marketing mix, financial policies, or appointment policies. Subsidization practices may weaken the SOEs' willingness to avoid inefficiencies. Most of the SOEs operate natural monopolies or so-called key industries, in which competition is restricted. For political reasons, SOEs may operate plants at suboptimal size. Finally, managers do not have sufficient incentives to avoid waste of resources.

The empirical evidence is much more ambiguous and lends only limited support to the hypothesis that SOEs are less efficient than private firms. The financial results of SOEs certainly show a dismal picture of losses. However, these losses may be a result of social and political demands on the enterprises. In terms of efficiency, these firms' performance is much less bleak. As efficient users of resources, they may have done as well as private firms producing the same product, in the same country.

SOEs' performance is affected by three sets of factors: First, objective factors such as input prices or the level of available infrastructure. Second, decisions made externally to the enterprises regarding its labor policies, investment and pricing. Third, the internal organization of the firm (McCawley, quoted in Hill, 1982, p. 1020). These three sets are obviously interrelated. Thus, the internal organization may suffer low morale because of decisions made externally to the enterprise. External influence also means that managers have to devote much time to the submission of reports and negotiations with controllers. If managers have little influence on input prices and on machinery used, they might resort to apathy. In most countries, SOEs have comparative disadvantages in terms of requirements to achieve noneconomic goals, to employ individuals of certain political affiliation or of certain tribes or to achieve a host of other social and political goals. The more they have to achieve these goals, the higher the probability that management will suffer from "widespread resentment, cynicism and loss of morale" (NEDO, 1976, p. 10).

In some countries, SOE managers are appointed, not because of their competence but because of their political or tribal affiliation and for the same reason they are not dismissed when they do not perform efficiently. To the extent that managers are indeed appointed because of political largesse, they owe their allegiance to the minister who appointed them and will follow his or her directions, not necessarily attempting to run efficient operations. This issue is discussed in Chapter 8.

Three things seem clear. First, poor monitoring, excessive intervention and attempts of civil servants to minimize managerial discretion lead to risk aversion, lack of initiative and waste. Second, the persistent tendency of government to use SOEs as conduits for dispensing subsidies or giving political patronage has been a major cause of losses and of inefficiency. Third, at least in some countries, a new managerial class has evolved, attempting to acquire more autonomy and increasing elbow room for independent action. These managers have different values then their private-sector counterparts but also deep-seated different outlooks and goals than the civil servants. In the eyes of their controllers, many SOE managers mirror private-sector behavior, taking advantage of opportunities for profitable growth and ignoring what civil servants see as the national interest. As SOE managers see it, their controllers do not understand the way business firms should be run. They are therefore unresponsive to central direction and resent any attempt to direct them in a way detrimental to the conduct of the firm with the same degree of business acumen displayed by firms in the private sector.

However, government is responsible to its citizens for the efficient conduct of its business and must, therefore, control the operations of the enterprises it owns. Let us turn to an analysis of how controls of SOEs operate in real life.

References

Aharoni, Yair, 1981b, "Performance Evaluation of State-Owned Enterprises: A Process Perspective," *Management Science* 27, no. 11: 1340–1347.

Aharoni, Yair, 1982, "State-Owned Enterprise: An Agent without a Principal," in Leroy P. Jones, ed., *Public Enterprise in Less-Developed Countries* (New York: Cambridge University Press), 67–76.

Ahlbrandt, Roger S., Jr., 1973, "Efficiency in the Provision of Fire Services," *Public Choice* 16 (Fall): 1–15.

Ahmed, Zia, ed., 1982, *Financial Profitability and Losses in the Public Enterprises of Developing Countries* (Ljubljana: I.C.P.E.).

Alchian, Armen A., 1965, "Some Economics of Property Rights," *Politico* 30 (December): 816–829.

Alchian, Armen A., 1977, *Economic Forces at Work* (Indianapolis: The Liberty Fund).

Atkinson, Anthony, and Joseph Stiglitz, 1980, *Lectures on Public Economics* (New York: McGraw-Hill Economics Handbook Service).

Baldwin, John R., 1975, The Regulatory Agency and the Public Corporation: *The Canadian Air Transport Industry* (Cambridge, Mass.: Ballinger).

Baran, Paul, and Paul M. Sweezy, 1968, *Monopoly Capital* (New York: Penguin).

Baumol, William J., 1959, *Business Behavior, Value and Growth* (New York: Macmillan).

Baumol, William J., and David F. Bradford, 1970, "Optimal Departures from Marginal Cost Pricing," *American Economic Review* 60, no. 3: 265–283.

Bennett, James T., and Manuel H. Johnson, 1979, "Public versus Private Provision of Collective Goods and Services: Garbage Collection Revisited," *Public Choice* 34: 55–63.

Bergson, Abram, 1968, *Planning and Productivity under Soviet Socialism* (New York: Columbia University Press).

Bergson, Abram, 1973, "On Monopoly Welfare Losses," *American Economic Review* 63, no. 5: 853–870.

Bergson, Abram, 1984, "Income Inequality under Soviet Socialism," *Journal of Economic Literature* 22, no. 3: 1052–1099.

Berle, Adolph A., Jr., and Gardiner C. Means, 1932, *The Modern Corporation and Private Property* (New York: Macmillan) (rev. ed., 1968).

Blair, John M., 1976, *The Control of Oil* (New York: Pantheon Books).

Blankart, Charles B., 1979, "Bureaucratic Problems in Public Choice: Why Do Public Goods Still Remain Public?" in R.W. Roskamp, ed., *Public Finance and Public Choice* (Paris: Cujas Publishers), 155–167.

Borcherding, Thomas E., Warner W. Pommerehne and Friedrich Schneider, 1982, "Comparing the Efficiency of Private and Public Production: The Evidence from Five Countries," *Zeitschrift für Nationalökonomie*, Suppl. 2, pp. 127–156.

Bös, Dieter, 1978, "Cost of Living Indices and Public Pricing," *Economica* 45: 59–69.

Bös, Dieter, 1981, *Economic Theory of Public Enterprise* (Berlin: Springer-Verlag).

Cameron, Kim, 1980, "Critical Questions in Assessing Organizational Effectiveness," *Organizational Dynamics* 9, no. 2 (Autumn), 66–80.

Campbell, John P., 1976, "Contributions Research Can Make in Understanding Organizational Effectiveness," *Organization and Administrative Sciences* 7, no. 1–2: 29–45.

Caves, Douglas W., and Laurits R. Christensen, 1980, "The Relative Efficiency of Public and Private Firms in a Competitive Environment: The Case of Canadian Railroads," *Journal of Political Economy* 88, no. 5: 958–976.

Chandler, Alfred D., Jr., 1977, *The Visible Hand: The Managerial Revolution in American Business* (Cambridge, Mass.: The Belknap Press).

Coase, Ronald H., 1937, "The Nature of the Firm," *Economica* 4: 386–405.

Cowling, Keith, and Dennis C. Mueller, 1978, "The Social Costs of Monopoly Power," *Economic Journal* 88: 727–748.

Crain, Mark W., and Asghar Zardkoohi, 1978, "A Test of the Property Rights Theory of the Firm: Water Utilities in the United States," *Journal of Law and Economics* 21: 395–408.

Dahrendorf, Ralf, 1959, *Class and Class Conflict in Industrial Society* (Stanford, Calif.: Stanford University Press).

Daniels, R.W., 1977, "The Regulation and Control of Public Utility Prices: British Experience 1960–1975," in Alexis P. Jacquemin and Henry W. de Jong, eds., *Welfare Aspects of Industrial Markets* (Leiden: Martinus Nijhoff), pp. 367–400.

Davies, David G., 1971, "The Efficiency of Public versus Private Firms: The Case of Australia's Two Airlines," *Journal of Law and Economics* 14, no. 1: 149–65.

Davies, David G., 1981, "Property Rights and Economic Behavior in Private and Government Enterprises: The Case of Australia's Banking System," *Research in Law and Economics* 3: 111–142.

De Alessi, Louis, 1969, "Implications of Property Rights for Government Investment Choices," *American Economic Review* 59, no. 1: 13–24.

De Alessi, Louis, 1973, "Private Property and Dispersion of Ownership in Large Corporations," *Journal of Finance* 28, no. 4: 839–851.

De Alessi, Louis, 1974a, "An Economic Analysis of Government Ownership and Regulation: Theory and the Evidence from the Electric Power Industry," *Public Choice* 19: 1–42.

De Alessi, Louis, 1974b, "Managerial Tenure under Private and Government Ownership in the Electric Power Industry," *Journal of Political Economy* 82, no. 3: 645–653.

De Alessi, Louis, 1977, "Ownership and Peak-Load Pricing in the Electric Power Industry," *Quarterly Review of Economics and Business* 17, no. 4: 7–26.

De Alessi, Louis, 1980, "The Economics of Property Rights: A Review of the Evidence," *Research in Law and Economics* 2: 1–47.

Demsetz, Harold, 1983, "The Structure of Ownership and the Theory of the Firm," *Journal of Law and Economics* 26: 375–390.

Dholakia, Bakul H., 1978, "Relative Performance of Public and Private Manufacturing Enterprises in India: Total Factor Productivity Approach," *Economic and Political Weekly Review of Management*, Feb. 25, pp. M.4–M.10.

Diamond, Peter A., and Jan A. Mirrlees, 1971a, "Optimal Taxation and Public Production, Part I: Production Efficiency," *American Economic Review* 61, no. 1: 8–27.

Diamond, Peter A., and Jan A. Mirrlees, 1971b, "Optimal Taxation and Public Production, Part II: Tax Rules," *American Economic Review* 61, no. 3: 261–278.

Dreyfus, Pierre, 1977, *La Liberté de Réussir* (Paris: Jean Claude Simoen). Republished 1981, as *Une Nationalisation Réussie: Renault* (Paris: Fayard).

Eckstein, Alexander, ed., 1971, *Comparison of Economic Systems* (Berkeley: University of California Press).

Ellman, Michael, 1979, *Socialist Planning* (London: Cambridge University Press).

Finsinger, Jörg, 1983a, "Competition, Ownership and Control in Markets with

Imperfect Information," in Finsinger, Jörg, ed., *Public Sector Economics* (Berlin: International Institute of Management), pp. 111–133.

Fisher, Peter S., 1982, "Alternative Institutional Structures for State and Local Government Ownership of Railroads," *Logistics and Transportation Review* 18, no. 3: 235–254.

Foreman-Peck, James, and Michael Waterson, 1985, "The Comparative Efficiency of Public and Private Enterprise in Britain: Electricity Generation between the World Wars," *Economic Journal* 95 Suppl.: 83–95.

Fubara, Bedford A., 1984, "Strategy Formulation and Political Intervention in State-Owned Companies in LDCs," *RVB Newsletter and Research Papers* 4, no. 1: 7–17.

Funkhouser, Richard, and Paul W. MacAvoy, 1979, "A Sample of Observations on Comparative Prices in Public and Private Enterprises," *Journal of Public Economics* 11, no. 3: 353–368.

Furubotn, Eirik G., and Svetozar Pejovich, 1972, "Property Rights and Economic Theory: A Survey of Recent Literature," *Journal of Economic Literature* 10: 1137–1162.

Furubotn, Eirik G., and Svetozar Pejovich, eds., 1974, *The Economics of Property Rights* (Cambridge, Mass.: Ballinger).

Gantt, Andrew H., and Guiseppe Dutto, 1968, "Financial Performance of Government-Owned Corporations in Less Developed Countries," *IMF Staff Papers* 15, no. 1: 102–148.

Gillis, Malcolm, 1980, "The Role of State Enterprises in Economic Development," *Social Research* 47, no. 2: 248–289.

Goodermote, Dean, and Richard B. Mancke, 1983, "Nationalizing Oil in the 1970s," *The Energy Journal* 4, no. 4: 67–80.

Gordon, Marsha, 1981, *Government in Business* (Montreal: C.D. Howe Institute).

Gordon, Robert A., 1945, *Business Leadership in the Large Corporation* (Berkeley: University of California Press).

Grayson, Leslie E., 1981, *National Oil Companies* (New York: John Wiley & Sons).

Gregory, Paul, and Gert Leptin, 1977, "Similar Societies under Differing Economic Systems: The Case of the Two Germanys," *Soviet Studies* 29, no. 4: 519–542.

Handoussa, Heba Ahmad, 1980, "The Impact of Economic Liberalization on the Performance of Egypt's Public Sector Industry" (Paper presented at the Second BAPEG Conference, April), Cambridge, Mass.

Harberger, Arnold C., 1954, "Monopoly and Resource Allocation," *American Economic Review* 44: 77–87.

Hellman, Richard, 1972, *Government Competition in the Electric Utility Industry* (New York: Praeger).

Hill, Hal, 1982, "State Enterprises in Competitive Industry: An Indonesian Case Study," *World Development* 10, no. 11: 1015–1023.

Hirsch, Werner Z., 1965, "Cost Functions of an Urban Government Service: Refuse Collection," *Review of Economics and Statistics* 47, no. 1: 87–92.

Jackson, Raymond, 1969, "Regulation and Electric Utility Rate Levels," *Land Economics* 45, no. 3: 372–376.

Jensen, Michael C., and William H. Meckling, 1976, "Theory of the Firm: Managerial Behavior, Agency Costs and Ownership Structure," *Journal of Financial Economics* 3, no. 4: 305–360.

Jones, Leroy P., 1981c, *Efficiency of Public Manufacturing Enterprises in*

Pakistan, Prepared for Pakistan Ministry of Production and Pakistan Division, World Bank.

Jones, Leroy P., and Ingo Vogelsang, 1982, *The Effect of Markets on Public Enterprise Conduct and Vice Versa* (Ljubljana: International Centre for Public Enterprises, October).

Kamerschen, David R., 1966, "An Estimation of the Welfare Losses from Monopoly in the American Economy," *Western Economic Journal* 4, no. 3: 221–236.

Kay, J.A., 1983, "A General Equilibrium Approach to the Measurement of Monopoly Welfare Loss," *International Journal of Industrial Organization* 1: 317–331.

Kemper, Peter, and John M. Quigley, 1976, *The Economics of Refuse Collection* (Cambridge, Mass.: Ballinger).

Kitchen, Harry M., 1976, "A Statistical Estimation of an Operating Cost Function" 56–76.

Larner, Robert J., 1966, "Ownership and Control in the 200 Largest Nonfinancial Corporations, 1929 and 1963," *American Economic Review* 56, no. 4, part 1: 777–787.

Larner, Robert J., 1970, *Management Control and the Large Corporation* (New York: Dunellen).

Leibenstein, Harvey, 1966, "Allocative Efficiency vs. X-Efficiency," *American Economic Review* 56, no. 3: 392–415.

Leibenstein, Harvey, 1976, *Beyond Economic Man* (Cambridge, Mass.: Harvard University Press).

Levy, Brian D., 1982, "World Oil Marketing in Transition," *International Organization* 36, no. 1: 113–133.

Lindsay, Cotton M., 1976, "A Theory of Government Enterprise," *Journal of Political Economy* 84, no. 5: 1061–1077.

Lipsey, R.G., and K. Lancaster, 1956/1957, "The General Theory of Second Best," *Review of Economic Sudies* 24: 11–32.

Little, Ian M.D., and James A. Mirrlees, 1974, *Project Appraisal and Planning for Developing Countries* (New York: Basic Books).

Littlechild, Stephen C., 1983b, "The Effect of Ownership on Telephone Penetration," *Telecommunications Policy*, no. 3: 246–247.

Maccoby, Michael, 1976, *The Gamesman* (New York: Simon & Schuster).

Mann, Patrick C., 1979, "Public Ownership in Water Service" (Paper presented at the State-Owned Enterprises Conference, Harvard Business School, Boston, Mass., March).

Mann, Patrick C., and John L. Mikesell, 1971, "Tax Payments and Electric Utility Prices," *Southern Economic Journal* 38, no. 1: 69–78.

Mann, Patrick C., and John L. Mikesell, 1976, "Ownership and Water-System Operation," *Water Resources Bulletin* 12: 995–1004.

Mann, Patrick C., and Edmond J. Siefried, 1972, "Pricing in the Case of Publicly Owned Electric Utilities," *Quarterly Review of Economics and Business* 12, no. 2: 77–89.

Manne, Henry G., 1965, "Mergers and the Market for Corporate Control," *Journal of Political Economy* 73, no. 2: 110–120.

Marris, Robin, 1964, *The Economic Theory of Managerial Capitalism* (London: Macmillan).

McEachern, William A., 1975, *Control, Compensation and Performance in the Large Corporation* (Lexington, Mass.: D.C. Heath).

McEachern, William A., 1976, "Corporate Control and Risk," *Economic Inquiry* 14, no. 2: 270–278.

Meyer, Robert A., 1975, "Publicly Owned versus Privately Owned Utilities: A Policy Choice," *Review of Economics and Staistics* 57, no. 4: 391–399.

Miller, Donald B., 1977, *Personal Vitality* (Boston: Addison-Wesley).

Mintzberg, Henry, 1983, *Power in and Around Organizations* (Englewood Cliffs, N.J.: Prentice-Hall).

Monsen, R. Joseph, 1969, "Ownership and Management: The Effect of Separation on Performance," *Business Horizons* 12: (August), pp. 45–52.

Monsen, R. Joseph and Kenneth D. Walters, 1983, *Nationalized Companies: A Threat to American Business* (New York: McGraw-Hill).

Moore, Thomas G., 1970, "The Effectiveness of Regulation of Electric Utility Prices," *Southern Economic Journal* 36, no. 4: 365–375.

Morgan, W. Douglas, 1977, "Investor Owned versus Publicly Owned Water Agencies: An Evaluation of the Property Rights Theory of the Firm," *Water Resources Bulletin* 13: 775–781.

National Economic Development Office (NEDO), 1976, *A Study of U.K. Nationalised Industries* (London: HMSO).

Neuberg, Leland Gerson, 1977, "Two Issues in the Municipal Ownership of Electric Power Distribution Systems," *Bell Journal of Economics*, 8, no. 1: 303-323.

Niskanen, William A., ed., 1971, *Bureaucracy and Representative Government* (Chicago: Aldine-Atherton).

Nove, Alec, 1973, *Efficiency Criteria for Nationalised Industries: A Study of the Misapplication of Micro-Economic Theory* (London: Allen & Unwin).

Nunnenkamp, Peter, 1981, "The Efficiency of State-Owned Enterprises in the Manufacturing Industry of Taiwan," *Academia Economic Papers* 9, no. 2: 87–124.

Nyman, Steve, and Aubrey Silbertson, 1977, "The Ownership and Control of Industry," in Alexis P. Jacquemin and Henry W. De Jong, *Welfare Aspects of Industrial Markets* (Leiden: Nijhoff), pp. 43–72.

Olson, Mancur, 1965, *The Logic of Collective Action: Public Goods and the Theory of Groups* (Cambridge, Mass.: Harvard University Press).

Otter, Casten von, 1984, "The Welfare State—The Public Sector Efficiency and Neo-Conservative Critique," *Economic and Industrial Democracy* 5, no. 2: 249–260.

Palmer, John, 1972, "The Separation of Ownership from Control in Large U.S. Industrial Corporations," *Quarterly Review of Economics and Business* 12, no. 3: 55–62.

Papandreou, Andreas G., 1952, "Some Basic Problems in the Theory of the Firm," in Bernard Francis Haley, ed., *Survey of Contemporary Economics*, Vol. 2 (Homewood, Ill.: Irwin), pp. 183–219.

Pashigian, B. Peter, 1976, "Consequences and Causes of Public Ownership of Urban Transit Facilities," *Journal of Political Economy* 84, no. 6: 1239–1259.

Peltzmann, Sam, 1971, "Pricing in Public and Private Enterprises: Electric Utilities in the United States," *Journal of Law and Economics* 14, no. 1: 109–147.

Pescatrice, Donn R., and John M. Trapani III, 1980, "The Performance and Objectives of Public and Private Utilities Operating in the United States," *Journal of Public Economics* 13, no. 2: 259–276.

Pfeffer, Jeffrey, and Gerald R. Salancik, 1978, *The External Control of*

Organizations: A Resource Dependence Perspective (New York: Harper & Row).

Pondy, Louis R., 1969, "Effects of Size, Complexity and Ownership in Administrative Intensity," *Administrative Science Quartely*, 14, pp. 47–60.

Poole, R.W., Jr., 1983, Objections to Privatization," *Policy Review*, vol. 24 (Spring), pp. 105–119.

Primaux, Walter J., Jr., 1975, "A Re-examination of the Monopoly Market Structure for Electric Utilities," in Almarin Philips, ed., *Promoting Competition in Regulated Markets* (Washington, D.C.: Brookings Institution), 175–200.

Primaux, Walter J., 1977, "An Assessment of X-Efficiency Gained Through Competition," *Review of Economics and Statistics* 59, no. 1: 105–108.

Pryke, Richard, 1971, *Public Enterprises in Practice: The British Experience of Nationalisation over Two Decades* (London: MacGibbon and Kee).

Pryke, Richard, 1981, *The Nationalised Industries: Policies and Performance Since 1968* (Oxford: Martin Robertson).

Ramamurti, Ravi, 1985b, "State-Owned Enterprises and Profits: An Empirical Study in an LDC" (Paper presented at the Forty-Fifth Annual Meeting of the Academy of Management, San Diego, August).

Ramanadham, V.V., 1984b, *The Nature of Public Enterprise* (London: Cromm Helm).

Ranis, Gustav, ed., 1971, *Government and Economic Development* (New Haven, Conn.: Yale University Press).

Reddy, Ram G., 1983, *Government and Public Enterprise: Essays in Honour of V.V. Ramanadham* (London: Frank Cass).

Reed, P.W., 1973, *The Economics of Public Enterprise* (London: Butterworth).

Rees, Ray, 1968, "Second-Best Rules for Public Enterprise Pricing," *Economica* 35: 260–273.

Roberts, David R., 1959, *Executive Compensation* (Glencoe, Ill.: Free Press).

Robson, William A., 1962, *Nationalised Industry and Public Ownership*, 2nd ed. (London: Allen & Unwin).

Sapolsky, Harvey M., 1972, *The Polaris System Development* (Cambridge, Mass.: Harvard University Press).

Savas, Emanual S., 1977a, "Policy Analysis for Local Government: Public vs. Private Refuse Collection," *Policy Analysis* 3, no. 1: 49–74.

Savas, Emanual S., 1979, "Public vs. Private Refuse Collection: A Critical Review of the Evidence," *Journal of Urban Analysis* 6: 1–13.

Savas, Emanuel S., 1982, *Privatizing the Public Sector* (Chatham, N.J.: Chatham House Publishers).

Scherer, Frederick M., 1980, *Industrial Market Structure and Economic Performance*, 2nd ed. (Chicago: Rand McNally).

Schnitzer, Martin, 1972, *East and West Germany: A Comparative Economic Analysis* (New York: Praeger).

Schwartzman, David, 1960, "The Burden of Monopoly," *Journal of Political Economy* 68: 627–630.

Selznick, Philip, 1949, *TVA and the Grass Roots* (Berkeley: University of California Press).

Shanks, Michael, ed., 1963, *The Lessons of Public Enterprise* (London: Jonathan Cape).

Sheehan, Robert, 1967, "Proprietor in the World of Big Business," *Fortune* 75: (June) 178–183.

Shelton, John, 1967, "Allocative Efficiency v. 'X-Efficiency': Comment," *American Economic Review* 57, no. 5: 1252–1258.

Shirley, Mary M., 1983, *Managing State-Owned Enterprises*, Staff Working Paper 577 (Washington, D.C.: World Bank).

Short, R. Peter, 1984, "The Role of Public Enterprises: An International Statistical Comparison," in *Public Enterprises in Mixed Economies: Some Macroeconomic Aspects* (Washington, D.C.: International Monetary Fund), pp. 110–196.

Smith, Adam, 1937, *The Wealth of Nations* (New York: Modern Library).

Spann, Robert M., 1977, "Public versus Private Provision of Governmental Services," in Thomas E. Borcherding, ed., *Budgets and Bureaucrats: The Sources of Governmental Growth* (Durham, N.C.: Duke University Press), pp. 71–89.

Stanbury, W.T., and Fred Thompson, eds., 1982, *Managing Public Enterprises* (New York: Praeger).

Stano, Miron, 1975, "Executive Ownership Interests and Corporate Performance," *Southern Economic Journal* 42, no. 2: 272–278.

Steers, Richard M., 1975, "Problems in the Measurement of Organizational Effectiveness," *Administrative Science Quarterly* 20, no. 4: 546–558.

Tendler, Judith, 1968, *Electric Power in Brazil: Entrepreneurship in the Public Sector* (Cambridge, Mass.: Harvard University Press).

Trebat, Thomas J., 1983, *Brazil's State-Owned Enterprises: A Case Study of the State as Entrepreneur* (New York: Cambridge University Press).

Turvey, Ralph, 1971, *Economic Analysis and Public Enterprises* (London: Allen & Unwin).

United Nations, Industrial Development Organization (UNIDO), 1983, *The Changing Role of Public Industrial Sector in Development*, v. 83–56863 (Vienna: UNIDO).

Villajero, Dan, 1961–1962, "Stock Ownership and the Control of Corporations," *New University Thought* 2: 33–77 and 3: 47–65.

Wallace, Richard L., and Paul E. Junk, 1970, "Economic Inefficiency of Small Municipal Generating Systems," *Land Economics* 46, no. 1: 98–104.

Wells, Louis T., Jr., 1973, "Economic Man and Engineering Man," *Public Policy* 21, no. 3: 319–342.

Williamson, Oliver E., 1964, *The Economics of Discretionary Behavior: Managerial Objectives in a Theory of the Firm* (Englewood Cliffs, N.J.: Prentice-Hall).

Worcester, Dean A., 1973, "New Estimates of the Welfare Loss to Monopoly, United States: 1959–69," *Southern Economic Journal* 40, no. 2: 234–245.

World Bank, 1981, *Accelerated Development in Sub-Saharan Africa* (Washington, D.C.: World Bank).

World Bank, 1983, *Work Development Report* 1983 (New York: Oxford University Press).

Yuchtman, Ephraim, and Stanley E. Seashore, 1967, "A System Resource Approach to Organizational Effectiveness," *American Sociological Review* 32, no. 6: 891–903.

Yunker, James A., 1975, "Economic Performance of Public and Private Enterprise: The Case of U.S. Electric Utilities," *Journal of Economics and Business* 28, no. 1: 60–67.

Zeitlin, Maurice, 1974, "Corporate Ownership and Control: The Large Corporation and the Capitalist Clan," *American Journal of Sociology* 79, no. 5: 1073–1119.

DEVELOPMENT POLICY

State Enterprises in Developing Countries

by Peter Nunnenkamp, Kiel*

The role of state-owned enterprises in the development process in the Third World is the subject of serious controversy. This article attempts to test empirically whether there is a relationship between the importance of public production in developing countries and their overall economic performance.

A considerable degree of scepticism prevails when governments assume the majority shares and control of business activities which otherwise would be left to private entrepreneurs. This is mainly due to experiences in advanced Western economies, where public ownership is frequently associated with ineffective management, significant burdens for the taxpayers and a considerable misallocation of resources. On the other hand, high expectations are placed on state enterprises. Especially in the Third World they are considered to stimulate economic growth and to promote industrialisation. Accordingly, public investment is assigned a prominent role in the industrial sector of many developing countries which otherwise pursue rather different economic policies.

Notwithstanding that the debate on the conflicting hypotheses about the role of public enterprises resulted in a vast amount of literature, economic research is still in an underdeveloped state in this field. Very little is known about the economic impact of public production, i.e. whether state enterprises succeeded in creating employment and in enhancing growth and industrialisation. The choice between "using rigorous methods to generate definite statements about trivial problems and using soft 'intuitive groping' to make questionable assertions about critical issues"[1] that is symptomatic for research on public enterprises, is largely due to the lack of data. Very few developing countries present detailed and comprehensive accounts on the activities of public enterprises. Even more of a problem is that the statistical information available is not fully comparable between different countries. The coverage of statistics differs because of inconsistent definitions of the public enterprise sector.

Although shortcomings remain, the data situation has improved a great deal due to a recent publication.[2] Thus it seems promising to focus on some critical issues concerning the economic costs and benefits of state enterprises by substituting rather simple statistical procedures for merely intuitive groping. After a short summary of the major reasons for state enterprises and some frequently neglected drawbacks probably arising from public production, and an overview of the role of state enterprises in the Third World in quantitative terms, the following analysis attempts to subject the aforementioned conflicting hypotheses on the economic impact of state enterprises to an empirical test. Applying cross-country correlation analysis, it is checked whether economic performance in terms of overall growth, gross fixed capital formation and employment generation was relatively favourable in countries where state enterprises play a prominent role.

* Institute of World Economics.

[1] Leroy P. Jones: Introduction, in: Leroy P. Jones (ed.): Public Enterprise in Less-Developed Countries, Cambridge 1982, p. 13.

[2] R. P. Short: The Role of Public Enterprises: An International Statistical Comparison, in: International Monetary Fund: Public Enterprise in Mixed Economies: Some Macroeconomic Aspects, Washington 1984.

By the same token, some evidence is presented on the economic costs of public production, for example in terms of budgetary burdens, inflation and debt creation.

State enterprises are assumed to fulfil a variety of economic and social objectives.[3] Apart from providing infrastructural facilities, the main emphasis is placed on their role in the industrial sector:

□ Governmental control of key industries ("commanding heights") via public enterprises is intended to reduce the influence of foreign companies and to prevent private monopolies. Furthermore, governments wish to foster industrialisation and influence the path and direction of development.

□ Non-competitive private companies faced with bankruptcy are nationalised in order to maintain the jobs. In some instances, disadvantaged population groups are given preferential employment in public enterprises (as in Malaysia), or regional imbalances are to be reduced.

□ It is expected that public enterprises will improve the supply of goods falling into the basic needs category at socially acceptable prices.

□ Public enterprises should help the upgrading of unskilled labour and contribute to a better supply of managerial skills, thereby reducing the widespread lack of human capital.

□ In the field of foreign trade, public enterprises should increase national self-sufficiency by import substitution and promote the expansion and diversification of national exports.

These and other objectives are given different weights in different countries. However, most developing economies with a significant public share in the industrial sector have one thing in common: public enterprises are assigned a pioneer role in promoting industrialisation and growth. They are supposed to play a central role especially in those areas where private entrepreneurs are still reluctant to invest due to perceived limitations of the market mechanism.

Markets may fail in different respects to produce economically optimal results.[4] Government intervention (of which public production is only one of many possibilities, though considered the most effective one by its proponents) may be required in cases of increasing returns to scale, public goods and externalities, and market imperfections. If production is subject to increasing returns to scale throughout the whole range of relevant activity levels, a monopolisation of unregulated private markets may be expected. This would reduce production below the macroeconomically optimal level. It is argued that performance would be inefficient in dynamic terms as well, "because incentives for innovation will be weaker than would likely prevail under a more competitive regime".[5]

Externalities are assumed to play a prominent role in developing countries.[6] External benefits prevailing at an early stage of development are largely of a pecuniary nature, i.e. interdependence among producers is mediated by the price mechanism. If a large-scale investment removes a bottleneck, for example, the investor's customers will derive benefit because of lower input prices. But the share of profits that escape the investor may be so high that the investment will not be realised altogether, its macroeconomic desirability notwithstanding. According to the infant industry argument, private losses incurred at the beginning of production may be offset by subsequent private profits only with considerable delay. This may retard economic development if producers are averse to taking risks and do not anticipate the profitability of activities in the longer run. Although this is not a case of market failure, government intervention is frequently required in order to overcome the lack of innovative Schumpeterian entrepreneurs which is considered characteristic for many Third World economies. By assigning to the state the role of investing in infant industries it is implicitly assumed that the "middle-class 'virtues' fundamental to entrepreneurial drive"[7] are significantly stronger in the public sector.

The industrialisation process may be negatively affected by imperfections in factor markets as well. If labour in the agricultural sector is paid according to its

[3] For an overview see, for example, Armeane M. Choski: State Intervention in the Industrialization of Developing Countries: Selected Issues, World Bank Staff Working Paper, No. 341, Washington 1979, pp. 6-12.

[4] For a more detailed elaboration, see Peter Nunnenkamp: Market-Failure versus Government-Failure: On the Role of Public Industrial Enterprises in Developing Countries, in: Vierteljahresberichte des Forschungsinstituts der Friedrich-Ebert-Stiftung, No. 98, December 1984, pp. 347-359.

[5] Charles Wolf jr.: A Theory of Nonmarket Failure: Framework for Implementation Analysis, in: Journal of Law and Economics, Vol. 22 (1979), pp. 107-112. The case for public production is not very strong, however. A monopolistic position is always threatened by domestic or foreign potential competitors. This constrains the monopolist's ability to cut production and raise prices and provides him with sufficient incentives for innovations.

[6] See, for example, Marcus Fleming: External Economies and the Doctrine of Balanced Growth, in: Economic Journal, Vol. 65 (1955), pp. 241-256.

[7] Deepak Lal: Public Enterprises, in: John Cody, Helen Hughes, David Wall (eds.): Policies for Industrial Progress in Developing Countries, Oxford 1980, p. 212.

average (rather than its marginal) productivity, domestic industrial production will be depressed due to a sub-optimal labour migration from agriculture to industry. Capital markets in developing countries often lack a sufficiently sophisticated infrastructure, so that the supply of funds for investment is eroded by hoarding and capital mobility is reduced.[8] Under these conditions it is probably most difficult for private producers to finance high-yielding but risky pioneer projects. Consequently, it is argued that investments that remove barriers to further economic development, but frequently require considerable amounts of capital, should be the public sector's responsibility.

Possible Drawbacks

The market-failure debate in economic theory contributed to a remarkable extension of public intervention into private markets in general and state ownership in particular. For quite some time it was taken for granted that politicians, bureaucrats and public managers would be able and willing to correct market failures in a way that guaranteed macroeconomic efficiency. Subsequently, this rather naive belief was challenged by the theory of government failure.[9] It is striking that many proponents of public production activities tend to ignore their critics, although the new perception of public sector operations resulted in hypotheses on the economic impact of state enterprises that sharply contrast with the traditional ones.

It is most unrealistic to assume that managers of state enterprises would above all strive to improve national welfare. They can, rather, be expected to maximise their own interests, just as private entrepreneurs do. As a promising way of increasing income, prestige and political leverage, public managers may expand the operations of the enterprises of which they are in charge. Probably, state enterprises extend production beyond macroeconomically optimal levels. The widespread practice of covering the losses of state enterprises out of the government budget allows them to invest in large-scale projects, even if this results in lasting excess capacity. In an attempt to maximise capacities or sales, public managers may also be interested in crowding out private activities rather than merely filling gaps in private initiative and offsetting market failure.[10]

The alleged positive role of state enterprises in economic development is further challenged by the concept of X-inefficiency.[11] There are various reasons why public production in particular is likely to take place below the production possibility curve. Firstly, incentive systems prevailing in the public sector do not reward efforts to reduce costs.[12] Consequently, overstaffing is to be expected and cost-intensive modern technologies favoured by public managers may be installed, notwithstanding macroeconomic inappropriateness. Secondly, the economic environment in which state enterprises are typically operating gives rise to X-inefficiency. Competitive pressure is rather weak in the public sector due to officially restricted market entry. Competition from abroad is limited by import restraints, particularly in the officially fostered key industries, that do not conform to the country's comparative advantages.

Indirectly, public production may further add to inefficiencies. The more industrialisation is regulated by the government, the more private resources are absorbed by rent-seeking activities.[13] Private economic agents compete in inducing the public sector to take measures that would be favourable to them. Since market prices of publicly produced goods frequently do not cover total costs, customers of state enterprises will use the opportunity of obtaining subsidised inputs to divert resources from production to rent-seeking. These resources are wasted from a macroeconomic standpoint. Empirical estimates indicate that inefficiencies caused by rent-seeking are substantial.[14]

A Quantitative Overview

The quantitative importance of state enterprises in developing countries may be indicated by their percentage shares in gross domestic product (GDP) and gross fixed capital formation.[15] In the mid-1970's,

[8] In many cases price distortions in labour and capital markets are due to government failure rather than market failure, however. Minimum wage legislation that raises labour costs beyond equilibrium rates is most common in developing countries. Frequently, private savers are discouraged from depositing their savings with financial intermediaries because of officially reduced interest rates.

[9] See, for example, the contributions in Horst Hanusch (ed.): Anatomy of Government Deficiencies, Berlin 1983.

[10] William A. Niskanen: Bureaucrats and Politicians, in: Journal of Law and Economics, Vol. 19 (1976), p. 633.

[11] Harvey Leibenstein: Allocative Efficiency versus X-Efficiency, in: American Economic Review, Vol. 56 (1966), pp. 392-415.

[12] Alan T. Peacock: On the Anatomy of Collective Failure, in: Public Finance, Vol. 35 (1980), pp. 33-43.

[13] James M. Buchanan: From Private Preferences to Public Philosophy: The Development of Public Choice, in: The Economics of Politics, Institute of Economic Affairs, Readings, Vol. 18, London 1978, pp. 13f.

[14] Anne O. Krueger: The Political Economy of the Rent-Seeking Society, in: American Economic Review, Vol. 64 (1974), pp. 291-303.

[15] See the data given in R. P. Short, op. cit. Average figures are weighted averages for 1974-77 or the closest period for which data are available, unless otherwise indicated.

state enterprises accounted for 8.6 per cent of GDP (based on data for about 30 countries) and 27 per cent of overall investments (about 50 countries). Whereas the output share was slightly below the respective figure in industrial countries (9.6 per cent), the investment share in developing countries dramatically exceeded the figure of 11 per cent in industrial countries. In contrast to industrial economies, where the relative size of the public enterprise sector did not change significantly in recent years, there has been a remarkable increase in the Third World. Between the late 1960's and the end of the 1970's the average output and investment shares of state enterprises increased by 4.5 and 10.5 percentage points respectively.

State enterprises are now of major quantitative significance in most of the countries for which data are available. Average output and investment shares are broadly similar in Asia and Latin America, but noticeably larger in Africa. According to different per capita income levels the picture shown in Table 1 emerges.

Although state enterprises are still most important in the traditional fields, i.e. so-called natural monopolies like public utilities, communication and non-road transport, they are now engaged in virtually all types of economic activity. Typically, natural resource industries are largely operated by state enterprises. Economies of scale and high risks, but also the economic rents obtainable in mining are the principal reasons for public dominance. In manufacturing the public engagement increased most rapidly in recent years. Especially in many African and Middle Eastern countries, the manufacturing sector is dominated by state enterprises. They are most prominent in heavy industries such as petroleum refining, chemicals, transport equipment, iron and steel, that are supposed to play a key role in economic development. State enterprises are expected to strengthen interindustrial linkages and to make use of economies of scale as well. Average plant sizes are dramatically higher in the public sector than in the private sector.[16]

Table 1

Output and Investment Shares of State Enterprises in Developing Countries of Different Income Levels

(per cent)

GDPC[1]	SHGDP[2]	SHINV[2]
< 400	10.3 (11)	30.6 (14)
400 – 999	14.2 (6)	24.6 (14)
1000 – 1500	12.3 (3)	19.5 (10)
> 1500	10.3 (6)	25.0 (11)

[1] Per capita income in US-$ (1981).
[2] Unweighted average shares in output and investment, respectively; in most cases figures are for the late 1970s. In parentheses: number of countries for which data are available.
Source: R. P. Short: The Role of Public Enterprises: An International Statistical Comparison, in: International Monetary Fund: Public Enterprise in Mixed Economies: Some Macroeconomic Aspects, Washington 1984, Table 1.

State Enterprises and General Economic Development

It is extremely difficult to assess the economic impact of public production empirically. The following correlation analysis may provide a first step in this direction. In subsequent research, it has to be supplemented by more sophisticated analyses that allow the impact of state enterprises to be isolated from other relevant influences. Two different coefficients were calculated: Spearman rank correlation coefficients and Pearson correlation coefficients.

The results presented in Table 2 indicate that state enterprises failed to fulfil their principal role, i.e. to enhance economic development in Third World countries. The relative importance of state enterprises in developing countries is reflected by their output and investment shares (SHGDP, SHINV). In view of the above-mentioned hypotheses raised by the proponents of public production, the following variables were selected as indicators of the countries' general economic performance: real growth in GDP and gross fixed investment (GROGDP and GROINV, respectively), the industrialisation level (INDLEV) and growth in employment (GROEMP). Consequently, 16 coefficients were estimated. Just one out of these is significant at the 10 per cent level of confidence (Pearson – in contrast to Spearman – shows a positive correlation between the share of state enterprises in GDP and the industrialisation level). In all remaining cases no significant relationship emerged between the quantitative importance of state enterprises and general economic performance. In sharp contrast to widespread expectations, the coefficients seem to be rather negative for both GROGDP and GROINV.

The evidence is disappointing as well, if the progress made in employment generation is considered. The share of state enterprises in overall employment is

[16] For the Indian example, see Peter Nunnenkamp: Die Rolle öffentlicher Industrieunternehmen im Exportsektor Indiens, Schriften des Zentrums für regionale Entwicklungsforschung der Justus-Liebig-Universität Gießen, Vol. 30, Hamburg 1985, Table 5.

[17] See R. P. Short, op. cit., pp. 27f.; Malcolm Gillis: The Role of State Enterprises in Economic Development, Harvard Institute for International Development, Development Discussion Paper, No. 83, Cambridge 1980, pp. 28ff.

generally considerably less than that in GDP.[17] The missing link between high public investments and GROEMP has to be attributed to the extremely high capital intensity typically prevailing in state enterprises' operations. This partly reflects the industrial distribution of public production, i.e. its prominence in sectors that are inherently capital-intensive. However, the Indian example also points to drastic intra-industry differences in factor proportions between public and private enterprises.[18] As in India, the cost of capital to state enterprises is lower than that to private producers in many developing countries, so that the same situation is likely to prevail elsewhere.

Thus a prominent role by state enterprises in the economy does not seem to be a sufficient condition (nor a necessary one) for a more favourable development record. In some instances, government failure (such as officially induced price distortions in factor markets) rather than market failure must be blamed for insufficient economic success.

World Market Orientation

Things look even worse if the state enterprises' role in external trade is considered (see Table 3). Sometimes it is argued that public production may improve the development prospects of Third World economies by reducing current account deficits. State enterprises are supposed to accelerate the growth in exports and to diversify the country's export basket by supplying non-traditional export items. On the other hand, they should improve on import-substitution policies.

The correlation coefficients presented in Table 3 indicate complete failure in all three respects:

□ High output and investment shares by state enterprises were related to low, rather than high, growth in real exports (GROEXP); all four coefficients are significantly negative (at a 4 per cent level of confidence or better).

□ The more prominent state enterprises figure in the economy, the less diversified are the country's exports, if the share of three major commodities in total world market sales is taken as an indicator of export concentration (COMCON).

□ As regards growth in real imports (GROIMP), the coefficients remained insignificant; moreover, they have "wrong" signs, so that state enterprises seem to have speeded up import growth rather than reduced it.

An in-depth study of the export performance of state enterprises in India indicated that their share of industrial production (about 20 per cent in the 1970's) and employment (about 15 per cent) exceeded their share of exports (5-6 per cent) by 150-300 per cent. Notwithstanding the rather weak world market orientation of the Indian private sector, state enterprises lagged further behind: in the 1970's only 3.3 per cent of public industrial production was exported. World markets served as a temporary outlet for excess public production at times of insufficient domestic demand and were neglected as soon as domestic demand provided for satisfactory capacity utilisation. The state

[18] See Peter Nunnenkamp: Die Rolle öffentlicher Industrieunternehmen im Exportsektor Indiens, op. cit., p. 106.

Table 2

State Enterprises and Economic Development: Correlation Results[1]

	Spearman				Pearson			
	SHGDP		SHINV		SHGDP		SHINV	
	coeff.	sig. (N)	coeff.	sig. (N)	coeff.	sig. (N)	coeff.	sig. (N)
GROGDP	–0.18	0.19 (25)	–0.11	0.23 (44)	–0.21	0.16 (25)	–0.13	0.19 (44)
INDLEV	0.10	0.34 (21)	0.04	0.41 (37)	0.30	0.10 (21)	0.16	0.18 (37)
GROINV	–0.11	0.32 (21)	–0.09	0.29 (41)	–0.01	0.48 (21)	–0.09	0.29 (41)
GROEMP	0.02	0.46 (24)	–0.01	0.47 (41)	0.15	0.24 (24)	0.05	0.37 (41)

[1] Spearman rank correlation coefficients and Pearson correlation coefficients, respectively; besides the coefficients, the second column presents the level of significance (one-tailed test) and the number of observations on which the calculation is based (in parentheses). Variables: SHGDP = share of state enterprises in GDP; SHINV = share of state enterprises in gross fixed investment (SHGDP and SHINV are mostly for the late 1970's); GROGDP = average annual growth in real GDP, 1970-81; INDLEV = industrialisation level, i.e. share of industry in GDP in 1981; GROINV = average annual growth in gross fixed capital formation at constant prices, 1970-81; GROEMP = average annual growth in employment, 1970-81.
Source: R. P. Short, see Table 1; World Bank: World Development Report; IMF: International Financial Statistics; own calculations.

enterprises' role in diversifying India's exports was negligible. Public production was neither sufficient nor necessary to open up new overseas markets by non-traditional exports.

Even in the case of homogeneous products and standardised production processes state enterprises failed to surpass the private sector's export performance. A more favourable picture was most likely to be expected in this area. State enterprises that operated on a moderately larger scale than private producers had the opportunity of making use of increasing returns to scale. Moreover, the marketing of homogeneous and standardised goods was rather easy and required less flexibility, thereby reducing the public sector's comparative disadvantages arising from bureaucratic decision-making.[19] Apparently, these factors were offset by export-retarding effects. Apart from considerable X-inefficiencies, the government-induced high capital intensity in the public sector and the priority given to heavy industries (such as steel, machinery and transport equipment) have probably impeded a more favourable export performance by state enterprises. The role of state enterprises within the framework of India's development plans completely neglected the country's comparative advantages in international markets. A similar pattern of public production is typical for many other developing countries, so that the Indian experience is likely to be repeated elsewhere.

Financing the Deficits of State Enterprises

Though there is hardly any evidence of economic benefits that may be attributed to state enterprises, they may have given rise to considerable economic costs. X-inefficiencies, misconceived industrialisation policies and highly capital-intensive production processes in the public sector can be presumed to absorb economic resources that could have been employed more productively in the private sector. According to information on the overall balances of state enterprises presented by Short, the return on public investment was rather low in commercial terms. Excluding the receipts of current government transfers, the self-financing ratio of state enterprises amounted to only 10 per cent in those developing countries for which data were available.

In the mid-1970's, the overall deficits of state enterprises in developing countries averaged almost 4 per cent of GDP.[20] Table 4 indicates that high public investment shares were strongly correlated with high deficits of state enterprises (DEFOV). Deficits had to be financed either by borrowing by state enterprises in domestic and international financial markets or by capital infusions by the government. Various drawbacks may arise from these options:

□ Borrowing from domestic commercial banks is likely to crowd out private investors because of credit rationing or rising capital costs. The same applies if state enterprises shift their deficits to the government budget and governments refinance by borrowing in domestic capital markets.

□ The money supply is affected if state enterprises have direct access to borrowing from the central bank (this is the case in several developing countries) or if governments refinance by money creation. Most probably, this would result in higher inflation rates. Table 4 provides some evidence that high public investment shares (in case of both Spearman and Pearson correlations) and high deficits of state enterprises (DEFOV and DEFCOR in case of Spearman correlations) were significantly related to high government budget deficits. However, correlations between state enterprises' deficits and the inflation rate remained insignificant (the 10 per cent level of confidence is considered as a minimum standard). Moreover, all coefficients have "wrong" signs in view of what might have been expected.

□ The international debt situation of developing countries is negatively affected if state enterprises step up their foreign borrowing or if credits raised in international markets in order to finance their deficits are channelled through central government accounts. As discussed below, this may trigger debt servicing difficulties.

The International Debt Burden

In the mid-1970's, for those countries providing a complete breakdown of sources of finance, about 25 per cent of the state enterprises' deficits were covered by direct foreign borrowing.[21] The share of international lending would probably have been much larger if indirect foreign borrowing by state enterprises were taken into account, i.e. foreign loans channelled through government accounts. The observation that the deficits of state enterprises were significantly related to

---

[19] For adding marketing and institutional aspects to the concept of comparative advantage, see Leroy P. Jones, Lawrence H. Wortzel: Public Enterprise and Manufactured Exports in Less-Developed Countries: Institutional and Market Factors Determining Comparative Advantage, in: Leroy P. Jones (ed.): Public Enterprise in Less-Developed Countries, Cambridge 1982, pp. 217-242.

[20] The exclusion of current government transfers increased the deficits by another percentage point; see R. P. Short, op. cit., pp. 29ff.

[21] See R. P. Short, op. cit., pp. 45ff.

Table 3

State Enterprises and External Trade: Correlation Results[1]

	Spearman				Pearson			
	SHGDP		SHINV		SHGDP		SHINV	
	coeff.	sig. (N)	coeff.	sig. (N)	coeff.	sig. (N)	coeff.	sig. (N)
GROEXP	–0.44	0.02 (21)	–0.40	0.01 (38)	–0.41	0.03 (21)	–0.29	0.04 (38)
COMCON	0.29	0.08 (24)	0.24	0.06 (46)	0.34	0.05 (24)	0.37	0.01 (46)
GROIMP	0.12	0.30 (21)	0.07	0.33 (38)	0.26	0.13 (21)	0.05	0.38 (38)

[1] See footnote to Table 2; additional variables: GROEXP, GROIMP = average annual growth in exports and imports respectively, at constant prices, 1970-81; COMCON = commodity concentration, i.e. share of 3 major commodities in total merchandise exports in 1981.
Sources: See Table 2; World Bank: World Tables; own calculations.

Table 4

State Enterprises, Government Budget Deficits and Inflation: Correlation Results[1]

	Spearman						Pearson					
	DEFOV		GOVDEF		INFL		DEFOV		GOVDEF		INFL	
	coeff.	sig. (N)	coeff.	sig. (N)	coeff.	sig. (N)	coeff.	sig. (N)	coeff.	sig. (N)	coeff.	sig. (N)
SHGDP	–0.17	0.26 (18)	0.04	0.44 (17)	–0.24	0.12 (25)	–0.26	0.15 (18)	–0.32	0.11 (17)	–0.11	0.31 (25)
SHINV	–0.66	0.001 (35)	–0.42	0.01 (32)	–0.17	0.13 (48)	–0.67	0.000 (35)	–0.46	0.004 (32)	–0.18	0.11 (48)
DEFOV	–	–	0.28	0.10 (22)	0.20	0.12 (36)	–	–	–0.02	0.46 (22)	0.19	0.13 (36)
DEFCOR	–	–	0.45	0.03 (19)	0.07	0.38 (23)	–	–	0.15	0.27 (19)	0.24	0.13 (23)

[1] See footnote to Table 2; additional variables: DEFOV = overall deficit of state enterprises as a share of GDP (surplus: +); DEFCOR = corrected deficit of state enterprises as a share of GDP, i.e. overall deficits minus current government transfers to state enterprises (surplus: +); GOVDEF = government budget deficit as a share of GPD (surplus: +); DEFOV, DEFCOR and GOVDEF are mostly for the late 1970's; INFL = average annual rate of inflation (consumer prices), 1970-81.
Sources: See Table 2.

Table 5

State Enterprises and Foreign Debt: Correlation Results[1]

	Spearman				Pearson			
	DEBGNP		DSR		DEBGNP		DSR	
	coeff.	sig. (N)	coeff.	sig. (N)	coeff.	sig. (N)	coeff.	sig. (N)
SHGDP	0.55	0.002 (25)	0.39	0.03 (23)	0.63	0.000 (25)	0.28	0.10 (23)
SHINV	0.44	0.001 (46)	0.37	0.01 (45)	0.31	0.02 (46)	0.33	0.01 (45)
DEFOV	–0.40	0.01 (34)	–0.14	0.22 (32)	–0.37	0.02 (34)	–0.14	0.22 (32)
FORBOR	0.30	0.08 (24)	0.48	0.01 (23)	0.10	0.31 (24)	0.41	0.03 (23)

[1] See footnote to Table 2; additional variables: DEFOV = overall deficit of state enterprises as a share of GDP (surplus: +); FORBOR = foreign borrowing by state enterprises as a share of GDP (DEFOV and FORBOR are mostly for the late 1970's); DEBGNP = public and publicly guaranteed debt as a share of gross national product, 1980-82; DSR = debt service ratio, i.e. debt service on public and publicly guaranteed debt as a share of exports, 1980-82.
Sources: See Table 2; World Bank: World Debt Tables; own calculations.

government deficits but not to domestic inflation indicates that government budget deficits were largely financed in international capital markets, rather than by domestic money creation.[22] In the period 1976-78, state enterprises accounted for one third of all international borrowing by developing countries.[23]

Against this background it might be supposed that state enterprises contributed to the deteriorating debt situation of many developing countries in the early 1980's. This view is supported by the correlation results presented in Table 5. The analysis considers two of the most frequently used debt indicators, the ratio of foreign debt outstanding to gross national product (DEBGNP) and the ratio of interest and amortisation payments on external liabilities to the country's exports (debt service ratio, DSR) as a measure of the debt service burden of developing countries. All coefficients have the expected signs and all but three are significant at the 10 per cent level of confidence or better. High deficits of state enterprises are associated with large amounts of accumulated debt relative to GNP. With increasing direct borrowing by state enterprises in international capital markets the debt service ratio increases. Both DEBGNP and DSR show a strongly positive relation to the output and investment shares of state enterprises. Moreover, a look at those 23 developing countries that provide data on the adjusted deficits of state enterprises (DEFCOR, i.e. DEFOV minus current government transfers) reveals that the probability of rescheduling increased for countries with a relatively high DEFCOR. For the nine countries that did not reschedule part of their foreign debt within the period 1975-84, DEFCOR averaged 2.5 per cent. The respective figure amounted to 3.2 per cent (3.6 per cent) for countries with one (more than one) rescheduling agreement.

Summary

In the above, the hypothesis of a positive role for state enterprises in the economic development of Third World countries was subjected to simple empirical tests. There is hardly any evidence that state enterprises fulfilled the assumed pioneer role within the framework of industrialisation plans in a way that would have benefitted developing countries' economies. In contrast to widespread expectations, a prominent role by public production within the economy was neither associated with relatively favourable growth and industrialisation records, nor with high employment generation. In the field of foreign trade, state enterprises seem, rather, to have added to the economic problems of developing countries. High output and investment shares by state enterprises were related to poor overall export performance and high export concentration on a few traditional commodities. This may have contributed significantly to balance of payments difficulties in many developing countries.

It goes without saying that the correlation analysis presented above provides a rather weak empirical test. Subsequent research should supplement this by more sophisticated procedures in order to isolate the effects of public production on economic development from other relevant factors. This article can therefore only serve as a first step towards reaching definite conclusions. However, it strongly questions the rather naive belief that public production per se will remove the bottlenecks to economic growth and industrialisation.

A reappraisal of what state enterprises can achieve has to consider the economic costs of public production as well. Market failure is a necessary rather than a sufficient condition for state intervention. In terms of economic welfare, public production activities can only be justified where welfare-increasing effects due to the correction of market failure exceed welfare losses due to government failure. The correlation analysis indicates that the economic costs of state enterprises were far from negligible. The striking deficits of state enterprises in many developing countries represented a major reason for high and rising government deficits. There is no evidence of inflationary effects arising from public production. However, crowding-out of private economic activities is likely to have occurred. Moreover, the lack of private initiative in industries that are typically given high priority in government planning cannot be attributed simply to market failure and private risk aversion. Both theoretical considerations and empirical findings tell us, for example, that for most developing countries it does not make sense to invest in capital-intensive industries because of comparative disadvantages. The economic benefits of state enterprises engaged in these industries are highly debatable. Public production may, rather, have resulted in a substantial misallocation of resources. Finally, state enterprises seem to have added significantly to one of the most severe problems many Third World economies are struggling with today. The financing of the state enterprises' deficits has contributed considerably to the accumulation of foreign debt and has increased the probability of debt servicing difficulties

---

[22] According to World Bank estimates (World Development Report 1985, Washington 1985, p. 62), a significant positive relationship prevailed between growing government deficits and the accumulation of foreign debt.

[23] See World Bank: Borrowing in International Capital Markets: Third Quarter 1979, Washington 1980.

[26]

Measured Sources of Inefficiency in the Performance of Private and Public Enterprises in LDCs

Robert Millward

1. INTRODUCTION

Impressions of the performance of enterprises often originate in informal case studies or anecdotes. Such sources are important if more comprehensive statistics are weak. There are three good reasons, however, for attempting precise measurements and for exploring the statistical generality of performance. First, is that measurement can reveal the source of enterprise inefficiencies in terms of the size of the organisation, the choice of technique, the product range. Second, it can also help to distinguish managerial performance from questions of government policy which, like low interest rates and subsidised product prices, may sometimes be treated as exogeneous to management. Third, and especially important in the assessment of the role of ownership, it provides a vital check on rhetoric.

The experience in performance measurement over the last decade in several Western countries bears this out. There has been a considerable theoretical literature recently on the incentive structures of different organisational forms much of which would predict that productivity and cost effectiveness would be lower in the public sector. If one looks at those parts of the economy populated by public enterprise—which I shall take loosely to be public production for sale with break-even as one of the objectives—the evidence does not bear that out. Estimates of production and cost functions in the 1970s covering railways, electricity, water supply and airlines relating mainly to North America indicated that private utilities had no general advantage in terms of productivity or cost effectiveness and indeed the evidence for US electricity was very distinctly in the other direction.[1] Further research in the last few years on US electricity and water supply and on the pre-nationalisation period for gas and electricity in the UK (where both private and public coexisted) has reinforced that conclusion (Färe, Grosskopf and Logan 1985, Fergenbaum and Teeples 1983, Foreman-Peck and Waterson 1985, Millward and Ward 1986). However, there were two areas where performance was distinctly different. If we can take the detailed evidence of the US electricity supply and urban bus transit industries as a general guide, prices in public firms are generally less than in private firms and, in particular, the pattern of prices is less closely geared to the marginal costs of particular activities than in private firms. In general, therefore, choice of product range and output level is different and this has sometimes manifested itself in a higher profitability for private firms. Moreover, if one moves away from the public enterprise sector towards services more closely associated with government departments and without the same break-even framework again a contrast has been found. Refuse collection is the main area studied and has proved to be more cost-effectively supplied by private contractors.

Two other issues emerge. First, the privatisation programme in the UK, at least with respect to the public enterprise sector, has proceeded in spite of, rather than because of, the evidence on performance. The evidence at present simply does not bear out any presumption of an inherently more inefficient management in public enterprises in the fuel and transport industries and related infrastructure. Ownership of course has to be distinguished from competition, whose favourable effects on the performance of both public and private firms has been better documented. The second point is that the potential bias in performance measures is huge. Partial productivity measures (labour productivity, valued added per fixed asset) on their own are useless. Differences in factor prices across enterprises must be controlled in the performance measure. Unit cost data is otherwise misleading and the level of factor prices may be truly exogenous to management but nevertheless important in assessing the broader economic efficiency of public production. Constraining the technology to fit well known formulations like Cobb-Douglas production functions can also lead to bias, especially when efficiency is connected with size.

For all these reasons there seems to be a case for looking closely at the evidence now available in LDCs. Much of this relates to the manufacturing sector, where public and private coexist. In Western countries public enterprises have not been common in manufacturing but rather in fuel and transport and comparisons have been meaningful only where the two coexist as in twentieth-century USA generally and pre-1940 UK. Moveover, individual towns and regions have often been serviced by only one utility whose level of output and other service levels have been exogenously determined. Relevant performance measures must, therefore, recognise that size and service levels are often not matters of management choice. Comparisons of productivity and cost effectiveness are then made with output given. In LDC manufacturing the role of enterprise size is different. Public firms are more often in direct competition in the sale of commodities and with the size of the firm something within the control of management. In what follows we shall, therefore, pay particular attention to the role of enterprise size. Finally, it should be said that most research for LDCs faces huge problems in data gathering. Nevertheless, a 'bloody-minded' examination of the evidence would seem worthwhile without detracting one inch from the merit of the studies in question. Kirkpatrick (1986) has already trodden some of this ground and concluded that earlier claims for the superiority of the private sector have been exaggerated. Here, we look more closely at the basis of the comparisons and ask whether anything at all can be legitimately deduced from the available evidence.

2. TECHNICAL EFFICIENCY AND PRODUCTION FUNCTIONS

A firm's choice of technique, as well as the scale of its activity, may be affected by government policy as well as by the input and product prices it faces. Measures of technical efficiency are not so much concerned with choice of technique as with reflecting whether, amongst firms producing the same output with the same technique, there are some using more of at least one input with no less of any other inputs. In identifying how ownership has affected technical efficiency so measured, an ideal setting is where public and private firms are similar with respect to product quality, service and level of output and with a large enough sample to give some statistical significance to the results.

In practice, in the absence of such ideal data, it is necessary to estimate how, for the sector in question, quality, service and output vary with input levels and, whether allowing for that variation, there is an observed difference between public and private. For LDCs there appears to be only one study to date which does that at all satisfactorily. The 1971 data assembled by Tyler (1979) for the Brazilian steel industry excludes traditional small-scale firms. Labour force and capital stock were the main inputs. Because of multiple products, a volume measure of output could not be used but it was felt that the twenty-two modern firms in the sample had a similar product range, so that the use of value added or sales figures would not be a distortion. Tyler constrained the technology to be Cobb-Douglas and estimated both an average production function and one for the frontier or best-practice firms.[2] As a guide to certain matters considered later it is useful to report his results for the best-practice firms as follows, where 'q' is output, 'k' is the capital stock, and 'm' employment (all measured in logs).

$$q = 5.0 + 0.23k + 0.61m$$

It is then possible to calculate for each firm an efficiency index showing how each firm's output compares with the best-practice firms using a similar volume of inputs. The average index for government firms (best-practice = 1.0) was 0.56 with private domestic at 0.61 and foreign-owned at 0.71. However, there was a considerable range over the government firms from best-practice technique downwards. Tyler regressed, across the whole sample, the efficiency index (E) on ownership dummies to yield:

$$E = 0.57 + 0.136F - 0.026G$$
$$\quad\quad\quad\quad (1{,}04) \quad (0.179)$$

where 'F' relates to foreign ownership, and 'G' to government firms; the 't' ratios are shown in brackets and the R^2 was 0.07. Thus, ownership had no statistically significant impact on technical efficiency. In fact, the output elasticities in the production functions imply decreasing returns to scale for best-practice firms and increasing returns for the rest so that the efficiency index is largely a function of the size of the firm.[3]

Kim (1981) estimated (average) production functions for thirty-five firms in four manufacturing industries in Tanzania, excluding all firms with less than ten employees and using, like Tyler, volume data on labour and money measures of fixed assets, as the main inputs. For the food and machinery industries government ownership had no statistically significant effect. Foreign-owned firms had a significantly higher level of efficiency in machinery and textiles whilst government firms had lower efficiency in textiles and chemicals. There are, however, some severe problems in interpreting Kim's results. The way product mix varies within each industry is not clear and each firm's output is measured in neither volume nor value terms but rather from cost data, that is as operating costs plus depreciation plus net profit plus taxes net of subsidies.[4] Thus, the performance measure appears to be picking up price and profit factors rather than simply technical efficiency, a comment that would apply to his summary regression of all industries where output is proxied by value added and measured as operating costs plus depreciation.

What can we conclude from these two studies? There is a tendency for technical efficiency to be less in government-owned firms than in private firms and, amongst the latter, foreign-owned firms come out better. But the tendency is not statistically significant. Technical efficiency seems to be linked to size in these modern sector firms and government firms range from best- to worst-practice.[5]

3. PRODUCTIVITY INDICES AND THE SIZE OF FIRMS

The technical efficiency index of a firm is essentially a total factor productivity comparison with best-practice firms operating at the same scale of activity and where different inputs are aggregated by using as weights the output elasticities in the estimated production function. Unless the production function is homogeneous these elasticities will vary with the output level. In some studies productivity measures have been calculated 'directly', that is without estimating production functions; the reasons are not always clear, though in some cases data limitations are the problem. This immediately raises the question of how inputs are to be aggregated; the traditional method is to weight with factor shares but these will reflect the output elasticities only if there are constant returns to scale and the firm is input price efficient. To circumvent this problem and thereby retain the properties of technical efficiency measures, an alternative has been to estimate partial productivity ratios and rank a firm as technically more efficient than another if at least one ratio is higher and no other ratios are lower. Like all direct productivity measures, this is equivalent to the production function approach only if constant returns to scale prevail. Otherwise, productivity ratios will be reflecting decisions about the size of the firm rather than simply technical efficiency.

Thus, Hill's study (1982) of automated weaving in 1976 in Indonesia concentrated on public and private firms using similar machinery and producing cloth of a similar type and quality. Cloth output per manhour in fully-mechanised operation was some 25 per cent higher in private firms and 90 per cent higher for semi-automated plants; the various measures of output per unit of capital were also higher in private firms. The state firms are much bigger than private firms; the number of power looms per firm averaged over the whole industry was 318 in public firms and seventy-five in private. Decreasing returns to scale appear to be present in that the larger firms have lower productivity so that the probem of public ownership is one of size rather than productivity. The same can probably be said of the 300 Tanzanian manufacturing firms studied by Perkins (1983). Like Hill, he is concerned in part to show that more mechanical techniques are not necessarily better. Restricting ourselves first to the five industries (sugar, flour milling, baking, cooking oil, timber sawing) where output can be measured in volume terms and where both public and private are in the sample, he compares for 1975 two common production techniques and finds that in the firms using a more 'appropriate' (labour intensive) technique, output per unit of capital is higher. For such firms in the cooking oil industry, labour productivity is also higher to that such firms are treated as being technically efficient; for the other industries labour productivity is generally less with the labour intensive technique so that the result is not clear cut. However, of the nineteen government firms in the sample for these five industries, seventeen were classed as technically inefficient in having both lower labour productivity and lower capital productivity than some other firms.

Overwhelming as these figures appear to be, Perkins does not report the general pattern of public and private nor the statistical significance of the results, and in two of the five industries there was at least one government firm which was technically efficient. After all, of the twenty-two firms in Tyler's sample for Brazilian steel there were only three best-practice firms (of which one was public) and the implication of his results is that all the rest were technically inefficient, that is, with their inputs output could have been higher. The government firms in manufacturing in Tanzania[6] have on average, a bigger workforce, a larger capital stock per employee and bigger output levels, suggesting there are decreasing returns to scale, with the problem of public firms one of size rather than technical efficiency. Finally, since unit costs for both government and private firms using the more capital intensive techniques are higher (as we shall see later) one might ask how the private firms can survive and whether the products in question are strictly comparable (for example, refined sugar, cement versus jaggery and burnt bricks) as well as the standardisation of attributes and the reliability of delivery.

It should be noted that part of Krueger and Tuncer's study (1982) of Turkish manufacturing is concerned with using partial productivity ratios in the above manner but, since data on the size of public and private firms is not given, it is difficult to know whether their measures are reflecting technical efficiency or choice of output levels. Some of their manipulations assume, as we shall see, constant returns, but they do not estimate returns to scale. For each industry there are data for the public and private sector firms with ten employees or more, on value added, number of employees and an estimate of the capital stock. Using this data for both 1963 and 1976 suggested that for the machinery and beverages industries labour productivity is higher in public firms and so also is capital productivity, so that the public firms would here be classed as technically more efficient. In both years the private firms were more efficient in food, paper products, chemicals, metal production, electrical machinery and transport equipment. In other cases the partial ratios are no guide. Krueger and Tuncer, however, also estimate, effectively, a composite input for each sector in each industry weighting each separate input by the average expenditure share on that input in the industry as a whole.[7] On that basis the public sector has a productivity advantage in textiles for 1976 (but not for 1963) and in wood production, tobacco and non-metallic mineral products for 1963 (but not for 1976); for petroleum and coal there is only an estimate for 1976 when the public firms had considerably higher labour productivity, but a lower capital productivity, which was enough to give private firms the advantage. Overall, Krueger and Tuncer feel the private sector has a higher productivity level.

The use of factor share weighted productivity measures means that price efficiency as well as technical efficiency is being picked up by these measures. More important in the present context is that unless there are constant returns to scale these measures could well be reflecting enterprise size as much as technical efficiency. In fact, looking over all these direct productivity indexes for Tanzania, Indonesia, and Turkey there are plenty of examples of public firms at both ends of the spectrum notwithstanding some tendency for public firms to be less technically efficient that private firms. The doubts about this latter tendency arise now, not simply from the lack of any statistical testing of its significance, but also from the absence of estimates of returns to scale which means again that the public sector problem could be one of size rather than technical efficiency.

4. OUTPUT VALUATION AND THE PRODUCT MIX

Perkins' study of Tanzanian manufacturing embraced four other industries, and the reason for our delayed consideration of these results is that they involve a more general difficulty about the measurement of output. In footwear and farm implements the sole government firms were technically efficient as was one of the four government firms in printing, leaving only garments as the industry where the (two) government firms were all inefficient. Apart from the continuing problems of interpreting these results in terms of size and returns to scale, a new problem is that in these cases in the absence of a single volume measure of output Perkins had to use value added and it is not clear how far this weighting of different product volumes by product price affects public firms relative to private.

The problem is a general one given the extensive use of output value as a proxy for output volume in several public/-private comprisons for LDCs. Where several products appear in a production function the technical efficiency index would aggregate them with the use of input elasticities as weights.[8] In the absence of production function information it is common to weight each product by revenue shares or, as in value added measure of output, by prices. It can be shown that these are precise proxies for input elasticities only where constant returns to scale prevail in all output dimensions and relative product prices equal relative marginal costs.[9] Otherwise, the output measure will be reflecting profitability differences between firms. Moreover, if the product mix *is* different as between public and private the measured output differences will be sensitive to the prices chosen. Thus, Kim (1981) also estimated for Tanzania productivity ratios for the manufacturing sector as a whole. For the early 1970s, as may be seen in the first row of Table 6.1, output per man is shown to be higher in the private sector. He estimated capital productivity in terms of gross output (proxied, as before, by cost data) per unit of operating capital (proxied by material and energy costs) and found the private sector figures to be double that of public firms, allowing the conclusion that public firms were unproductive in all dimensions. However, using his other data on value added and fixed capital yields a higher figure for public firms, as may be seen in Table 6.1. Moreover, Perkins' data for the same years, as well as the annual averages for 1970–74 as shown in Table 6.1 suggest on a different price basis that labour productivity was slightly higher in public firms and capital productivity slightly lower. Killick's (1983) data for Ghana also raises some worries about the product mix. Value added per person in state manufacturing firms is estimated as 45 per cent of that in private manufacturing firms in 1962/63, 39 per cent in 1965/66

Table 6.1: Tanzania manufacturing industry annual averages 1970–74

	Public	*Private*	*Total*	*Ratio*
Labour Productivity				
a) Value added per employee current prices T'000sh. (Kim)	20.6	22.2	—	0.93
b) Value added per employee T'000sh. at 1966 prices (Perkins)	9.8	—	9.2	1.06
Capital Productivity				
a) Value added per unit of fixed capital at current prices (Kim)	2.16	0.49	—	4.28
b) Value added per fixed asset at 1966 prices (Perkins)	0.45	—	0.47	0.95
Capital/Labour Ratios				
a) Fixed capital per worker T'000sh. at current prices (Kim)	9.5	45.5	—	0.21
b) Fixed assets per employee T'000sh. at 1966 prices (Perkins)	21.7	—	19.3	1.21

Source: Kim (1981) and Perkins (1983). Kim's data relates to 1970–5 and the fixed capital figures are based on data on depreciation allowance and rentals on fixed assets.

and 55 per cent in 1969/70. However, data for 1969 suggests that 83 per cent of the gross output of public enterprises was produced in industries in which state concerns contributed 75 per cent or more of total output. In six industries public firms accounted for all the output whilst for the entire manufacturing section of the economy wholly owned state concerns accounted for only 15 per cent of output. Apart from the problem of returns to scale, this Ghanian data does not include anything on capital productivity and, whilst capacity utilisation appeared low in public enterprises, Killick reported that the relative achievements of public and private were not known.[10] Finally, doubts about the uniformity of the product mix are also reported by Krueger and Tuncer for Turkey. Public firms are more important than private in the Turkish tobacco industry; within beverages there is a state monopoly in alcoholic beverages but not soft drinks; also the authors report that the output mix in petroleum and coal was substantially different in the two sectors.

Where there is no guarantee of a similar product mix, some studies seek to draw comparisons about public and private by examining their respective growth rate of productivity over time. But any conclusions about the dynamism of one sector relative to the other is completely meaningless unless the product mix *is* the same. For otherwise, whether the public sector, for example, exhibits a larger productivity growth than the private sector is more likely to be reflecting technical progress and consumer demand changes for the products which happen to be produced by the public sector. The best example is Dholakia's study (1978) for India from 1960/61 to 1975/76 covering the public and private sectors of manufacturing industry as a whole. Dholakia calculated a composite factor input along the lines of Krueger and Tuncer and found that in the private sector it grew by 70 per cent whilst net output, in real terms, rose by 75 per cent. But the increase in the scale of activity in the public sector was considerably different with output rising by 570 per cent, composite input by 260 per cent and, hence, total factor productivity rising nearly 90 per cent, as compared to virtually no change in the private sector. In the absence of any explicit guide to product mix, it is difficult to attribute these differences simply to ownership. This applies also to Krueger and Tuncer's observation that total factor productivity in the public sector of Turkish manufacturing 1963–76 was growing at an annual average rate of 2.65 per cent compared to 1.84 per cent in the private sector. Any conclusions about the role of ownership in such a context is just as dependent on the uniformity of the product mix as is the comparison of absolute productivity levels, though in the Turkish case the supplementary disaggregated results provide something absent in Dholakia.

5. COST EFFECTIVENESS

In the absence of data on labour and capital inputs, it is often possible to use cost information in performance measures. They will, of course, reflect not simply technical efficiency but also the extent to which choice of technique has been adapted to the factor prices facing the firm (input price efficiency). The broad approach would be to evaluate across the firms in an industry how costs vary with output and factor prices and whether, allowing for such variation, there is a difference between public and private firms. To date, studies of costs in firms in LDCs have not used this cost function approach but have simply calculated costs per unit of output in public firms and compared this with costs per unit of output in private firms in the same industry. Unless, therefore, factor prices are the same in all firms this will distort the performance comparison even for firms who are equal in technical and input price efficiency. If decreasing returns to scale operate, problems of size will again be confused with problems of efficiency.

In Perkin's (1983) study of Tanzanian manufacturing only 22 per cent of government firms were technically efficient by his criterion, though as we have seen in five of the nine industries where public and private coexist there was at least one technically efficient government firm. To assess 'economic' efficiency he calculates unit costs in each industry, embracing labour, capital, fuel and maintenance. Dividing the unit costs of government firms in each industry by that of the lowest cost producer in that industry yields a figure which, even for the lowest cost government firms ranges from 1.1 in flour mills to 3.1 for farm implements, and for the highest cost government firms ranges from 1.4 in footwear to 7.8 in cooking oil. What is particularly missing here (apart again from some indication of returns to scale and of the general spread of public and private performance) is an assessment of how far high wage rates raises the costs of government firms and how far cheap capital has given them an advantage. From the point of view of managerial performance what we want to know is whether, at the factor prices facing them, public firms' costs are higher than would be the case if a private firm faced these prices. Whether the level of prices and interest rates are at an economic level is a separate, albeit important, matter, one of government policy and resource allocation. Finally, it is of note in Perkins' results that for all manufacturing firms, private as well as public, the more labour intensive technique turns out to be cheaper except in sugar and the pit-sawing section of the sawn timber industry. Perkins notes that the more capital intensive techniques are presumably less profitable, which raises the question of why they are chosen. He argues later that '... the preferred project is the one that can be secured, developed, approved, delivered and staffed most quickly and easily' (p. 228). This suggests that 'costs' have a wider dimension than that measured, as also does output (cf. above).

Some of the same reservations apply to the unit cost estimates of Funkhouser and MacAvoy (1979) for various industries in 1971 in Indonesia. They estimated costs per ton or kilo in fertilisers, cement, shipping, rubber and palm oil, and cost per unit of value added in finance and construction. They found that, in general, the variation in unit costs with output was similar in the public and private sectors but with the latter at a lower level. Again there appears to be some tendency for public firms to be out of scale since, when comparisons are made solely between matching pairs of the same size, the cost difference disappears. A major difficulty with the results, however, is the absence of any data on input prices and the fact that the unit cost data relate simply to operating costs. The omission of capital costs would be unimportant only with homogeneous production functions but there is no evidence to support that assumption.[11]

Finally, we might note that Gupta's study (1982) of the fertiliser industry in India 1968–77 is directed at developing total factor productivity measures, but on close inspection these appear to be virtually measures of unit costs or even profitability. There was no usable data on the size of the labour force so that the wage bill was taken as a proxy, and for public firms there was an adjustment to reflect private sector wage rates. Estimates of the capital stock were made but the capital input in each firm in a given year was calculated as the capital stock multiplied by the rate of return obtainable in the private sector. The capital cost so calculated plus the wage bill constitute Gupta's estimate of the aggregate factor input in each firm. Dividing output by this measure of input yielded productivity figures for the public and private sectors of the industry. Over the whole period the public sector figures averaged less than 40 per cent of the private sector or 70 per cent if adjustments are made for certain exogeneously imposed constraints on public firms (such as source of feedstock). Clearly, here, the ratio of input to output is a measure of unit costs with labour and capital costed at private sector prices. It would be reflecting technical efficiency only if factor prices were the same in all firms, constant returns to scale prevailed and all firms chose the cost-minimising factor combination for those factor prices. As a measure of cost effectiveness, reflecting that is both technical and price efficiency, it is equivalent to the cost function approach only, as we have seen in the other studies, if constant returns to scale prevailed and factor prices were the same in each firm. In fact the study is also interesting in its measures of output. Gupta points out that the fertiliser '... industry produces a variety of products and the product mix differs from unit to unit' (p. 169). In parts of the study he builds up a measure of output by converting the different products to basic nutrients, to which are assigned weights reflecting a number of considerations, including the cost of production. Clearly such a measure has some similarities with the ideal aggregation process discussed earlier. But, Gupta uses this measure only in estimations of raw material productivity (which turn out to favour public sector firms). For the total factor productivity measures, value added is used with prices taken from the private sector. In conjunction with the measure of input his comparison of public and private is reflecting not necessarily technical efficiency, nor even cost effectiveness, but rather the differences in profitability.

6. CONCLUSIONS

In LDCs, concern about public firms has often been expressed in terms of financial losses and drains on development budgets.[12] This has been reinforced by the claim that the economic performance of public firms is inferior to that of private concerns. Here, we have looked at the performance of public and private concerns in LDCs in terms of technical efficiency and cost effectiveness and the following limited conclusions seem warranted:

(a) There is no evidence of a statistically satisfactory kind to suggest that public enterprises in LDCs have a lower level of technical efficiency than private firms operating at the same scale of operation. On a less formal level the tendency in Turkey, Indonesia and Tanzania seems to be nevertheless pointing in that direction.
(b) Data from Brazil, Tanzania and India suggests that the technical efficiency of public enterprises is not uniform but ranges from worst- to best-practice.
(c) Several industries under investigation, specifically Indonesian weaving and Tanzanian manufacturing, appear to exhibit decreasing returns to scale, as does Brazilian steel in the best-practice firms. At the same time public enterprises are often bigger than the average firm so the returns to scale might simply be reflecting a poor performance by public firms. Unfortunately, these two effects have been unscrambled only in Tyler's study of Brazilian steel where the effect of ownership was found to be statistically insignificant. Again, on a less formal level, the tendency seems to be pointing to the problems of public firms being related as much to choice of an excessive scale of operations as to technical efficiency *per se*.

(d) A particular data problem relates to product mix and to ensuring that the use of output value as a proxy for output volume is not distorting comparisons of public and private. This undermines some of the conclusions that might be made for the whole of the manufacturing sectors in Tanzania, India and Ghana. Neither is it possible to circumvent this issue by comparing rates of productivity growth over time. Little can be deduced from the higher growth rate of productivity in the public enterprise section of Indian and Turkish manufacturing if there are significant differences in product mix between public and private sectors.

(e) No satisfactory studies of cost effectiveness have yet emerged. The research for Indonesia and Tanzania includes no formal allowance for differences in factor prices between public and private firms (nor for returns to scale), whilst the results for the Indian fertiliser industry seen to be reflecting profitability as much as anything else.

In summary, the comparative performance of public and private firms in LDCs is a relatively unexplored area once one moves away from simple profitability studies. There is some very limited scattered evidence that productivity may be lower in the public sector but public enterprises can be found at the top as well as the bottom of the range and more studies are needed to permit any general conclusions.

NOTES

1. For literature surveys see Borcheding. Pommerehne and Schneider, 1982; and Millward and Parker, 1983. The latter also contains an extensive discussion of the general problem of performance measurement.
2. Other formulations including translog. and Constant Elasticity of Substitution (CES) were estimated but did not prove superior to Cobb-Douglas.
3. Broadly similar results were found for the plastics industry which had no government firms, and the split of ownership between

foreign and domestic had no statistically significant effect on performance.

4. Labour is measured in man-hours and there is an additional variable, employment, to represent enterprise size but Kim provides no guide to an interpretation. Across all four industries, size raises output but since the latter is measured via costs, and since man-hours is a further variable, the coefficient on employment is really saying that a decline in man-hours per employee will raise costs. Note, also, the marginal product of capital is estimated to be negative in the food and beverages industries, whilst the marginal product of labour is negative in machinery.
5. Gupta, 1982, also estimates a production function for the Indian fertiliser industry, 1968–77. Apart from the coefficient on the ownership dummy, detailed results are not provided. In addition, as we shall see later, there are some doubts about the measures of labour and output.
6. See Table 6.1 and note the contrast with Kim's estimate of capital intensity.
7. They calculate the growth rate of labour per unit of output in shifting from private to public, weighted by labour's share, and add this to the growth rate of capital per unit of output weighted by capital's share.
8. That is, the coefficient on each product will be the elasticity of (composite) input with respect to that product. In the absence of such information one might use partial productivity ratios (passengers per employee, freight per employee) but this has not been common since with more than one imput no simple efficiency criteria exists.
9. See Millward and Parker, 1983, footnote 24.
10. Killick, 1983, pp. 72–74 and Tables 1 and 12.
11. Cf. Foreman-Peck and Waterson, 1985.
12. See Choksi, 1979; and Killick, 1983.

REFERENCES

Borcherding, T.E., Pommerehne, W.W. and Schneider, F. (1982), 'Comparing the efficiency of private and public production: the evidence from five countries', *Zeitschrift für Nationalökonomie*, Supplement 2.

Choksi, A.M. (1979), 'State intervention in the industrialisation of developing countries: selected issues', *World Bank Staff Working Paper*, No. 341.

Dholakia, B.H. (1978), 'Relative performance of public and private manufacturing enterprises in India: total factor productivity approach', *Economic and Political Weekly*, Review of Management, February, pp. M4–M11.

Färe, T., Grosskopf, S. and Logan, J. (1985), 'The relative performance of publicly owned and privately owned electric utilities', *Journal of Public Economics*, Vol. 26, pp. 89–106.

Fergenbaum, S. and Teeples, R. (1983, 'Public versus private water delivery: a hedonic cost approach', *Review of Economics and Statistics*, Vol. 65, pp. 672–8.

Foreman-Peck, J. and Waterson, M. (1985), 'The comparative efficiency of public and private enterprises in Britain: electricity generation between the World Wars', *Economic Journal*, Supplement to Vol. 95, pp. 83–95.

Funkhouser, R. and MacAvoy, R.W. (1979), 'A sample of observations on comparative prices in public and private enterprises', *Journal of Public Economics*, Vol. 11, pp. 353–68.

Gupta, M. (1982), 'Productivity performance of the public and the private sector in India: a cast study of the fertiliser industry', *Indian Economic Review*, Vol. XVIII, Nos. 2–4, pp. 165–186.

Hill, H. (1982), 'State enterprises in a competitive industry: an Indonesian case study', *World Development*, Vol. 10, No. 11, pp. 1015–23.

Killick, T. (1983), 'The role of the public sector in the industrialisation of African developing countries', *Industry and Development*, No. 7, pp. 57–88.

Kim, K.S. (1981), 'Enterprise performance in the public and private sectors: Tanzanian experience 1970–5', *Journal of Developing Areas*, Vol. 15, April, pp. 471–84.

Kirkpatrick, C.H. (1986), 'The World Bank's views on state owned enterprises in LDCs: a critical comment', *Revista Internazionale di Scienze Economiche e Commerciali.*

Krueger, A.O. and Tuncer, B. (1982), 'Growth of factor productivity in Turkish manufacturing industries', *Journal of Development Economics*, Vol. 11, pp. 307–25.

Millward, R. and Parker, D. (1983), 'Public and private enterprise: comparative behaviour and relative efficiency', Ch. 5 in Millward, R. *et al.* (eds), *Public Sector Economics*, London: Longmans.

Millward, R. and Ward, R. (1986), 'The costs of public and private gas enterprises in late 19th century Britain', *ESRC Quantitative Economic History Study Group Conference*, September, Birbeck College, London.

Perkins, F.C. (1983), 'Technology choice, industrialisation and development experiences in Tanzania', *Journal of Development Studies*, Vol. 19, No. 2, November, pp. 213–43.

Tyler, W.G. (1979), 'Technical efficiency in production in a developing country: an empirical examination of the Brazilian plastics and steel industries', *Oxford Economic Papers*, Vol. 31, November, pp. 477–95.

Name Index

The International Library of Critical Writings in Economics

1. Multinational Corporations
   Mark Casson
2. The Economics of Innovation
   Christopher Freeman
3. Entrepreneurship
   Mark Casson
4. International Investment
   Peter J. Buckley
5. Game Theory in Economics
   Ariel Rubinstein
6. The History of Economic Thought
   Mark Blaug
7. Monetary Theory
   Thomas Mayer
8. Joint Production of Commodities
   Neri Salvadori and Ian Steedman
9. Industrial Organization
   Oliver E. Williamson
10. Growth Theory (Volumes I, II and III)
    R.Becker and E. Burmeister
11. Microeconomics: Theoretical and Applied (Volumes I, II and III)
    Robert E. Kuenne
12. The Economics of Health (Volumes I and II)
    A.J. Culyer
13. Recent Developments in Macroeconomics (Volumes I, II and III)
    Edmund S. Phelps
14. Urban and Regional Economics
    Paul C. Cheshire and Alan W. Evans
15. Modern Public Finance (Volumes I and II)
    A.B. Atkinson
16. Exchange Rate Economics (Volumes I and II)
    Ronald MacDonald and Mark P. Taylor

17. The Economic Value of Education: Studies in the Economics of Education
Mark Blaug

18. Development Economics (Volumes I, II, III and IV)
Deepak Lal

19. The New Classical Macroeconomics (Volumes I, II and Ill)
Kevin D. Hoover

20. The Economics of the Environment
Wallace E. Oates

21. Post Keynesian Theory of Growth and Distribution
Carlo Panico and Neri Salvadori

22. Dynamic Labor Demand and Adjustment Costs
Giorgio Galeazzi and Daniel S. Hamermesh

23. The Philosophy and Methodology of Economics (Volumes I, II and III)
Bruce J. Caldwell

24. Public Choice Theory (Volumes I, II and III)
Charles K. Rowley

25. Evolutionary Economics
Ulrich Witt

26. Economics and Psychology
Shlomo Maital and Sharone L. Maital

27. Social Choice Theory (Volumes I, II and Ill)
Charles K. Rowley

28. Non-Linear Dynamics in Economic Theory
Marc Jarsulic

29. Recent Developments in Experimental Economics (Volumes I and II)
John D. Hey and Graham Loomes

30. Monopoly and Competition Policy (Volumes I and II)
F.M. Scherer

31. The Economics of Technical Change
Edwin Mansfield and Elizabeth Mansfield

32. The Economics of Exhaustible Resources
Geoffrey Heal

33. The Economics of Institutions
Geoffrey M. Hodgson

34. The Economics of Transport (Volumes I and II)
Herbert Mohring

35. Implicit Contract Theory
Sherwin Rosen

36. Foundations of Analytical Marxism (Volumes I and II)
John E. Roemer

37. The Economics of Product Differentiation (Volumes I and II)
Jacques-François Thisse and George Norman

38. Economic Growth in Theory and Practice: A Kaldorian Perspective
John E. King

39. Markets and Socialism
Alec Nove and Ian D. Thatcher

40. Recent Developments in the Economics of Education
Elchanan Cohn and Geraint Johnes

41. The Theory of Inflation
Michael Parkin

42. The Economics of Location (Volumes I, II and III)
Melvin L. Greenhut and George Norman

43. Financial Intermediaries
Mervyn K. Lewis

44. The Political Economy of Privatization and Deregulation
Elizabeth E. Bailey and Janet Rothenberg Pack

45. Gender and Economics
Jane Humphries

46. Macroeconomics and Imperfect Competition
Jean-Pascal Bénassy

47. Labor Economics (Volumes I, II, III and IV)
Orley C. Ashenfelter and Kevin F. Hallock

48. The Economics of Altruism
Stefano Zamagni

49. The Economic Analysis of Rent Seeking
Robert D. Tollison and Roger D. Congleton

50. Economics and Biology
Geoffrey M. Hodgson

51. The Economics of Ageing
John Creedy

52. Fiscal and Monetary Policy (Volumes I and II)
Thomas Mayer and Steven M. Sheffrin

53. The Economics of Information (Volumes I and II)
David K. Levine and Steven A. Lippman

54. Transaction Cost Economics (Volumes I and II)
Oliver E. Williamson and Scott E. Masten

55. Agricultural Economics
George H. Peters

56. International Debt (Volumes I and II)
Graham Bird and P. Nicholas Snowden

57. Economics and Discrimination (Volumes I and II)
William A. Darity, Jr

58. Business Cycle Theory
Finn E. Kydland

59. International Trade (Volumes I and II)
J. Peter Neary

60. The Money Supply in the Economic Process
Marco Musella and Carlo Panico

61. Small Firms and Economic Growth (Volumes I and II)
Zoltan J. Acs

62. Producer Cooperatives and Labor-Managed Systems (Volumes I and II)
David L. Prychitko and Jaroslav Vanek

63. Ethics and Economics (Volumes I and II)
Alan P. Hamlin

64. The Economics of the Family
Nancy Folbre

65. The Economics of Training (Volumes I and II)
Orley C. Ashenfelter and Robert J. LaLonde

66. Chaos Theory in Economics: Methods, Models and Evidence
W. Davis Dechert

67. General Equilibrium Theory (Volumes I, II and III)
Gérard Debreu

68. Economic Growth: Theory and Evidence (Volumes I and II)
Gene M. Grossman

69. Long Wave Theory
Christopher Freeman

70. The Economics of Communication and Information
Donald M. Lamberton

71. The Foundations of Public Finance (Volumes I and II)
Peter Jackson

72. The Theory of the Firm
Mark Casson

73. The Economics of Uncertainty (Volumes I and II)
John D. Hey

74. The Economics of Global Warming
Tom Tietenberg

75. The Development of Ecological Economics
Robert Costanza, Charles Perrings and Cutler Cleveland

76. Economic Growth in the Long Run: A History of Empirical Evidence (Volumes I, II and III)
Bart van Ark

77. The Economics of Productivity (Volumes I and II)
Edward N. Wolff

78. The Economics of Population: Key Modern Writings (Volumes I and II)
Julian L. Simon

79. Political Business Cycles
Bruno S. Frey

80. Cultural Economics: The Arts, the Heritage and the Media Industries (Volumes I and II)
Ruth Towse

81. Law and Economics (Volumes I, II and III)
Richard A. Posner and Francesco Parisi

82. Independent Central Banks and Economic Performance
Sylvester Eijffinger

83. Culture, Social Norms and Economics (Volumes I and II)
Mark Casson

84. Industrial Policy and Competitive Advantage (Volumes I, II and III)
David B. Audretsch

85. The Economics of Housing (Volumes I and II)
John M. Quigley

86. Economic Demography (Volumes I and II)
T. Paul Schultz

87. Trade and the Environment: Economic, Legal and Policy Perspectives
Alan M. Rugman and John J. Kirton with Julie A. Soloway

88. The Economics of Fiscal Federalism and Local Finance
Wallace E. Oates

89. Price Theory and its Applications
Bernard Saffran and F.M. Scherer

90. Women in the Labor Market (Volumes I and II)
Marianne A. Ferber

91. Market Process Theories (Volumes I and II)
Peter Boettke and David Prychitko

92. Input–Output Analysis (Volumes I, II and III)
Heinz Kurz, Erik Dietzenbacher and Christian Lager

93. Mathematical Economics (Volumes I, II and III)
Graciela Chichilnisky

94. The Foundations of Regulatory Economics (Volumes I, II and III)
Robert B. Ekelund, Jr.

95. The Economics of Marketing
Martin Carter, Mark Casson and Vivek Suneja

96. Service Industries in the Global Economy (Volumes I and II)
J.R. Bryson and P.W. Daniels

97. Economic Justice (Volumes I and II)
Giorgio Brosio and Harold M. Hochman

98. Foreign Exchange Intervention: Objectives and Effectiveness
Sylvester C.W. Eijffinger

99. Economic Anthropology
Stephen Gudeman

100. Consumer Theory
Kelvin Lancaster

101. The Economics of Famine
Jean Drèze

102. Microeconomic Theories of Imperfect Competition
Jean J. Gabszewicz and Jacques-François Thisse

103. The Economics of Executive Compensation (Volumes I and II)
Kevin F. Hallock and Kevin J. Murphy

104. The Foundations of Long Wave Theory (Volumes I and II)
Francisco Louçã and Jan Reijnders

105. The Economics of Commodity Markets
David Greenaway and C.W. Morgan

106. Corporate Governance (Volumes I, II, III and IV)
Kevin Keasey, Steve Thompson and Mike Wright

107. Economic Welfare: Concepts and Measurement (Volumes I and II)
John Creedy

108. Economic Forecasting
Terence C. Mills

109. Recent Developments in Game Theory
Eric S. Maskin

110. The Economics of Increasing Returns
Geoffrey Heal

111. The Economics of Corruption and Illegal Markets (Volumes I, II and III)
Gianluca Fiorentini and Stefano Zamagni

112. The Economics of Price Discrimination
George Norman

113. The Economic Theory of Auctions (Volumes I and II)
Paul Klemperer

114. The Economics of Regional Policy
Harvey W. Armstrong and Jim Taylor

115. Economic Integration and International Trade
Carsten Kowalczyk

116. The Political Economy of Science, Technology and Innovation
Ben Martin and Paul Nightingale

117. The Economics of Science and Innovation (Volumes I and II)
Paula E. Stephan and David B. Audretsch

118. Innovation, Evolution of Industry and Economic Growth (Volumes I, II and III)
David B. Audretsch and Steven Klepper

119. The Economics of Energy (Volumes I and II)
Paul Stevens

120. Privatisation in Developing Countries (Volumes I and II)
Paul Cook and Colin Kirkpatrick

121. The Economics of Tourism (Volumes I and II)
Clem Tisdell

122. The Economics of Unemployment (Volumes I, II, III and IV)
P.N. Junankar

123. Privatisation and Corporate Performance
David Parker

Future titles will include:

International Finance
Robert Z. Aliber

Welfare Economics
William J. Baumol and Charles A. Wilson

The Economics of Defence
Keith Hartley and Todd Sandler

Economic Theory and the Welfare State
Nicholas Barr

The Theory of Trade Policy Reform
Carsten Kowalczyk

The Economics of Property Rights
Svetozar Pejovich

Income Distribution
Michael Sattinger

The Economics of Politics
Dennis C. Mueller

The Economics of Sport
Andrew Zimbalist

The Political Economy of Development
Amitava Krishna Dutt

The Regulation and Supervision of Banks
Maximilian J.B. Hall

Public Procurement
Sue Arrowsmith and Keith Hartley

The Economics of Advertising
Kyle Bagwell

Forms of Capitalism: Comparative Institutional Analyses
Ugo Pagano and Ernesto Screpanti

The Economics of Business Strategy
John Kay

The Economics of Crime
Isaac Ehrlich

The Economics of Organisation and Bureaucracy
Peter Jackson

Realism and Economics: Studies in Ontology
Tony Lawson

The International Economic Institutions of the Twentieth Century
David Greenaway and Robert C. Hine

The Economics of Structural Change
Harald Hagemann, Michael Landesmann and Roberto Scazzieri

The Economics of the Mass Media
Glenn Withers

Alternative Theories of the Firm
Richard Langlois, Paul Robertson and Tony F. Yu

International Financial Integration
Sylvester C.W. Eijffinger

The Economics of Budget Deficits
Charles Rowley

The Economics of Intellectual Property
Ruth Towse and R.W. Holzhauer

Path Dependence
Paul David

The Economics of Contracts
Lars A. Stole

New Developments in Exchange Rate Economics
Lucio Sarno and Mark P. Taylor

The Political Economy of Monetary Union
Paul De Grauwe

New Institutional Economics
Claude Ménard

The Economics of Barter and Countertrade
Bernard Yeung and Rolf Mirus

Comparative Law and Economics
Gerrit de Geest and Roger Van Den Bergh

Cost-Benefit Analysis
Arnold C. Harberger and Glenn P. Jenkins

The Economics of Migration
Klaus F. Zimmermann and Thomas Bauer

The Economics of Networks
Michael Katz and Carl Shapiro

The Economics of Technology Transfer
Sanjaya Lall

Regulation, Economics and the Law
Anthony I. Ogus

The Economics of Labor Unions
Alison Booth

The Economics of Poverty and Inequality
Frank A. Cowell

The Economics of Business Strategy
John Kay

The Economics of Free Trade
Robert W. Staiger

Forecasting Financial Markets
Terence C. Mills